The Texas Guide

The Texas Guide

Gary James

Fulcrum Publishing
Golden, Colorado

The information in *The Texas Guide* is accurate as of November 1999. However, prices, hours of operation, addresses, phone numbers, websites, and other items change rapidly. If something in the book is incorrect or if you have ideas for the next edition, please write to the author in care of Fulcrum Publishing, 16100 Table Moutain Parkway, Suite 300, Golden, Colorado 80403.

The Texas Guide provides many safety tips about weather and travel, but good decision making and sound judgment are the responsibility of the individual. Neither the publisher nor the author assumes any liability for injury that may arise from the use of this book.

Library of Congress Cataloging-in-Publication Data
James, Gary.
     The Texas guide / Gary James.
            p.   cm.
     Includes index.
     ISBN 1-55591-371-7 (pbk.)
      1. Texas—Guidebooks. I. Title.
   F384.3.J36 2000
   917.6404'63 21—dc21   99-040044

Printed in Italy
0 9 8 7 6 5 4 3 2 1

Cover photograph: North Franklin Peak in Franklin Mountains State Park with storm and rainbow at first light; sotol plants in foreground. Photo copyright © 1999 Laurence Parent.
Back cover photograph: Dallas skyline at night. Photo by Gary James
Cover and interior design: Michelle Taverniti
Maps: Marge Mueller, Gray Mouse Graphics
Editorial: Daniel Forrest-Bank, Don Graydon
Composition: Bill Spahr

Fulcrum Publishing
16100 Table Mountain Parkway, Suite 300
Golden, Colorado 80403
(800) 992-2908 • (303) 277-1623
www.fulcrum-books.com

Contents

Acknowledgments

This is the place where all authors pull out a long list of names and thank the people who have made their existence possible. I'm no different. I'd like to thank my mom and dad, who worked hard for a living all their lives in the dust bowl of West Texas, and who thought a career in radio and television was only a passing fad for their oldest son. They told me I could never make a living at it. Sometimes I think they're right.

I would like to thank Jerry Barron and Eddie Don Harris, two high school classmates who convinced me I would never make it as a professional football player; former Houston fire chief Robert Clayton, who convinced me I would never make it as a golf pro; and my entire family, who convinced me I would never make it as a rock star. That didn't leave much else, so I did what any blue-blooded Texan would do. I studied journalism, and eventually met up with the likes of Tom Jarriel, Chuck Pharris, Bob Harper, and Ray Miller; they were the ones who shaped my life (and I certainly plan to get even with them for that some day). Others who have been most helpful along the way include my great friend Mary Goldman, who got me this gig with Fulcrum Publishing, and Lyn Salerno, one of the people at KPRC, Channel Two TV in Houston, who was a joy to work with over the years.

One more colleague deserves mentioning—Bob Lewis. He has been one of my greatest friends, and you'll hear more about him in the pages ahead. Bob started his career in Fort Worth and wound up in Big Spring. I started in Big Spring and wound up in Houston. Bob was, and still is, important to me because he convinced me that I was good enough to travel the state and report back what the "real people" were thinking. He and several other people at KPRC-TV, like Jack Harris, Jack McGrew, and Ray Miller, came up with the idea for the longest-running, regionally syndicated television program in the state: *Eyes of Texas.*

Bob didn't stay around long enough to work on the show. He moved on to West Texas and discovered that he enjoyed radio more than television. If you listen to the radio as you travel around Texas, you might even catch part of a conversation with Texans that Bob broadcasts regularly on more than a hundred stations around the state. You won't hear his real name on the show, but you might catch his stage name— Tumbleweed Smith. He's one of hundreds and hundreds of wonderful people I've met in my travels. Some of them, like Bob, will tickle your tummy. Others may touch your heart. And all of them will make you wish you had more time on this earth to meet every Texan. Thanks to all of them, too, for making my life's work so interesting.

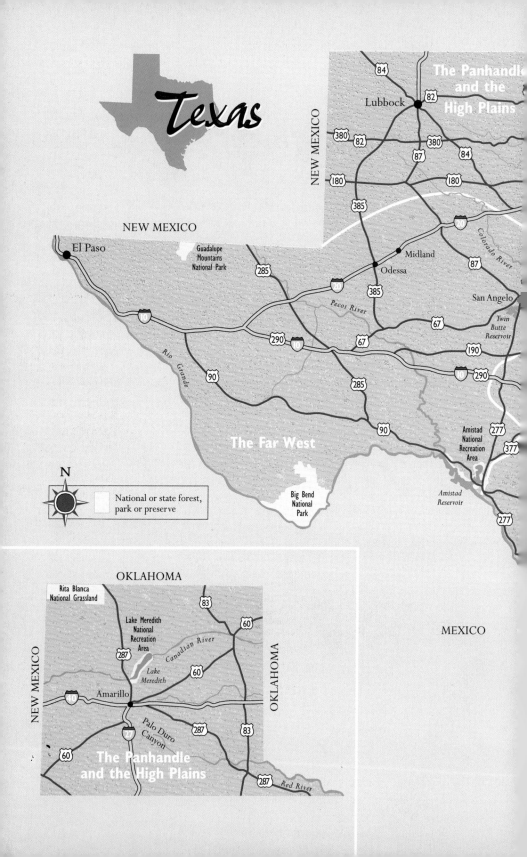

Texas

The Panhandle and the High Plains

NEW MEXICO

84
82
Lubbock
380 82
87 380 84
180 180
385

Colorado River

NEW MEXICO

El Paso

Guadalupe Mountains National Park

285

10

Midland
Odessa

10

385

San Angelo

87

Twin Butte Reservoir

290 10

Pecos River

67

67

190

Rio Grande

90

10 290

285

N

National or state forest, park or preserve

The Far West

90

Amistad National Recreation Area

277
377

Big Bend National Park

Amistad Reservoir

277

OKLAHOMA

Rita Blanca National Grassland

83
60

Lake Meredith National Recreation Area

Canadian River

287

60

Lake Meredith

NEW MEXICO

40

Amarillo

OKLAHOMA

MEXICO

27

Palo Duro Canyon

287

83

60

The Panhandle and the High Plains

287

Red River

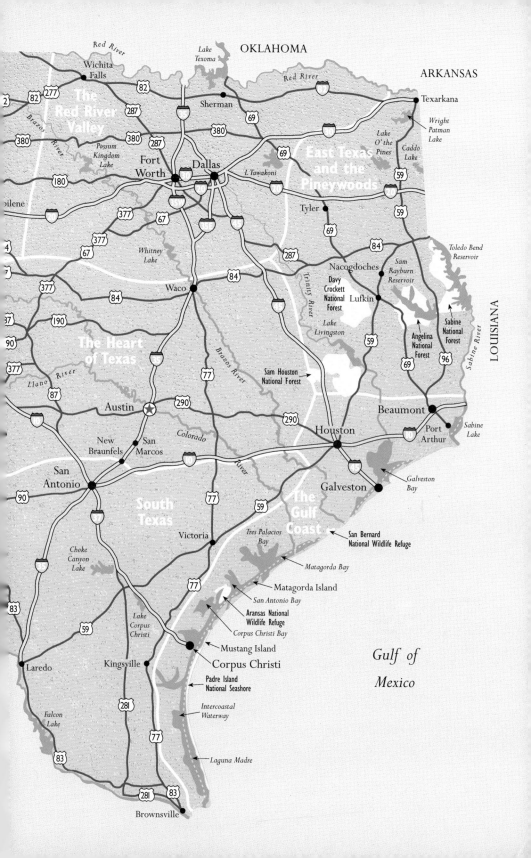

Introduction

The great philosopher Yogi Berra once said, "If you ever reach a fork in the road, be sure and take it." That's my philosophy too—especially when you travel in my state. Texas is a land filled with forks in the road. Take one path and you'll disappear in the Pineywoods of East Texas. A turn in another direction will take you to the hot, dry deserts of West Texas. Turn again and you'll enjoy the blistering, white beaches of South Padre Island, or travel north and you might just find snowy canyons in Palo Duro. Go south and you'll discover the palm trees and the freshly grown fruit and vegetables in the area called the Valley, or just stay put in Central Texas and you'll be enveloped by some of the loveliest hills, lakes, and scenery anywhere. There are many forks to take when you travel through the Lone Star State, and each one introduces you to something new . . . something different . . . and, yes, somewhere exciting . . . to places and people you'll never forget.

Have I told you that Texas is my favorite place to be? Well, it's true. I've seen it all—as a photojournalist traveling the world and as producer of the most successful regionally produced television show in the country, *Eyes of Texas*—but my roots are in the blowing desert winds of West Texas, and almost 40 of my 58 years on this planet have been spent in the eastern part of the state: fishing in the lakes of the Pineywoods, collecting seashells on the sandy beaches of the Gulf of Mexico, and photographing the thorny bushes of the Big Thicket.

If it's trivial to say that Texas is, indeed, all things to all people, then forgive me, but there is no doubt that this state offers a bit of everything to everybody: towering skylines and modern freeways smothered by rush-hour traffic; lonely prairies occupied by scorpions, prairie dogs, and horny toads (that's native talk for horned lizards); inland lakes busting with bass and crappie; and the wide-open spaces of Big Bend Country, where ghost towns have turned into tourist havens and dinosaurs once ruled.

Texas is a paradise for vacationers and an accommodating host for some of the biggest conventions in the world. Texas still boasts of being the largest state, but because of Alaska that boast now comes with a qualifier: It's the largest of the contiguous forty-eight states. It has more than 3,100 towns and cities spread out over more than a quarter of a million square miles. It is farther from Texarkana in the Northeast to El Paso in the Far West than it is from El Paso to Los Angeles. When my wife, Punkie, and I lived in Beaumont, we occasionally drove to Big Spring to visit our families, and one of the main things I remember about our drives was the enormity of Texas. The journey took almost ten hours, and as we approached Big Spring from the east, a road sign revealed that another 308 miles stood between us and El Paso. Now *that's* a big state.

Just a few more words about the variety here. Where else can you choose between enjoying the classical sounds of some of the best symphonic music in the world, or watching a goat-roping demonstration? How about hiking in the rugged Guadalupe Mountains, or deep-sea fishing in the Gulf? You can put on a coat and tie and enjoy some of the finest gourmet food in the world at Tony's, an exclusive restaurant in Houston, or jump into your jeans for a hayride and a chuckwagon meal at Indian Cliffs Ranch near El Paso in the Far West.

The comparisons never stop. Texas can reinvent itself to your satisfaction. If you like the great outdoors, welcome to Texas. If you enjoy the arts, welcome to Texas. If you're looking for the company of crowds, welcome to Texas. And if you want to be alone to contemplate and soak in scenery for all seasons, welcome to Texas.

Happy travelin', neighbors!

Background Information

History

Columbus received credit for finding the New World in 1492, but his discovery was old news to Texas. Pictographs in the rocks around San Angelo and in Seminole Canyon not far from Del Rio indicate that Paleo-Indians lived in this country thousands of years ago. They probably were descendants of Asian groups that migrated across the Bering Strait Land Bridge to North America. Artifacts indicate these people were nomadic and few in number. They hunted with arrows and spears of flint. They harvested fruits and nuts from the land, and freshwater fish from streams and rivers.

Around the beginning of the first century A.D., a woodland Indian culture that came to be known as Pre-Caddoan developed in East Texas. These people established permanent homes, and they produced pottery out of that gummy East Texas mud. The Caddo Indians who evolved from that original culture were social and civilized people, with their own chiefs, priests, and craftspeople. A certain gender equality must have existed in their communities, as Caddo women participated in many community affairs.

Probably the most intriguing mystery of the state's prehistoric period is the origin of the Malakoff-Trinidad heads: stone carvings in the shape of human heads, found in Henderson County in the 1920s and '30s. They were dug from the bottom of a gravel pit that dates back at least 40,000 years, suggesting that an advanced culture may have predated the Paleo-Indians.

THE LANDLORDS:
SPAIN, FRANCE, AND MEXICO

Columbus never set foot in the land that would become Texas, but Cabeza de Vaca and two other Spanish explorers did in the 1530s. They brought with them a Moorish slave—Esteban—who historians say was the first African to arrive in this land. The explorers had sailed from Cuba to explore the Gulf Coast, but shipwrecked near present-day Galveston and lived among various Indian tribes for a number of years. In his travels, Cabeza de Vaca couldn't escape the stories about great wealth somewhere to the north. Today we believe those stories were concocted by the Indians to persuade the Spaniards to move on and leave them alone.

Meanwhile the French were also interested in this land, and opposed the Spanish claims to the area. In 1682, René Robert Cavelier, Sieur de la Salle, sailed into the Gulf of Mexico and claimed the Gulf Coast for France. He immediately returned home and then came back with four ships full of potential colonists. On the way, two of the ships were lost at sea, but the lucky survivors came ashore at Lavaca Bay, about halfway between the present-day sites of Galveston and Corpus Christi. There la Salle established Fort St. Louis.

La Salle never saw his homeland again. During the third of the exploratory expeditions he made inland, he was killed by one of his own men. Today a rose granite statue of la Salle stands on the sands of old Indianola on the Texas coast, and another stone likeness stands in downtown Navasota, in Grimes County, where he was killed.

Eventually Fort St. Louis was abandoned, but not before France claimed the Rio Grande as the western boundary of the Louisiana Territory. This move infuriated the Spanish, who sent expeditions to explore the Texas coast and the interior and established two missions in East Texas. Diseases brought by the Spanish devastated the tribes of peaceful Caddo Indians, who blamed the priests' holy water for the illnesses and returned to their traditional religion.

The Spanish missionaries moved out of East Texas around 1700 and enjoyed more success to the west. In 1718 they established what became the most famous mission in the Southwest, San Antonio de Valero—later nicknamed the Alamo when the military took it over in 1800. The establishment of San Antonio de Valero and five more missions in the San Antonio area marked the beginning of a new era in Spanish expansion, but it wasn't an easy task. In the heart of Texas, the Apaches ruled, and the whole area of South Texas, beset by Indian raids, was barely under Spanish control.

Another Indian people, the Comanches, began moving south to the Great Plains from the Rocky Mountains. They ran roughshod over the Apaches, who retreated to the lower Texas plains and in turn attacked the peaceful Jumano and Coahuiltecan tribes. Squeezed between the Comanches to the northwest and the Spanish to the south, the Apaches

Mission Concepcion, one of San Antonio's historic missions.

eventually made peace with the colonizers in the San Antonio area.

Meantime, an all-out war was developing to the northwest. In 1757, 200 miles from San Antonio, the Comanches attacked and destroyed the mission of San Saba de la Santa Cruz. A major battle ensued, with the Comanches and their Plains Indian allies on one side and the Spanish, the Apaches, and a number of Mexican Indians on the other. The Comanches, using French rifles and field tactics, soundly defeated the Spanish—the most humiliating loss the Spanish ever suffered against the northern Indians. Spain's control of Texas began slipping away. Spain and France both were beginning to wonder if this land was worth all the misery. These nations began easing out of the picture, leaving much of the land to the Texans themselves: a blend of Mexicans, Indians, and southwestern frontiersmen who just wanted to be left alone.

When Napoleon of France sold the Louisiana Territory to the United States in 1803, President Thomas Jefferson claimed all the land extending to the Rio Grande, including the area of present-day Texas. The region divided by the Rio Grande was occupied at that time by many Mexican-born Spaniards fed up with Spanish rule. In 1810 revolutionary mestizos (Mexican-born Spaniards who were also part Indian) began

a decade-long struggle to free the region and all of Mexico from Spanish rule. A year later the revolutionists sent emissary Jose Bernardo Gutierrez to Washington, D.C., to obtain guns and support from the United States. He got neither, but what happened next gave birth to Texas.

Upon his return from Washington, Gutierrez joined West Point graduate Augustus Magee at Nachitoches, Louisiana, to form a Republican Army of the North. The army began storming across Texas in August 1812, and Texas as an independent nation was created. It didn't last. Spain recaptured the territory at the battle of Medina River in 1813 and negotiated with the United States a border between Texas and Louisiana. The new official border had little effect on Anglos grabbing land in Texas, as Spain didn't have the resources to guard the border. And with the U.S. economy in a squeeze, many Americans were happy to move to Texas in the search for new opportunity.

In 1821, Mexico granted an Anglo-American named Moses Austin a franchise to settle 300 families in the area between the Brazos and Colorado Rivers. Mexico believed these new Texans would serve as a buffer of sorts to protect Mexico from the deadly Plains Indians. But the advantage went to the Anglos—

rough, tough settlers determined to build permanent homes for themselves in Texas.

In 1825, Mexico authorized Austin to bring 900 more families into Texas, and in 1831 he was contracted to bring in 800 European and Mexican families. By the end of that year, Austin had been responsible for bringing almost 5,700 people to Texas. The Anglos who settled Central and North Texas came mostly from Missouri, Kentucky, and Tennessee, whereas most of those coming to East Texas immigrated from Mississippi, Louisiana, Arkansas, and Alabama. Colonists from Mexico gravitated toward the fertile south of Texas, where cotton farming and cattle ranching became popular.

THE REVOLUTION

The people who settled Texas were not particularly happy with Mexican rule, but they weren't excited about the possibility of being controlled by the United States either. Simply put, they wanted to be left alone. Most of the immigrants pledged their allegiance to Mexico, but they did so with the understanding that they would live under a republican form of government, as outlined in the Mexican Constitution of 1824.

In 1830 the Texans cheered as General Antonio Lopez de Santa Anna instigated an army revolt and installed himself as president of Mexico. Encouraged by Santa Anna's victory, the Texans held a convention in San Felipe and declared Texas a separate Mexican state. But Santa Anna, announcing himself to be the new dictator of Mexico, refused the Texans' declaration. His refusal sparked the bloody Texas Revolution.

The first shots were fired in Gonzales, about 60 miles east of San Antonio. When the Mexican army demanded the town surrender a cannon given to the local militia for defense against Indian attack, the citizens refused. On October 2, 1835, they flew a flag over the cannon, with words that read "Come and Take It". A small band of Mexican soldiers accepted the invitation and were repelled. They retreated to San Antonio, with the Texans in hot pursuit, and in 5 days the Texans captured San Antonio. In subsequent skirmishes they gained control of garrisons at Nacogdoches, Goliad, and Anahuac.

By the end of 1835, the Texans thought that the war was over and they had won. A small minority, led by Governor Henry Smith, wanted to break away completely from Mexico, but the majority of Texans remained loyal to Mexico. They simply wanted to throw their support behind Mexican liberals in an effort to restore constitutional government.

Reality came to bear on the Texans in February 1836. Santa Anna, infuriated with the Texans, ordered Mexican troops to march on Texas, leading them himself. A force of about 4,000 troops swarmed into San Antonio and trapped a small Texas fighting force inside the walls of a tiny fortress known as the Alamo. The battle lasted 12 days.

William Travis commanded the Texas troops, who were outnumbered forty to one. Battle-hardened warriors like Indian fighter Jim Bowie and sharpshooter Davy Crockett helped fend off the Mexicans but had little effect on the defeat everyone knew was coming. Santa Anna flew a red flag, the Mexican symbol for "no quarter, no mercy, no surrender." He had been quoted throughout his military career as saying, "If you kill your enemies, then you never have to forgive them."

The defenders held off Mexican attacks without a single Texan death until the walls were finally breached March 6. Travis had said he would defend the Alamo to the death, and he kept his word. He was killed early during the final attack. Bowie, on his sickbed, was killed as he fought off Mexican riflemen. Crockett may have died in the battle, or he may have been executed afterward. All the Texans were executed on the spot, and their bodies were burned and buried in a common grave outside San Fernando Cathedral. Afterward, Santa Anna announced a glorious victory in San Antonio. His aide, Colonel Juan Almonte, privately noted: "One more such glorious victory and we are finished." Mexico lost some 1,500 soldiers in the battle.

The irony is that most of the defenders of the Alamo were Mexicans. Most of them considered Mexico their native country. Most of them wanted to change the system, not abandon it. The Texans flew a Mexican flag throughout the battle. But Santa Anna's arrogance and cruelty created a bitter memory that would never go away.

Before the siege of the Alamo ended, a council that had convened at the Texas town of Washington declared Texas an independent republic. After the fall of the Alamo, General Sam Houston and his ragtag Texas army went on the run, heading for the United States—or at least that's what Santa Anna thought.

While Santa Anna's crack army of about 1,300 soldiers rested on the marshy banks of the San Jacinto River near Harrisburg (later Houston), the men led by General Houston took them on.

On April 23, 1836, 800 Texas soldiers—armed with flimsy weapons and the knowledge that if they lost this battle, the Republic of Texas was dead—overran the Mexican encampment. The battle lasted only 20 minutes. The Texans killed every Mexican soldier in sight. Santa Anna was captured the next day and was held prisoner until he signed treaties that guaranteed withdrawal of all Mexican troops from Texas and recognition of a new nation: the Republic of Texas.

ANNEXATION

Texas was an independent republic for 10 years, and the period wasn't particularly successful. The Texans had trouble governing themselves, were disorganized, and frankly, couldn't stomach their own authority. They had defeated the Mexican government but they still had the Indians to deal with. The economy never quite came around, and the southern border of Texas, where it touched Mexico, remained unstable.

General Sam Houston was elected president and, with his vice president, Lorenzo de Zavala, enacted a voter-ratified constitution. In 1837 the Texans, looking for protection from the dangers of another Mexican revolution, formally requested that Texas be annexed to the United States. But that didn't sit well with U.S. abolitionists, who feared Texas would be a slave-holding state. The request was withdrawn. Houston's old friend President Andrew Jackson formally recognized the republic as an independent nation later that year.

Houston, who had lived among the Cherokees for a number of years, worked to establish humane Indian policies. As president of Texas, he gave land to Indians fleeing persecution in the eastern United States, and he was in the process of making peace with the Comanches on the western frontier when his 2-year term ended.

Mirabeau Lamar, second president of the Republic of Texas, reversed Houston's Indian policies. In 1838 he kicked the Cherokees out of the land Houston had set aside for them in East Texas, and killed one of Houston's close friends, Cherokee chief Philip Bowles. In 1840 he created an ugly incident in San Antonio that would be remembered forever. He in-

vited twelve Comanche chiefs to meet and exchange war prisoners. Lamar became angry because the Indians brought only one prisoner, so he ordered his troops to open fire. Many of the chiefs were killed, and in response the Indians began a series of raids on Anglo settlements in Texas that would last for 35 years.

Lamar fared better in foreign affairs. He persuaded France to recognize the republic in 1839, and Holland, Belgium, and Great Britain followed suit. When Lamar's term ended, Houston returned to office and reopened negotiations with the Comanches, and eventually the warring Indians settled down. But then in 1842, Mexico tried to retake Texas. Fourteen hundred Mexican troops marched into San Antonio and captured the town. Captain Jack Hayes of the newly established Texas Rangers gathered 600 Texas volunteers and managed to push the Mexicans back into Mexico.

Toward the end of Houston's second term, the United States began showing an interest in bringing Texas into the Union. U.S. leaders feared Texas was becoming too intimate with Great Britain—and might even become part of the British empire. Instead of admitting Texas as a state, the United States wanted to annex it only as a territory. But when James Polk won the presidency on a platform of westward expansion, Texas statehood soon followed. In 1845, Texas became the twenty-eighth state in the Union.

STATEHOOD AND BEYOND

The annexation of Texas put the United States in a position to grab land all the way to the Pacific Ocean over the next few years. Mexico still considered Texas its property, and the movement of U.S. troops all the way south to the Rio Grande brought on war with Mexico. By 1847, Mexico had conceded defeat. The Treaty of Guadalupe Hidalgo made the Rio Grande the southern border of Texas, and turned the territories of Nuevo Mexico and Alta California over to the United States. Those territories would become the states of Colorado, New Mexico, Nevada, Arizona, California, and parts of Utah and Wyoming. The Texas population began expanding, with immigrants arriving from many nations to take advantage of cheap land. Between 1850 and 1860 the Texas population almost tripled.

Governor Hardin Runnels, elected in 1857, pushed for reinstitution of slave trading in Texas. Under

Sam Houston, slavery had been illegal. Now Texas was about to choose sides in anticipation of a civil war. Many southern states wanted to secede from the Union, and all of them favored slavery. After Houston succeeded Runnels as governor, Texas sided with the Union for the time being. It wasn't long, though, before Texas found itself in the middle of an intense conflict between Unionists and secessionists.

When President Lincoln offered to send federal troops to Texas to put down the ensuing rebellion, Houston declined, with these words: "I love Texas too well to bring strife and bloodshed upon her." Over Houston's objections Texas became a Confederate state on March 2, 1861. When Houston refused to swear allegiance to the Confederacy, he was kicked out of office. He retired to Huntsville, where he died 2 years later.

In the Civil War, the primary job of Texas was to supply cloth and ammunition to the rest of the Confederacy. No battles were fought on Texas soil. Following the Civil War, Texas entered a period of lawlessness. Federal troops occupied the state, but most of them were stationed along the Rio Grande to protect the border from Mexico. The Indian frontier was left defenseless, and outlaws and thieves seemed to be attracted to the state.

That's when Texas got its Wild West reputation. In the years between 1865 and 1868, the state recorded more than a thousand murders. Some cities, such as El Paso and Fort Worth, were downright dangerous. You had to be rough, tough, and fast on the draw to stay alive on the Texas frontier in those days. Gunslingers like John Wesley Hardin, Luke Short, Clay Allison, and Black Jack Ketchum made lasting reputations.

Texas Rangers take credit for eventually forcing the Plains Indians out of the state, but in truth they had already started leaving by the latter half of the nineteenth century. Buffalo hunters probably did more to run off the Indians than did the Rangers. Buffalo camps were set up all along the Indian frontier, and the animals were killed randomly and without control, simply for their hides. With far fewer animals available as food, the Indian tribes moved on.

THE CHISHOLM TRAIL

The cotton industry in East Texas suffered greatly after the war, but the cattle business in South and West Texas boomed. In 1871 alone, almost three-quarters of a million head of cattle were moved from Texas to railheads in Kansas. The route was along the Chisholm Trail, named for Indian trader Jesse Chisholm. The first cattle drive took place in 1867, when cowboys from the O. W. Wheeler ranch moved 2,400 head of longhorn steers from San Antonio to Abilene, Kansas. At the North Canadian River, in Indian Territory (Oklahoma) in the dead of winter, they picked up some wagon tracks and followed them to Kansas. Those were Jesse Chisholm's tracks. He had been hauling trade goods to Indian camps since 1864.

There was so much money to be made from these early cattle drives that some notable early Texans took on the challenge. Captain Richard King delivered his cattle to Kansas personally and brought the profits back to Texas to enlarge his own spread, the King Ranch, which he built into an 825,000-acre empire in South Texas.

The Chisholm Trail finally went out of use in 1885. The railroad had reached Texas, and barbed wire had closed up the grazing land. During its existence as a cattle route, the Chisholm Trail had been used to move more than 5 million cattle and 1 million mustangs. It was the greatest movement of livestock in world history.

OIL

Long before Europeans arrived in this country, early residents had discovered oil seeping from the ground. It was used for medicinal purposes, mostly as a high-powered laxative. Survivors of the DeSoto expedition of 1543 used the gooey stuff to caulk boats, but it took a man from San Augustine, Lyne Barret, to recognize its real potential. He drilled the first well in 1866 in Nacogdoches County at a place that came to be called Oil Springs. Oil was only a lubricant and cooking fuel back in those days, and there wasn't much demand. Barret continued drilling and produced modest yields in Brown and Bexar Counties.

In 1894 a larger oil reservoir was discovered in Corsicana, and the first commercial refinery was built in Texas. Interest in oil was increasing. The Corsicana refinery developed a locomotive fuel, and at the beginning of the twentieth century, the Corsicana field was pumping out 500,000 barrels of oil a year.

Then in 1901 a find at Spindletop near Beaumont sent Texas on its way to becoming the oil capital of the United States. In its first year Spindletop yielded more than 3 million barrels of oil. In 1902 output climbed above 17 million barrels. An even larger reservoir was discovered near Kilgore in East Texas in 1930. It yielded 100 million barrels of oil in its first year. Many more Texas oil fields have been discovered since then, particularly in the Permian Basin of West Texas, but none larger than the Kilgore strike.

THE TWENTIETH CENTURY

In the early 1900s, the excesses of corrupt Mexican politicians brought on another revolution in that country. Thousands of refugees fled across the border into Texas to escape the violence. Pancho Villa, a cattle rustler and bandit, became an important figure in the revolution. The U.S. public became so enamored with Villa's escapades that Hollywood sent film crews to accompany him on raids against the Mexican militia. But by 1915, Villa had given up his unsuccessful battle for Mexico and returned to raiding villages in Texas. This prompted President Woodrow Wilson to send 100,000 National Guard troops to the Texas border. They stayed, protecting the border, until the Mexican revolution fizzled out a year later.

Pancho Villa's enemies say he was nothing but a thug and a bandit, but his supporters say he carried out his raids in order to draw the United States into the revolution. The colorful Villa is still remembered today by old-timers in West Texas, who love to talk about his exploits.

Permian Basin Petroleum Museum in Midland.

During the depression years of the 1930s, Texas fared well, boosted by its oil industry. World War II, from an economic standpoint, was good to the industrial sector. Shipbuilding and aircraft manufacturing became important new industries in the state, and the petroleum companies expanded as demand for fuel increased.

After World War II the state's industrial base diversified even more as large companies moved in to take advantage of inexpensive electricity and land. In 1959, Texas Instruments developed the first silicon microchip, elevating Texas to the field of high-tech enterprise. Since then Texas has worked hard to attract more high-tech industries and has succeeded in a number of places, including Austin, Dallas, and Houston.

Now, after all these years, the state has awakened to what could become its greatest industry ever: tourism. The rest of this book stands as a testimonial of the myriad reasons why Texas has become so attractive to travelers.

The People

If you happen to be driving on a lonely Texas highway, particularly out west or in the Panhandle, and the driver of a vehicle with a Texas license plate waves at you as you pass, be sure to wave back. Many local drivers are friendly and courteous, and you'll discover that many of them still wave at passing cars. If that happens, wave back. It'll make you feel good.

The people of Texas are friendly, and they come from just about everywhere. The state's demographic history involves not a simple line moving west, but a convergence of lines of migration from every direction. Hispanics moved into the state from the south. Most Europeans came from the east. French Canadians came from the north, and Asians came from the west.

Since the mid–nineteenth century, most immigrants have been of European descent. Today about two-thirds of the 17 million people who live in Texas have their roots in Europe. A fourth of the population is Hispanic (that is, of Spanish, Mexican, or mestizo descent), and African Americans make up about 12 percent. The fastest-growing population is Hispanic, although a large number of Asians have found homes in Texas in recent years, mostly in urban areas.

Tragically, the thing we call the "Frontier Spirit" brought on the demise of the original Texans, the

Native Americans. The massive move west took their land and left little space for them to survive. The Indians we read about in books and see in the movies—the Comanches, the Apaches, and the members of the Plains tribes—didn't really live in Texas at all. Their homes were up north, and they came to Texas to hunt. The real natives in Texas were the Caddos, a civilized and sophisticated confederation of about twenty-five tribes that included the Tonkawas of Central Texas, the Coahuiltecans and Jumanos of South and Southwest Texas, and the Karankawas of the Gulf Coast. Many of them died at the hands of the Spanish and the French who once occupied this land. Today only two officially recognized tribes live year-round in Texas, the Tiguas in West Texas and the Alabama-Coushattas in East Texas. Members of one migratory tribe, the Kickapoos, spend part of each year at Eagle Pass.

Texans of German decent make up the state's fourth largest ethnic group, behind the English, Hispanics, and African Americans. The early German immigrants settled mostly in Central Texas. They came to escape war and persecution in Europe and brought with them the social organization and many of the customs and dialects of their homeland. German-style beer halls are still fairly common in Central Texas, along with some of the finest German food you'll ever taste.

The French occupy fifth place in number among ethnic groups in the state because of the Acadian French influence from Louisiana. Cajun celebrations and festivals fill the air in the Golden Triangle Area (Beaumont–Port Arthur–Orange) much of the year. The immigration of Central Europeans also made its mark as communities of Poles, Czechs, and Wends arose in Central and East Texas. Norwegians brought farming skills and settled mostly in Dallas, Henderson, and Bosque Counties.

African Americans played significant roles in Texas history. Several all-black infantry and cavalry units were instrumental in fighting off the Indians during the Indian wars. The Comanches feared them, calling them buffalo soldiers. Black cowboys helped tame the West, and one of them, Bill Pickett, invented the art of bulldogging, a standard event in all rodeos. A black Texan, Scott Joplin, was the father of ragtime music, and many people say that the original rock 'n' roll got its start in the backstreet bars of Houston,

with musicians like Blind Lemon Jefferson and Lightning Hopkins.

Hispanics have had more influence in Texas than just about any other group. They've also been around the longest. Texas was under Spanish or Mexican rule for about 150 years. The Hispanic influence reaches into language, food, architecture, music, fashion, and more. Some influences are so deeply woven into the fabric of Texas that you can't separate one from the other.

The Texas cowboy is based on the Spanish vaquero. Original Texas architecture was borrowed from the Spanish and Mexican heritage. Texas food wouldn't be identified as Texan without the Mexican influence. And the Tex-Mex food you order in El Paso is not the same as the Tex-Mex food in Austin or in the area of South Texas known as the Valley. That in itself says something about the great size of the state.

English is the most widely spoken language here, with Spanish a distant second—but don't be surprised if you hear a little German spoken in the Hill Country and a lot of Cajun French in Southeast Texas. It's good to know some Spanish if you're coming to Texas, but the Spanish you hear on the border may be a little hard to understand. Most of it is part English and part Spanish. We call it Tex-Mex. A lot of my Mexican friends from the interior of Mexico can't understand it either.

The Texas vocabulary varies somewhat from what you're probably used to. In many of the small towns, motels are "tourist courts," and air-conditioning is "refrigerated air." And a lot of words like "yonder" and "git" and "winder" (as in "window") make their way into Texas talk. Many East Texans talk with a southern drawl, while a lot of West Texans have a nasal twang when they speak. Don't trouble yourself, though. All those Texans think *you* talk funny too. And the two most common words you'll hear during your stay are "ma'am" and "sir." Have I told you that Texans are the friendliest people in the world?

The Land
The Rocky Mountain region, the Great Western High Plains, the Great Western lower plains, and the Gulf Coast forested plains all converge on Texas, and the result is a unique study in diversity. The western part of the state is wide open, while the southeast is a mixed bag of sandy beaches and swampland. Central Texas

has rolling hills and underground springs, and the Pineywoods of East Texas offer lush blackland soil rich in nutrients and dense forests of pine and hardwood trees.

A few oddities of nature dot the state. The southern part of the Pineywoods has a patch of land that resembles a primeval forest. We call it the Big Thicket. And a lone stand of maple trees (Lost Maples State Park) sits in the middle of the Hill Country. The state has 13 major rivers, more than 150 freshwater lakes, almost 100 mountains that are more than a mile high, and 23 million acres of forestland. There are 254 counties in the state, and the largest of them, Brewster, covers 6,000 square miles.

Animals

Probably the most famous Texas animal is the armadillo, found virtually all over the state. Armadillos look like they are from the age of the dinosaurs, and they probably are descendants, but they aren't dangerous. During the Great Depression, armadillo meat was a popular food supplement, and in the 1950s armadillo shells were sold at almost every highway curio shop.

Texas has some black bears, but not nearly as many as in the past. Most of them are now confined to the mountains of the trans-Pecos region out west and the river bottoms of East Texas. Big Bend National Park reports that the black bear is making a comeback in the region, and the same is true there for the mountain lion.

Deer are prolific in Texas. Big and small, their numbers are estimated at well over 3 million. Most of them are the white-tailed deer found in almost every region. And don't be shocked if you spot the elegant pronghorn, a type of antelope, in the Panhandle or the High Plains. They are fairly common.

Prairie dogs used to be prolific in the plains and prairies of Texas, but they made such a nuisance of themselves that ranchers began killing them off. Now about the only places to see these burrowing rodents are in parks dedicated to the creatures.

The bottlenose dolphin and the manatee are native to the Gulf Coast. Other marine mammals that visit the Texas coast include several other species of dolphins, the right whale, the minke whale, and the dwarf sperm whale.

The American alligator is the largest reptile in Texas and can usually be found in the bayous of East Texas

and the salt marshes along the Gulf Coast. Texas is home to more than a hundred species of snakes, with sixteen considered poisonous to humans. Copperheads live in the western part of the state, western cottonmouths spend their time in the east near water, and rattlesnakes live all over the state—pretty much "wherever they want to live," as Texans say. There are lots of nonpoisonous snakes in Texas, but I wouldn't stick my hand out to pet any of them.

Five of the world's nine species of sea turtles are occasionally seen along the coast. Largest of the group is the leatherback, which sometimes reaches 7 feet in length.

Texas has more species of birds than any other state. We like to think it's because they find the state a comfortable place to live, especially in winter. And of course Texas is overrun with bird watchers most of the year—many of them packing expensive photographic gear that makes mine look amateurish, and I'm supposed to be a professional.

The best areas for bird-watching are along the Gulf Coast and in the Lower Rio Grande Valley. Every spring, tiny communities in the Rio Grande Valley become sizable urban areas as birders come to view the remarkable variety of flying creatures. Late fall is also a popular time for bird-watching. The salt marshes make especially good viewing areas for some of the larger birds, like egrets, cranes, ducks, geese, and herons. The most famous flying creature to spend time in Texas is the whooping crane. From November to April, boat captains in the area of the Aransas National Wildlife Refuge on the Texas coast make a nice living carrying tourists out for a glimpse of the dinosaur-like birds.

Other winter residents along the coast include the snow goose and the Canada goose, as well as mottled ducks and ibis. Other birds of the Texas coast include pelicans, gulls, sandpipers, loons, and marsh hawks. My favorite is the pink-feathered roseate spoonbill, often mistaken for a flamingo.

All kinds of bass, sunfish, crappie, and catfish are native to the state. Crayfish, better known as crawfish, thrive in the bayous of East Texas. The Gulf of Mexico is rich with sea life. Sportfishing is very big, and boats leave almost every day from places like Galveston, heading for the coral reefs for some bottom fishing for snapper. Yellowfin tuna, blue marlin, wahoo, tarpon, and even some sailfish provide sport to the serious saltwater fisher. And almost every section of the state has its own special lake where fishing is good. Texans are serious about their fishing.

Climate

The Texas climate is varied, but with one predominant characteristic: sunshine. From the Gulf to the Guadalupes, the sun shines most of the year, so bring plenty of warm-weather gear and lots of sunscreen. You'll need plenty of lip protection if you spend much time in West Texas, which is hot and very, very dry. East Texas is humid, and there is not much you can do about it except look for places that are air-conditioned.

Winter comes late and leaves early. Only January and February can really be called winter. That's when cold fronts often sweep rapidly through the state, bringing sudden drops in temperature. Snow may powder the High Plains, but down along the border snowflakes are seldom seen.

Spring is March and April, when bluebonnet and Indian paintbrush and 5,000 other species of wildflowers color the state. The highway department also plants them along the thoroughfares. Temperatures are warm.

It's hard to tell when spring becomes summer, because it's so subtle. The days become long. The river fishing is great. Swimmers hit the pools and the beaches, and Texans revel in the season of the sun.

October through December features the blue skies and cool nights of fall. This too is a season of color. You may need a sweater or light jacket in the evening.

We've all heard about Texas twisters and hurricanes, but they don't happen nearly as often as most people believe. Texas ranks well below Florida and Oklahoma, and usually behind Indiana, Iowa, Louisiana, and Mississippi, in number of tornadoes. If you see one on your trip, turn away from it and seek safety. Tornadoes are fascinating to watch, but don't fool yourself. They can be deadly.

In West Texas and the Panhandle, you can often spot dusters—whirlwinds shooting up into the sky. They are just as much fun to watch as tornadoes and not nearly so destructive. As for hurricanes, we always have plenty of warning from the National Weather Service. My advice is not to stick around if a hurricane is coming. Once it's passed, that's another story.

Longhorn cattle grazing in a field of wildflowers in the Texas Hill Country.

Beachcombing is a blast after hurricanes. You'd be surprised what washes up on the beach. And fishing is absolutely fantastic after a storm.

October to December and March to May are the best times to visit the trans-Pecos and Big Bend area. The summer months of June through August are usually too hot for the average visitor, with daytime temperatures that reach the 100s. The mountain climate is quite temperate this time of year, but avoid the heat of desert hiking. Fall is best for river-running down the Rio Grande. Spring is super for bird-watching and for viewing the wildflowers.

Overall, the best months for travel are usually late October through November, March and April, and late May and early June. Trips during those times usually avoid extreme heat and cold and heavy rainfall. But no guarantees.

Texas has no real peak tourist season. The state tends to receive about the same numbers of visitors year-round, probably because it has different things to offer travelers at different times. South Texas is the exception. It is more heavily traveled in winter due to the influx of people escaping those cold winters up north. More than 100,000 residents of northern states are winter Texans.

Visitor Information

General Information

TRAVEL INFORMATION CENTERS

The Texas Department of Transportation operates travel information centers that are designed to be rest areas as well. Uniformed travel counselors welcome visitors and provide a wealth of free literature and suggestions to make every trip more pleasant. You can pick up a free Texas map at any one of these facilities, and the counselors can help you chart routes to any place in the state. They'll point out the most convenient short-line directions or leisurely scenic drives to your destination, and supply printed information about points of interest and recreation areas along the way.

The **Travel Information Center (1-800-452-9292, www.dot.state.tx.us.)** provides information, literature, and emergency road conditions any time of day. And just about every city has a chamber of commerce or tourist agency to serve travelers. The information centers are open daily 8 A.M.–5 P.M. except Thanksgiving, Christmas, New Year's Day, and the eves of these holidays. You just can't enter Texas without passing by one of these travel information centers:

Amarillo: on I-40 from Oklahoma and New Mexico
Anthony: on I-10 from New Mexico
Austin: in the capitol complex
Dennison: on U.S. 75/69 from Oklahoma
Gainesville: on U.S. 77/I-35 from Oklahoma
Harlingen: at the junction of U.S. 77 and U.S. 83
Langtry: on U.S. 90/loop 25 along the Texas–Mexico border
Laredo: on I-35 from Mexico
Orange: on I-10 from Louisiana
Texarkana: on I-30 from Arkansas
Waskom: on I-20 from Louisiana
Wichita Falls: on I-44/U.S. 277/281 from Oklahoma

THE INTERNET

The Internet has become a wonderful source of information for travelers, once you know how to use it. Almost every agency and many commercial enterprises in Texas have a website and/or an e-mail address. Those that don't almost apologize when you ask whether they are on the Internet. I've included as many e-mail addresses and websites as possible in this guidebook. Many of the places I visited are developing a site or in the process of getting an e-mail address.

A terrific starting point on the Web for those who enjoy outdoor activities like camping, fishing, boating, hiking, and hunting is **www.texas outside.com.**

A great deal of information on lakes, lodging, and golf courses is available at **www.touringtexas. com/tourmain.htm.** The site has links to more than eighty-five Texas cities and towns and more than a hundred government and business Web pages. Sites with some Texas golf information include **www. txgolf.com, www.golfsw.com,** and **www.net caddie.com.**

The website **www.texassleepaways.com** provides a bed-and-breakfast directory. More ideas for places to stay are available at **www.hat.org.** The "hat" in the name stands for Historic Accommodations of Texas.

The state Parks and Wildlife Department runs **www.tpwd.state.tx.us,** definitely one of the busiest Web pages in Texas. The site can feed you information about parks, camping, hunting, fishing, boating, historic sites, nature trails, conservation—and even jobs, in case you like this place enough to move here. The state Department of Economic Development operates **www.traveltex.com,** another source of information about places to visit.

Spend some time on the Web before you get on the road to Texas. It will save you time once you get there.

OTHER GOOD INFORMATION SOURCES

The Texas Department of Economic Development publishes the *Texas Accommodations Guide,* and it's free. Contact the department at **P.O. Box 12728, Austin, 78711; 1-800-888-8839** or **512-462-9191.**

The organization Historic Accommodations of Texas publishes *Great Stays of Texas,* filled with descriptions of bed-and-breakfasts, beautiful illustrations, and historical points of interest. It's available for about $10 through the organization at **P.O. Box 1399, Fredericksburg, 78624; 1-800-428-0368.**

In the metropolitan areas of the state, *Key Magazine* offers information about some of the more popular eating establishments. The magazine can be contacted at **1220 Waverly, Houston, 77008; 713-880-9200.**

For information about camping or parks anywhere in the state, you can contact the state **Parks and Wildlife Department, 4200 Smith School Rd., Austin, 78744.** Numbers to call are **1-800-792-1112** or **512-389-4800;** you can make camping reservations at **512-389-8900** (Mon.–Fri., 9 A.M.–6 P.M.). Most Texas state parks require an admission fee, plus a range of fees for camping and other accommodations.

The Texas Department of Transportation publishes a list of all campgrounds operated by federal, state, county, municipal, and other government authorities, like the Army Corps of Engineers. The free publication *Texas Public Campgrounds* can be obtained by sending a request to **Department of Transportation, P.O. Box 5064, Austin, 78763-5064.**

Other sources of camping information are the **Texas Association of Campground Owners, 6900 Oak Leaf Dr., Orange, 77630; 409-886-4082;** and the **Texas KOA Kampgrounds Owners Association, 602 Gembler Rd., San Antonio, 78219; 210-547-5201.**

For lots of good detail about bicycling in the state, I recommend Andy White's *Best Bike Rides in Texas* (Globe Pequot Press, 1995). Many of the more popular golf courses in the state are covered in *The Texas Golf Guide, Second Edition* (Republic of Texas Press, 1999).

Tips for Visitors

Area codes—Texas is growing so fast it seems impossible to keep up with the changes and additions to telephone area codes. Be prepared to double-check with operators if you have trouble reaching numbers you call. In the past 5 years, all of the major cities and surrounding areas have added new area codes, and more are on the way.

Time zones—With the exception of far West Texas, the state operates on central standard time. That's 1 hour behind the East Coast and 2 hours ahead of the

West Coast. The area of Texas that is west of Van Horn—which includes El Paso—is on Mountain Standard Time, 1 hour behind the rest of the state. (When it's 6 P.M. in New York, it's 5 P.M. in most of Texas, 4 P.M. in El Paso, and 3 P.M. in California.) All of Texas observes daylight saving time from the first Sunday in April to the last Sunday in October.

Information for disabled visitors—Most public buildings are accessible to the handicapped and include special parking. Increasingly, tourist attractions and facilities offer the same.

Getting There

Texas has 250,000 miles of roads, 13,000 miles of rail lines, and 35 major airports. You'll need a car to really do justice to all the places you'll want to see in Texas. Public transportation has not caught on here in a big way, except in the major metropolitan areas. Texas, with one of the finest highway systems in the nation, is made for motorists. But for travelers without their own cars, there are some alternatives in the form of buses, trains, and rental cars.

By bus—Regional bus companies connect just about all the towns of Texas, and larger cities are linked by Greyhound-Trailways Bus Lines. Most intercity buses are air-conditioned and equipped with rest rooms. If you plan to travel by bus, consider buying a pass that permits large blocks of travel during a specific period or in a specific region; ask the bus companies for details. The larger cities, including Houston, Dallas, Fort Worth, Austin, Corpus Christi, and San Antonio, have special downtown bus lines for visitors and shoppers.

By train—Rail is another alternative for travel. Two Amtrak lines run through the state: the Texas Eagle (Chicago to San Antonio, with a Dallas-to-Houston connection) and the Sunset Limited (Los Angeles to Miami). These two trains have stops at twenty terminals in Texas: Alpine, Austin, Beaumont, Cleburne, Bryan/College Station, Corsicana, Dallas, Del Rio, El Paso, Fort Worth, Houston, Longview, Marshall, McGregor, San Antonio, Sanderson, San Marcos, Taylor, Temple, and Texarkana. For schedule information or bookings inside the United States, call **Amtrak** at **1-800-872-7245.** The Texas High Speed Rail Author-

Wildflowers along I-45, south of Huntsville.

ity is developing plans for a 200-mile-per-hour bullet train to link San Antonio, Dallas, Fort Worth, and Houston, with stops in San Marcos, Austin, and Waco—but you won't see it until at least 2010.

By car—All major auto rental agencies have offices in Texas, and most offer airport locations to make it convenient to step off a plane and into a car. The most economical way to rent is by the week or month. Some agencies provide an extra discount to customers who reserve a car at least a week in advance. With some planning, you can rent a compact car for as little as $20 a day or $105 a week.

Secondary roads that intersect major highways are often designated Farm Roads or Ranch Roads. There can be long distances between gas stations in some parts of West Texas and South Texas, so check your gauge and the distances before heading out on long open stretches.

You'll spot many historical markers as you drive along the highways. I suggest you stop at a local bookstore, go to the Texas section, and pick up a little volume called *Why Stop? A Guide to Texas Historical Roadside*

Markers (Gulf Publishing, 1992). The book discusses every historical marker in the state, and it makes for fun reading as you and your family travel those long Texas highways.

DRIVING LAWS

Speed limits, caution zones, stops, and directions are marked along 76,000 miles of Texas highways by more than a half million signs. The maximum speed limit for cars and light trucks on rural interstate highways is 70 miles per hour. Lower limits are posted on all other highways and streets.

Passing is illegal when there is a continuous yellow stripe on the driver's side of the center line. It is illegal to pass from either direction a school bus that is stopped or about to stop and has its red warning lights flashing.

A right turn is permitted on a red light after a full stop, unless a traffic sign says otherwise. And seat belts are a must. Texas law requires seat belts to be worn by drivers and front-seat riders in passenger vehicles. That includes trucks with safety-belt capability. The law also requires children under the age of two to be secured in an approved safety seat or seat belt, whether they are in the front or the back.

All motor vehicles operated in Texas must have a liability insurance policy in effect, and evidence of the policy must be in the car. And of course it's illegal to throw trash on the highway. I hate those "Don't mess with Texas" signs, but they seem to work. The legal drinking age in Texas is twenty-one years, and you cannot consume alcoholic beverages while driving a vehicle no matter how old you are. Violation of any of these laws can result in a substantial fine—even jail if you drink and drive.

HIGHWAY REST AREAS

Many years ago Texas pioneered the concept of miniature parks along highways, an idea that has since been adopted nationwide. Today it pays off for travelers in the state. Including the twelve travel information centers listed in General Information, Texas provides more than a thousand rest areas, picnic areas, and scenic turnouts that invite motorists to pause and take a break from driving. Parks are equipped with shaded arbors, tables, benches, and cooking grills. You are welcome to rest in these places, but Texas law says you can't stay in one spot for more

Horse grazing in a field of bluebonnets, outside Navasota.

than 24 hours or put up any kind of structure (in other words, a tent).

More than a hundred of the rest areas include information panels (called infoboards) that describe attractions along the way: museums and historical points of interest; state and national parks; caverns that are open for tours; fishing and other recreation opportunities; and major attractions such as San Antonio's River Walk, Houston's Astrodome/Astroworld, or Galveston's Strand. By checking out the infobords, you may discover a point of interest or a fun-filled family attraction you've overlooked.

Visiting Mexico

The enchantment and flavor of Mexico draw tourists to the border when they come to Texas. You'll find many crossings all along the border, from a new high bridge that spans the Rio Grande at Laredo to a tiny ferry crossing at Los Ebanos in the Valley. Mexican shops and markets are colorful and fascinating. The prices are attractive. The people are friendly. Crossing the border is easy and simple, if you know what to expect. There are no fees other than for auto insurance or special permits such as hunting and fishing licenses, bridge tolls, and U.S. Customs duties. Every U.S. citi-

zen must carry proof of citizenship when crossing into Mexico. Immigration officers now require a passport, birth certificate, voter registration card, or any other document that proves citizenship. This is a change from the past, so be prepared.

You'll need a Mexican tourist card if you travel beyond the border area or if you stay longer than 72 hours. The free cards can be obtained from the Mexican immigration authorities or from Mexican government tourist offices in the United States. Proof of citizenship is required.

Mexico requires an automobile permit if you plan to drive into the interior beyond the border cities. You can get the $10 cards at the border, and you must pay with a major credit card. You'll need a title of ownership for the vehicle, plus written permission from the owner if you don't own the car.

It's unlawful to operate a motor vehicle in Mexico without automobile insurance issued by a Mexican insurance company. Your own insurance company can usually make arrangements or provide the number of a company that can provide coverage. Short-term Mexican auto insurance is available from several agencies and travel services on the Texas side of the border. Sanborn's is a reliable American company specializing in such short-term coverage. Auto accidents are considered criminal offenses, and, regardless of fault, vehicles that are involved are usually impounded.

The following listing is only a general summary of travel regulations between the United States and Mexico, and specific rules change constantly. For more information or to check on the latest rule changes, contact the immigration and customs authorities of both countries.

Foreign-made articles taken into Mexico—Foreign-made items, such as cameras, watches, and jewelry made in a country other than the United States, must be registered with U.S. Customs before you enter Mexico. Without proof of prior possession, you may be required to pay import fees when you return.

Mexican currency—If you are visiting only the border cities, you are not likely to need Mexican currency. U.S. dollars are readily accepted. If you do need to exchange currency, any bank or large hotel can do it for you.

Pets—Both Mexico and the United States have restrictions on animals, and you'll do well to leave your pet at home or board it in a kennel before crossing the border. If you must have that special pet by your side, be sure to bring recent veterinary paperwork with you.

Hunting and fishing in Mexico—Contact Mexican authorities for current regulations, hunting and fishing licenses, and procedures for bringing firearms and ammunition into the country. Any game that is legally taken in Mexico may be brought into Texas, but it must be accompanied by a statement issued by U.S. Customs at the border that the game originated in Mexico. There are no restrictions on bringing fish caught in Mexico into Texas, but you must declare them at the border.

Returning to Texas—When you return, a U.S. Customs officer will verify your nationality and ask whether you bought anything while you were in Mexico. Each U.S. citizen may bring back up to $400 in Mexican purchases, duty free, every 30 days. U.S. duties will be assessed at the border on everything

above the $400 exemption. U.S. law permits only 1 liter of duty-free alcoholic beverages to be brought back by each adult citizen during a 30-day period without payment of duties and taxes. Also, Texas law requires payment of a state tax on all alcohol brought in from Mexico. So take your calculator with you. Those bargain prices on liquor purchased in Mexico may not be such a good deal by the time you get it back to the States.

Prohibited imports—Certain articles are either prohibited from being brought into the United States or are subject to various quarantines, limitations, or special permits. They include narcotics or drugs; weapons; some trademarked items; most fruits, vegetables, plants, animals, birds, and meats; and products made from the hides, shells, feathers, or teeth of endangered species. Check with the U.S. Embassy before you go.

How This Book Is Organized

The Texas Guide is divided into seven geographical regions: The Heart of Texas; South Texas; The Gulf Coast; East Texas and the Pineywoods; The Red River Valley; The Panhandle and the High Plains; and The Far West. Each regional section contains a detailed map and is further divided into special destination areas that offer the most rewarding trips for visitors. For each principal destination area, you'll find an overview of the area's history and appeal, followed by listings and descriptions of major attractions, places to visit both indoors and out, the area's various towns, scenic drives, and festivals and other events. There's a detailed look at recreational possibilities for each area, plus a rundown on good places to eat and good places to stay.

Every region of Texas is very special to me because I've been there and I've got wonderful memories of people I met or places I visited. With your patience, I might just pause now and then to tell you a tale or two along the way.

Major Attractions

In Austin there's the state capitol and the Sixth Street shopping and entertainment district. In Waco it's the famous suspension bridge and Baylor University. San Antonio has its River Walk, Dallas its State Fair Park, and Fort Worth its stockyards. Every place has its major attractions, and each section of this book will start off with a look at the best of them.

Seeing and Doing

One of the unique features about this book is not just telling you something about the state, but showing you what Texans do for pleasure. Whether it's strolling through the wildflowers at Lady Bird Johnson Wildflower Research Center in Austin, taking a mission tour in San Antonio, shopping at Houston's Galleria Shopping Mall, or spending a fun-filled day at Six Flags Over Texas in Arlington, there's no limit to all the exciting things to see and do in this unique state.

Festivals and Events

With all the events, you'll wonder if a day goes by when Texas isn't celebrating something. I've counted well over 200 festivals and special events throughout the state every year, ranging from the world's largest rodeo, in Houston, to the Oatmeal Festival in Bertram. Some of the more entertaining events may be worth planning your vacation around. Others may be happening while you're passing through, and may be worth the detour.

In Lubbock they have the National Cowboy Symposium every September. In San Antonio the Texas Folklife Festival takes over the Institute of Texan Cultures in Hemisfair Park in late July. San Marcos has its own Mardi Gras, and Abilene stages a celebrity quail hunt in February. And that's only the beginning. There's the Scottish Festival and Highland Games in Arlington every June, and a water carnival in hot, dry Fort Stockton in July. And don't forget the Hotter 'n Hell Hundred bicycle race at Wichita Falls in August. There's something for everyone, and it is all documented as we visit the various parts of the Lone Star State.

Recreation

Most travel books deal with history, attractions, and places to eat and sleep. *The Texas Guide* does too—but we also like enjoyable exercise, so the book features a lot of outdoor activities as well. One of the greatest things about hiking, biking, bird-watching, camping, trail riding, fishing, and golfing in Texas is that you have the opportunity to choose exactly what appeals to you: rugged mountains, thorny deserts, flowing rivers, sandy beaches—and a whole lot more. Texas is filled with state parks, and those parks offer all kinds of recreation. All you have to do is find them and enjoy them.

The Texas Guide shows you some of the finest hiking routes anywhere. If your thing is horseback riding, try Big Bend for a journey through some of the most gorgeous scenery imaginable. Bird watchers will count more species of birds here than just about anywhere else. Avid fishers will delight in some of the out-of-the-way places in East Texas where they can drop their lures. Golfers can tee it up at the highest course in the state (I'm talking about elevation), in Marfa, or at one of the plush public championship courses in Sugar Land. If you care to run the river in a canoe or raft, you can do that at Lajitas in Big Bend. If you prefer bicycle riding, I'll tell you about biking in the Hill Country, and in many other places as well. This section also includes dude ranches and such, where many activities are out-of-doors.

Where to Eat and Where to Stay

At the end of every main destination, and also mixed in with many sections on the smaller towns, I'll give you my take on some of the better and more interesting places to eat and to spend the night. I haven't spent decades traveling this state without coming up with some of my own favorites and special finds. You'll get a quick and casual look at a wide variety of cafes and restaurants, hotels, and bed-and-breakfasts—all sorts of places that will get you happily fed and rested, Texas-style.

The Towns of Texas

Although most parts of the state are anchored by a big city or two, Texas remains a state of individual towns and communities. In the The Heart of Texas region, for instance, we spend a good bit of time in Austin, but much of the information is about the towns you'll encounter on the road: Elgin and Round Rock, Leakey and Luckenbach, Independence and Washington—all those places that give depth and character to the Texas experience. For each destination area, the book makes separate stops at a host of towns to look at the special attractions of each.

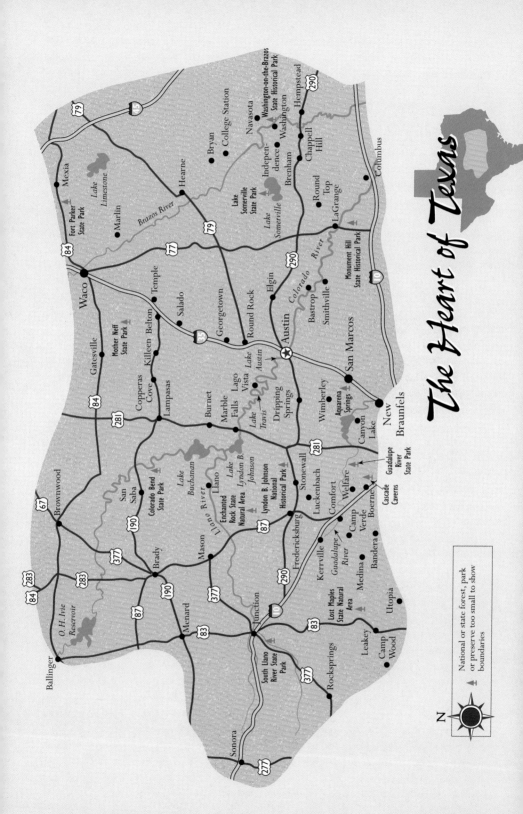

The Heart of Texas

N

National or state forest, park or preserve too small to show boundaries

Ballinger
O.H. Ivie Reservoir
84 283
283
377
87
Brownwood
67
190
San Saba
377
Brady
190
Menard
83
377
Junction
10
South Llano River State Park
377
Rocksprings
Sonora
377

Mexia
Fort Parker State Park
84
Lake Limestone
Marlin
Brazos River
Waco
Gatesville
84
281
Mother Neff State Park
Temple
Killeen
Belton
Copperas Cove
Lampasas
Salado
Burnet
Marble Falls
Lake Buchanan
Colorado Bend State Park
Llano River
Llano
Mason
Lake LBJ
Lyndon B. Johnson
Enchanted Rock State Natural Area
Lyndon B. Johnson National Historical Park
87
Fredericksburg
290
Kerrville
Guadalupe River
Camp Verde
Medina
Bandera
Lost Maples State Natural Area
Leakey
Camp Wood
Utopia

79
45
Hearne
Bryan
College Station
Navasota
Washington-on-the-Brazos State Historical Park
Washington
Hempstead
290
Independence
Brenham
Chappell Hill
Columbus
Round Top
LaGrange
Lake Somerville State Park
Lake Somerville
77
79
Georgetown
Round Rock
35
Elgin
290
Colorado River
Bastrop
Smithville
Monument Hill State Historical Park
10
Austin
Lago Vista
Lake Austin
Lake Travis
Dripping Springs
Wimberley
Aquarena Springs
San Marcos
New Braunfels
Canyon Lake
281
Stonewall
Luckenbach
Comfort
Welfare
Guadalupe River State Park
Boerne
Cascade Caverns

The Heart of Texas

Tubers on the Guadalupe River near San Marcos.
Photo courtesy of the Texas Department of Tourism.

The Heart of Texas

If someone set out to visit all the sights worth seeing in Texas, it's likely that he or she would start in the part of the state we call the Heart of Texas. It's a region that includes the state capital, Austin, and all or part of twenty-five counties near the geographical center of the state. It's bordered on the east and south by a geological fault zone known as the Balcones Escarpment, on the west by the Edwards Plateau, and on the north by rolling plains and prairies. The elevation is typically about 1,000 feet, and it never goes above 1,400 feet.

Most of this region is also known as the Hill Country, for the lovely rolling hills that give it so much grace and beauty. For purposes of this guidebook, the Heart of Texas is divided into five main areas, with the Hill Country as one of them. This permits separate, detailed treatment for the other four areas: Austin; the North-Central area that includes Waco; the Independence Trail country; and the towns of San Marcos and New Braunfels.

The Heart of Texas is a transition zone between humid East Texas and semiarid West Texas. It's the best of all the worlds in Texas, and it's the place most Texans would like to call home. In the heat of those miserable Texas summers, breezes bring some relief, and when it's unseasonably cold in West and North Texas, the hills in the Heart of Texas act as shields from the blowing northerly winds.

The source of this region's magic is hidden below the surface. Over the years geological forces twisted the limestone bedrock until it broke free, creating an upthrust that we call the Balcones Escarpment. All of that shifting also caused the natural spring waters of the Edwards Aquifer underground to gurgle upward, creating dozens of rivers, streams, and pools. Rolling hills and rocky ledges all come natural in this part of Texas, and when the reds and blues and yellows of the wildflowers bloom in season, there is no prettier picture anywhere.

The tourists come in large numbers to this part of Texas year-round, because the weather is usually nice all the time. Blue skies and gentle breezes dominate, and the thermometer seldom dips below 40, even in winter. Fall and spring, when the highway borders explode with the colors of wildflowers, are the best times to come. In autumn the maples, sycamores, and oaks take on golden, orange, and yellow tones. Except for Interstate 35 and Interstate 10, most roads in the region are narrow and hilly and have remained largely unchanged for a hundred years. And aside from the growth of Austin, most of the communities in the Heart of Texas remain small and rustic. They are like windows to the past.

History

People have been living in this region for thousands of years, but most of them were always on the move. There is little evidence of their culture except for a few rock paintings and thousands of arrow and spear points. The Comanches moved down into this area from the northern plains in the 1700s and displaced the earlier Indian tribes. The Comanches were fierce and fearless, and superb horsemen. They competed with the Spanish, Mexicans, and Texans for control of the territory, and lost the battle about 200 years ago.

Between 1840 and 1850, a large number of settlers, mostly frontiersmen from the southern United States, were attracted to the region, particularly to Williamson, Hays, Comal, and Gillespie Counties. By the 1860s the largest Anglo-American immigration was from Arkansas and Tennessee.

German immigrants were drawn here too. Ships loaded with Germans fleeing persecution in the Old Country arrived on the Gulf Coast as early as 1840. They formed wagon trains and spent weeks on the trail before reaching land that had been set aside for them here. The towns of Fredericksburg, Comfort, Boerne, and New Braunfels still have strong German cultures guiding the lives of their residents.

By 1870, Gillespie County was 86 percent German, and Comal County was 79 percent German. Each community in the German portion of the Hill Country developed its own distinctive subculture, particularly in a religious sense. The Pedernales Valley in Gillespie County became an enclave of Lutherans and Catholics who loved dancing and ethnic clubs. The Llano Valley in Mason and western Llano County was dominated by Methodists who disapproved of dancing, drinking, and card playing. The Guadalupe Valley of Kendall County became the domain of freethinkers who maintained the only rural stronghold of agnosticism in Texas.

In the northern part of the Heart of Texas, the Waco Indians ruled until about the 1830s, when the Cherokees moved in and moved them out. The Waco were agricultural people and not aggressive enough to survive in this country. Their name lasted, however, and the city of Waco eventually grew out of that original settlement. The town developed around a ferry service that carried westward immigrants across the Brazos River in the mid–nineteenth century. In 1870 a toll bridge was built across the Brazos—the second longest in the world at the time. It became indispensable for cattlemen driving herds up the Chisholm Trail.

The Independence Trail area got its name from the Texas Revolution of 1835–1836, and simply indicates a region of significant historical events in the creation of an independent Texas. The town of Washington, in the upper northeastern corner of what is now Washington County, was a major political and commercial center in early Texas and was the site of the founding in 1836 of the Republic of Texas.

San Marcos and nearby New Braunfels live and thrive on water: San Marcos sits on the Edwards Aquifer and offers some of the cleanest, freshest spring water found anywhere. San Marcos is a college town that clings more to the future than to the past, although evidence suggests that people were living here 8,000 years ago. Today about 3 million people a year visit San Marcos for the sun, the fun, and the scenery.

New Braunfels sits on both the Guadalupe River and the Comal River (shortest in the state). The town was founded in 1845 when Prince Carl of Solms-Braunfels led the first group of German immigrants to land along the Guadalupe. New Braunfels has managed to retain its Old World style despite the heavy influx of tourists.

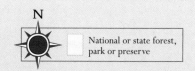

National or state forest,
park or preserve

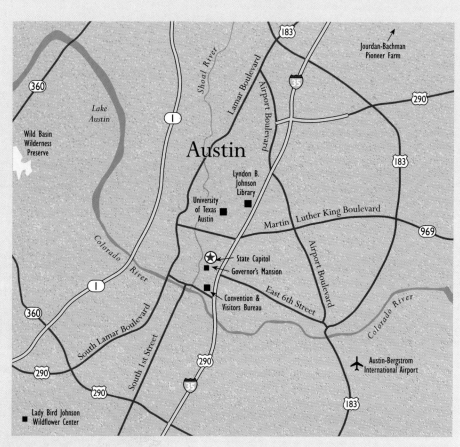

N

183

Jourdan-Bachman
Pioneer Farm

35

290

360

Shoal River

Lamar Boulevard

Airport Boulevard

183

Lake
Austin

1

Wild Basin
Wilderness
Preserve

Austin

Lyndon B.
Johnson
Library

University
of Texas
Austin

Martin Luther King Boulevard

969

Colorado River

1

State Capitol

Governor's Mansion

Airport Boulevard

360

Convention &
Visitors Bureau

East 6th Street

Colorado River

South Lamar Boulevard

South 1st Street

290

290

290

35

Austin-Bergstrom
International Airport

183

Lady Bird Johnson
Wildflower Center

Austin ✪

Austin

Austin, political capital of Texas, originally was a tiny encampment called Waterloo. (This seems only fitting, as General George Custer spent time here.) The encampment later was named for the state's founding father, Stephen F. Austin. The town was the capital of the Republic of Texas until 1842, when the threat of Mexican troops resulted in relocation of the capital to Houston, then later to the town of Washington. Austin regained its status as capital for good in 1844; statehood followed in 1845.

If you spend much time in the state capitol building, largest in the United States, be prepared to talk politics. The capitol was built with money obtained by selling about 3 million acres of Panhandle grazing land to a Chicago syndicate, which went on to create the famous XIT Ranch near Dalhart. The pink granite used in construction of the capitol was harvested in Burnet (BURN-it), northwest of Austin. The capitol has recently been restored to near-original splendor, and it is a must-see on your visit to Austin.

Austin also claims to be the live-music capital of the world, with entertainment 7 days a week in many of its restaurants and clubs. It is a progressive city—growing, some say, faster than it should. Austin bustles not only as the center of state government, but also as a western capital of the high-tech industry. The city is home to the main campus of the University of Texas.

Austin is rich in natural resources as well. The Colorado River flows through town, and Barton Springs swimming pool, a huge, ice-cold natural pond fed by underground springs, is only a few minutes from downtown. There are plenty of opportunities for outdoor recreation, from a walk on the local hike-and-bike trail to a turn on Town Lake in a rowboat.

The capital is a city of paradoxes. Its culture is down-home yet sophisticated, laid-back but bustling with energy. During the past decade, Austin has been named the third best place to live in the United States, the second fastest-growing city in the United States, the nation's best-read and most computer-literate city, the city with the fittest population, and home to the most restaurants and bars per capita in America.

Austin's love affair with nature manifests itself many ways, from Barton Springs to the Lady Bird Johnson National Wildflower Research Center and its showcase of native plants. Another symbol of the city's reverence for things natural is the 500-year-old Treaty Oak, in a tiny park on Baylor Avenue between Fifth and Sixth Streets. The tree is the lone survivor of a grove of oaks where, legend has it, Stephen F. Austin

Congress Avenue and the Texas State Capitol in Austin. Photo courtesy of Texas Highways magazine.

signed the first boundary treaty with the Indians of the area.

Historic structures and ethnic foods serve as reminders of Austin's multicultural makeup. You can visit such places as the German Free School Building, French Legation Museum, Scholz Beer Garden, Jourdan-Bachman Pioneer Farm, and Lorenzo de Zavala State Archives. Hispanic culture has made a major mark on Austin cuisine as reflected by the immense popularity of Tex-Mex restaurants.

The Austin area has its share of microbreweries and brewpubs, and there are awarding-winning wineries in and around the city. You can quench your thirst with a variety of specialty brews served in some trendy brewpubs on Sixth Street and in other parts of town. The European wine-making tradition was introduced to the Hill County in the nineteenth century and is now enjoying a renaissance of sorts as more and more wineries make their home in the Austin area.

All around Austin are smaller towns, each with something to offer the visitor. Bastrop is one of the oldest communities in the state. Round Rock is where

outlaw Sam Bass met his Maker. Twenty miles north of Austin is Georgetown, with its quaint downtown shopping district, a historic courthouse square, and Southwestern University.

Getting Around

BUSES
Austin is blessed with one of the better city bus systems in the state, with more than fifty neighborhood bus routes, eleven express and feeder routes, and three special downtown routes nicknamed the Armadillo Express. Even if you have a car, using **Capital Metro (512-474-1200)** will save you a lot of money in parking.

CABS
Yellow Cab (512-472-1111) and **American Cab (512-452-9999)** offer 24-hour taxi service.

TOURS
Gray Line Tours (512-345-6789, 1-800-472-9546) gives narrated rides past many points of interest in Austin, including the capitol building, the governor's mansion, LBJ Library, Barton Springs, Town Lake, East Sixth Street, and the O. Henry home.

Visitor Information

Austin Convention and Visitors Bureau
Open Mon.–Fri. 8:30 A.M.–5:00 P.M., Sat. 9 A.M.–5 P.M., Sun. 1–5 P.M. **201 E. 2nd St., Austin, 78701; 1-800-926-2282, 512-474-5171, fax 512-404-4383; gspain@austintexas.org; www.austin360.com/acvb**; also, try **www.citysearch.com**.

Major Attractions

State Capitol
Pink granite quarried in the Hill Country makes this building unique. Builders at first planned to use limestone for construction, but fortunately changed their minds and chose the more permanent granite. It was built in 1888. Renovations in recent years make the inside as attractive as the outside.

The capitol building, 7 feet taller than the nation's capitol in Washington, D.C., is the focal point of downtown. It rests on 46 acres of immaculate, landscaped grounds that offer shade trees and flowering gardens to visitors. Other state office buildings flank the main structure, and daily tours are conducted of all the facilities.

The capitol complex visitor center is housed in the renovated General Land Office building, which was constructed around 1857. Exhibits include a pictorial history of the capitol's renovation and a 20-minute informational video. Open Mon.–Fri. 8 A.M.–10 P.M., Sat.–Sun. 8 A.M.–5 P.M.; last tour at 4:15 daily. Free. **112 E. 11th St. (11th St. and Congress Ave.), Austin, 78711; 512-463-0063; www.capitol.state.tx.us.**

Information about points of interest in the capitol, the city, and other parts of the state is available at the **Travel Information Center (1-800-452-9292, www.dot.state.tx.us.)** operated by the state Department of Transportation, also in the old General Land Office building. Open Tues.–Fri. 9 A.M.–5 P.M., Sat. 10 A.M.–5 P.M.

Lady Bird Johnson National Wildflower Research Center

Hike a meadow, view an exhibit, meet Ralph the talking lawnmower. These are just a few of the things you can do as you walk through acres and acres of wildflower gardens. This beautiful place was the dream of Lady Bird Johnson, the former first lady. With her gift of $125,000 and 60 acres of land in 1982, the center was born. It is dedicated to the preservation and reestablishment of native plants throughout the country. Tours are best in spring, during the wildflower blooming season.

The center has a 232-seat auditorium for special shows and a stone observation tower that affords an overview of twenty-three magnificent gardens. You can eat lunch or enjoy a cappuccino at the Wildflower Cafe or select a gift at the little Wild Ideas store.

Because the center is not limited to Texas, you can also get information about growing wildflowers in your part of the country. It is a national information center for wildflowers, and the people who work here are a wonderful source of facts and ideas. There is a great deal to see and do here, but the scenery is most important: Give yourself plenty of time to stop and smell the primroses.

The Lady Bird Johnson Wildflower Center is a private, nonprofit organization supported by mem-

Wildflowers at the Lady Bird Johnson National Wildflower Research Center in Austin.

bership dues; gifts from individuals, foundations, and businesses; and facility revenues. Beginning at $25, membership includes free admission to the gardens, a discount from the center's store and mail-order catalog, a subscription to the bimonthly newsletter *Wildflower*, and reciprocal privileges at more than 100 arboretums and botanical gardens.

Open daily except Monday and major holidays. Grounds: Tues.–Sun. 9 A.M.–5:30 P.M. Visitors gallery: Tues.–Sat. 9 A.M.–4 P.M., Sun. 1–4 P.M. Wild Ideas store: Tues.–Sat. 9:00 A.M.–5:30 P.M., Sun. 1–4 P.M. Wildflower Cafe: Tues.–Sat. 10 A.M.–4 P.M., Sun. 11 A.M.–4 P.M. Admission $3.50 adults, $2.00 students and senior citizens, $1.00 children under 5. Call **512-292-4200** for group rates or to make reservations for guided tours. The gardens, grounds, and buildings are smoke-free; no pets or alcoholic beverages permitted. **4801 LaCrosse Ave., Austin, 78739; 512-292-4100, fax 512-292-4627; www.wildflower.org.**

Wild Basin Wilderness

A total of 227 acres of beautiful land southwest of

Austin were set aside in the mid-1970s for preservation through active management, nature education, and research. It's a place to take leisurely and relaxing walks and to learn about plants and animals that live in this region.

The wilderness is ideally located on Bee Creek on the Balcones Escarpment, where the woodlands and the grasslands of the Hill Country join. Public trails pass through woodland, grassland, and streamside habitats. The Wild Basin is home to some threatened and endangered species of plants, animals, and birds, including the golden-cheeked warbler and the black-capped vireo, as well as hundreds of other species.

Wild Basin offers environmental education programs during the spring and fall and field trips for schoolchildren. You can also take guided tours that specialize in such topics as birding, animal tracking, geology, wildflowers, reptiles and amphibians, insects, and stargazing. Enjoy the special features of the place, such as the environmental education center, Bee Creek pool, and the elm grove.

At this outdoor wonderland, you'll find all kinds of short trails for roaming and sightseeing. An easy-access trail provides a route for visitors whose mobility is impaired. It's ideal for less strenuous walks, with no steep inclines and benches every 300 feet. The Laurel Trail features evergreen Texas mountain laurels along the way; they bloom in spring. The Falls Trail winds its shady way through Spanish oak and Ashe juniper to a waterfall and plunge pool. There are even more short trails to entice you. The Woodland Trail grants a cool and winding stroll along a wet-weather creek. The Ledge Trail, wide and level, traverses a grassland in the center of Wild Basin.

Wild Basin is a good example of privatization in action, as most of the operating budget is raised through membership dues, corporate donations, fundraising events, and grants. The wilderness, open daily from sunrise to sunset, is **on Loop 360, about 1 mile north of Bee Cave Rd. (Ranch Road 2244) southwest of Austin; 512-327-7622; hike@ wildbasin.org; www.wildbasin.org.**

The Hill Country Flyer

Ride a steam locomotive through the Hill Country. It's an unforgettable ride through a gorgeous landscape. Today the Hill Country Flyer transports passengers. But in 1881, it was built to help tap the mineral riches of this land, including the pink granite used to build the state capitol.

It was first known as the Austin & Northwestern Railroad. The railroad became part of the Southern Pacific line before it was sold to the city of Austin in 1986. It was restored by the Austin Steam Train Association and returned to service in 1992 as an excursion train. Locomotive 786 has quite a history with Southern Pacific: From 1916 until 1956 it hauled freight and passengers to and from the capital city.

With the Hill Country Flyer, the hearty rhythms of steam passenger trains echo once again through the limestone hills of Central Texas. The train takes you from Austin's northwest edge deep into the heart of the Hill Country, through 33 miles of pristine scenery and Texas history.

From Cedar Park, home of the springtime Cedar Chopper's Festival, the train rambles through the town of Leander, then drops down the rocky ledges of Short Creek Canyon to make a crossing of the crystal-clear South San Gabriel River. As the line climbs up the river's oak- and cedar-studded valley, draped with wildflowers in the spring and glorious with color in the fall, you may glimpse local fauna ranging from white-tailed deer to Texas longhorns—maybe even a few emus.

Beyond Liberty Hill and Bertram, the Flyer tops a rocky ridge and descends into Hamilton Creek Valley and the historic town of Burnet. There you get a leisurely stopover for lunch and shopping, or maybe just a stroll around the town square. Burnet's century-old jail will take you back to old Texas for a minute or two. Nearby is the old army post of Fort Groghan, established during the Indian wars, and the Confederate Air Force keeps a few restored warplanes at the Burnet Airport. There's a good chance you'll stumble onto an old-fashioned western gunfight on the town square while you're in town. (See the The Hill Country chapter in this section for more details on Burnet.)

The Hill Country Flyer runs every Saturday and Sunday, March through December. It leaves Cedar Park, about 10 miles northwest of Austin on U.S. Hwy. 183, at 10 A.M. and arrives in Burnet at 12:30 P.M., leaves Burnet at 3:00 P.M., and arrives back in Cedar Park at 5:30 P.M. There are open-window coaches and comfortable vintage cars from the 1920s. Round-trip fares: $24 adults, $10 children 13 and under.

Also available are air-conditioned cars or stream-lined parlor-sleepers from the 1950s that offer lounge or compartment seating; fares are $38 adults, $19 children.

The Twilight Flyer runs on selected Saturday evenings for a relaxed, romantic 2-hour journey for adults, with complimentary hors d'oeuvres and beer, wine, and soft drinks. It leaves Cedar Park at 7 P.M. Fares for regular coach are $20 for one person, $38 for two. Air-conditioned coaches are $26 for one, $38 for two.

Austin & Texas Central Railroad, Box 1632, Austin, 78767; 512-477-8468, fax 512-477-8633; www.main.org/flyer.

Travis County Farmers Market

Homegrown, homemade, and the true taste of Texas. That's what you get at the Travis County Farmers Market. This market on more than 3 acres of land will show you what's good and what's in season. It's as fresh as you'll ever see it—unless you grow it yourself. You'll find tomatoes, peaches, potatoes, peppers, and peas; rosemary, spinach, squash, apples, and watermelon. And much more: jalapeño mustard, hot 'n' peachy jams, locally made jellies, fresh-baked bread, and homemade pies. They even make their own tamales at the farmers market. If you'd like to ship some of this taste of Texas back home, they can make that happen too.

In a city filled with good restaurants, the market is a great place to make time for an unusual meal. Fresh brisket, barbecue chicken, and pork ribs are daily features, and you can eat there or take your food with you. Texas barbecue is usually drenched in sauce, so if you're interested in the meat more than the sauce (like I am), be sure and ask for the sauce on the side. For something lighter, how about a sandwich on fresh homemade bread, with vine-ripe tomatoes, and fresh peach pie to follow?

If you're not particularly hungry and want to save some bucks, pass up the sit-down meals. You can have free nibbles as you make your way around the market, and, frankly, a lot of the merchants will be downright disappointed if you don't sample their food.

There's more than just food at the farmers market. Out back is a 5,000-square-foot barn brimming with antiques, collectibles, and primitive furnishings made right here in Texas. Take time to browse through some of those Texas primitives. You'll be intrigued with the craftsmanship and with just how simple and practical furniture was made back when Texas was young.

Kids can have a great time at the market too. There are four raised-bed gardens on the property where youngsters can see fruits and vegetables as they are growing. They can learn how to grow corn, or see pumpkins getting fatter by the day in the pumpkin patch.

Every morning the aroma of fresh coffee and homemade breads fills the air. Holidays are special, of course, with pumpkins packing the place at Halloween, and November and December bringing poinsettias, grapevine wreaths, and Christmas trees. But any time of year is a good time to visit because there's always something going on and there's always something good to eat. It's a shame they didn't have the Travis County Farmers Market when I was going to school in Austin. It would have saved me a lot of indigestion at Dirty's Drive-in.

Here are phone numbers for some of the fine tenants at the market: **Celia's Tacos, 512-419-7221; Cocinito de Lucero, 512-450-1006; Farmers Market Trading Company, 512-459-4664; Hill Country Landscape and Garden Center, 512-459-3833; Republic of Texas Provision Company, 512-302-9911; Rinehart's Real Texas Barbecue, 512-453-0604; Sweetie Pies Bakery & Sandwiches, 512-451-7431.**

Travis County Farmers Market is located at **6701 Burnet Rd., Austin, 78757; 512-454-1002.**

Jourdan-Bachman Pioneer Farm

Imagine stepping back in time for a day. You can do that at the Jourdan-Bachman Pioneer Farm. It's an outdoor living-history museum that shows visitors what rural life was like on a typical Hill Country farm years ago. The farm offers a composite look at three family lifestyles typical of the area in the late nineteenth century, using historically correct farm animals, crops, clothing, furnishings, buildings, implements, and food. Costumed interpreters are there to answer questions and present a picture of the past as they go about their daily chores.

The farm's programs change throughout the year. Visit in the fall and help pick cotton and watch as it is spun into yarn. Gather around a campfire on a winter day and sing old-time favorites played on the pump organ. Experience the sights and smells of cooking on a wood-burning stove or in a Dutch oven, or just enjoy the peace of a rural setting. Sometimes the folks at the farm might be stuffing sausage or making soap. Other times you might get a chance to milk a cow, plow a field, or learn to shoe a horse. It's a wonderful way to learn history.

Special times of the year mean special programs. Around Halloween you can check out the haunted hayride. The craft of candlemaking comes alive in the Christmas season.

The Jourdan-Bachman Pioneer Farm is open year-round on Sundays 1–5 P.M., and in addition is open June–Aug. Mon.–Thurs. 9:30 A.M.–3:00 P.M., and Sept.–May Mon.–Wed. 9:30 A.M.–1:00 P.M. Admission: $3 adults, $2 children 3–12, $2 for groups of 10 or more. **11418 Sprinkle Cut-Off Rd.; 512-837-1215, fax 512-837-4503.**

Sixth Street

When I was in college a thousand years ago, Sixth Street in Austin was off-limits to most students. It was a rough part of town—not a place to be after hours. I worked at a local radio station and my chores every

Stevie Ray Vaughan statue on display at Town Lake in Austin. Photo courtesy of the Texas Department of Tourism.

morning included checking out the overnight police activity. Sixth Street had more than its share. What a difference time makes! Sixth Street today may very well be the largest drawing card Austin has, with the exception of the state capitol.

The Sixth Street area has two sides—east and west—bisected by Congress Avenue, with two distinct characters depending on the time of day. During daylight hours, Sixth Street west of Congress Avenue is crowded with businesspeople and tourists looking for a meal, a meeting, or collectibles to buy. The dozen eateries west of Congress on Sixth range from an ethnic bakery to a cafe specializing in Southwestern cuisine. People shop for antiques at the **Pecan Square Emporium** or pick up Willie Nelson's latest CD at Austin's favorite music store, **Waterloo Records,** at **6th and N. Lamar; 512-474-2500.**

At night, Sixth Street east of Congress Avenue comes alive. College kids, travelers, and locals flock to a cluster of clubs and restaurants to be entertained, and to find out why Austin claims to be the live-music capital of the world. Between all the shops and restaurants are nightclubs with scores of musicians waiting to be discovered. Willie Nelson, Jerry Jeff Walker, and Asleep at the Wheel's Ray Benson come and go to test the Austin music scene. In the heart of the city, at Riverside Drive and South First Street, a statue of Stevie Ray Vaughan stands tall in his trademark hat and cape. Music is everywhere. Austin has its own Walk of the Stars, on Trinity between East Sixth and East First. The American sounds of country, bluegrass, western swing, folk, and conjunto music are always present.

The 110-year-old **Driskill Hotel** crowns Sixth Street **(Sixth and Brazos, 512-474-5911, www.driskillhotel.com).** Any politician who has ever been involved in Texas politics has made a deal at the Driskill, and a couple of turn-of-the-twentieth-century ghosts still roam its hallways. The old relic is undergoing an $8 million renovation.

Seeing and Doing

Children and Families

Austin Children's Museum

Children of all ages can touch, play, and climb to their heart's delight. Music activities relate to three themes:

how different people live, the human body, and science and technology. Open Tues.–Sat. 10 A.M.–5 P.M., Sun. noon–5 P.M. **201 Colorado St.; 512-472-2499, fax 512-472-2495; www.austinkids.org.**

Austin Zoo

A zoo that offers children a hands-on encounter with many different animals; also pony rides, a picnic area, and a party barn. Open Wed., Sat., and Sun. 10 A.M.–6 P.M. **10807 Rawhide Trail; 1-800-291-1490, 512-288-1490; www.austinzoo.com.**

Galleries and Art Museums

Austin Museum of Art at Laguna Gloria

Home of Texas Fine Arts Association, on the shores of Lake Austin. Exhibits of twentieth-century American art, classes, films, and lectures. Open Tues.–Sat. 10 A.M.–5 P.M., Sun. 1–5 P.M. **3809 W. 35th St.; 512-458-8191, fax 512-454-9408; www.amoa.com.**

Dougherty Arts Center

Offers visual and performing-arts programs, as well as a fine-arts school with classes and workshops. Open Mon.–Thurs. 9 A.M.–9:30 P.M., Fri. 9 A.M.–5:30 P.M., Sat. 10 A.M.–2 P.M. **1110 Barton Springs Rd.; 512-397-1458, fax 512-397-1451; www.ci.austin.tx.us/dougherty.**

Elisabet Ney Museum

Studio of German sculptress who immigrated to Texas in the 1870s. Open Wed.–Sat. 10 A.M.–5 P.M., Sun. noon–5 P.M. **304 E. 44th St.; 512-458-2255; elisabet@earthlink.net.**

Umlauf Sculpture Garden

About 150 examples of the works of sculptor Charles Umlauf. Indoor exhibits are in a modern museum, and outdoor sculptures are scattered throughout a tree-shaded garden. Open Thurs.–Sun. 1–4:30 P.M. Located near Zilker Park at **605 Robert E. Lee Rd.; 512-445-5582.**

Gardens and Arboreta

Fiesta Gardens

On Town Lake. Displays of exotic flora and a lagoon. **512-480-8318.**

Old Bakery and Emporium, on Congress Avenue in Austin.

Museums and Historic Sites

Daughters of the Republic of Texas Museum

Memorabilia of the days of the Republic of Texas. **510 E. Anderson Ln.; 512-339-1997.**

French Legation

Built in 1840 by Comte Alphonse de Saligny, the French charge d'affaires to the Republic of Texas. The entire complex is a gem of Creole architecture and displays a superb collection of period furniture. (A little cultural aside: The charge d'affaires used to let his farm animals, mostly pigs, run loose in the streets of Austin. He ignored the city's complaints. Lawmakers finally made the practice illegal.) Open Tues.–Sun. 1–5 P.M. **802 San Marcos St.; 512-472-8180; dubois@french-legation.mus.tx.us; www.french-legation.mus.tx.us.**

George Washington Carver Museum

Ever-changing exhibits on black history and culture in Austin and Travis County. Open Tues.–Thurs. 10 A.M.–6 P.M., Fri. and Sat. noon–5 P.M. **1165 E. Angelina St.; 512-472-4809; paralee22@aol.com; www.carvermuseum.com.**

Governor's Mansion

Stately mansion built in 1856. The governor lives in a private second-floor apartment, but the other elegant rooms and antique furnishings may be seen on public tours Mon.–Fri., leaving every 20 minutes from 10:00 to 11:40 A.M. **1010 Colorado St.; 512-463-5518; www.governor.state.tx.us/mansion. htm.**

Harry Ransom Humanities Research Center

Extensive collection of rare books, manuscripts, photographs, documents, and art. On display is one of the Gutenberg Bibles, and one of the very first photographs. **Two locations on the University of Texas campus; 512-471-8944.**

Lyndon B. Johnson Library and Museum

Archival material relating to LBJ and the office of the presidency in general; colorful highlights of his political campaigns and his life in Texas. Exhibits include a moon rock and a replica of the Oval Office. Open daily 9 A.M.–5 P.M. **2313 Red River St.; 512-916-5137, fax 512-916-5171; www.lbjlib.utexas. edu.**

Moonlight Towers

Unusual lighting towers that stand 165 feet high, with mercury vapor lamps that cast a glow over a radius of more than half a mile. Towers similar to these once lit up American cities before the turn of the twentieth century. Austin is now the only U.S. city with such a tower system. For locations of the towers, contact the **Austin Visitor Center; 512-478-0098; www. austintexas.org.**

O. Henry Home

Residence of William Sydney Porter, the short-story writer who wrote under the name of O. Henry and lived in Austin from 1884 to 1895. Open Wed.–Sun. noon–5 P.M. **409 E. 5th St.; 512-472-1903; www.ci. austin.tx.us/parks/ohenry.htm.**

State Cemetery

Monuments mark the final resting place for almost 2,000 patriots, statesmen, and heroes of Texas. Open Mon.– Sat. 8 A.M.–5 P.M., Sun. and holidays 9 A.M.–6 P.M. **909 Navasota St.** (7 blocks east of I-35 at E. 7th St.).

Texas Federation of Women's Clubs Building

State headquarters. Offers books and historical information about Texas women, a collection of dolls that represent all of the women who were wives of Texas governors, and portraits of famous Texas women. Open Wed.–Thurs. 1–4 P.M., group tours by appointment. **24th and San Gabriel Sts.; 512-476-5845.**

Texas Memorial Museum

A popular field trip for schoolchildren. This museum displays geological and archaeological artifacts from all over the Southwest. It has dinosaur bones, precious gems, and a historical display on Lady Liberty, the original statue that stood atop the capitol. Open Mon.–Fri. 9 A.M.–5 P.M., Sat. 10 A.M.–5 P.M., Sun. 1– 5 P.M., closed major holidays. Located on the campus of the University of Texas, **2400 Trinity St.; 512-471-1604; tmmweb@uts.cc.utexas.edu; www. utexas.edu/depts/tmm.**

Texas Military Forces Museum

At Camp Mabry in Austin. Established in 1892 as a summer base for the Texas Volunteer Guard; now home to the Texas National Guard. The museum features military artifacts. Open Wed. 2–6 P.M., Thurs.– Sun. 10 A.M.–4 P.M., closed holidays. **W. 35th St. and MoPac Freeway (Loop 1); 512-406-6967, fax 512-706-6750; www.agd.state.tx.us/museum/ htm.**

Texas State Library (Lorenzo de Zavala State Archives)

Everything you ever wanted to know about Texas history; includes the state archives. Open Mon.–Sat. 8 A.M.–5 P.M., closed holidays. Located just east of the state capitol at **1201 Brazos St.; 512-936-INFO; www.tsl.state.tx.us.**

Wells Branch Homestead

An 1850s cabin complete with tools and utensils of the day, and old-timers to explain what life was like in early Texas. Visit during the Christmas Craft Bazaar (Nov. 30–Dec. 1). In the Wells Branch subdivision in the northern suburbs of Austin; **512-251-9814; www.wellsbranchmud.com.**

Nature Centers

Austin Nature Center

Natural history and botany exhibits. Open Tues.–Sat. 9 A.M.–5 P.M., Sun. 1–5 P.M. **301 Nature Center Dr.; 512-327-8180; www.aconnect.ci.austin. tx.us.**

Nightlife

Dance Two-Step

Try stepping out at one of the legendary country-western dance halls, such as the **Broken Spoke (3101 S. Lamar Blvd., 512-442-6189); Old Santa Fe Saloon (505 E. 6th St., 512-496-4296); The Lumberyard (16511 Bratton, 512-255-9622);** or **Dance Across Texas (2202 Ben White Blvd., 512-478-0098).**

Other Sights

The University of Texas

From its original 40 acres near the state capitol, the school has grown to become a major U.S. academic institution. Today the main campus has 357 acres and 120 buildings. The information center in Sid Richardson Hall, open weekdays 8 A.M.–4:30 P.M., has campus information and maps. The center is located at the **corner of Manor Rd. and Red River; 512-471-3434; www.utexas.edu.**

Parks

Hamilton Pool Preserve

Long a treasured swimming hole for locals, this grotto-like pool has captured the attention of visitors too. Includes picnic areas and nature trails; guided tours by reservation. Sixteen miles west of downtown Austin, **off State Hwy. 71; 512-264-2740.**

Zilker Park

Home of the popular **Barton Springs swimming pool** (open late March through October), Zilker Hillside Theater, and Austin Area Garden Center, with a beautiful showcase of flowers and a pioneer log cabin on the property. The park also offers tours of dinosaur tracks at Zilker Botanical Gardens. Don't miss the park's Japanese Garden. The park, run by the Austin Parks and Recreation Department, is at **2000 Barton Springs Rd.** (leave I-35 at Riverside Drive West, turn west onto Barton Springs Rd., then go about 2.5 miles to the park entrance); **512-499-6700; www.ci.austin.tx.us.**

Performing Arts

"Austin City Limits"

See a taping of the longest-running show on PBS. For tickets, call **512-471-4811, ext. 310,** or write to **P.O. Box 7158, Austin, 78713; www.pbs.org/klru/ austin.**

Scenic Drives

Marble Falls Scenic Drive

Whatever you do, don't leave the Austin area without seeing at least some of the marvelous scenery. I suggest a side trip between Austin and **Marble Falls**—especially if you are fortunate enough to be here in spring when the bluebonnets and Indian paintbrush line the highways. The drive covers almost the same route as the Hill Country Flyer, but on a farm road instead of a railroad track.

From Austin, drive about 10 miles northwest on U.S. Hwy. 183 to Cedar Park. From there, head west on Road 1431 to Marble Falls, a distance of about 30 miles. It's one of my favorite scenic drives—narrow and winding, but if you don't get in a hurry, you'll see spectacular displays of spring colors in the fields of wildflowers and rolling hills alongside Lake Travis.

Before you return to Austin, stop by **Michel's Drug Store** in downtown Marble Falls **(216 Main St., 830-693-4250)** to sample a treat from an old-fashioned soda fountain and catch up on the latest gossip. Or if you've got time for a meal, and have the money, I recommend **Russo's Texitaly** (that's native talk for Italian food in Texas), just south of Lake Marble Falls on a bluff off U.S. Hwy. 281, overlooking the town **(830-693-7091).** Russo's offers good food and a fantastic view in a place where old-time songwriter Oscar Fox was inspired to write "Hills of Home."

Marble Falls and Lake Travis are part of the Highland Lakes region, which is covered in detail in The Hill Country chapter.

Lake Travis at sunset, west of Austin. Photo courtesy of the Texas Department of Tourism.

Shopping

The Drag

Yes, it's called the Drag, and it's the **area bordering the west side of the University of Texas campus** that is a popular dining and see-and-be-seen district for students. Of course it's loaded with bookstores, college and otherwise (Austin's bookstore sales are highest per capita of the fifty largest U.S. cities).

Made in Austin

Here are some shops around town that make for pleasant shopping trips: **Clarksville Pottery,** featuring handcrafted pottery from dinnerware to door hangings **(4001 N. Lamar Blvd. and 9722 Great Hills Trail, 512-454-9079, clarksville@jumpnet.com, www.citysearch.com). Stonehouse Gallery,** offering Tex-Mex merchandise from jewelry to furniture **(5013 Duval, 512-453-0190, www.city search. com). Josephine,** a boutique with the latest Austin fashions and glamorous accessories **(3709 Kerbey Ln., 512-452-7575). Yard Dog,** an art shop with rural southern folk art **(1510 S. Congress Ave., 512-912-1613). Simply Divine,** offering all-cotton clothing for women and children **(1606 S. Congress Ave., 512-444-5546, www.citysearch.com). Your Living Room,** a furniture store stocked with merchandise made by Texas artists **(220 S. Congress Ave., 512-320-9909, yourlivingroom@msn. com). Buzz Design Studio,** a warehouse studio and hangout for a variety of Austin artists who design beds, chairs, bowls, jewelry, whatever **(108 W. 2nd St., 512-302-3732).**

Old Bakery and Emporium

Built as a bakery by Swedish immigrant Charles Lundberg in 1876; now it's a craft shop selling handicrafts and some baked goods. Open Mon.–Fri. 9 A.M.–4 P.M.; additional hours during summer and December, Sat. 10 A.M.–3 P.M. **1006 Congress Ave.; 512-477-5961; www.citysearch.com.**

Tours

AERIAL TOURS

Hot-Air Ballooning

Aerial trips are available throughout the Hill Country and the Highland Lakes region from **Austin**

Aeronauts (512-440-1492) and **Balloonport of Austin (512-835-6058).** Dawn flights are the most popular.

BOAT TOURS

Capitol Cruises

Excursions on Town Lake and Lake Austin, both within the city limits, for family outings, sunset cruises, bat-watching (in season), or private parties; catering available. Also pontoon, paddleboat, canoe, and kayak rentals. Cruises depart from the Hyatt Regency dock on Town Lake, **208 Barton Springs Rd.; 512-480-9264; capcruis@onr.com; www.io.com/~capcruis.**

Lone Star Riverboat

Sightseeing trips on Town Lake aboard a genuine paddle wheeler—a 90-minute cruise past the mouth of Barton Creek and Zilker Park through a wilderness area of limestone cliffs, huge bald cypress and native pecan trees, and waterfowl including great blue herons. Captain Mike also offers boat trips to the South Congress Avenue Bridge when the Mexican free-tail bats are flying, between April and October. Sightseeing trips March–Nov.; charter cruises year-round. Departs from the Hyatt Regency dock on Town Lake. **512-327-1388; captmike@flash.net; www.city search.com/aus/lonestar.**

WALKING TOURS

The Austin Convention and Visitors Bureau Tours

The **Congress Avenue Tour** includes downtown Austin and Sixth Street. It's a 90-minute guided tour that departs from the south steps of the capitol, and you'll hear a lot of stories about Texas politics on the way. The **Bremond Block Tour** is a guided walk past a rare collection of old homes in one of Austin's historic districts; it includes a stroll by the governor's mansion. The **Driskill Hotel Tour** covers the corridors and open spaces of one of the city's oldest and most majestic hotels. The **Hyde Park Tour,** a self-guided outing, looks at Victorian and bungalow-style homes along tree-shaded streets in another historic neighborhood. For details and booklets on these walking tours, call the **Convention and Visitors Bureau, 512-478-0098.**

Wagering

Manor Downs

Quarterhorse racing with pari-mutuel betting; spring and fall. About 12 miles east of Austin, **off U.S. Hwy. 290; 512-272-5581.**

Wildlife Viewing

Bat-Watching

Austin is home to the largest urban bat population in the world. Between April and October, bat enthusiasts gather on the Congress Avenue Bridge over Town Lake at sunset to watch almost a million Mexican free-tail bats emerge in search of an evening meal. On the north bank of Town Lake, Bat Conservation International has built an observation deck. If you prefer more comfortable viewing, try the cafe or the Shoreline Grill in the **Four Seasons Hotel (98 San Jacinto Blvd., on Town Lake),** where the waiters announce bat flights as the animals pass by.

Wineries and Breweries

Celis Brewery

Belgian brewmaster Pierre Celis produces three brews: Celis White, Celis Pale Bock, and Celis Golden. Tours Tues.–Sat. 2 P.M. and 4 P.M. Reservations recommended. **2431 Forbes Dr.; 512-835-0884; www.celis.com.**

Slaughter Leftwich Winery

Transforms grapes grown at a vineyard near Lub-

Bats coming out at dusk at the Congress Avenue Bridge in Austin. Photo courtesy of Texas Highways *magazine.*

bock into award-winning wines. The native-stone facility has a panoramic view of Lake Travis and the Hill Country. Wine-tasting room open daily 1–5 P.M. Tours year-round Sat.–Sun. 1–5 P.M., plus Thurs.–Fri. July–Aug. From Austin, take Ranch Rd. 2222 west to Ranch Rd. 620, then south past Mansfield Dam. From there it is 1 mile to the winery at **4209 Eck Ln.; 512-266-3180.**

Festivals and Events

January

Red-Eye Regatta

A New Year's Day boat race featuring fifty first-class keel-boat crews competing at the Austin Yacht Club at Lake Travis; **512-266-1336.**

February

3M Half-Marathon

Early February. A 13-mile footrace from Gateway Plaza at Loop 360 and U.S. Hwy. 183 that drops through the city and finishes at House Park Field on Shoal Creek Blvd. This is one of the events listed by *Runner's World* magazine as among the 100 best races; **512-472-3254; www.3m.com/races.**

Carnaval Brasileiro

Austin's version of Rio de Janiero's Fat Tuesday, this festive extravaganza specializes in conga lines and lavish costumes. At the City Coliseum; **512-320-1553.**

Motorola Austin Marathon

Mid-month. From Gateway Plaza to Auditorium Shores; race has an overall drop of 400 feet, with scenic views of the Hill Country; **512-343-1164, fax 512-343-5407; www.runtex.com.**

March

Austin Downtown Conjunto Festival

Celebrates Tex-Mex border culture with 2 days of music and festivities **at Mexic-Arte Gallery, 5th St. and Congress Ave.; 512-480-9373.**

Austin International Poetry Festival

Poets from around the world unite to read their works and present a workshop; **512-416-7435; www. hyperweb.com/aipf.**

Greater Austin Open

A tournament on the Nike Tour in professional golf. See future stars compete for prize money at the Hills of Lakeway, one of Jack Nicklaus's challenging golf courses in the Hill Country (overlooking Lake Travis, west of Austin); **512-261-7200; www.golf.com/tour/ nike/austin.**

Jerry Jeff Walker's Birthday Celebration

Three-day celebration of Austin's greatest name in music; dances, rodeo events, and a Saturday-night performance **at the Paramount Theater, 713 Congress Ave.; 512-472-5470; www.thepara mount.org.**

South by Southwest Music Festival

Free concerts and general craziness for a whole week while bands from all over converge in Austin to play their music and to be discovered. This event gives unknown bands an audience and an avenue to move on to better things; **512-467-7979, fax 512-451-0754; sxsw@sxsw.com; www.sxsw.com.**

Travis County Livestock Show and Rodeo

Livestock exhibits, auctions, cook-offs, and oh yes, a rodeo **at the Texas Exposition and Heritage Center, 7311 Decker Ln.; 512-928-3710; www. austinrodeo.com.**

Zilker Kite Festival

More than 200 handmade kites, varying in size from a postage stamp to 60 feet long, fill the city's skies at this spring ritual; **512-478-0905.**

April

Capitol 10,000 Road Race

Listed as one of the top 100 road races in *Runner's World* magazine, this is Austin's biggest race, with thousands of participants. **Starts at 15th St. and Congress Ave.; 512-445-3598.**

Eeyore's Birthday Party
Usually the last week of the month. An outdoor festival honoring the Winnie the Pooh donkey and featuring costume contests, face painting, maypole wrapping, and live music. **In the area of Lamar Blvd. and Martin Luther King Jr. Blvd.; 512-448-5160.**

Hill Country Wine and Food Festival
First or second weekend in the month. Sample some of the best wines in Central Texas; a must for wine enthusiasts. The festival is headquarted at the **Four Seasons Hotel; 512-329-0770.**

Safari
An environmental festival with tours through discovery labs, bird exhibits, and wildlife exhibits. **Austin Nature and Science Center, 300 Nature Center Dr.; 512-327-8181.**

Schlotzsky's Bun Run 8K and 5K Fun Walk/Run
A very popular run/race for everyone in Austin's favorite park, with challenging, rolling hills and a festive finish.

Spamarama
Usually the last weekend of the month. Zany festival celebrating potted pork meat, Spam dish contests, food, sports, and live music. **On the shores of Town Lake; 512-280-7961.**

Wildflower Days at the Lady Bird Johnson Wildflower Center
Blooming season for most of Texas's most popular wildflowers produces a river of colors in early spring and a perfect time to wander through the wildflower fields. **4801 LaCrosse Ave.; 512-292-4100; www.wildflower.org.**

May

Cinco de Mayo
This celebration of Mexico's defeat of the French on May 5, 1862, includes mariachi bands and tejano music, dancing, eating, crafts exhibits, and a menudo cook-off. At **Fiesta Gardens on Town Lake; 512-499-6720.**

Fiesta Laguna Gloria
The state's largest art show, held as a fund-raiser for the Laguna Gloria Art Museum; usually the third weekend in May. **3809 W. 35th St.; 512-458-8191; www.amoa.org.**

Flora Rama
Sharpen your gardening skills at one of the largest flower and garden vendor gatherings in the state; more than 100 booths. **Zilker Botanical Gardens, 2220 Barton Springs Rd.; 512-477-8672.**

Old Pecan Street Festival
Held every May and September, this event includes a mix of musical acts, street performers, specialty foods, and children's events. **Along 6th St.** (the modern name for the route formerly known as Pecan Street); 512-478-1704.

Zilker Park Bluegrass Festival
Bluegrass bands, workshops, food, and music, plus children's activities. **In Zilker Park on Barton Springs Rd., east of Loop 1; 512-218-1567.**

June

Cedar Chopper's Festival
Mid-month. Arts and crafts, a carnival, and a parade topped off with a county and western dance Saturday night. **In the city of Cedar Park, 15 miles northwest of Austin on U.S. Hwy. 183.**

Clarksville/West End Jazz and Arts Festival
A celebration of Austin's West End, a predominantly African American neighborhood; **512-477-9438.**

Green Mesquite Rhythm & Blues Festival
Usually first weekend in June. A celebration of Austin's homegrown blues acts; **512-479-0485.**

Hyde Park Historic Homes Tours
Turn-of-the-century homes open their doors to the public on Father's Day every year. **Just north of the University of Texas campus in Hyde Park; 512-458-4319.**

The New Texas Festival
Throughout the city; a celebration of the vocal arts,

featuring concerts, visiting artists, and free music; a unique and exciting musical experience; **512-476-5775.**

July

Austin Aqua Festival

Parades, pageants, and water-related contests. Town Lake, just south of downtown; **512-472-5664.**

Bastille Day at the French Legation

French music and fencing matches as the city's oldest existing structure is opened up to food, wine, pastries, and fashions. **At 8th and San Marcos Sts.; 512-472-8180.**

Freedom Festival

Annual Fourth of July celebration; live music and an impressive fireworks and laser demonstration. In Zilker Park.

Frontier Days

Locals reenact the Sam Bass shoot-out and recall the good ol' days with music, dancing, and a carnival. Old Settlers Park, in the northern Austin suburb of Round Rock; **512-255-5805.**

August

KHFI/Z102 Great River Raft Race

A fun and frivolous festival featuring all kinds of home-made watercraft cruising on Town Lake; **512-474-9233.**

September

Diez y Seis

Mid-month. A week-long celebration of Mexican independence, featuring folk dancing, tejano and conjunto music, mariachi bands, a pageant, and plenty of Mexican food; **512-482-0175.**

Pioneer Farm Fall Festival

An 1880s cotton farm celebrates the pioneer spirit as artisans demonstrate their skills, and fiddlers (and others) provide old-time entertainment. **Jourdan-Bachman Pioneer Farm, 11418 Sprinkle Cut-Off Rd.; 512-837-1215.**

October

Austin Heart of Film Festival

Showcases films and offers screenwriters educational

Wild turkey in a stream near Marble Falls.

workshops. **The Driskill Hotel, 116 E. 6th St.; 512-478-4795.**

German American Day

A celebration of German heritage in Texas. **German Free School Building, 507 E. 10th St.; 512-482-0927.**

Halloween on Sixth Street

A 7-block street party where everybody puts on costumes and enjoys the flavor of Sixth Street; **512-476-5461.**

Hoop-It-Up

Mid-month. Annual three-on-three basketball competition with more than 900 teams engaging in all kinds of play. Located in **downtown Austin on Sixth St.; 1-800-926-2282, 512-474-5171 (Austin Convention and Visitors Bureau).**

International Children's Festival

Dance, music, theater, and hands-on activities engage children and represent traditions from around the world. **Fiesta Gardens, on Town Lake; 512-472-2494.**

The Mediterranean Festival

Annual eating frenzy as chefs serve traditional dishes of Ethiopia, Palestine, Lebanon, and Greece, and teach customs of their respective countries. **St. Elias Eastern Orthodox Church, 408 E. 11th St.; 512-476-2314.**

Texas Wildlife Exposition

Celebrate the great outdoors and learn new fishing, boating, and hunting tips from the experts. At headquarters of the **State Parks and Wildlife Department, 512-389-4472.**

Wells Branch Homestead Festival

Pioneer costumes and demonstrations of blacksmithing, quilting, lace-making, soap making, and candlemaking; hosted in an 1850s log cabin that serves as a working museum. **Wells Branch Homestead, 2106 Klattenhoff Dr.; 512-251-9814; www.wellsbranchmud.com.**

December

Austin Symphony "Holiday Pops"

Picnics and live music to ring in the New Year. Palmer Auditorium, **corner of Riverside Dr. and S. 1st St.; 512-476-6064.**

Trail of Lights at Zilker Park

The ultimate Christmas celebration in Austin, filled with candy canes, snowmen, Christmas trees, and decorations; attracts large crowds to the park; **512-476-5461.**

Victorian Christmas Celebration

Annual holiday observance at the O. Henry Home, **409 E. 5th St.; 512-472-1903; www.ci.austin.tx.us/parks/ohenry.htm.**

Yulefest

Zilker Tree Lighting Ceremony, a tree-lighting that lasts all month, and Yule Run, a 3-mile Fun Run through Zilker Park; **512-397-1468, 512-480-3015.**

Recreation

You'll find a multitude of choices for recreational activities around Austin. Among them are water sports on Lake Travis, canoeing and paddle-boating on Town Lake, picnicking and camping at the Lower Colorado River Authority parks, and biking and hiking along Barton Creek. There's more: swimming in an outdoor paradise at McKinney Falls State Park, boating down Lake Austin, golfing at one of Austin's many first-class courses.

Biking

Barton Creek

A 7-mile scenic ride through a surprisingly untouched area within Austin where you can appreciate wild plants and birds along the route. Keep your eyes on the road, because you share the trail with hikers. **Located in Zilker Park** (south side of Town Lake on Barton Springs Rd., in west Austin).

McKinney Falls State Park

Biking areas are set aside in one of the Hill Country's outdoor paradises. Thirteen miles south of the state capitol building, **off U.S. Hwy. 183; 512-243-1463.**

Rocky Hill Ranch Mountain Bike Resort

A refreshing break from the noise and stress of the city, this resort has 30 miles of trails guaranteed to please all levels of mountain bikers. The trail system, spread over the resort's 1,200-plus acres, is graded for individual rider skill levels: green trails for beginners; blue trails for the advanced biker, offering challenging slopes, stream crossings, and technical riding; and black trails for the experts, with very challenging slopes, crossings, and technical riding. Bring your camping gear and stay in one of hundreds of camping spots ranging from pine forests to creekside playgrounds. **On Farm Road 153 about 2 miles south of Buescher State Park** (which is about 10 miles southeast of Bastrop, near Smithville); **512-237-2241.**

Town Lake

An easy ride around Town Lake in the center of Austin. Enjoy the lake, Barton Creek, and the beautiful scenery, especially in early spring. Watch out for joggers and hikers.

Veloway

A popular landmark with a 3-mile surface that's terrific for biking and in-line skating. Located next to the National Wildflower Research Center at **4801 LaCrosse Ave.; 512-480-9821.**

Bird-Watching

Grab your binoculars. The Austin–Hill Country area is on the migration path of countless species of birds and is the nesting area of many more. **Austin Audubon Society, 512-926-8751.**

Golfing

Here's a selection of public golf courses worth taking a swing at in Austin and the surrounding area.

AUSTIN

Barton Creek Resort and Country Club

8212 Barton Club Dr.; 512-329-4000, 512-329-4001.

Bluebonnet Hill Golf Club

9100 Decker Ln.; 512-272-4228.

Circle C Ranch Golf Club

11511 Road 1826; 512-288-4297.

Hancock Park Golf Course

811 E. 41st St.; 512-453-0276.

Jimmy Clay Golf Course

5400 Jimmy Clay Dr.; 512-444-0999.

Lions Municipal Golf Course

2901 Enfield Rd.; 512-477-6963.

Morris Williams Municipal Golf Course

4305 Manor Rd.; 512-926-1298.

River Place Golf Course and Country Club

4207 River Place Blvd.; 512-346-6784.

Riverside Golf Course

1020 Grove Blvd.; 512-389-1070.

OTHER TOWNS IN THE AREA

Blackhawk Golf Club

225 Kelly Ln., Pflugerville; 512-251-9000.

Crystal Falls Golf Course

3400 Crystal Falls Pkwy., Leander; 512-259-5855.

Forest Creek Golf Club

99 Twin Ridge Pkwy., Round Rock; 512-388-2874.

Kurth-Landrum Golf Course

Southwestern University campus, Georgetown; 512-863-1333.

Lockhart State Park Golf Course

Four miles southwest of Lockhart, off U.S. Hwy. 183; 512-398-3479.

Lost Pines Golf Club

In Bastrop State Park; 512-321-2327.

Luling Golf Club

On U.S. Hwy. 80, 2 miles north of I-10; 830-875-5114.

Mustang Creek Golf Course
Two miles north of Taylor, off U.S. Hwy. 79 north; 512-365-1332.

Pine Forest Golf Club
2509 Riverside Dr., Bastrop; 512-321-1181.

Point Venture Country Club
422 Venture Blvd., Leander; 512-267-1151.

Hiking
Take your choice of some of the following great hiking opportunities in and around Austin.

Barton Creek
A day-hike through a surprisingly wild area within Austin, about 16 miles round-trip through a rugged, wooded canyon. Barton Creek is the city's longest and least-developed hiking trail. It is also frequented by mountain bikers, so keep an eye open as you round the corners. Use care crossing the creek if it's running high. Best time to hike is from fall through spring; there is drinking water at the trailhead. **Located in Zilker Park** (south side of Town Lake on Barton Springs Rd., in west Austin). Maps for hikers are provided by the **Austin Parks and Recreation Department, 512-499-6700.**

Buescher State Park
A fairly easy day-hike, about 8 miles round-trip through a dense forest of pines; similar to the hike through the Lost Pines at Bastrop State Park. Buescher Park, however, is a lot more secluded than Bastrop Park, so if you like doing things by yourself, this may be the place. The trail starts in a woodland of oak and juniper, but then the pines come into play not far from the trailhead. You'll pass a small pond, and later cross over a footbridge in a valley at about the halfway point on the hike. It's a beautiful walk, but, like the Bastrop hike, insects can be a nuisance in spring and summer. Be sure to carry water. Pick up a trail map at park headquarters. The park is about 10 miles southeast of Bastrop, **off Hwy. 71,** and 2 miles north of Smithville; **512-237-2241.**

Hamilton Pool
An easy day-hike along a cypress-lined creek; about 2 miles round-trip. Water is available at Hamilton Creek,

but purify it if you take it from the creek. Maps are available at the Hamilton Pool headquarters. The walk takes you by a pool of water fed by a 45-foot waterfall and into a narrow canyon lined with bald cypresses. Cliff swallows nest high up on the overhanging cliffs, and ferns sprout from seeps in the canyon walls. Hamilton Pool is a popular place, especially during the summer; be prepared to contend with crowds if you go on weekends. About 30 miles northwest of Austin, **off State Hwy. 71; 512-264-2740.**

Lake Georgetown
A 16-mile hiking and backpacking route named the Good Water Trail encircles Lake Georgetown in Cedar Breaks Park and Russell Park. Immediately northwest of Georgetown (about 20 miles north of downtown Austin), **off I-35; 512-863-3016.**

Lost Pines
A moderate walk or overnight hike in the Lost Pines of Texas, about 8 miles round-trip through dense forest. The well-marked trail makes a large, beautiful loop through lush loblolly pines, which are rare in this part of the state. Ticks, chiggers, and mosquitoes are common, especially from spring through summer, and summer can be very hot. The best time for hiking is fall through spring. Take plenty of water with you, because there's no place to fill up along the way. You can get a map at park headquarters. If you want to spend the night, you'll need a camping permit from the park. **Located in Bastrop State Park,** just east of Bastrop **on State Hwy. 21; 512-321-2101; www.tpwd.state.tx.us/park/bastrop.**

McKinney Falls State Park
A 3-mile hiking trail within the park, with interpretive trails, rock shelters, and shady rest stops along the way. The park is 13 miles south of the state capitol building, **off U.S. Hwy. 183; 512-243-1643; www.tpwd.state.tx.us/park/mckinney/mckinney.htm.**

Town Lake
An easy hike around Town Lake in the center of Austin. About 4.5 miles round-trip, though options permit the hike to be extended to 10 miles. Water is available at the trailhead by the auditorium and Zilker Park. As you hike, forget the bridges, highways, and

Hamilton Pool, west of Austin. Photo courtesy of the Texas Department of Tourism.

traffic noises. Instead enjoy the lake, Barton Creek, and the beautiful redbud trees that bloom in early spring. Watch out for joggers and cyclers.

Parks and Camping

Bastrop State Park

Bastrop's 3,500 acres include a golf course and a 10-acre lake, as well as 72 campsites (18 with water only, 54 with water and electricity) plus a primitive camping area for backpackers. The park also offers 12 cabins, a 4-bedroom lodge, rest rooms, showers, a trailer dump station, dining hall with a kitchen for day use, a group camp with 4 dorms, playground, picnic area, and swimming pool. Fishing, 8.5 miles of hiking trails, and a scenic drive. One mile east of Bastrop, about 25 miles southeast of Austin **on State Hwy. 21; 512-321-2101** or **512-389-8900 (camping reservations); www.rtis.com/reg/bastrop/statepk.htm.**

Buescher State Park

Buescher is a 1,700-acre park with a 25-acre lake and 65 campsites (25 with water only, 40 with water and

electricity). There are 4 screened shelters, rest rooms, showers, a trailer dump station, a group picnic area, a group trailer area, a recreation hall with kitchen, and playground. Picnicking, swimming, fishing, 8-mile hiking trail, and a scenic drive. Located about 10 miles southeast of Bastrop, and 2 miles north of Smithville, **off State Hwy. 71 (P.O. Box 75, Smithville, 78957); 512-237-2241.**

Lake Austin and Lake Travis

Includes seven parks with campsites in the immediate Austin area. **Pace Bend Park** has 420 campsites and water/electric hookups, showers, trailer dump stations, and a boat ramp. **Mansfield Dam Recreation Area** has 36 campsites, a trailer dump station, and a boat ramp. **Sandy Creek Park** has 31 campsites, a trailer dump station, and a boat ramp. **Cypress Creek Park** has 10 campsites and a boat ramp. **Arkansas Bend Park** has 12 campsites and a boat ramp. **Bob Wentz Park** at Windy Point offers 6 campsites. **Lake Austin Metropolitan Park** has 20 campsites with water/electric hookups, showers, a trailer dump station, and a boat ramp. Lake Austin Metropolitan Park is managed by the **Austin Parks Department, 512-346-1831.** The other parks are operated by **Travis County, 512-472-7483,** by cooperative agreement with the Lower Colorado River Authority. (For more details on camping and other activities at Lake Travis and the other Highland Lakes, see The Hill Country chapter.)

Lake Bastrop

The lake 2 miles east of Bastrop State Park is divided into two recreation areas: the South Shore and the North Shore. The **South Shore** unit is still being developed, but it is available for groups by reservation; facilities include a picnic area, tables, grills, water, electricity, chemical toilets, a boat ramp, and bank fishing. The **North Shore** has 66 campsites (44 with water and electricity), 8 screened shelters, flush toilets, showers, a trailer dump station, snack store, and a boat ramp. Swimming and fishing. Located immediately northeast of Bastrop; **512-303-7666** or **512-389-8900 (camping reservations).**

Lake Georgetown

Includes three parks: **Jim Hogg Park** has a camping area, trailer area, electrical outlets, sanitary facilities, drinking water, showers, a trailer dump station, and a boat ramp. **Cedar Breaks Park** offers a camping area, picnic facilities, trailer area, electrical outlets, sanitary facilities, drinking water, showers, a trailer dump station, a boat ramp, and hiking trails. **Russell Park** has picnic facilities, sanitary facilities, drinking water, showers, a group shelter, swimming site, boat ramp, and hiking trails. Parks are **on the lake just northwest of Georgetown, some 20 miles north of Austin; 512-863-3016.**

Lake Granger

There are four parks on this lake: **Willis Creek Park** has 27 campsites, water/electric hookups, and a trailer dump station. **Friendship Park** has 13 campsites, showers, and swimming. **Taylor Park** has 48 campsites, water/electric hookups, a trailer dump station, and showers. **Wilson H. Fox Park** is the largest, with 58 campsites, water/electric hookups, a trailer dump station, showers, and swimming. Stilling Basin at the lake is open year-round, 24 hours a day, for fishing. **The lake is 15 miles northeast of Taylor between Farm Road 1331** (which goes east from Circleville) **and Farm Road 971** (which goes east out of Granger). Taylor is about 25 miles northeast of Austin, on U.S. Hwy. 79; **512-859-2668.**

Lockhart State Park

Lockhart offers 20 developed campsites (10 with water/electricity, 10 with water/electricity/sewage), primitive campsites, rest rooms, showers, a group picnic area, recreation hall with kitchen for day use, a playground, and a swimming pool and bathhouse. Also picnicking, fishing, and a 9-hole golf course. The park is 4 miles southwest of Lockhart, which is some 25 miles south of Austin, **on U.S. Hwy. 183; 512-398-3479.**

McKinney Falls State Park

McKinney has 84 campsites (14 with water only, 70 with water and electricity), rest rooms, showers, trailer dump stations, a group camp with 6 screened shelters, a group dining hall with kitchen, a youth-group primitive area, playgrounds, an interpretive trail, a 3-mile hike/bike trail, and historic structures. Also picnicking and fishing. The park is 13 miles southeast of downtown Austin **off U.S. Hwy. 183; 512-243-1643; www.tpwd.state.tx.us/park/mckinney/mckinney.htm.**

Rock Climbing

Limestone cliffs and rock formations west of Austin provide great opportunities for rock climbing.

You can also do your climbing indoors. **Pseudo Rock** offers a 5,000-square-foot climbing wall you can play on all day for $8. The climbers who work at Pseudo Rock are the best sources for information on outdoor climbing sites near Austin. Pseudo Rock is at **Second St. and San Jacinto Blvd.; 512-474-4376, fax 512-474-1973; www.world-quest.com/edge/pseudorock/index.html.**

Where to Eat

Unless you plan a long stay in the capital city, you're not likely to experience all the tastes of the town. But if your stomach can handle it, try some of the Tex-Mex food and a couple of steak houses. Save your urge for seafood until you get to the Gulf Coast.

The "hot kisses" at the **City Grill** rate as some of the most popular appetizers in town. They are stuffed jalapeño peppers and, yes, they're hot. The steaks are tasty, and the surroundings are elegant. **Corner of Fourth and Sabine Sts.; 512-479-0817.**

The heat of those jalapeño peppers is also worshipped at the more casual **Texas Chili Parlor,** where politicians and businesspeople alike hang out. The chili is famous, and is as tasty as it is hot—observe the ratings: X is for tenderfoots, XX is a barn burner, and XXX is considered volcanic. They also serve burgers and chicken dishes here, all moderately priced. **1409 Lavaca; 512-472-2828.**

The **1886 Lunchroom** at the Driskill Hotel is a great place to eat in style if you like the atmosphere of a grand old hotel. It's crowded at lunch, so go early. **116 E. 6th St.; 512-474-5911.** The next best thing to home cooking is **Threadgill's,** the definitive "Southern food" restaurant in the city, founded by Eddie Wilson. This is not just a restaurant. It's also a music hall, and a museum to boot. **6416 N. Lamar Blvd.; 512-451-5440.**

Guero's restaurant is located, appropriately enough, in an old feed store. The place serves up Tex-Mex food to customers, and my favorite is the peppery tortilla cheese soup. **1421 S. Congress Ave.; 512-447-7688.**

Basil's may be the best Italian eatery in town. 'Nuff said. **900 W. 10th St.; 512-477-5576.** And **Scholz Beer Garden** gets my vote for the best nachos, cheeseburgers, and beer in town, and the fare is inexpensive too. Scholz also serves up some good German dishes and barbecue. **1607 San Jacinto Blvd.; 512-474-1958.**

When James Michener was in Texas researching his novel about the state, he asked me to recommend a good place to eat barbecue. I did, and it turned out he didn't like it. He's from the Northeast, and people in that part of the country order barbecue for the meat, not the sauce. In Texas, unless you tell them otherwise, the meat is drenched in sauce. Funny thing is that today I like barbecue Northeastern style; like Michener, I get my sauce on the side. But however you order it, the Austin area has a lot of great barbecue restaurants. One that comes to mind is the **Salt Lick (on Camp Ben McCullough Rd. west of Austin, at 18001 Farm Road 1826, 512-894-3117).** Its sauce has an almost Oriental cast to it. And in the communities around Austin, you might try **South Side Market and BBQ** in Elgin **(1212 U.S. Hwy. 290 west, 512-285-3407); Louie Mueller BBQ** in Taylor **(206 W. 2nd St., 512-352-6206),** which has great atmosphere, if you can stand the smoke; **Bastrop BBQ and Meat Market** in Bastrop **(19 Main St., 512-321-7719); City Market** in Luling **(633 Davis, 830-875-9019); and Kreutz Market** in Lockhart **(208 S. Commerce, 512-398-2361),** where you can still get Cokes and Dr. Peppers in the small bottles. In Smithville, **Charlie's Joint (110 Main St., 512-237-3317)** is the place of choice for barbecue lovers. Most folks agree that Charlie's is weird, but the cookin' is just fine.

Where to Stay

You can relax like a king or camp out like a kid in the Austin area. It depends on your personal preferences and on how much you want to spend. The capital region offers a full range of lodging facilities, with all the standard hotel/motel chains, plus a few resorts and bed-and-breakfast establishments. You might want to send for the *Texas Accommodations Guide* as you plan your trip. It's published annually by the Hotel Review

Company—and it's free. Contact the company at **900 Congress Ave., Suite 201, Austin, 78701; 512-474-2996.** Meanwhile, here are some places for your consideration.

Austin–Lake Travis Bed-and-Breakfast
Hill Country executive home with southwestern decor. **4446 Eck Ln.; 512-266-3386.**

Austin's Wildflower Inn
New England country decor with beautiful garden. **1200 W. 22nd St.; 512-477-9639, fax 512-474-4188; kjackson@io.com.**

Barton Creek Resort
8212 Barton Club Dr.; 1-800-336-6158; www.bartoncreek.com.

Chequered Shade Bed-and-Breakfast
Countryside atmosphere for hiking, biking, wildlife-watching; 20 minutes west of Austin at **2530 Pearce Rd.; 512-346-8318.**

The Driskill Hotel
A grand old hotel in downtown Austin. **604 Brazos at E. 6th St.; 1-800-252-9367, fax 512-474-2214; www.driskillhotel.com.**

The Gardens on Duval Street
Elegant home in central Austin. **3210 Duval; 512-477-9200; www.io.com/~kjackson/index.htm.**

Hyatt Regency Austin on Town Lake
208 Barton Springs Rd.; 1-800-233-1234; www.hyatt.com/pages/ausraa.html.

La Casita
Bed-and-breakfast in a Hill Country guest cottage. In Granite Shoals at **1908 Redwood Dr.; 1-800-798-6443.**

Lake Austin Spa Resort
1705 Quinlan Park Rd.; 1-800-847-5637; info@lakeaustin.com; www.lakeaustin.com.

Lakeway Inn and Conference Resort
101 Lakeway Dr.; 1-800-525-3929; www.lakewayinn.com.

Rainbow Courts
Family owned and operated since 1918. In Rockdale
at **915 E. Cameron; 512-446-2361.**

Towns in the Area

Here's a look at attractions in some of the towns
around Austin: Elgin, Bastrop, Smithville, Dripping
Springs, Round Rock, and Georgetown. The towns
are presented clockwise around Austin, beginning with
Elgin to the east.

Elgin
Getting There: Elgin is on U.S. Hwy. 290, about 25
miles east of Austin. **Visitor Information: Elgin
Chamber of Commerce, 15 N. Main St., Elgin,
78621; 512-285-4515; www.elgintx.com.**

Established as a flag stop on the Houston and Texas
Central Railroad in 1872, Elgin (ELL-gun) owes its
existence to a major flood of the Colorado River in
1869. The railroad moved to Elgin when its first building site flooded.

The economy is light industrial, and at one time
Elgin was the Brick Capital of the Southwest. Today
it's known for its quaint Main Street and for hot sausage. Four companies make the sausage and sell it in
town; one is **Cross-town BBQ** at **211 Central Ave.;
512-281-5594.**

SEEING AND DOING

The Nofsinger Home
Built in 1906 of brick from a local clay pit, offers an
interesting view of the past. The home now serves as
the Elgin City Hall. Tours available. **310 N. Main St.;
512-285-4515.**

Bastrop
Getting There: Bastrop is on State Hwy. 71, about
25 miles southeast of Austin. **Visitor Information:
Bastrop Chamber of Commerce, 927 Main St.,
Bastrop, 78602; 512-321-2419, fax 512-303-0305;
www.bastroptexas.com.**

More than 125 structures listed on the National
Register of Historic Places are in this community
located along the original Old San Antonio road (El
Camino Real). Main Street is lined with century-old
structures housing antique shops, restaurants, and
specialty stores. A lot of the people making big money
in the high-tech business in nearby Austin live in
Bastrop.

SEEING AND DOING

Alum Creek
Here's where you'll find one of the best weekend flea
markets in the state, featuring mostly Texas relics,
genuine antiques, and early pioneer artifacts. Five
miles east of town **on U.S. Hwy. 71; 512-321-2101;
www.rtis.com/reg/bastrop/statepk.htm.**

Central Texas Museum of Automotive History
Eight decades of automotive history in about eighty-
five vintage cars, from Model Ts to a Dusenberg. Some
are old, some are rare, all are beautiful. Open April–
Oct. Wed.–Sat. 9 A.M.–5 P.M., Sun. 2–5 P.M.; and Nov.–
March, Fri.–Sat. 9 A.M.–5 P.M., Sun. 2–5 P.M. Twelve
miles south of Bastrop **on State Hwy. 304; 512-237-
2635; www.tourtexas.com/rosanky.**

Colorado Riverwalk
Stroll back into history along Bastrop's downtown
riverwalk, a joint project of the city, the Lower Colorado River Authority, and the Texas Parks and Wildlife Department.

Lock's Drug
Visiting Lock's is like stepping back into history. Furnished and equipped like a nineteenth-century doctor's
office and drugstore; includes an old-fashioned ice
cream parlor. **1003 Main St.; 512-321-2422.**

FESTIVALS AND EVENTS
Check with the **Bastrop Chamber of Commerce**
at **512-321-2419** for details on these events.

April—Yesterfest; Salinas Art Festival.
May—Iron Bridge Market Days.
July—Old Iron Bridge Patriotic Fest.
August—Homecoming Festival.
October—Iron Bridge Market Days.
November—Opera House Arts & Crafts Show.
December—Christmas Parade and Home Tour.

RECREATION

Bastrop State Park
A total of 3,500 acres of quiet, rolling parkland shaded by the Lost Pines, the only forest of pines in Central Texas. Camping, fishing, swimming, and hiking are only a few of the attractions; it even has its own golf course. One mile east of Bastrop on State Hwy. 21; 512-321-2101.

WHERE TO STAY

The Colony Bed-and-Breakfast
Historic two-story home with a lot of antiques. 703 Main St.; 512-303-1234.

Smithville
GettingThere: Smithville is on State Hwy. 71, about 13 miles southeast of Bastrop (and 40 miles southeast of Austin). Visitor Information: info@smith villeonline.com; www.smithvilleonline.com.

Smithville is the sort of small town that everybody likes. Shading oak trees dominate the city's streets, and the gently rolling waters of the Colorado River keep life comfortable.

Smithville has always been a railroad community. The Taylor, Bastrop and Houston Railroad came through in 1887 and the town boomed. Today an old caboose stands near a restored railroad ticket office at the Smithville Railroad Historic Park (102 W. 1st St., 512-237-2313). They're proud of their past in this town, and they're holding on to it.

SEEING AND DOING

Heritage House
Exhibits a wealth of historical archives and antiques. 602 Main St.; 512-237-4545.

WHERE TO EAT

Backdoor Cafe
One of the big attractions downtown, with its down-home meals. Owner Rob Remlinger cooks up two entrees a day, posts a menu outside, and has quite a reputation as a gourmet cook. 117 Main St.; 512-237-3128.

WHERE TO STAY

Moon Shadow Cabins in the Pines
Cabins, plus nature trails to explore. 147 O'Grady Rd., west of town off U.S. Hwy. 71; 512-360-5414; www.moonshadowcabins.com.

Dripping Springs
Getting There: Dripping Springs is on U.S. Hwy. 290, about 20 miles west of Austin. Visitor Information: www.drippingsprings.com.

Dripping Springs is mostly a ranching area and also serves as a bedroom community for Austin.

SEEING AND DOING

New Canaan Farms
Interesting for several reasons. You can take a tour of the facility where they make jam and jelly. You can also view a turn-of-the-twentieth-century kitchen, plus wildlife photographs by Cody Carlson. Also on the site is a large oak tree where Lyndon Johnson made his first political speech, when he was 22. Eight miles west of Dripping Springs on U.S. Hwy. 290; 512-858-7669.

Round Rock
GettingThere: Round Rock is at the intersection of I-35 and U.S. Hwy. 79, about 6 miles north of Austin. Visitor Information: Round Rock Chamber of Commerce, 212 E. Main St., Round Rock, 78664; 512-255-5805, fax 512-255-3345; www.austinmall.com/rr.

The town was named for a large, round rock in the bed of the brushy creek that runs through town.

SEEING AND DOING

Old Settlers Park
A favorite place in the area. At Palm Valley, 4 miles east of Round Rock on U.S. Hwy. 79, the highway to Taylor.

Palm House Museum
A restored founding-family home with authentic period furnishings, an elegant parlor, and a Swedish kitchen. It also houses the Chamber of Commerce. 212 E. Main St.; 512-255-5805.

Round Rock Cemetery

Holds the remains of Sam Bass, a notorious outlaw who was ambushed and killed in downtown Round Rock in July 1878. He was 27 years old. The cemetery is **1 mile west of town off Sam Bass Rd. (U.S. Hwy. 79).**

FESTIVALS AND EVENTS

Call **1-800-747-3479** or check with the **Round Rock Chamber of Commerce** at **512-255-5805** for details on these events.

February—Three-Legged Willie Distance Classic.
March—Sportsfest.
April—Daffodil Days; Easter Egg Hunt.
July—Old Settlers Annual Reunion and Fiddlers Competition; Texas State Fast Draw Competition.
September—Sam Bass BBQ Cook-off.
October—Old Settlers Bluegrass & Acoustic Music Festival; Outlaw Trail 100 Bicycle Tour; Haunted Hayrides.
November—A Chocolate Affair.
December—Christmas Family Night.

Georgetown

Getting There: Georgetown is on I-35, about 20 miles north of downtown Austin. **Visitor Information: Georgetown Convention and Visitors Bureau, corner of Main and 7th Sts., P.O. Box 346, Georgetown, 78627; 512-930-3545, fax 512-930-3587; www.georgetown.org.**

Georgetown was originally a stop for cattle drovers along the Chisholm Trail and later became an agricultural trade center. It is the site of Southwestern University, a prestigious Methodist school founded in 1840 and the oldest chartered university in Texas. The town square is right out of yesterday, and Georgetown is home to three historical districts that showcase more than 180 homes and other buildings.

SEEING AND DOING

Inner Space Cavern

The state's most accessible cavern; subterranean beauty of stalactites, stalagmites, and flowstones, plus remains of prehistoric mastodons, wolves, and ice-age animals. On I-35 at the south edge of Georgetown. **P.O. Box 451, Georgetown, 78627; 512-863-5545; www.innerspacecavern.com.**

Mar-Jon Candle Factory

Tour a factory that displays the world's largest collection of decorative candles. During the week visitors can watch candlemakers at work. **4411 S. I-35, Georgetown, 78627; 1-800-955-6973, fax 512-863-9597; www.thecandlefactory.com.**

Red Poppies

Georgetown claims to be the red poppy capital of Texas. Resident Henry Purl Compton collected poppy seeds in Europe during World War I and brought them back home. Poppies are now a big part of the city landscape, and a sea of poppies greets visitors every spring.

Walburg Mercantile Store

Don't ask me how a genuine master chef from Germany and a professional yodeler ever got together in this place, but we can all thank our lucky stars for it. Herbert Schwab prepares the best German food I've ever tasted, and he does it with a flair. Ronnie Tippelt yodels like a master from the Old Country, and his band entertains in the huge beer garden out back on Friday and Saturday nights between April and mid-November, weather permitting. And if you're really lucky, you'll be there when Wally the waitress dances to Ronnie's music. What a place! They start serving the German food at 5 P.M. Wednesday and Thursday, noon on Friday, 5 P.M. on Saturday, and noon on Sunday. Eight miles north of Georgetown on I-35, then 5 miles east on Farm Road 972 to the community of Walburg; **512-863-8440; www.austin360.com/eats/walburg/index.html.**

FESTIVALS AND EVENTS

Check with the **Gergetown Chamber of Commerce** at **512-930-3545** for details on these events.

March—Quilt and Stitchery Show at the Community Center.
April—Sertoma Bluebonnet Classic Car Show in San Gabriel Park; The Annual Red Poppy Trail to show off the poppies.
May—Mayfair in San Gabriel Park; Georgetown Fly-in and Static Air Show.
July—Fourth of July Family Festival.
August—Fiesta San Jose.

October—Heritage Weekend; Squarecrows Festival; Palace Theater Classic Car Parade and Sock Hop.
November—Annual Wurstbraten at Zion Lutheran Church.
December—Courthouse Holiday Lights display; Holiday Home Tour **(1-800-436-8696).**

RECREATION

Lake Georgetown

Built by the Army Corps of Engineers, the lake offers bird-watching, boating, swimming, hiking, and picnic and camping areas. Discover more than 250 plant and animal species native to Central Texas while walking along the hiking trails. Immediately northwest of town; **512-863-3016.**

WHERE TO STAY

Page House

A historic home with a garden. **1000 Leander Rd.; 512-863-8979.**

The Hill Country

Nobody has ever been quite sure exactly where the Texas Hill Country begins and ends. The problem is that everybody wants to live in the Hill Country. It's a tourist bonanza for any town that can advertise that it's a part of the Hill Country. For this book, we bound the Hill Country section on the east by Austin and neighboring towns, on the south by Bandera and the road to Rocksprings, on the west by Junction as it winds its way north to Mason, and on the north by Lampasas. There are a lot of folks who would widen those boundaries, and I'm usually one of them, but I've tried to divide up the state as simply as possible for new visitors. I give places like San Antonio, San Marcos, and New Braunfels their own chapters later in the book because they deserve their own full sections and descriptions.

The limestone hills of Central Texas gave the Hill Country its name. Elevation averages about 1,300 feet above sea level, and soft breezes and low humidity make this place a paradise. Beyond the mild climate, there's an intriguing culture in the Hill Country. It's a combination of small-town quaintness and Texas self-sufficiency. Most of the towns date back to the mid-1800s and were settled by Europeans of German, Polish, and Czech descent. The folks can be clannish and not so easy to know, but once you establish a friendship with them, they are friends for life.

When I first started traveling for the TV program *Eyes of Texas,* I spent a lot of time in the Hill Country, photographing its natural beauty and talking to the people. I was required to perform an unusual ritual each time I went to Fredericksburg or Bandera to film a story. First I had to stop at the local store or post office and introduce myself around to all the locals. Then I had to explain that I was from the big city (Houston) and that I was there to shoot pictures of the people and the town. Then I had to stand around and smile as the old-timers made fun of me and took potshots at Houston and all those folks who live in big cities.

After a while I would take out my camera and start taking pictures. The first ten or fifteen minutes were never any good because everybody was looking at the camera and waving and doing all the things people do when they are uncomfortable. About an hour into the visit, they would begin ignoring me, and the pictures would get good. The faces looked natural, and the flavor of the community unfolded.

Today I can go to a Hill Country town and some old-timer will step up and tell me right where to stand while I take his picture. Everybody's an expert at taking pictures these days. That's good for photographers but not so good for the towns, because a lot of the communities that were so natural and so special 15 years ago are now just one more tourist attraction in a state filled with tourist attractions.

Some of the cities, however, have remained special. Fredericksburg and Bandera fit that category. They are still great places to visit, and they've managed to hold onto their past quite well. In the 1980s I met a young man named Roy Bellows, who was struggling to make a living as a blacksmith in Fredericksburg. He was one of the new breed. His work was geared more toward art than shoeing horses. Roy managed to keep an old skill alive in a new era, and he's still around, at the same workshop on East Schubert Street **(830-997-7806).** Roy is constantly out there, forging

Getting There

The closest major airports are **San Antonio International Airport** in San Antonio and **Robert Mueller Municipal Airport** in Austin, and both offer rental cars and other such travel necessities.

It's easy to drive to the heart of the Hill Country from Austin. Almost every road heading west, north, or south will take you there. I-35 north from Austin is the highway to Waco, but if you work your way west and north on some of those smaller farm-to-market roads (Farm Roads) and state highways, you will eventually wind up in the Hill Country town of Lampasas. U.S. Hwy. 183 northwest out of Austin also takes you to Lampasas, but west of 183 are the Highland Lakes and the roads to Hill Country cities like Burnet, Llano, and Buchanan Dam. U.S. Hwy. 290 west of Austin takes you to Johnson City, Fredericksburg, and Kerrville—more Hill Country towns. South and west of Austin is some of the most fantastic scenery of all, with narrow, winding roads that take you through the likes of Buda, Driftwood, Blanco, and, eventually, Luckenbach. To drive deep into the Hill Country from San Antonio, just head northish on any thoroughfare—State Hwy. 16, I-10, U.S. Hwy. 281, I-35—and you'll get there.

Texas longhorns grazing in a pasture in the Texas Hill Country.

you through the Highland Lakes—one more very special part of the Hill Country.

Getting Around

Gray Line Tours (512-345-6789, 1-800-472-9546) offers Hill Country day-trips from Austin to the LBJ Ranch in Stonewall and to Fredericksburg for food and shopping for $42 a person. Gray Line in San Antonio also offers a Hill Country tour. It takes you to Fredericksburg for shopping and great ethnic food and a visit to the Chester Nimitz Museum, then to Stonewall, birthplace of Lyndon B. Johnson, and to the LBJ Ranch, and finally on to Luckenbach—except on Wednesdays, when the community is closed. That's right; the whole town is closed. That trip costs $35 for adults, $17.50 for children 5 to 12, and free for kiddos under 5.

Visitor Information

Buchanan Dam Chamber of Commerce
P.O. Box 282, Buchanan Dam, 78609; 512-793-2803.

Burnet Chamber of Commerce
705 Buchanan Dr., Burnet; 512-756-4297; www.burnetchamber.org.

Fredericksburg Convention and Visitors Bureau
106 N. Adams St., Fredericksburg, 78624; 830-997-6523, fax 830-997-8588; www.fredericksburg-texas.com.

Highland Lakes Tourist Association
P.O. Box 1967, Austin, 78767.

shapes out of iron and heat. But he says he can hardly get anything done for all the tourists who stop by to watch him work and to ask questions. He loves it.

The scenery in the Hill Country is spectacular, especially along the rivers like the Blanco, the Frio, the Guadalupe, and the Medina. Road tours, whether by car or bicycle, can put you into the middle of it all. Traveling State Hwy. 16 out of Bandera up to Kerrville, then west on Farm Road 337 to Frio Canyon and towns like Leakey and Utopia, makes for wonderful sightseeing. The Willow City Loop outside Fredericksburg is another favorite tour. The drive from Austin to Burnet takes

Kerrville Convention and Visitors Bureau
1700 Sidney Baker St., Suite 200, Kerrville, 78028; 830-792-3535, 1-800-221-7958, fax 830-792-3230; kerrcvb@ktc.com; www.ktc.net/kerrcvb.

Lago Vista Chamber of Commerce
20624 Ranch Road 1431; 512-267-7952; lago vista@prismnet.com; www.lagovista.org.

Major Attractions

Enchanted Rock State Natural Area

This park north of Fredericksburg is named for the giant granite rock on the site that may be more than a billion years old. The huge dome of the 500-foot-high Enchanted Rock takes in about 640 acres. Indian lore says it was once the site of human sacrifice. Some tribes were afraid to set foot on it; other used its height as a gathering place. For generations this rock was held in awe and reverence. Some early residents believed ghost fires flickered on the dome on moonlit nights. Some people even today think the rock is haunted, while others gather on it during moonlit nights in the belief it can be a source of spiritual power. Now and then at night the rock fills the air with creaks and groans, probably from contraction of the granite as it cools down.

The park is used year-round for picnicking and primitive camping in designated areas, but it's really best for rock climbing, rappelling, and hiking. The park presents some of the best challenges in the Southwest for rock climbing and rappelling, especially in the area known as Buzzard's Roost. Hiking trails wind in and out of the rock's many cliffs and crevices. A 4-mile loop trail negotiates some of the rock outcroppings, and a fairly difficult trail leads to the dome's crest. This trail takes you to a splendid view of the 1,600-acre park. The park has sites for tents, but not for RVs.

Enchanted Rock Park is listed as an archaeological district on the National Register of Historic Places. The state of Texas is proud of this place and sometimes restricts the number of daily visitors to help protect it from such problems as tree loss due to root exposure caused by the trampling of so many feet.

Two creeks, Sandy and Walnut, flow around the base of the dome. Some of the vegetation is typical of this part of the state: live oaks, mesquite, Texas persimmon, Mexican buckeye, prickly pear, and a variety of grasses. There are also some trees not ordinarily found in the Hill Country, like blackjack oak, hickory, and post oak. Some of the animals you might see while enjoying Enchanted Rock are turkeys, armadillos, white-tailed deer—and plenty of jackrabbits.

Enchanted Rock is open daily 8 A.M.–10 P.M. It's located **18 miles north of Fredericksburg on Ranch Road 965; 915-247-3903; www.wild texas.com/parks/ersna.htm.**

The Highland Lakes

One of the finest tourist attractions the Hill Country has to offer came on the heels of catastrophes many years ago. Following a series of deadly floods, Austin persuaded the state to dam the Colorado River in several places northwest of the city. (This isn't the river in Colorado; this one starts and ends in Texas.)

Ecologists are still screaming about how the dams destroyed ecosystems, but most Hill Country residents love the lakes that resulted. They have seven lakes to play in, and hundreds of miles of waterfront real estate to buy, sell, or rent. You'll find the "outdoor crowd" in the Highland Lakes. This is where campers, bikers, hikers, and hang gliders turn out.

From north to south, the seven lakes are Buchanan, Inks, LBJ, Marble Falls, Travis, Austin, and Town. Only Buchanan, LBJ, and Travis are of significant size. Lake Austin and Town Lake are within the confines of the city of Austin. The Lower Colorado River Authority operates a number of free or low-fee lakeshore campgrounds in the Highland Lakes area. The best time to visit is April, when the wildflowers are in bloom. The Highland Lakes town of Burnet has a Bluebonnet Festival the second weekend in April.

The Highland Lakes region extends northwest from Austin for 60 miles or so, and is accessible by a network of roads that encircle the lakes. Towns in the region include Burnet, Granite Shoals, Horseshoe Bay, Lago Vista, and Marble Falls. Sources of information on the region include the **Highland Lakes Tourist Association (P.O. Box 1967, Austin, 78767),** the **Burnet Chamber of Commerce (705 Buchanan Dr., Burnet; 512-756-4297, www.burnetcham ber.org),** and **www.highlandlakes.com.**

The following descriptions of each lake will give you an idea of the range of things you can see and do.

See the section on camping, later in this chapter, for details on campsites at each of the lakes.

Inks Lake

One of the more scenic reservoirs in the Highland Lakes system, 803-acre Inks Lake provides excellent year-round fishing. Lake records include a Guadalupe bass just under 3 pounds and a 33-pound striped bass. Inks Lake, also popular for boating and other water sports, has docks, marinas, and leisure homes. There's a golf course at Inks Lake State Park near Buchanan Dam. Inks Lake is south of Buchanan Dam on Park Road 4; **www.tpwd.state.tx.us/park/inks/inks.htm.**

Lake Austin and Town Lake

These two Highland Lakes are within the city of Austin. Check the Austin chapter for things to see and do at the lakes.

Lake Buchanan

This is the highest and broadest of the Highland Lakes, a 23,000-acre impoundment. Water sports and fishing are superb, with generous space for boating, skiing, and sailing. There are a number of beaches, docks, marinas, lakeside leisure-home developments, and public and commercial campgrounds. The lake's record fish catches include a 2.2-pound Guadalupe bass, a 3-pound white bass, and a 27-pound striped bass. The lake is located about **halfway between Burnet and Llano on State Hwy. 29; www.high landlakes.com/chamber.**

Lake Lyndon B. Johnson

A 6,300-acre lake edged by steep hills and granite domes, Lake LBJ has marinas, boat rentals, and launching ramps. Fishing records on the lake include an 11-pound hybrid striped bass, a 12-pound large-mouth bass, a 23-pound striped bass, and a 6-pound smallmouth bass. Water-skiing and sailing are popular.

Lake LBJ is just south of Kingsland, which is on Farm Road 1431 on the east side of the lake. Farm Road 2900 and other roads lead to recreational areas on the lake's west shoreline; **www.cxo.com/~kingsland.**

Lake Marble Falls

Scenic blue waters wind among the hills in this 780-acre impoundment. The lake divides up the landscape with the town of Marble Falls, and makes for some beautiful scenery in doing so. Fishing is good year-round, with record catches for largemouth bass at 5 pounds, smallmouth bass at 4 pounds, and striped bass at 18 pounds. Boating, sailing, swimming, and water-skiing are also popular here. The lake has boat ramps, city parks, picnic facilities, and a lakeside swimming pool; **www.highlandlakes.com/lakemarblefalls.**

Lake Travis

This is the second largest of the Highland Lakes, with a reservoir that covers almost 19,000 acres. Lake Travis is the closest large lake to Austin and, as you might expect, the busiest.

The lake, with a shoreline largely dedicated to camps, marinas, resorts, and leisure-home developments, is popular for boating, water-skiing, scuba diving, and sailing. The fishing records include Guadalupe bass, 3.6 pounds; striped bass, 30 pounds; hybrid striped bass, 13 pounds; largemouth bass, 8 pounds; white bass, 2 pounds. In addition to commercial facilities, six public parks offer camping. The most popular of the parks is McGregor, a day-use park with a beach that is often referred to as Hippie Hollow. The park is off Farm Road 620 east of Mansfield Dam and has long been a favorite hangout for swimming and hiking, and for sun worshipping au naturel.

Another favorite hangout, this one for people who would rather bend their arms than do outdoor exercises, is the back porch at the **Oasis Restaurant (off Farm Road 620, at 6550 Comanche Trail; 512-266-2442).** The word is that McGregor Park attracts a lot of topless sun worshipers, and that if you look real hard and use your imagination, you can see them from a vantage point at the Oasis. Or you can just go on down to the park and enjoy the view firsthand if you're not embarrassed. The sun worshipers aren't.

Windy Point County Park is 1.5 miles past McGregor Park, off Farm Road 620. It receives a steady year-round breeze, and is a popular spot for windsurfing, swimming, diving, and picnicking.

You can take sailing lessons on Lake Travis from the **Texas Sailing Academy** at **Commander's Point Yacht Basin (just off Farm Road 620 near Mansfield Dam; 512-266-2333). Emerald Point Marina (5973 Hiline Rd.; 512-266-1535)** provides slips for 500 boats, and a heated fishing pier. You can also arrange rentals and other boating services at other dock areas around the lake, such as Lake Travis Marina, Paradise Cove Marina, Dodd Street Marina, Eagle Ridge Marina, Yacht Harbor Marina, and Skip's Boat Rentals. The **Austin Yacht Club (5906 Beacon Dr., on the south side of Lake Travis, 512-266-1336)** hosts sailing regattas on Lake Travis each spring and fall.

Divers can explore the remains of several sunken boats in the lake. **Scuba International (512-219-9484)** and **Pisces Scuba (512-258-6646)** are just two of the outfits that rent diving equipment. There are several resort airstrips near the lake.

For maps and more details on facilities, contact headquarters of the **Lower Colorado River Authority, 3700 Lake Austin Blvd., Austin; P.O. Box 220, Austin, 78767; 512-385-7131; utaylor@flash.net; www.laketravis.com.**

Lyndon B. Johnson National Historical Park

This park honoring the 36th president of the United States, who died in 1973, actually has three different locations: his boyhood home, the Johnson Settlement down the street from the home, and the Johnson Ranch near Stonewall.

The one-story house where LBJ lived as a child is at G and Ninth Streets in Johnson City. A visitor center at the site offers exhibits, a bookstore, and audio-visual programs. Tours are conducted every half hour throughout the day. Open daily 8:30 A.M.–5:00 P.M. except Thanksgiving, Christmas, and New Year's Day. **830-868-7128.**

My sister, Pat, was married to a Secret Service agent who guarded the Johnsons after they left the White House. Pat, her husband, and their children lived in one of the family houses across the street from LBJ's boyhood home—and tourists often confused the two homes. Pat recalls explaining to tourists who found her working in the garden that she wasn't a Johnson relative. Finally, after deciding it was just too time-consuming to explain, she started smiling and waving back to tourists who wandered by the place. Some of you who have been to LBJ's boyhood home may think you waved at a member of the former first family, so I won't burst your bubble by describing my sister.

A couple of blocks from the home is the second part of this very special park, Johnson Settlement. This old ranch complex was owned by LBJ's grandfather and great-uncle from 1867 to 1872, and was a gathering point for several cattle drives. Many cabins and other structures date from the 1850s. Experts are on hand from time to time to show how soap was made, how cotton was woven, and how things were generally done before the industrial revolution reached Texas. Pastures with grazing Texas longhorn cattle reflect the frontier heritage.

Some 20 miles west of Johnson City, near Stonewall on U.S. Hwy. 290, is Johnson Ranch, the family cemetery, and the former Texas White House, where Lady Bird Johnson still resides. Tours are by National Park Service buses only, which take visitors on 90-minute visits to the ranch and cemetery. The ranch is open daily 10 A.M.–4 P.M. except Christmas. **P.O. Box 329, Johnson City, 78636; 830-868-7128; www.nps.gov/lyjo.**

Lost Maples State Natural Area

Tucked away in a remote canyon, at certain times, lies an autumn color display that rivals any in New England. If the weather has been kind, big-tooth maples blaze red, yellow, and orange, attracting thousands of color-crazed viewers in late October and early November. The maples date back to a time when the region was a lot wetter and cooler. Steep canyon walls along the Sabinal River protect the flora from dry winds and high summer temperatures. When the maples hit their peak colors, usually in the last two weeks of October, this normally quiet park gets real crowded, especially on weekends. After October 1, the park's maple hotline (**1-800-792-1112**, Texas only) offers a recorded color forecast to help you time your visit.

The most popular hike among the 10 miles of trail at the park is the easy Maple Trail (half a mile round-trip). It starts at the picnic area and winds along the Sabinal River through stands of maple, pecan, sycamore, and walnut. If you cross the river, you can link up with the East Trail, a 4-mile route that proceeds north along the river, then west to a primitive camping area, and on down along a steep ridge to an overlook before returning to the visitor center. The West Trail is a 3-mile loop between the top of Can Creek and Mystic Canyon.

The visitor center, with exhibits on local natural and cultural history, is open daily 8:30 A.M.–5 P.M.

Lost Maples State Park near Medina in the Hill Country. Photo courtesy of Texas Highways magazine.

The main campground has drive-in sites, and there are also eight primitive camping areas.

Lost Maples is 4 miles north of Vanderpool on Ranch Road 187, which is approximately 60 miles northwest of San Antonio. **P.O. Box 156, Vanderpool, 78885; 830-966-3413; www.tpwd. state.tx.us.**

Vanishing Texas River Cruise

If you like water, if you enjoy exploring, and if you love seeing something unusual, this is the adventure for you. It's a boat trip in search of bald eagles. The American bald eagle is rare these days, but about twenty to thirty of them winter at Lake Buchanan in the Highland Lakes region. The eagle-watching trips run daily between mid-November and late March, with peak viewing times in January and February.

It's a 2.5-hour trip that offers even more than eagle-watching. You are likely to also see great blue herons, egrets, terns, cormorants, and pelicans. The boat leaves from the northeast shore of the lake, off Farm Road 2341, passing some of the rugged cliffs

that surround the lake and traveling near the 50-foot-high falls of Fall Creek.

The trip actually runs year-around, and there's always something to see. From April to June, the cruise focuses on wildflowers. From July through October, it's scenery and wildlife. The boat operates every day except Tuesday, and sunset dinner cruises are also offered. **P.O. Box 901, Burnet, 78611; 512-756-6986; www.vtrc.com.**

Bandera Dude Ranches

Bandera bills itself as the Cowboy Capital of the World, but perhaps it should be the Dude Ranch Capital. There are eight dude ranches in the Bandera area, all catering to family vacations for city folks looking for a ranch experience.

The typical dude ranch offers trail rides, hayrides, barbecues, and recreation. Lodging is generally in rustic cabins, and meals are ranch-style. Guests aren't obliged to participate in the group activities and can make use of the facilities on their own, but most of them join in. After all, that's what they came for. Kids love these places.

Dixie Dude Ranch has been a working ranch since 1901 and probably offers the most authentic ranching experience. It has plenty of room for experienced horse riders, but it also offers trail rides for the less experienced. The Dixie is located **9 miles south of Bandera on Farm Road 1077; P.O. Box 548, Bandera, 78003; 830-796-7771, 1-800-375-7771, fax 830-796-4481; ranchweb.com/dixie/index.html.**

Mayan Ranch may be the best-known dude ranch in Bandera. The Mayan's 326 wooded acres are adjacent to the Medina River, and the scenery is spectacular. There's swimming, horseback riding, hiking, tennis, and even country dancing classes. The ranch is about **1.5 miles west of town; 830-796-3312.**

Silver Spur Dude Ranch was built in more recent times. It's a family-owned guest ranch with slightly more modern facilities. The Silver Spur is just beyond the Dixie Dude Ranch **on Farm Road 1077; P.O. Box 1657, Bandera, 78003; 830-796-3037, fax 830-796-7171; texastom@aol.com; www. ranchvacation.com/silvspur/default.htm.**

Other guest ranches in the Bandera area are the **Flying L Guest Ranch (P.O. Box 1959, Bandera, 78003; 830-796-3001, 1-800-282-5134, sales@**

flyingl.com, www.flyingl.com); **LH7 Ranch Resort** (P.O. Box 1474, Bandera, 78003; 830-796-4314, fax 830-796-7156); **Lost Valley Resort Ranch** (P.O. Box 2170, Bandera, 78003; 830-460-7958); **Diamond H Ranch** (5322 Highway 16 North, Bandera, 78003; 830-796-4820); and **Twin Elm Guest Ranch** (P.O. Box 117, Bandera, 78003; 830-796-3628).

Towns in the Area

You might say that the major attractions of the Hill Country are the many towns that call it home. Dotted throughout the Hill Country are towns big and small, each with its own enticements for the visitor. Get out your map and follow along as we tour the communities of this region. We'll start in Fredericksburg and then work our way out and around the Hill Country, in this order: Fredericksburg, Kerrville, Stonewall, Luckenbach, Llano, Burnet, Marble Falls, Lago Vista, Bandera, Medina, Welfare, Comfort, Camp Verde, Utopia, Leakey, Camp Wood, Rocksprings, Junction, Sonora, Brady, Mason, and Menard.

Fredericksburg

Getting There: Fredericksburg sits at the junction of U.S. Hwy. 290, U.S. Hwy. 87, and State Hwy. 16, some 70 miles northwest of San Antonio and roughly the same distance west of Austin. **Visitor Information: Fredericksburg Convention and Visitors Bureau, 106 N. Adams St., Fredericksburg, 78624; 830-997-6523, fax 830-997-8588; fbgchmbr@ktc.com; www.fredericksburg-texas.com.**

Fredericksburg is a great place for many things—including shopping. The town has more than its share of arts and crafts shops, and a lot of residents are turning out a great many original products, so allow time to browse through some of the shops. But that's really only the beginning of this fascinating place.

SEEING AND DOING

Admiral Nimitz Historical Center
The center is named after the U.S. admiral who accepted the Japanese surrender in World War II aboard the USS *Missouri*. Nimitz was born in Fredericksburg,

where his grandfather built the Steamboat Hotel in about 1852. This landmark structure—looming like a ship in the middle of the Hill Country—now houses the center's **Museum of the Pacific War.**

Also at the center is the **Garden of Peace,** a gift from the people of Japan; and the outdoor **History Walk,** lined with rare aircraft, tanks, and guns. The Nimitz Center also has the **Plaza of the Presidents,** recognizing U.S. presidents from Franklin D. Roosevelt to George Bush who served in the military during World War II. The plaza was dedicated September 2, 1995, the fiftieth anniversary of Nimitz's acceptance of the Japanese surrender.

The Nimitz Center is open daily 8 A.M.–5 P.M. except Christmas. **304 E. Main St.; P.O. Box 777, Fredericksburg, 78624; 830-997-4379; nimitz@ktc.com; www.nimitz-museum.org.**

Dulcimer Factory
John and Shirley Naylor make some of the finest dulcimers you'll ever lay eyes on, but the real fun is watching them work, play, and talk about their favorite musical instrument. **715 S. Washington St.; 830-997-6704.**

Fort Martin Scott
This is the site of the first federal fort established in Texas, 3 years after Texas joined the Union in 1845. It was constructed to guard frontier communities from Indians, but the German settlers had already reached a treaty of friendship with the Comanches so the fort wasn't really needed. The informal treaty between the settlers and the Comanches was never broken.

The fort, with twenty-one buildings, was active until 1853 and became a center of commerce for settlers, Indians, and soldiers. The only original structure still standing is an old guardhouse, now restored. The visitor center exhibits a miniature model of Fort Martin Scott along with artifacts, old documents, and interesting details about trade in those days. Beef cost 4 cents a pound. Other popular food items were sugar, rice, coffee, and bear grease.

The fort is open from March through Labor Day, Wed.–Sun. 9 A.M.–5 P.M.; and from Labor Day through February, Fri.–Sun. 9 A.M.–5 P.M. Located **2 miles east of Fredericksburg on U.S. Hwy. 290; 830-997-9895.**

Fredericksburg Herb Farm

This organic herb garden features rows of carefully tended flowering, culinary, and ornamental herbs harvested for gourmet vinegar, olive oils, seasonings, teas, blossom potpourris, bath potions, and body fragrances. You'll find hundreds of herb varieties, plus a country store, tearoom with herbal desserts, and a bed-and-breakfast. Open Mon.–Sat. 9:30 A.M.–5:30 P.M. and Sun. 1–4 P.M. **402 Whitney St.; 1-800-259-HERB, 830-997-8615; herbfarm@ktc.com; www.fredericksburgherbfarm.com.**

Fredericksburg Sunday Houses

Sunday houses were tiny dwellings maintained near a church as a weekend place of residence. They became popular in the late 1800s among farmers and ranchers around Fredericksburg. Their homes were too far away to allow time to ride into town on Sunday to go to church. So those who could afford it built these second homes in town.

Sunday houses remained a fixture for many years, until rural communities could afford to build their own churches. These former Sunday houses still dot the landscape in and around Fredericksburg and are easy to spot because they are very small and have very steep roofs. The Germans built the homes with steep roofs mainly out of habit: They had come from a country that needed steep roofs to shed winter snows. The houses had a more practical benefit in Texas, however. The steep roofs provided room for a loft, and that's where the children usually slept. Many of these houses have now been incorporated into the bed-and-breakfast craze, and serve as great places to stay as you travel through the country. The **Metzger Sunday House (231 W. Main St., 830-997-5612)** is just one of the Sunday house bed-and-breakfasts available in Fredericksburg. The **Fredericksburg Convention and Visitors Bureau (830-997-6523)** offers a list of the town's bed-and-breakfast operators.

Hallford's Pick Your Own Orchard

At this 100-acre orchard, you pick your own and pay by the box—a great experience for kiddos if you are there at the right time. And the right time is almost any time. They have twelve varieties of peaches, three varieties of nectarines, oriental persimmons, plums, blackberries, and tomatoes. Peaches of some kind or

other ripen from mid-May through mid-October. Persimmons ripen from October through December. The orchard is **on Farm Road 1631, 1 mile northeast of Fredericksburg; 830-997-3064, 1-800-880-4041.**

If you can't get to the orchard, you can buy from the **Peach Basket** at **334 W. Main St. in Fredericksburg.** You can also buy from the **Gillespie Co. Fruit Growers Co-op, on U.S. Hwy. 290 near the intersection of Farm Road 1623,** open daily 8:30 A.M.–7 P.M. And those Fredericksburg peaches are really good. I have friends who find an excuse to drive to the Hill Country every year just to load up on the peaches.

Check with the **Fredericksburg Convention and Visitors Bureau (830-997-6523)** for a list of other peach orchards in Gillespie County, and for other useful brochures and maps.

Pioneer Museum Complex

Operated by the Gillespie County Historical Society, the complex offers an 8-room furnished pioneer home and store, plus a barn, smokehouse, and log cabin. Of particular interest is a restored Sunday house. Open April–Oct., daily except Tues., 10 A.M.–5 P.M., and Sun. 1–5 P.M.; rest of the year, Sat. 10 A.M.–5 P.M. and Sun. 1–5 P.M. **309 W. Main St.; 830-997-2835; www.ktc.net/gchs/pioneer.htm.**

Vereins Kirche Museum

This reconstructed church was the first public building in Fredericksburg. It's an eight-sided structure that served as a school, meeting hall, and house of worship. Today it holds archives and local history. Open March–Sept., Mon.–Fri. 10 A.M.–3 P.M.; and Oct.–Feb., Mon.–Fri. 10 A.M.–3 P.M. **Market Square on W. Main St. in midtown Fredericksburg; 830-997-6523.**

Wineries

Bell Mountain/Oberhellman Vineyards offer tours and tastings with a Bavarian flavor on Saturdays at 11 A.M., 1 P.M., and 3 P.M. from the first Saturday in March through the second Saturday in December. Their stock includes a delicious wine that has a hint of jalapeños in it. Only in Texas! The winery is **14 miles north of Fredericksburg on State Hwy. 16; 830-685-3297.**

Pedernales Vineyards is open for tours and tasting Mon.–Sat. 9 A.M.–5 P.M. It's **5 miles south of town on State Hwy. 16; 830-997-8326.**

RECREATION

Lady Bird Johnson Municipal Park
An excellent 190-acre municipal park featuring a fully equipped RV site and facilities for swimming, tennis, volleyball, and badminton, plus an 18-hole golf course that's seldom crowded and is fun to play **(ladybird golf@fbg.net).** Also a shaded picnic area with grills, group pavilion, and a small lake for boating and fishing. Located **on State Hwy. 16, 3 miles south of Fredericksburg; 830-997-4202.**

Kerrville

Getting There: Kerrville is about 60 miles northwest of San Antonio on I-10. **Visitor Information: Kerrville Chamber of Commerce; 830-896-1155; www.kerrvilletx.com.**

Kerrville, like Fredericksburg, is a great place to shop for things Texan. It's also one of the state's most popular health and recreation centers; there are more than two dozen boys-and-girls camps nearby. It's also an active retirement area for senior citizens. Kerrville, and nearby Ingram and Hunt, have some delightful RV camps along the Guadalupe River.

Kerrville has been home to some pretty special people over the years. Jimmie Rodgers, the king of country music, had a home in Kerrville and lived here for a while. Ace Reid, one of my favorite cartoonists, grew up in Kerrville and never left. Ace's daily cartoon "Cowpokes" was published in hundreds of newspapers around the country, but he says he got most of the inspiration for his cartoons about a couple of goofy cowpokes simply by spending time at Frank's Bar in Kerrville. Unfortunately, the bar and Ace Reid are no longer around.

SEEING AND DOING

Cowboy Artists of America Museum
Here's a showcase for contemporary cowboy artists, including Joe Beeler, James Boren, and Melvin Warren. Permanent and rotating collections, plus special exhibitions and workshops. Open Mon.–Sat. 9 A.M.–5 P.M., Sun. 1–5 P.M., closed holidays. **1550 Bandera** **Highway (State Hwy. 173), Kerrville; P.O. Box 1716, Kerrville, 78029; 830-896-2553, fax 830-896-2556; webmaster@caamuseum.com; www.caamuseum.com.**

Hill Country Arts Foundation
Artists conduct classes here, and attractions include an art gallery, plus gift shop, studios, and theater in a scenic setting on the banks of the Guadalupe River. Outdoor theatrical productions are staged June through August. The visual arts center is open Mon.–Sat. 10 A.M.–4 P.M., Sun. 1–4 P.M. **507 State Hwy. 39 west, in Ingram, about 10 miles west of Kerrville; 830-367-5122, fax 830-367-5725; hcaf@ktc.com; www.hcaf.com.**

Hill Country Museum
Hill Country antiques, artifacts, and memorabilia in the former home of one of the men who first settled this area, Captain Charles Schreiner. **226 Earl Garrett St.; 830-896-8633.**

James Avery, Craftsman
Avery's focus is on jewelry made of gold and silver, and he's one of the best in the Southwest. Tours by appointment. **On Harper Rd.; 830-895-1122.**

Kerrville Camera Safari
The Wilson Haley Ranch is a drive-through ranch featuring native and exotic animals, from armadillos to zebras; also a petting zoo. Open 9 A.M.–sunset daily. Located **at the intersection of I-10 and State Hwy. 16, Kerrville; 830-792-3600; www.texashillcountry.com/kerrvill/areattr.safari.html.**

Mooney Aircraft Corporation
Fine aircraft on display; tours by appointment. Louis Shreiner Field. **Five miles south of Kerrville on State Hwy. 27; 1-800-456-3033, 830-896-6000, fax 830-896-8180; www.mooney.com.**

Old Ingram
Business buildings of the old section of Ingram now house art studios and galleries, along with antique shops, boutiques, and restaurants. **On loop off State Hwy. 39 and State Hwy. 27, about 10 miles west of Kerrville.**

Riverside Nature Center

Special programs for children blend cultural history with the area's natural history. The center has a wildflower meadow, walking path, and a butterfly garden. Open Tues.–Sat. 10 A.M.–2 P.M. **150 Francisco Lemos St.; 830-257-4837; mca@ktc.com; www.ktc.net/riverside.**

Stonehenge in the Hills

It's a replica of the original Stonehenge in England, built by an eccentric Texan named Al Shepperd. The Shepperd family invites travelers to walk through their version of Stonehenge anytime. They call it Stonehenge II, and it's 60 percent as tall and 90 percent as large in circumference as the original. It's located **about 20 miles west of Kerrville and 2 miles north of Hunt, on Farm Road 1340.** They don't give out their phone number, but you don't need reservations. Stonehenge II is open to tourists year-round.

RECREATION

Kerrville-Schreiner State Park

Five hundred beautiful Hill Country acres on the upper reaches of the Guadalupe River, with camping, shelters, RV hookups, rest rooms, picnicking, fishing, swimming, nature study, and hiking. Located **on the south edge of Kerrville off State Hwy. 173; 830-896-2093.**

YO Ranch

The YO is a working ranch where you can watch real cowboys at work and play, and where you can spend the night in comfort in century-old, antiques-filled cottages. The ranch, catering mostly to adults, also offers photography tours through its exotic-wildlife park for pictures of everything from emus to giraffes. The YO has the largest registered herd of longhorn cattle in the country. If you're really in the mood for a hoot, take part in the 3-day longhorn cattle drive staged across the ranch every Memorial Day weekend. Besides herding longhorns, you'll join in the campfire entertainment and chuckwagon cookouts. The cattle drive costs $175 a person if you bring your own horse—more if you rent one. Located at **Mountain Home, 18 miles northwest of Kerrville; 830-640-3222; www.dallassites.com/yoranch.**

Stonewall

Getting There: Stonewall is on U.S. Hwy. 290, about 9 miles east of Fredericksburg. **Visitor Information: Stonewall Chamber of Commerce, at LBJ State Park off U.S. Hwy. 290, Stonewall, 78671; 830-644-2735; www.tpwd.state.tx.us.**

Near Stonewall is the Johnson Ranch, the Johnson family cemetery, and the former Texas White House for Lyndon Baines Johnson. See the information on the LBJ National Historical Park earlier in this chapter for more details.

SEEING AND DOING

Grape Creek Vineyard

Bring a picnic lunch, buy a bottle of wine, and enjoy a relaxing picnic in the winery's pecan grove on South Grape Creek. You also can spend the night at the Inn on Grape Creek, a bed-and-breakfast overlooking the vineyard. The winery offers tours and tastings Tues.–Sat. 10 A.M.–6 P.M., Sun. noon–6 P.M. **Four miles west of Stonewall on U.S. Hwy. 290; 830-644-2710.**

Sauer-Beckmann Living History Farm

Costumed interpreters carry out the daily activities of a turn-of-the-twentieth-century Texas-German farm family year-round. Cows are milked, pigs are slopped, and eggs are gathered. Meals are cooked, butter is churned, and cheese is made. On a seasonal basis, visitors may see gardening, canning, butchering, and sausage making. The farm brings alive an authentic piece of history for people of any age. The farm is **in LBJ State Park in Stonewall; 830-644-2252; www.tpwd.state.tx.us/lbj.**

Wildseed Farms

This is a working farm where wildflowers are grown—not just bluebonnets, but wildflowers of all varieties. The country store at the farm has information on growing wildflowers, plus Texas memorabilia for purchase. You can also wander through a field of wildflowers—in season, of course. Operator John Thomas is called Johnny Wildseed in these parts. He is one of the largest wildflower seed producers in the country, having operations in Fredericksburg and near Houston, and hundreds of acres of farmland bursting with blooms. Says John: "I just wanted to put a little beauty in this world." He did! Wildseed Farms is open 9:30 A.M.–6 P.M. daily. **On U.S. Hwy. 290, 7 miles west of Stonewall on the road to Fredericksburg; P.O. Box 3000, Fredericksburg, 78624; 1-800-848-0078, 830-990-8080, fax 830-990-8090; www.wildseedfarms.com.**

Luckenbach

Getting There: It's easy to miss Luckenbach. It's not on a major highway, and souvenir seekers are forever stealing the city-limits signs. From Fredericksburg, go east on U.S. Hwy. 290 for about 6 miles and turn right (south) onto Farm Road 1376. Luckenbach is another 4.5 miles.

Luckenbach, population 25, was settled in the mid-1800s by German pioneers. It was a relatively obscure spot until the 1970s, when a genuine Texas character named Hondo Crouch put it on the map. Hondo opened a general store and beer joint in town and invited people like Jerry Jeff Walker and Willie Nelson to come by and jam now and then. The more they jammed, the more famous the name "Hondo Crouch" became. Waylon Jennings and Willie Nelson brought Luckenbach its first taste of fame when they sang, "In Luckenbach, Texas, ain't nobody feelin' no pain." Jerry Jeff Walker recorded his classic *Viva Terlingua* album right here in Luckenbach.

SEEING AND DOING

The truth is that Luckenbach has very little except a reputation, and that reputation keeps it alive (except on Wednesdays, when the whole town is closed). There is one unpainted general store/beer joint, a rural dance hall, and a sometimes blacksmith shop. But if you're in the area on a Sunday afternoon, Luckenbach is worth visiting. Musicians gather, and banjo pickers, guitar strummers, and fiddlers break into action beneath Luckenbach's grand old oak trees. Whittlers whittle and washer-pitchers pitch washers, while other locals play dominoes in the country store.

Hondo Crouch is no longer here, but a bust is on display outside the general store. Hondo's widow, Schotzie, owns an automotive parts business in nearby Fredericksburg, and she is almost as much a character as Hondo was. Her specialty is restoring Model T Fords, and she knows more about Model T parts that anybody I've ever met. But if you're interested in a Model T, bring plenty of money. The last time I

Children watching white-tailed deer in Kerr County, near Kerrville. Photo courtesy of Texas Highways *magazine.*

checked, a Model T restored by Schotzie Crouch went for about $15,000.

Llano

Getting There: Llano is near the northern tip of the Highland Lakes region, on State Hwy. 71 about 65 miles northwest of Austin. **Visitor Information: Llano Chamber of Commerce; 915-247-5354; contact@llanochamber.org; www.llanochamber.org; or info@llano.net; www.llano.net.**

Founded in 1855 on the spring-fed Llano River as a rough frontier village, the present-day farm and ranch community bills itself as the Deer Capital of Texas. Llano hosts many hunters seeking white-tailed deer during the fall and winter season. There is year-round fishing in the picturesque Llano River and nearby Highland Lakes. The Chamber of Commerce offers an entertaining and educational walking tour of the downtown area, a designated National Historic District. The chamber also has details on camping and picnicking available at Llano's city/county parks, some with RV hookups. Among the offerings are lake and pool swimming, fishing, boating, playgrounds, hiking trails, and a 9-hole golf course.

Burnet

Getting There: Burnet (BURN-it) sits at the intersection of U.S. Hwy. 281 and State Hwy. 29, in the Highland Lakes region, about 50 miles northwest of Austin. **Visitor Information: Burnet Chamber of Commerce, 705 Buchanan Dr.; 512-756-4297; www.burnetchamber.org.**

Called the Bluebonnet Capital of Texas by some, this is a year-round tourist destination. It offers shopping for antiques on a historic town square, and beautiful scenery in or out of season supplied by outcroppings of granite and underground caverns, and the fact that Burnet is the heart of the Highland Lakes region. There are plenty of camping facilities and excellent fishing on nearby Highland Lakes, and hunters have little problem taking deer, wild turkey, and dove in season.

SEEING AND DOING

Buchanan Dam Visitors Center

Spectacular view of the largest of the Highland Lakes, in a building near the dam. The building houses the local Chamber of Commerce and a museum that traces construction of the dam. Visitors can feed huge schools of fish that congregate below the observation deck. Open daily 9 A.M.–5 P.M. **About 12 miles west of Burnet on State Hwy. 29; 512-793-6588.**

Fall Creek Vineyards

This 65-acre estate on the northwest shore of Lake Buchanan offers French tradition combined with California technology to create premium wines. Open for tours and tasting Mon.–Fri. 11 A.M.–3 P.M., Sat. noon–5 P.M. In addition, open Sun. noon–4 P.M. mid-March to mid-Nov. for tasting and sales only. From Burnet, drive about 12 miles west on State Hwy. 29, then north on State Hwy. 261 to Bluffton, then northeast on Farm Road 2241 to the town of Tow. **1111 Guadalupe St.; 512-476-4477, fax 915-379-4741; www.fcv. com.**

Fort Croghan Museum

Restored powder house, carriages, old guns, furniture, and relics from frontier days, in a stone and log building. Open Mon.–Sat. 8 A.M.–5 P.M.; Sun. 1–4 P.M. **703 Buchanan Dr., off State Hwy. 29 west; 512-756-8281.**

Highland Lakes CAF Air Museum

Headquarters for the Confederate Air Force Hill Country Squadron features World War II fighter planes, firearms, photographs, and memorabilia. **At Burnet Municipal Airport, 3 miles south of Burnet on U.S. Hwy. 281; 512-756-2226.**

Inks Lake National Fish Hatchery

Open Mon.–Fri. 8 A.M.–4 P.M. The hatchery is **10 miles west of Burnet on State Hwy. 29; 512-793-2474.**

Kingsland Archaeological Center

This archaeological showcase is operated by the Lower Colorado River Authority. More than 100,000 artifacts have been recovered, some dating back 10,000 years to the first people to migrate to the banks of the Colorado River. The center has a continuing education program and offers walking tours of the excavation site. From Burnet, drive 14 miles south on U.S. Hwy. 281, then right (west) on Farm Road 1431 for about the same distance to Kingsland. The center is **a couple of miles east of Kingsland on County Road 126; 512-598-5261.**

Longhorn Cavern State Park

Two miles of underground fantasy where prehistoric cavemen once lived. This was also the site of secret gunpowder manufacture for the Confederate Armies in the Civil War, and later became an outlaw hideout. Cave tours are supplemented by nature trails, a snack bar, and a museum displaying Indian artifacts. Open daily except Christmas Eve and Christmas. **From Burnet, take U.S. Hwy. 281 about 5 miles, then turn right (west) onto Park Road 4 and travel about 5 miles to the park; 512-756-4680; www.tpwd.state.tx.us/park/longhorn/longhorn.htm.**

RECREATION

Burnet County Park

Excellent fishing camp on the east side of Lake Buchanan, about 10 miles northwest of Burnet. Access is **via State Hwy. 29 west and Ranch Road 2341 north.**

Marble Falls

Getting There: Marble Falls is on U.S. Hwy. 281, on Lake Marble Falls, some 40 miles northwest of Austin. **Visitor Information: Marble Falls Chamber of Commerce; 830-693-4449.** Also the **Marble Falls/Lake LBJ Chamber of Commerce; 1-800-759-8178; www.instar.com/mall/marblefalls/index.html.**

Hunting, fishing, camping, and recreation abound in this Hill Country community named for a series of waterfalls over marble outcroppings in the Colorado River. Water-skiing and sailing are also part of the fun, and this is one of the most popular white-tailed deer hunting areas in the state.

SEEING AND DOING

Fox Memorial Marker

A monument overlooking the Colorado River and the Hill Country is dedicated to Oscar J. Fox, composer of the classic song "Hills of Home." He was born Oscar Julius Fuchs (pronounced Fox) on a ranch outside Marble Falls in 1879. Fox was a music teacher who never wrote a lyric, but set poems to music—poems collected by another Texan, John Avery Lomax, from the cowboys and other people he met. Fox published "The Hills of Home" in 1925, and eventually wrote a treasury of Texas songs, including "Old Paint," "The Old Chisholm Trail," "Whoopee Ti Yi Yo, Git Along, Little Dogies," "Will You Come to the Bower?" and "The Cowboy's Lament." The marker is in a roadside park **on U.S. Hwy. 281 just south of Marble Falls.**

Granite Mountain

You can view the mountain from a roadside picnic area, but you can't go on the mountain itself because of the quarrying taking place there. The mountain is a huge dome of pink and red granite, valued worldwide. Quarrying began in the 1880s for construction of the Texas capitol. An unending flow of the superb material has continued ever since, but the bulk of the dome seems untouched. The roadside viewing area is **on Ranch Road 1431 just north of Marble Falls.**

Lake Marble Falls Cruise

Travel the magnificent blue waters of Lake Marble Falls aboard the *General Johnson* as it winds along the scenic Hill Country. There are dinner/sightseeing cruises on Friday and Saturday. For reservations call **830-693-6126.**

Scenic Drives

Ranch Road 1431 both northwest and southeast out of Marble Falls offers breathtaking scenery over wind-

ing curves and hills, with frequent glimpses of Highland Lakes. On the western shore of Lake Marble Falls, both **Ranch Road 2147** and **State Hwy. 71** provide scenic drives to be remembered.

Lago Vista

Getting There: Lago Vista is on Farm Road 1431, offering exceptional scenery through the Hill Country. To get to Lago Vista from Austin, drive about 10 miles northwest on U.S. Hwy. 183 to Cedar Park, then head west on Farm Road 1431 for another dozen miles or so to the town. **Visitor Information: Lago Vista Chamber of Commerce; 512-267-7952; lagovista@prismnet.com; www.lago vista.org.**

Originally a lakeside resort with homes, condos, and golf courses, Lago Vista was incorporated in 1984. The town takes in more than 11 miles of Lake Travis shoreline. There's year-round golfing, boating, fishing, hunting, and tennis.

SEEING AND DOING

Lago Vista Airpower Museum

Shows off a collection of more than 150 model aircraft of many nations from World Wars I and II, the Korean and Vietnam Wars, and the Gulf War. Also at the museum are some intriguing full-size aircraft, including an L-4 Grasshopper and RF-4C Phantom Jet. Located **in Hangar 9 at Lago Vista Airport, off Road 1431, right at Bar-K Ranch Road to the airport; 512-267-7141, 512-267-7952.**

Bandera

Getting There: Bandera is on State Hwy. 16, about 40 miles northwest of San Antonio. **Visitor Information: Bandera Convention and Visitors Bureau, 1808 State Hwy. 16 south; P.O. Box 171, Bandera, 78003; 830-796-3045, 1-800-364-3833, fax 830-796-4121.**

The first settlers to Bandera were woodcutters who came in the 1840s to make shingles from the bald cypress trees growing along the Medina River. A Mormon contingent later moved into the territory, and, still later, Polish immigrants established the town of Bandera. Eventually Bandera settled into ranching. (See the Bandera Dude Ranches section in Major Attractions earlier in this chapter.)

Camp Verde General Store, south of Kerrville.

SEEING AND DOING

Frontier Times Museum

Western relics, western art, and more than 40,000 objects from old Bandera are on display, including such oddities as a two-headed goat and a South American shrunken head. Open daily 10 A.M.–4:30 P.M., Sun. 1–4:30 P.M. **506 13th St.; 830-796-3864.**

St. Stanislaus Catholic Church

Built in 1876, it serves a Polish settlement that dates back to 1855. It's one of the oldest Polish parishes in the United States. At **Seventh and Cypress Sts.; 830-460-4712.**

Scenic Drives

Beautiful Hill Country landscapes appear in every direction from Bandera. **State Hwy. 173** takes you north to Camp Verde and Kerrville. To the south, the same highway rolls to the southern edge of the hills and enters the lower South Texas plains. **State Hwys. 16 and 46** east afford a scenic trip through Pipe Creek on the way to Boerne. To the west, **Farm Road 470,** taking off from State Hwy. 16 just a couple miles outside Bandera, offers rolling hills and green valleys threaded by sparkling creeks.

Sims Spur Company

The largest spur manufacturing company in the United States. Open Mon.–Fri. 8 A.M.–5 P.M.; guided tours by appointment. **1108 Main St.; 830-796-3716.**

RECREATION

Hill Country State Natural Area

This 5,300-acre park has remained largely undevel-

oped. Primitive camping in designated areas, as well as horseback riding, backpacking, and hiking, are permitted. **On Farm Road 1077, 10 miles west of Bandera; 512-796-4413; www.tpwd.state.tx. us.park/hillcoun/hillcoun.htm.**

Medina

Getting There: Medina sits on State Hwy. 16, a bit more than 50 miles northwest of Austin (and about a dozen miles up the road from Bandera).

Medina is the Apple Capital of Texas, home to the annual **Texas International Apple Festival (830-589-7224)** in late July or early August. Give the credit for this fame to Love Creek Orchards.

SEEING AND DOING

Love Creek Orchards

Established by Houston oilman Baxter Adams, who gave up city life when the great Texas oil depression struck in the early 1980s. Adams bought some land in the Hill Country and became an apple grower. Today the orchards are the focal point of the community, especially from July to October when the apples are harvested. Adams offers guided tours through his plant on Saturdays if you make an appointment. Tours leave at 10 A.M. from the **Cider Mill Store on Main St. (830-589-2588); P.O. Box 1401, Medina, 78055; 1-800-449-0882, fax 830-589-2880; lovecreek/ hillcnty@flash.net.**

Scenic Drive

Ranch Road 337 is an attraction in itself. The stretch of road from Medina to Vanderpool covers about 25 miles and is one of the most scenic routes through the hills and valleys of the Hill Country.

Welfare, Comfort, and Camp Verde

Getting There: Take I-10 northwest from San Antonio for about 45 miles to its intersection with State Hwy. 27. Welfare is just off the interstate, followed to the west by Comfort, Center Point, and then Camp Verde, which is on State Hwy. 173 near its intersection with Farm Road 480.

These names may sound like a lyric from an old Tex Ritter railroad song, but they're really just the designations for a group of towns in the beautiful rolling hills south of Kerrville. Along I-10 approaching Kerrville from the east, the town names jump up at you.

SEEING AND DOING

First comes Welfare—a name most likely derived from the German word *wohlfarht,* meaning "pleasant trip." It seems only fitting, however, that the most popular eating place for miles around Welfare is a place called the **Po-Po Restaurant (830-537-4194).** It's just off the interstate, and signs direct you to it. They serve good fried chicken here, but don't be in a hurry. The service is unhurried.

A couple of miles west of the interstate, on State Hwy. 27, you'll come to Comfort, one of the most historic German communities in the Hill Country. It was settled in 1852 by a bunch of freemasons, freethinkers, and political activists. It was the only community in Texas that sided with the Union in the Civil War. A **monument near the center of town** honors about thirty settlers killed by Confederate soldiers as they tried to escape to Mexico.

Comfort has a number of historic buildings and a terrific old structure downtown that has been converted into a shopping mall of sorts. It's the 1880 **Faust Hotel,** originally designed by noted architect Alfred Giles. About a dozen antique shops take up the first floor, called the **Marketplatz (at High and Main Sts., 830-995-2000).** If you're looking for something really old, stroll through the **Ingenhuett General Store (830 High St., 830-995-2149).** You'll find all the things that general stores sell, plus information about the town and the area from the friendly people there.

You just have to stop and see the **Little People Car Company** in Comfort. This father-and-son operation restores and rebuilds pedal cars, the kind that were popular in the '20s and '30s. The average car sells for $300 to $400. If you have small children or grandchildren, you wouldn't want to go there early in your visit to Texas, because you might spend all your money. Situated **on High St. near Sixth St. downtown.**

Comfort used to be home to a strange little trade in armadillos. An enterprising local resident noticed that travelers were fascinated with the animals, which are common locally. Armadillos look like something out of the dinosaur age, but they're small and not at all dangerous. You'll see a lot of them dead along Texas roads because they're not very bright, and they don't see well. The Comfort businessman found quite a profit in killing armadillos, mounting them, and then selling them to tourists as lamp stands, ashtrays, or just plain conversation pieces. His conscience and the local animal rights organization finally got to him, and he shut the business down.

Camp Verde is next—15 miles or so west of Comfort, via State Hwy. 27 and Farm Road 480. Camp Verde was established in 1855 as a frontier post, and gained lasting fame as the site of the Confederate army's camel experiment. The Confederacy hoped to use camels instead of horses or mules for overland communications and transportation across the dry, rugged country westward to Fort Yuma, California. The experiment failed. The cranky camels were even harder to deal with than jackasses, and the project was abandoned in 1869.

Camp Verde General Store and Post Office is an authentic country store with all kinds of merchandise for modern use, plus fascinating photographs of the old military days. **On State Hwy. 173, just south of Farm Road 480; 830-634-7722. A roadside park** on the banks of Verde Creek affords a beautiful view of the countryside. The park is **directly across from the Camp Verde General Store.**

Utopia

Getting There: To find Utopia, simply head west out of San Antonio on U.S. Hwy. 90 for about 50 miles, turn north at Sabinal onto County Road 187, and drive for 20 miles or so. Suddenly you're in Utopia.

Historians believe Utopia was named by frontier circuit-riding preachers who found the place absolutely heavenly. Precisely why they found it heavenly, we're not sure, but the climate sure is nice. This is the home of **Utopia Water (830-775-2521),** sold around the state. The boss fills the bottles right out of the spring by his farmhouse and ships them to market.

SEEING AND DOING

Sabinal Canyon Museum

Displays local arts and crafts, including historic photos and handmade quilts. Open Sat. 10 A.M.–4 P.M. and Sun. 1–4 P.M. or by appointment. **On the main street, 3 blocks north of the post office; 830-966-2326.**

Utopia Organic Gardening

A family business that sells fruits and vegetables grown without the use of chemical pesticides or fertilizers. **Just off Farm Road 187 at 2 School St.; 830-966-3724.**

Leakey

Getting There: Leakey (LAY-key) is on U.S. Hwy. 83, some 90 miles west of San Antonio.

Leakey is one of the most picturesque parts of the Edwards Plateau, with rolling hills and a dramatic canyon cut by the Frio and Nueces Rivers. Ranching is the dominant industry; camping, hunting, and bird-watching are popular with visitors.

In March, Leakey is one of the great spots in the United States to watch hummingbirds. Many people in town have hummingbird feeders, and the birds have discovered that fact. Now the hummingbird arrivals have turned into big events. The **Frio County Chamber of Commerce (830-232-5222)** can tell you when the hummingbirds will be flying into Leakey.

SEEING AND DOING

Real County Historical Museum

Memorabilia of the history of the Real County area. **Just off Courthouse Square, east of U.S. Hwy. 83; 830-232-5330.**

Scenic Drive

You can explore the rich beauty of **Frio Canyon** around Leakey. Begin the trip about 10 miles north of Leakey on Farm Road 336, then travel south through Leakey on U.S. Hwy. 83 for about 20 miles, then turn west onto State Hwy. 127 and proceed until you cross the Sabinal River into Sabinal.

Texarome Perfume Factory and Cedar Mill

Texas cedar wood and its derivatives are some of the most widely used ingredients in fragrance formulas worldwide. The factory is open daily for public viewing; **1.5 miles east of Leakey on Farm Road 337.**

Wildlife Art Museum

Features taxidermy, sculpture, paintings, and canvas. Open Mon.–Sat. 9 A.M.–5 P.M. In Leakey **on Farm Road 337, 3 blocks east of the courthouse.**

RECREATION

Garner State Park

A total of 1,400 acres on the Frio River, this is one of the most popular family-oriented recreational parks in the state. The park rents comfortable stone and timber cabins that accommodate up to six people. The camping area provides shaded sites for tents, trailers, and screen shelters. It has rest rooms with showers, and a grocery store for supplies. Other facilities include a snack bar and restaurant in the summer, pedal boats, miniature golf, swimming, fishing, boating, hiking, and nature trails. The park is **10 miles south of Leakey on U.S. Hwy. 83; 512-389-9900, 1-800-792-1112; www.tpwd.state.tx.us/park/garner/garner.htm.**

Camp Wood

Getting There: Camp Wood is on State Hwy. 55, 40 miles north of Uvalde (which is on U.S. Hwy. 90 about 70 miles west of San Antonio, 70 miles east of Del Rio). **Visitor Information: Nueces Canyon Chamber of Commerce, P.O. Box 369, Camp Wood, 78833; 830-597-6241.**

Franciscan missionaries settled here in 1762. The town was named after the army post established almost a hundred years later. Historical markers north of town on State Hwy. 55 give details on the fort and the mission.

In March 1924, **Charles Lindbergh** made an unscheduled stop in Camp Wood, 3 years before his famous solo flight from New York to Paris. Lindbergh was attempting to fly to California by following the tracks of the Southern Pacific Railroad, but he was following the wrong set of tracks. The set he was following belonged to the Uvalde and Northern Railroad, a short-line railroad that carried supplies up the Nueces River. When the tracks ended at the community of Camp Wood, Lindbergh landed his plane in a pasture north of town. After making repairs, he was airborne again—but only briefly. Engine trouble forced him to land on the city's main street. After a few days and more repairs, he tried to take off again—this time striking a telephone pole with a wing and crashing into Walter Pruett's hardware store. Lindbergh spent several more days in Camp Wood before he was able to get in the air again. Old-timers still talk about the event as if it were yesterday. In 1976 the town renamed a park and a street after Lindbergh and his flying partner, Leon Klink, and the state placed a historical marker in the park.

SEEING AND DOING

Scenic Drive

This is a motorist's paradise. A **67-mile loop drive** to the northeast that begins and ends in Camp Wood spans some of the finest scenery in the region, with massive timbered hills, steep cliffs, and small secluded valleys and streams. From Camp Wood, drive 4 miles northwest, then turn north onto Farm Road 335, following the Nueces River, and go 20 miles to State Hwy. 41. Go 12 miles east on Hwy. 41, turn right (south) onto Farm Road 336 and follow it for 20 miles to Leakey, and then go west for 18 miles on Farm Road 337 to return to Camp Wood.

RECREATION

Camp Wood's location on the edge of the Nueces River Canyon offers spectacular scenery and sparkling streams. **Lake Nueces Park** has camping facilities (some with full RV hookups), swimming, boating, and fishing. It's **on Hwy. 55, 3.5 miles south of town; 830-278-3216.**

Rocksprings

Getting There: Rocksprings sits at the intersection of U.S. Hwy. 377 and State Hwy. 55, about 130 miles northwest of San Antonio and 75 miles northeast of Del Rio. **Visitor Information: Rocksprings Chamber of Commerce; 830-683-6466.**

Rocksprings, established in the 1890s, is the highest part of the Hill Country (elevation 2,450 feet). The town was named for its prized supply of water, some of the best on the Edwards Plateau. This country is dry in the summer, mild and sunny in winter. It's a year-round vacation spot offering camping, picnicking, hiking, and rock collecting. In season, hunters take white-tailed deer, wild turkey, and upland game birds. Fishing is excellent on the South Llano and Nueces Rivers.

SEEING AND DOING

Angora Goat Breeders Association Museum

Photos and records of the early history of Angora goat raising in this country. This is the nation's only registry office for the industry. Open Mon., Wed., Fri., 9 A.M.–

noon and 1–4 P.M. **On Austin St., downtown; 830-683-4483.**

Devil's Sinkhole State Natural Area

A magnificent hole in the ground where millions of Mexican free-tail bats gather from late April through October. The best periods to view the bats in great numbers are in May and then again in August, September, and October. At sunset and sunup, the shadowy flying mammals take flight out of the cave in a feeding frenzy that lasts about half an hour. The sinkhole is on private property and not open to the public unless you receive advance permission to join a scheduled tour. **Off State Hwy. 377, 8 miles northeast of Rocksprings; 830-563-2342.**

RECREATION

Kickapoo Cavern State Park

This is an undeveloped park that offers primitive camping and several caves to explore under supervision. **About 37 miles south of Rocksprings on Farm Road 674; 830-563-2342.**

Junction

Getting There: Junction is at the junction of U.S. Hwy. 83, U.S. Hwy. 377, and I-10—about 110 miles northwest of San Antonio via I-10 (and about 50 miles northwest of Kerrville). **Visitor Information: Junction Chamber of Commerce; 915-446-3190; kimblecococ@sat.net.**

Settled in 1876, Junction is a trade and retail center noted for the production of fine wool and mohair. Camping, fishing, canoeing, and hunting are popular in the area. As you drive at night, even on the freeways, be careful to avoid hitting deer, which feed alongside the highways.

SEEING AND DOING

Kimble County Historical Museum

Displays artifacts from the days of the early settlers. Open Mon.–Fri. 9:30 A.M.–noon and 2–5 P.M., and on weekends by appointment. **At Fourth and College Sts.; 915-446-4219.**

O. C. Fisher Museum

A replica of the Washington, D.C., office of a longtime congressman from this district. Open weekdays. **Kimble County Library, 208 N. 10th St.; 915-446-3615.**

Scenic Drives

Take your pick. Almost any road heading out of Junction is scenic. One of the best drives is to travel **south on U.S. Hwy. 377** along the South Llano River. A highway rest stop about 22 miles from town offers a magnificent overlook. Another view I love is just **off I-10** as you approach Junction from the southwest. Take exit 457 and pull into the parking lot of the **Day's Inn (915-446-3730)** situated on a hill. From there, look out at a beautiful picture of the Texas Hill Country, the city, and the place where the North and South Llano Rivers meet.

RECREATION

South Llano River State Park

A 500-acre wooded park with abundant wildlife. The bottomland is roost to the winter turkey, and the roosting area is closed to visitors from October to March. Facilities include camping, hiking, wildlife observation, and picnicking. You can go canoeing, tubing, and swimming in the spring-fed river. (Adjacent to the park is the 2,100-acre Walter Buck Wildlife Management Area.) **Four miles south of Junction, off U.S. Hwy. 377; 915-446-3994; www.tpwd.state. tx.us/parks/slano/slano.htm.**

Sonora

Getting There: Sonora is just off I-10, about 170 miles northwest of San Antonio (and 60 miles west of Junction).

On the western slope of the Edwards Plateau, this community began as a trading post on the old San Antonio to El Paso Road. It is a leading wool and mohair center and a popular hunting spot. The longest fenced cattle trail in the world once extended northeast for about 100 miles from Sonora to a railhead at Brady.

SEEING AND DOING

Caverns of Sonora

These caverns were discovered in 1955 by spelunkers from Dallas, who tried to keep them a secret. When word did get out and the caverns were opened to the world, people quickly labeled them some of the most strikingly beautiful ever seen.

The 8-mile-long cave has seven levels, but new passageways are still being found. The lower levels are the best. They're still actively producing formations. Some are luminous and phosphorescent; some are crystalline and transparent. All have names inspired by their shapes: the Mummy, the Passing Quarterback, the Ice Cream Cone. The Christmas Tree Room has stalagmite formations known as coral trees.

The privately operated tours through the caverns cover about a mile and a half and take 2 hours. The 70-degree temperature is pleasant, though in winter the humidity goes up to 98 percent. The walk involves a lot of elevation changes. There are a number of rest stops, but tours are strenuous. Daily tours begin every half hour from 8 A.M. to 6 P.M. from May through September, and from 9 A.M. to 5 P.M. the rest of the year. From Sonora, drive **about 8 miles west on I-10, then south for 7 miles on Caverns of Sonora Road (Ranch Road 1989).**

The cavern operators present a Covered Wagon Dinner Theater from mid-June to mid-August in a small natural amphitheater **(915-387-2880).** Costumed storytellers recall the early days of the area and offer musical entertainment as visitors sit at picnic tables for dinner. The site also has a camping area with RV hookups.

Brady, Mason, and Menard

Getting There: Looking at a map, it appears that all roads lead to Brady. Five U.S. or state highways converge in or next to the city. **Brady** is about 115 miles northwest of Austin, via State Hwy. 71, and it's about 140 miles northwest of San Antonio, via I-10 and U.S. Hwy. 87. **Mason** is 28 miles south of Brady on U.S. Hwy. 87. **Menard** is 33 miles west of Brady on U.S. Hwy. 190. **Visitor Information: Mason Chamber of Commerce, 108 Fort McKavett St.; 915-347-5758; www.bradytx.mason, www. masontexas.net.**

Brady was a cowboy town along the Dodge Cattle Trail, and historical markers note that it is the geographical center of Texas. The city has some very nice parks, a city-owned lake and golf course, year-round fishing, and seasonal hunting.

Brady is the place where the Bowie brothers got their reputations. Jim and Rezin Bowie spent 8 days fighting off Tawakoni Indians with knives they had made themselves, and of course the Bowie knife eventually became famous.

Mason and Menard grew up in the mid-1800s. Mason developed under the protection of Fort Mason, where Robert E. Lee had his final command in the U.S. Army before joining the Confederacy. Menard was an early trading post established near the ruins of a Spanish mission, Santa Cruz de San Saba.

Mason has become a hot spot for rock hunters in recent years. The area has a prime supply of topaz and other brightly colored stones there for the taking. But of course don't cross any fences or trespass on private property.

Part of Mason's distinct Texas flavor comes from the rock fences scattered around town. Some of them were built many years ago by ranchers who took the time to find the rocks and stack them perfectly. Others were created more recently, by people who have made a living out of building rock fences.

SEEING AND DOING

Brady

Heart of Texas Historical Museum. Early ranch and home exhibits, farm implements, pioneer weapons, vintage photos, and memorabilia housed in a restored county jail. Open afternoons Sat., Sun., and Mon. One block west of the town square, **at the corner of High and Main Sts.; P.O. Box 1401, Brady, 76825; 915-597-3491; www.bradytx.com/sites/museum.html.**

Santa Fe Center. Restored train depot serves as an art gallery and studio. Operated by the Brady/McCulloch County Chamber of Commerce. **Depot and N. Bridge Sts.; 915-597-3491.**

Mason

Fort Mason. Restored officers quarters mark the location of Fort Mason. Other than that, there are only crumbling foundations of the 23 other buildings that once stood on this site. The fort was abandoned in 1869. **Five blocks south of the courthouse in Mason.**

Fort Mason City Park. A 125-acre park with picnic facilities among large pecan trees. Fully equipped RV camping site, rodeo arena, athletics fields, walk-

Log cabin in a field of wildflowers in the Hill Country, near Menard.

ing trails, a playscape, and a 9-hole golf course. **U.S. Hwy. 87, 1 mile south of Mason; 915-347-5798.**

Mason County Museum. A collection of Mason County historical matter housed in a school building dating from the 1870s. The school was built from stone largely taken from the ruins of Fort Mason. Open Mon.–Fri. 9 A.M.–5 P.M. **300 Moody St.**

Sequist Home. About the most impressive historic home in town in Mason. Built in the 1880s, it has 17 rooms, 14 fireplaces, and outstanding period furnishings. Tours by appointment. **400 Broad St.; 915-347-5541.**

Menard

Fort McKavett State Historic Site. Fort McKavett was established in 1852 as Camp San Saba but later renamed for Captain Henry McKavett, killed at the battle of Monterey in the Mexican War. The fort was abandoned during the Civil War, then reoccupied by Colonel Ranald Mackenzie in 1868. By 1876 there was a sizable community here: stone barracks for eight infantry companies, twelve officers quarters, a hospital, guardhouse, bakery, post office, large headquarters building, storehouse, and stables. But the fort's importance declined after 1874, and it was abandoned for good in 1883. There has been extensive restoration of the ruins here, and if you explore only one old fort in the Hill Country, I recommend this one. Open Wed.–Sun. 8 A.M.–5 P.M. **From Menard, take U.S. Hwy. 190 west for 12 miles, then travel south on Farm Road 864 for a couple of miles to the fort; 915-396-2358; mckavett@airmail.net; www.tpwd.state.tx.us.**

Menard County Museum. Local history exhibits and frontier artifacts. Open Sat. and Sun., 1–5 P.M. **100 Frisco Ave.; 915-396-2365.**

Menard Country Store. Locally produced handicrafts and food. Open daily except Tues., 9 A.M.–5 P.M. **U.S. Hwy. 83 north at Magnolia St.; 915-396-2506.**

Ruins of Real Presidio de San Saba. The Presidio was a Spanish fort established in 1751 to protect Mission Santa Cruz de San Saba. The mission was a failed effort to "civilize" the Indians. Instead, in 1758, a strong force of Comanches and other Indians overran the mission, killing priests and others and burning the buildings. The mission was never rebuilt. The ruins of the old fort are **2 miles west of Menard, off U.S. Hwy. 190.**

RECREATION

Brady Reservoir
A 2,000-acre lake on Brady Creek that offers a wide range of water sports and fishing year-round. Facilities include boat ramps, docking, resorts, camps, and leisure homes. Fishing records include largemouth bass, 9.5 pounds, and smallmouth bass, 4.75 pounds. **About 3 miles west of Brady on Farm Road 3022.** For information, call the **Brady Lake Store** at **915-597-1823.**

Festivals and Events

January

Kingsland Welcomes Winter Texans Supper
Early January. **Kingsland/Lake LBJ Chamber of Commerce, 915-388-6211.**

San Saba Youth Livestock Show
Mid-month. **915-372-5141.**

March

Easter Fires Pageant
Late March. Reenactment of the founding of Fredericksburg and the 1847 peace treaty with the Indi-

ans. The name of the pageant comes from the tale that settlers made up to quiet the fears of their children when they saw Indian signal fires. The smoke and fire was from the Easter Bunny boiling eggs in large kettles. For more information call the **Fredericksburg Convention and Visitors Bureau** at **830-997-6523.**

Easter Hill Country Bike Tour
Late March. Bike tour, plus Easter sunrise services and Easter egg hunt. **Schreiner College Campus, State Hwy. 27 east, Kerrville; 830-792-3535.**

Llano Air Show
Late March. **Llano Chamber of Commerce, 915-247-5354.**

Peach Blossom Time
St. Francis Xaviar Parish Festival, **Stonewall; 830-644-2735.**

April

Bluebonnet Trail
Mid-month. Throughout the Highland Lakes region. **512-793-2803.**

Highland Lakes Squadron of the Confederate Air Force Fly-in
Mid-month. **Kate Craddock Field, Burnet; 512-756-2226.**

Hill Country Heritage Days
Usually the third weekend in April. **Johnson City; 830-868-7684.**

May

Blanco Classic Car Show and Market Days
Mid-month. **Blanco; 830-833-5101.**

Cow Camp Cook-off & Arts and Crafts Festival
Early May. **San Saba; 915-372-5141.**

Howdy Roo Chili Cook-off
Early May. **Marble Falls; 830-693-4449.**

June

Kerrville Folk Festival

First week in June. Showcases musicians playing a little bit of everything from blues to gospel to bluegrass and more, with eleven 6-hour evening concerts. **Quiet Valley Ranch, State Hwy. 16 south, Kerrville; 830-257-3600; info@kerrville-music.com; www.kerrville-music.com.**

Stonewall Peach Jamboree

Usually third weekend in the month. Peach show, peach pie and cobbler contest, peach pit–spitting contest, and a bunch of other peachy contests. There's also a rodeo, dance, parade, fiddler's contest, and carnival. **830-644-2735.**

Texas State Muzzle Loading Championship

Marksmen from all over compete with flintlock rifles and pistols, muskets, and muzzle-loading shotguns. **Brady Lake, west of Brady; 915-597-3491.**

July

Aqua-Boom Festival

Early July. **Kingsland; 915-388-6211.**

Night in Old Fredericksburg

Mid-month. Entertainment for all ages; food and drink and *gemutlichkeit* (fun and fellowship). Also horse racing at a nearby pari-mutuel track. **830-997-6523.**

Spring-Ho Festival

Celebrating the underground springs that made Lampasas a popular health resort before the turn of the century. **Lampasas; 512-556-5301.**

Texas International Apple Festival

Late July. More than twenty countries enter their finest apples in competition against those harvested in Medina. Texas sweet apple cider is a star of the show. Music, a quilt contest, and activities for kids. **Medina; 830-589-7224.**

August

Bluegrass Music Festival

Mid-month. **Llano.**

Gillespie Country Fair

Late August. This 100-year-old fair has a downtown parade, livestock show, arts and crafts show, carnival, and agricultural exhibits. **Fredericksburg; 830-997-2359.**

Kerrville Wine & Music Festival

Late August. Concerts, wine tasting, seminars, arts and crafts, and camping. **Quiet Valley Ranch, State Hwy. 16 south, Kerrville; 830-257-3600; www.kerrville-music.com/wmfest.html.**

Lakefest Drag Boat Races

Second weekend in August. **Marble Falls.**

September

World Championship Barbecue Goat Cook-off

Teams from all over the nation, and a few other countries, come to compete. **Richards Park, Brady; 915-597-3491.**

October

Crop Walk

Late October. To benefit the fight against world hunger. **Schreiner College Campus, State Hwy. 27 east, Kerrville; 830-896-2551.**

Down by the Riverside Festival

Early October. Educational exhibits and activities for the whole family. **Louise Hays Park, Kerrville; 830-257-4837.**

Fort Croghan Day

Mid-month. **Burnet; 512-756-4297.**

Haunted House

Late October. **Johnson City; 830-868-7684.**

Kerrville Fly-in/FAA Southwest Regional Fly-in

Mid-month. Some of the finest examples in the world of past, present, and future sports aircraft appear at this gathering of the Experimental Aircraft Association. **830-792-3535.**

Oatmeal Festival

Late October. This most enjoyable event begins with a barbecue supper in Oatmeal, Texas, on Friday night, then moves on to a trail ride to Bertram Saturday morning. There's an oatmeal cook-off, if you can believe it, plus an oatmeal-eating contest and an over-ripe-cantaloupe toss before the dance exhibition and open-air dance Saturday night. Sunday brings an afternoon of gospel music. **In Bertram, just east of Burnet; 512-355-2197.**

Oktoberfest

Early October. All the ingredients of an authentic German festival, with singing, dancing, and oompah bands, plus wurst, sauerkraut, and German baked goods. **Fredericksburg; 830-997-6523.**

Pumpkin Street Festival

Late October. **Burnet; 512-756-4297.**

Run in the Hills

October 4. Events: 8-kilometer run and 2.5-mile fun walk through the beautiful Hill Country. **Schreiner College Campus, State Hwy. 27 east, Kerrville; 830-895-5100.**

November

Harvest Festival

Early November. **Kingsland; 915-388-6211.**

Lights Spectacular

Late November through beginning of January. The Blanco County Courthouse is a sight to behold when it's decorated with 100,000 white bulbs, forming a curtain of light cascading from the second-story ledge to the ground. Highlights during December include a parade, a choir concert, and a lamplight tour of LBJ's boyhood home. **Johnson City; 830-868-7684.**

December

Fantasy of Lights for the Old & Young

First and second weekends in the month. Music, lights, and dancing as Burnet's town square and nearby Hamilton Creek Park light up for Christmas. Santa makes an appearance, and the local theater puts on a show. **Burnet; 512-756-4297.**

Twilight Country Christmas Tour

Mid-month. A twilight tour of homes and businesses that are all decked out for the holidays. **Kerrville; 830-896-6705.**

Recreation

Biking

The Hill Country is made for bike riding. I've picked out a few favorites for you to try. And for more, take a look at Andy White's *Best Bike Rides in Texas* (Globe Pequot Press, 1995).

Burnet to Bertram

Some of the most gorgeous scenery in the Hill Country can be seen on this trip through **Burnet, Bertram, Oatmeal, and Marble Falls,** especially in the spring. Here's a ride that can be as long as 56 miles or as short as 30 miles. Headquarters is in the town square at Burnet, about 60 miles northwest of Austin.

From Burnet, take the old Austin road (State Hwy. 330) and then Farm Road 243 to Bertram. That leg of the journey is about 15 miles. At Bertram turn south onto Ranch Road 1174, which leads you on a 7-mile winding route to the community of Oatmeal (check out the giant oatmeal can in the city park).

Then it's back on your bike and about 10 more miles on Road 1174 on a scenic descent before the road intersects Farm Road 1431. Travel west on Road 1431, which normally carries a lot of vehicle traffic, for about 10 miles to Marble Falls. From Marble Falls, travel north on State Hwy. 340 (Mormon Mill Road) for about 12 miles on the return trip to Burnet.

There are a couple of ways to shorten the ride if you like, but if you do, you'll miss either Bertram or Oatmeal. My choice would be to miss Bertram if my legs just wouldn't take the entire 56-mile trip.

The Hill Country Bike Ride

This 67-mile loop ride starts in **Hunt,** which is on State Hwy. 39, about 15 miles west of Kerrville. This land is pretty special, with its rolling hills, its rippling streams, and its rugged canyons.

From Hunt, pedal southwest, following the south fork of the Guadalupe River, on Hwy. 39 for about 32 miles, all the way to U.S. Hwy. 83. Then travel

Enchanted Rock in the Hill Country. Photo courtesy of Texas Highways *magazine.*

north for 9 miles to the intersection of Hwys. 83 and 41. Check out Garven's Store at the intersection. Take a right (east) on Hwy. 41 and pedal for 7 miles until you reach Farm Road 1340. Turn right onto Road 1340 and follow the north fork of the Guadalupe River for 19 miles back to Hunt, where you should arrive tired but happy.

LBJ Country Bike Ride

This 36-mile ride begins at the Lyndon B. Johnson State Historical Park off of U.S. Hwy. 290, about 21 miles west of **Johnson City.** There is some climbing involved in this tour through the land made famous by the nation's 36th president. The ranch roads are narrow, and so are the country lanes. Traffic is usually light, but watch out for those cars that sneak up on you.

Begin the ride by leaving LBJ State Historical Park from Park Road 52. Turn west onto Ranch Road 1, which runs parallel to the Pedernales River. Then turn north onto RM 1623 and cross the river, then go west onto RM 2721.

At almost 7 miles into the trip, turn right onto Klein-Ahrens Road. You'll cross seven cattle guards in the next 5 miles. At 12 miles into the ride, turn right at the unmarked intersection. This is Grape Creek Road. Eight-tenths of a mile later, at another unmarked intersection, is Ranch Road 1631.

Turn left onto Road 1631, and it takes you to Cave Creek in less than 5 miles. Then it's left again, onto Cave Creek Road, for about 4 miles, then right onto Gellerman Lane. Cross U.S. Hwy. 290 on Gellerman and find Upper Albert Road after 4.5 miles. Take Upper Albert Road to Albert; then pedal north on Lower Albert Road for 10 miles back to the park.

The Lost Maples Ride

Here is a 50-mile bike ride that will challenge you with long steep climbs and dramatic descents along the way. The ride starts at Lost Maples General Store, 1 mile north of **Vanderpool** on Farm Road 187. Vanderpool is some 65 miles northwest of San Antonio. The roads on this ride are lightly traveled for the most part, and you can stop for food and water along the way in Leakey and Utopia.

The toughest part is at the beginning, with lots of hills on the 12-mile ride east on Ranch Road 337 from the general store at Vanderpool to Leakey. From Leakey, travel south for 11 miles on Ranch Road 1120 (with a brief turn onto U.S. Hwy. 83) to Rio Frio. Then it's east for 14 miles on Ranch Road 1050 to Utopia. See if you can find some of that sparkling Utopia spring water for sale while you rest in this community. Then turn north onto Farm Road 187 for the 13-mile section back to the general store. This last leg should be particularly scenic because you parallel the Sabinal River all the way.

Hang Gliding

Packsaddle Mountain got its name from its distinctive shape. This was the site of the last Indian battle in the area, and legend has it that frontiersman James Bowie spent a lot of time here in a fruitless search for a hidden stash of gold.

These days, the east rim of the 1,600-foot peak is a launching ramp for hang gliders. In summer you can hardly drive down State Hwy. 71 without seeing hang gliders doing their thing on the mountain, which is **just outside Kingsland, by Lake LBJ** in the Highland Lakes region.

Hiking

Enchanted Rock

A relatively easy day-hike around the immense granite outcrop that is this park's namesake—about 5 miles round-trip. The elevation varies from 1,300 to 1,800 feet. The best season is fall through spring. There's water at the trailhead. The rock offers a spectacular view unlike any other of the Hill Country. And there's a bonus: rock climbing is allowed. Located **18 miles north of Fredericksburg on Ranch Road 965; 915-247-3903.**

Inks Lake

A mellow day-hike through the granite hills of Inks Lake State Park. This hike is about 5 miles round-trip. There are maps at the park office and water at the trailhead. In spring you'll see plenty of wildflowers. The park is several miles south of Buchanan Dam **on Park Road 4 (and about 20 miles northwest of Marble Falls); 512-793-2223.**

Lost Maples State Natural Area

Two trails in Lost Maples State Natural Area are among the Hill Country hiking highlights. The **Lost Maples Trail** provides a day-hike through wooden canyons and among big-tooth maple trees. The hike is almost 5 miles round-trip. The **Mystic Canyon Trail** is 4.5 miles round-trip. You can enjoy these hikes any time of year. If you come in October or November, you can view the spectacular display of fall colors—though you'll have to share it with crowds of other visitors. There's water at the trailhead, and maps at the park office. Located **4 miles north of Vanderpool on Ranch Road**

187 (and about 60 miles northwest of San Antonio); 830-966-3413.

Pedernales Falls State Park

Hiking opportunities include a couple of day-hikes at this park near Johnson City. The **Pedernales Falls Trail** offers an easy hike through undeveloped Hill Country, typical rolling countryside with limestone hills and scrub forest of oak and juniper. The Pedernales River winds its way through this area. Most of the 6.5-mile hike is on old ranch roads. The **Wolf Mountain Trail** is a fairly easy 7-mile hike similar to the one to Pedernales Falls. It offers crystal-clear river water and spectacular views of a canyon with rocky bluffs, ruins of an old ranch house, and tall oaks, elms, and cypresses. There is water at the trailhead, and the park office provides maps for hikers. The park is **10 miles east of Johnson City on Ranch Road 2766; 830-868-7304.**

Golfing

Some of the many possibilities among the public courses in the Hill Country:

BANDERA

Flying L Guest Ranch
P.O. Box 1959, Bandera, 78003; 830-460-3001; sales@flyingl.com; www.flyingl.com.

Lost Valley Resort Ranch
P.O. Box 2170, Bandera, 78003; 830-460-8008.

BRADY

Brady Municipal Country Club
Hwy. 87, Brady, 76825; 915-597-6010.

BUCHANAN DAM

Highland Lakes Golf Course
Box 567, Buchanan Dam, 78609; 512-793-2859.

BURNET

Delaware Springs Municipal Golf Course
At the south city limits, **on U.S. Hwy. 281; 512-756-8471.**

FREDERICKSBURG

Lady Bird Johnson Municipal Golf Course
P.O. Box 111, Hwy. 16, S. Lady Bird Park, Fredericksburg, 78624; 1-800-950-8147.

HORSESHOE BAY

Horseshoe Bay Resort and Club
Public, but very expensive, this 54-hole resort has three Robert Trent Jones courses: Ram Rock, Slick Rock, and Apple Rock. P.O. Box 8283, Horseshoe Bay, 78654; 830-598-6561.

JUNCTION

Junction Golf Club
P.O. Box 656, Junction, 76849; 915-446-2968.

KERRVILLE

Scott Schreiner Golf Course
1 Country Club Dr., Kerrville, 78028; 830-257-4982.

KINGSLAND

Packsaddle Golf Club
P.O. Box 179, Kingsland, 78639; 915-388-3863.

LAGO VISTA

Highland Lakes Country Club
20552 Highland Lakes Dr., Lago Vista, 78645; 512-267-1685.

Lago Vista Country Club
416 Rim Rock Rd., Lago Vista, 78645; 512-267-1179.

LLANO

Llano Golf Club
Route 10, Box 34, Llano, 78643; 915-247-5100.

MARBLE FALLS

Blue Lake Golf Club
Route 3, Box 246, Marble Falls, 78654; 830-598-5524.

Meadowlakes Country Club
220 Meadowlakes Dr., Marble Falls, 78654; 830-963-3300.

ROCKSPRINGS

Rocksprings Country Club
Private but open to out-of-town golfers, this is the only sand green golf course in Texas. P.O. Box 175, Rocksprings, 78880; 915-683-4224.

Parks and Camping

HIGHLAND LAKES AREA
All the lakes in the Highland Lakes chain northwest of Austin have campgrounds. Most of the campgrounds at Lake Buchanan, Inks Lake, Lake LBJ, and Lake Marble Falls are privately operated, though there is camping at Inks Lake State Park. Most of the campgrounds at Lake Travis are operated by Travis County.

Here are some of the major parks in the Highland Lakes:

Lake Buchanan
Black Rock Park. Primitive camping, boat ramp. Farm Road 261, off State Hwy. 29; 512-473-4083.

Cedar Lodge. Cabins, cottages, full RV hookups. Farm Road 261; 512-793-2820.

Crystal Cove Resort. Cabins, full RV hookups. Off Farm Road 261; 512-793-6861.

Poppy's Point. Boat ramp, full RV hookups. Off Farm Road 261; 512-793-2819.

Shaw Island. Primitive camping. Four miles off Farm Road 261; 512-473-4083.

Silver Creek RV Park. Full RV hookups. On Ranch Road 2341; 512-756-2381.

Inks Lake
Inks Lake State Park. Campsites, screened shelters, boat ramps, hiking trails, and 9-hole golf course. Park Road 4, off State Hwy. 29; 512-793-2223.

Rock-A-Way Park. Tent sites, boat ramp. Privately operated. **512-793-2314.**

Shady Oaks. Tent and RV sites. Privately operated. **Near Inks Dam; 512-793-2718.**

Lake LBJ
These privately operated facilities are all in Kingsland: **Kingsland Lodge.** Campsites, cabins, full RV hookups. **915-388-4830.**

LA-Z-L RV Park. Boat ramp, full RV hookups. **915-388-3473.**

Longhorn Resort. Cabins, marina, RV hookups. **915-388-4343.**

Plainsmen Lodge. Cabins, boat dock, RV hookups. **915-388-4344.**

Rio Vista Resort. Tent sites, boat docks, RV hookups. **915-388-6331.**

Lake Marble Falls
These two facilities south of Marble Falls are privately operated:
Kampers Korner. Full RV hookups. **830-693-2291.**

River View RV Park. Full RV hookups. **830-693-3910.**

Lake Travis
These six parks are operated by **Travis County (512-472-7483).**

Arkansas Bend. Tent sites, boat ramp. **Near Lago Vista; 512-473-9437.**

Bob Wentz Park at Windy Point. Tent sites, boat ramp. **Near Mansfield Dam; 512-473-4083.**

Cypress Creek. Tent sites, boat ramp. **Farm Road 2769 and Old Anderson Mill; 512-473-4083.**

Mansfield Dam Park. Tent sites. **At Mansfield Dam; 512-473-4083.**

Pace Bend Park. Tent sites, RV hookups, boat ramp.

Four and a half miles east of U.S. Hwy. 71; 512-473-4083.

Sandy Creek Park. Primitive camping. Lime Creek **near Farm Road 1431; 512-473-4083.**

These three facilities are privately operated:
At the Park. Full RV hookups. **Near Pace Bend Park; 512-264-1395.**

Hudson Bend Camper Resort. Full RV hookups. **Near Mansfield Dam; 512-266-8300.**

Krause Springs. Northwest shore **near Spicewood; 830-693-4181.**

OTHER AREAS

For reservations at any of the state-operated campgrounds among the following facilities, call **512-389-8900.**

Blanco State Park
A great view of the Blanco River, providing a fun place to swim, fish, and ride a boat. There are 31 campsites (21 with water and electricity, 10 with water, electricity, and sewage service). At the south city limits of Blanco **on Park Road 23,** off U.S. Hwy. 281, 14 miles south of Johnson City; **830-833-4333.**

Brady Parks
Try **Brady Lake Park (915-597-1823);** 20 wheeled-camper sites, 40 tent sites. Also **Richards Park (915-597-2152);** 102 wheeled-camper sites, and a 15-acre camping area. In **Brady,** about 115 miles northwest of Austin, via State Hwy. 71.

Enchanted Rock State Park
Walk-in camping at 46 tent sites (no RV or vehicle camping allowed). Rock climbing areas, plus more than 7 miles of hiking and backpacking trails. Camping is great here, but the place is very popular; best to reserve a spot. The park is 18 miles north of Fredericksburg **on Ranch Road 965; 915-247-3903.**

Fort Mason City Park
Campsites and RV sites, along with picnic facilities, walking trails, and a playscape for the kiddos. **U.S.**

Hwy. 87, 1 mile south of Mason (41 miles north of Fredericksburg).

Garner State Park

Includes 357 campsites, trailer and RV hookups, dump station, 40 screened shelters, 17 cabins, group facilities, rest rooms, showers, picnic area, fishing, swimming, hiking and biking trail, a park store, and some facilities for the handicapped. Thirty-one miles north of Uvalde **on U.S. Hwy. 83** (and some 80 miles northwest of San Antonio); **830-232-6132.**

Hill Country State Natural Area

Camping (including **equestrian camping**), group facilities, fishing, swimming, hiking and biking trails, horseback riding, and a park store. **On Farm Road 1077,** 10 miles west of Bandera; **512-796-4413; www.tpwd.state.tx.us.park/hillcoun/ hillcoun.htm.**

Kerrville-Schreiner State Park

This state park has 120 campsites, trailer/RV hookups, dump station, screen shelters, group facilities, rest rooms, showers, picnic facilities, fishing, swimming, boat ramps, 7 miles of hiking and nature trails, a park store, and some facilities for the handicapped. About 5 miles south of Kerrville off State Hwy. 16 **on State Hwy. 173; 830-257-CAMP.**

Lady Bird Johnson Municipal Park

This 190-acre park is run by the city of Fredericksburg. It has 112 campsites, a 20-acre lake for fishing, and a nice 18-hole golf course **(830-997-4010)**. On Live Oak Creek, 3 miles southwest of Fredericksburg **on State Hwy. 16; 830-997-4202.**

Lake Nueces Park

Lake Nueces Park has 25 campsites and all the trimmings. **On State Hwy. 55,** 3.5 miles south of Camp Wood (which is between Uvalde and Rocksprings); 830-278-3216.

Llano City/County Parks

Camping, hiking, boating, swimming, and other activities are available at these parks within Llano. **On U.S. Hwy. 71, about 65 miles northwest of Austin, near the northern end of the Highland Lakes region;** 915-247-5354.

Lost Maples State Natural Area

This natural area has 38 campsites, trailers with hookups, dump station, rest rooms, showers, picnic facilities, fishing, swimming, hiking, nature trails, interpretive exhibits, and a park store. **Four miles north of Vanderpool on Ranch Road 187 (about 60 miles northwest of San Antonio); 830-966-3413.**

Pedernales Falls State Park

One of the state's most beautiful parks, its 4,800 acres stretch out along both banks of the Pedernales for about 6 miles and for an additional 3 miles along the rugged gorge known as the Pedernales Falls. Camping, trailer hookups, dump station, group facilities, rest rooms, showers, picnic facilities, fishing, swimming, hiking, biking, horseback riding, nature trails, and a park store. **Eight miles east of Johnson City on Ranch Road 2766; 830-868-7304.**

South Llano River State Park

Camping, trailer hookups, dump station, rest rooms, showers, picnic tables, fishing, swimming, hiking and biking trails as well as nature trails, and a park store. Four miles south of Junction, **off U.S. Hwy. 377; 915-446-3994.**

Utopia Community Park

With camper sites and screened shelters, this park is on the Sabinal River—plus you get to say you spent the night in Utopia. **On County Road 187, some 20 miles north of Sabinal** (which is about 50 miles west of San Antonio on U.S. Hwy. 90); **830-966-2300.** Also in Utopia: **Good Shepherd Campground,** a family-owned facility; **830-966-2325.**

Where to Eat

Fredericksburg

The city is known and revered for its German traditions and its German food.

Altdorf Biergarten and Restaurant

Specializes in German food, although they also offer steaks and Tex-Mex. Open Mon.–Fri. for lunch and dinner, Sat. for lunch only. In an 1860s limestone building at **301 W. Main St.; 830-997-0878.**

Cookie Jar & Muffin Mania

A good place to start off the day. **106 E. Main St., 830-997-3499.**

Der Lindenbaum

One of the best German restaurants in town. Specialties of the house include pork and beef meatballs in a caper sauce, breaded steak with cheese, and locally made sausages and kraut. Open daily 10:30 A.M.–10 P.M. **312 E. Main St.; 830-997-9126.**

Dietz Bakery

The oldest bakery in town, and they still make everything fresh daily. **218 E. Main St.; 830-997-3250.**

Fredericksburg Fudge

They sell a lot of fudge—and it comes in lots of varieties. **105 N. Llano St.; 830-997-0533).**

Friedheims's Bavarian Restaurant & Bar

Features authentic Bavarian-style cuisine, including potato dumplings and imported sauerkraut. Open Tues.–Sun. for lunch and dinner. **905 W. Main St.; 830-997-6300.**

HillTop Cafe

Serves Greek, Texan, and Cajun. Open Wed.–Sat. for lunch and dinner, Sun. for brunch. Eleven miles northwest of Fredericksburg **on U.S. Hwy. 87; 830-997-8922.**

Opa's Smoked Meats

Sausage fans ought to tour this third-generation smokehouse, where they have all types of cured meat. Open Mon.–Sat. **410 S. Washington St. (U.S. Hwy. 87 south); 830-997-3358.**

Peach Tree Gift Shop and Tea Room

210 S. Adams St. (State Hwy. 16 south); 830-997-9527.

Rabke's Table Ready Meats

Another area favorite, this deli market and deer processing facility lies a few miles north of Fredericksburg, **in Willow City; 830-685-3266.**

Kerrville

Acapulco Restaurant

Serves about the best Mexican food in town. **1718 Sidney Baker St.; 830-257-6222.**

Alpine Lodge

Offers a number of schnitzels and sausage platters, but mostly American food like steak and fried chicken. **1001 Junction Hwy.; 830-257-8282.**

Bill's BBQ

Serves brisket, links, ribs, chicken, and occasionally cabrito. Open Tues.–Sat. until the meat runs out. **1909 Junction Hwy.; 830-895-5733.**

Joe's Jefferson Street Cafe

Down-home cooking with things like homemade bread, pastries, and chicken-fried steak. **1001 Jefferson St.; 830-792-9170.**

Raleigh House

Located in Ingram, just west of Kerrville, the Raleigh House was my favorite place to eat in the area for years, back when Martha Johnson was running the place. She opened when she had the notion and closed when she felt like it. But if you got there when she was in the right mood, her food was wonderful: down-home cooking with great desserts, and fresh rolls with a hint of orange. Well, that was a few years back. Martha is 92 now, and she finally retired and closed the restaurant—but not before publishing two wonderful cookbooks filled with recipes from her days at the Raleigh House. You can still get her cookbooks by writing to **1431 Lois St., Kerrville, 78027.** And, oh yes, one of those books has the recipe for those wonderful orange rolls.

Other Towns

BANDERA

In Bandera, where cowboys rule, steaks are the food of choice. **Harvey's Old Bank Steakhouse** serves up hearty breakfasts, steaks, and other Texas dishes. They also have a pleasant outdoor eating area **(309 Main St., 830-796-8486)**. **Busbee's BBQ** is one of the better barbecue places in town **(319 Main St., 830-796-3153)**. Maybe the best-kept secret in the Bandera area is the **Pipe Creek Junction Cafe** (about 12 miles east of Bandera on State Hwy. 16, 830-535-4742). On the outside it looks like a country store, but inside is a restaurant with a menu that will perk you up. They serve catfish, rabbits, frog legs, and fried chicken livers, all served with home-made bread. Save room for their buttermilk pie.

BLANCO

If you want the best cooking in Blanco (14 miles south of Johnson City), you'll have to go to the bowling alley. The **Blanco Bowling Club Cafe (830-833-4416)** on the square serves great down-home meals, and you get to see just about everybody in town. This is where everybody eats, meets, and recreates in Blanco. **On the square, across from Blanco County's first courthouse.**

COMFORT

When you're hungry, you can try the **Cafe on High Street (next to the Comfort Common Bed-and-Breakfast, 830-995-3470)** or **Arlene's Cafe (also on High St., 830-995-3330).** About 45 miles northwest of San Antonio is the **Cypress Creek Inn (on State Hwy. 27 on the western edge of town, 830-995-3977),** a popular spot right down by the river that has been serving down-home meals for almost half a century. And just off I-10 between Comfort and Welfare is **Po-Po Restaurant (830-537-4194).** They serve great fried chicken, if you can ever get anyone to wait on you.

LEAKEY

The **Frio Canyon Cafe, Feed Store and Exxon (830-232-5200)** in Leakey offers good local flavor. In town at the top of the hill **on U.S. Hwy. 83 south.**

LLANO

If you're in Llano at lunchtime, you might try **Inman's Kitchen (809 W. Young St., 915-247-5257),** or the **Main Street Tea Room & Jeannie's Desserts (111 W. Main St. on the courthouse square, 915-247-4561).** The **Badu House** is more of a sit-down place that specializes in steaks, chicken, and seafood **(601 Bessemer St., 915-247-4304).**

MARBLE FALLS

The **Bluebonnet Cafe (830-693-2344)** is still about the most popular eating establishment in Marble Falls. Chicken and dumplings is among the Tuesday specials. The cafe is **just north of the bridge on U.S. Hwy. 281.**

Where to Stay

Fredericksburg

Fredericksburg claims to be the original home of the bed-and-breakfast business in this country. It's certainly true that when such establishments caught on in the United States, many of the early ones were opened up right here, in Fredericksburg. They were ideal. They blended in beautifully with the little Sunday houses that farm families used to keep in town, and with the other quaint buildings scattered around the area. In fact many of the bed-and-breakfasts are now located in Sunday houses. About 250 bed-and-breakfasts flourish in a 50-mile radius of Fredericksburg. Like most other cities, Fredericksburg also has plenty of standard motels, if you'd rather just check in and check out.

Bed-and-Breakfast of Fredericksburg is the oldest B&B rental agency in town. J. D. Horn handles the rental of a number of bed-and-breakfasts around town, including Immigrant's Landing, on Main Street, once a restaurant and antique store; and Lost Creek Bed-and-Breakfast, a rustic log cabin that camouflages the air-conditioning and the TV and makes you feel like you're really spending a night in the Old West. **240 W. Main St.; 830-997-4712, 1-800-997-1124; bandbfbg@ktc.com; www.bandbfbg.com.**

Das College Haus

Three individual suites in a turn-of-the-twentieth-century home. Call **Country Lodging Service** at 830-990-8455.

Das Kleine Nest

A honeymoon cottage with its own wedding chapel out back. Call **Gastehaus Schmidt** at 830-997-5612.

Inn on Grape Creek

Bed-and-breakfast overlooking Grape Creek Vineyard between Fredericksburg and Stonewall. **830-644-2710.**

Luckenbach Inn
This bed-and-breakfast is an 1800s log cabin that has two bedrooms and a separate guest cottage out back. The inn also offers an eight-course gourmet meal Friday nights, by reservation. Nine miles outside town on the road to Luckenbach. Call **Bed-and-Breakfast of Fredericksburg** at **1-800-997-1124** or **830-997-4712; theinn@luckenbachtx.com.**

Kerrville area

Casa del Rio Cottage
Stone cottage on the Guadalupe River. **State Hwy. 39 west of Hunt; 830-238-4424.**

Guadalupe River RV Resort
Ten two-bedroom furnished cottages plus RV access. **2605 Junction Hwy.; 830-367-5676.**

Holiday Inn–YO Ranch Hotel
Red tin roofs and white Texas limestone walls, and very nice inside. Recognized as one of the state's best accommodations. **2033 Sidney Baker; 830-257-4440, fax 830-896-8189; holinyo@ktc.com; www.holiday-inn.com/hotels/keitx.welcome.html.**

Inn of the Hills River Resort
Cabanas and native stone walls, with suites overlooking the Guadalupe River. **1001 Junction Hwy.; 1-800-292-5690, 830-895-5000; resv@innofthehills.com; www.innofthehills.com.**

Johnson Creek Bed-and-Breakfast
Cabin in a rustic setting. **State Hwy. 27 east of Mountain Home; 830-367-5312.**

Lazy Hills Guest Ranch
A 750-acre ranch resort with 25 rooms. **State Hwy. 27 north of Ingram; 830-367-5600.**

Marianne's Bed-and-Breakfast
Cottage on an 18-acre ranch features pets for children and authentic German food. **State Hwy. 27 at Center Point; 830-634-7489.**

Mo-Ranch Conference Center
This Christian conference center on the north fork of the Guadalupe River has 82 hotel-style rooms. **Farm Road 1340, west of Hunt; 830-238-4455.**

Lake Buchanan
These accommodations are on the west side of Lake Buchanan in the Highland Lakes region.

Cottonwood Cove
Cabins with fishing dock. On the northwest shore, in the town of Tow. **915-379-2641.**

Driftwood Shores Resort
Cabins, RV hookups, boat dock. **915-379-2406.**

Eagles Nest Lodge
Cottages, covered boat ramp, and fishing dock. **915-379-3131.**

Other Towns

BANDERA

Dixie Dude Ranch
Playground, golf, horseback riding, fishing, western entertainment. **830-796-4481; www.ranchweb.com/dixie/index.html.**

Flying L Guest Ranch
Tennis, golf, horseback riding, children's activities.

Mayan Dude Ranch
Hayrides, cowboy breakfasts, barbecue. **830-796-3312, 830-460-3036; sales@flyingl.com; www.flyingl.com.**

BURNET

Last Chance Resort
Eighteen units plus waterfront condos. **512-756-7766.**

COMFORT

Comfort Common Bed-and-Breakfast
818 High St.; 830-995-3030.

Gast Haus Lodge
A restored old hotel that once was a stage stop. Four units, plus fishing in Cypress Creek. **830-995-2304.**

CONCAN

Yeargan's River Bend Resort
On the west bank of the Frio River just off U.S. Hwy. 83, north of Garner State Park; 830-232-6616.

HORSESHOE BAY

Horseshoe Bay Country Club Resort
In the Highland Lakes region. Almost 200 hotel-style accommodations with condos and townhouses, plus a great marina and three championship golf courses. If you've got the money, this is a terrific place to stay, especially if you're a golfer or enjoy being around inland lakes. **U.S. Hwy. 281 south to Farm Road 2147, then west about 5 miles; 512-598-2511.**

LAMPASAS

Moses Hughes Ranch Bed-and-Breakfast
1850s ranch house on a creek west of Lampasas. 915-556-5923.

LEAKEY

River Haven
Cabins with a view of the Frio River, and horseback riding is nearby. Great tubing country. **830-232-5400; rhc@sig.net; www.lcstech.com/rhaven.**

LLANO

The Badu House
Historic bed-and-breakfast inn with turn-of-the-century ambiance. **601 Bessemer St.; 915-247-4304.** I have to tell a story here. An old friend of mine, Ann Ruff, worked with her husband to save the old Badu House and to restore it. After the job was done, and after the death of her husband, Ann went into writing, and spent the last years of her life traveling the state and cataloging in book form the best, worst, funniest, saddest, weirdest places in Texas. After I had spent 25 years pro-

ducing a TV program about Texas, I had few friends who could best me in what we called "Texas Talk"—that is, telling someone something they didn't know about a city or a person in Texas. Ann Ruff could best me.

MASON

Hasse House
Historic home with period furniture and wood-burning stove. **Six miles east of Mason on State Hwy. 29; 915-347-6463.**

RIO FRIO

Rio Frio Bed-and-Breakfast
Eight furnished cottages on the east side of the Frio River. **Just south of Leakey on Farm Road 1120; 830-232-6633; friobnb@sig.net; www.lcstech.com/friobnb.**

SONORA

Devil's River Inn
Longtime motel on the main highway through town, not far from the Caverns of Sonora. **915-387-3516.**

UTOPIA

Bluebird Bed-and-Breakfast
Twelve miles west of Utopia on Farm Road 1050; 830-966-3525.

VANDERPOOL

Texas Stagecoach Inn
Karen Camp is in charge of this old-fashioned place, and it's one of my favorites in the Hill Country. Karen has five individual units you can pick from. It's worth the trip just to talk to Karen; she's one of those people who loves history, and she's playing a large part in preserving it. **1-888-965-6272, 830-966-6272, fax 830-966-6273; stagein@swtexas.net; www.bbhost.com/txstagecoachinn.**

Waco and the North-Central

Waco and the North-Central Texas land along the Brazos River was Indian country until the mid-1800s, controlled by the Waco Indians. But the Brazos begins far from here, rising at the confluence of its Salt Fork and Double Mountain Fork near the eastern boundary of Stonewall County, way up in the Panhandle. The Brazos winds its way southeastward down to Waco and then more southerly till it empties into the Gulf of Mexico, a journey of more than 840 miles.

The Brazos is probably the river that Frenchman René Robert Cavelier, Sieur de la Salle, wrote about in his travels, though he called it the Maligne. Many legends have grown up explaining the name Brazos, and the most common involves an expedition in the 1700s by Spanish explorer Coronado. His men were lost and wandering around in this country, about to die from lack of water, when friendly Indians guided them to a stream. The story goes that Coronado named the stream *Los Brazos de Dios*—The Arms of God.

Although the Brazos was well known to Spanish explorers and missionaries, the first permanent settlements on the river were created by Anglos. Originally the Brazos was navigable for about 250 miles from the Gulf of Mexico. It was an important waterway before the Civil War, and today you still can find evidence of giant locks that were built on the river to aid navigation. Even before Texas statehood in 1845, the Brazos was a source of water for power and irrigation.

The Brazos River Authority was established in 1929 to manage the waters of the Brazos. The river is now dammed to form reservoirs at nine places: Aquilla, Belton, Georgetown, Granger, Proctor, Somerville, Stillhouse Hollow, Waco, and Whitney.

A ferry service sprang up on the Brazos in the mid-nineteenth century to provide passage across the river for the hundreds and hundreds of immigrants who showed up, moving west. Some were following rumors of a gold discovery in California. Others simply felt the eastern United States was too crowded. The ferry business, a very profitable enterprise, was replaced in 1870 by a toll bridge—at that time the longest suspension bridge in the United States and the second longest in the world. It was quite an achievement out here in the wide-open spaces of Texas, and right then and there Waco established itself as one of the great cities of the West.

Getting Around

Ground transportation in the city includes the city's bus system, **Waco Transit Services (254-753-0113)**; the **Yellow Cab Company (254-756-1861)**; and **Waco Streak Limousine (254-772-0430)**.

Visitor Information

Waco Chamber of Commerce

254-752-6551, fax 254-752-6618; info@waco-chamber.com; www.waco-chamber.com.

Waco Convention Center

100 Washington Ave., P.O. Box 2570, Waco, 76702-2570; 1-800-321-9226, 254-750-5810, fax 254-750-5801; www.wacocvb.com.

Waco Special Events Recording
254-752-9226; www.waco-texas.com.

Major Attractions

Texas Ranger Hall of Fame and Museum

That enterprising young man who built the first commercial ferry service across the Brazos River in 1849 was Shapley P. Ross, who early in his career established a reputation as an Indian fighter. Later he became Captain Ross of the Texas Rangers, and is best remembered today as one of the men who built that organization into a famous outfit. The Hall of Fame and Museum in Waco traces the history of the Texas Rangers.

The Rangers originally were private investigators hired by ranchers along the frontier to protect them and their livestock from Indians. Stephen F. Austin hired the first ten Rangers in 1823. The Rangers played a major role in the Texas fight for independence from Mexico, and eventually developed into a state paramilitary force that fought Indians and patrolled the Mexican border.

It was said that a Texas Ranger could "ride like a Mexican, trail like an Indian, shoot like a Tennesseean, and fight like the Devil." Not all the Ranger stories over the years were heroic, but the image of a Ranger even now is the image many people still possess of the "typical" Texan—tall and slim, with the look of Gary Cooper and the demeanor of Steve McQueen. An often-told story tells about the Ranger who steps from a train in a riot-torn town and is asked, "You mean they sent only one Ranger?" To which he replies, "You got only one riot, don't you?"

Texas Ranger Hall of Fame and Museum in Waco. Photo courtesy of Texas Highways *magazine.*

> **Getting There**
> Waco is the launching point for the things you'll want to see and do in this region. The city is built along I-35. Travel north 90 miles and you'll be in the Dallas–Fort Worth Metroplex. Take I-35 south and you'll reach Austin after about 100 miles. U.S. Hwy. 190 southeast will take you to Houston in about 4 hours, and State Hwy. 6 northwest will get you to another legendary cowboy town, Abilene. **Waco Regional Airport (254-750-8656)** *is served by many airlines, including* **Continental (1-800-525-0280)** *and* **American Eagle (1-800-433-7300).**

The Texas Ranger Museum and the Hall of Fame are part of a 35-acre park built around a replica of Fort Fisher, a Ranger outpost established in 1837. This replica serves as headquarters of Ranger Company F. The museum chronicles Ranger history with paintings, dioramas, audiovisual presentations, a library, and impressive gun collections. The Colt display follows the development of the pistol that won the West.

Open daily 9 A.M.–5 P.M. Mule-drawn wagon tours leave from the museum Mon.–Fri. 10 A.M.–5 P.M. No reservations necessary. **Fort Fisher exit, I-35, at University Parks Dr.; 254-750-8631; trh@eramp.net; www.texasranger.org.**

Waco Suspension Bridge

It took 2.7 million bricks and $135,000 to build Waco's suspension bridge in 1870. It was 475 feet long and spanned the width of the Brazos River. It was a massive undertaking for its time, and a great gamble. But upon completion, the bridge brought the cattle drives of the Chisholm Trail right through town to take advantage of the river crossing. A year later, railroad tracks were finally laid into town, and Waco took its place as a significant city of the Southwest.

For twenty years, a toll was charged for each person crossing the bridge and for each head of cattle. In 1889, McLennan County bought the bridge and transferred the deed to the city, on condition the bridge would be maintained as a free public highway.

The bridge is directly **across from the Waco Convention Center at 100 Washington Ave.** and spans the Brazos River between University Parks Dr. and Martin Luther King Blvd.

Today the bridge is open only to pedestrian traffic and is surrounded by lovely parks: Indian Spring Park is on the west bank; Martin Luther King Jr. Park is on the east bank. A landscaped riverwalk connects the bridge to Fort Fisher and the Texas Ranger Hall of Fame on the other side of the freeway. Opposite Fort Fisher is Cameron Park, a 416-acre playland with a picnic area, riding and hiking trails, and a wildflower preserve.

Cameron Park

Here are 368 acres of woods, walking and biking trails, riverside picnic areas, a wildflower preserve, a children's playground designed for access by the physically challenged, and a zoo. The land was donated to Waco as a memorial to Waco businessman and philanthropist William Cameron.

The **Cameron Park Zoo** is a natural-habitat facility with a cascading waterway and shaded walks. It includes an African savanna, gibbon island, Sumatran tigers, and a treetop village. From March through June, **Miss Nellie's Pretty Place** showcases wildflowers along its winding paths and picturesque pool.

As you wander about, you'll enjoy finding **Proctor Springs,** with its pools of water and lush vegetation. Scenic overlooks sprout here and there: Emman's Cliff, Lawson's Point, Circle Point, Lover's Leap.

Cameron Park Clubhouse (2601 Sturgess St.) is available for group rental, with a kitchen and two large meeting rooms, as well as a grassy picnic area. Picnic areas throughout the park have covered pavilions, grills, and tables (reserve by calling **254-750-5980**). Trails for hiking or biking meander through the park, over creeks and along the river. The park offers sports enthusiasts fishing, boating, and open areas for volleyball, plus something called a disk golf course—a creation that involves baskets scattered throughout the park for people to aim Frisbees into.

The park is adjacent to the Brazos River, **5 blocks west of I-35 on University Parks Dr. Cameron**

Park: 254-750-5980; www.wacocvb.com/ cameron.htm. Cameron Park Zoo: 254-750-8400, fax 254-750-8430; www.waco-texas. com/zoo.

The Governor Bill and Vara Daniel Historic Village

More than twenty wood-frame buildings at Daniel Historic Village give a glimpse of life in an 1890s Texas cotton farming community. Structures include a school, livery stable, church, hotel, cotton gin—even a saloon.

The original creation of the village was the work of Bill Daniel—known to everyone as Governor Bill. Governor Bill Daniel never was governor of Texas. But during the Kennedy years, he was governor of Guam, and his brother, Price Daniel, really was governor of Texas.

Bill is of the friendly sort and will talk your arm off if you let him, and he has always been one of the real characters in the state. He attended Baylor University in Waco, but his home has always been in Liberty County, northeast of Houston. For many years he and his wife, Vara, collected artifacts and memorabilia of things past. He built a historical village at his ranch in Liberty County to hold his collection. Eventually he gave the whole village to Baylor University, which explains why this fascinating village is now in Waco, along the banks of the Brazos River.

The village is open Sat.–Sun. 1–5 P.M. and Tues.– Fri. 10 A.M.–4 P.M. **On the campus of Baylor University, off I-35 (exit 335B); 254-710-1160; www.baylor.edu/~museum_studies.**

Baylor University

Baylor University, the state's oldest institution of higher learning and the largest Baptist-sponsored university in the world, was chartered when Texas was a republic—on February 1, 1845, in Independence, Washington County. After many years and much squabbling among Baptist leaders, Baylor University was moved to Waco in 1886.

Among the campus locations that reward a visit is the **Armstrong Browning Library,** with the world's largest collection of materials relating to Robert and Elizabeth Barrett Browning. The library's fifty-six stained-glass windows display the poetry of the Brownings. An extensive Wedgwood china collection is also on display. Open weekdays 9 A.M.–noon and 2–4 P.M., Sat. 9 A.M.–noon. **At 7th and Speight Sts.; 254-710-3566.**

Also on campus is the **Strecker Museum,** the oldest continuously operated natural history and cultural museum in Texas. Open Tues.–Fri. 9 A.M.–noon and 1:30–4 P.M., Sat. 10 A.M.–4 P.M., Sun. 2–5 P.M. **Sid Richardson Bldg., S. 4th St.; 254-710-1110.**

Baylor University is located **off I-35 and University Parks Dr. (exit 335B); 254-710-1011 (main university switchboard); www.baylor. edu.** The **Weithorn Information Center** is open Mon.–Fri. 8 A.M.–5 P.M.; **1301 S. University Parks Dr.; 254-710-1921.**

Seeing and Doing

Crafts Centers

Homestead Heritage
Center of Traditional Crafts
The days when a craftsman's skills really counted for something are recalled at the Center of Traditional Crafts **(just north of Waco off I-35, at Elm Mott exit 343; 254-829-0417).** The center features **Homestead Heritage Furniture (254-829-2060),** where people craft custom furniture using traditional methods of hand joinery, creating such pieces as full-length longleaf-pine armoires, dining room sets, and four-poster beds. At the **Potter's House (254-757-2229),** potters turn out bowls, bottles, and vases on an old-fashioned wheel. At the **Heritage Forge Blacksmith Shop,** smithies use eighteenth-century techniques to shape raw steel into decorative ironwork.

Gardens and Arboreta

The Earle-Harrison House and Pape Gardens
Antebellum Greek Revival–style home with 5 acres of lawns, pond, and gardens. Open Mon.–Fri. 9 A.M.–5 P.M., Sat.–Sun. 1:30–5 P.M. **1901 N. 5th St.; 254-753-2032.**

Museums and Historic Sites

Crash at Crush
A highway marker identifies the location of one of the most grotesque publicity stunts ever concocted. Just before the turn of the twentieth century, when railroads were king, a man named William George Crush talked the Missouri, Kansas, and Texas Railroad into letting him stage a head-on train wreck for the public. They advertised it as the Crash at Crush and charged for the event. Excursion trains brought in about 20,000 sightseers. It was spectacular all right, but at least five spectators were killed and scores injured when the trains collided Sept. 15, 1896. You'll see the marker **along U.S. Hwy. 35, about 15 miles north of Waco.**

Dr. Pepper Museum
The 1906 "Home of Dr. Pepper." Exhibits, memorabilia, and a working turn-of-the-twentieth-century soda fountain, featuring floats, shakes, and *sweet* fountain Dr. Pepper. The soft drink, very popular in Texas, was originally formulated at the Old Corner Drug Store in downtown Waco. It was the pet project of chemist R. S. Lazenby, who named the beverage after his girlfriend's father in an effort to impress him. This building was formerly the main facility for producing Dr. Pepper, but it's now a museum that traces the history of this and other Texas soft drinks, including the famous Big Red. Dr. Pepper isn't bottled in Waco anymore, but there are bottling plants in two other Texas cities, Dublin and Irving. **300 S. 5th St.; 254-757-1024; dp-info@drpeppermuseum. com; www.drpeppermuseum.com.**

Fort Fisher City Park
Fort Fisher stood here in 1837. Now, century-old oak and pecan trees shade more than 100 riverside campsites and RV hookups. **I-35 at University Parks Dr.; 254-750-8630, 1-800-922-6386.**

Historic Waco Foundation
The foundation **(810 S. 4th St., 254-753-5166)** maintains four historic homes in the city, featuring authentic period furniture, china, and decorative arts from the late 1800s. **Fort House,** 1868, in Greek Revival style, is open Sat.–Sun. 2–5 P.M. **(503 S. 4th St., 254-753-5166). East Terrace,** 1872, an Italianate villa, is open Mon.–Fri. 11 A.M.–3 P.M., Sat.–Sun. 2–5 P.M. **(100 Mill St., 254-753-5166). Earle-Napier-Kinnard House,** 1869, in Greek Revival style, is open Sat.–Sun. 2–5 P.M. **(814 S. 4th St., 254-756-**

A collection of vintage rifles at the Texas Ranger Hall of Fame and Museum in Waco. Photo courtesy of the Texas Department of Tourism.

0057). **McCulloch House,** 1872, in Greek Revival style, is open Sat.–Sun. 2–5 P.M. **(407 Columbus Ave., 254-756-2828).**

Mount Carmel

It's still much too soon to think of this as simply a tourist attraction, but travelers want to know about the Branch Davidians and the siege at Mount Carmel. More than seventy members of the group died April 19, 1993, in the burning of the compound after a 51-day federal siege following the deaths of four federal agents. It is said to be the largest armed conflict between the U.S. government and its citizens since the Civil War. The visitor information center at Fort Fisher has a detailed map of the route to the Mount Carmel compound and some information about the conflict. Little is left today of the compound—just tank tracks and piles of rubble, surrounded by 12-foot-high barbed wire fences; visitors are not permitted beyond the fences. Mount Carmel is **14 miles northeast of Waco, off Farm Road 2491.** The **Taylor Museum of Waco History** in Waco includes an exhibit about David Koresh, the Branch Davidians, and the tragedy

at Mount Carmel. The museum is at **701 Jefferson Ave.; 254-752-4774.**

Texas Sports Hall of Fame

Memorabilia of sports greats such as Lee Trevino, Nolan Ryan, George Foreman, and Babe Didrikson Zaharias. Includes the Tom Landry Theater and interactive displays. Open daily 10 A.M.–5 P.M. **1108 S. University Parks Dr.; 254-756-1633; www.wacocvb.com/tshof.htm.**

SHOPPING

Austin Avenue

Take a walk down Austin Avenue in downtown Waco for some of the most enjoyable shopping experiences around. While you're at it, check out the restored vaudeville theater, the **Hippodrome (724 Austin Ave., 254-752-9797).** Now for the shopping: **Antiques on Austin (1525 Austin Ave., 254-753-1795). Austin Avenue Emporium (800 Austin Ave., 254-757-2180). The Cottage Shop,** antiques **(708 Austin Ave., 254-756-0988). Gladys' Bookstore (710 Austin Ave., 254-754-7868). The Hub,** men's clothing **(506 Austin Ave., 254-754-8611). Once Upon a Time,** fantasy collections **(1509 Austin Ave., 254-754-8009). Sironia Boutique (1509 Austin Ave., 254-754-8009). Variety Store,** antiques **(716 Austin Ave., 254-755-7035). Wanda Fannin's,** specialty clothing **(1509 Austin Ave., 254-754-6168).**

TOURS

Brazos Trolley

Here's a deal. For 50 cents, you can catch the trolley for its regular route past many of Waco's major sites, including the Texas Ranger Museum, Texas Sports Halls of Fame, Fort Fisher, Baylor University, Strecker Museum, the Dr. Pepper Museum, the suspension bridge, several historic homes, and the Cameron Park Zoo. However, the trolley only operates Sat.–Sun. 10 A.M.–6 P.M. **254-753-0113.**

Wineries and Breweries

Bosque Brewing Company

Open Mon.–Sat. 8 A.M.–5 P.M., with group tours available by reservation. **300 S. 6th St.; 254-754-5154.**

Festivals and Events

January

Autorama

Usually third weekend of the month. **Waco Convention Center, 100 Washington Ave.; 254-750-5810.**

Mid Tex Farm & Ranch Show

Mid-month. Waco. **Convention Center, 100 Washington Ave.; 254-750-5810.**

February

Harley Davidson Show

Early February. Waco. **Convention Center, 100 Washington Ave.; 214-216-5520.**

March

Brazos River Festival

Late March. Activities include reenactment of a Civil War battle at Cameron Park in Waco, an art show, and the Cotton Pageant. **254-776-1825.**

Daniel Village Pioneer Heritage Days

Early April. **Daniel Historic Village, on the campus of Baylor University; 254-755-1160.**

Native American Pow Wow

Late March. **Ferrell Center, on University Parks Dr. on the campus of Baylor University; 254-755-1915.**

July

Brazos Night

July 4. Fireworks and independence celebrations throughout Waco. **254-750-5871.**

September

The Great Texas Raft Race

Labor Day. You can enter anything homemade that floats and moves by paddle power. Crews range from 2 to 100 people. The race begins at the McLennan Community College landing on the Bosque River and ends 3.5 miles downstream at Fort Fisher Park on the Brazos River. **254-753-5222.**

Thursday evening summer concerts, a regular event in Waco. Photo courtesy of the Texas Department of Tourism.

October

Heart O' Texas Fair & Rodeo
Early October. 254-776-1660.

November

Daniel Village 1890s Texas Thanksgiving
Late November. **Daniel Historic Village, on the campus of Baylor University; 254-755-1160.**

Homestead Heritage Crafts & Children's Fair
Late November. **254-776-9972.**

December

Christmas on the Brazos
Early December. A holiday tour showcasing some of Waco's historic homes decorated for the holidays. **254-753-5166.**

Recreation

Golfing

Battle Lake Golf Course
In the town of Mart, **Eighteen miles southeast of Waco on State Hwy. 164. Route 1, Box 82, Mart, 76664; 254-876-2837.**

Cottonwood Creek Golf Course
The best public course in Waco. **5200 Bagby, Waco, 76711; 254-752-2474.**

James Connally Golf Course
P.O. Box 154638, Waco, 76715; 254-799-6561.

Western Oaks Country Club
1600 Western Oaks Dr., Waco, 76712; 254-772-8100.

Hiking

Fairfield Lake State Park
An easy day-hike of about 5 miles round-trip travels through the woods and fields above Fairfield Lake. As with most Texas hikes, the best period for the outing is fall through spring; it can be hot and uncomfortable the rest of the year. The trail takes you around the southern edge of the lake through stands of post oak, eastern red cedar, elm, white ash, and hickory, with some open grassy areas. Interpretive signs identify many of the trees and plants on the first half of the trip. A pond and many trailside benches make this an enjoyable hike. You can get maps at the park office. Water is available at the trailhead, and primitive camping is allowed. **About 7 miles northeast of Fairfield on Farm Road 3285 (Park Road 64).** Fairfield is on U.S. Hwy. 84, about 65 miles east of Waco. **903-389-4514.**

Parks and Camping

Fairfield Lake State Park
Provides 135 campsites (36 with water only, 99 with water and electricity), and a primitive camping area for backpackers. **About 7 miles northeast of Fairfield on Farm Road 3285 (Park Road 64); Route 2, Box 912, Fairfield, 75840; 903-389-4514, 1-800-792-1112; www.tpwd.state.tx.us/park/fairfield/fairfield.htm.**

Fort Fisher City Park
Provides 110 campsites and 20 tent sites, with riverwalk, fishing, and the Texas Ranger Hall of Fame and Museum. **I-35 at University Parks Dr., P.O. Box 2570, Waco, 76702-2570; 254-750-8630.**

Hords Creek Lake
Three parks—**Flat Rock, Friendship,** and **Lakeside**—offer camping areas, trailer areas, dump stations, and launching ramps. About **12 miles west of Coleman on State Hwy. 153.** Coleman is about 20 miles northwest of Brownwood. **HCR 75, Box 33, Coleman, 76834-9320; 915-625-2322.**

Lake Waco
This 7,200-acre lake has four parks with camping facilities: **Airport Park, Speegleville I Park, Midway Park, Speegleville III Park.** There are opportunities to swim, boat, fish, water-ski, or picnic at seven parks along 60 miles of shoreline. **State Hwy. 6, west edge of Waco; Route 10, Box 173-G, Waco, 76708-9602; 254-756-5359.**

Mother Neff State Park

Offers 21 campsites (15 with water only, 6 with water and electricity). Includes Tonkawa Indian Cave and 1.5 miles of hiking trails. **Twenty-two miles northwest of Temple on State Hwy. 36, then 5 miles north on State Hwy. 236.** The entrance is on the left. **Route 1, Box 58, Moody, 76557; 254-853-2389.**

Where to Eat

El Conquistador

Serves up Tex-Mex. **901 North Loop 340; 817-772-4596.**

Elite Cafe

The house specialty here is chicken-fried steak. That's the food specialty. The other specialty is providing a place to eat that has recaptured the atmosphere of a diner out of the 1950s. Owner David Tindsley bought the old place some years back, restored it, and reopened it as one of the special eating places around Waco. Open for breakfast, lunch, and dinner. Call for hours. Just off I-35 at the south end of Waco. **2132 S. Valley Mills Dr.; 254-754-4941.**

George's

The students from Baylor University hang out here for the chicken-fried steak and for the "Big O"—a giant-size globe of beer. **1925 Steight Ave.; 254-753-1421; www.georgesrestaurant.com.**

Lone Star Tavern

In my opinion, the Lone Star Tavern is the second best steak house in the state of Texas. (For my favorite, read a little further on to find out about the Stagecoach Inn in Salado). Don't let the outside fool you; it's on the casual side, like the service. Inside, you order by circling the steak of your choice on a menu. The smallest you can order is 16 ounces—a full pound—and they go on up to 32 ounces. It's a great meal for steak lovers. Open Mon.–Fri. for lunch and dinner, and Sat. for dinner only; no reservations. **One mile east of Loop 340 at 4713 Corsicana Highway; 254-799-0918.**

Nick's

A Greek–American restaurant that has served Greek dishes, as well as steak and seafood, for three generations. Open Mon.–Fri. for lunch and dinner, Sat. for dinner only. **4508 W. Waco Dr.; 817-772-7790.**

Where to Stay

Howard Johnson Riverplace Inn

You can get a view of the Brazos River from here. **I-35, exit 335C; 254-752-8222.**

Old Main Lodge

Probably the best-known motel in town. Located near the Baylor University campus, where it has been forever. **I-35, exit 335A; 254-753-0316, 1-800-528-1234.**

Waco Hilton

An upscale national-chain hotel. **113 S. University Parks Dr.; 254-754-8484.**

Towns in the Area

Waco is just the start. Following is a look at some of the other towns and treats of the North-Central area. Communities include Ballinger, Belton, Brownwood, Copperas Cove, Gatesville, Killeen, Lampasas, Marlin, Mexia, Salado, San Saba, and Temple. The following listings begin with Mexia, east of Waco, then move through the towns south of Waco and then west of the city.

Mexia

Getting There: Mexia is on U.S. Hwy. 84, about 35 miles east of Waco. **Visitor Information: Mexia Chamber of Commerce, 315 N. Sherman St., P.O. Box 352, Mexia, 76667; 254-562-5569; chamber@mycroft.mexia.com; www.glade.net/~chamber.**

Mexia is named after Mexican General Jose Antonio Mexia, whose family donated the townsite. Mexia was an ardent follower of Mexican dictator Santa Anna, but later turned against him. He paid the price—Mexia was executed by a firing squad. The town has probably the most commonly mispronounced name of any community in Texas. It's muh-HEY-uh.

Wildlife viewers at Colorado Bend State Park. Photo courtesy of the Texas Department of Tourism.

SEEING AND DOING

Confederate Reunion Grounds State Park

From 1889 until 1946, this park was the site for reunions of military veterans of the Confederate States of America. The park includes an 1872 Heritage House, an 1893 dance pavilion, a two-story log cabin, and a Confederate cannon. The park also provides nature trails, and fishing in the Navasota River. **Six miles south of Mexia, off State Hwy. 14, where Farm Road 2705 and Farm Road 1623 intersect; 254-562-5751.**

Old Fort Parker State Historic Site

Fort Parker was established in 1834 as a private fort to protect a handful of families from Indians. In 1836, Indians overran the fort, killed many members of the John Parker family, and kidnapped others—including Cynthia Ann Parker, who grew up with the Indians. She had a son, Quannah Parker, who grew up to become the last great warrior chief of the Comanche tribe. The fort is open Wed.–Sun. until dusk. **Eight miles south of Mexia, off State Hwy. 14; 254-729-5253.**

RECREATION

Fort Parker State Park

Covers 1,500 acres of wooded and open parkland on the Navasota River, providing natural beauty and var-

ied recreational opportunities, with 25 campsites, 12 screen shelters, and wilderness camping available. **Five miles south of Mexia, off State Hwy. 14 (and 55 miles east of Waco); 254-562-5751.**

Golfing

Olde Oaks Golf and Country Club. P.O. Box 88, Mexia, 76667; 254-562-2391.

Marlin

Getting There: Marlin is on State Hwy. 6, about 25 miles southeast of Waco. **Visitor Information: Marlin Chamber of Commerce, 245 Coleman St., Box 369, Marlin, 76661; 254-883-2171, fax 254-883-2171; www.marlintexas.com.**

In the early 1890s, hot artesian water was discovered beneath the ground here and made the town a spa and health resort for many years. Today the water is again leading the way as residents investigate the promise of geothermal energy. A hospital and the Chamber of Commerce office are heated by hot spring water.

SEEING AND DOING

Falls County Museum

Focuses on local and pioneer history. Open Mon.–Fri. 1–4 P.M. **141 Railroad St.; 254-883-9101.**

RECREATION

Falls of the Brazos Park

Offers fishing, canoeing, swimming, and camping. **About 5 miles southwest of Marlin, off State Hwy. 7 at the Brazos River; 254-883-3203.**

Temple

Getting There: Temple is on I-35, 35 miles south of Waco and 55 miles north of Austin. **Visitor Information: Temple Chamber of Commerce, 2 N. 5th St.; 254-773-2105; www.ci.temple.tx.us.**

Established in 1880, Temple grew up along the Gulf, Colorado and Santa Fe Railroad line. Today it is a retail trade and agricultural center and is one of the Southwest's leading medical centers because of facilities such as Scott and White Hospital and Clinic, King's Daughters Hospital, Olin E. Teague Veterans Center, and Texas A&M University's School of Medicine.

SEEING AND DOING

Czech Heritage Museum

Czech heritage is strong in this community. The museum's collection includes a 1530 Bible, an 1895 handmade dulcimer, antique clocks, and Old World costumes, plus extensive archives on Czech immigration to Texas. Open weekdays 8 A.M.–5 P.M. **520 N. Main St.; 254-773-1575.**

Ferguson House

Home of the most famous, or should I say infamous, team of governors this state has ever known: Ma and Pa Ferguson. Pa Ferguson was elected governor in 1914 and again in 1916. But Farmer Jim—that's what they called the governor—got out of favor with the education establishment and ended up being impeached and barred from running again. So Ma Ferguson ran for the job, and was elected governor in 1924—the first woman governor of the state. Now I have to tell you that the house is not open to the public. But if you just want to take a look, it's at **518 N. 7th St. at W. French St.**

The Grove Country Life Museum

Among the old-time establishments you can see at the museum are the W. J. Dube General Store, with memorabilia of the past, and the Planters State Bank, recalling early banking. Adding to this look at life in the past is a blacksmith shop and a saloon. Open Sat.–Sun. 10 A.M.–6 P.M. **Fifteen miles northwest of Temple on State Hwy. 36.**

Railroad and Pioneer Museum

Housed in a restored depot, the museum's exhibits show the early days of railroading in the area. Open Tues.–Fri. 1–4 P.M., Sat. 10 A.M.–4 P.M. **S. 31st St. and Avenue H; 254-298-5561.** The **Texas Train Festival** is held each year, usually one weekend in mid-September. Activities range from a model train show and swap meet at the civic center to crafts demonstrations at the Railroad and Pioneer Museum. **254-773-2105.**

Wildflower Trails

In 1989 the state legislature designated Temple the Wildflower Capital of Texas. Tours and weekend events are held every year during March and April. **254-773-2105.**

Railroad and Pioneer Museum in Temple. Photo courtesy of the Texas Department of Tourism.

FESTIVALS AND EVENTS

August—Texas Train Festival

Usually third week of the month. Music, ethnic food, train displays, plus reenactment of a train robbery and a Civil War battle. Various locations in Temple, including the restored Santa Fe Depot at S. 31st St. and Ave. H.

RECREATION

Golfing

Greenbriar Golf and Country Club. In the town of Moody, **approximately 15 miles north of Temple, Route 2, Box 465, Moody, 76557; 254-853-2927.**

Sammons Park. 2220 W. Avenue D, Temple, 76504; 254-778-6850.

Miller Springs Natural Area

When Lake Belton, 8 miles west of Temple, overflowed its spillway in 1992, nature carved out a canyon and created a giant wetland below. This place is now preserved as a natural area offering hiking, birdwatching, and wildlife photography. The Miracle Mile boardwalk, wheelchair accessible, provides views of the wetlands and restored native prairie. Open dawn to dusk. Located **on the north side of the Lake Belton dam; 254-770-5720.**

Temple Lake Park

This place should be renamed Temple's Park at the Lake because its 172 acres are situated on Lake Belton. The park features camping, picnicking, fishing, boating, and swimming. **Nine miles northwest of Temple at the end of Farm Road 2305; 254-780-2461.**

WHERE TO EAT

Bluebonnet Cafe
This local institution has been serving southern-style food for 50 years. Temple residents boast that the Bluebonnet has the best chicken-fried steak in Texas. Of course, you'll find that chicken-fried steak is like barbecue in this country: Every community thinks it has the best, and they are all good. **705A 25th St.; 254-773-6654.**

Classic Cafe
Serves lunch and dinner 7 days a week out of a historic office building. **4 S. Main St.; 254-774-8701.**

WHERE TO STAY

Holiday Inn
802 N. General Bruce Dr.; 254-778-4411.

Salado
Getting There: Salado is halfway between Austin and Waco—roughly 45 miles from either city, via I-35. **Visitor Information: Salado Chamber of Commerce; 254-947-5040; www.salado.com.**

I used to get kidded by people about all the TV stories I did about Salado. But how can you help it? It seems like every building has a historical marker out front. It's really more of a village than a town, and it's loaded with charm. Salado was incorporated in 1867, and took its name from the creek that ran through town. People called the creek *Salado,* meaning "salty." Salado had its own college in the 1860s, and it was prominent along the Chisholm Trail. But when the railroad laid its tracks around the town, Salado's prominence declined.

Today's visitors find a fascinating variety of shops, galleries, and places selling antiques and crafts. Fashion designer Grace Jones draws customers from all over the country to her store in an old converted bank building. Outstanding craftspeople and artists live in Salado.

There's a terrific golf course that some say is the most beautiful in Texas. You'll see signs leading to **Mill Creek Golf and Country Club** when you take **exit 285 off I-35** at Salado. Mill Creek is a championship

golf resort with 18 holes now, and plans for 18 more in a couple of years. Mill Creek is semiprivate, which means it's open to the public, for a price. It's worth it. **254-947-5698.**

SEEING AND DOING

Central Texas Area Museum
A small but excellent showcase of local history. Open daily 10 A.M.–5 P.M. A taped drive-yourself tour of points of interest in the area is available for rent at the museum. **423 S. Main St., across from the Stagecoach Inn.**

Pace Park
This park provides a tree-shaded picnic area alongside Salado Creek. The site was an Indian campground long before recorded history. You can still see ruts from wagon trains on the Chisholm Trail in the bedrock of the creek just north of the park. Pace Park is about **2 blocks east of Main St.**

Stagecoach Inn
The inn was a prominent stopover on the Chisholm Trail in the nineteenth century. Now it's a steak house—a *great* steak house. The guest book from the original Stagecoach Inn listed names like General George A. Custer, Robert E. Lee, Sam Houston, and Jesse James. The book was stolen years ago. **I-35, exit 285; 1-800-732-8994, fax 254-947-0671; www.touringtexas.com/stage-off.**

FESTIVALS AND EVENTS

August—Salado Art Fair in Pace Park
One of the best arts and crafts shows in the state. **254-947-5040.**

November—Scottish Festival: The Gathering of the Clans
On the second weekend of the month, representatives of about 200 clans come from all over the United States. Dancing, bagpipe music, contests, and British car show. **254-947-5232.**

December—Country Christmas Weekend Homes Tour
Half a dozen historic homes are decorated and open

for touring, usually the first weekend in the month. 254-947-5567.

RECREATION

Stillhouse Hollow Lake

This 6,400-acre impoundment of the Lampasas River features broad areas of open water between rocky, steep shorelines. It's one of the few Texas lakes where anglers may take smallmouth, largemouth, and Kentucky spotted bass on the same outing. There are five public parks on the lake that offer marina service, camping, picnicking, and boat launching ramps. **Eight miles southwest of Belton or due west of Salado; 254-939-2461.**

WHERE TO EAT

Stagecoach Inn

This ranks as my very favorite steak house in Texas. It's a little more upscale than the Lone Star Tavern in Waco, and more expensive too—but the steaks are the greatest. The age-old tradition of the wait staff reciting the menu for the day is still carried on. Meals are served in a historic building where the likes of Sam Houston, George Custer, and Charles Goodnight of the Goodnight Loving Trail often spent the night. Open 7 days a week. **I-35, Salado exit; 254-947-5111, 1-800-732-8994.**

Tyler House

This well-known eating establishment offers gourmet continental cuisine amid antiques and fine art. Open Tues.–Sat. for lunch and dinner; reservations recommended. **Just north of Salado Creek, which runs through downtown Salado; 254-947-5157.**

WHERE TO STAY

Country Place Bed-and-Breakfast

Farm Road 2268 outside town; 254-947-9683.

Inn at Salado

N. Main St. at Pace Park; 254-947-5999.

Inn on the Creek

Center off Royal St. at Salado Creek; 254-947-5554.

Rose Mansion

Off Royal St. in the Victorian Oaks subdivision; 254-947-5999.

Belton

Getting There: Belton sits at the intersection of I-35 and U.S. Hwy. 190, 40 miles south of Waco and 55 miles north of Austin. **Visitor Information: Belton Chamber of Commerce, P.O. Box 659, Belton, 76513; 254-939-3551; www.dcbelton.org.**

SEEING AND DOING

Bell County Museum

Focusing on the history of the county, this museum is housed in one of the restored Carnegie Library buildings scattered around the state. **201 N. Main St.; 254-933-5243.**

Ding Dong, Texas

About halfway between Belton and Lampasas, south of U.S. Hwy. 190 on Farm Road 440, is one of the most colorful towns in Texas, at least in name. It was settled in the late 1800s by a rancher who believed in hard work. He worked his sons hard too, so on Saturday nights the sons and the other cowboys from the ranch usually let off steam in a nearby town. The farmer's wife worried about her sons' safety, so they agreed to always ring the bell at the country church on their way home, to show they were all right. The community that grew up by the church became officially named Ding Dong, Texas. It's only a place to drive by today. There are no signs announcing it, but it's one of those intriguing places that perpetuate the Texas mystique.

Summer Fun USA

Tube down 725 feet of river rapids or slide from a 40-foot tower into a Texas-size pool. There's a sandy beach for volleyball and horseshoe pits. The place is open weekends beginning in mid-May, then daily from Memorial Day through Labor Day. **1410 Waco Rd.; 254-939-0366.**

University of Mary Hardin-Baylor

Established in 1845, just before Texas statehood, as a women's college. The university, now coeducational, is at **College and 10th Sts.; 254-939-5811; www.umhb.edu.**

RECREATION

Lake Belton

A scenic 12,000-acre impoundment of the Leon River and several creeks, noted for numerous arms and coves along 110 miles of shoreline. Thirteen public parks offer camping, picnicking, and boating. Northwest of Belton via State Hwy. 317, then west on Farm Road 2271. **99 Farm Road 2271, Belton, 76513-9717; 254-939-1829.**

WHERE TO STAY

Belle of Belton

An 1890s mansion delightfully decorated in antiques. **1019 N. Main St.; 254-939-6478.**

Killeen

Getting There: Killeen is on U.S. Hwy. 190 between Temple and Lampasas, about 55 miles southwest of Waco.

SEEING AND DOING

First Cavalry Division Museum

A military museum displaying 150 years of cavalry uniforms, equipment, and weapons. **Building 2218 on Headquarters Ave. at Fort Hood; 254-287-3626.**

Fort Hood

Killeen is home to the largest army post in the world. Fort Hood covers 339 square miles **off U.S. Hwy. 190 beginning just north of Killeen and extending north almost all the way to Gatesville.**

Second Armored Division Museum

On display is the history of the unit that George Patton made famous, including some of the general's personal items. **Building 418 on Battalion Ave. at Fort Hood; 254-287-8811.**

RECREATION

Golfing

Municipal Golf Course. 406 Roy Reynolds Dr., Killeen, 76543; 254-699-6034.

Copperas Cove

Getting There: Copperas Cove is on U.S. Hwy. 190, 19 miles east of Lampasas and about 30 miles west of Temple. **Visitor Information: covechamber@n-link.com; www.copperascove.com.**

Originally one of the watering holes along the Chisholm Trail, Copperas Cove is a farming and ranching community near Fort Hood army base.

SEEING AND DOING

Topsey Exotic Ranch and Drive Through Park

This ranch/park near town is home to 70 exotic species, including camels and lions that roam the place. You can visit too and photograph the animals from your car. **Eight miles northwest of Copperas Cove via Farm Road 1113; 254-547-3700.**

Lampasas

Getting There: Lampasas sits at the junction of U.S. Hwys. 190, 281, and 183. That places it about 60 miles northwest of Austin via Hwy. 183, and some 90 miles from Waco via I-35 and Hwy. 190. **Visitor Information: Lampasas Chamber of Commerce, 501 E. 2nd St.; 512-556-5172; www.ci.lampasas.tx.us.**

The Indians drank mineral spring water in Lampasas long before the frontiersmen arrived. The water still flows to the tune of about 3 million gallons daily throughout the region, and there are a couple of places you can see it: at Hancock Park, at the intersection of U.S. Hwys. 190 and 281 south, and at Hanna Springs, at the end of North Street out of downtown Lampasas.

Lampasas connects the Texas Hill Country to the High Plains. There is prime hunting, and fishing in the nearby Lampasas and Colorado Rivers. Lampasas also brags about its native stone courthouse, which is on the National Register of Historic Places.

The northern boundaries of **Lake Buchanan** are within an easy drive south of Lampasas. Buchanan is the largest of the Highland Lakes, described in detail in The Hill Country chapter.

SEEING AND DOING

Keystone Square Museum

Housed in an early frontier building, displaying historic artifacts plus information on the Texas Rangers. Open Sat. 10 A.M.–2 P.M. **304 S. Western St.; 512-556-2224; www.lampasas-tx.com/keyston_square_museum.htm.**

FESTIVALS AND EVENTS

April—Bluebonnet Fair & Farm Heritage Days

Early April. **Courthouse square; 512-556-5172.**

April—Earth Day Celebration at Colorado Bend State Park

Late April. A special occasion when Gorman Falls and Gorman Caves are opened to visitors. **915-628-3240.**

July—Spring-Ho Festival

Early July. **W. M. Brook Park; 512-556-5172.**

December—Carol of Lights

Early December. **Courthouse square; 512-556-2760.**

RECREATION

Hancock Park

A 109-acre municipal facility that includes Hancock Springs, the city water supply, includes picnic areas and playgrounds, a swimming pool, a pavilion, and an 18-hole golf course. Southwest of Lampasas **at the intersection of U.S. Hwys. 190 and 281 south.**

W. M. Brook Park

Offers an outdoor theater, picnic areas, and playgrounds. South side of the city, **at the intersection of U.S. Hwys. 190, 281, and 183,** directly across from Hancock Park.

WHERE TO EAT

Cheese Chalet

Offers thirty different cheeses and a variety of meats; a nice deli-style restaurant. Open Mon.–Sat. for lunch and dinner. **523 E. 3rd St.; 512-556-6611.**

Lisa's Schnitzel House

A popular place for authentic German food. Open Tues.–Sat., dinner only. **311 E. 3rd St.; 512-556-2660.**

WHERE TO STAY

Moses Hughes Ranch Bed-and-Breakfast

A native stone ranchhouse on a Hill Country creek. Seven miles west of Lampasas on Farm Road 580; 254-556-5923.

San Saba

Getting There: San Saba is 36 miles west of Lampasas, via Hwy. 190. **Visitor Information: San Saba Chamber of Commerce; 915-372-5141.**

San Saba was settled in the 1850s and named for the scenic river on which it is located. The San Saba and Colorado Rivers are popular with campers and fishers. The town is known for its wonderful crop of pecans every year.

RECREATION

Colorado Bend State Park

Offers scenic settings along the banks of the Colorado River. The park provides primitive camping, chemical toilets, 5.5 miles of hiking trails, and picnic facilities (no drinking water is provided). Fantastic fishing. You'll think you've walked into a rain forest when you visit **Gorman Falls** at the park. Park personnel lead tours to the falls, the only way visits are permitted. Tours go year-round, Sat. 10 A.M. and 2 P.M., and Sun. 10 A.M., weather permitting. From San Saba, **take U.S. Hwy. 190 east 5 miles to Farm Road 580, then right 13 miles to Bend; follow the signs to the park; 915-628-3240.**

Mill Pond Park

Includes a tiny spring-fed lake, waterfalls, a swimming pool, and picnic sites. More than 5 million gallons of water flow up through the rocks beneath the lake daily. Facilities include baseball fields, a pavilion, tennis courts, and playground equipment. RV hookups also available. **Five blocks east of the courthouse square.**

Risien Park

Bordered on one side by the San Saba River. Includes picnic facilities, playground equipment, a pavilion, volleyball courts, and an amphitheater—all beneath beautiful pecan trees. **On the east edge of San Saba on U.S. Hwy. 190.**

Ballinger

Getting There: Ballinger is on U.S. Hwy. 67, about 35 miles northeast of San Angelo, and 56 miles south of Abilene (via U.S. Hwy. 83). Ballinger is about 185 miles east of Waco. **Visitor Information: Ballinger Chamber of Commerce, P.O. Box 577, Ballinger, 76821; 915-365-2333, fax 915-365-3445; www.ballinger.**

SEEING AND DOING

Carnegie Library
Built in 1909, this library is one of the few in the state in continuous use as a library. Listed on the National Register of Historic Places. Open weekday afternoons. **204 N. 8th St.; 915-365-3616.**

Cowboy and His Horse
The famous statue honoring Charles H. Noyes, a cowboy killed in a range mishap, is on the courthouse lawn downtown **at the intersection of U.S. Hwys. 83 and 67.** The Noyes Family commissioned the work by sculptor Pompeo Coppini.

Pioneer Plaza
Features a fountain, gazebo, and a restored Star Tobacco sign, circa 1909. **106 S. 7th St.**

FESTIVALS AND EVENTS

April—Texas State Festival of Ethnic Cultures and Arts and Crafts Show
Late April. **City Park, Crosson and 3rd Sts.; 915-365-2333.**

June—Big Sky Road Riders Rally
Mid-month. Motorcycle buffs from all over West Texas come to Ballinger to show off and talk shop. **City Park, Crosson and 3rd Sts.; 915-365-2333.**

August—Open Bass Tournament
Mid-month. **On Lake O. H. Ivie, 25 miles southeast of Ballinger, by the Concho River; 915-365-2333.**

RECREATION

City Park and Lake
Offers camping, fishing, water-skiing, and picnicking on Elm Creek.

Brownwood

Getting There: Brownwood is on U.S. Hwy. 67/377, 117 miles southwest of Fort Worth, and about 125 miles west of Waco (via U.S. Hwy. 84). **Visitor Information: Brownwood Chamber of Commerce, P.O. Box 880, Brownwood, 76804; 915-646-9535, fax 915-643-6686; cmitchel@ci.brownwood.tx.us.**

SEEING AND DOING

Brown County Museum of History
Provides seven rooms of historical exhibits in an old castle-like jail building. Open Wed. 1–4 P.M., Sat. 11 A.M.–4 P.M. **200 N. Broadway St.**

Camp Bowie Memorial Park
Honors the men of the famed 36th Infantry Division. Vintage military equipment is displayed. Camp Bowie industrial area **at the intersection of Crockett Dr. and Morris Sheppard Dr.**

Douglas MacArthur Academy of Freedom
Affiliated with Howard Payne University, the academy specializes in history and government in the context of western civilization. The academy is dedicated to General Douglas MacArthur, and memorabilia and some of his personal souvenirs are displayed. Tours Mon.–Sat. when school is in session. **Austin Ave. at Coggin St.; 915-646-2502; www.ci.brownwood.tx.us/academy.htm.**

FESTIVALS AND EVENTS

March—Home and Garden Show
Mid-month. **Various locations; 915-646-9535.**

July—Bayou Blast
Early July. Citywide celebration of Brownwood's history. **Riverside Park; 915-646-9535.**

RECREATION

Golfing
Coleman Country Club. In the town of Coleman, **30 miles west of Brownwood. P.O. Box 128, Coleman, 76834; 915-625-2922.**

Lakewood Recreation Center. Only 9 holes here, but this is a good example of what small communities can do to entertain themselves. This challenging course has water hazards and fast bent-grass greens. **In the town of Rising Star approximately 25 miles north of Brownwood on U.S. Hwy. 183; Route 1, Rising Star, 76471; 254-643-7792.**

Lake Brownwood State Park
Offers swimming, fishing, boating, hiking, and camping. Provides 87 campsites, 17 cabins, 10 screen shelters, nature trails, some hiking trails, and a lighted fishing pier. The park is **23 miles northwest of Brownwood via State Hwy. 279 and Park Road 15; Route 5, Box 160, Brownwood, 76801; 915-784-5223.**

WHERE TO EAT

Section Hand Steakhouse
This family restaurant offers good steaks and a big salad bar. Open every day for lunch and dinner. **4412 U.S. Hwy. 377 S.; 915-643-1581.**

Underwood's Cafeteria
They have been serving barbecue since the 1950s, although their contemporary menu has expanded. You'll find Underwood Cafeterias all over West Texas. **402 W. Commerce; 915-646-6110.**

Gatesville
Getting There: Gatesville is on U.S. Hwy. 84, about 35 miles west of Waco. **Visitor Information: Gatesville Chamber of Commerce; 254-865-2617; www.ci.gatesville.tx.us.**

One of my favorite museums, the Buckhorn on the courthouse square in Gatesville, has long since closed its doors, but a brand-new facility is home to the Coryell County Museum.

SEEING AND DOING

Coryell County Courthouse
You might check out the courthouse while you're in Gatesville. It was built in 1897 of hand-cut, hand-carved limestone, a fine example of Romanesque Renaissance Revival architecture in Texas. The clock tower is copper-domed, and the glass in the rotunda skylight has a Texas star pattern. At each entrance are columns in Roman Corinthian style, and over the east entrance is the figure of an owl, for wisdom. The statues on the roof represent justice. Many people think this is the most glorious courthouse in Texas. I disagree. I think the Shackelford County Courthouse in Albany, near Abilene, has it beat (see the Abilene chapter).

Coryell County Museum
The Coryell is filled with city and county history, including old pictures and old structures, like the county's first jailhouse, double-walled for security. The prize here is a collection of thousands of spurs collected by local high school coach Lloyd Mitchell. One set was obtained from a real northeastern dude, Jackie Kennedy Onassis. **718 Main St.; 254-865-5007.**

FESTIVALS AND EVENTS

January—Taste of Gatesville Plus Celebration
Mid-month. **Various locations; 254-865-8050.**

August—Health and Wellness Fair
Early August. **Activities Complex, on U.S. Hwy. 84 at the eastern city limits; 254-248-6338.**

October—Coryell Market Days
First weekend in the month. **Activities Complex, on U.S. Hwy. 84 at the eastern city limits; 254-865-5007.**

The Independence Trail

The town of Washington in this part of the state calls itself the Birthplace of Texas, and for good reason. It's an important part of the region called the Independence Trail—a region instrumental in the Texas fight for independence from Mexico. Look for the numerous road signs in this region that designate places along the Independence Trail.

Even as the soldiers of Texas were fighting to defend the Alamo in San Antonio against the onslaught of Santa Anna's forces, lawmakers gathered at the Texas town of Washington to declare an independent republic. The year was 1836. The delegates to the meeting created and signed a declaration of independence that was inspired by the U.S. Declaration of Independence. Then the delegates abandoned town and ran like hell, because in the weeks after the Alamo tragedy, the Mexican army was hunting for them.

You can visit the town today and get in touch with the hope for independence that was in the air back in those days. The town was originally called Washington and then, after the Civil War, took on the name Washington-on-the-Brazos, for the river that flows through it—although many Texas leaders had referred to it as Washington-on-the-Brazos even before the Texas war for independence. Today this early era of Texas history truly comes alive at Washington-on-the-Brazos State Historical Park.

There also are plenty of bonuses for touring the Independence Trail region. Washington is off the beaten path, still a tiny village in a quiet setting. The region's landscape makes you want to linger. This part of Texas is rich in rolling hills, towering oaks, and fertile blackland, with many horse ranches and dairy farms. In my opinion, nowhere in Texas in the spring do the bluebonnets, paintbrushes, and Indian blankets put on such a show as they do when they display their blues, reds, and yellows along the Independence Trail.

Visitor Information

Bryan/College Station Convention and Visitors Bureau
715 University Dr. E.; 409-260-9898; info@cschamber.org; www.bcschamber.org.

Chappell Hill Chamber of Commerce
P.O. Box 113, Chappell Hill, 77426.

Hearne Chamber of Commerce
201 Magnolia St.; 409-279-2351; www.hearne.com.

Hempstead Chamber of Commerce
733 12th St.; 409-826-8217.

La Grange Area Chamber of Commerce
129 N. Main St.; 1-800-524-7264, 409-968-5756, fax 409-968-8000; chamber@lagrange.org; www.lagrangetx.org.

Navasota Chamber of Commerce
117 S. La Salle (Business State Hwy. 6); 409-825-6600, 1-800-252-6642; www.rtis.com/reg/navasota.

Round Top Chamber of Commerce
On the square in Round Top; 409-249-4042.

Washington County Chamber of Commerce
Information about the county and about Washington-on-the-Brazos. **314 S. Austin St., Brenham; 409-836-3695.**

Major Attractions

Washington-on-the-Brazos State Historical Park

This 154-acre park contains part of the original town site of Washington and a reconstruction of Independence Hall, where the Texas Constitution was drawn up. Also on the site is the former home of Anson Jones, last president of the Republic of Texas. A pecan grove picnic area helps make the park an inviting place to visit.

The park's **Star of the Republic Museum** traces the history of the Texas Republic. The museum's research library, administered by Blinn College, is accessible to the public. The library is open daily 10 A.M.–5 P.M. from March through August, and the same hours Wed.–Sun. from September through February.

The park is open daily 8 A.M. to sundown. **Twenty miles northeast of Brenham; take State Hwy. 105 to the town of Washington, then Farm Road 912 to the park; 409-878-2214; www.tpwd.state.tx.us/park/washingt.**

Farm Road 1155 north of the park winds through beautiful pastoral landscapes of the Brazos River Valley, along a route used by the early settlers.

Blue Bell Creameries

Blue Bell was founded in 1907 as the Brenham Creamery Company. The name was changed to Blue Bell in 1930, after the wildflower that grows in this area and blooms in summer.

The creamery at first produced only two gallons of ice cream a day. Today that wouldn't even take care of employee snacks. Blue Bell has grown a great deal since it started, but the growth has taken place within the spirit of a small dairy. When the employees tell you it's really still just the little creamery in Brenham, you believe it.

At the operation in Brenham, you can visit the old-timey gift shop and see antique delivery trucks still

---

Getting There

A good staging area for a visit to the Independence Trail region is the city of Brenham, about a 90-minute drive from either Austin or Houston on U.S. Hwy. 290. You can fly into **Austin's Robert Mueller Municipal Airport** and drive west to Brenham, or fly into **George Bush Intercontinental Airport** north of Houston and head northwest on U.S. Hwy. 290 to Brenham.

Washington-on-the-Brazos is northeast of Brenham, only about 20 miles up State Hwy. 105. A 25-mile drive north of Washington brings you to the towns of Bryan and College Station, often referred to together as Bryan/College Station, home of Texas A&M University.

There's also easy access from Brenham to the community of Independence, 12 miles north of Brenham on Farm Road 390. South and southwest of Brenham are the historic towns of La Grange and Columbus.

---

posting the Blue Bell name. Inside you'll be treated to free tastes of the latest Blue Bell flavors. Tours of the plant are given daily. (Groups of 15 or more need reservations; all tours during spring break are by reservation only.)

The creamery is east of downtown Brenham on Farm Road 577. Take U.S. Hwy. 290 east to the outskirts of town, turn left onto Road 577, and travel 2 miles to the creamery; 409-830-2197, 1-800-327-8135; www.bluebell.com.

Antique Rose Emporium

William Shakespeare may have been right when he said "a rose by any other name would smell as sweet." But since then, grafting and inbreeding have robbed a lot of roses of their fragrance. At some point, the experts decided that people wanted roses that looked good more than roses that smelled good.

But Mike Shoup of Independence, Texas, doesn't necessarily feel that way. He is a rose fanatic, and an expert gardener. He enjoys the old roses more than

Antique Rose Emporium in Independence. Photo courtesy of Texas Highways magazine.

hundred people, it's one of the smallest incorporated cities in Texas. It was established in 1835 as Jones Post Office. Twenty years later Round Top Academy was founded, with a tuition of $10 a session, and the town eventually became Round Top. The twentieth century passed fairly uneventfully in Round Top until the 1960s, when a wealthy woman from Houston, Mrs. Charles Bybee, set about developing **Henkel Square (409-249-3308)** as an authentic evocation of old Texas. It was a slow process, deliberately done over a period of many years. Mrs. Bybee was dedicated to preserving this bit of Texas, and she did. Henkel Square, with its display of restored structures from the early 1800s, is a wonderful example of what can be done to preserve and protect a small town's history.

Once Henkel Square was on its feet, other projects appeared. Today the tiny community bubbles over with tourists most of the year. Music teacher **James Dick** has his own private academy here, 5 blocks north of Henkel Square. A fort built in the 1820s by Indian fighter John Henry Moore has been reconstructed here. A restored nineteenth-century plantation farm has become the **Winedale Historical Center,** a living history museum **(4 miles east of Round Top via Farm Roads 1457 and 2714; 409-249-3505).**

Monument Hill State Historical Park

A 48-foot marker of stone, bronze, and polychrome honors the men of the Mier Expedition who were executed by Mexicans in 1842. The marker is on top of a hill with a spectacular view of this part of Texas.

The marker commemorates a tragic episode in Texas revolutionary history. In 1842 a group of Texas soldiers crossed the Rio Grande into the community of Mier, not far from Laredo, where they fought a losing battle with Mexican soldiers and eventually surrendered. Mexican dictator Santa Anna wanted to execute the Texans, but his generals convinced him this would be too harsh. So he decided to execute one out of every ten. Every man was ordered to draw a bean from a container; those who drew the black beans were executed. Seventeen Texans met death before a firing squad.

You can take a self-guided tour of the park, and there is a wheelchair-accessible interpretive trail. You can also enjoy a nature trail, picnic sites, and a playground. Open daily 8 A.M.–5 P.M. **Two miles south**

the new ones being developed. The old roses are hardy and don't require much attention, and their fragrances are much more pronounced. So in his spare time, Mike started collecting old roses from cemeteries, along the streets, and in vacant lots—wherever he could find them. Many of the old roses were originally brought to this area by early pioneers.

At first people thought Mike was crazy. Here was this college-trained young man who went around digging up old flowers. But he had the last laugh. Today Mike and his wife run the Antique Rose Emporium outside Independence, and they ship roses all over the world.

Mike's commercial garden is open to the public Tues.–Sat. 9 A.M.–6 P.M., and Sun. 11 A.M.–5:30 P.M. If you end up buying a rose, he'll be happy to pass on a few tips on how to best care for it. **On Farm Road 50 just south of Farm Road 390 on the outskirts of Independence; 1-800-441-0002.**

Round Top

Round Top is a town—one that in my estimation is a major attraction. With a population of fewer than a

of La Grange off U.S. Hwy. 77; 409-968-5658; www.cvtv.net/business/monument.html.

On a neighboring site within walking distance is the **Kreische State Historical Park,** with the ruins of a stone brewery and home built by pioneer Heinrich L. Kreische. His brewery was one of the first in Texas, turning out more than 700 barrels of beer a year in the mid-1800s. Tours are given Sat.–Sun., 2 P.M. and 3:30 P.M.

Towns in the Area

This tour of the region begins in Brenham, then visits the towns north of Brenham—Independence, Washington, Navasota, Bryan/College Station, and Hearne—followed by the towns generally south of Brenham—Chappell Hill, Hempstead, Round Top, La Grange, and Columbus.

Brenham

Getting There: Brenham is along U.S. Hwy. 290, about 65 miles northwest of Houston and 75 miles east of Austin.

When the town of Brenham is mentioned, the first thing that comes to mind, for Texans, is Blue Bell Ice Cream. This is where the good stuff is made (see Major Attractions earlier in this chapter). But there's much more to the Brenham area than peaches and cream.

SEEING AND DOING

Brenham Heritage Museum

Houses the city's history in a renovated 1915 federal building. **105 S. Market St.; 409-830-8445.**

Burton's Farmers Gin

Built in 1914, and now a national historic landmark, this cotton gin remains in operation to show tour groups how it refined cotton when the plant reigned supreme in the Brazos Valley. **Twelve miles west of Brenham on U.S. Hwy. 290; 409-289-FEST.**

Ellison's Greenhouses

The only wholesale greenhouse facility in the state that allows the public to tour its working operations. Prebooked tours are offered Mon.–Thurs., with walk-in tours Fri.–Sat. Five acres of greenhouses produce

roses, daisies, lilies, mums, and much more year-round. In November and December you'll see a sea of poinsettias. **1808 S. Horton St. off Farm Road 577; 409-836-0084.**

Monastery of St. Clare Miniature Horse Farm

Home to a group of Franciscan Poor Clare Nuns who support the monastery by raising miniature horses and by selling handmade ceramics and other crafts. Open daily 2–4 P.M. except Holy Week and Christmas. **Nine miles northeast of Brenham on State Hwy. 105; 409-836-9652.**

RECREATION

Nueces Canyon Equestrian Center

A major horse center that specializes in cutting-horse shows, also offers hayrides, horseshoe pitching, volleyball, horse demonstrations, lake fishing, and an RV park. **9501 U.S. Hwy. 290, 8 miles west of Brenham; 409-289-5600.**

Independence

Getting There: Independence is on Farm Road 390, about 12 miles north of Brenham.

Independence is home to the Antique Rose Emporium, described in Major Attractions earlier in this chapter. Visitors also enjoy seeing Old Baylor Park, site of the original campus that led to present-day Baylor University in Waco and the University of Mary Hardin-Baylor in Belton. Four large stone pillars mark the original site of Baylor's administration and classroom building. Half a mile west of Independence on Farm Road 390.

SEEING AND DOING

Sam Houston Homesite

Commemorated with a large granite marker. **On Farm Road 390 in Independence, 1 block east of the Texas Baptist Historical Center.**

Scenic Drive

One of my favorite scenic drives is **Farm Road 390 east and west** from Independence. It offers attractive scenery and exceptional vistas, especially colorful around mid-April during the bluebonnet season.

Texas Baptist Historical Center

In the Independence Baptist Church, organized in 1839. It's the third oldest Baptist church in Texas, and the place where General Sam Houston was converted in 1854. Includes artifacts dating back to the Civil War. Open Wed.–Sat. 10 A.M.–4 P.M. **At the junction of Farm Road 390 and Farm Road 50 in Independence.**

Washington

Getting There: Washington is on State Hwy. 105, about 35 miles south of Bryan/College Station. (It's also roughly 70 miles northwest of Houston and 90 miles east of Austin.) **Visitor Information: Washington County Chamber of Commerce, 314 S. Austin St., Brenham; 409-836-3695.**

Washington was a busy place even before it became the site of the 1836 meeting to declare Texas an independent republic. The Andrew Robinson family created a settlement in the area in 1821. Robinson soon opened a ferry concession providing the only transportation across the Brazos. The ferry service spurred growth of the town, and the arrival of steamers up the Brazos made Washington a legitimate river port. Its importance was only magnified by the meeting of delegates to draft a declaration of independence for Texas.

Then history took a turn. In 1858, as railroad lines reached the edge of the city, the Houston and Texas Central Railroad wanted to be paid a premium to link up with the town. Washington refused to come up with $11,000, so the railroad bypassed it, directing its lines instead to a more understanding and appreciative community, Hempstead. The prosperous port town of Washington sank into decline.

Washington today is a tiny community near Washington-on-the-Brazos State Historical Park, which includes part of the original townsite of Washington. For a description of the park and its offerings, see Major Attractions earlier in this chapter.

Navasota

Getting There: Navasota is at the junction of State Hwys. 105 and 6, 18 miles southeast of College Station and about 60 miles northwest of Houston. **Visitor Information: Navasota Chamber of Commerce, 117 S. La Salle (Business State Hwy. 6); 409-825-6600, 1-800-252-6642; www.rtis.com/reg/navasota.**

SEEING AND DOING

Harlock History Center

The history of the region is on record in this two-story home, constructed in 1892. **1215 E. Washington St., State Hwy. 105; 409-825-7615.**

La Salle Monument

It was 130 years before the first Anglo settler reached this country that the French explorer René Robert Cavelier, Sieur de la Salle, arrived in what would become Texas. He had made a mistake. La Salle was looking for the mouth of the Mississippi River, but a series of misadventures brought his three ships to Matagorda Bay. He established a coastal colony called Fort St. Louis. Two years later, while doing some inland exploring, he was murdered by one of his own men. The deed was committed at the site of present-day Navasota. The monument is **in the middle of the thoroughfare in the 300 block of Washington Ave. downtown.**

Weaver Apiaries

Before the turn of the twentieth century, a man named Weaver and his bride received ten hives of honeybees as a wedding present. Today, four families of Weavers are in the bee business. In addition to producing honey, they are the country's largest exporter of queen bees. Call for tours. **Ten miles south of Navasota off State Hwy. 6.; Route 1, Box 256, Navasota, 77868; 409-825-7312, fax 409-825-7351; bweaver@myriad.net; www.beeweaver.com.**

Bryan/College Station

Getting There: The towns of Bryan and College Station, usually linked as Bryan/College Station, are on State Hwy. 6, halfway between Waco and Houston. The towns are about 75 miles southeast of Waco and about 80 miles northwest of Houston. **Visitor Information: Bryan/College Station Convention and Visitors Bureau, 715 University Drive East; 409-260-9898; info@cschamber.org; www.bcschamber.org.**

SEEING AND DOING

Messina Hoof Wine Cellars

The wine-making traditions of Messina, Italy, and

Hoof, Germany, are blended at the vineyards of this Texas winery. There are picnic facilities and fishing at the lake on the property, and grape stomping at certain times of year. Tours weekdays 1 P.M.; Sat. 10:30 A.M., 12:30 P.M., 2:30 P.M., and 3:30 P.M.; and Sun. 12:30 P.M. and 2:30 P.M.; reservations necessary. There is a retail store and a tasting room; open Mon.–Fri. 9 A.M.–5:30 P.M., Sat. 10 A.M.–5 P.M., Sun. noon–4 P.M. **Next to the airport on Wallis Rd., south of State Hwy. 21, 6 miles northeast of Bryan; 409-778-9463; www.messinahof.com.**

Texas A&M University

Visitors find plenty to see and do on the campus of the oldest institution of higher learning in Texas. Stop at the campus information center for details and maps on the attractions; open Mon.–Fri. 9 A.M.–5 P.M. The center is on the first floor of the eleven-story **Rudder Tower, across from the university's G. Rollie White Coliseum; 409-845-5851; www.tamu.edu.**

The university is famous for its military cadet corps and Reserve Officer Training Corps, whose graduates served by the thousands in World Wars I and II, as well as in the Korean, Vietnam, and Gulf Wars. The university's **Sam Houston Sanders Corps of Cadets Center** has exhibits honoring the university and its cadets **(409-862-2862)**. Also on campus is the **Albritton Bell Tower,** with forty-nine bells cast in France **(Old Main Dr. and Wellborn Dr.).** The art exhibits of the **J. Wayne Stark University Center Gallery** are open Tues.–Fri. 9 A.M.–5 P.M. and Sat.–Sun. noon–6 P.M.; the **Forsyth Gallery** is open Mon.–Fri. 9 A.M.–8 P.M. and Sat.–Sun. noon–6 P.M.; both galleries are in Memorial Student Center, adjacent to Rudder Tower. The **Centennial Wood Carvings,** a series of six hand-carved walnut panels depicting the history of the University, are also on display in the Memorial Student Center. The university's **Floral Test Garden** has hundreds of varieties of seeds and bulbs cultivated to test the adaptability of the local climate **(Houston and Jersey Sts.).**

You can take your pick of a number of tours at the university. **Texas A&M Creamery:** how ice cream and cheeses are made **(409-260-9898)**. **University Vet School:** tours of clinic for large and small animals **(1-800-777-8292). Cotton and Its History (409-260-9898).**

Texas World Speedway

Stock cars and motorcycles compete for speed on this multimillion-dollar track. A 27,000-seat stand looks over a 3-mile grand prix racecourse, recognized as one of the nation's finest. **Ten miles south of College Station on State Hwy. 6; 409-690-2500; tws@texasworldspeedway.com; www.texasworldspeedway.com.**

RECREATION

Gibbons Creek Reservoir

This cooling pond for a power generating plant is a popular spot to fish for bass, catfish, and crappie. Open 5:30 A.M.–9:30 P.M., closed Wed. and major holidays. The reservoir is **22 miles east of Bryan on County Road 164.**

Hearne

Getting There: Hearne is at the intersection of U.S. Hwy. 79 and State Hwy. 6, about 55 miles southeast of Waco and about 85 miles northeast of Austin. **Visitor Information: Hearne Chamber of Commerce, 201 Magnolia St.; 409-279-2351; www.hearne.com.**

SEEING AND DOING

"Aunt Jemima"

Rosie Lee Moore served for many years as the woman who portrayed the cook Aunt Jemima for the Quaker Oats Company. Moore, of Robertson County, Texas, was working for the advertising department at Quaker Oats when she was chosen as the latest in the line of women to promote the company's products as Jemima. She died in 1967, and is buried at **Hammond Colony Cemetery, 6 miles northwest of Hearne on County Road 229; 409-850-1967.** During the late 1960s, the traditional Aunt Jemima image gave way to an artist's conception of a more modern black woman. The image may have changed over the years, but the message of a warm, caring, motherly woman serving up delicious breakfasts has remained the same.

Camp Hearne

German prisoners of war were held at this camp during World War II, and plans are under way to preserve

Rustic architectural beauty along scenic Farm Road 390, north of Brenham.

the facility, which is not now open to the public. A model of the camp is on display at the **Hearne Chamber of Commerce (201 Magnolia St., 409-279-2351)** and can be viewed weekdays 9 A.M.–4 P.M.

The Columns Antiques

Antiques are now displayed and sold from this gracious southern-style mansion, built by an early settler named Easterwood. The mansion is one of the most photographed homes in Texas. **206 W. Davis St.; 409-279-6051.**

Dream Catcher Guest Ranch

A unique setting for business retreats, family reunions, weddings, and tourist visits, including western-style adventure with horse-drawn wagon rides, trick roping, fiddling around, hayrides, and campfires. An out-of-the-ordinary experience at a working cattle ranch where the sounds of wagon trains and the pony express still echo from the past. Browse in nearby antique shops and dine in quaint country restaurants. Also, you can bicycle the beautiful back roads of Texas. The ranch is near the town of Franklin, about a dozen miles northeast of Hearne. **Route 2, Box 115, Franklin, 77856; 409-279-2050.**

Chappell Hill

Getting There: Chappell Hill is on U.S. Hwy. 290, about 45 miles northwest of Houston and 90 miles east of Austin. **Visitor Information: Chappell Hill Chamber of Commerce, P.O. Box 113, Chappell Hill, 77426.**

SEEING AND DOING

Browning Plantation

A restored 1857 mansion open for tours. **Two miles from Chappell Hill;** at the only traffic light on U.S. Hwy. 290 in Chappell Hill, go south on Farm Road 1190 to a T in the road, then look for a sign directing you to the plantation. **409-836-6144.**

Chappell Hill Historical Museum

At the site of the former Chappell Hill Female College. Open Wed.–Sat. 10 A.M.–4 P.M., Sun. 1–4 P.M. **At Church and Poplar Sts.; 409-836-3933.**

Stagecoach Inn

Built in 1850 by the town's founders, Jacob and Mary Chappell Haller. **Main and Chestnut Sts.; 409-836-9515.**

Hempstead

Getting There: Hempstead is on U.S. Hwy. 290, about 35 miles northwest of Houston and 100 miles east of Austin. **Visitor Information: Hempstead Chamber of Commerce, 733 12th St.; 409-826-8217.**

Hempstead was once known as Six Shooter Junction. The most notable gun battle shocked the nation in 1905 when U.S. congressman John Pinckney, his brother, and two others were gunned down in the Waller County Courthouse while arguing political issues with some prohibitionists. The courthouse was riddled with seventy-five gunshots.

SEEING AND DOING

Frazier's Ornamental and Architectural Concrete

Stop by if you're in the market for birdbaths or water fountains. Frazier has acres of concrete yard statuary, from entry pieces to tabletop creations. Open daily except Wed. **On business U.S. Hwy. 290 near the eastern city limits; 409-826-6760.**

Liendo Plantation

Built in 1853 by one of the largest landowners in Texas, this cotton plantation was originally a Spanish land grant assigned to Justo Liendo, the plantation's namesake. The plantation was occupied by Elisabet Ney and her husband, Dr. Edmond Montgomery, from 1873 to 1911, and both are buried on the grounds. Liendo is listed on the National Register of Historic Places. Tours first Sat. of each month at 10:00 A.M., 11:30 A.M., and 1 P.M. **On Farm Road 1488 northeast of Hempstead:** Take U.S. Hwy. 290 to the eastern edge of town, turn left onto Farm Road 1488 and travel about a mile, then turn right onto Wyatt Chappell Road and travel about three-quarters of a mile to Liendo Plantation; **1-800-826-4371.** The plantation also operates a tearoom in a small house in Hempstead (on State Hwy. 6 about a mile west of the U.S. Hwy. 290 bypass; look for the big sign).

Watermelons!

Another thing about Hempstead: This place produces great watermelons. You can buy them in most grocery stores—or at roadside stands (it's more fun that way). These delicious Hempstead watermelons are usually harvested in June and July.

Round Top

Getting There: Round Top is on State Hwy. 37, about 15 miles northeast of La Grange and about an equal distance west of Brenham. **Visitor Information: Round Top Chamber of Commerce, on the square in Round Top; 409-249-4042.** For more on Round Top, also see Major Attractions earlier in this chapter.

SEEING AND DOING

Bethlehem Lutheran Church

The center of Lutheran faith in Fayette County, this church was dedicated in 1866. It's built of stone construction with distinctly German architecture, and houses an unusual pipe organ made of hand-shaped cedar. **In Round Top 1 block west of State Hwy. 237.**

Henkel Square

Inside a split-rail fence on the town square, several restored structures dating from 1820 are displayed. Also a superb collection of Anglo and German American furnishings. Open noon–5 P.M. **On Farm Road 1457, facing the courthouse square; 409-249-3308.**

International Festival Institute

Founded by pianist James Dick, the institute features music students in residence from all over the world. One concert weekend is scheduled every month from August through April and for 6 weeks in June and July. The concerts of orchestral, chamber, and solo works are in Festival Concert Hall on the institute's 80-acre campus. Tours are available. **Five blocks north of Henkel Square in Round Top, on State Hwy. 237; 409-249-3129, fax 409-249-3100; festinst @fais.net; www.fais.net/~/festinst.**

Moore's Fort

The fort was built in 1828 by Indian fighter Colonel John Henry Moore at the bend in the Colorado River that is the present-day site of the town of La Grange. The fort was moved to Round Top and restored. **On State Hwy. 237 at the northern edge of Round Top.**

Royer's Cafe

Bud and Karen Royer operate a mail-order homemade

pie business, and opened the cafe as an afterthought. Their whole family stays busy making pies and shipping them out, and the cafe has caught on too. **On the square in town, at 105 Main St.; 877-866-7437.**

Winedale Historical Center

A restored nineteenth-century farm with plantation homes, log cabins, fireplace kitchen, smokehouse, and barns. The center, operated by the University of Texas at Austin, studies the ethnic cultures of Central Texas. Open Sat. 9 A.M.–5 P.M., Sun. noon–5 P.M.; group tours Mon.–Fri. with at least 2 days' notice. **Four miles east of Round Top via Farm Roads 1457 and 2714. Round Top Historical Society; 409-249-5058; www.rtis.com/reg/roundtop/wine dale.htm.**

La Grange

Getting There: La Grange is on State Hwy. 71, some 55 miles southeast of Austin and about 93 miles west of Houston. **Visitor Information: La Grange Area Chamber of Commerce, 129 N. Main St.; 1-800-524-7264, 409-968-5756, fax 409-968-8000; chamber@lagrange.org; www.lagrangetx.org.**

La Grange is an early German community with an 1890s courthouse, an old county jail, an 1886 MKT Depot, historical markers, and the St. James Episcopal Church, circa 1885. Near La Grange is the Monument Hill State Historical Park and Kreische State Historical Park, described earlier in this chapter in Major Attractions.

SEEING AND DOING

Fayette Heritage Museum and Archives

Showcases art and genealogical collections. Open Tues.–Fri. 10 A.M.–5 P.M., Sat. 10 A.M.–1 P.M., Sun. 1–5 P.M. **855 S. Jefferson St.; 409-968-6418; www.lagrange.fais.net/museum.local.**

Painted Churches

Four rural churches in the La Grange area offered a lasting canvas for the European settler-artists who decorated the structures to resemble the churches of their homelands. The churches feature Gothic steeples, ornate altars, intricately painted and stenciled ceilings with arches, and colorful stained-glass windows.

Open daily 8 A.M.–5 P.M. for self-guided tours. The churches are at High Hill, Praha, Dubina, and Ammansville. **409-968-5756.**

Columbus

Getting There: Columbus sits along I-10, about 70 miles west of Houston and 120 miles east of San Antonio. **Visitor Information: Columbus Chamber of Commerce; 409-732-8385.**

This city is a treasure trove of Victorian and turn-of-the-century homes. Some of these private residences are open to the public during the Springtime Festival on the third weekend in May and during Christmas on the Colorado following Thanksgiving weekend. Other times of year, the views you can get simply by walking or driving around the town are certainly rewarding, even if you can't go into the houses. A **Walking/Driving Tour** features historic Columbus homes, businesses, tearooms, and arts and crafts shops beginning at the 1886 Stafford Opera House on the square, and including the Alley Log Cabin (1224 Bowie St.), the Colorado County Courthouse on Milam Street, the Dilue Rose Harris House Museum (602 Washington St.), the Live Oak Art Center (1014 Milam St.), the Mary Elizabeth Hopkins Santa Claus Museum (604 Washington St.), and the Senftenberg-Brandon House Museum on Walnut Street. Drive to any of these historic structures and park in front; a sign will tell you where to dial your radio to hear about the history of the place.

SEEING AND DOING

Columbus Opry

Grand ol' Opry-style country music, every Sat. 7:30–10 P.M. **Oaks Theater, 715 Walnut St.; 409-732-6510; www.intertex.net/madspil/colopry.htm.**

Texas Pioneer Trail

Columbus is one of many pivotal points along the Texas Pioneer Trail—an area covering Washington, Fayette, Colorado, and Austin Counties. It's the region known as the Cradle of Texas, where Stephen F. Austin's "old three hundred"—the first organized settlers to the area—planted their roots in the early 1820s. You can visit historic and scenic sights as the trail crisscrosses an area extending north from Brenham and nearby Washington-on-the-Brazos, south to Oakland, west of La Grange, and east to San Felipe. Maps and information are available from the **Columbus Chamber of Commerce, 409-732-8385.**

Festivals and Events

March

Hearne Dogwood Trails

Usually mid-March to mid-April. Every spring a miraculous thing happens to the countryside in Robertson County. Millions of creamy white blossoms unfold and fill the skies with the closest thing to a snowfall that the region ever gets. These are blooms from the flowering dogwood trees that grow wild in the sandy, acid soils of the post oak savannah. It's a sight to behold. **Hearne Chamber of Commerce, 409-279-2351.**

Texas Independence Day Celebration

On the Sunday nearest to March 2. Washington-on-the-Brazos State Park hosts this giant anniversary party commemorating the birth of the Republic of Texas, with appearances by the Brazoria Militia and the Texas Army, and a reenactment of the signing of the Texas Declaration of Independence. Artisans and musicians participate. **409-836-3695.**

April

Bluebonnet Festival

Usually the first weekend in April. Chappell Hill. **409-836-3695.**

Winedale Spring Festival and Texas Crafts Exhibition

First weekend in April. A folk fair with pioneer activities, crafts, exhibits, and music and entertainment at an old-fashioned barn dance. At the Winedale Historical Center near Round Top. An antiques fair and local arts and crafts fair is usually going on simultaneously at Round Top, so you can take in both shows. **409-278-3530.**

May

Maifest

Early in May. A German folk festival with parades, food, and a German maypole. Fireman's Park in Brenham.

Navasota Nostalgia Days

First weekend in May. Historical homes tour, parade, and arts and crafts. **409-825-6600.**

Springtime Festival

Third weekend in May. Includes the annual Magnolia Homes Tour. Several historic homes are open for public inspection, and so is the Stafford Opera House and Museum. Also an arts and crafts show, surrey rides, and a production at the Opera House. In Brenham; **409-732-5881.**

September

Fall Food Festival

Saturday before Labor Day. The Peaceable Kingdom School sponsors this food festival. Mt. Fall School Road, off Pickens Road, north of State Hwy. 105 between Navasota and Brenham. **409-878-2353.**

Fayette County Country Fair

Labor Day weekend. La Grange. **409-968-5756.**

Washington County Fair

Mid-month. One of the state's most exciting county fairs includes a livestock exhibit and sale, country store, carnival, rodeo, and name entertainers. In Brenham.

October

Texas Renaissance Festival

On seven weekends in October and November. Features jousting, juggling, and dancing. On 237 wooded acres south of Plantersville, near Navasota, on Farm Road 1774. **409-894-2516; www.texrenfest.com.**

Winedale Oktoberfest

Usually first weekend in October. An emphasis on German traditions. **409-278-3530.**

December

Christmas in the Park

Nov. 30–Dec. 31. Seasonal ceremonies at Central Park

with a lighting ceremony, hayrides, and refreshments throughout the month. In Bryan/College Station.

Recreation

Golfing

BRYAN

Bryan Municipal Golf Course
206 W. Villa Maria, Bryan, 77801; 409-823-0126.

COLLEGE STATION

Texas A&M Golf Course
Five par 3s, but it's a challenging course. **On campus; 409-845-1723.**

HEARNE

Hearne Municipal Golf Course
405 Northwood, Hearne, 77889; 409-279-3112.

HEMPSTEAD

Fox Creek Golf Course
Route 3, Box 128F, Hempstead, 77445; 409-826-2131.

Hiking

This region does not lend itself to a lot of hiking, but there are many interesting places to take little walks. So for those of you who miss those regular morning walks back home, you might try to rise a little early and get out and walk around some of these vacation spots. Here are a few suggestions from a short fat man who's done it.

Bryan/College Station

The campus of Texas A&M University is full of sidewalks and walking trails and is a good place to get some leg exercise in the morning or late afternoon. A golf course on campus provides scenery along the way.

In **La Grange,** take a walk around Monument Hill off U.S. Hwy. 77. In **Columbus,** try a walk around the downtown and courthouse square. As for **Round Top,** a stroll through Henkel Square or the Winedale Historical Center can be nice. These are suggestions

for people who qualify more as walkers, not hikers, but the following are a couple of legitimate hikes.

Lake Somerville State Park

Here's an easy day-hike of about 8 miles round-trip through the backcountry of the park. Much of the trail follows a broad service road, so the trail also is a good one for mountain bikes and horses. The trail along the shore of Lake Somerville passes several primitive camp areas. You can get maps at the park office. There is water at the trailhead, which is near headquarters of the park's Nails Creek Unit. **About 20 miles northwest of Brenham on State Hwy. 36; 409-289-2392.**

Lone Star Trail and Little Lake Creek

This hike of almost 10 miles round-trip is a taste of what the East Texas Pineywoods are like. There are a lot of pines, thick brush, and some marshland, and elevation averages about 270 feet. It can be humid in these parts and the best period to hike is from fall to spring. Take plenty of bug spray, and watch out for poison ivy. The trailhead is not easy to find and the trail is not particularly easy to follow. Out of Navasota, go east on State Hwy. 105 about 22 miles to Farm Road 149. Turn north (left) and go about 1.5 miles, then turn left onto a poorly paved road that is labeled Forest Road 211. In 2 miles the pavement ends, and there are signs marking the trailhead. **In the western reaches of Sam Houston National Forest, about 35 miles northeast of Navasota; 409-344-6205.**

Parks and Camping

Fayette Lake

Primitive overnight camping is permitted by this cooling pond for a coal-fired electric generating plant. It's a popular bass fishing spot. **Access is 10 miles east of La Grange on State Hwy. 159; 409-247-5011.**

Lake Somerville

Has an 85-mile shoreline with a number of camping areas, including Overlook Park, Welch Park, Big Creek Park, Rocky Creek Park, and Yegua Creek Park. All campsites have drinking water and sanitary facilities. Overlook and Yegua Creek are the more popular areas. Overlook is right on State Hwy. 36 as you get to the lake from Brenham, which is about 20 miles to the southeast. Yegua Creek is about 2 miles south of Overlook Park on Farm Road 1948. More information is available at headquarters at the north end of the dam, off State Hwy. 36; **409-596-1622.**

Lake Somerville State Park, located on the lake, also has camping facilities. The park's **Birch Creek** unit and **Nails Creek** unit offer camping, trailer hookups, dump station, cabins, shelters, showers, picnic area, fishing, swimming, boating, hiking, biking, and horseback riding. Birch Creek is on the west side of the lake, at the end of Park Road 87; **409-535-7763.** Nails Creek is on the southwest side of the lake, accessible from Farm Road 1697; **409-289-2392.**

Peaceable Kingdom School

Picnicking and primitive camping are available on 152 acres of mixed woodlands and meadows. Three rental cabins, a shelter, and plenty of campsites that share a solar shower, cold-water sink, and outhouse. On Saturday from 11 A.M. to 2 P.M., the school serves gourmet herbal home-cooked lunches. **Mt. Fall School Road, off Pickens Road, north of State Hwy. 105 between Navasota and Brenham; 409-878-2353.**

Where to Eat

Brenham

Fluff Top Roll

Specializes in homemade soups, stews, chili, and hearty breakfasts. **210 E. Alamo St.; 409-836-9441.**

K&G Steakhouse

This establishment has been serving steaks in Blue Bell country since 1966. They also have a lunch buffet. **2209 S. Market St.; 409-836-7950.**

Must Be Heaven

Features sandwiches, soups, and a large selection of quiches. **107 W. Alamo St.; 409-830-8536.**

Bryan/College Station

Kaffee Klatsch

Located in a restored old building in the town's garden district, they serve everything from gumbo to homemade chicken salad. Open Mon.–Sat. for lunch only. **106 North Ave.; 409-846-4360.**

Chappell Hill

At **Bevers Kitchen** you'll get down-home food in a restored historic home. Open Mon.–Thurs. for lunch only, and Fri.–Sat. for lunch and dinner. **Downtown on Main St.; 409-836-4178.**

Columbus

Hackemack's Hofbrauhaus

A good spot for all-out German food. **About 10 miles north of Columbus on Farm Road 109; 409-732-6321.**

Schoebel's Restaurant

Serves down-home country food with a little bit of traditional German food too. If you're looking for someone in Columbus, chances are you'll find them at Schoebel's come lunchtime. **202 Milam St.; 409-732-2385.**

La Grange

Bon Ton Restaurant

They serve all meals all the time. **On Business Route 71 on the western edge of town; 409-968-5863.**

Round Top

Round Top tops my list of favorite places to eat in this area. Bud and Karen Royer opened up a cafe on the square in Round Top and also started a mail-order pie business, and then it got out of hand. The pies became very popular, and the cooking was good too. So now **Royer's Cafe** is as busy as Bud and Karen allow it to be. They make their own breads, rolls, and pies. They ship out every pie they can sneak by the customers, and the grilled tuna steak is as good as I've tasted anywhere. Open Wed.–Sat. for lunch and dinner, and Sun. for lunch only. **105 Main St.; 877-866-7437.**

Where to Stay

Brenham

The **Washington County Chamber of Commerce** has a brochure listing about a dozen bed-and-breakfast establishments. The publication includes a map, rates, and detailed descriptions of each one. **314**

S. Austin St., Brenham, 77833; 409-836-3695, fax 409-836-2540.

Bryan/College Station

Take your pick from a long line of motels along University Drive. The **College Station Hilton and Conference Center** may offer you slightly more upscale lodging for a slightly more upscale price. **801 University Dr. E.; 409-693-7500, fax 409-846-7361; info@hiltoncs.com; www.hiltoncs.com.**

Chappell Hill

Although the **Browning Plantation** is on the Historic Homes tour, it's also a bed-and-breakfast. **Route 1, Box 339; 409-836-6144.**

Columbus

A couple of choices in Columbus are the **Gant Guest House (926 Bowie St., 409-732-5135)** and the **Raumonda,** a two-story Victorian house **(1100 Bowie St., 409-732-5135).**

Navasota

There's the **Best Western Navasota Inn (State Hwy. 6 bypassing the town; 409-825-7775, 1-800-780-7234, www.bestwestern.com).** Or you can stop over at the **Castle Inn Bed-and-Breakfast** and spend the night in an 1893 mansion **(1403 Washington Ave., 409-825-8051).**

Round Top

There's no long line of motels, but you can spend the night in a restored nineteenth-century cottage furnished with early Texas antiques: the **Gaust House Round Top Bed-and-Breakfast (409-249-3308).**

River Centers: San Marcos and New Braunfels

When Prince Carl of Solms-Braunfels led several thousand German immigrants to this country in 1844, he selected the land in and around present-day Comal County because it looked more like Germany than any other place he could find. Huge trees shaded the village. Clear streams provided drinking water. The land was fertile along the Comal and Guadalupe Rivers, and there was plenty of room to grow.

What the stately prince from Germany never imagined was that this prize land would belong to the tourists one day, and that the rivers that powered grist mills in the beginning would ultimately power inner tubes, sending hundreds of freewheeling sun worshipers spinning down the waters. The town still carries the prince's name, but times have changed, indeed, in New Braunfels.

San Marcos is a river city too. It got its name from the San Marcos River, discovered by Spanish explorers on St. Mark's Day in the 1700s. The Spaniards stuck around and tried to establish missions to educate and Christianize the Indians, but the plan never worked. By the 1840s the Spaniards were gone and settlers had dealt with the Indians in other unfortunate ways. The San Marcos River has always been an important source of water for people living here. Archaeologists say humans may have inhabited this area 12,000 years ago. Evidence from the bottom of Aquarena Springs, source of the San Marcos, shows that this may be one of the oldest Indian sites in North America.

Southwest Texas State University is situated in San Marcos. You can jump on I-35 in San Marcos and drive to Austin in less than an hour. But both San Marcos and New Braunfels have grown up around rivers, and the rivers—the San Marcos, the Comal, and the Guadalupe—are what keeps this area friendly to visitors.

Visitor Information

Boerne Chamber of Commerce

1 Main Plaza, Boerne, 78006; 830-249-8000, fax 830-249-9639.

Canyon Lake Chamber of Commerce

P.O. Box 1435, Canyon Lake, 78133; 830-964-2223, fax 830-964-3209; clcc@gvtc.com; www.canyonlakechamber.com. Also, Canyon Lake Visitors Bureau, at Hancock Plaza, 830-935-2025.

Greater New Braunfels Chamber of Commerce

Includes information about Gruene. Open Mon.–Fri. 8 A.M.–5 P.M., Sat. 9:30 A.M.–4 P.M., Sun. 10 A.M.–2 P.M. 390 S. Seguin Ave.; 1-800-572-2626, 830-625-2385, fax 210-625-7918; www.newbraunfels.com.

San Marcos Chamber of Commerce

Three locations: 202 North C. M. Allen Parkway; 512-393-5900. 215 W. San Antonio St., No. 105; 512-353-1103 (Hispanic). 1811 North I-35; 512-

Getting There

If you are flying in, **San Antonio International Airport** *is the best choice. All major airlines go through San Antonio. New Braunfels is only about a 20-minute drive from San Antonio by way of Loop 410 north to I-35. San Marcos is on I-35, 15 miles north of New Braunfels and about 40 miles north of downtown San Antonio. As usual for most of the state's points of interest, you'll need your own vehicle to visit, because the majority of the sites are out of the way for buses, trains, or taxis.* **Gray Line of San Antonio** *offers bus tours daily from San Antonio to the San Marcos Outlet Mall for a day of shopping—and it will take a day. There are more than 100 outlet stores. The trip includes a brief stopover at the historic community of Gruene. Adults $20.* **210-225-1706, 1-800-472-9546, fax 210-226-2515.**

393-5930 (travel information center), 1-888-200-5620, fax 512-353-3030; www.sanmarcostx.com.

Wimberley Chamber of Commerce
P.O. Box 12, Wimberley, 78676; 512-847-2201; info@wimberley.org; www.wimberley.org.

Major Attractions

Aquarena Springs

At Aquarena Springs, headwaters of the San Marcos River, is Spring Lake, a water-oriented nature park. Visitors can view aquatic plants, fish, and occasionally an underwater ballet while riding in a glass-bottom boat. Or they can enjoy the submarine theater, which is lowered beneath the water for a 30-minute show featuring mermaids and Ralph the swimming pig. The park has what it calls a "sky spiral" that lifts passengers in a revolving dome 250 feet above the park to give a panoramic view of San Marcos and the surrounding hills, and a Swiss sky ride that crosses over the springs to a

feature known as the Hanging Gardens.

Some history has been preserved. The remains of a 1753 Spanish mission are on the grounds, as is a replica of a frontier village. Now and then, artisans display their work and show off their skills in the frontier village. You can view artifacts dating back 12,000 years in the archaeology museum, and use interactive kiosks that explain the early Texas experience in San Marcos.

Open daily, Memorial Day to Labor Day 10 A.M.–8 P.M., and the rest of the year 10 A.M.–5 P.M. **I-35 exit 206 in San Marcos; 512-396-8900, 1-800-999-9767.**

Schlitterbahn Waterpark

The Schlitterbahn (German for "slippery rock") in New Braunfels is the best artificial white-water excitement in the state. At the 15-year-old park, water in the chutes and slides comes directly from the Comal River and is recycled back into it. It's the state's largest waterpark, with more than 65 acres of family fun. Be prepared to wait in line in peak season.

Most of the rides were designed to handle inner tubes, so floaters can exercise a degree of control over speed and direction. Probably the most exciting ride is the Raging River Tube Chute, which fires tubers through 1,600 feet of turns, twists, and spins before it empties into the river. Tubers then float down the river back to the park—and start all over.

There are several milder water rides for small children. Altogether there are 9 tube chutes, 17 water slides, 5 large hot tubs, 5 swimming pools, a playground, a picnic area, a miniature golf course, 2 restaurants, 20 snack bars, and a hotel.

Schlitterbahn has added something new: the **Boogie Bahn,** constructed by Flow Rider of California, king of artificial wave makers. Boogie Bahn hosts the annual Flow Rider Bodyboarding Championships in late May. For this event the waves are pumped up to 8 feet in height.

You can also do some quieter and less exciting tubing in the nearby Guadalupe River. The river doesn't have nearly the carnival atmosphere that Schlitterbahn has, but it too attracts large crowds in the summer.

Schlitterbahn is open 10 A.M.–8 P.M. on weekends in late April, early May, and September, and daily from mid-May through August. Activities are reduced the rest of the year except for special events like the annual Texas

Bikini Invitational. Dates change from year to year, so be sure and check before you go. **On the banks of the Comal River, across from Landa Park; 830-625-2351, fax 830-620-4873; fun@schlitter bahn.com; www.schlitter-bahn.com.**

Gruene Historical District

Gruene was a major cotton processing center in the early part of the century, but in 1925 boll weevils destroyed the cotton business. Most people left town and Gruene was empty until the 1970s, when a few enterprising area businesspeople thought they could make some money converting the town into a tourist attraction.

Factory Outlet Mall in San Marcos, featuring bargains and name brands. Photo courtesy of Texas Highways *magazine.*

They moved into a lot of old buildings and restored them, and they attracted a lot of artisans, who opened shops. But the crowning achievement was the resurrection of an 1878 tavern called **Gruene Hall.** Today it is the oldest continuously running dance hall in Texas. They feature live music every Thursday through Sunday, and the crowds range from the working class to the deep pockets.

Movie stars working the area usually make time to relax a little at Gruene Hall. Outsiders love the Texas atmosphere. Country singer George Strait spent 6 of his early years as a singer here, performing with the Ace in the Hole Band. Local favorite Jerry Jeff Walker wanders in now and then to perform, and even Willie Nelson shows up occasionally. You never know who you'll see at Gruene Hall. That's part of the attraction. On the outskirts of New Braunfels, **on the Guadalupe River, on North Loop 337; 830-625-2385; web master@gruene.net; www.gruene.net.**

Factory Outlet Stores

If you enjoy shopping, this is truly a paradise. Within 20 minutes, you can travel on the freeway between the factory outlet stores in San Marcos and New Braunfels and shop till you drop. The stores at the outlet centers aren't off-brand operations. Brooks Brothers, Eddie Bauer, Nike, and Black and Decker have shops in San Marcos, just to name a few. Bugle Boy, Reebok, and Spaulding have shops at the New Braunfels factory outlet, along with many more nationally known companies.

The **New Braunfels Factory Outlet Stores,** known locally as the Mill Creek Stores, were here first. The place has fifty factory outlets specializing in dis-

counted clothing and housewares. Discounts range from 20 percent to 70 percent; most of the merchandise is first-rate; the remainder is "factory seconds" with minor flaws. That means you just need to look everything over carefully before you buy.

The New Braunfels stores are open Mon.–Sat. 9 A.M.–9 P.M., Sun. 10 A.M.–6 P.M. **Off I-35, exit 188 in New Braunfels; 830-620-6806.**

The **San Marcos Factory Outlet Stores** are newer, and there are a whole lot more of them—about seventy. But the operation is about the same, and the discounts are about the same—now and then they'll drop prices as much as 75 percent to attract buyers.

The San Marcos stores are open Mon.–Sat. 9 A.M.–9 P.M., Sun. 11 A.M.–6 P.M. **Off I-35, exit 200 in San Marcos; 1-800-628-9465, 512-396-2200; www. primeoutlets.com/sanmarcos/index.html.**

The **Tanger Factory Outlet Center** nearby has an additional thirty stores, including a Sara Lee Bakery outlet. **At I-35, exit 200; 512-396-7446.**

Tourists gaze at the "Sherwood Forest" formation in Natural Bridge Caverns near San Antonio. Photo courtesy of the Texas Department of Tourism.

Natural Bridge Caverns and Wildlife Ranch

This is one of the most popular limestone caves in the state, and one of the hardest to find. During my travels around the state, I was forever passing signs saying "This Way to Natural Bridge Caverns." The problem is that there are too many signs—always leading you to believe that Natural Bridge Caverns is just around the corner, and it's not. All the brochures for the caverns say that "you can't miss the signs." But they don't say anything about missing the park. I finally called for directions. Here's what I found out: The caverns are located about halfway between San Antonio and New Braunfels, off Farm Road 3009. From I-35, take the Garden Ridge–Schertz exit.

Once you get there, it's a terrific experience. The entrance to the caverns is spanned by a 60-foot-long bridge created naturally by limestone. Different rooms in the cave are named for their predominant formations. The Castle of White Giants features limestone columns. The Chandelier has a ribbon formation of stone hanging from the ceiling. Sherwood Forest has tall, thin, treelike formations.

Hour-long tours are offered. Outside the cave is a picnic area, snack bar, interpretive center, and gift shop. Open daily June–Aug. 9 A.M.–6 P.M., and the rest of the year 9 A.M.–4 P.M. **26495 Natural Bridge Caverns Rd.; 830-657-6101; www.natural-bridgetexas.com.**

The nearby **Natural Bridge Wildlife Ranch** raises exotic animals from around the world on 200 acres. A paved 3.5-mile safari drive-through allows visitors to view many of the animals. Open daily June–Aug. 9 A.M.–6:30 P.M., and the rest of the year 9 A.M.–5 P.M. Ranch entrance is on Farm Road 3005, off I-35 exit 175. **26515 Natural Bridge Caverns Rd.; 830-438-7400; nbwrinf@gvtc.com; www.tourtexas.com.**

Seeing and Doing

New Braunfels

CHILDREN AND FAMILIES

The Children's Museum

A hands-on children's exhibit that includes a TV studio, a puppet palace, and other creative areas. Open Tues.–Fri. 9 A.M.–5 P.M., Sat. 10 A.M.–5 P.M., Sun. noon–5 P.M. **I-35 at the McQueeney exit 187; 1-888-928-8326; watteam@watteam.org; www.watteam.org/museum/html.**

River Camps

River camps and resorts have been popular in these parts for decades, with clear, cool—and I do mean cool—spring-fed pools, tubing chutes, rapids, and scenic settings for family recreation. There are plenty of picnic spots and camps along River Road (but be sure to stay off private property). This is a party place for young people at certain times, and it is a family vacation spot in the summer. Old River Road leads out of New Braunfels and follows the Guadalupe River to Canyon Lake.

MUSEUMS AND HISTORIC SITES

Alamo Classic Car Museum

One of the finest private collections of classic vehicles in the state, representing more than eight decades of automotive history. Open daily 10 A.M.–6:30 P.M. **I-35, exit 180 or 182; 830-606-4311.**

Conservation Plaza

Owned by the New Braunfels Conservation Society, the plaza is a collection of old structures from the area that have been restored and moved to this place in the city for all to admire. Includes the Lindheimer Home, the Buckhorn Barber Shop, the Wagenfuehr Home, and the Baetge House. Furnishings include early Texas and German furniture. Other structures include the Rose Conservatory, Haelbig Music Studio, Church Hill School, and the Jahn Cabinet Shop and Home. Open Tues.–Fri. 9 A.M.–5 P.M., Sat.–Sun. 2–5 P.M. **1300 Church Hill Dr.; 210-625-8766.**

Faust Hotel

A restored 1920s hotel with all the history preserved. **240 S. Seguin Ave.; 830-625-7791.**

Hummel Museum

Features the largest collection of Hummel figurines in the world. Sister Maria Innocentia Hummel, a German nun, created figurines during the 1930s of pudgy German children dancing, hiking, or cavorting with farm animals. Sister Hummel's unique figurines were introduced to the United States by occupation forces returning from Germany following World War II, and are still in great demand today. The museum contains paintings and drawings by the nun, as well as hundreds of her figurines. The gift shop sells Hummel-inspired art. Open Mon.–Sat. 10 A.M.–5 P.M., Sun. noon–5 P.M. **199 Main Plaza; 830-625-5636, 1-800-456-4866.**

Museum of Texas Handmade Furniture

Housed in an 1858 home, the museum displays a large collection of antique furniture handcrafted in Texas in the 1800s. Open Memorial Day to Labor Day, Tues.–Sat. 10 A.M.–4 P.M. and Sun. 1–4 P.M.; Labor Day to Memorial Day, Sat.–Sun. 1–4 P.M. **1370 Church Hill Dr.; 830-629-6504.**

Sophienburg Museum

On this hilltop site, Prince Carl of Solms-Braunfels built a log fortress. The museum displays many of the nobleman's personal effects, Indian artifacts, and household items of pioneer days. Open Mon.–Sat. 10 A.M.–5 P.M., Sun. 1–5 P.M. **401 W. Coll St. at Academy Ave.; 830-629-1572.**

OTHER SIGHTS

Buck Pottery

Hand-thrown pottery that Dee Buck makes as you watch. In the barn behind the mercantile store in Gruene. **1296 Gruene Rd.; 830-629-7975.**

PARKS

Landa Park

An exceptionally scenic city park built along the state's shortest river—the Comal, only 2.5 miles long. The park features towering old trees, spring-fed swimming pools, tubing, picnicking, boating, bicycling, hiking—even golf on a course that's not very difficult but is one of the prettiest around. The Comal has the largest springs in the state, producing more than 8 million gallons an hour. **830-629-7275.**

WINERIES AND BREWERIES

Guadalupe Valley Winery

There's no vineyard here. The grapes are purchased

from Texas vineyards and processed in a restored cotton gin (listed on the National Register of Historic Places). The tasting room and gift shop are open Mon.–Sat. 10 A.M.–5 P.M., Sun. noon–5 P.M. Tours offered in the summer, Sat.–Sun. noon–4 P.M.; also Sept.–May, third Sat. of the month. Group tours of ten or more given year-round by appointment. **1720 Hunter Rd. in Gruene; 830-629-2351.**

San Marcos

MUSEUMS AND HISTORIC SITES

Belvin Street Historic District

Nineteenth-century homes shaded by huge live oaks. These private residences are open to the public during the Tours of Distinction the first weekend in May. **Southwest San Marcos along Belvin St. between the 700 block and the 1000 block.**

OTHER SIGHTS

National Fish Hatchery and Technology Center

A research facility to preserve endangered fish species of the Southwest. Open Mon.–Fri. 7:30 A.M.–4 P.M. **I-35 at McCarty Ln. exit; 512-353-0011.**

San Marcos River Walkway

This walkway unites three city parks along the San Marcos River, and is accented by lush landscaping. Access is from Juan Veramendi Plaza. **C. M. Allen Parkway at Hopkins St.**

Wonder World

This attraction includes a cave created by an earthquake along the Balcones Fault. You'll also find a wildlife park, animal feeding and petting areas, an observation tower, and a gift shop. A miniature train travels through the wildlife park. Open daily March–Oct. 8 A.M.–8 P.M., and the rest of the year 9 A.M.–5 P.M. **On Bishop St. inside the city limits; 512-392-3760.**

WINERIES AND BREWERIES

Moyer Champagne Winery

The only champagne-like wine made in Texas. Open

for tours Fri.–Sat.; tasting and sales every day. **San Marcos Factory Shops, off I-35 exit 200; 512-396-1600.**

Towns in the Area

Wimberley

Getting There: Wimberley is on Rural Route 12 about 15 miles northwest of San Marcos. **Visitor Information: Wimberley Chamber of Commerce, P.O. Box 12, Wimberley, 78676; 512-847-2201; info@wimberley.org; www.wimberley.org.**

This picturesque village near San Marcos has become a resort and retirement community. Visitors are cheered by cool, shady pools protected by towering cypress trees on Cypress Creek and the Blanco River. There are green meadows and majestic hills, and white-tailed deer. This spot fosters vacation hideaways and youth camps.

When I was traveling for the *Eyes of Texas* TV show, people were constantly asking me for suggestions on the best places to retire in Texas. Wimberley topped my list because of its climate, scenery, and proximity to Austin and San Antonio. Old-timers can spend the rest of their lives in this country and be perfectly happy, but flat-bellies enjoy it too, because there are places for hiking, fishing, climbing, camping, boating, golf, and tennis.

Downtown Wimberley is an attractive shopping area with the atmosphere of a mall, located in a 4-block area of the village. Hill Country scenes captured on canvas are just some of the souvenirs you can take back home with you from the arts and crafts galleries you'll run across.

SEEING AND DOING

Fisher Store

An old-timey general store in the town of Fisher, 9 miles west of Wimberley, all decked out in early Texas furnishings and waiting for visitors. **At Ranch Road 32 and Farm Road 484; 512-244-1546.**

Pioneertown

A village of the Old West has been re-created at 7-A Ranch Resort on the Blanco River, with a general store, saloon, hotel, and opera house. A medicine show

and old-time melodramas head up the activities in summer. Open daily 10 A.M.–10 P.M. in summer; Sat.–Sun. 1:00–5:30 P.M. in winter. **One mile south of the Wimberley town square; 512-847-2517.**

Scenic Drive

The winding ridge route known as the **Devil's Backbone** offers exceptional views of the Hill Country. This is a 24-mile drive between San Marcos and Blanco, and one of the state's most scenic drives. It begins at the intersection of Ranch Road 12 and Ranch Road 32, 5 miles south of Wimberley, and goes along Road 32 toward Blanco. It's a winding drive through some hilly Hill Country. At one point, there is a razor-backed ridge—the Devil's Backbone—with a beautiful view. There are a lot of summer camps in these hills.

RECREATION

The Blue Hole

The Blue Hole has been rated as one of the top ten swimming holes in Texas and was oft photographed for TV commercials. It's part of a private family-oriented club, so you'll need a membership to get in, but they offer reasonably priced weekly and monthly memberships. There is camping and an RV park. **County Road 173, on Cypress Creek outside Wimberley; 512-847-9127.**

Hiking

Many of the roads leading into and out of this town point to hiking opportunities, particularly along Cypress Creek and the road that follows the Blanco River.

Canyon Lake

Getting There: Canyon Lake is about 20 miles west of San Marcos and 15 miles northwest of New Braunfels. River Road in New Braunfels follows the Guadalupe River to Canyon Lake. **Visitor Information: Canyon Lake Chamber of Commerce, P.O. Box 1435, Canyon Lake, 78133; 830-964-2223, fax 830-964-3209; clcc@gvtc.com; www.canyonlakechamber.com.** Also, **Canyon Lake Visitors Bureau, at Hancock Plaza; 830-935-2025.**

In 1964 the Corps of Engineers dammed up the Guadalupe River and created a major flood-control

Old Town Plaza in Wimberley. Photo courtesy of Texas Highways *magazine.*

facility in the San Antonio–New Braunfels area. Canyon Lake has become a busy recreational spot, attracting about 2 million visitors a year who water-ski, sail, windsurf, fish, swim, and scuba dive within its 8,000-acre area. The lake has 80 miles of shoreline and is fairly near I-35, so I don't have to tell you it's a very popular overnight stop for tourists and winter Texans alike.

There are eight public recreation areas along the shoreline, and six of them provide for camping. (See the Camping section later in this chapter.)

Canyon Lake is at the other end of River Road that takes you out of New Braunfels. You can camp along the Guadalupe River and enjoy river activities, or you can continue to Canyon Lake for other water sports.

SEEING AND DOING

The Church on the Hill

This tiny church on a hill **at Canyon Lake** near the dam makes you feel right at home. It's St. Thomas Catholic Church, but the services are nondenominational when they are held for the tourist crowd every morning and evening. It's inspirational, especially at dusk when the service is held outdoors, weather permitting. **830-964-3497.**

Boerne

Getting There: Boerne (BURN-ee) is on I-10, about 35 miles northwest of San Antonio and 40 miles west of New Braunfels. **Visitor Information: Boerne Chamber of Commerce, One Main Plaza, Boerne, 78006; 830-249-8000, fax 830-249-9639.**

Boerne was laid out in 1849, established by German pioneers in 1851, and named for a German political writer of the day. People who fish love the lakes and streams around Boerne. Hunters feast on whitetail bucks and migratory game birds.

SEEING AND DOING

Agricultural Heritage Center

An indoor and outdoor exhibit featuring antique farm machinery and an operating blacksmith shop. Open Wed. and Sun. 1:30–4 P.M., and upon request for tour groups. Closed last 16 days of Dec. and first 15 days of Jan. **Adjacent to Boerne City Park on State Hwy. 46 east; 830-249-8000.**

Cascade Caverns

A popular visitor attraction since 1932. Well-lighted, comfortable walking trails, and huge underground rooms with crystal pools, including a 90-foot waterfall. Has camping facilities for RVs, trailers, and tents.

Guided tours every half hour. Open daily from Memorial Day to Labor Day 9 A.M.–6 P.M.; in winter Mon.–Fri. 10 A.M.–4 P.M., Sat.–Sun. 9 A.M.–5 P.M. **At I-10 exit 543; 830-755-8080.**

Cave Without a Name

When this cave was opened in 1939, they had a contest to name it, and the winner was a young man who said, "This cave is too pretty to name." There are dozens of imaginative formations growing from the walls and dangling from the roofs of several rooms. Open daily except Tues. **Six miles northeast of Boerne, off Farm Road 474; 830-537-4212.**

Cibolo Wilderness Trail

A 65-acre greenbelt in Boerne with walking trails, estuary, and year-round environmental awareness programs. **On River Rd. at State Hwy. 46; 830-249-4616.**

Kronkosky Hill

This is the original home of the Albert Kronkosky family, built about 1911. Today it's a private school, St. Albert's, and a convent for Benedictine Sisters. The most prominent structure on campus is Kronkosky Tower, now a school library. This tower looks out of place in Texas, but it affords a good view of the countryside. Visitors are welcome on the grounds during the day. On the highest hill in Boerne, at **202 Kronkosky St.; 830-249-3579.**

Kuhlman-King Historical House

Home and museum, open Sun. 1–4 P.M. and upon request for groups. **402 E. Blanco St.; 830-249-2030.**

Scenic Drive

One of my favorites. The drive starts by the city park in Boerne and travels to the outskirts of New Braunfels. It's about 40 minutes of parks, rivers, and ranchland **along State Hwy. 46** from Boerne to New Braunfels. (Observe the speed limit; I think some communities here pay for city government with traffic fines.)

Sister Creek Vineyards

Tastings and tours daily, noon–5 P.M. **1142 Sisterdale Rd.; Farm Road 1376, 12 miles north of Boerne in Sisterdale; 830-324-6704.**

RECREATION

Guadalupe River State Park

Almost 2,000 acres of scenic Hill Country landscapes with beautiful vistas and wildlife. The juniper thickets offer a nesting habitat for rare golden-cheeked warblers. **Thirteen miles east of town on State Hwy. 46; 830-438-2656.**

Festivals and Events

February

Mardi Gras

Early February. Local answer to New Orleans's fabulous event, with a masquerade ball, costume contest, face painting, and a bike decorating contest. In San Marcos. **512-353-1103.**

March

Go Western Gala

Mid-month. Sponsored by Canyon Lake Chamber of Commerce. **830-964-2223.**

April

First Saturday Market Day

First Saturday of the month, April Dec. A giant flea market with more than 200 vendors. **Lions Field at Ranch Road 2325, in Wimberley.**

May

Viva! Cinco de Mayo

Early May. A tribute to Mexico and Mexican citizens with menudo cook-off, downtown parade, carnival, and a beauty pageant. Dancing every night. In San Marcos. **512-353-8482.**

June

Berges Fest

Father's Day weekend. German heritage is emphasized with street dancing and oompah music. **Boerne main plaza; 830-249-8000.**

Texas Water Safari

Second Saturday in June. San Marcos is the starting point for a grueling marathon canoe race along 260 miles of the San Marcos and Guadalupe Rivers to the Gulf of Mexico. Crews must paddle and carry their boats nonstop through rough water, log jams, dams, and other hazards to arrive in Seadrift, on the coast, within a 100-hour time limit. **512-357-6113.**

July

Fourth of July Rodeo

Centered around Independence Day. Students compete in calf roping and barrel racing; old-fashioned family entertainment. In Wimberley. **512-847-2201.**

September

Comal County Fair

Late September. One of the oldest county fairs in the state, featuring a parade, carnival, and all the other things that go with county fairs. **New Braunfels fairgrounds; 830-625-1505, 1-800-445-2323.**

Republic of Texas Chilympiad

Third weekend in September. Hundreds of teams from all over the country compete for the best, or most unusual, chili dishes, with ingredients including armadillos and rattlesnakes. Entertainment, arts and crafts, and a dance every night. **Hays County Civic Center, I-35, exit 201; 512-396-5400.**

October

Canyon Lake Shrimpfest

Early October. **On Canyon Lake; 830-964-2223.**

Gospel Music Festival

One weekend early in the month. Featuring gospel groups from all over the state. It's four-part harmony outdoors, and it doesn't get any better than this. **Blue Hole Recreation Club, east of Wimberley on County Road 173 at Cypress Creek; 512-847-9127.**

Moving Waters Native American Pow Wow

Early October. Native American arts and crafts show, competitive dance contest, Native foods, and teepee

contest. **River Valley Resort, Canyon Lake; 830-964-3613.**

November

Wurstfest

Ten days, beginning the Friday before the first Monday in November, in New Braunfels. Billed as the Best of the Wurst, this is New Braunfels' answer to German festivals, and it is probably the most popular event of its kind in the state. My old friend Jerome Nowotny said it best when asked to comment on the Wurstfest: "My, my, they have a lotta beer!" Most of the events are held at Landa Park and include art shows, music, dancing, historical exhibits, food vendors, and the Tour de Gruene Bicycle Classic, a 28-mile road race. **P.O. Box 310309, New Braunfels, 78131; 1-800-221-4369; wurstfest@new-braunfels.com; www.new-braunfels.com/wurstfest.**

December

Christmas Parade of Lights

Mid-month. Texas Yacht Club Parade along the shoreline of Canyon Lake. **1-800-528-2104.**

Recreation

Anybody who loves the great outdoors will love this area—particularly those who enjoy water sports. From New Braunfels through San Marcos, and on to Boerne, Wimberley, and Canyon Lake, you'll find the camping, biking, and river experiences of a lifetime.

Biking

San Marcos and New Braunfels have a permanent love affair with biking. The cities often feature bicycling events. During the Mardi Gras in February at San Marcos, there is a bike decorating contest. New Braunfels stages the **Tour de Gruene 28-mile Bicycle Classic** in November and tops it off with an antique bicycle show. The backroads and out-of-the-way spots are fun to explore on two-wheelers.

The Devil's Backbone

The Devil's Backbone is the nickname for a stretch of highway between Blanco and San Marcos near Can-

Honey Creek at Guadalupe River State Park, outside Boerne.

yon Lake. It's a favorite training ground for members of the Southwest Texas State University cycling team. This 30-mile ride features some steep climbing and some long, gradual descents. Be alert: Farm Road 12 may surprise you with the amount of traffic it has, and that goes double for Farm Road 32, especially on weekends.

Start at "old town" Wimberley at the junction of Farm Road 12 and Hays County Road 173. Head south on Road 12 across Cypress Creek for half a mile, then turn left onto Farm Road 2325, heading toward Blanco. At 4 miles into the trip, go left onto County Road 181 (the Fischer Store Road). Road conditions are a little rough for the next few miles.

At 12 miles into the ride, you'll reach a stop sign at the intersection of Road 181 and Farm Road 484. Turn left onto Road 484, then left again after a quarter mile onto Farm Road 32. After a total ride of 17 miles, you'll be on the razor-backed ridge known as the Devil's Backbone. The road is wider here, and so is the view. This stretch of 3 miles has big hills and great views, and you'll come across a rest area on the left with some beautiful Hill Country scenery.

At 24.5 miles, turn left and you will be back on Farm Road 12 for the slow descent back to Wimberley and the end of a 30-mile trip.

Gruene Hall and the River Road Ride

Try this 30-mile ride and you'll know why this country is so popular with bikers. If you take this trip in summer, there will be a lot of people to contend with. But if you come after summer, you might just be all alone. A ride along River Road is absolutely wonderful anytime after Labor Day and before Memorial Day.

Begin at Gruene Hall at the intersection of Hunter Road and Gruene Road in town. Almost immediately, Gruene Road bends sharply to the left and then descends quickly to the Guadalupe River. After about 1 mile, bear right on Rock Street. Travel half a mile down Rock Street, then turn right onto River Road.

At 2 miles into the trip, you'll cross Loop 337—but stay on River Road. The next 10 miles is the most scenic, with campgrounds and riverbanks shaded by cypress and live oak trees along the Guadalupe River.

At about 15 miles into the trip, you'll reach a caution light and the intersection with Farm Road 2673, in the community of Sattler. River Road jogs there just a bit, but continue north onto South Access Road and begin a steady climb to Canyon Lake Dam. At 17 miles, turn right (south) onto Farm Road 306. Now you're heading back to your starting point. At 19.5 miles into the ride, you'll cross the Guadalupe again, and right after that you'll cross the intersection with Farm Road 2673. Continue on Road 306, which takes you back to Gruene to complete the trip.

Then relax and reward yourself with some of that simple country music at Gruene Hall.

Golfing

BOERNE

Tapatio Springs Golf Resort

A resort in the country outside Boerne, this is one of my favorite golfing facilities. This semiprivate course is not particularly long, but it is hilly and unbelievably beautiful. **W. Johns Rd., Boerne, 78006; 830-537-4197.**

CIBOLO

Northcliffe Country Club

5301 Country Club Blvd., off I-35 between New Braunfels and San Antonio; 830-606-7351.

NEW BRAUNFELS

Landa Park Golf Course

A short but beautiful public course that helps decorate the park and the Comal River. Come early, because it's always crowded with local players. **800 Golf Course Dr., New Braunfels, 78130; 830-608-2174.**

SAN MARCOS

Aquarena Springs Golf Course

A short, almost wide-open public course. **1 Aquarena Springs Dr. (on Spring Lake), San Marcos, 78666; 512-245-7593.**

Hiking

Cibolo Wilderness Trail

An easy 2-mile day-hike along a cypress-lined stream. Elevation is about 1,300 feet, and the most comfortable seasons are fall through spring. Special attractions are the bald cypress trees and the native prairieland. **Boerne City Park, at Cibolo Creek and State Hwy. 46 in Boerne; 830-249-4616.**

Guadalupe River State Park

Hiking trails through Hill Country land that is rich in beauty. **Thirteen miles east of Boerne on State Hwy. 36; 830-438-2656.**

Landa Park

Short hiking trails wind throughout the park in the shade of towering oaks. **On the Comal River in New Braunfels.**

In the Air

When you're ready to get off the ground, you can go bungee jumping with **Bungy Over Texas,** which has a crane set up over the San Marcos River north of New Braunfels. You can take a flying leap for $30 **(830-269-JUMP, perrin@utdallas.edu, dallas.net/ ~iperrin/ne49.html).** Skydiving is another thrill-sport you can try. **Sky Dive San Marcos (512-488-2214)** takes first-timers on tandem jumps that include a 30-second freefall and 5-minute parachute drop— all for a mere $135. They'll take experienced jump teams too.

Parks and Camping

Blue Hole Recreation Club

Private, but reasonably priced weekly and monthly memberships available for camping. They also have an RV park. **East of Wimberley on County Road 173 at Cypress Creek; 512-847-9127.**

Canyon Lake

Six public parks on Canyon Lake provide for camping: **North Park, Jacobs Creek Park, Canyon**

Landa Park and "The Chute," a popular swimming hole and recreation area in New Braunfels. Photo courtesy of Texas Highways magazine.

Park, **Potters Creek Park**, **Cranes Mills Park**, and **Comal Park.** All parks have campsites, trailer areas, boat ramps, drinking water, rest rooms, and (except for North Park) dump stations.

Information on both the public and private facilities is available from the **Canyon Lake Project Office, HC Route 4, Box 400, Canyon Lake, 78133; 830-964-3341.**

These privately operated campgrounds around the lake also may fit your needs:

Canyon Lake Campground & RV Park. 830-899-2544.
Guadalupe's Best RV Park & Campground. 830-907-2267.
Maricopa Ranch Resort. Hwy. 306; 830-964-3731.
Mountain Breeze. 830-964-2484.
O'Henry's Hideaway. 8511 River Rd.; 1-800-496-4248, 830-964-1443.
River Valley Campground. On River Rd.; 830-964-3613.
Riverside Resort. Hwy. 306; 830-964-3629.
Rockin' R River Rides & Campground. 1-800-553-5628.

Guadalupe River State Park

Noted for its ruggedness and scenic beauty, the park has 105 campsites (37 with tent camping only, 48 with water and electricity, 20 walk-in tent sites), with rest rooms, showers, trailer dump stations, amphitheater, picnicking, playground, swimming, fishing, and hiking trails. **Thirteen miles east of Boerne on State Hwy. 36; 830-438-2656.**

River Camps

From New Braunfels to Canyon Lake along River Road, private campgrounds are ready for your business. The **Greater New Braunfels Chamber of Commerce (830-625-2385, 1-800-572-2626)** can provide literature on the campgrounds.

Tennis

John Newcombe's Tennis Ranch

This place looks like a Hill Country dude ranch, except with tennis racquets instead of saddles. Three-time Wimbledon singles champ John Newcombe

established this place many years ago. Like him, most of his instructors are Australian. You can come for a lesson or for a lengthy stay. Accommodations range from dorms to motel rooms to family cottages. They also offer junior programs and summer and holiday camps. **On State Hwy. 46 about 5 miles west of New Braunfels; P.O. Box 310469, New Braunfels, 78131; 1-800-444-6204 (in Texas), 830-625-9105, fax 830-625-2004; newktennis@aol.com; www.Instar/newks.**

T Bar M Conference Center and Tennis Ranch

A 250-acre resort with 12 outdoor tennis courts, 2 indoor courts, 3 outdoor pools, a gymnasium, and jogging trails. Accommodations include a 40-room motel and about 35 condos. **Two miles west of Loop 337 around New Braunfels, right on State Hwy. 46 just before the Newcombe tennis ranch; 830-625-7738.**

Water Sports

A stretch of the Guadalupe River from Canyon Lake south to New Braunfels is a great place for white-water canoeing, rafting, and kayaking. There are places to get out of the river along the way if the rapids get too tricky. Trips can last anywhere from 3 to 9 hours, depending on where you put in and what kind of craft you choose.

Because most of the land along the Guadalupe is privately owned, you can only put in and take out at designated areas. Many of the outfitters who rent the rafts will provide maps. The map entitled "Guadalupe River Scenic Area" can be obtained from the **Greater New Braunfels Chamber of Commerce (1-800-572-2626, 830-625-2385),** and it lists locations for vendors, food sources, campgrounds, and rapids along the river.

River outfitters include **Gruene River Co. (1404 Gruene Rd., 830-625-2800, grueneriverco@gruene.net, www.gruene.net/riverraftco); Guadalupe River Station (7430 River Rd., 830-964-2850, www.txhillctry.com/river-road/station.html); Rainbow River Trips (830-964-2227, 1-800-874-3745, samnjudy@gvtc.com, www.texashillcntry.com/rainbowcamp); Rockin' R River Rides (830-629-9999, 1-800-55FLOAT, rockinr@sat.net, www.rockinr.**

com); **Texas Canoe Trails (830-620-6503);** and **Texas Homegrown (830-629-3176, www.gruene.net/homegrown/net).**

Landa Park offers the largest springs in the state for tubing and boating; on the Comal River in New Braunfels. **Prince Solms Park** is also a place you can put in on the Comal River for tubing; it's a small park just east of Landa Park. Open daily March–Oct. **830-625-2028.**

RIDING THE SAN MARCOS

Water-sports enthusiasts from Austin and San Antonio come to San Marcos to try their skills at canoeing, kayaking, or riding inner tubes down the crystal-clear, 72-degree waters of the San Marcos River. **Spencer Canoes (512-357-6113)** and **T. G. Canoes (512-353-3846)** rent canoes and kayaks. Lions Club Tube Rental and River Taxi **(512-392-8255)** rent large inner tubes for floating the river. They operate on weekends in the spring, and daily from Memorial Day to Labor Day in San Marcos City Park. From San Marcos City Park on Bugg Lane, tubers can spend about 40 minutes floating all the way to Rio Vista Park at Cheatham Street and the San Marcos River. That's where you'll find a lot of Southwest State University students that time of year—tubing on the river. (By the way, the restaurant of choice for students in the area is the **River Pub Grill,** at **701 Cheatham St.)**

Guadalupe River State Park is a place to canoe, as well as fish, swim, and hike. **Thirteen miles east of Boerne on State Hwy. 36; 830-438-2656.**

Where to Eat

From traditional German cooking to fast-food franchises, this area has it all. New Braunfels seems to have more sit-down restaurants, while San Marcos is more into drive-through for the college crowd, but every city has some special places.

New Braunfels

Krause's Cafe

This local establishment has been here since 1938. The cafe has a basic menu with a few German dishes and a

large selection of pies. Open for all meals Mon.–Sat. **148 S. Castell St.; 830-625-7581.**

Langston House

Serves continental food in a restored old mansion. Open for lunch and dinner Tues.–Sun. **190 S. Seguin Ave.; 830-625-1898.**

New Braunfels Smokehouse

Specializes in smoked meats, with the usual selections plus a few German choices like bratwurst. They also have sandwiches and homemade desserts, and a gift shop and mail-order facilities. Open 7 days a week. **At State Hwy. 81 and State Hwy. 46; 1-800-537-6932, 830-625-2416; meats@nbsmokehouse. com; www.nbsmokehouse.com.**

Wolfgang's Keller

Specializes in German, French, and American dishes. Open for dinner Tues.–Sun. **In the cellar of the Prince Solms Inn; 1-800-625-9169.**

San Marcos

Capers on the Lake

Features a reasonably priced menu of pastas, salads, seafood, and Mexican food. **At Aquarena Springs, at I-35, exit 206; 512-392-5929.**

Fuschak's Pit Barbecue

Every Hill Country town has its "local" barbecue restaurant, and Fuschak's is it for San Marcos. **920 State Hwy. 80 at the eastern city limits; 512-353-2712.**

Katy Station Restaurant

Located in a restored railroad depot, this upscale steak house also serves chicken and seafood. **400 Cheatham St.; 512-353-5888.**

Pepper's at the Falls

A popular family restaurant serving American food. **100 Sessom Dr., on the San Marcos River; 512-396-5255.**

Woody's Meat Market

Features steaks. **2601 Hunter Rd.; 512-392-1199.**

Other Towns

BOERNE

Cafe Ye Kendall Inn
This place does it all, but their steaks are particularly good. Open 7 days a week for lunch and dinner. **On the town square; 830-249-2138.**

Country Spirit
You can get a good steak here. Open Wed.–Mon. for lunch and dinner. **707 S. Main St.; 830-249-3607.**

Peach Tree Kountry Kitchen
A Victorian tearoom with home-cooked meals. Open Tues.–Sat. for lunch only. **448 S. Main St.; 830-249-8583.**

GRUENE

Gristmill Restaurant
This is my number-one pick for a sit-down meal. It's housed in the old cotton gin and has some tables overlooking the river. The menu is not elaborate; the smoked sausage, chicken-fried steaks, and grilled chicken are the most popular. They also serve burgers. Open 7 days a week for lunch and dinner from Mar. through the first weekend in Dec.; closed on Mon. the rest of the year. **1287 Gruene Rd. behind Gruene Hall; 830-625-0624.**

WIMBERLEY

John Henry's
Enjoy fajitas or a mesquite-grilled steak on the deck overlooking Cypress Creek. Open 7 days a week for lunch and dinner. **On the town square; 512-847-5467.**

Where to Stay

New Braunfels

Faust Hotel
Restored old hotel decorated with antiques. **240 S. Seguin Ave., south of the downtown plaza; 830-625-7791.**

Gruene Mansion Inn
A Victorian mansion and several outbuildings, including a carriage house, river barn, and corn crib, have been converted into small apartments. On the bluff overlooking the Guadalupe River, this mansion is listed in the National Register of Historic Places. **1275 Gruene Rd.; 830-629-2641.**

Prince Solms Inn
Eight-room lodging in an 1898 two-story home named for the town's founder, Prince Carl of Solms-Braunfels. **295 E. San Antonio St.; 1-800-625-9169, 830-625-9169; www.texasbedandbreakfast.com/ princesolmsinn.htm.**

San Marcos

Aquarena Springs Inn
A two-story inn with 25 rooms and a restaurant. Also there is a 1928 vintage resort with 19 rooms overlooking Spring Lake and the golf course. **At Aquarena Springs; 512-396-8901; www.vpfss. swt.edu/aquainn.htm.**

Crystal River Inn
A bed-and-breakfast with 10 rooms in a restored 1883 home and two other buildings. Close to the courthouse and the Belvin Street Historic District. **326 W. Hopkins St.; 1-888-396-3739, 512-396-3739; cri@haysco.net; www.crystalriverinn.com.**

Other Towns

BOERNE

Borgman's Sunday House Bed-and-Breakfast
A one-story Sunday House with 12 units. **911 S. Main St.; 830-249-9563.**

Guadalupe River Ranch
On 360 acres; 34 rooms. **Take Farm Road 474 northeast of Boerne for 8 miles to the ranch entrance; 830-537-4341; grranch@gvtc.com; www.guadalupe-river-ranch.com.**

Tapatio Resort and Country Club
Has 89 rooms, lovely scenery, plus an 18-hole golf course. **On Johns Road, 4 miles west of Boerne;**

follow the signs; 1-800-999-3299, 830-537-4611.

Ye Kendall Inn

This old stagecoach inn built in 1859 was a gathering place for lawmen, army officers, cattle drovers, and frontier celebrities. It remains the focal point of Boerne, and all parades in the town travel around the downtown plaza and past the old hotel. Restored with six units. **On the town square, 128 W. Blanco St.; 1-800-364-2138, 830-249-2138.**

CANYON LAKE

Good sources of information on homes, condos, or resort rooms for rent at Canyon Lake are the agencies that handle such rentals. Places to contact include: **Abbott's Rental (830-964-2625); Lakeview Lodge (830-899-7007); Property Management Professionals (830-964-2921); Scenic River Properties (1-800-765-7077); Clearwater Management (803-964-2224); Cedar Terrace Condos (830-899-7375); Maricopa Ranch Resort** (830-964-3731); and **Stage Stop Ranch (1-800-782-4378, 830-935-4455).**

WIMBERLEY

7A Ranch Resort

This resort has 26 rustic cottages and a half mile of river frontage for swimming and fishing. **Off Ranch Road 12 on River Road, west of Wimberley; 512-847-2517.**

Singing Cypress Gardens

Bed-and-breakfast with gardens and frontage on Cypress Creek. Within walking distance of town square. **400 Mill Race Ln.; 1-800-827-1913, 512-847-9344; info@scgardens.com; www.scgardens.com.**

Southwind

Two rooms with private bath on a wooded hilltop. **Three miles out of town on Farm Road 3237; 512-847-5277.**

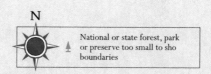

National or state forest, park
or preserve too small to sho
boundaries

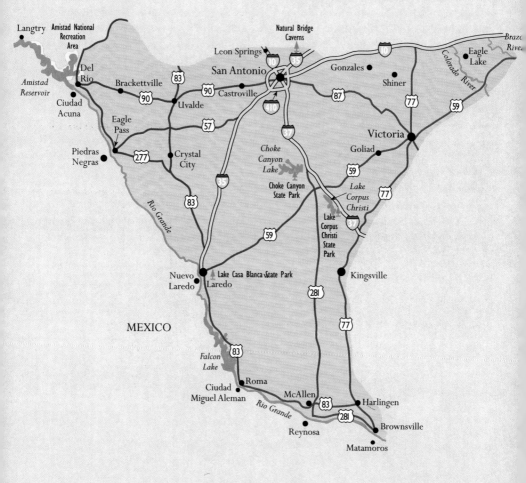

Langtry
Amistad National
Recreation
Area

Natural Bridge
Caverns

Leon Springs

Brazo
Rive

Eagle
Lake

Colorado River

Del
Rio

San Antonio

Gonzales

*Amistad
Reservoir*

Brackettville

83

Shiner

Castroville

77

90

90

Uvalde

87

59

Ciudad
Acuna

410

Eagle
Pass

57

7

Victoria

277

*Choke
Canyon
Lake*

Goliad

Piedras
Negras

Crystal
City

59

*Lake
Corpus
Christi*

Choke Canyon
State Park

35

77

83

59

Lake
Corpus
Christi
State
Park

77

Rio Grande

Nuevo
Laredo

Lake Casa Blanca State Park

Kingsville

Laredo

MEXICO

281

*Falcon
Lake*

83

77

Roma

Ciudad
Miguel Aleman

McAllen

Harlingen

83

Rio Grande

281

Reynosa

Brownsville

Matamoros

South Texas

South Texas

Armadillos strolling down a Texas highway, a familiar South Texas scene.
Photo courtesy of Texas Highways magazine.

South Texas

Draw an inverted triangle with the northern points being Del Rio to the west and Columbus and Sealy to the east, and the southern point being Brownsville in the Valley. These are my boundaries of South Texas. A lot of this is Rio Grande country—where Texas and Mexico meet. It's a land rich in Texas lore and the cowboy/vaquero atmosphere that carried this state into the twentieth century.

Ranching is big business in South Texas, and so is oil and winter tourism. The real estate industry has joined in to help boost the economy. There's money to be made in hunting too. Out-of-towners and large corporations have bought up large plots of brushland, and they treat important clients to some of the finest hunting in the state. When I was a kid growing up in West Texas, it didn't take any money to go dove hunting—just a watering pond and a little creative hiding out along a flyway. Nowadays, hunting for doves, quail, geese, or white-tailed deer is a sport for the richer. A lot of South Texas ranchers lease out their land to hunters in season; it's easier to make a buck this way than by rounding up cattle.

Some of the blackland around Uvalde may well be the richest farmland in the state. Farmers grow just about everything there, from cotton to jalapeño peppers. Farther south, the region known as the Valley is famous worldwide for its vegetables. The sweet onion known as the 10-15 was tested and developed there by agricultural experts from Texas A&M, and those ruby red grapefruit that are so much in demand today all over the country got their start and continue to be improved in the Valley.

It would be hard to separate Texas from Mexico were it not for the Rio Grande. From Brownsville to Del Rio, the land looks much the same on both sides of the river. Most of the residents on the Texas side have Mexican ancestry and most are farmers. The houses are a little nicer in Texas than in Mexico. The economy is better on the American side. There are still a lot of bargains to be found on the Mexican side, in cities like Matamoros, Reynosa, and Nuevo Laredo, and if you are wise enough to speak a little Spanish,

that makes the trip even more enjoyable. Don't be disappointed, though, if you do speak the language but don't understand some of it. They speak border Spanish down there, and sometimes even Mexicans from the interior of Mexico don't understand the language. It's part Texan and part Mexican. They call it Tex-Mex.

Some of the most attractive terrain in all of Texas is found in South Texas. Some of the puniest is there too. The rolling hills and the post oaks paint a pretty picture of the state around San Antonio, and palm trees and rich farmland light up the Valley. The land in between offers little more than scrub oaks, mesquite bushes, and hot dry summers—but that's where the oil is, so everybody's happy.

History

San Antonio and the entire Alamo Country may not be where Texas began, but it's where Texas got its reputation. At San Antonio, Texans took a stand against the tyranny of Mexican rule. This is where a tiny band of disorganized soldiers gave their lives at the Alamo and set the stage for Texas to win its independence from Mexico in 1836. The people in Alamo Country share a rich history and warm lifestyles, offering touches of German and Alsatian cultures as well as the more dominant Mexican and Texan.

Spain founded many of its earliest Texas settlements in South Texas and introduced cattle ranching to North America here. Brahma cattle crossed over into Texas with the very first explorers near Del Rio. The animals we know as Texas longhorns arrived with Spanish expeditions. Santa Gertrudis cattle were developed on the King Ranch outside present-day Kingsville. The very first great cattle trail was not the Chisholm Trail that we read so much about in history books. It was the Shawnee Trail, stretching from Brownsville at the southernmost tip of Texas up to Kansas City in the 1840s. South Texas remained a stronghold of Hispanic culture until well into the twentieth century. Even today most South Texas counties have predominately Hispanic populations.

From the Valley to Val Verde County along the Rio Grande, and northward to San Antonio, visitors are constantly reminded just how close they really are to another country. Touches of Old Mexico are everywhere, from the fiery cuisine to wide-brimmed sombreros, and hanging in the air everywhere are the sounds of mariachi, conjunto, and Tejano music. The Mexican flavor of South Texas is like taking a deep breath. Once you taste the Tex-Mex food and listen to the border music, you never want to be without it again.

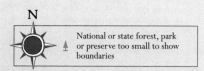

N

National or state forest, park
or preserve too small to show
boundaries

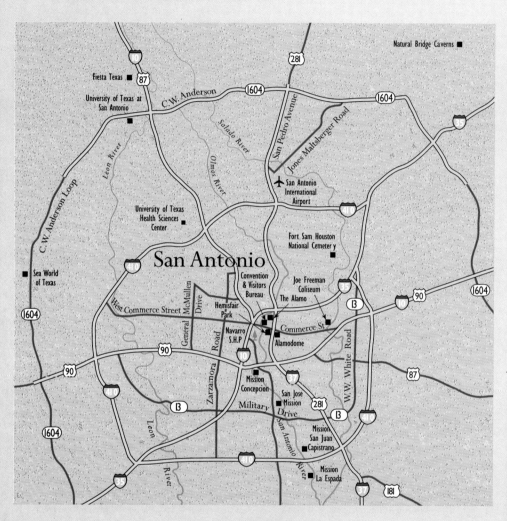

Natural Bridge Caverns ■

Fiesta Texas ■

University of Texas at
San Antonio ■

C.W. Anderson

San Pedro Avenue

Jones Maltsberger Road

Saladi River

Olmos River

Leon River

C. W. Anderson Loop

San Antonio
International
Airport

University of Texas
Health Sciences
Center ■

San Antonio

Fort Sam Houston
National Cemetery ■

Sea World
of Texas ■

West Commerce Street

General McMullen Drive

Convention
& Visitors
Bureau

Hemisfair
Park

Joe Freeman
Coliseum

The Alamo

Commerce St.

Navarro
S.H.P.

Alamodome

Zarzamora Road

W.W. White Road

Mission
Concepcion ■

Military

San Jose
Mission ■

Drive

San Antonio River

Leon

River

Mission
San Juan
Capistrano ■

Mission
La Espada ■

San Antonio

San Antonio

You could write a book on just the things to do and see in San Antonio. Many people have. The Alamo City is probably the most talked-about city in the state, even more than Dallas or Houston. It is far and away the most cosmopolitan. Houston built its reputation on industry; Dallas built its reputation on promotion. San Antonio is known for history and tourism. Its chief product is Texas and the Texas lifestyle. When people come to Texas to see Texans and to soak up the lifestyle of the Old West, they come to San Antonio. More than a third of the people who come to Texas visit San Antonio. Year in and year out, the Alamo City always tops the list of places visited in the state. Will Rogers called San Antonio one of four unique cities in America, ranking it right up there with Boston, New Orleans, and San Francisco.

San Antonio is a bicultural blend of Old World and New World. It is the largest city in the United States (population about 1 million) with a Hispanic majority. Everybody seems laid-back in San Antonio. In the early evening, many of the residents are downtown enjoying one of the city's most popular gathering places, the San Antonio River Walk (see Major Attractions, later in this chapter).

Spanish explorers arrived at what is now south San Antonio in 1691 and found friendly Indians living on the banks of a winding river. The arrival coincided with a special occasion to the Spaniards, St. Anthony's Day, so they named the spot San Antonio. By 1794 this tiny village was the capital of Spanish Texas. Spain brought in fifty-five colonists to offset the Indian population, and by the early 1800s San Antonio had a line of missions established. Their goal was to civilize the Indians.

Following the Mexican Revolution in 1821, San Antonio became part of the Republic of Mexico. About the same time, Stephen F. Austin came to town and negotiated a land grant from Mexico that allowed him to bring 300 Anglo-American colonists into Texas. In 1836, when Texas declared its independence from Mexico, there were only about 3,500 Anglos in Texas. In that year, the famous battle of the Alamo was fought and lost. Later in 1836, Texans were inspired by the massacre at the Alamo to fight it out with dictator Santa Anna and an elite force of Mexican soldiers in the swampland near a place called San Jacinto. The battle lasted only eighteen minutes, but the Texans, shouting "Remember the Alamo," kept killing the Mexican soldiers for almost a full day. Many military historians consider the battle of San Jacinto the most decisive military victory in U.S. history.

San Antonio has always been a military town. It began with the arrival of Spanish conquistadors in 1718 and continues even now. In 1898 Teddy Roosevelt trained here with the Rough Riders for the war with Spain in Cuba. Brooks and Kelly Air Force Bases opened here in 1917. Randolph Air Force Base opened in 1930, and Lackland Air Force Base followed in 1941. A lot of military types come here to serve, and stay to retire. They enjoy the climate, the laid-back atmosphere, and the small-town attitude, even though San Antonio ranks among the ten largest cities in the United States. Some people claim San Antonio is larger in population than Dallas, but Dallas adamantly refutes that claim, charging it is merely gossip spread by the folks in Houston.

The biggest boost to the economy of San Antonio is tourism. The city is home to four of the state's top

Getting There

San Antonio is the launching spot for travel in South Texas. Harlingen, far to the south in the Valley, offers some commercial air service, but all major airlines fly in and out of **San Antonio International Airport.** Ten U.S.-based airlines and three Mexico-based airlines provide service to more than fifty cities. All major car rental companies have offices at the airport. San Antonio International Airport is located about **8 miles north of downtown at I-37 and Loop 410** (about 20 minutes by car). San Antonio is at the confluence of **major freeways** that crisscross the state. I-35 comes from Austin, about 85 miles to the northeast, then travels south 160 miles to Laredo and the Mexican border. I-10 will carry you to the Alamo City from Houston 200 miles to the east, then westward all the way to El Paso at the western tip of the state. I-37 heads south from San Antonio.

Amtrak offers train service three times a week to and from New Orleans and Los Angeles, and daily to and from Chicago. The San Antonio terminal is on St. Paul's Square at **1174 E. Commerce St.; 210-223-3226. Greyhound Trailways (210-226-7371)** has service between San Antonio and the Hill Country.

politan area just south of the Texas Hill Country and in the northernmost part of South Texas. Average highs and lows look like this: January, 62°/42°; March, 72°/50°; May, 85°/65°; July, 94°/74°; September, 89°/69°; and November, 70°/49°. Long lunch breaks are common. Downtown is filled with sidewalk cafes and open-air restaurants. The people all seem to have a festive outlook, and with good reason: they have fiestas or celebrations of some sort every month of the year.

Getting Around

Star Shuttle (210-366-3183) operates a shuttle service between the airport and many downtown hotels. A trip by **taxi** from the airport to downtown costs about $12.

Gray Line bus tours (210-226-1706) leave from the Alamo every day of the week. So do a variety of other van and bus tours, plus horse and carriage rides. **Paseo del Rio Boats (210-222-1701)** load daily for rides from near the Market Street Bridge, across from the Hilton Palacio del Rio Hotel on the River Walk.

Visitor Information

San Antonio Chamber of Commerce
602 W. Commerce St. at Alamo; 210-229-2100, fax 210-229-1600; www.sachamber.org.

San Antonio Convention and Visitors Bureau
121 Alamo Plaza; 1-800-447-3372, 210-270-8700; sacvb@sanantoniocvb.com; www.sanantoniocvb.com.

San Antonio River Association
211 Broadway St.; 210-227-4262.

Visitor Information Center
317 Alamo Plaza; 210-299-8155.

Major Attractions

The Mission Trail

San Antonio is the only city in the United States with five Spanish missions inside its city limits. All were built along the San Antonio River. The Alamo was the first, established in 1718, and today is the most popu-

ten attractions—the Alamo, the River Walk, the Mission Trail, and Sea World. If you're the type who likes to avoid tourists, this still may be the place. With the relaxed attitude of the locals, it is not so easy to differentiate between the people who live here and the people who visit here.

The dress of the day for the average male is a *guayabera*—a short-sleeve shirt, open at the neck, worn in tropical capitals from Mexico City to Manila. I used to call them barber-shop shirts because all the barbers wore them where I grew up in West Texas. The climate is what you might expect for a metro-

lar because of its fascinating past. The Alamo is a separate state historical site (see below) and is located right in the middle of downtown, at 300 Alamo Plaza.

The other four missions—Concepcion, San Francisco de la Espada, San Jose, and San Juan Capistrano—are south of downtown, along a 5.5-mile Mission Trail (not a walking trail, but a driving route). Each of these four missions still serves as an active Roman Catholic parish. San Jose is considered the queen of the missions in San Antonio because of its outstanding architecture. In this respect, the least impressive of the bunch is the Alamo.

San Antonio Missions National Historical Park (2202 Roosevelt Ave., 210-534-8833, fax 210-534-1106, www.nps.gov/saan/) is part of the National Park system and includes the missions other than the Alamo:

Concepcion

Originally founded in East Texas in 1716 as one of six missions developed as buffers against the threat of French incursion from the east. The mission was transferred to its present site in 1731. **807 Mission Rd.**

San Francisco de la Espada

The smallest mission, with the simplest architecture. **10040 Espada Rd.**

San Jose

One of the country's finest examples of Spanish Mission architecture. Its entrance is beautifully sculpted, and Rosa's Window completes the eighteenth-century design. **6539 San Jose Dr.**

San Juan Capistrano

San Juan has a distinctive bell tower that makes for a striking photo. **9101 Graf Rd.**

(*Note:* Between the missions of San Francisco de la Espada and San Juan Capistrano lies the Espada Aqueduct, originally dug by Spanish missionaries in the 1730s. The updated aqueduct functions today as an irrigation system for the city.)

Hemisfair Park

This is the site of the 1968 World's Fair. The event was not considered very successful, but it did cause the city to revive an area that was in steep decline. Today it houses the Tower of the Americas—a fancy skyscraper that looks like a large needle and, with its revolving restaurant on top, is the focal point of San Antonio's downtown skyline. Also on the grounds of Hemisfair Park is the Instituto Cultural Mexicano, a convention center, a theater for the performing arts, and the John Wood County Courthouse. You'll find walking paths, a water garden, and some fine examples of early Texas architecture.

Hemisfair Park is home to the Institute of Texan Cultures, where the history of just about everything that ever happened in Texas is documented. With its dioramas, exhibits, and historical photographs, the institute acknowledges the contributions of each culture in Texas, from Native Americans and Spanish and German settlers to Dutch dairy farmers, Jewish pioneers, and Asian rice farmers. The institute, operated by the University of Texas, hosts the annual Texas Folklife Festival. The institute, at **801 S. Bowie St.,** is open every day but Monday; **210-458-2300.** Hemisfair Park, at **600 Hemisfair Plaza Way,** is bounded by Alamo St., I-37, Durango St., and Market St.; **210-207-8590.**

The Alamo

The history of the Alamo reads like the script for a Hollywood movie—but even better, because it's true. More than a century and a half ago, a small band of self-proclaimed Texans held off the finest soldiers in the Mexican army for almost two weeks. They closed themselves in behind the walls of the fort, originally a mission, and fought to the death.

Well-known Texas and American leaders and some folk heroes died here. Colonel William Barrett Travis, a fiery redhead from South Carolina, commanded the fort and made it clear that he was prepared to die defending the Alamo. He did. Jim Bowie died here too, and frontiersman Davy Crockett came all the way to Texas from Tennessee to fight and die alongside the Texans. When the smoke cleared, it was victory for the Mexicans, but the price was high. A total of 189 Texans were killed in the 13-day siege, but some 1,500 Mexican soldiers died in the battle. Most importantly, the battle bought time for General Sam Houston, who later won the war at San Jacinto.

The Alamo is open year-round and offers history talks and tours. **300 Alamo Plaza; 210-225-1391; www.thealamo.org.**

The Alamo in San Antonio, Texas's most famous mission. Photo courtesy of Texas Highways magazine.

The River Walk

One of the city's most popular attractions is partly natural, partly human-made. It is a series of cobblestone and flagstone paths extending for 21 blocks along the San Antonio River from the Municipal Auditorium on the north end to the King William Historic District at the south. The river itself is located one level below the busy streets of downtown, so you have to walk downstairs to get to it. There is access to the River Walk from Alamo Plaza, Rivercenter Mall, and city streets including South Alamo, South Broadway, Preso, Navarro, St. Mary's, Market, Commerce, and Crockett. Once you are there it becomes a world all its own, with motorized boats carrying tourists up and down the river while sidewalk cafes and specialty shops decorate the paths.

Architect Robert Hugman designed the River Walk back in the 1930s, and no doubt shortened his life in his constant battles with city fathers over what the walk would become. Hugman envisioned it as it is today: a pleasant and magical escape from the roar of city traffic. The original planners wanted it to have more of a circus atmosphere, thinking this would attract more money for the city. Hugman, however, won his battle to keep the River Walk gardenlike and beautiful, and we should all be thankful for that. Mer-

chants thank him too, because the River Walk is also one of San Antonio's greatest commercial successes.

The original River Walk, with more than 2 miles of walkways and thirty-five bridges, was built by the Works Progress Administration (WPA) in the 1930s. But following completion, it lay idle, almost abandoned, until the 1968 Hemisfair, when the city finally allowed commercial development along the river. Today the River Walk is the center of just about every cultural happening in the city. Restaurants, cafes, bars, hotels, boutiques, and the Rivercenter shopping mall line the walk. Barges and river taxis carry visitors up and down the waterway. The Arneson River Theater features live theatrical and musical performances during the warmer months and serves as focal point for presentations at many of the city's festivals.

In spite of its groomed look, the San Antonio River is a natural, spring-fed, dirt-bottom river that starts just outside the city limits and flows 180 miles to the Guadalupe River near the Gulf Coast. Every year following New Year's Day, the River Walk area is drained for general cleaning. To keep the River Walk tourist traffic from coming to a halt, the city sponsors a River Bottom Festival and Mud Parade in celebration of—you guessed it—the empty riverbed. They'll invent a festival at the drop of a hat here in San Antonio.

Here are some of the places to notice as you stroll along the River Walk, beginning with the Fourth Street Bridge at the north end of the walk and ending at the King William Historic District:

Fourth Street Bridge
One of thirty-five bridges spanning the San Antonio River.

Richmond Street Bridge
Take note of the multihued tile work along the railings.

Augusta Street Bridge
One of just three original iron and wood bridges left in the city. **115 E. Travis St.**

Ben Milam Cypress Tree
On the river's left bank. This is the River Walk's oldest tree, named for a Texan killed during the Bexar Siege of 1835. The old cypress concealed a Mexican sniper who is said to have shot Milam.

Floodgate No. 3
Built by River Walk architect Robert Hugman to tame the waters of the river.

The Esquire Bar
A local hangout that attracts a somewhat rough-and-tumble crowd. **155 E. Commerce St.**

La Mansion del Rio
The river's oldest and most distinctive hotel. **112 College St.; 1-800-292-7300, fax 210-226-0389; www.lamansion.com.**

Nix Medical Center
This 24-story, 1929-vintage building boasts the city's finest gargoyle-studded facade. **414 Navarro St.**

Hyatt Regency
Designed by architect O'Neil Ford, this 16-story hotel encloses one of the nation's largest atrium lobbies. **123 Losoya St.; 210-222-1234; www.hyatt.com.**

Restaurant Row
Eating establishments line both sides of the walk between Crockett and Commerce Streets.

Clifford Building
A classic example of turn-of-the-twentieth-century San Antonio architecture, this structure with its distinctive tower is probably the most looked-at building in town. Today the Royalty Coin Shop occupies the building. **423 E. Commerce St.**

Arneson River Theater
Part of the original WPA project that created the River Walk, the Arneson is an amphitheater that is featured in most of the city's festivals.

La Villita
San Antonio's oldest neighborhood. The name, in Spanish, means Little Town, and many believe this is the original village of San Antonio. Frontier fighter Jim Bowie lived here before he left for his meeting with destiny at the Alamo. Adobe homes still line the

Hemisfair Tower in San Antonio, where you can view the city from above or eat a fancy meal in a revolving restaurant on top of the needle. Photo courtesy of the Texas Department of Tourism.

narrow streets, many of them housing artisans and specialty gift shops. **At S. Alamo and Villita Sts.; 210-207-8610.**

King William Historic District

If you get this far on the River Walk, you'll want to walk around the most historic residential district in the city—25 blocks of late-nineteenth-century homes and neighborhoods established by German merchants. Walking tours of the district and home tours can be arranged by calling the **King William Association** at **210-227-8786.**

Seeing and Doing

Art Galleries and Museums

McNay Art Museum

The Spanish-style home built for oil heiress Marion Koogler McNay is now a museum displaying works of many of the world's most noted artists, including Degas, Picasso, Gauguin, van Gogh, El Greco, Cezanne, Dufy, Klee, and Chagall. Open daily except Mon. **6000 N. New Braunfels Ave., next to the San Antonio Art Institute; 210-805-1728; www.mcnayart.org.**

Southwest Craft Center

Two galleries, space for arts and crafts classes, and a restaurant are housed in what was once a school for girls, San Antonio's first. The French-style buildings were built in the 1850s. The galleries are open Mon.–Sat. 10 A.M.–4 P.M. **300 Augusta St.; 210-224-1848.**

Gardens and Arboreta

San Antonio Botanical Gardens

Set on 33 acres, the amazing attraction of this place is its collection of plants from all regions of the state. There is also an herb collection, a children's garden, and a giant greenhouse where you can visit a desert room, a palm room, and a fern room. Also featured is the Lucile Halsell Conservatory, a 90,000-square-foot complex of underground greenhouses that use the earth's insulation to limit plant exposure to the elements. Only the pyramidal glass roofs are visible from above ground. The gardens are open Tues.–Sun. and

holidays 9 A.M.–6 P.M. **555 Funston Place, just north of Fort Sam Houston; 210-207-3255; www.sa-attractions.com.**

Museums and Historic Sights

Fort Sam Houston

Fort Sam, founded in 1876, was training quarters for major American military figures from John J. Pershing to Dwight D. Eisenhower. It's now a far cry from the active base it was for so many years, but it is a nice place for visiting and recalling military memories. The quadrangle that dates back to the fort's beginning is worth seeing for its free-running menagerie of white-tailed deer, ducks, rabbits, geese, and exotic varieties of chickens. Building 123 has a museum with exhibits tracing the history of the Buffalo Soldiers, the Rough Riders, and the birth of military aviation in this country. The museum is open Wed.–Sun. 10 A.M.–4 P.M. The museum is **on Stanley Rd. within the confines of the fort, which is at Grayson St. and New Braunfels Ave.; 210-221-1886.**

Hertzberg Circus Collection

Tom Thumb's carriage and a miniature replica of an old-fashioned circus are displayed, where Big Top memorabilia abound. Open daily except Sun. 9 A.M.–5 P.M.; in addition, open holidays and Sun., June–Labor Day 1–5 P.M. **210 W. Market St.; 210-207-7819.**

Instituto Cultural Mexicano

Funded by the Mexican government, this institute has become one of San Antonio's most popular attractions. It offers exhibits on Mexican history and culture. Open every day but Mon. **600 Hemisfair Park; 210-227-0123.**

Ripley's Believe It or Not!

More than 500 one-of-a-kind oddities and artifacts are on display from the beautiful and often bizarre collection of Robert Ripley—including the world's smallest painting and authentic dinosaur eggs. Step into a Texas hurricane and see what a 200-mile-per-hour wind feels like. Also in the same facility is the Plaza Theater of Wax, featuring more than 225 life-like wax figures of folks like Elvis Presley and Whoopi Goldberg. Open daily 9 A.M.–7 P.M., Fri.–Sat. until 10 P.M. **301 Alamo Plaza; 210-224-9299.**

San Fernando Cathedral

Canary Islanders laid the original cornerstone for the nation's oldest cathedral in 1738. Even today, descendants of some of those Canary Islanders take mass here. The cathedral dome serves as the city's geographical center, and out front are buried the remains of those who died at the battle of the Alamo. **115 Main Plaza; 210-277-1297, fax 210-271-0149; sfc2000 @flash.net; www.sanfernandocathedral.org.**

Spanish Governor's Palace

Built in 1749 as the residence for the man in charge of the nearby Presidio, the palace today is a museum that allows visitors to see what life was like when the city was a Spanish colony. Open Mon.–Sat. 9 A.M.–5 P.M.; Sun. 10 A.M.–5 P.M. **Camaron St. at Military Plaza; 210-224-0601.**

Texas Rangers Museum

Texas Rangers memorabilia and trail-drive artifacts decorate the rooms in this place where the Texas mystique is very much alive. **3805 Broadway St.; 210-822-9011.**

Other Sites

Barney's

You won't find my favorite San Antonio museum in most books. An old friend of mine, Barney Smith, runs the place, and as far as I know, he has the largest collection of toilet seats in the country. That's right: toilet seats from everywhere, in all shapes and sizes and with all kinds of designs. He won't tell you his favorite because, he says, all of them are pretty special. They tell stories of people he has met over the years and events that have happened in his life. His collection is in his garage, and Barney is there most every day. If you want to be sure, call him before you drive on over. **239 Abiso St., near Alamo Heights; 210-824-7791.**

The Hall of Horns, Fins, and Feathers

In the 1960s, this was a saloon and showplace created by Lone Star Brewery. Back then you could wander in, get a free glass of beer, and stare at a gigantic display of animal deformity. It was, I must admit, captivating to see. These were animal freaks of nature, stuffed and mounted: a Texas longhorn with one of its horns twisted around and piercing an eye, a two-headed calf, and hundreds upon hundreds of horns of all shapes and sizes. The beer is gone, but the collection of horns—and now fins and feathers—lives on. **600 Lone Star Blvd.; 210-270-9467.**

IMAX Theater Rivercenter

The 45-minute docudrama *Alamo: The Price of Freedom* runs daily on a giant screen with an enhanced sound system. In the evening, old-fashioned action movies are featured. Open daily at 10 A.M. **849 E. Commerce St. in Rivercenter Mall.** For a schedule of films, call **210-225-4629; imax@imax-sa.com; www.imax.com/theatres/san-antonio.html.**

Parks

Brackenridge Park

The city's largest and most varied park. The **San Antonio Zoo (www.sazoo-aq.org)** is located in the 343-acre park. Also at the park, a former rock quarry is the setting for a Japanese tea garden complete with miniature bridges and carp ponds. Brackenridge Stables offers horses for rent. You can view the park from above on a skyride, or travel on the Brackenridge Eagle, a 3.5-mile miniature railway. The park is near downtown at **3903 N. St. Mary's St.; 210-737-0097.**

Fiesta Texas

Officially called Six Flags Fiesta Texas, this is a 200-acre park showcasing the heritages of the state. Shows, rides, restaurants, and shops are choreographed into four theme areas: Hispanic, German, 1920s Southwest, and 1950s rock 'n' roll. They didn't just build a park here; they completely changed the geography, bringing in huge earthmovers and then landscaping the place and putting up the buildings. When they were finished, it was like visiting another world. Take my word for it, Fiesta Texas is something to behold. Open daily in summer, only on weekends in spring and fall, closed Dec.–Feb. except for special holiday programs. **17000 West I-10, off Loop 1604, in San Antonio; 1-800-473-4378.**

Friedrich Park

This park of more than 200 acres has hiking and nature trails and is forested with plum, oak, walnut, and cedar trees. There are even some stone ruins of early frontier settlements. About 12 miles northwest of San

Antonio. Take I-10 west to Camp Bullis Road, then go left under the freeway and back right on the I-10 feeder (it's a two-way street at this point). You are then about a mile and a half from the park entrance, and there are plenty of signs pointing the way. **210-698-1057; www.wildtexas.com/parks/fwp.htm.**

San Pedro Park

Oldest park in the city, and the second oldest park in the United States (after Boston Commons). Built in 1852, the park features a museum, zoo, tropical garden, pavilion, and bathhouse. **1300 San Pedro Ave., next to San Antonio College; 210-207-3000.**

Sea World of Texas

This is the largest of all the Sea World parks around the country, and home to Shamu the killer whale. The park has a giant aquarium, a penguin showroom, and a carnival midway. The park is open weekends and some weekdays in the spring, daily during the summer, and weekends in the fall through November 1. **10500 Sea World Dr., 16 miles northwest of downtown off State Hwy. 151 at Ray Ellison Dr. and Westover Hills Blvd.; 210-523-3611; www.seaworld.com.**

Shopping

San Antonio is blessed with an assortment of shopping centers large and small, but the jewel is the downtown **Rivercenter,** a three-level mall at one end of the River Walk, next to the two Marriott hotels. The three floors feature some 125 shops and restaurant arranged U-shape around a fountain plaza.

El Mercado, the biggest Mexican marketplace in the United States, brings south-of-the-border commerce to San Antonio. Row after row of booths sell local handicrafts and imported goods. Get there in the morning if you can, because an authentic farmers market is open then. The shops are open daily 10 A.M.– 6 P.M., and later in the summer months. **514 W. Commerce St.; 210-225-2755; www.hotx.com/elmercado.**

Botica Guadalupana is the oldest pharmacy in the city; it sells traditional Mexican herbal remedies **(106 Produce Row, 210-534-4900). Del Bravo Record Shop** has a large selection of Tejano, conjunto, and other Latin music **(554 Old U.S. Hwy. 90 west, 210-433-8351). Antique Conglomerate**

El Mercado in San Antonio. Photo courtesy of the Texas Department of Tourism.

is a complex of about a dozen antiques shops **(5525 Blanco Rd., north of downtown). Sheplers** bills itself as the largest western-wear store in the world **(6201 NW Loop 410, 210-681-8230, www.sheplers.com). Little's Boots** has supplied three generations of San Antonians with custom-made boots **(110 Division St., 210-923-2221).** The best ready-made boots in town are sold at **Lucchese Boot Company (4025 Broadway St., 210-828-9419). Eisenhauer Road Flea Market** is the city's largest flea market. It's open daily, year-round **(3903 Eisenhauer Rd., 210-653-7592).**

Sports

Alamodome

Built for $187 million in 1993, this is San Antonio's monument to sports and entertainment. It covers 18 acres and seats up to 77,000 people for every kind of event from a trade show to a Super Bowl. It is home to the city's NBA franchise, the San Antonio Spurs. **I-37 at Montana St.; 1-800-884-3663; www.alamodome.com.**

Mexican Rodeos

Charreada, or Mexican-style rodeo, predates the rodeos that most Texans are familiar with. Charreada traces its roots back to Spain's vaquero tradition. The **San Antonio Charro Association (210-532-0693)** performs frequently for festivals throughout the year. Members of the association practice most weekend afternoons at their charro ranch on Padres Drive, next to **Mission County Park (6126 Padre Dr.),** and visitors are welcome to watch.

Festivals and Events

January

River Bottom Festival and Mud Parade

Live music and the coronation of a Mud King and Mud Queen celebrate the annual draining and cleaning of the San Antonio River along the River Walk.

February

Carnaval del Rio

A totally Texas music festival that covers the regional spectrum, from blues music to zydeco and conjunto; a 3-day event sponsored by the Paseo del Rio Association. **213 Broadway St.; 210-227-4262.**

Cine Festival

North America's oldest and largest Chicano/Latino film festival; sponsored by the Guadalupe Cultural Arts Center. **1300 Guadalupe St.; 210-271-3151.**

San Antonio Stock Show and Rodeo

While winter besets most other parts of the country, the Texans in San Antonio prepare for more than two weeks of riding, roping, and generally raising Cain during annual rodeo festivities. **210-225-0612; livestock@sarodeo.com; http://hotx.com/ sarodeo.**

March

Paseo de Marzo

A spring fair with Mexican food, music, and dance **at Market Square.**

St. Patrick's Day Festivities

Parades, green beer, and a variety of entertainment as the Irish celebrate their place in the Lone Star State. The San Antonio River is usually dyed green for the occasion.

Spring Renaissance Fair

A medieval European–style event held the weekend after the St. Patrick's celebration. **At Market Square, 514 W. Commerce St.**

April

Fiesta San Antonio

A celebration of the day when Texas won its independence from Mexico in 1836. This celebration rivals New Orleans's Mardi Gras in color and good old-fashioned fun. Every part of the city gets in on the action. Military bases hold special events, the art community puts on shows, and there's a boat parade on the San Antonio River. In the La Villita district, more than a hundred booths offer exotic foods and other things. **122 Heiman St.; 210-723-4378; fiesta@ fiesta-sa.org; www.fiesta-sa.org.**

Viva Botanica

The spring flower show, held the second weekend in April at the San Antonio Botanical Gardens, **555 Funston Place; 210-207-3255.**

May

Cinco de Mayo

A purely Mexican holiday commemorating Mexico's independence from Spain. Events throughout the city. Call the **San Antonio Hispanic Chamber of Commerce** at **210-255-0462.**

Tejano Conjunto Festival

Spectators from as far away as Europe make pilgrimages to this 5-day music festival featuring the best conjunto performers in the country.

June

Fiesta Noche del Rio

Every Thursday, Friday, and Saturday night during the summer, local actors, singers, and dancers perform in shows featuring Spanish and Mexican culture. Events throughout the city. Call the **San Antonio Hispanic Chamber of Commerce** at **210-255-0462.**

July

Fourth of July

A 5-day bash with music during the day and fireworks every evening at La Villita, Fort Sam Houston, Lackland Air Force Base, and Sea World.

Texas Folklife Festival

This powerful annual celebration takes place in the latter part of July and the early part of August. All the ethnic groups in Texas, and there are plenty, set up booths and sell their heritage through song and dance and demonstrations. You might find a fiddle maker from Devine, or a windmill collector from Monahans. If you're lucky you might hear an old-timer telling stories about the past. Whatever you find, it will be heartwarming and a genuinely touching experience. My favorite people at the festival have always been the gospel singers, like the Duckens Family of Temple, and my favorite entertainment area is the one marked "Cajun." Texas has its own special breed of Cajuns who hail from the Golden Triangle area around Beaumont, Port Arthur, and Orange; their roots are in Louisiana, but their homes are in East Texas. Although I don't particularly care for their coffee, I dearly love the way they party. On the grounds of the **Institute of Texan Cultures in Hemisfair Park; 210-458-2300; www.texancultures.utsa.-edu/folklife.htm.**

August

Semana de las Misiónes

Mission week starts with a special program in early August at Mission San Jose, followed by celebrations at each of the city's five Spanish missions on the following five days. **210-932-1001.**

September

Diez y Seis

Mexican Independence Day, with celebrations at Market Square, La Villita, Guadalupe Plaza, and the Arneson River Theater, with lots of food and music. **210-255-0462.**

Great Country River Festival

Usually the last weekend in September. A country and western music celebration. **Arneson River Theater and the River Walk; 210-227-4262.**

October

Greek Funstival

Usually the last week in October, celebrating Greek culture and its influence in San Antonio. **St. Sophia Greek Orthodox Church, 2504 N. St. Mary's St.; 210-735-5051.**

Oktoberfest

Sausage, beer, and German music, celebrating the influence of sausage, beer, and German music on San Antonio. **422 Pereida St.; 210-221-1521.**

November

Lighting Ceremony and Holiday River Parade

Friday night after Thanksgiving. Annual lighting ceremony in preparation for Christmas along the San Antonio River. More than 50,000 lights adorn trees and bridges. Santa Claus doesn't make his annual appearance on Main Street; he floats down the river, of course. **210-227-4262.**

December

Fiesta de las Luminarias

On weekends during December, the River Walk glows with thousands of luminarias made with paper bags, sand, and lighted candles. Carolers sing from floating barges, and lights twinkle in the trees.

Las Posadas

A Christmas tradition in San Antonio. Local leaders take part in a massive floating parade along the river. Singers move along the river, acting out the holy family's search for lodging the night Christ was born.

Recreation

Biking

The Alamo Regional Group of the **Sierra Club (P.O. Box 644, San Antonio, 78209; 210-222-8195)** sells a guide called *Outdoor San Antonio and Vicinity* that contains several bicycling maps. Another good source of information is the **San Antonio Wheelmen (P.O. Box 34208, San Antonio, 78265; 210-826-5015, www.cains.com/wheelmen),** a group that meets monthly and organizes group rides.

Caving

San Antonio is right at the edge of the Hill Country, an area honeycombed with limestone caves, so spelunking is a popular activity. The Alamo Regional Group of the **Sierra Club (P.O. Box 644, San Antonio, 78209; 210-222-8195)** says there are 172 caves worth exploring within a 70-mile radius of the city. Serious spelunkers will want to contact the Bexar Grotto of the **Speleological Society (210-699-1388, 210-377-3948)** for a schedule of trips.

Golfing

San Antonio is a golfer's town. Its year-round warm temperatures attract some of the best golfers in the country, and the courses offer some of the finest golf in the Southwest.

Brackenridge Golf Course

The oldest course in the state, built in 1915. **2315 Ave. B, Brackenridge Park; 210-226-5612; rdominquez@expressnews.net; www.express news.com/cityguide/sports/golf/brack enridge.**

Cedar Creek

Another championship course with views and triple-tiered greens. **8250 Vista Colina; 210-695-5050.**

Pecan Valley Golf Course

Another old course in town, but this one is a long 7,100 feet and it's a tough one. You've got to hit the ball long to clear the water hazards. **4700 Pecan Valley Dr.; 210-333-9018.**

The Quarry

One of the city's newest public courses. It's like playing golf along the edge of the Grand Canyon, but it's not difficult to score well if you hit the ball straight. **444 E. Basse Rd.; 1-800-347-7759, 210-824-4500; proshop@quarrygolf.com; www.quarry golf.com.**

There are other challenging public courses in the area, including **Olmos Basin (7022 McCullough Ave., 210-826-4041); Mission del Lago (1130 Mission Grande, 210-627-2522); Riverside (203 McDonald, 210-533-8371);** and **Willow Springs (202 Coliseum Rd., 210-226-6721).** Active and retired military can play at either of two 18-hole courses at **Fort Sam Houston (Grayson St. and New Braunfels Ave., 210-222-9386).**

Volksmarching

Group walking as a sport started with the International Volkssport Association in Germany in the 1960s. The sport spread to Fredericksburg, Texas, in the late 1970s. In San Antonio, there are three organized groups: the Randolph Runners, the Selma Pathfinders, and the Texas Wanderers. Folks of all ages walk in the volksmarches and receive a patch or other symbol for each one they complete. **210-659-2112.**

Where to Eat

Ask me where to eat in San Antonio, and I'll tell you to go down to the river. The San Antonio River Walk is landscaped with restaurants and cafes, from the very expensive to the very reasonable. I'm going to throw out a few names now, but don't limit your taste buds to just these places. There are great eating places all over San Antonio.

My choice for the best Mexican breakfast in town is **Mi Tierra,** a family restaurant nestled among the shops in Market Square at **El Mercado (218 Produce Row, 210-225-1262).** For American/Texan food, try the **Alamo Cafe;** there are two in San Antonio **(9714 San Pedro St. and 10060 West I-10; 210-691-8827),** and they specialize in chicken-fried steak and Tex-Mex food. They make their tortillas on the premises.

BIGA (206 E. Locust St., 210-225-0722) is a San Antonio original, started by ex-Londoner Bruce Auden. The menu changes daily, but the pasta is always excellent and the fresh homemade breads and pastries are worth the visit. **Cappy's (5011 Broadway St., 210-828-9669),** a renovated lumber warehouse, serves everything from salads to seafood to burgers. **Earl Abel's (4210 Broadway St., 210-822-3358)** is a classic 1950s American eatery, a meat-and-potatoes type of place. You'll usually find a lot of seniors there because they have specials going on all the time. **Luby's** has eighteen locations in San Antonio, the city where the chain got its start. Among them is the one at **911 N. Main St. (210-225-7720, www.lubys.com).**

The River Walk has a **Hard Rock Cafe (111 W. Crockett St., 210-224-7625).** The **Liberty Bar** features mesquite-grilled meats in a building that some say was once a brothel **(328 E. Josephine St., 210-227-1187).** **Mama's** is about the friendliest place in town and will serve you meatloaf and chocolate cake, if you like that combination **(9907 San Pedro St., 210-342-3219).** **Polo's Restaurant** serves perhaps the most exotic meals in town and maybe the most expensive; you can dine on lamb, antelope, Texas rabbits (in the historic Fairmount Hotel at **401 S. Alamo St., 210-225-4242).** In Alamo Heights, the **Twin Sisters Bakery and Cafe** is a popular breakfast and lunch place **(6322 N. New Braunfels Ave., 210-822-0761).** The **Zuni Grill** turns out some unique meals, including pecan-crusted chicken and Texas goat cheese with spinach **(511 River Walk, 210-227-0864).**

The **Chinatown Cafe** is one of my favorite Asian eating places **(Broadway and Nacogdoches Sts., 210-822-3522).** The **County Line** is my pick for barbecue **(606 W. Afton Oaks Blvd., 210-496-0011).** And then there is the **Pig Stand (1508 Broadway St., 210-222-2794),** which claims to be the oldest continually operating restaurant in the city and features '50s-style barbecue, including those famous pig sandwiches. My wife, Helen, says Pig Stands in Texas started her on the road to being overweight. She says she used to pig out with a neighbor at a Pig Stand in Beaumont while I was out covering all the news that was fit to report on radio.

I could spend another couple of pages talking about the terrific eating places in San Antonio. There's the **Lone Star Cafe (237 Losoya St., 210-223-9374); Schilo's,** a German American deli **(424 E. Commerce St., 210-223-6692);** and the **Babylon Grill (910 S. Alamo St., 210-222-0110).**

Don't visit San Antonio without eating Mexican. That's what I think they do best around here, and there are plenty of places to choose from, including **Aldaco's Mexican Cuisine,** the friendliest spot on St. Paul Square **(1141 E. Commerce St., 210-222-0561); Big Ern's Taco Palace,** a popular taco joint

(2030 Goliad Rd., 210-333-3542); and **Los Barrios,** not so much for the food but for the atmosphere, with its location in the middle of a largely Hispanic neighborhood **(4223 Blanco, 210-732-6017).**

For seafood, the **Water Street Oyster Bar** is a favorite **(999 E. Busse St., 210-829-4853).** So is the **Bayous on the River Walk,** featuring Cajun/Creole seafood **(off N. Presa St., 210-223-6403).**

The **Grey Moss Inn** specializes in grilled steaks **(about 12 miles northwest of San Antonio on Scenic Loop Rd., in the community of Helotes, 210-695-8301).** So does the **Little Rhein Steakhouse,** an 1847 stone house on the River Walk. The steaks here are the best, and the most expensive, San Antonio has to offer **(231 S. Alamo St., 210-225-2111).**

Where to Stay

Bed-and-Breakfast Hosts of San Antonio offers a complete listing of such places in the San Antonio area. **166 Rockhill St.; 210-824-8036.**

If you've got the money, I suggest staying downtown by the river. On the other hand, if you don't mind driving, you can lodge inexpensively in the San Antonio area. I used to spend the night in New Braunfels, just north of the city, because I could always find a reasonably priced room there; it's only about a 30-minute drive to the north edge of downtown. But for vacationers, the best is probably a room near the river. Here are some of the best-known:

Built in 1859, the **Menger** is San Antonio's oldest hotel and probably its most famous. Its register boasts names like O. Henry, Robert E. Lee, Sarah Bernhardt, Mae West, and Teddy Roosevelt. A friend of mine insists there are ghosts in the bar at the Menger, and plenty of stories claim this place is, indeed, haunted. **204 Alamo Plaza, near the Alamo; 1-800-345-9285, fax 210-228-0022; menger@ipsa.net; www.mengerhotel.com.**

Other hotels include the **St. Anthony (300 E. Travis St., 210-227-4392, fax 210-222-1896, stanthonyhotel@travelbase.com, www.stanthonyhotel.com);** the **Sheraton Gunter Hotel (205 E. Houston St., 210-227-3241);** the **Emily Morgan,** another hotel that faces right onto the Alamo complex **(705 E. Houston St., 210-225-**

8486); the **Crockett Hotel (320 Bonham St., at Crockett St., 210-225-6500);** and **La Mansion del Rio (112 College St., 1-800-292-7300, fax 210-226-0389, www.lamansion.com),** housed in a mission-style structure on the river.

In 1910, rooms at the **Fairmount Hotel (401 S. Alamo St., 210-225-4242)** were 75 cents a night. In the 1980s I had a film crew there with our trusty *Eyes of Texas* cameras documenting the move of the hotel building from its original location on East Commerce Street to South Alamo Street. The price of rooms has gone up considerably since 1910, and the move of the Fairmount is listed in the *Guinness Book of World Records* as the "world's largest building move."

Some of the more popular lodges along the River Walk are the **Hilton Palacio del Rio (200 S. Alamo St., 210-222-1400); Holiday Inn River Walk North (110 Lexington Ave., 1-800-465-4329); Holiday Inn RiverWalk (217 N. St. Mary's St., 210-224-2500); Marriott River Walk (711 E. River Walk, 210-224-5555);** and the granddaddy of all the hotels along the river, the **Marriott Rivercenter (101 Bowie St., at Commerce St., 210-223-1000),** with 1,000 rooms—and believe it or not, it's usually difficult to find an available room.

Towns in the Alamo Country Area

There's no question about it: San Antonio is the dominant city of South Texas. But there are many other towns in Alamo Country with an interesting history and visitor attractions that are within reasonable driving range east, south, and west of San Antonio. This section looks at a selection of Alamo Country towns: how to get there, the special offerings of each, and how to get more information. We visit Gonzales, Shiner, Eagle Lake, Victoria, Goliad, Kingsville, Crystal City, Uvalde, Castroville, and Leon Springs. The towns are organized in roughly a broad clockwise sweep beginning just east of San Antonio.

Gonzales

Getting There: Gonzales is about 80 miles east of San Antonio. From San Antonio, take I-10 for 55 miles to the second Luling exit, then travel southeast on

U.S. Hwy. 183 about 20 miles to Gonzales. **Visitor Information: Gonzales Chamber of Commerce, 414 St. Lawrence; 830-672-6532; www.gonzalestexas.com.**

The Gonzales area is noted for being the place where the first shot of the Texas Revolution was fired. Gonzales was given a cannon by sympathetic supporters of the Texas fight for independence from Mexico, but when the cannon arrived, the Mexican government sent soldiers to confiscate it. The Texans made a flag that displayed the words "Come and take it." When the soldiers tried, one blast from the cannon caused them to retreat. It was a minor victory for the Texans that didn't last long but, like the Alamo, the "Come and take it" cannon at Gonzales became a rallying point for the Texans during the war. You can visit the site by traveling a couple miles south of Gonzales on U.S. Hwy. 183, then west for 6 miles on State Hwy. 97 to the monument. In later, more peaceful, times, Gonzales became cattle country. The first brand was recorded here in 1829, and the Chisholm Trail came through in 1866.

SEEING AND DOING

Gonzales Pioneer Village Living History Center
On display is a collection of artifacts gathered by relatives of some of the old-timers around here. **On U.S. Hwy. 183, north of U.S. Hwy. 90A near the northern city limits.**

FESTIVALS AND EVENTS

October—"Come and Take It" Celebration
In early October. A 4-day funfest honoring the first shot of the Texas Revolution with a festival, street dance, and parade. **830-672-6532.**

November–December—Winterfest
Thanksgiving weekend and the following weekend. A celebration of the cultures that make up Gonzales. **Confederate Square, in the 400 block of St. George St.; 830-672-6532.**

RECREATION

Lake Wood Recreation Area
One of the best-kept secrets in Alamo Country, this is

a quiet, scenic campground. It has picnicking, camping, boating, fishing, and canoeing in the lake or the nearby Guadalupe River. **About 5 miles west of Gonzales, off of U.S. Hwy. 90A on Farm Road 2091 south; 830-672-2779; lakewood@gvtc. com; http://gvtc.com/lakewood.**

Palmetto State Park
Located in an area once known as the Ottine Swamp, this park looks like a tropical botanical garden. It's a 263-acre park composed mostly of swampy woodlands along the San Marcos River. There are 37 campsites, many with water and electricity, plus swimming, fishing, and short nature and hiking trails. **From Gonzales, take U.S. Hwy. 183 north for 12 miles, then go west on Park Road 11 for 2 miles to the entrance; 830-672-3266.**

WHERE TO EAT
Hernandez Cow Palace Restaurant is a family steak house **(314 W. U.S. Hwy. 90A, 830-672-4777).**

WHERE TO STAY
St. James Inn displays all the flavor of early Texas in a quaint, restored old home. **723 St. James St.; 830-672-7066.**

Shiner
Getting There: Take I-10 east of San Antonio for about 55 miles to U.S. Hwy. 183, then go south for 20 miles to Gonzales. Shiner is 18 miles east of Gonzales on U.S. Hwy. 90A. **Visitor Information: www.shinertexas.com.**

Cotton is still king in this area, although beef and dairy cattle are beginning to play larger roles in the economy. Since the beginning in 1887, this has been a trade center for Czech and German farmers.

SEEING AND DOING

Spoetzl Brewery
The oldest independent brewery in Texas, this is one of only a few remaining breweries whose product is made, bought, and consumed entirely in Texas. Spoetzl produces 25,000 barrels of Shiner beer annually and markets it in the surrounding area. You can tour the brewery in the winter Mon.–Fri. at 11:00 A.M. and 1:30 P.M. In the summer, tours begin at 10:00 A.M.,

11:00 A.M., 1:30 P.M. and 2:30 P.M. **603 E. Brewery St.; 361-594-3383; shiner@dcci.com; www. shiner.com.**

WHERE TO EAT
The **Country Corner Cafe** is a popular gathering place for locals **(305 E. 5th St., 361-594-2822).**

WHERE TO STAY
The **Kasper House B&B** provides comfortable country relaxation. **305 N. Ave. C; 361-594-4336.**

Eagle Lake
Getting There: From San Antonio, take I-10 east 125 miles to Columbus, then turn right (south) onto State Hwy. 71 and go 11 miles to U.S. Hwy. 90A. Travel east on Hwy. 90A for 8 miles to Eagle Lake. **Visitor Information: Eagle Lake Chamber of Commerce; 409-234-2780; www.main.elc.net.**

SEEING AND DOING

Attwater Prairie Chicken Refuge
This 3,400-acre sanctuary for coastal prairie chickens is near the San Bernard River. These birds at one time were in danger of being wiped out, but now they are thriving again, and are wonderful critters to watch. You can arrange tours by calling the **Eagle Lake Chamber of Commerce (409-234-2780)** or the **refuge (409-234-3021).** The refuge is about **halfway between Eagle Lake and Sealy on Farm Road 3013.**

RECREATION

Hunting
The goose-hunting capital of the state, Eagle Lake is where all the goose- and duck-hunting fanatics wind up every season, stumbling around in wet rice fields for hours waiting for that flock of snow geese or Canadian blues to come down for a closer look at their decoys. You can book hunts through the **Jimmy Reel Goose Hunting Club (P.O. Box 83, Eagle Lake, 77434).** A couple of the more popular places to stay for hunters (or honeymooners) are the **Eagle Hill Inn and Retreat (307 E. State St., 409-234-3551)** and the **Farris 1912,** a restored railroad hotel **(201 N. McCarty Ave., 409-234-2546).**

WHERE TO EAT
Hunters gather to tell stories and enjoy family cooking at the **Blue Goose Restaurant (in Altair, 8 miles west of Eagle Lake on U.S. Hwy. 90A; 409-234-3597).**

WHERE TO STAY
The **Farris 1912** is a restored railroad hotel that has become a popular lodge for goose hunters in season. There are 15 rooms in the hotel and 4 suites in the Bentley House next door. **201 N. McCarty Ave.; 409-234-2546.**

Victoria
Getting There: Victoria is about 100 miles southeast of San Antonio, and it can be an interesting drive if you are in no rush. Take U.S. Hwy. 181 south for 60 miles to Kenedy, then go left briefly on State Hwy. 72 and turn right onto Farm Road 239, taking it for 32 miles to Goliad, where you turn left onto U.S. Hwy. 59 for the final 22 miles to Victoria. A more direct route from San Antonio is to go east on I-10 for 55 miles to Luling, then right (south) on U.S. Hwy. 183 for 52 miles to Cuero, and finally left (east) on U.S. Hwy. 87 for 28 miles to Victoria. **Visitor Information: Victoria Convention and Visitors Bureau, 700 Main St.; 361-573-5277; viccvb@ icsi.net; www.visitvictoria.org.**

Victoria was a crossroads for early explorers Cabeza de Vaca and la Salle. Agriculture and oil and gas are the main industries here. The city also is an architectural treasure, with almost a hundred structures listed in the National Register of Historic Places.

SEEING AND DOING

Nave Museum
This memorial honors Texas painter Royston Nave, who was appreciated more in northeastern U.S. art circles than in his home state. Most of his inspiration came from this part of Texas. **306 W. Commercial St.; 361-575-8227; www.viptx.net/museum/ nave.**

Riverside Park and Rose Garden
This 560-acre park bordering 4 miles of the Guadalupe River has a rose garden with a thousand-plus bushes representing more than 100 varieties. There's also an

Palmetto State Park near Gonzales. Photo courtesy of the Texas Department of Tourism.

18-hole public golf course. **On Red River St.; 361-572-2763.**

Texas Zoo
More than 200 animals, all strictly from Texas, are displayed in their native habitats. I think this is one of the best zoos in the state. If you come to Texas, you've got to see an armadillo. If you don't find one on the road, you can see one at the Texas Zoo. **110 Memorial Dr., in Riverside Park; 361-573-7681; www. viptx.net/texaszoo.**

FESTIVALS AND EVENTS

May—Bach Festival
Late in the month. The festival honors the music of Bach and other composers. **361-572-2787; info@victoriabachfestival.org; www.victoria-bachfestival.org.**

October—International Armadillo Confab and Exposition
One weekend late in the month. This lighthearted event honors the local animal with races, a chili cook-off,

arts and crafts, and the Miss Vacant Lot Beauty Contest. **Riverside Park; 361-573-5277.**

RECREATION

Coleto Creek Reservoir and Regional Park
Recreation areas provide picnicking, camping, boating, and fishing. **Along U.S. Hwy. 59, 12 miles southeast of Victoria, between Victoria and Goliad; www.visitvictoria.org/coleto.htm.**

Lake Texana State Park
The 575-acre park is named for the town of Texana, a major community in this area in the 1830s but long since gone. Activities include camping, boating, waterskiing, jet-skiing, canoeing, swimming, and sailing. Hiking and birding are exceptionally good here, and so is the fishing. The park is **23 miles northeast of Victoria on U.S. Hwy. 59 (and 6.5 miles east of Edna on State Hwy. 111); 361-782-5718.**

WHERE TO EAT
For an eating place with local flavor, try **Maggie's Meat Market and Restaurant (2001 John Stockbauer Dr., 361-573-0428).** The **Ramsey Restaurant** is a family eating place **(1403 N. Navarro St., 361-572-3287). Napoleon's Restaurant** is an upscale steak house **(2101 N. Laurent St., 361-575-0691).** Also popular here are **Mi Familia Restaurant,** with Tex-Mex food **(2804 Port Lavaca Dr., 361-572-0304),** and **Tejas Cafe,** a sandwich shop **(2902 N. Navarro St., 361-572-9433).**

WHERE TO STAY
Among the motels along the route to Houston is **Westerner Motor Hotel. 3004 Houston Hwy.; 361-575-4531.**

Goliad

Getting There: From San Antonio, take I-10 east for 55 miles to U.S. Hwy. 183 at Luling, then go south about 80 miles to Goliad. **Visitor Information: Goliad County Chamber of Commerce, Market and Franklin Sts.; 361-645-3563, 1-800-848-8674; gedc@icsi.net; www.goliad.org.**

A lot of Texas history originated here. Explorers moved through on their way to other territory. Missions and forts were built, and still stand today. This

community played a large role in the Texas Revolution. The Mexican army slaughtered about 400 Texans here, and the event built up hatred and resentment for the Mexican government that lasted until the final shot was fired. Today, Goliad's economy is based on oil, agriculture, and tourism.

SEEING AND DOING

Fannin Battleground State Historic Site
A 13-acre park where Colonel James Walker Fannin and his force of about 400 men were captured and executed during the war with Mexico. This is a day-use park with activities restricted to historical studies and picnicking. **Take U.S. Hwy. 59 east of town for 9 miles, then go south on Park Road 22 for less than a mile; 361-645-2020; www.tpwd. state.tx.us/park/fannin/fannin.htm.**

General Zaragoza Birthplace
A building commemorating the birth in Goliad of Mexican hero Ignacio Zaragoza, who put his small Mexican force up against Maximilian's French army in 1862 and routed the French. The battle took place on May 5, and that date is now celebrated in both Mexico and the Mexican American communities in Texas as Cinco de Mayo. **On U.S. Hwy. 183 about 2 miles south of Goliad; 361-645-2282.**

Goliad State Historical Park
Features the ruins of Mission Nuestra Señora del Espiritu Santo de Zuniga, established in 1722. This mission once controlled the land between the Guadalupe and San Antonio Rivers and possessed huge herds of cattle used to supply settlements in Mexico and Texas. This park on the San Antonio River offers camping, fishing, hiking, boating (but no ramps for river access), and historical studies. There is a nature trail with varied areas for viewing birds and wildlife. **U.S. Hwy. 183 about 1 mile south of Goliad; 361-645-3405; www.goliad.org/park/gsp.htm.**

Presidio de la Bahia
A fort built in 1749 to protect the missions and to guard a 300-square-mile section of land called New Spain. It became what is thought to be the most fought-over fort in Texas. **On U.S. Hwy. 183, 2 miles south**

of Goliad; 361-645-3752; www.goliad.org/presidio.htm.

FESTIVALS AND EVENTS

May—Fiesta Zaragoza

First weekend in May. A celebration honoring the famous general. **At Goliad County Fairgrounds; 361-645-3563.**

June—Goliad Longhorn Stampede

Don't miss this event if you are in the area. Longhorn breeders and trail riders reenact a part of their history by driving about 100 longhorn steers from Fannin to Goliad. The first reenactment was held in 1976 and resulted in an actual stampede; longhorns can be stubborn. This event is often called the "fastest parade in history," with good reason. Call the **Goliad County Chamber of Commerce at 361-645-3563.**

RECREATION

Choke Canyon State Park

One of two state parks in the general Goliad area, though it is some distance from that town. Consists of two units, **South Shore** and **Calliham,** on the 26,000-acre Choke Canyon Reservoir, a water supply for Corpus Christi. The park offers camping, picnicking, boating, hiking, wildlife viewing, birding, fishing, an area for horseback riding, a lake beach, plus a pool that is open in summer. To get there from Goliad, **take U.S. Hwy. 59 southwest for 54 miles to the town of George West, then go north on U.S. Hwy. 281 for 10 miles.** The **South Shore unit (361-786-3538)** is 3.5 miles west of Three Rivers on State Hwy. 72. The **Calliham unit (361-786-3868)** is 12 miles west of Three Rivers on Hwy. 72. You can also get to Three Rivers by driving about 65 miles south of San Antonio on I-37.

Lake Corpus Christi State Park

The other state park in the general Goliad area, also some distance from that town. The 21,000-acre lake was created by damming the Nueces River. Activities include camping, picnicking, boating, water-skiing, fishing, hiking, swimming, and bird-watching. From Goliad, take U.S. Hwy. 59 southwest for 30 miles, then go left on U.S. Hwy. 181 for 11 miles to Skimmer, then right on State Hwy. 359 to Mathis. The park is **on Farm Road 1068, 4 miles southwest of Mathis.** You can also get to Mathis by driving about 35 miles north of Corpus Christi on I-35. **361-547-2635.**

WHERE TO EAT

Expect excellent food at **Empresario Restaurant (141 S. Courthouse Square, 361-645-2347). Irma's Cafe** serves up all the flavor of a hometown cafe **(802 E. Pearl St., 361-645-8545).**

WHERE TO STAY

Antler's Inn is a popular stop for deer hunters. **On U.S. Hwy. 59 west; 361-645-8215.**

Kingsville

Getting There: Take I-37 south from San Antonio for 114 miles to Robstown, then go south on U.S. Hwy. 77 for 30 miles to Kingsville. **Visitor Information: Kingsville Tourist Information Depot, 1501 N. 77 Bypass at Corral St.; 361-592-4121.** Also, **Kleberg County Convention and Visitors Bureau, 101 N. 3rd; 361-592-8516;** and the **Kingsville Chamber of Commerce, 635 E. King St.; 361-592-6438; www.kingsville.org.**

Kingsville was named for Captain Richard King, who created the world-famous **King Ranch.** King was a steamboat captain who supplied the U.S. Army with goods and weapons in the Mexican War. In the 1850s he bought 75,000 acres that had been a Spanish land grant called the Santa Gertrudis, and he kept acquiring land over the years until the ranch grew into an empire of 825,000 acres crossing four county lines, creating one of the world's largest ranches. The King Ranch is where Santa Gertrudis cattle were developed. Another man, Robert Kleberg Sr., played no small part in the development of the ranch and the town. He drilled for water and found it in 1899, and from that time on, Kingsville had a permanent source of water. Limited tours of the ranch are offered daily. **In Kingsville; 361-592-8055, fax 361-595-1344; www.kingranch.com.**

SEEING AND DOING

King Ranch Museum

Shows off a collection of western memorabilia from the ranch and the region. **405 N. 6th St.; 361-595-1881.**

Fannin Battleground Monument, east of Goliad.

King Ranch Saddle Shop

A 120-year-old shop that has outfitted governors, presidents, and foreign leaders over the years. **201 E. Kleberg Ave.; 361-595-5761; www.krsaddle shop.com.**

L. E. Ramey Golf Course

A challenging 18-hole public course with unique landscape and human-made lakes. Open daily. **One mile south of Kingsville on U.S. Hwy. 77; 361-592-1101.**

FESTIVALS AND EVENTS

June—George Strait Team Roping and Concert

At Kingsville's Exposition Center and Dick Kleberg Park. **361-592-8516.**

WHERE TO EAT

The **Barn Door** is popular for barbecue **(on U.S. Hwy. 77 south, 361-296-3132).** Burgers and steaks are on the menu at the **Mesquite Grill (621 W. Corral St., 361-592-1182).** For the family, try **Barth's Restaurant (3034 S. U.S. Hwy. 77, 361-595-5753)** or **Lee's Family Dining (406 N. 6th St., 361-516-0195).**

WHERE TO STAY

The **B Bar B Ranch Inn** is on an 80-acre working ranch **(on U.S. Hwy. 77 outside Kingsville; 361-296-3331).** In the coastal community of Riviera is **Bailey's Lodge on Baffin Bay (16 miles south of Kingsville on U.S. Hwy. 77; 361-595-4666).** For local flavor, try the **Coachway Inn in Luling. On U.S. Hwy. 90 on the outskirts of Kingsville; 830-875-5635.**

Crystal City

Getting There: Take I-35 south of San Antonio for 42 miles, then go right (west) on U.S. Hwy. 57 for 52 miles to La Pryor, then south on U.S. Hwy. 83 for 19 miles to Crystal City. **Visitor Information: Greater Crystal City Chamber of Commerce, near the Popeye statue downtown; 830-374-3581.**

Crystal City is a packing, processing, and shipping center for large quantities of onions, carrots, tomatoes, peppers, and spinach from the Valley. Spinach was the inspiration for the town's best-known attraction, its **Popeye statue.** A statue of the spinach hero was erected downtown in 1937 by the Del Monte Company, which had a large processing plant in Crystal City. It's a favorite spot for snapshots with children.

WHERE TO EAT

You'll find real Tex-Mex food at the **Compean Cafe (504 E. Zavala St., 830-374-2761). Popeye's Buffet Cafe** is a popular local hangout **(on the old Uvalde Highway in Crystal City, 830-374-5641).**

Uvalde

Getting There: Take U.S. Hwy. 90 west of San Antonio about 80 miles. You'll pass through some of my favorite communities on the way, including Castroville, D'Hanis, Sabinal, and Knippa. **Visitor Information: Uvalde Chamber of Commerce, 330 E. Main St.; 830-278-3361; www.uvalde.org.**

Uvalde is the home of former Texas governor Dolph Briscoe and of "Cactus Jack" Garner, vice president of the United States when FDR was running the country. Uvalde was also home to Pat Garrett after he killed Billy the Kid, and other lesser-known western characters spent time in these parts. J. K. "King" Fisher lived in this area in the 1880s. He was an outlaw and then a lawman, though many historians say he never did give up his lawbreaking ways. Bat Masterson called Fisher the best man with a gun in the West. But he wasn't good enough. Fisher and another notorious Texan, Ben Thompson, were killed in a gunfight in a San Antonio dance hall in 1884.

Uvalde sits at the crossroads of two highways that span the entire United States: U.S. Hwy. 90, which runs from Florida to California, and U.S. Hwy. 83, which reaches from Canada to Mexico. The city is sometimes referred to as Tree City, USA, because of an ordinance protecting oak trees that grow in the middle of some of the streets. (Goliad also has a lot of protected oaks that cause detours in street traffic.)

SEEING AND DOING

Garner Museum

Honors hometown boy John Nance Garner, who went to Congress in 1903 when Theodore Roosevelt was president and became vice president to FDR. Garner is famous for his description of the office of vice president. He said, "It isn't worth a bucket of warm spit." **333 N. Park St.; 830-278-5018.**

Jardin de los Heroes Park

Honors Vietnam veterans; includes a playground and picnic facilities. **801 W. Main St.**

Scenic Drive

A good round-trip route from Uvalde is U.S. Hwy. 83 north through Concan, past Garner State Park to Leakey, then west on Farm Road 337 to Camp Wood, and finally south on State Hwy. 55 back to Uvalde, for a drive of a little under 100 miles.

Uvalde Grand Opera House

A two-story brick building that's been an office building and a theater. Today it's a museum and is listed in the National Register of Historic Places. **104 W. North St.; 830-278-4184.**

Uvalde Memorial Park

Provides a golf course **(Memorial Golf Course, 329 E. Garden St., 830-278-6155),** lighted tennis courts, and walking trails. **337 E. Main St. on the banks of the Leon River.**

FESTIVALS AND EVENTS

August—Regional Sailplane Competition

Early in the month. Uvalde's excellent soaring weather is one of the reasons that sailplane pilots from across the United States come here for this competition. The sailplanes travel hundreds of miles, but you can watch the takeoffs and landings. **Uvalde Flight Center, Municipal Airport, Farner Field Rd.; 830-278-3361.**

October—Cactus Jack Festival

The second weekend of the month. It features a rodeo and parade, dances, entertainment, and an arts and crafts fair. **Memorial Park / Fairgrounds on U.S. Hwy. 90; 830-278-3361.**

RECREATION

Fort Inge County Park

The site of a U.S. Cavalry post built in 1891. The park features hiking trails, camping, picnicking, and bird-watching. Along the Leon River, **on Farm Road 140, 1.5 miles south of Uvalde.**

Garner State Park

A 1,430-acre park along the Frio River, and one of the most-visited parks in the state. It offers fishing, swimming, camping, hiking, and biking. It also has paddleboats for rent, picnic areas, and cabins. **On U.S. Hwy. 83, 31 miles north of Uvalde, just outside the community of Concan; 830-232-6132; www.tpwd.state.tx.us/park/garner/garner.htm.**

Park Chalk Bluff

A magnificent campground with a 400-foot limestone bluff. This is a restful place to stay, and is not quite as crowded as Garner State Park. It typifies South Texas scenery and offers some solitude in a normally busy area. Two of the Southwest's greatest Indian fighters, Henry Robinson and Henry Adams, met their ends here at the hands of about twenty renegade Indians. From Uvalde, **take U.S. Hwy. 83 north for about 2 miles, then State Hwy. 55 west for about 15 miles; 830-278-5831.**

WHERE TO EAT

You'll find good Mexican food at **Don Marcelino Restaurant (2210 E. Main St., 830-278-8998),** and family dining at the **Town House Restaurant (2105 E. Main St., 830-278-2428).** Cactus Jack Cafe & Tortilla Factory serves up great Mexican food and atmosphere **(2217 Main St., 830-278-4422).**

WHERE TO STAY

There's an atmosphere of both Texas and Mexico at **Casa de Leona Bed-and-Breakfast. 1149 Pearsall Rd., outside of Uvalde; 830-278-8550.**

Castroville

Getting There: About 15 miles west of the San Antonio city limits on U.S. Hwy. 90. **Visitor Information: Castroville Chamber of Commerce, 802 London St.; 1-800-778-6775, 830-538-3142; castrochamber@freewwweb.com/castroville.net; www.castroville.net.**

Castroville was founded in 1844 by a group of Alsatians, a mixture of German and French people, brought to the United States by Henri Castro. Many of the homes are German-style country cottages with steeply pitched roofs because the people who came here were accustomed to heavy winter snows. I rate this community as the most interesting in the state, after Fredericksburg, for its history, its beautiful location along the Medina River, and its architecture. There is not a lot of outdoor activity here, but the

history will captivate you. The people here are not unfriendly, but they are not necessarily friendly either. They just leave you alone and that's okay, because you don't need a guide to lead you to the wonderful old buildings in town. They're everywhere.

SEEING AND DOING

Landmark Inn State Historic Structure

A revived old hotel that was here when stagecoach travelers stopped on their way to and from San Antonio. There's no radio and no TV, but there are rocking chairs and ceiling fans, and the ruins of an old water-powered grist mill alongside the Medina River. Operated by the state as a hotel. **402 Florence St.; 830-931-2133.**

Mount Gentilz Cemetery

Known as Cross Hill, the rise above the cemetery offers a panoramic view of the Medina Valley. **Along U.S. Hwy. 90 west as you are leaving town.**

St. Louis Catholic Church

Don't let the big church building fool you. That's the "new" church built in 1868. Next door to the big structure is a tiny building that looks like a storage shed beside the church; it's the original chapel built by the colonists. **Downtown square; 830-538-2267.**

FESTIVALS AND EVENTS

August—St. Louis Day

Held in late August every year. A feast honoring the town's patron saint, and a homecoming for Castroville residents who have moved away.

RECREATION

Castroville Regional Park

Covers 126 wooded acres along the Medina River, and offers picnic, camping, and fishing areas and an Olympic-size swimming pool. The experts say bass fishing here is very good. In the southwestern part of Castroville, at **703 Paris St.; 830-538-2224.**

Medina Lake

A 5,000-acre lake with campgrounds, marinas, and cottages for rent. From Castroville, take Farm Road 471 north for about 17 miles to Farm Road 1283, then drive west for 5 miles to Park Road 37; **www.tp wd.state.tx.us/fish/infish/lakes/medina/ lake_id.htm.**

WHERE TO EAT

The **Alsatian Restaurant** serves up good food from an interesting menu **(403 Angelo St., Castroville, 830-931-3260). Sammy's** is a favorite eating place, specializing in chicken-fried steaks and such **(202 U.S. Hwy. 90, Castroville; 830-538-2204). Habys Alsatian Bakery** features apple fritters, strudel, and homemade breads, pies, cookies, and coffee cakes **(207 U.S. Hwy. 90, Castroville; 830-931-2118). Hermann Sons Steak House** is one of my favorite steak houses in the state **(on U.S. Hwy. 90, just east of Hondo, which is 20 miles west of Castroville; 830-426-2220).**

WHERE TO STAY

The **Landmark Inn** is a former stage stop, now owned and operated by the state as an inn. **402 Florence St.; 830-931-2133.**

Leon Springs

Getting There: Take I-10 northwest out of San Antonio about 20 miles to the Leon Springs exit. The town is about 5 miles beyond Loop 1604 on the Interstate. **Visitor Information: webmaster@ leonsprings.com; www.leonsprings.com.**

This little community near San Antonio is certainly worth mentioning because of the work of Stephen Tello and others at a very special place called **Primarily Primates.** Have you ever wondered what happens to the trained animals in Hollywood who are past their prime, or to zoo animals that get hurt, become irritable, or just can't get along with crowds anymore? The sad truth is that sometimes they were just discarded or put to sleep until people like Stephen Tello and organizations like Primarily Primates came along. Today, 550 monkeys and apes, plus many other animals, get loving care and comfortable quarters for living out their lives in this facility. Animal rights activist Bob Barker has helped support Primarily Primates since its inception. The place isn't officially open to the public, but a phone call will usually result in an invitation to visit (and the opportunity to contribute to this fine cause). **P.O. Box 15306, Leon Springs, 78212; 830-755-4616, fax 830-755-2435; www.primarilyprimates. org.**

The Valley

The South Texas Valley—the Rio Grande Valley—is synonymous with vegetable and citrus crops. Most of the citrus grown and developed in Texas comes from the Valley. Most of the vegetables grown and developed in Texas come from the Valley.

You've heard of those famous Vidalia onions in Georgia? Well, they got their start in the Valley. You've read about those sweet, tasty ruby red grapefruit? Well, they started in the Valley. And I'm certain you've tasted the crunchy, sweet Texas onion called the 10-15. That's right, they were developed by a bunch of agricultural geniuses from Texas A&M. I've got to admit there are a lot of smart farmers at Texas A&M—and that compliment is coming from a graduate of the University of Texas.

The Rio Grande Valley was pretty much ignored until the turn of the twentieth century, after river levees and underground irrigation systems had been developed. Before that, periodic floods made farming next to impossible. Although the soil was rich and fertile and had plenty of promise, the naturally high evaporation rate made it difficult to farm the Valley without irrigation. Now farmers enjoy a 330-day growing season. The land produces fifty-six varieties of fruits and vegetables—everything from sugar cane to cucumbers.

Most of the Valley lies at the same latitude as the Florida Keys. The average low temperature for January is 51 degrees. The average high for the same month is 70 degrees. The annual rainfall is usually about 25 inches. September is the wettest month. The hurricane season begins in May, peaks in August, and fades out by the end of October. With an eye to the weather, the best time of year to visit the Valley is between October and May.

Snowbirds, or winter Texans, flock to the Valley between November and April. As many as 125,000 people take up residence here in the winter, seeking relief from the harsh winters of the upper midwestern and northeastern United States. And it's not just the weather that brings them here. There are two national wildlife refuges, a state park, the beaches of South Padre Island, and the border towns for passing the time.

Birding is a real sport in this country. Up to 400 species of birds can be seen in the Valley throughout the year, especially during fall and winter. Several local organizations organize birding trips and distribute free information on Valley birdlife, including the **Frontera Audubon Society (956-968-3257), the Rio Grande Audubon Society (956-464-3029),** and the **Lower Rio Grande Sierra Club (956-969-2113).**

A field of cabbages in the Valley. Photo courtesy of the Texas Department of Tourism.

In the 1970s I made my first trip to the Valley—for a job interview at a TV station in Harlingen. I was wined and dined, treated to dinner at a palatial Mexican restaurant. The people were friendly, and the pay was a whole lot better than Houston. But a friend of mine who was born in the Valley said, "Don't take the job." The Valley lives and dies by the crop season, he explained. When the crops come in fine, everybody is rewarded. But when the crops don't come in because of drought or flood or any reason, everybody suffers. (I must have visited during a good crop season.)

The history, the beauty, and the friendliness of the Valley pay off for tourists. Visiting it is a wonderful experience. In this chapter, we take a look at some of the principal cities of the Valley, beginning with Brownsville (in Texas) and Matamoros (just over the Rio Grande border in Mexico). Then it's off to Harlingen, Texas, and then to McAllen, Texas, and neighboring Reynosa, Mexico.

Brownsville and Matamoros

Brownsville is the oldest town in the Rio Grande Valley. Explorers were here as early as 1519. Karankawa Indians were particularly unpleasant to outsiders; they were cannibals. But by the 1740s the Karankawas had moved on, and the first Spanish village was established. Almost a hundred years later it was named Matamoros, in honor of a priest who died in Mexico's struggle for independence from Spain. On the northern bank of the Rio Grande a community called Fort Texas was established; then it became Fort Brown and, eventually, Brownsville.

The Civil War was good for both communities. Enterprising businessmen in Brownsville and Matamoros made a lot of money playing tag with the Union navy as they shipped Texas cotton to Europe by way of Mexican ports to the south. The last battle of the Civil War was fought at Palmito Ranch, just east of Brownsville. Ironically the Confederates won that battle, then found out the war was over.

Today Brownsville and Matamoros are the largest cities along the Rio Grande, offering low-cost vacationing and shopping on both sides of the river. Life is relatively quiet here. The subtropical climate is tem-

A lion resting at the Gladys Porter Zoo in Brownsville. Photo courtesy of Texas Highways magazine.

pered by cool Gulf breezes and encourages a leisurely lifestyle.

Getting Around

Just across Gateway International Bridge at the tourist information booth, you can hire licensed, English-speaking tour guides in Matamoros. They'll usually charge about $25 per car. Ask to see the wallet-size permit the approved guides carry from the Mexican Tourism Department.

A 2-hour narrated trolley tour of Brownsville showcases the city's main attractions, passing historic homes and visiting one of the city's museums. All tours start at the **Visitor Information Center** (see below).

Visitor Information

Brownsville Chamber of Commerce
956-542-4341; www.brownsvillechamber.com.

Brownsville Visitor Information Center
Will load you down with advice and free literature. Open Mon.–Sat. 8 A.M.–5 P.M., Sun. 9 A.M.–4 P.M. **At the junction of Farm Road 802 and U.S. Hwy. 77/83; 1-800-626-2639, 956-546-3721, fax 956-546-3972; visinfo@brownsville.org; www. brownsville.org.**

Visas, tourist cards, and other international documentation for Mexico can be arranged at Brownsville's **Mexican consulate. 724 Elizabeth St.; 956-541-7601.**

Getting There

Brownsville is located at the extreme southern tip of Texas, where U.S. Hwys. 77 and 83 meet the Rio Grande. If you are driving from the north, U.S. 77 will take you there. If you are approaching from the west along the Texas border with Mexico, U.S. 83 will take you to Brownsville.

For airline passengers, there is the **Brownsville/South Padre Island International Airport (700 S. Minnesota Ave., 956-542-4373)**, but Continental Airlines is the only major airline that flies in. A larger selection of carriers, including Southwest, American Eagle, and Sun Country, is available at **Valley International Airport** outside Harlingen, about 30 miles north of Brownsville.

Gateway International Bridge joins Brownsville and Matamoros and leads to Avenida Alvaro Obregon, the main tourist strip. **Valley Transit Company** buses run regularly from Brownsville to Matamoros; the one-way fare is about $3. You can also walk to the shopping district in Matamoros from the bridge in about 15 minutes. **Gray Line Tours (956-761-4343)** offers sightseeing/shopping tours of Matamoros.

Mexico's national rail system operates a first-class service called El Tamaulipeco between Matamoros and Monterrey. The train leaves the Matamoros station **(phone 6-67-06)** at Avenue Hidalgo and Calle daily at 10 A.M.

Seeing and Doing

ART GALLERIES AND MUSEUMS

Don Breeden Art Gallery

Wildlife paintings are the specialty of the artist-owner of this Brownsville gallery. **2200 Boca Chica Blvd.; 956-542-5481.**

MUSEUMS AND HISTORIC SITES

Fort Brown

Fort Brown was constructed to protect the citizens. It was instrumental in starting the war with Mexico. Texas believed its southern boundary was here on the Rio Grande. Mexico believed the boundary was much farther north, at the Nueces River. It took a full-blown war to settle the dispute. What is left are the remains of the original fort that was built here. **600 International Blvd., east of Gateway International Bridge.**

Museo del Maiz/Corn Museum

A museum that honors the corn crop that was a critical factor in the growth of Mexican civilization. **Constitution at Fifth in Matamoros.** To call Matamoros from Brownsville, **dial 011-52-891 and then the five-digit local number, 6-3763.**

Palmito Ranch Battlefield

Site of the final battle of the Civil War. A marker is **on State Hwy. 4 about 14 miles east of Brownsville.**

OTHER SIGHTS

Port of Brownsville

A 17-mile-long ship channel that connects to the Gulf of Mexico and hosts ships from all over the world. There is also a large shrimp fleet here. **Five miles east of Brownsville, off State Hwy. 48; 956-831-4592, fax 956-831-5006; marketing@portofbrownsville.com; www.portofbrownsville.com.**

PARKS

Brazos Island State Park

This park is actually an undeveloped beach on the Gulf of Mexico—a beautiful beach, but no facilities. Permitted activities include camping, fishing, surfing, and the usual things people do at beaches. There is a half-mile-long stone jetty at the north end that provides pretty good Gulf fishing. The park is **22 miles east of Brownsville on State Hwy. 4.**

Gladys Porter Zoo

Professionals rank this one of the ten best zoos in the country. The design and landscaping give the appearance that visitors are in the cages and the animals are in the open spaces. There are more than 1,800 mammals, birds, and reptiles from five continents in this 31-acre zoo. **Ringgold and 6th Sts., Brownsville;**

956-546-7187, fax 956-541-4940; webmaster@
gpz.org; www.gpz.org.

Sabal Palm Grove Wildlife Sanctuary

This is one of the best-preserved sabal palm forests in
the United States. It is a 172-acre site owned by the
National Audubon Society, with nature trails and self-
guided tours. **From International Boulevard in
Brownsville, go 5.7 miles southeast on Farm
Road 1419; 956-541-8034.**

South Padre Island

More on this island in The Lower Coast chapter in The
Gulf Coast region. South Padre Island begins **25 miles
northeast of Brownsville; www.south-padre-
island.com**

SHOPPING

Barbara de Matamoros

An upscale shop on the Mexican side that features
everything from ceramics to fashions to papier-mâché
macaws on a perch. **37 Avenida Alvaro Obregon,
4 blocks south of Gateway International Bridge;
phone 2-5058.**

Mercado Juarez

There are two markets here in Matamoros—one old
and one new. Each has many small shops under a low
roof. This is where you'll find the typical Mexican
market, where you can quibble over prices and walk
away with a bargain—but don't be so sure. You are
dealing with professional salespeople here. **In
Matamoros at Calle Nueve.**

SPORTS

Bullfights in Matamoros

The season generally runs May through September.
The **Brownsville Visitor Information Center
(956-546-3721)** has details.

Festivals and Events

FEBRUARY

Charro Days

Parades, fiestas, dances, floor shows, sport events, and

even a Mexican rodeo highlight this celebration of two
countries. *Charro* refers to Mexican horsemen, whose
formal attire was the traditional black or striped pants
covered with fancy chaps, a bolero jacket, and a
sombrero. **In Brownsville and Matamoros; 956-
546-3721; www.brownsville.clever.net/
charro.html.**

SEPTEMBER

Diez y Seis

A big Mexican Independence Day celebration, an
international fiesta that turns into a bicultural weekend of fireworks and parades. **In Brownsville and
Matamoros; 956-546-3721.**

Recreation

BIRD-WATCHING

Brownsville is a paradise for bird watchers. Almost
400 bird species, including many tropical birds found
nowhere else in the state, share the refuges here, and
there are plenty. The **Brownsville Visitor Information Center (956-546-3721)** has a birder's guide
for sale.

GOLFING

Rancho Viejo Resort and Country Club

Two 18-hole championship golf courses that will challenge any golfer. Located **9 miles north of Brownsville on U.S. Hwy. 77 at Rancho Viejo Dr.;
830-350-4000.**

Where to Eat

BROWNSVILLE

Boca Chica Boulevard

Eating at **Palm Court Restaurant** is like eating in
an open court, and they feature all kinds of food (**2235
Boca Chica Blvd., 956-542-3575); Antonio's**
serves good fajitas (**2921 Boca Chica Blvd., 956-
542-6504); and Miguel's** serves great fajitas (**2474
Boca Chica Blvd., 956-541-8641).**

Los Camperos Char Chicken

The specialty is smoked, charbroiled chicken served

with corn tortillas and red and green salsas. **1440 International Blvd.; 956-546-8172.**

Maria's Better Mexican Food
Winter Texans and locals alike come here for breakfast gorditas made with thick homemade flour tortillas. **1124 Central Blvd.; 956-542-9819.**

MATAMOROS

Blanca White's Matamoros Long Bar
This place has good food and a restrained atmosphere. **North of El Graniero at Avenida Alvaro Obregon.**

The Drive Inn
A border institution since 1916. It serves steaks, seafood, and Mexican dishes. Still the best place to eat in Matamoros. **Calle 6 and Hidalgo; phone 2-0022.**

El Graniero
Matamoros prides itself on serving the best tacos along the border. There are several stands popular with locals, and this is one of the nicer ones. **On Avenue Obregon near Calle Gardenias.**

Garcia's
Matamoros has several great seafood restaurants, and this is one of them. Good food, but a bit touristy. **Six blocks south of Gateway International Bridge, on Avenida Alvaro Obregon; phone 3-1833.**

Pancho Villa's
Specializes in steaks and chicken, but also offers seafood. Pictures of Pancho Villa and other Mexican revolutionaries line the walls. **55 Avenida de la Rosa; phone 6-4840.**

Texas Bar
A wild and crazy place for fun as well as food. **Calle 5 and Gonzalez.**

Where to Stay

BROWNSVILLE

Holiday Inn Fort Brown Hotel and Resort
Housed where the original Fort Brown used to stand;

convenient to Gateway International Bridge. **1900 E. Elizabeth St.; 956-546-2201.**

Rancho Viejo Resort & Country Club
Fancy quarters, and championship golf and tennis centers. **1 Rancho Viejo Dr.; 956-350-4000.**

Harlingen

Harlingen was named for a city in the Netherlands. The chaos of the Mexican Revolution and its aftermath made bandit raids commonplace in the early 1900s. Some say there were more sidearms than citizens until the National Guard and the Texas Rangers stepped in to calm things down. Today Harlingen links the Valley to the rest of Texas. It is a processing, distribution, and marketing center for the major citrus orchards and vegetable farms.

Near Harlingen are two other towns that merit a visit: Weslaco, about 20 miles west of Harlingen via U.S. Hwy. 83, and Nuevo Progreso, on the other side of the Rio Grande from Weslaco.

Getting There
Harlingen is at the intersection of U.S. Hwy. 77 and U.S. Hwy. 83, 28 miles north of Brownsville. Several airlines, including Southwest, American Eagle, and Sun Country, fly into **Valley International Airport, north of downtown Harlingen at the intersection of N. 7th St. and Sul Ross Ave.; 956-430-8600.**

Visitor Information

Harlingen Chamber of Commerce
Open Mon.–Fri. 8 A.M.–5 P.M. **311 E. Tyler St.; 1-800-531-7346, 956-423-5440, fax 956-425-3870; hcoc@harlingen.com; www.harlingen.com.**

Harlingen Visitor Center
A social headquarters for winter visitors from mid-November to mid-April. **2021 W. Harrison St.; 956-428-4477.**

Rio Grande Valley Chamber of Commerce
At U.S. Hwy. 83 Expressway and Farm Road 1015, in Weslaco; 956-968-3142.

Golfing at one of many championship courses in the Brownsville–Harlingen–McAllen area. Photo courtesy of Texas Highways *magazine.*

Texas Travel Information Center

Open daily 8 A.M.–5 P.M. year-round except Easter, Thanksgiving, Christmas Eve, Christmas Day, and New Year's Day. **2021 W. Harlingen St. (at the junction of U.S. Hwy. 77 and U.S. Hwy. 83); 956-428-4477.**

Weslaco Area Chamber of Commerce and Tourism Center

1710 E. Pike Blvd.; P.O. Box 8398, Weslaco, 78599; 956-968-2102; www.chamber@weslaco.com.

Seeing and Doing

MUSEUMS AND HISTORIC SITES

Marine Military Academy and Texas Iwo Jima War Memorial

The young men at this private military prep school wear uniforms similar to the U.S. Marines and follow the customs and traditions of the Corps. If you've ever wanted to see a Marine Corps precision drill or a Marine parade, this is the place. The young cadets are serious about preserving the proper dignity of the Marine Corps. On campus is the Iwo Jima War Memorial. It's the original working model used to cast the famous bronze memorial than stands in Arlington National Cemetery. **320 Iwo Jima Blvd., Harlingen; 956-423-6006; www.mma-tv.org.**

Rio Grande Valley Historical Museum Complex

This is four museums in one: all the history of Harlingen in one spot. The **Historical Museum** features the cultural and natural history of the Lower Rio Grande Valley. **Paso Real Stagecoach Inn** is a lodging place that was in use until 1904 (35 cents a night for room and board). The **Medical Museum** documents Harlingen's first hospital. The **Lon C. Hill Home** was built in 1905 by the man who founded the town. The complex is **at Harlingen Industrial Air Park; 956-430-8500, fax 956-430-8502; rgvmuse@hiline.net; www.hiline.net/rgvmusu.**

NATURE CENTERS

Valley Nature Center

Exhibits of native birds and other nature items from

the area. Outside is a 4-acre park. **301 S. Border Ave. in Gibson Park, in the town of Weslaco, about 20 miles west of Harlingen via U.S. Hwy. 83; 956-969-2475; www.hiline.net/vnature.**

PARKS

Pendleton Park

Offers tennis courts, swimming, sports fields, a playground, picnic tables, and a 27-hole municipal golf course. **At the corner of Morgan and Grooms Sts.**

SEASONAL FAVORITES

Sugar Tree Farms

This place is a good example of how many farmers in the area market their fruits and vegetables. You can buy by the pound, the sack, or the gift pack, and they will even ship for you. **4701 W. Expressway 83, Harlingen; 956-423-5530.**

SHOPPING

Nuevo Progreso

A little-publicized Mexican community on the other side of the Rio Grande from Weslaco. There's not much "action" here, but the trip is laid-back and pleasant. You can park on the U.S. side and walk across the bridge. The marketplace begins just as you get into Mexico. Nuevo Progreso also has some great eating places. **Take Farm Road 1015 south to Gateway International Bridge.**

WAGERING

Valley Greyhound Racetrack

They have races about 300 nights a year, and matinees on Wednesday and Saturday. **On Ed Carey Dr., about 1.5 miles southwest of Harlingen; 956-428-0161.**

Festivals and Events

OCTOBER

Riofest

A cultural festival featuring arts and artisans at work. **In Harlingen, at Fair Park; 956-425-2705.**

Recreation

BIRDING

Laguna Atascosa National Wildlife Refuge

A 45,000-acre coastline sanctuary behind Padre Island. It is the southernmost refuge in the United States and is located on what is called the Great Central Flyway, along which birds migrate annually between Canada and the Gulf of Mexico. More than 300 species have been spotted here. **On Farm Road 106, about 25 miles east of Harlingen; 956-748-3607.**

GOLFING

Tony Butler Municipal Golf Course

A 27-hole facility featuring traps, water hazards, and tropical vegetation. Annually the course plays host to the Rio Grande Valley Amateur Championship. **Exit U.S. Hwy. 83 at M Street in Harlingen and turn into Victor Park; follow the access road to the course; 830-430-6685.**

Treasure Hills Country Club

An 18-hole championship course designed by Robert Trent Jones, featuring hilly terrain and numerous trees. This is a semiprivate club with tee times required; it reciprocates with other clubs. **3009 N. Augusta National Dr., Harlingen; 830-425-3171.**

Where to Eat

HARLINGEN

Lone Star

Known for its barbecue, the Lone Star also serves some seafood and Tex-Mex. **4201 W. Business U.S. Hwy. 83; 956-423-8002.**

Pepe's Mexican Restaurant

The specialties are Mexican-style food, including tortilla soup and sizzling fajitas. **117 S. Sunshine Strip; 956-423-3663.**

Vannie Tilden Bakery

Pastry delights or tacos for breakfast—but also come back for lunch. They serve some of the best chicken and dumplings in the Valley. **203 E. Harrison St.; 956-423-4062.**

NUEVO PROGRESO

Arturo's
A very fancy restaurant that offers Mexican and American food. **In Nuevo Progreso, about 1 block south of Gateway International Bridge.**

WESLACO

Ciro's
Serves up some terrific seafood, including unusual shrimp dishes, plus red snapper and other fish—as well as steaks, fajitas, and even kosher ribs. **318 W. Pike Blvd.; 956-969-2236.**

Milano's Italian Restaurant
Does what it says—serving Neapolitan-style cuisine since 1955. **2900 W. Pike Blvd.; 956-968-3677.**

Where to Stay

HARLINGEN

Harlingen Inn
Comfortable, and convenient to the expressway that cuts through the Valley. **6779 U.S. Hwy. 83; 956-425-7070.**

Ross Haus Bed-and-Breakfast
Country living in one of the Valley's old homes. **205 S. 4th St.; 956-425-1717.**

WESLACO

Best Western Palm Aire
One of the newest in a long line of lodging spots in this area. **Farm Road 1015 at U.S. Hwy. 83; 956-969-2411.**

McAllen and Reynosa

Many Midwesterners and Canadians spend their winters in the McAllen area, strolling through citrus groves and otherwise enjoying the climate. The economy is based on tourism and on the citrus and vegetable crops.

Getting There
To get to McAllen from Brownsville, take U.S. Hwy. 77/83 north for 28 miles to Harlingen, then go west on U.S. 83 for 30 miles. Reynosa is across the Rio Grande from McAllen.

Mario's Tours offers day-trips to Reynosa, with stops including the market, main square, a cemetery, the Pemex oil refinery, a residential area, and a factory that manufactures products in Mexico for sale in the United States. Mario's also runs a 3-day tour to Monterrey. **956-632-7834.**

Visitor Information

McAllen Convention and Visitors Bureau
10 N. Broadway St.; P.O. Box 790, McAllen, 78505; 956-682-2871, fax 956-631-8571.

McAllen Visitor Center
Information and literature on attractions, accommodations, dining, and events in McAllen and Reynosa. Open Mon.–Fri. 8:30 A.M.–5:00 P.M. **10 N. Broadway St.; 1-800-250-2591; www.mcallen.org.**

Seeing and Doing

ART GALLERIES AND MUSEUMS

Gabii's
Featuring folk art and crafts and Mexican designer dresses. **In Reynosa at 1097 Avenida Los Virreyes.**

McAllen International Museum
Mexican folk art, colorful masks, paintings, and sculptures featuring local artists. **1900 Nolana St., McAllen; 956-682-1564, fax 956-686-1813; mim@hiline.net; www.mcallenmuseum.org.**

MUSEUMS AND HISTORIC SITES

Los Ebanos Ferry
This is the last hand-pulled ferry on the Rio Grande, and is more of a tourist attraction than anything else. Just park your car and ride the ferry over and back. Operates daily 8 A.M.–4 P.M. **About 20 miles west of McAllen on U.S. Hwy. 83, then south on Farm Road 886 to the river.**

Old Clock Collection
This collection includes about 2,000 antique clocks, some dating back to 1690. Kids will love the cuckoo clocks. **308 W. Park St., in the town of Pharr, 5 miles east of McAllen; 956-787-1481.**

Shrine of La Virgen de San Juan del Valle

You don't have to be a Catholic to appreciate this impressive shrine. It was built at a cost of $5 million, raised mostly through small donations. **Ten miles east of McAllen on U.S. Hwy. 83 to San Juan.** You can see it **overlooking San Juan on a hill north of downtown on Business U.S. Hwy. 83 and Raul Longoria Rd.**

NIGHTLIFE

Square Dancing

McAllen claims the title of Square Dance Capital of the World because so many people here are interested in the pastime. From January to March every year, the **McAllen Convention and Visitors Bureau (956-682-2871)** sponsors the world's largest beginners square dance class. That keeps interest in square dancing keen, and it's no wonder you can find a square dance somewhere in the area almost every night.

OTHER SIGHTS

Reynosa

Half a million people live in this counterpart to McAllen on the Mexican side of the Rio Grande. Reynosa is quieter than Matamoros, but offers much of the same for visitors: several fine restaurants, occasional Sunday-afternoon bullfights, and gift shops with a wealth of handicraft items in the Zona Rosa. The Zona Rosa is the tourist district. (Be careful with your Spanish. If you tell the cabbie you want to go to the Zona Roha (Roja), you'll wind up in the red-light district.)

SEASONAL FAVORITES

Eggers Acres

Pick your own fruit off trees in season at this family citrus market. It's run by the granddaughter of the man who discovered the famous ruby red grapefruit. **Five miles west of McAllen on Shary Rd.; 956-581-7783.**

Klement's Grove

Another pick-your-own-fruit place—or you can buy it already picked and bagged. **On Farm Road 1924, 3 miles west of McAllen; 956-682-2980.**

SHOPPING

Zaragoza Market

A typical tourist-oriented border market, with dozens of small shops where you can haggle over prices to your heart's delight. **In Reynosa, just south of the Main Plaza.**

Festivals and Events

JANUARY

Rio Grande Valley International Music Festival

A week of musical events featuring well-known guest performers and symphony orchestras. **In McAllen; 956-686-1456.**

MARCH

Springfest

Nine days early in the month. Parades, beauty pageants, auto shows, and ethnic entertainment. **In McAllen; 956-682-6221.**

Recreation

BIRDING

Bentsen–Rio Grande Valley State Park

A 588-acre protected delta land, a favorite of bird watchers. Park naturalists conduct daily bird-watching and wildlife tours from December through March. Facilities include campsites, 3 miles of hiking trails, and two nature trails. **Fifteen miles west of McAllen via U.S. Hwy. 83, Farm Road 2062, and Park Road 43; 1-800-792-1112, 956-585-1107; www.tpwdstate.tx.us/park/bentsen/bentsen.htm.**

Santa Ana National Wildlife Refuge

A birder's paradise, this is a 2,000-acre refuge that preserves a part of the Rio Grande delta as it was before the land was cleared for cultivation. It is also filled with critters you've probably never seen before, like the ocelot and the jaguarundi. There are plenty of trails to walk. Between late November and the end of April, the refuge offers a tram tour. **About 16 miles southeast of**

McAllen, near the town of Alamo; the entrance is about a half mile east of the intersection of U.S. Hwy. 281 and Farm Road 907; 956-787-3079, fax 956-787-8338; santaana@hiline.net; www.hiline.net/santaana.index.shtml.

FISHING AND HUNTING

Three local clubs lead fishing (bass) and hunting trips (dove, duck, geese, quail, deer) to the nearby Mexican state of Tamaulipas: **Antlers, Fur, and Feather Guide Service (956-687-8188)**; Club Exclusive/Big Bass Tours (600 E. Beaumont St., McAllen, 1-800-531-7509, 956-687-8513, fax 956-687-8514, www.bigbasstours.com); and **Mexican Whitewings Unlimited (956-631-7286)**.

Where to Eat

McALLEN

Iannelli Ristorante Italiano

Serves up pasta perfection. N. 10th St. and LaVista; 956-631-0666.

Johnny's Mexican Food

A no-frills restaurant with a Tex-Mex menu. 1010 W. Houston Ave.; 956-686-9061.

Lotus Inn

Specializes in Hunan and Mandarin cuisine. 1122 N. 10th St.; 956-631-2693.

The Patio at Jones and Jones

Upscale eating place, for when you get tired of all that Mexican food on the border. 2100 S. 10th St.; 956-687-1171.

Tom and Jerry's

A chicken-fried steak and burger place in an old house with a screened porch and a patio. It's a great change of pace. 401 N. 10th St.; 956-687-3001.

REYNOSA

La Cucaracha

Popular steak and seafood place with entertainment and dancing nightly. **About 3 blocks southwest**

Visitors at Santa Ana National Wildlife Refuge near McAllen. Photo courtesy of the Texas Department of Tourism.

of Gateway International Bridge; phone 2-0174.

La Mansion del Prado

Upscale eating establishment. Note the intricate tile work throughout the restaurant. **About 5 blocks southeast of Gateway International Bridge; phone 2-9914.**

Sam's

The two-meat dinner here runs about $7, and they've been serving it up since 1932, so they must be doing something right. You'll be serenaded by mariachis. To me it's always been the best Mexican food on the border, and they serve the sweetest onions in the Valley. **Allende at Ocampo, 1 block west of Gateway International Bridge; phone 2-0034.**

Where to Stay

McALLEN

Embassy Suites Hotel

Comfortable quarters near a fancy shopping mall; a favorite place to stay for wealthy Mexicans who come to the Valley for shopping and relaxation. 1800 S. 2nd St.; 956-686-3000.

The Rio Grande Border

The South Texas border region offers some of the most interesting history in the state, including battles won and lost with Mexico long years ago. The facts and some of the legends about the border live on today in movies still being made in Hollywood.

After Texas won its independence from Mexico, the victory was really only on paper, because fighting continued along the Rio Grande. The United States decided to build a string of forts along the river to protect settlers from not only Indians but also from Mexican bandits. These bandits would wade or swim the river in a shallow spot, rob settlers near the border, and then disappear back into Mexico. Travelers today on U.S. Hwy. 83 and U.S. Hwy. 277 along the Rio Grande find ruins of old forts in almost every town—but there is much more to discover than old forts along the border.

U.S. Hwy. 90 west of Del Rio along the Mexican border can be one of the dullest drives in the state, but then suddenly out of nowhere it turns into one of the most spectacular. This is Amistad country, site of one of the state's great lakes: Amistad International Reservoir. Amistad (Spanish for "friendship") was a joint effort by the United States and Mexico in the late 1960s. The lake, covering 65,000 acres, is operated by the International Boundary and Water Commission.

This region is also home to the renowned Indian pictographs, from thousands of years ago, at Seminole Canyon. And it's famous too for the much more recent slice of history carved out by Roy Bean, the infamous self-proclaimed judge who dispensed his own brand of justice from a saloon in Langtry.

Major Attractions

Amistad International Reservoir

The Amistad dam impounds an international body of water that reaches 78 miles up the Rio Grande, 25 miles up Devils River, and 16 miles up Pecos River, with some 851 miles of shoreline. More than a million people visit this area every year.

GETTING THERE

From San Antonio, take U.S. Hwy. 90 west for 153 miles to Del Rio, then continue west on Hwy. 90 for another 10 miles to the lake. Or from San Angelo, take U.S. Hwy. 277 due south for about 150 miles, and you'll reach the lake shortly before you get to Del Rio.

VISITOR INFORMATION

The headquarters for Amistad International Reservoir and Amistad National Recreation Area has maps of the lake and information on fishing, boating, hunting, and park regulations. **At the intersection of U.S. Hwy. 90 and U.S. Hwy. 277, about 4 miles north of Del Rio; 830-775-7491.** Information is also available from **Superintendent, Amistad National Recreation Area, HCR3 Box 5J, Del Rio, 78840; 830-775-7491; www.nps.gov/amis.**

BOATING

You can rent boats, including houseboats, from **Lake Amistad Resort and Marina (about 15 miles northwest of Del Rio on U.S. Hwy. 90 at the Diablo East Recreation Area, 830-774-4157).** Boats are also available at **Rough Canyon Marina (about 21 miles north of Del Rio on U.S. Hwy. 277, then left on Recreation Road 2 for 7 miles, 830-775-8779). Rough Canyon Inn and Country Store (a couple of blocks from Rough Canyon Marina, 830-774-6366)** also rents boats.

CAMPING

There are primitive campsites at Governor's Landing, San Pedro Flats, Old 277 North, Old 277 South, and Spur 406. All designated camping areas provide chemical toilets and cooking grills, but not drinking water or showers. Camping is also permitted anywhere along the shore except next to marinas and in posted noncamping areas. There are no fees, but camping is limited to 14 days in a calendar year. Near Diablo East Marina are three commercial campgrounds: **American RV Resort Campground (830-775-6484); Amistad RV Park (830-775-6491);** and **Holiday Trav-L Park (830-775-7275).** Not far from Rough Canyon Marina is **Rough Canyon Trailer Park/Campgrounds (830-775-6707).** Near the junction of U.S. Hwy. 277 and U.S. Hwy. 90 is **Fisherman's Headquarters (830-774-4172).**

DIVING

The period of November through April offers the finest scuba diving, with the best visibility being about 25 feet. The most popular dive site at Amistad is Diablo East, where a cove near View Point Cliffs has been marked off for diving and swimming only. The depth exceeds 100 feet. A dive platform is anchored at 40 feet, and there is a boat wreck for divers to explore. Other good spots include **Castle Canyon,** the **U.S. Hwy. 90 bridge,** the cliffs area in **Cow Creek Canyon,** and **Indian Springs,** 6 miles up Devils River via Rough Canyon. Spear fishing is permitted with a valid license, but only for gar, drum, buffalo carp, and other rough fish. You must register at park headquarters **(830-775-7491)** before venturing off on a dive.

FISHING

The lake is stocked with smallmouth bass, striped bass, white bass, crappie, northern pike, freshwater drum, five species of catfish, and Rio Grande and African perch, just to name a few. When I was a teenager, they used to catch 100-pound catfish in this lake. Watch for the buoys that divide U.S. from Mexican waters. You can fish on both sides of the international boundary, and there is no closed season, but a Texas fishing license is required in U.S. waters and a Mexican license is required in Mexican waters. You can get U.S. and Mexican licenses at the marinas or at most bait shops in Del Rio.

WHERE TO STAY

Places to stay include **Amistad Lodge,** overlooking the lake **(off U.S. Hwy. 90 between Black Brush Point and Diablo East, about 5 miles west of Del Rio, 830-775-8591); Angler's Lodge (on U.S. Hwy. 90, 830-775-1586); Lakeview Inn (closer to the dam, on U.S. Hwy. 90, 830-775-9521); Laguna Diablo Resort (at Rough Canyon, at 1 Sanders Point Rd. off U.S. Hwy. 277, 830-774-2422);** and **Rough Canyon Inn (off U.S. Hwy. 277, 830-774-6266).**

Seminole Canyon State Historical Park

The canyon is named for the Seminole Indians who frequented the area at the time of the Anglo-American expansion in the mid–nineteenth century. At least 200 Indian rock-art sites have been discovered in this canyon and elsewhere in the lower Pecos River region. Some of the wall paintings date back 4,000 years and perhaps more. The Indians made paint by grinding minerals into powder and then mixing the powder with animal fat. They used plants or hands and fingers for brushes, and the resulting pictographs cover a wide range of subjects and designs. The **Rock Art Foundation** promotes the study and preservation of lower Pecos River rock-art sites **(3861 Fredericksburg Rd., San Antonio, 78212; 210-525-9907, fax 210-525-9909, admin@rockart.org).**

GETTING THERE

Seminole Canyon Park is about 45 miles west of Del Rio, off U.S. Hwy. 90.

VISITOR INFORMATION

The park visitor center is 9 miles west of Comstock on Hwy. 90; open Wed.–Sun.; **1-800-792-1112, 915-292-4464.** Also, **Seminole Area Chamber of Commerce, 915-758-2352.**

Seminole Canyon State Historical Park covers 2,100 acres in and around the canyon. Trails lead to the canyon's two primary pictograph sites. A park ranger guides the short trail to **Fate Bell Shelter,** a major site with cave shelters beneath a semicircular canyon ledge. Several levels of Indian paintings have been discovered here. The main rock-art period is marked by sticklike figures that are shown hunting. The other trail offers a 6-mile round-trip walk to a

A majestic view of the Rio Grande from one of the state's oldest communities, Roma. Photo courtesy of the Texas Department of Tourism.

Rio Grande overlook opposite **Panther Cave.** This is a worthwhile hike, but to get the best look at the Panther Cave pictographs, you really should go by boat (see below). Biking is also permitted along this trail.

The best way to explore the Pecos River–Rio Grande–Devils River area is by boat. You can see pictographs that aren't accessible on foot. **Panther Cave,** just below the mouth of the Pecos River, is probably the best site. It got its name from a panther painting that's more than 15 feet long. You can rent a boat at Amistad International Reservoir (see Boating in that section) or join a guided tour. Four operators are licensed to conduct tours in the area: **High Bridge Adventures (915-292-4495); American Water-sports (915-775-6484); Lake Amistad Tours (915-775-7100);** and **Jim Zintgraff (210-525-9907).**

The park camping area has thirty-one drive-in sites (for reservations, call **512-389-8900**). Camping and RV opportunities outside the park include **Baker's Crossing Campground (in Comstock, 915-292-4503);** the **Owls Nest RV Park (near Comstock, 915-292-4460);** and the **Casa Blanca Motel,** which accepts RVs **(on U.S. Hwy. 90 at Comstock, 915-292-4431).**

Langtry

If you are looking for a quick taste of the Old West, my vote goes to Langtry. The place was established in the 1880s when two railroad lines came together at nearby Dead Man's Gulch. A tent city here at the time, called Vinegaroon, had a reputation for lawlessness. Texas Rangers came to town and commissioned the local store owner to serve as justice of the peace. And that started the era of **Judge Roy Bean** in West Texas.

Roy Bean was probably the biggest crook in the territory, and he quickly proclaimed himself the law west of the Pecos. Bean renamed the town Langtry, after his idol, English actress Lillie Langtry, and opened a saloon called the Jersey Lilly. Judge Roy held court in his saloon and often fined defendants by making them buy a round of drinks for the house. In 1896 he defied Texas and Mexico by staging a championship prize fight on a sandbar in the middle of the Rio Grande; at the time, professional boxing was illegal on both sides of the border.

Bean died in 1904. Seventy years later, John Huston came to Langtry to film part of his movie *The Life and Times of Judge Roy Bean,* starring Paul Newman. The

Jersey Lilly Saloon is now restored and open for public viewing, behind the Judge Roy Bean Visitor Center.

GETTING THERE
Langtry is 60 miles northwest of Del Rio on U.S. Hwy. 90.

VISITOR INFORMATION
Judge Roy Bean Visitor Center, 1 mile south of Hwy. 90 on Loop 25; 915-291-3340, fax 915-291-3366.

BUD'S PLACE BARBECUE AND BEER
It's open daily and not bad, considering there is no competition in the area. **A block south of the visitor center.**

CACTUS GARDENS
Next to the Judge Roy Bean Visitor Center is a nature trail through a well-planned Chihuahuan desert garden that offers much more than cacti. It is filled with native plants, some of which were used for medicinal and utilitarian purposes in early Texas.

SCENIC OVERLOOK
U.S. Hwy. 90 at the Pecos High Bridge offers a glimpse into the canyon of the Pecos River. Travelers can pause and picnic in a roadside park on the east rim of the canyon, **about 18 miles east of Langtry.** The view is spectacular.

Towns in the Area

This chapter highlights the principal Rio Grande border towns from Roma in the south to Del Rio in the north. The towns include Roma, Texas, and Ciudad Miguel Aleman, just across the river in Mexico; Laredo, Texas, and neighboring Nuevo Laredo, Mexico; Eagle Pass, Texas, and nearby Piedras Negras, Mexico; Bracketville, Texas; and finally Del Rio, Texas, and its neighbor across the river, Ciudad Acuna.

Roma and Ciudad Miguel Aleman
Getting There: Roma is 90 miles southeast of Laredo along U.S. Hwy. 83 (and about 100 miles northwest of Brownsville). Ciudad Miguel Aleman is across the Rio Grande from Roma. **Visitor Information:**

Roma is included in the Texas Historical Commission's publication *Los Caminos del Rio.* You can get information about Roma and other communities along the Texas southern border by contacting the commission at **1511 Colorado St., Austin, 78701; 512-463-6100; www.thc.state.tx.us/loscam.html.**

Some of the most interesting architecture in the state is located in the tiny community of Roma. It was settled many years ago not only by Mexicans from the south, but also by Germans and Spaniards. They brought with them architectural knowledge from Europe, and the structures built here are unbelievable stone buildings. Some of these structures are still lived in, others are in ruins, but all are intriguing to examine. Roma also offers one of the most impressive vistas of the Rio Grande along the entire border—so impressive that scenes around the town were used in the 1952 Elia Kazan film *Viva Zapata,* starring Marlon Brando.

Ciudad Miguel Aleman is another story. It is a sleepy little village on the Mexican side with a great story to be told about it. Many years ago, Mexico elected a president who promised to rid the country of red-light districts along the border. The president's name was Miguel Aleman, and when he was elected, he chose to clean up a border community north of here first. So his army packed up the ladies of the evening, closed the brothels, and moved the ladies downriver to this spot. The women he forcibly uprooted vowed they wouldn't forget Aleman. Eventually the brothels reopened in this spot and a town grew around them, and the ladies made good their promise by naming the town after the man who made them move.

SEEING AND DOING

Roma Historical Museum
Exhibits trace the influence of American, Spanish, and Mexican cultures on this area. Open Mon.–Fri. 9 A.M.– 4 P.M. **At Estrella and Lincoln Sts.; 956-849-1555.**

RECREATION

Falcon State Recreation Park
The 572-acre park on the shores of Falcon Reservoir offers cabins, boating, camping, picnicking, and fishing. The area is crowded much of the year with winter Texans who own RVs and enjoy moving around. Experienced canoeists and kayakers enjoy the 20-mile stretch

of the Rio Grande from Falcon Dam to Roma. There is also prominent birdlife in the park. **Fourteen miles northwest of Roma on U.S. Hwy. 83; 956-848-5327.**

Nuevo Guerrero

The ruins of a Mexican village that was destroyed when Falcon Lake was impounded. The residents of the original village were moved at government expense to higher ground. The original village has become a wonderful fishing spot at Falcon Lake and is visible only part of the year, when the lake level drops. Nearby on the southwest edge of the lake are facilities for camping, boating, picnicking, and fishing. To get to Nuevo Guerrero, **travel 18 miles northwest of Roma on U.S. Hwy. 83, then go left on Farm Road 2098 to the Rio Grande and Falcon Reservoir; Nuevo Guerrero is across the lake on the Mexico side.**

WHERE TO EAT

Che's Restaurant & Bar

The place for freshwater catfish right out of the Rio Grande. **In La Borde House at Rio Grande City, 14 miles east of Roma on U.S. Hwy. 83; 956-487-5101.**

WHERE TO STAY

La Borde House

A lovely New Orleans–style hotel and restaurant in Rio Grande City, 14 miles east of Roma on U.S. Hwy 83. **610 E. Main St.; 956-487-5101.**

Roma Inn

Provides comfortable overnight lodging. **On the eastern city limits, on U.S. Hwy. 83, Roma; 956-849-3755.**

Laredo and Nuevo Laredo

Getting There: From San Antonio, take I-35 south for 150 miles to Laredo. Nuevo Laredo is across the Rio Grande from Laredo. **Visitor Information: Laredo Convention and Visitors Bureau, 501 San Agustin, Laredo, 78040; 1-800-361-3360; www. lcvb@icsi.net; www.cityoflaredo.com.** Also, **Texas Travel Information Center,** a roadside center operated by the Texas Department of Transportation, **on I-35 about 6 miles north of Laredo; 956-722-8119.**

Laredo and Nuevo Laredo are probably the best known of the border towns in Texas—and the most popular because of the huge marketplace on the Mexican side. You can leave your car on the U.S. side and walk to the market, but it's likely you'll need a cab for the return trip because you'll be loaded down with trinkets and gifts.

SEEING AND DOING

Fort McIntosh

This fort, established by the army in 1848, was in continuous use until May 1946. It was one of those border forts built to protect settlers from Indians and banditos. Today it is surrounded by college students attending Laredo Junior College. **On the banks of the Rio Grande; laredo.cc.tx.us/campus_history.htm.**

Nuevo Laredo

A bustling Mexican city of more than a quarter million people that has bargain shopping, inexpensive dining, professional baseball, and occasional bullfighting. There is no need to drive a car to Nuevo Laredo. You can park and walk to almost any place you want to go, including the market. Some of the best shopping can be found at **Deutsch's,** for its custom-made gold and silver jewelry **(320 Guerrero); Marti's,** for its designer clothes, jewelry, and perfumes **(2933 Victoria);** and the **Nuevo Mercado de la Reforma,** the New Market **(just south of the international bridge),** named such because it replaced the old one that burned down when someone accidentally tossed a match into a fireworks shop. Bargain-hunting here is fun, and the merchants expect to haggle on prices.

Republic of the Rio Grande Building

Seven different flags have flown over this quaint one-story building. Inside, the story is told of how Texas came to be a separate nation for a brief time in its history. **1000 Zaragoza St. on San Agustin Plaza, Laredo; 956-727-3480.**

St. Augustine Church

Established in 1767; the present church was constructed in 1872. **On San Agustin Plaza, Laredo; 956-722-0441.**

FESTIVALS AND EVENTS

February—George Washington's Birthday Celebration

In February at various locations in both cities. The people of the two Laredos have been celebrating Washington's birthday since 1898. Whether or not it is just an excuse for a fiesta does not matter. It's a big event, with concerts, dancing, fireworks, entertainment, and parades. One highlight is the Jalapeño Festival, which includes a contest to see who can eat the most of what locals call border grapes, and a Some Like It Hot recipe contest. **956-722-9895.**

July—Borderfest

This is a 3-day weekend affair around the Fourth of July, celebrating U.S. independence and Laredo's heritage under seven flags and seven cultures. **At the Laredo Civic Center; 956-722-9895.**

RECREATION

Lake Casa Blanca State Park

This 371-acre park offers picnicking, camping, a dump station, a boat ramp, and a fishing pier. The lake is among the state's best for black bass fishing. **Ten minutes from downtown Laredo off U.S. Hwy. 59; 956-725-3826.**

WHERE TO EAT

Cadillac Bar (El Dorado)

Probably the best-known restaurant in Nuevo Laredo. **At Beldon y Ocampo; phone 12-00-15.**

Charlie's Corona

Serves international cuisine. **3902 San Bernardo Ave., Laredo; 956-725-8227.**

Cotulla-Style Pit Bar-B-Q

Barbecue and fajitas, but famous for its mariaches—that's what they call breakfast tacos here, which are tortillas filled with choices of more than two dozen types of food. Seriously, you haven't enjoyed a real breakfast taco until you've tried these. **4502 McPherson Ave., Laredo; 956-724-5747.**

Favorato's

Offers steaks, seafood, and Italian entrees. **1916 San Bernardo Ave., Laredo; 956-722-9515.**

Laredo Bar & Grill

A swanky northside eating establishment. **102 Del Court, Laredo; 956-717-0090.**

Mexico Tipico

Serving tortas (sandwiches), Mexican food, and grilled meats, including *cabrito*. **934 Guerrero, Nuevo Laredo; phone 2-1525.**

Tack Room

Upscale restaurant in Laredo for folks fed up with food on the run. Good steaks, good spare ribs, but expensive. **1000 Zaragoza St. at La Posada Hotel; 956-722-1701.**

Victoria 3020

This restaurant is in a mansion and specializes in exotic Mexican dishes from the interior, like shrimp in tequila-based sauce and spiced chicken breast steamed in a banana leaf. **3020 Victoria at Matamoros, Nuevo Laredo; phone 3-3020.**

WHERE TO STAY

La Posada

Without doubt the most convenient place to stay if you come to Laredo for border shopping. **At 1000 Zaragoza St. adjacent to the International Bridge; 956-722-1701.**

Eagle Pass and Piedras Negras

Getting There: From San Antonio, take I-35 south for 42 miles, then go west for 100 miles on U.S. Hwy. 57 to Eagle Pass. Piedras Negras is across the Rio Grande from Eagle Pass. **Visitor Information:** Eagle Pass lists two **Chambers of Commerce:** one at **400 Garrison St.; 830-773-3224;** and the other at **370 N. Monroe St.; 830-757-0499; epsofc@admin. hilco-net.com; www.eaglepasstexas.com.**

The little community of Eagle Pass will never compare in excitement to the other towns along the border, but I find it interesting because of an aspect of its Indian history. For many years a tribe of Kickapoo Indians lived under the bridge at Eagle Pass, living in poverty and sheltering themselves in cardboard huts. It was a disgrace, and a sad sight to see. Today a 125-acre site has been developed 8 miles south of Eagle Pass as a permanent home for the Kickapoo.

El Mercado Shopping Center in Laredo. Photo courtesy of Texas Highways *magazine.*

SEEING AND DOING

Fort Duncan Museum
On Bliss Street in the headquarters building of the old fort, another one that was built in the 1840s to protect settlers. **At Fort Duncan Park, Eagle Pass; 830-773-1714.**

Piedras Negras
The name of the town means "black rocks"—a reference to the coal uncovered in this area long ago. This was coal-mining country from the late 1880s to the early 1900s. The main shopping plaza and most popular restaurants are within an easy walk of the international bridge. The **central market** is on **Zaragoza Street.** There are usually bullfights here one Sunday a month from Memorial Day to Labor Day.

WHERE TO EAT

Club Moderno
Continental and Mexican cuisine. The Derby Club in the same building has off-track betting. **At Zaragoza and Allende in Piedra Negras.**

Don Cruz Restaurant
A varied menu, but the Mexican food is the best. I suggest the red snapper Vera Cruz—style. **On Morelos between Teran and Allende in Piedras Negras.**

WHERE TO STAY

Dream Motel
A local mom-and-pop establishment in Eagle Pass. **1395 Del Rio Hwy.; 830-773-6990.**

Bracketville
Getting There: From San Antonio, travel 120 miles due west on U.S. Hwy. 90 to Bracketville. The town is also 32 miles east of Del Rio.

Bracketville grew up around Fort Clark, still another of those Texas frontier forts. Kinney County is larger than the whole state of Rhode Island but has only one town in addition to Bracketville: Spofford. This is ranching country and a popular place to hunt deer, javelina, wild turkey, quail, and dove. Bracketville has two claims to fame: Fort Clark, home of the renowned black Seminole scouts, and Alamo Village.

SEEING AND DOING

Alamo Village
This replica of the nineteenth-century Alamo mission is the largest movie set ever built outside Hollywood. It took 5,000 people 2 years to build, using the original Spanish plans and adobe bricks made on-site by craftsmen from Mexico. In the mid-1950s, John Wayne came to Texas to film the epic *The Alamo.* He wanted to use the real Alamo in San Antonio for the movie, but the request was denied by the Daughters of the Republic of Texas, who maintain the Alamo. They weren't about to allow a movie company to take over what they see as a shrine. So the Alamo was reconstructed at Bracketville, with the help of area rancher Happy Shahan. Once the filming was complete, Shahan took it one step further. He added an Old West town that has been used by scores of production companies since then in filming movies, commercials, and TV shows. Every Labor Day, the Cowboy Horse Races are held here. Alamo Village is open to visitors daily throughout the year. During the summer, there's usually live entertainment and simulated gun duels. Located **on the Shahan Ranch, 6 miles north of Bracket-ville on Ranch Road 674; 830-563-2580; www. webmovie.com/tx/alamo.htm.**

Seminole Indian Scout Cemetery
This cemetery tells one of the saddest stories in the

history of Texas. Buried here along with some of their descendants are about a hundred black Seminoles who served as scouts for the U.S. Army at nearby Fort Clark during the Indian wars. Their history dates back to the early 1800s, when a group of slaves ran away from Georgia and South Carolina and became sharecroppers for Seminole Indians in Florida. By the mid-1800s they had mixed in with the tribe, and the men in the group were known for being great warriors. When the army was trying to rid West Texas of Indians, it decided that the best way to do it was to get other Indians to run them off. That's where the black Seminoles came in. They were hired by the army and participated as scouts in twenty-six successful campaigns against the Indians between 1871 and 1881. Three of them earned Medals of Honor. When all the army heroes died, their bodies were moved to Washington, D.C., to be buried, but not so for the Seminole Indian scouts, who were still second-class citizens. So they were buried in this tiny cemetery outside Bracketville; even the Medal of Honor winners weren't allowed to be buried in Washington. The black Seminole Indian scouts who helped win that war in the mid-1800s rest at this cemetery under the West Texas soil today, and many of the graves are marked only with wooden headstones. The cemetery is **about 5 miles south of Bracketville on Farm Road 3348.**

RECREATION

Fort Clark Springs

Here is the only frontier fort in Texas that has been turned into a resort, complete with golf course, swimming

Fort Clark, once a military outpost, now a subdivision in Bracketville. Photo courtesy of Texas Highways magazine.

pool, and a motel and RV park. Some of the original buildings have been restored, and you can tour the grounds during the day. **On the eastern edge of Bracketville, off U.S. Hwy. 90; 830-563-2495; fcsaprdi@aol.com; www.fortclark.com.**

WHERE TO STAY

Fort Clark Springs Resort

An early Texas fort transformed into a resort. **On U.S. Hwy. 90, in Bracketville; 830-563-9210.**

Del Rio and Ciudad Acuna

Getting There: From San Antonio, travel 153 miles due west on U.S. Hwy. 90 to Del Rio. Ciudad Acuna is across the Rio Grande from Del Rio. **Visitor Information: Del Rio Chamber of Commerce, 1915 Ave. F; 830-775-3551; delriotx@del rio.com; www.chamberdelrio.com.**

Del Rio, with a 1990 population of 30,700, is the largest city between San Antonio and El Paso. Del Rio came into being because the San Felipe Springs gushed out more than 90 million gallons of water a day. It was the wettest spot in all of West Texas and grew up rapidly as settlers moved west looking for land and water. Originally the town was called San Felipe del Rio, and the name survived for more than two centuries, until the 1880s, when the U.S. Post Office suggested shortening it to Del Rio to avoid confusion with another Texas town, San Felipe de Austin.

Dr. John R. Brinkley was a celebrated Texas figure who made Del Rio his home. The good doctor came to Texas after he fell out of favor with the medical establishment in Kansas for advertising on the radio. Brinkley introduced his own version of the modern wonder drug Viagra to the world back in the 1930s. It is said that between 1933 and 1938, he earned $12 million from his particular medical specialty—somehow using goat glands to make impotent men sexually active again. He didn't have much success, but he sure brought in a lot of customers. He advertised to the world over a 100,000-watt radio station that he built just across the Rio Grande in Mexico. Eventually the luster of Brinkley's claims wore thin, and he retired to Little Rock, Arkansas. During his days in Del Rio, Brinkley imported hundreds of palm trees to the city; many of them still line the boulevards.

Del Rio's neighbor across the border is the Mexican city of Acuna, with a population of roughly 120,000. Its marketplace is not as large as many of the others along the border, but Acuna ranks in my books as the friendliest place on the border to spend your money.

SEEING AND DOING

Ciudad Acuna

The city was named for a romantic poet of the Mexican Revolution. Tourist shopping is near the international bridge. Many of the shopkeepers speak English, and most deal in American currency. There's a lot of junk for sale in the marketplace, but there are a few treasures as well; your mission, should you decide to accept, is to find them. **www.villadelrio.com/acuna.html.**

Liquor, jewelry, and brass items are just a few of the things you'll find at **Lando Curios (290 Hidalgo, phone 2-1269).** La Rueda sells modern Mexican designer clothes for women **(215 Hidalgo E., phone 2-1260).** At **Pancho's Market,** the wares include leather goods, liquor, jewelry, and clothing, and there's a lounge in the rear for the weary shopper **(299 Hidalgo E., phone 2-0466).**

Val Verde Winery

This is the oldest winery in Texas, begun in 1883 by Frank Qualia, an Italian immigrant; it is still operated by his family. They have tours of the facility and wine-tasting events. **100 Qualia Dr., Del Rio; 830-775-9714.**

Whitehead Memorial Museum

Seven buildings that depict the history of the territory. Included are the Perry Mercantile building, an 1870s structure that was moved here, and a replica of the Jersey Lilly, the saloon and court that was operated by Judge Roy Bean. Texas is loaded with replicas of the Jersey Lilly Saloon. The real one is at Langtry, about 60 miles northwest of Del Rio on U.S. Hwy. 90 (see the chapter on Amistad). But the graves out back of the replica of Jersey Lilly Saloon at Del Rio are the real thing; the famous judge and his son are buried there. **1308 S. Main St., Del Rio; 830-774-7568; www.whitehead-museum.com.**

FESTIVALS AND EVENTS

October—Fiesta de Amistad

An annual event usually in late October that serves as one of the area's major attractions. It is a binational fiesta featuring an international parade, beginning in Del Rio and winding up in Ciudad Acuna. **830-775-3551.**

RECREATION

San Felipe Springs and Moore Park

These springs were an important watering stop on the historic Chihuahua Road, which connected Texas with Chihuahua City, Mexico, in the early days. About 90 million gallons of clear spring water flows daily, creating a lush oasis in a semiarid setting. San Felipe Country Club golf course surrounds the springs, and Moore Park provides a large swimming pool. **On the north side of Del Rio, at 100 Swift St.; 830-774-8755.**

WHERE TO EAT

Asadero la Posta

Great meats, including steaks, ribs, and fajitas. There is a great fajita plate with onions, quesadilla, and guacamole that sells for about $5; try to beat that anywhere else. **348 Allende, Ciudad Acuna; phone 877-1-64-27.**

Cripple Creek Saloon

Log cabin-style building, with barrel-house piano music as the kitchen dishes up steaks, swordfish, and whatever else tickles your fancy. **On U.S. Hwy. 90, 2 miles west of Del Rio; 830-775-0153.**

Crosby's

It started in the 1930s and is still going strong, and is one of the best places to eat across the river in Ciudad Acuna. Old photos from the Mexican Revolution line the walls. This is the place to try *cabrito.* **195 Hidalgo; phone 877-2-20-20.**

Lando Restaurant and Bar

Upscale eating place with a good reputation. **270 Hidalgo, Ciudad Acuna; phone 877-2-59-75.**

Memo's

A longtime restaurant owned by local celebrity Blonde Calderon, a band leader and piano player for country and western singer Ray Price for many years. Nowadays he jams every Tuesday night at Memo's while his staff serves up some of the finest Tex-Mex food in Del Rio. **804 E. Losoya St.; 830-775-8104.**

WHERE TO STAY

1890 House

This restored home, now a bed-and-breakfast, is representative of the history of the region. **609 Griner St., Del Rio; 830-775-8061.**

La Quinta Inn

A national-chain motel in Del Rio. **2005 Ave. F; 830-775-7591.**

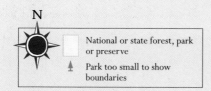

N

| National or state forest, park or preserve
🌲 | Park too small to show boundaries

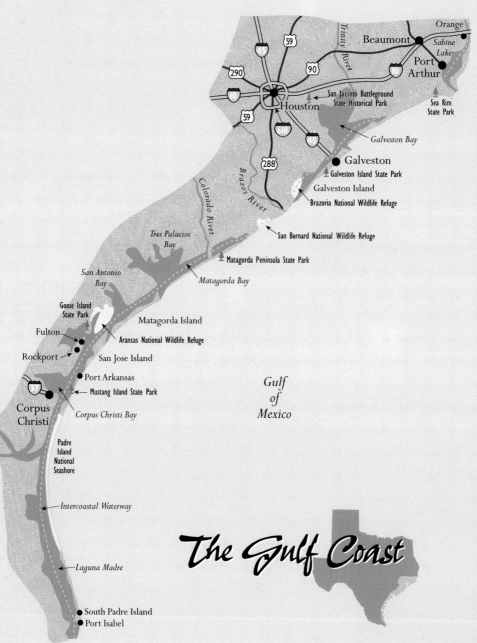

Orange

Beaumont

Sabine Lake

Port Arthur

Trinity River

59

290

90

10

Houston

59

San Jacinto Battleground State Historical Park

Sea Rim State Park

610

45

Galveston Bay

288

Galveston

🌲 Galveston Island State Park

Galveston Island

Brazoria National Wildlife Refuge

Brazos River

San Bernard National Wildlife Refuge

Colorado River

Tres Palacios Bay

🌲 Matagorda Peninsula State Park

Matagorda Bay

San Antonio Bay

Goose Island State Park

Matagorda Island

Fulton

🌲 Aransas National Wildlife Refuge

Rockport

San Jose Island

Port Arkansas

Mustang Island State Park

37

Corpus Christi

Corpus Christi Bay

Gulf of Mexico

Padre Island National Seashore

Intercoastal Waterway

Laguna Madre

The Gulf Coast

South Padre Island

Port Isabel

The Gulf Coast

Aransas National Wildlife Refuge along the Texas Middle Coast.
Photo courtesy of Texas Highways magazine.

The Gulf Coast

Mentioning the word "Texas" conjures up images of cattle, cowboys, and wide-open spaces, but there is a lot more to this state than most people think—even those of us who live in the state. Take me, for example. I was raised in West Texas, where neighbors are few and far between, and mesquite bushes are called trees. Every kid in West Texas had to have a car by the time he was 15, whether he was poor or rich. Even with cars, most of us didn't know that a world of sandy beaches and shrimp fishermen existed in Texas, because that world was more than 500 miles away, unreachable over a weekend in a '39 Mercury. But there it was anyway: the southeastern border of Texas—624 miles long, and all of it coastline, from Port Arthur to the Mexican border. It's the Gulf Coast of Texas.

This part of Texas on the Gulf of Mexico can be outright treacherous during hurricane season—and so calm the rest of the time that surfers have difficulty catching a wave. But the water is warm most of the year, and so is the climate, so anybody vacationing along the Gulf Coast can look forward to swimming, boating, and now and then a little windsurfing. The temperatures rarely drop below the 30s, making the Texas Gulf Coast a paradise most of the time.

Winter is little more than a minor inconvenience to Texans along the Gulf Coast. Most of the days are sunny, with occasional tropical breezes. Even the vegetation along the Gulf Coast takes on an air of the tropics, with towering date and palm trees, banana trees, and citrus trees. The region's climate is the lure for thousands of winter Texans.

You have choices, too. If you enjoy laid-back fishing villages, you'll find most of them on the Upper Coast. If you like solitude and sandy beaches, the Lower Coast is the place to go. There is one sizable city right on the coast—Corpus Christi—and one giant city a bit inland—Houston.

Most of the developed areas of the Texas shoreline are along the Upper Coast between Galveston and Port Arthur, but all of the coastline makes use of the Intracoastal Waterway, a series of channels that carry commercial and private boat traffic. The commercial traffic is heaviest on the Upper Coast, while the channels from Corpus Christi south are dominated by pleasure craft.

There is much concern about what commercialism is doing to the Texas coast and its sea life. More than 90 percent of all fish species found in the Gulf of Mexico spend at least part of their life cycles in estuary systems along the Gulf Coast. Many Texans are involved in efforts to preserve what remains of the beaches, wetlands, and salt marshes along the coast.

This section of the book divides the Gulf shoreline into five areas. The first three areas—**Houston; Galveston;** and the **Golden Triangle,** which includes Beaumont, Port Arthur, and Orange—are all part of the Upper Coast. This upper region is the most humid part of the Gulf Coast, and gets the most rainfall. The inner shoreline is thick with salt grass. This is also the state's main rice-producing region.

The fourth area is **Corpus Christi and the Middle Coast,** which runs from Matagorda Island southwest to Corpus Christi. The area is a mixture of grasslands and marshes, and is home to a number of rare critters that walk, swim, or fly. Many of them, like the whooping crane, are endangered and closely protected. The Middle Coast is the place to visit if you are into birding and wildlife.

The fifth area is the **Lower Coast,** which runs from Corpus Christi to the Mexican border and includes South Padre Island. The Lower Coast is much more arid, with fewer marshes and grasslands and more palm trees and sand dunes. This section is considered one of the ten most ecologically pristine coastal areas in the United States.

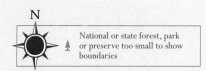

National or state forest, park or preserve too small to show boundaries

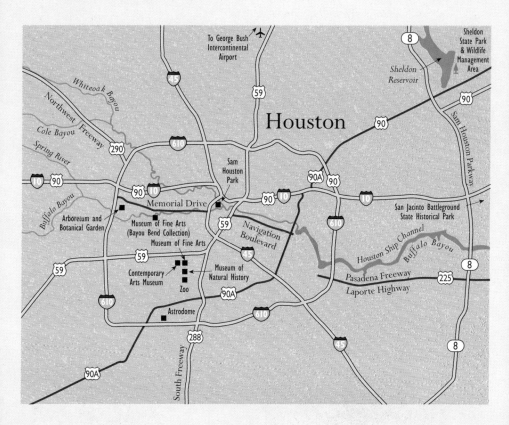

To George Bush Intercontinental Airport

Sheldon State Park & Wildlife Management Area

Sheldon Reservoir

Whiteoak Bayou

Northwest Freeway

Cole Bayou

Spring River

Sam Houston Parkway

Houston

Sam Houston Park

San Jacinto Battleground State Historical Park

Buffalo Bayou

Memorial Drive

Arboretum and Botanical Garden

Museum of Fine Arts (Bayou Bend Collection)

Museum of Fine Arts

Navigation Boulevard

Houston Ship Channel

Buffalo Bayou

Contemporary Arts Museum

Museum of Natural History

Pasadena Freeway

Laporte Highway

Zoo

Astrodome

South Freeway

Houston

Houston

With a population of some 1.7 million people, Houston is the largest city in Texas, the largest city in the Southwest, and the fourth largest city in the United States. Houston has the nation's third busiest port, and is home to what some have called the eighth wonder of the world, the Astrodome stadium. Houston wasn't even a town when the Allen brothers first settled it in August 1836. But this tiny riverboat landing on Buffalo Bayou developed into the industrial and financial hub for much of the state. It had the makings of a great port, and it had a cowboy culture and a Mexican culture that grew to become synonymous with Texas.

Many years ago I interviewed a kindly man named A. J. Farfel, who was one of the real movers and shakers in Houston. He was soft-spoken and loving, and always carried a few extra dollars in his pocket in case he ran into someone who was down and out and needed a break. I never heard him raise his voice to anyone, but when he spoke, people listened. You always hear about the "good ol' boy" businessmen who ran Houston back in the days when it was developing.

Well, I believe A. J. Farfel was the man the "good ol' boys" listened to. One of the listeners was county judge Roy Hoffeinz, a politician part of his life and a full-time promoter of other people's money. He's the man who talked the people of Houston and Harris County into paying for a fully air-conditioned, enclosed domed sports facility, the first in the nation—the Astrodome.

Sam Houston Park, Houston's first city park.

Getting There

George Bush Intercontinental Airport is the main airport in these parts, with daily service to more than 100 U.S. destinations and 26 international destinations. Allow 45 minutes to an hour to get to the airport from downtown Houston if the traffic is not heavy—and then more time running through one or more of the airport's four terminals. The airport is about **20 miles north of downtown between I-45 and U.S. Hwy. 59; 281-230-3000.**

Once the city's main airport, **William P. Hobby Airport** is now relegated to secondary status, with daily flights to seventy-two U.S. cities. Southwest Airlines still flies out of Hobby, making it a popular businessperson's airport. Allow 30 minutes to get to Hobby Airport, which is **south of downtown off I-45; 713-640-3000.**

Amtrak's Sunset Limited comes through 3 days a week on its way to either Los Angles or New Orleans. The Amtrak passenger station is at **902 Washington Ave., downtown; 1-800-USA-RAIL, 713-224-1577.**

dome proved that a large facility could be entirely air-conditioned. No matter the weather outside, it is always 72 degrees in the Astrodome. Houston today is built on that premise. A large part of downtown is air-conditioned and underground. An extensive system of tunnels beneath the skyscrapers of downtown Houston offers shopping in air-conditioned comfort, away from the noise and congestion. It's a 6-mile system of **underground pedestrian tunnels**—plus skywalks between buildings—that includes many shops and more than 100 restaurants. The best time to visit this system that connects fifty-five buildings with three hotels is during the work week, when the most stores are open. Tours are available by calling 713-840-9255.

Getting Around

BUSES

City Buses, commonly called **Metro,** operates more than 100 bus routes in the city and parts of surrounding Harris County, including the NASA/Clear Lake area. The basic fare is 85 cents. Free transfers are available for bus changes and short stopovers. A free transit map of greater Houston is available from the **Greater Houston Convention and Visitors Bureau** at 801 Congress St.; 713-227-3100.

FERRIES

Lynchburg Ferry is a watery shuttle for motorists and pedestrians, crossing the mouth of the San Jacinto River. It has been in operation since 1822. It is 25 miles east of downtown Houston off I-10, at **1001 S. Lynchburg Rd.; 281-424-3521.**

TAXIS

Houston has about twenty taxi companies. **Yellow Cab** is the largest **(713-236-1111). Fiesta Cab** employs Spanish bilingual drivers **(713-225-2666).**

TOURS

Gray Line Tours offers general tours of the city and special packages focusing on the Clear Lake/Space Center area; **713-223-8800, 1-800-334-4441, fax 713-223-0533.**

On the third Sunday of each month, a 3-hour **walking tour sponsored by the American Institute of Architects** covers more than fifty

Opened in 1965, it's still there today, just south of downtown, and still a drawing card to the city.

Houston is humid and hot most of the year. It is also given to torrential downpours. The humidity is a bummer, but Houstonians look at it this way: if Houston wasn't humid, there would probably be twice as many people living here. Humidity is highest in October and lowest in July. The good news is that temperatures rarely reach freezing in the winter, and in the summer, temperatures don't often climb above the mid-90s. But 90 degrees in the Houston humidity is very hot and uncomfortable.

A. J. Farfel said that if air-conditioning had not been invented, Houston would still be a tiny riverboat landing. I think he was right. Judge Hoffeinz's Astro-

buildings and public places in the downtown area; **713-622-2081.**

Visitor Information

Foreign Consulate Offices

Houston has more foreign consulates than any other city in the state. Individual county consulates will provide the necessary visas if you are planning a trip outside the United States. For information on traveling in Mexico, call the **Mexican Government Tourist Office, 2707 N. Loop 610 West, Suite 450; 713-880-5153.**

Greater Houston Convention and Visitor Information Center

Maps, brochures, and schedules of Houston-area events can be obtained at the center. Spanish-, French-, and German-speaking specialists are on staff. **801 Congress St.; 713-227-4422, 1-800-231-7799; houstongde@aol.com; www.houstonguide.com.**

Houston on Tape

A recorded audiotape that includes information on how to get around the city, where to have fun, and facts and little-known tips about sightseeing, festivals, museums, nature centers, getaways, parades, and more. Available for $3 at **Sound On Tape, 1000 Campbell Rd., Suite 208-108, Houston, 77055; 713-339-1315; jweaver@soundontape.com; www.soundontape.com.**

Major Attractions

Sam Houston Park

If you are looking for a quick history of Houston—if such a thing is possible—Sam Houston Park is the first place to stop. It's Houston's first city-owned park, created by a bunch of concerned citizens in the 1950s because one of the city's earliest homes was about to be demolished.

The Heritage Society of Harris County was created, and today some of Houston's earliest architectural history is preserved at the park. Several of the homes at the park must have been elegant showplaces in their day, and were built by some of Houston's earliest leaders, but you'll also find a one-room log cabin on display that was built in 1826, plus the frame home

of Houston's first black business leader, Jack Yates.

The tours are regular, the docents are delightful, and Sam Houston Park is one of my favorite escapes in downtown Houston, right in the shadows of the skyscrapers. **1100 Bagby St.; 713-655-1912; www.heritagesociety.org/park.html.**

Houston Museum of Natural Science

The museum showcases exhibits on space science, geology, archaeology, and natural history. Expect to share the place with schoolkids. The museum includes **Burke Baker Planetarium,** considered to be among the most sophisticated science teaching devices in the world **(713-639-4629, www.hmns.org/hmns/planetarium/bbppress.html).** The 232-seat planetarium can reproduce celestial patterns as they would be seen from any point on earth. You can fly into a black hole, and zoom through constellations faster than the speed of light.

The **Cockrell Butterfly Center** is a six-story glass-cone house at the museum that has about 2,000 live butterflies flying around in a tropical rain forest **(713-639-4600, www.hmns.org/hmns/butterfly.html).** The **Lillie and Roy Cullen Gallery of Earth Science** displays a collection of more than 600 rare mineral specimens and hundreds of gemstones.

The **Hall of Health** offers a transparent anatomical mannequin that displays lungs, heart, teeth, and other parts of the body. The hall has some hands-on exhibits. The museum's **Wortham IMAX Theater** features exciting films that are projected onto a screen that is six stories tall **(713-639-4629, www.hmns.org/hmns/imax.html).**

The Houston Museum of Natural Science is at **1 Hermann Circle Dr.; 713-639-4600; webmaster@hmns.org; www.hmns.mus.tx.us.**

San Jacinto Battleground State Historical Park

The park is the site of the battle in 1836 that won Texas its independence from Mexico. The **San Jacinto Monument** is 570 feet high and is said to be the tallest masonry monument in the world **(281-479-2421, info@sanjacinto-museum.org, www.sanjacinto-museum.org/index-html).** You can view the battleground from an observation deck at the top of the tower.

San Jacinto Monument at dusk, southeast of Houston. Photo courtesy of the Texas Department of Tourism.

Also at the site is the **San Jacinto Museum of History.** While at the park, you can view *Texas Forever,* a 35-minute movie that documents the famous battle, narrated by Charlton Heston. In the ship channel near the battleground is the battleship *Texas,* a veteran of both world wars. It is permanently moored here and serves as a naval museum.

The San Jacinto Battleground Park is **15 miles east of downtown Houston, near State Hwy. 225 and State Hwy. 134, at the town of LaPorte; 281-479-2431; www.tpwd.state.tx.us/park/battlesh/battlesh.htm.**

Seeing and Doing

Art Galleries and Museums

Menil Museum

A nationally renowned collection of art put together by John and Dominique de Menil. Includes Byzan-tine, medieval, and tribal art housed in a large building designed by Italian architect Renzo Piano. **1515 Sul Ross Ave.; 713-525-9400.**

Museum of Fine Arts

Features the city's finest collection of art objects, paintings, and sculpture, visited by more than half a million people each year. **1001 Bissonnet St.; 713-639-7300; www.mfah.org.**

Children and Families

Children's Museum

Hands-on exhibits for children from the ages of 4 months to 14 years in areas of science, history, culture, and the arts. **1500 Binz; 713-522-1138.**

J-Mar Farms

A petting farm with an Indian village, pony rides, hay-rides, fishing, cow milking, and more. **I-45 exit 91 near Conroe, 40 miles north of Houston; 1-800-636-8595, 409-856-8595; www.mcia.com/j-mar.htm.**

Gardens and Arboreta

Houston Arboretum and Nature Center

More than 5 miles of nature trails and 155 acres of woodlands just west of Memorial Park on Houston's west side. An educational facility for children and adults, as well as a preserve for native plants and animals. **4501 Woodway Dr.; 713-681-8433.**

Houston Garden Center

Garden trails and a rose garden. On the northern edge of Herman Park, next to the Texas Medical Center complex. **1500 Herman Dr.; 713-529-3960.**

June's Garden

This is a nice place to visit in Humble if you enjoy being in the company of growing plants and flowers. It was created by June Hodges, who is particularly attracted to day lilies. Her whole house and property is covered with growing things, and June can be persuaded to tell you about every flower, if you have an appointment—June is a tough old bird who won't allow you on her property unless you call first. **In Humble, 20 miles north of Houston, off U.S. Hwy. 59; 281-446-8709.**

Mercer Arboretum and Botanical Gardens

A 214-acre facility that features formal gardens, a picnic area, and 5 miles of garden and nature trails. **22306 Aldine Westfield Rd. in Humble, 20 miles north of downtown Houston at Farm Road 1960 and U.S. Hwy. 59; 281-443-8731.**

Historic Sites

Allen's Landing Park

The site where the Allen brothers started their first trading post in 1836. **Main and Commerce on Buffalo Bayou.**

Bailey's Prairie

Little more than a nice drive through hundred-year-old, moss-draped oak trees these days, this is one of those Texas places with a great story to take back home with you. The land once belonged to a crusty nineteenth-century rancher named Brit Bailey. He specified in his will that when he died, he wanted to be buried standing up because even in death, he wouldn't lie down for any man. And he wanted to be holding a bottle of his prized corn whiskey in one hand, his favorite coon-hunting dog by his side. The family followed Brit's instructions—including ending the life of the faithful dog so he could join his master. The unusual grave is tucked away in the trees on private property today. But word is that his spirit wanders around the community on a regular basis at night, looking for his bottle of whiskey—stolen from the grave. Don't expect to see the grave, but keep an eye out for a ghost. **South of Houston at State Hwy. 35 and Farm Road 521, between Angleton and West Columbia.**

Bayou Bend on the Azalea Trail in Houston. Photo courtesy of Texas Highways *magazine.*

Bayou Bend Collection

Housed in a twenty-eight-room Latin colonial structure that was home to the late Miss Ima Hogg, daughter of James Stephen Hogg, the first native-born governor of Texas. It is a remarkable collection of paintings and furniture from the colonial period, plus 14 acres of gardens bounded on three sides by Buffalo Bayou. A tour of this facility is especially memorable when the azaleas are blooming in the spring. **1 Westcott St.; 713-639-7758; www.riveroaksgardenclub.org/html/bayou bend.html.**

Christ Church Cathedral

Founded 1839, this is Houston's oldest church on its original site. It has hand-carved woodwork and stained-glass windows, including one designed by Tiffany. **1117 Texas Ave.; 713-222-2593.**

Market Square Historic District

This is Houston's original business district and has fifty-three historic buildings. **Bounded by Congress, Preston, Travis, and Milam Sts.**

Taylor-Stevenson Ranch

A working historical ranch that duplicates an early black-owned spread. It has all the things you might expect at a Texas ranch, plus historical emphasis on blacks, Hispanics, Native Americans, and women in the West. **About 2 miles south of the Astrodome at 11822 Almeda Rd.; 713-433-4441.**

Museums

Forbidden Gardens

A highly unusual 40-acre museum that replicates China's history, including the Forbidden City in Beijing, the sounds of a Chinese zither, and a look at a time when emperors ruled China. **23500 Franz Rd. in Katy, off I-10, 25 miles west of Houston; 281-347-8000.**

Fort Bend County Historical Museum

One of the state's best small museums, this place has a special exhibit on Jane Long, the Mother of Texas. **500 Houston St. in Richmond, 25 miles southwest of downtown Houston on U.S. Hwy. 59; 281-342-6478.**

Holocaust Museum Houston

Designed as a testimonial to those who died and a place to honor those who survived. **5401 Caroline St.; 713-942-8000, fax 713-942-7953; www.hmh.org.**

Museum of Printing History

One of the best bargains in the city, and one of my favorite museums. It lists among its greatest treasures one of nine remaining originals of the Hykamanto Dharani Scroll that was printed in Japan more than 1,200 years ago. Newspaper headlines tell of such events as the battle of Waterloo and Abraham Lincoln's assassination. **324 W. Clay; 713-522-4652.**

Nature Gardens

Armand Bayou Nature Center

A 1,900-acre center in southeast Harris County with plant and animal life in three major ecosystems: a hardwood forest, a tallgrass prairie, and an estuarine bayou. Also includes the Jimmy Martyn Farm, a working farm operated as it was at the turn of the twentieth century. Also has hiking, canoeing, birding, and self-guided tours. **8500 Bay Area Blvd. in Pasadena, about 15 miles southeast of downtown Houston on State Hwy. 225; 281-474-2551; abnc@ghgcorp.com; www.ghgcorp.com.**

Sea Center Texas

A marine aquarium and education center developed by the Texas Parks and Wildlife Department, Dow North American, and the Gulf Coast Conservation Association. The marine fisheries center here has the capacity to produce 20 million fingerlings annually, mostly red drum and spotted sea trout, for release into Texas coastal waters. The complex also has a visitor center, two "touch tanks" for getting close to certain animals, and a 50,000-gallon aquarium. **Plantation Dr. and Medical Dr. in Lake Jackson, 60 miles south of Houston on State Hwy. 288; 409-292-0100; www.tpwd.state.tx.us/news/magazine/seacen.htm.**

Other Sights

George R. Brown Convention Center

Opened in 1987, it is Houston's largest facility built to lure conventions to the city. It has nearly half a million square feet of exhibit space, with forty-three meeting rooms and three major halls, and a 31,000-square-foot ballroom. **1001 Convention Center Blvd.; 713-833-8000.**

Lyndon B. Johnson Space Center

Headquarters of America's manned space program, including the famous Mission Control that guided pioneering astronauts into space and that now directs the space shuttle projects. In Clear Lake, 20 miles southeast of downtown Houston. **2101 Nasa Rd. 1; 281-483-0123; www.jsc.nasa.gov.**

Oil Ranch

A dude ranch with hayrides, cookouts, a petting zoo, and an Indian village. **1 Oil Ranch Rd. in Hockley, 30 miles northwest of Houston on U.S. Hwy. 290; 409-931-3879.**

Orange Show

A colorfully bizarre collection of things built and collected by a Houston eccentric over a period of more than 25 years. It's a labyrinth of outdoor and indoor passages, stairs, and platforms amid whirligigs, wrought-iron assemblages, colored tiles, antiques, and junk. I met Jeff McKissack back when he was more a nuisance than an eccentric, at least according to his neighbors. Jeff had a thing for oranges. He thought oranges would save the world, so everything he built on his residential lot in southeast Houston honored, even worshiped, oranges. He announced to me that if everybody would eat oranges, all the world's crises would end. Jeff's neighbors wanted him gone because his lot, they said, looked like a junkyard. But he never moved. And guess what happened when he died: Art enthusiasts arrived on the scene and declared him an artist, and now Jeff McKissack's Orange Show is a part of Houston's culture scene. **2402 Munger St.; 713-926-6368.**

Space Center Houston

An education and entertainment complex that serves as the visitor center for NASA. It is a space adventure into the past and the future, filled with movies, interactive exhibits, and behind-the-scenes tram tours. This place is billed as "the closest thing to space on earth." In Clear Lake, 20 miles southeast of downtown Houston.

1601 Nasa Road 1; 281-244-2105, fax 281-283-7724; larrya@spacecenter.org; www.spacecenter.org.

Texas Medical Center

Organized in 1945, an immense complex of hospitals, medical and nursing schools, and research institutions whose purpose is the coordination of health education, patient care, and research. There are more than 100 buildings occupying 650 acres in southwest Houston. There are so many skyscrapers at the Texas Medical Center that locals refer to it as Uptown. **1155 Holcombe Blvd.; 713-790-1136; tmcinfo@tmc.edu; www.tmc.edu.**

Unicorn Ranch

A working cattle ranch open for parties and corporate retreats. **2855 Clemons Switch Rd. in Pattison, 50 miles west of Houston off I-10; 713-375-6939, fax 281-375-6939; unicorn@ain.net.**

Parks

Six Flags Astroworld/Water World

Part of the Astrodome complex and the Six Flags family and one of the nation's great amusement centers, with more than 100 shows plus rides and attractions for the whole family. **Kirby Dr. at Loop 610; 713-799-1234; sixflags.com/parks/sfaw/index.html.**

Splashtown USA

Catch a wave and a waterfall, or splash around in the Blue Lagoon. There is something for everybody at this 46-acre park. **I-45 exit 68 in Spring, about 18 miles north of Houston; 281-355-3300.**

Performing Arts

Alley Theatre

One of the few resident professional theaters in the country. The theater produces about a dozen plays annually; attracts acting, writing, and directing talent from all over; and has a reputation as one of the nation's top regional theaters. **615 Texas Ave.; 713-228-8421; www.alleytheatre.com.**

Miller Outdoor Theater

Offers free performances to the public throughout the year, from ballet to Shakespeare, musical comedy to symphonic concerts. Outdoor theater at **100 Concert Dr. in Herman Park.**

Wortham Theater Center

Home to Houston Grand Opera and Houston Ballet. **500 Texas St.; 713-237-1439.**

Shopping

British Market

A mini–department store of goods from the British Isles. In the Village, near Rice University, at **366 Rice Blvd., Houston; 713-529-9889.**

Brookwood Garden Center

This is a part of Brookwood Community, a place where mentally retarded people make their way in life, living here and working here. The center is one of the finest garden nurseries you'll find in the Houston area. **In Brookshire on I-10, about 28 miles west of Houston; 281-375-2149.**

Chinatown

Shops with Asian goods and foods for sale. **In the downtown Houston area bounded by St. Emanuel, Chartres, Lamar, and Rusk Sts.**

Factory Outlet Center in Conroe

A large complex of factory stores with name-brand products and good prices on clothing and whatever. **I-45 at 1111 League Line Rd., 40 miles north of Houston.**

The Galleria

One of Houston's most luxurious shopping centers; fashioned after a shopping plaza in Milan, Italy. **5075 Westheimer Rd., Houston; 713-621-1907.**

Houston Flea Market

A huge flea market with tons of items for sale on weekends **(6616 Southwest Freeway; 713-782-0391).** **Trader's Village** is another flea market, but a lot of this one is located indoors **(7979 N. Eldridge Parkway, Houston; 713-890-5500).**

Houston Sport Exchange

Root for your favorites, and purchase caps and clothes

Galleria Shopping Mall, a fancy shopping mall in southwest Houston. Photo courtesy of Texas Highways magazine.

for just about any college or pro team out there. **5015 Westheimer Rd.; 713-552-1882.**

Lilypons

A wonderful getaway for people who enjoy lilies of all varieties. You can buy them or just enjoy them. **In Brookshire off I-10, 30 miles west of Houston; 281-934-8525.**

Montrose

An ever-changing area of small specialty stores and restaurants near the museum district, with some great restaurants and sidewalk cafes. It is a good place to find antiques at a bargain if you know what you're looking for. **On the near-western edge of downtown at Elgin St. and Montrose Ave.**

Old Town Spring

One of the greatest shopping places you'll ever find. This is an old restored railroad village of the early 1900s, with about 150 shops featuring antiques, art, crafts, clothing, and restaurants. It's a great place to get away on weekends. **I-45 at Spring Cypress Rd. in Spring, about 18 miles north of Houston; 1-800-653-8696, 281-353-9310; ots@oldtownspringtx.com; www.oldtownspringtx.com.**

Rice Village

A public square–style shopping area that appeals to students and staff from the Texas Medical Center and to tourists. **Near Rice University, at Kirby Dr. and University Blvd.; www.ricevillage.com.**

Shudde Brothers Hatters

Try them for that special hat. **905 Trinity St., Houston; 713-223-2191.**

Stelzig's

I suggest Stelzig's, the oldest western-wear store in Houston, if you are in need of western wear to take back home with you, whether it's boots, a western shirt, or even a saddle. **3123 Post Oak Dr., Houston; 713-629-7779.**

Tootsies

High-fashion women's clothing and accessories. **4045 Westheimer Rd.; 713-629-9990.**

Whole Earth Provision Company

Flashlights, kayaks, ropes, backpacks, anything and everything for campers, plus children's books, luggage, and more. **2934 S. Shepherd St.; 713-526-3883.**

Sports

Compaq Center
Part of the Greenway Plaza Business complex, this is the home of the Houston Rockets basketball team and also hosts major rock concerts. **10 E. Greenway Plaza; 713-961-9003.**

Houston Raceway Park
A 440-acre drag-racing complex with major competition throughout the year. **2525 S. Farm Road 565 on the outskirts of Baytown, which is about 30 miles east of Houston; 281-383-2666, fax 281-383-3777; feedback@houstonraceway.com; www.houstonraceway.com.**

Tours

Astrodome Convention Center
The complex includes the Astrodome, Astrohall, and Astroarena. Tours daily unless preempted by an event. This is also home to the Houston Livestock Show and Rodeo every February. **Kirby at Loop 610; 713-799-9544; astros.com/dome/htm.**

BOAT TOURS

Clear Lake Queen
Two-and-a-half-hour narrated excursion ride on Clear Lake. Weekends. **At Clear Lake Park on State Hwy. 1, near NASA, 20 miles southeast of downtown Houston; 281-333-3334.**

Paddle Wheeler Southern Empress
Dining, dancing, and dinner cruises Thurs.–Sat. Lakeview Marina. **Take I-45 north from Houston for 40 miles to Conroe, then go west for 7.5 miles on State Hwy. 105 to the marina. Southern Empress cruises: 409-588-3000. Lakeview Marina: 409-588-3190.**

Port of Houston
The 50-mile-long Houston ship channel connects Houston to the Gulf of Mexico. More than 5,000 ships visit this port annually. Visitors can get up-close and personal with the port in the *Sam Houston,* a boat that makes the trip 4 days a week. This very interesting tour takes an hour and a half. **111 E. Loop 610 north; 713-670-2416; mktresrh@neosoft.com; www.portofhouston.com.**

Wagering

Gulf Greyhound Park
The largest, most successful greyhound racing track in the country operates year-round, and features a four-level air-conditioned grandstand. **Off I-45, 46 miles south of Houston at exit 15 at Lamarque; 1-800-ASK-2-WIN; gulfpark@gulfgreyhound.com; www.gulfgreyhound.com.**

Sam Houston Race Track
Class 1 race track offering pari-mutuel wagering on live thoroughbred and quarterhorse races. It has a 30,000-capacity grandstand with luxury suites. **On the Sam Houston Tollway near Farm Road 249, in north Houston; 281-807-RACE; general@shrp.com; www.shrp.com.**

Old Town Spring, a popular shopping spot north of Houston. Photo courtesy of Texas Highways magazine.

Wildlife Viewing

Liles Safari Ranch
Showcases 120 wooded acres that are home to hundreds of exotic animals, Texas wildlife, and birds. In **Kingwood, about 25 miles north of downtown Houston, on U.S. Hwy. 59; 281-359-1946.**

Wineries and Breweries

Anheuser-Busch Brewery
The brewing process from grains to the finished product is explained in a 45-minute tour, followed by a sipping of the suds. **775 Gellhorn Dr., at I-10 east and Loop 610; 713-675-2311.**

Festivals and Events

February
Chinese New Year Festival
The timing for this festival varies according to the Chinese lunar calendar. Mostly held in Chinatown. **713-780-8112.**

Houston Livestock Show and Rodeo
Mid-February to early March. Billed as the world's largest rodeo and livestock show. Held in the Astrodome complex. **P.O. Box 20070, Houston, 77225; 713-791-9000, fax 713-794-9528; www.hlsr.com.**

March
Azalea Trail
Organized by the River Oaks Garden Club. Floral splendor created by azaleas and other flowers all over the city, and displayed at many of Houston's fine old homes. **2503 Westheimer Rd.; 713-523-2483; www.riveroaksgardenclub.org/html/azaleatrail.html.**

April
Houston International Festival
Civic festival spotlighting the city's literary, visual, and performing arts. Also includes an international film festival at Greenway Plaza. **713-654-8808; info@hif.org; www.hif.org.**

Westheimer Colony Arts Festival
One weekend each April (and also one weekend in October). Visitors can browse through a variety of booths from the 100 to the 1100 block of Westheimer, shop for artwork of all kinds, and mingle with the people who live and work in the Montrose district. **713-521-0133.**

May
Cinco de Mayo
This is a celebration of Mexico's victory over the French in 1862, featuring food, music, and dancing. **In the area around the Brown Convention Center.**

Heights Home Tour
Mother's Day weekend. Six to ten homes in the Heights district are opened for public inspection; it's one of the city's oldest neighborhoods. **713-868-0102.**

Pin Oak Charity Horse Show
An annual highlight of the equestrian set, featuring competition from all over the United States and a few foreign countries for saddle-bred, hunter-jumper, walking, and other types of horses. **At the Great Southwest Equestrian Center west of Houston; 281-578-7009.**

June
Juneteenth Blues Festival
Houston's largest annual celebration honors the June 19, 1865, announcement of the abolition of slavery. Most of the activities are based around music, particularly gospel and blues. **Outdoor Theater at Sam Houston Park and various other downtown locations; 713-626-8000.**

August
Houston Jazz Festival
Around town, Houston's jazz culture is celebrated. For information, call the **Greater Houston Convention and Visitors Bureau** at **713-227-3100.**

September
Fiestas Patrias
Around town, a celebration of Hispanic heritage in the city. For information, call the **Greater Houston Convention and Visitors Bureau** at **713-227-3100.**

October
Greek Festival
Usually starts the first Friday in October at the Greek

Orthodox Cathedral (**3511 Yoakum St.**); a 3-day celebration of Greek culture and traditions. The food is terrific. For information, call the **Greater Houston Convention and Visitors Bureau** at 713-227-3100.

Westheimer Colony Art Festival

Aspiring and established artists display and sell their creative work on the streets and in some stores in the Westheimer shopping district. **713-521-0133, fax 713-521-0013; bcart@netroplis.net; www. bayoucityartfestival.com.**

November

Thanksgiving Day Parade

A steady procession of floats, marching bands, and visiting celebrities makes this one of downtown Houston's big events of the year.

December

Christmas Celebrations

Highlighting seasonal events throughout the month are free candlelight tours of Sam Houston Park; *The Nutcracker* performed by the Houston Ballet in Jones Hall; and concerts by the Second Baptist Church Choir.

Recreation

Biking

Houston's cycling community is very active because the city and surrounding areas are so flat. The **Houston Bicycle Club (713-729-9333)** will provide information on local cycling events. **Alexander Deussen County Park** has bicycle trails (**12303 Sonnier; 281-454-7057**). So does **Brazos Bend State Park (in Needville, south of Richmond; 409-553-5101).**

Alkek Velodrome, site of the 1989 Texas Track Championships, has a 33,000-meter track banked 9 to 33 degrees. It's a great challenge. **19008 Saums Rd.; 281-578-0858.**

The **Houston Parks and Recreation Department (713-845-1000)** has a system of hiking and biking trails that run for more than 30 miles through the city. Most frequently used are **Memorial Park** (along Buffalo Bayou) and **Brays Bayou** (on the southwest side of the city).

Fishing

Texas City Dike Lighted Pier

Popular fishing spot for many years in these parts. The dike extends 5 miles into Galveston Bay and has a 600-foot fishing pier beyond the tip of the dike. It offers the deepest water for pier fishing in the state and produces speckled trout, redfish, flounder, and tarpon. There are beach facilities, boat launching and service facilities, and camping and some motel accommodations. **At Texas City, 38 miles southeast of Houston on I-45, on the Texas City Dike road on the way to Galveston; 409-948-8172.**

Golfing

There are a number of municipal 18-hole golf courses open to the public in Houston, including **Brock Park** (on the east side at **8201 John Ralston Rd., 713-458-1350**); **Hermann Park** (Medical Center area at **6201 Golf Course Dr., 713-526-0077**); **Wortham** (on the southeast side at **7000 Capitol Ave., 713-921-3227**); **Jersey Meadows** (in Jersey Village at **8502 Rio Grande St., 281-896-0900**); **Memorial,** former home course for the Houston Open, now reconstructed into a championship course once more, with prices to match (on the near west side at **1001 Memorial Loop E., 713-862-4033**); and **Sharpstown** (west of downtown at **6600 Harbor Town St. off Bellaire Blvd., 713-988-2099**). **Bear Creek Golf World** is another popular golf complex, with three courses to choose from (on the west side at **16001 Clay Rd., off State Hwy. 6, 281-859-8188**).

Houston has several great championship golf courses open to the public. My favorite is my home course, **Greatwood.** Greatwood has the best drainage, and that's worth considering because it rains so much there. I think Greatwood also has the best greens, fast and undulating (in the southwestern suburbs at **Grand Parkway and U.S. Hwy. 59, 281-343-9999**). There are other good courses, including **Old Orchard,** with 27 holes partly in the woods and partly in the open (to the west at **13134 Farm Road 1464 outside Richmond, 281-277-3300**);

Southwyck, a fairly open course with plenty of water, and frequent wind (to the south at **2901 Club House Dr. in Pearland, 713-436-9999**); the **Tournament Players Course,** where the pros play every year **(1730 S. Millbend Dr. in The Woodlands, 281-367-7285);** and **Cypresswood** (to the north at **21602 Cypresswood Dr. in Spring, 281-821-6300**).

The most talked-about course in Houston, **Tour 18,** is a dream, if you want to play a round on a course with holes built to resemble those at some of the great courses in the country (outside Humble, northeast of downtown at **3102 Farm Road 1960, 281-540-1818**). As a 13 handicapper, I can tell you that Tour 18 is fun to play, if you've got the time. It took me about five hours to complete a round, but the sensation of playing a part that mimics the Masters in Augusta or Pebble Beach in California is something you'll remember for the rest of your life.

Hiking and Jogging

The **Houston Parks and Recreation Department (713-845-1000)** has a system of hiking and biking trails that run for more than 30 miles through the city. Most frequently used are **Memorial Park** (along Buffalo Bayou) and **Brays Bayou** (on the southwest side of the city). The **YMCA (713-659-5566)** and **YWCA (713-868-9922)** have facilities for jogging.

Horseback Riding

The **Houston Polo Club** has practice matches on Wednesday and Friday afternoons, free and open to the public. Regular Sunday matches cost $15. The summer season is from April to July, and the fall season is from September to November. **8552 Memorial Dr.; 713-622-7300.**

Houston has a number of fine facilities for equestrian sports and for other activities involving horses and livestock. My favorite is the **Houston Farm and Ranch Club (1 Abercrombie Rd., on State Hwy. 6 west of town near I-10; 281-463-6650).** Dick Atkins's people operate a charitable foundation out there, working with the youth of Houston and Harris County and with handicapped youngsters. The **Great Southwest Equestrian Center** has a big facility too, and stays busy most of the year (near Katy, at **2501 S. Mason Rd., 281-578-7669,**

mansion@gsw-equestrian-center.com, www.gsw-equestrian-center.com). Other facilities include the **Bay Area Equestrian Center (Farm Road 518 in Pearland, 281-996-1515)** and **Westheimer Stables (13250 Westheimer Rd., 281-497-2293).**

In the Air

Texas Air Aces

Wannabe pilots, ages 9 to 99, can try their hands in air-to-air combat. It's the real thing, not a simulator. Amateur pilots fly in the front seat of a T-34 aircraft while a professional supervises the mission from the rear seat. It costs some money, but you walk away with the experience of a lifetime and a videotape of yourself in action. Hooks Airport, north of Houston, at **8319 Thora Ln., Hangar A5, Spring, 77379; 1-800-544-2237, fax 281-251-7197; taace@swbell.net; www.airaces.com.**

Parks and Camping

Among Houston's campgrounds and RV parks are **All Star RV Resort** (to the southwest at **2700 W. Main St. in League City, 281-981-6814**); **Alexander Deussen County Park (12303 Sonnier St., 281-454-7057); KOA Houston Central (1620 Peach Leaf St., 281-442-3700); Red Dot RV Park (15014 Sellers Rd., 281-448-3438); Houston Leisure Park (1601 S. Main St., 281-426-3576);** and **Traders Village RV Park (7979 N. Eldridge Pkwy., 281-890-5500).**

Brazos Bend State Park

A total of 4,800 acres of coastal plain includes Brazos River bottomlands, beautiful live oak woodlands, oxbow lakes and marsh, and abundant wildlife. You may even see a Russian boar. I promise you'll see alligators. Keep young pets and children away from the water's edge; you'll discover why. A few years back the State Parks and Wildlife Department instigated a "desocializing program" for the alligators at Brazos Bend. The animals were getting entirely too comfortable around people, and officials feared that sooner or later one of the gators would attack a human being, so the bureaucracy swung into motion. The State of Texas spent a lot of money studying the problem, created a bunch of committees, and eventually figured out how to handle the problem. They took sticks and clubs to the area where the alligators hung out, made lots of noise, banged the sticks and clubs on the ground, and generally acted as if they didn't like the animals. That did the trick, and it only cost the state about $200,000. Is this a great country or what? But the alligators are still there. Brazos Bend also has tent and RV camping, picnic sites, screened shelters, fishing piers, hiking and biking trails, and wildlife observation platforms. There are 15 miles of hiking and biking trails at Brazos Bend, and six lakes for fishing. Within the park is the **George Observatory**, featuring a 36-inch telescope **(www.hmns.mus.tx.us/ hmns/george_observ.html).** On Saturday nights it is open to the public for stargazing. The park is at **21901 Farm Road 762 in Needville, 40 miles southwest of Houston (take U.S. Hwy. 59 southwest to Rosenberg, then travel south on State Hwy. 36 to Needville); 409-553-5101, 409- 553-3243; www.tpwd.state.tx.us/expltx/eft/ bbsp/bbsp-index.htm.**

Buffalo Bayou

Bisecting Houston, beginning in rural west Harris County at Barker Reservoir and meandering 50 miles east through the suburbs, the downtown, and all the way to the ship channel. The most attractive section is in **Memorial Park, 1001 Memorial Loop East,** on the near west side of the city, where the bayou's banks are lined with flora and the dirt jogging trails are filled with exercise nuts. The city allows canoeing in the bayou in Memorial Park and farther east in **Cleveland Park,** and plans are under way for greenbelts along the bayou all the way to the ship channel.

Sylvan Beach Park

A 32-acre county park at the site of a famous resort dance pavilion of the 1920s. It's an air-conditioned modern facility today, overlooking Galveston Bay fishing pier, with a boat launch ramp, playground, picnic areas, and a Heritage Societies showcase of Texas memorabilia. **1 Sylvan Beach Dr. in LaPorte, 25 miles east of Houston on State Hwy. 225; 281-470-1381.**

Wilderness Park

A 182-acre municipal park bordered by Buffalo Camp Bayou and the Brazos River. The park has an interpretive quarter-mile nature loop, a 4-mile hiking trail

with loads of Brazos River views, and picnicking and fishing. Wildlife includes deer, wild pigs, small mammals, and alligators. **On State Hwy. 332, 1 mile west of Lake Jackson, 60 miles south of Houston; 409-297-4533.**

Tennis

Most of the public parks in Houston have tennis courts where facilities are available on a first-come, first-served basis. Houston also has three tennis centers that take reservations: **Homer L. Ford Center (5225 Calhoun Blvd., 713-747-5466); Memorial Tennis Center (1500 Memorial Loop Dr., 713- 861-3765); and Southwest Tennis Center (9506 Gessner Rd., 713-772-0296).**

Where to Eat

Houston has all the chain restaurants, and because the city is not strictly zoned, you may just find an eating place on every corner. However, there are a few special places I prefer over the others. It all depends on your taste and your pocketbook.

Amalia's

A good place for chicken and beef fajitas. **2520 S. Voss Rd.; 713-784-1292.**

Antone's

Outlets all around the city; great poor-boy sandwiches. Not fancy but tasty; and check out the wines and cheese while you're there. The original Antone's is at **8110 Kirby Dr.; 713-667-3400.**

Armando's

An upscale Mexican food place, and definitely authentic. **2300 Westheimer Rd.; 713-521-9757.**

Brennan's

A branch of the famed New Orleans restaurant, but this one offers some Texas/southwestern dishes as well as Cajun delights. **3300 Smith St.; 713-522-9223.**

Cadillac Bar

A replica of the famous restaurant at Nuevo Laredo, offering roast quail, frog legs, and cabrito. **1802 Shepherd Dr.; 713-862-2020.**

Cafe Adobe

For spinach enchiladas. Near downtown: **2111 Westheimer Rd.; 713-528-1468.** And in Sugar Land: **2329 State Hwy. 6; 281-277-1700.**

Cafe Annie

Comes up with Southwest food guaranteed to impress you: how about some crabmeat tostadas? **1728 Post Oak Blvd.; 713-840-1111.**

Christy's Seafood

For the best jumbo fried shrimp in the area—and that includes Galveston—Christy's can't be beat. As far back as I can remember, Christy has always personally shopped for his own shrimp and negotiated deals for the best shrimp around. He was always in his restaurant, mingling with the customers, even before it became fashionable to do so. This is the only seafood place I've ever been where you can pay to have shrimp for dinner, and when you finish, you feel like you've eaten more shrimp than french fries or hush puppies. **6029 Westheimer Rd.; 713-978-6563.**

The Cloister

Lunch only. Years ago as an enticement to get the downtown crowd to use church facilities, Christ Church opened its cloister to the public for some Cajun lunches. Now it's a packed house every day at noon. **1117 Texas Ave., at Christ Church Cathedral; 713-222-2593.**

Goode Company Barbecue

One of Houston's many such places that claim to be the best in town. This one is good, no doubt, and entertaining too. On weekends you might find old-time country singers, in the tradition of Pappy Self and Bob Wills, performing in the outdoor pavilion. Jim Goode also has restaurants in the same neighborhood that specialize in seafood and Mexican food, and a gift shop that sells Texas memorabilia. **5109 Kirby Dr.; 713-522-2530.**

Goodson's Cafe

This place started out as a home-style restaurant in Tomball, a little community northwest of Houston. Back then the chicken-fried steaks were larger than the plates, and at lunchtime every day the tiny frame building was usually crammed full of truckers and other hard-workers. Ma Goodson was in the back frying up the steaks, and a robust lady with a German accent waited tables. Nobody ever talked back to her, and they ate what they got. After Goodson's Cafe got its reputation, Ma retired and sold it to somebody else, who moved the operation into Houston. Chicken-fried steak is still their specialty. The servings are not nearly as big as they used to be—but the steaks are better. One thing that has always grated on me, however, is that there is a message on the menu that says my old TV show *Eyes of Texas* has endorsed the restaurant. Nope. We did a story on the place, but we don't endorse any eating places. **Corner of Gessner Rd. and I-10 W.; 713-973-2233.**

Irma's

I do have some strong feelings about this place. A lady named Irma and her sons run it. It is located in a run-down part of Houston and is open only from 8 A.M. until 3 P.M., but to me it is the absolute best place in town for Mexican food. The food, especially breakfast, is wonderful. They don't have menus and they don't write down your order tickets. When you pay up, Irma just asks you what you had and trusts you to be honest. A lot of high-ranking police officers, firefighters, and politicians hang out regularly at Irma's. **22 N. Chenevert St.; 713-222-0767.**

James Coney Island

I promised I wouldn't talk about chain restaurants, but I've got to mention this one. It was started by a Houston native and has since been bought out by another chain, but the hot dogs are still the best in town. You can have the chili cheese Coney all the way, a New York Jumbo with sauerkraut, or, my favorite, the Chicago Jumbo with sweet relish—but don't eat them in the car. It'll take weeks to get rid of the aroma. Various locations around Houston.

Lai Lai Dumpling House

My favorite oriental dumpling house. **9262 Bellaire Blvd. near Gessner Rd.; 713-271-0080.**

Larry's Mexican Restaurant

I figure any restaurant that can survive several generations of families must have something going for it. That's Larry's. I have friends who remember going to Larry's when they were kids. It's still there, and it's still packed most weekends. The hot sauce is too hot for my taste, but my friends love it. **116 E. U.S. Hwy. 90A in Richmond; 281-342-2881.**

Lopez

A hole-in-the-wall Mexican restaurant that has a waiting line every time you go there. I'm not sure what makes it so good, but all my neighbors think it's the best around. I eat the nachos and drink dark beer. **11542 Wilcrest Dr.; 281-495-2436.**

Merida Restaurant

Serves up Yucatecan specialties. **2509 Navigation Blvd.; 713-225-0403.**

Nam's

My favorite Vietnamese food. **2727 Fondren Rd.; 713-789-6688.**

Nash D'amico's Pasta and Clam Bar

As good as it gets in the community around Rice University. **5510 Morningside Dr.; 713-526-3400.**

Nielsen's Delicatessen

Best rare roast beef sandwiches in town, and a potato salad that will knock your lights out. But you may have to eat standing up; seating is limited. Located in an old converted gas station at **4500 Richmond Ave.; 713-963-8005.**

Otto's

Anybody who likes barbecue has heard about Otto's. You often see celebrities there, like George and Barbara Bush. But I like the hamburgers better than the barbecue. They are simple and tasty. The atmosphere is very informal. **5502 Memorial Dr.; 713-864-2573.**

Pappa's

A family-owned business that grew into an empire. This name is all over town in restaurants that specialize in almost every type of food. Pappa's started out as a seafood place. Then came Pappasita's Mexican food, Pappa's Barbecue, Pappa's Steakhouse, and Pappadeaux's Cajun Seafood. You won't find a better steak in the city than at Pappa's Steakhouse, but the price is steep. **5839 Westheimer Rd.; 713-917-0090.**

Pho Tau Bay

One of those unassuming noodle houses in Houston's

little Saigon district that serves up great Vietnamese food. **2800 Travis St.; 713-524-3213.**

PT's Cajun Barbecue

A converted Exxon gas station that serves up crawfish by the tray, zydeco music, and a Cajun atmosphere. PT's attracts a lot of families on Sunday afternoons and many people from the nearby Johnson Space Center. Expect good food and great atmosphere, but don't show up expecting iced tea. They'll tell you right out that the only thing they serve to drink is beer or Coke. **11902 Galveston Rd., near Ellington Field; 281-481-8736.**

Sandy McGee's

Helen and the little ol' ladies at Greatwood golf course found this place for me. They are forever searching for unlikely places to eat lunch. Sandy McGee's was primarily a catering place when they first discovered it, but Sandy served light lunches part of the week. The place has since expanded into two full-blown cafes: in Rosenberg, 35 miles southwest of Houston (**1207 6th St., 281-341-9151**), and Richmond, 30 miles southwest of Houston (**314 Morton St., 281-344-9393**).

Shanghai Red's

There's wonderful seafood and a terrific atmosphere here, but go at night if you can—it's fun to watch the big ships pass by. On the Houston ship channel, at **8501 Cypress St.; 713-926-6666.**

Taste of Texas Steakhouse

Ed and Nina Hendee worked their way through college as waiters and after graduating decided that serving food to people was a pretty good business, so they opened their own place. They've made careers out of serving prime steaks to hungry people, and the food is good. **10505 Katy Freeway (I-10 West), on the west side of Houston; 713-932-6901.**

Thai Pepper

Houston's most authentic Thai restaurant uses fresh herbs and spices and no MSG. **2049 W. Alabama St.; 713-520-8225.**

Tokyo Gardens

Houston's oldest Japanese restaurant and sushi bar. **4701 Westheimer Rd.; 713-622-7886.**

Tony's

One of the best gourmet restaurants anywhere that advertises "continental" cuisine, and one of the most expensive. Reservations yes, and men must wear coats at lunch and ties at dinner, but this place has been one of the hubs of Houston's social scene for more than a decade. **1801 Post Oak Blvd.; 713-622-6778.**

Vargo's

Another one of those famous Houston steak houses, located in a quiet pastoral setting on the edge of the Memorial subdivision. This used to be the only upscale steak house in town; it's still one of the best. **2401 Fondren Rd.; 713-782-3888.**

Vicker's Inn

Owned and operated by one of the best cooks and biggest characters in all of Southeast Texas, Tom Barrett. Visit him in his kitchen any morning and he will be grumbling about the business and complaining about the lack of help, but come back at lunch or dinner and he will be serving some of the most delicious dishes you'll ever taste. His steaks are from the best cut of meat in the country. **122 S. 1st St. in La Porte, 25 miles east of Houston; 281-471-6505.**

What's Cookin'

An old-time German restaurant that serves every kind of beer you can imagine. Near Kemah, 30 miles southeast of Houston near NASA, at **930 Farm Road 518; 281-334-3610.**

Where to Stay

Hotel and motel accommodations are concentrated in a half dozen major areas of the city: central Houston; the west side; the Astrodome area, which includes the Texas Medical Center; the two major airports, Bush Intercontinental on the north and Hobby International on the south; and the southwest, including Sugar Land and Fort Bend County. The **Bed-and-Breakfast Society of Texas** maintains a registry of two dozen establishments in Houston **(713-523-1114).** Among the places that accept direct bookings are **Angel Arbor Bed-and-Breakfast (848 Heights Blvd., 713-868-4654)** and **Sara's Bed-and-Breakfast (941 Heights Blvd., 713-868-1130).**

Some of the better-known hotels include **Adam's Mark** (in southwest Houston at **2900 Briarpark Dr., 713-978-7400**); **Doubletree Hotel** (downtown at **400 Dallas St., 713-759-0202**); **Hotel Sofitel** (near Bush Intercontinental Airport at **425 N. Sam Houston Parkway E., 281-445-9000**); **Hyatt Regency** (downtown at **1200 Louisiana St., 713-654-1234**); **La Colombe D'or** (in the museum district at **3410 Montrose Ave., 713-524-7999**); **Westin Galleria** (in the Galleria at **5060 W. Alabama St., 713-960-8100**); the **Wyndham Warwick** (in uptown Houston at **5701 Main St., 713-526-1991**); and the **Woodlands Inn and Country Club** (in The Woodlands, north of downtown at **2301 N. Millbend Dr., 281-367-1100**).

Galveston

My old boss, Ray Miller, had a love affair with Galveston. He spent little time away from work, but when he did, he always headed for Galveston's West Beach. Ray had a beach house in this city-on-an-island before it was fashionable. He loved the beach and the history of the region. Once upon a time, Galveston was the most important city in all of Texas, the place where everybody coming to Texas wound up. They either arrived by sea from other lands or came here by covered wagon to do business, because much of the business conducted in Texas back in the old days started right here in Galveston. The pirate Jean Lafitte spent time in the waters off Galveston, looting ships. Thomas Edison was in Galveston in 1900 to take the very first movies of a city that had been ravaged by a hurricane. It was the worst natural disaster in American history. More than 6,000 people were killed.

Galveston was headquarters for the Confederate army in the state during the Civil War, and toward the end of the war, it was headquarters for the Union army. The building that housed both headquarters was Ashton Villa, built by the James Brown family in 1859 back when Galveston was the leading seaport of the Southwest. In the late 1960s a group of Galveston businessmen decided it was time to tear down the old structure and make room for something really worthwhile, like a parking lot. That's when Ray Miller stepped in. For months he used his influence as a newsman, trying to save Ashton Villa from the wrecking ball. He succeeded with the motto that "if Ashton Villa is not worth saving, then nothing Galveston has is."

Getting Around

TOURS

Classic Carriage Tours

It is usually easy to find a horse-drawn carriage, mostly in the Strand Historic District, to take you along some of the streets of the city. **1604 Ave. M; 409-762-1260.**

The Colonel Paddle Wheeler

Offers day cruises, dinner cruises, and moonlight cruises. This is an authentic reproduction of an 1860s stern-wheeler named in honor of Colonel W. L. Moody, a Virginian who came to Texas to practice law. **At Pier 22; 409-763-4666.**

Galveston Island Trolley

Loops from the Moody Civic Center at Seawall Blvd. and 21st St. to the Strand area and back. **409-763-4311.**

Treasure Island Tour Train

Open-air train that carries passengers on a leisurely 17-mile trip around new and old Galveston. Departs 7 days a week from **Moody Civic Center (Seawall Blvd. and 21st St.); 409-761-2618.**

Visitor Information

Galveston Island Convention and Visitors Bureau

2106 Seawall Blvd. at 21st St.; 1-888-425-4753, 409-763-4311; cvb@galvestontourism.com; www.galvestontourism.com, www.galveston.com.

Port Bolivar Chamber of Commerce
1760 U.S. Hwy. 87; 409-684-5940.

The Strand Visitors Center
Operated by the Galveston Historical Foundation, this should be one of your first stops when you hit the Strand Historic District. **2016 Strand St., Galveston, 77550; 409-765-7834; foundation@galveston-history.org; www.galveston-history.org.**

Major Attractions

Texas Seaport Museum
This museum is the place to get a feel for the sweeping maritime history of Galveston. Visitors have access to a computer database with information on more than 130,000 immigrants who entered Texas through the Port of Galveston.

Highlight of the museum is the *Elissa,* a completely restored sailing vessel that used to make regular trips into Galveston harbor in the late 1800s. The *Elissa* is the third oldest ship afloat today, giving way only to England's *Cutty Sark* and to the *Star of India* berthed in San Diego. The *Elissa* still sails every summer and ranks as my favorite attraction in Galveston. A wide-screen theater at the museum features stories of the sea and a film on restoration of the *Elissa.*

Seawolf Park on Pelican Island in Galveston. Photo courtesy of Texas Highways *magazine.*

The Texas Seaport Museum and the *Elissa* are at **Pier 21 off Water St.; 409-763-1877, fax 409-763-3037; tsm@phoenix.net; www.phoenix.net/~tsm.**

The Railroad Museum
Here you'll find the largest collection of vintage railroad locomotives and cars in the Southwest—and all of that is on the outside of the building. Inside the old Santa Fe Railroad station are displays that include thirty life-size sculptures of rail travelers frozen in a moment in time in the 1930s.

The museum also features model trains for kids of all ages. And check out the luxurious private railroad car that dates back to the 1920s. The Railroad Museum is at **123 Rosenberg St. at the west end of the Strand Historic District; 409-765-5700, fax 409-765-8635; railroad@tamug.tamu.edu; wwwtamug.tamu.edu/rrmuseum.**

Seeing and Doing

Historic Sites

Ashton Villa
An 1859 mansion that has survived all the storms and all the wars. A tour of the house is like tracing the history of the island. **2328 Broadway St.; 409-762-3933.**

The Bishop's Palace
A grandiose home often considered the crowning achievement of Galveston architect Nicholas Clayton, whose work left a lasting stamp on the city. **1402 Broadway St.; 409-762-2475.**

East End Historic District
Another fashionable residential subdivision of the city. The best way to enjoy this 40-block district is to stop first at the Convention and Visitors Bureau or the Strand Visitors Center and pick up a riding and walking tour map. **From 11th to 19th Sts. between Mechanic and Broadway Sts.**

The Samuel May Williams Home
One of the oldest homes on the island. Built in 1839 in Maine, then taken apart and shipped to Galveston and reassembled. **3601 Ave. P; 409-765-1839.**

Silk Stocking Historic District

The name comes from a period when only the wealthy ladies could afford silk stockings. This is where many of them lived. There are excellent examples of nineteenth-century architecture. **Along 24th and 25th Sts. between Avenue L and Avenue O.**

Strand Historic District

This is Galveston's original downtown business district. Once it was known as the "Wall Street of the Southwest," but today the banks and brokers are gone and the tourist shops and restaurants have taken charge. **From 20th to 25th Sts. between Water and Mechanic Sts.; www.galveston.com/attract/strand.**

The 1894 Grand Opera House

A fine old building that has seen the likes of Sarah Bernhardt, George Burns, and Gracie Allen. Check out the current shows; this is one of the best theater bargains in the state. It features double curved balconies, and no seat is farther that 70 feet from the stage. It is a wonderful place to be entertained. **2020 Post Office St. near 21st St.; 409-765-1894.**

Museums

The Lone Star Flight Museum

Thirty-four splendidly restored vintage aircraft from the two world wars. **2002 Terminal Dr. at Scholes Field; 409-740-7722, fax 409-740-7612; www.lsfm.org.**

Moody Mansion and Museum

A forty-two-room mansion that was built in 1895 and survived the Great Storm of 1900, it was occupied by one of Galveston's most prosperous and powerful families. **2628 Broadway St.; 409-762-7668.**

Nature Centers

Moody Gardens

A world-class education and recreation complex that includes a white-sand beach, seaside safari, rain forest, and an IMAX theater. Near Scholes Field airport at **1 Hope Blvd.; 1-800-582-4673; www.moodygardens.com.**

The Strand, once dubbed the "Wall Street of the Southwest," in Galveston. Photo courtesy of Texas Highways magazine.

Parks

Seawolf Park

Fishing from the rocks or from a 380-foot fishing pier. This park also has two World War II combat ships to explore: the USS *Stewart*, a destroyer escort, and the USS *Cavalla*, a submarine. From the upper level of the *Stewart* you can see the port of Galveston and the many ships working the ship channel, and watch the Bolivar ferry on its route from Point Bolivar to its landing on Galveston Island. **Take the 51st St. causeway to Pelican Island; 409-744-5738; www.brazosport.cc.tx.us/~nstevens/park.html.**

Festivals and Events

February

Mardi Gras Festival

Two weeks of fun and frolicking Galveston-style with masked balls, art exhibits, costume contests, entertainment for all ages, and ten parades—they never get tired of walking in Galveston. **409-765-7834.**

March

Galveston Film Festival

Film screenings and panel discussions held at the Galveston Arts Center as motion-picture producers of Texas honor Texas movies. For information, call the **Galveston Island Convention and Visitors Bureau** at **409-763-4311.**

April

Blessing of the Shrimp Fleet

Usually the first weekend following Easter. A 2-day festival that focuses on the Cajun shrimping traditions along the Gulf Coast. For information, call the **Galveston Island Convention and Visitors Bureau** at **409-763-4311.**

May

Historic Homes Tours

Two weekends early in the month. A half dozen nineteenth-century homes are opened to the public for tours. **409-765-7834.**

June

Crawfish Fest

First or second weekend of the month. A serious crawfish cook-off featuring nationally known chefs like Alex Patout and Enola Prudhomme.

November

Galveston Island Jazz Festival

Mid-month. Jazz greats come to the island for a 3-day festival on old Galveston Square. For information, call the **Galveston Island Convention and Visitors Bureau** at **409-763-4311.**

December

Dickens on the Strand

Usually the first Saturday and Sunday of December. Maybe the biggest event of the year, it's a Christmas celebration with an English flavor. The Strand Historic District is turned into an authentic re-creation of its namesake in London as it was during the nineteenth century. **409-765-7834; foundation@galveston-history.org; www.dickensonthestrand.com.**

Recreation

Bird-Watching

Galveston and the whole Gulf Coast is known for its wide variety of bird species, attracting birders from all over. Roseate spoonbills, herons, whitewing doves, and white and brown pelicans are only a few of the birds that spend time on the coast. **Bolivar Flats** is famous for waders and shorebirds, including flocks of avocets. From the ferry landing on the Bolivar Peninsula, across from Galveston, drive east of U.S. Hwy. 87 to the junction of Loop 108. Turn right toward the Gulf of Mexico and you will come to a wide, flat expanse of beach with shallow water and very little surf: Bolivar Flats. For more information, call the **Bolivar Peninsula Chamber of Commerce** at **409-684-5940.**

Diving

There are many good spots near the offshore oil rigs that range from 1 to 50 miles away. A 500-acre live coral reef known as the **Flower Garden Banks** is 120 miles offshore. **Fling Charters** has a 100-foot boat that provides 2- and 3-day diving trips to the Flower Gardens **(1203 N. Ave. J, in Freeport, 40 miles southwest of Galveston, 409-233-4445).**

Fishing

There is fishing in the bay, the piers, the jetties, the surf, and offshore in the Gulf. More than fifty varieties of saltwater fish swim in the warm waters. Charter and party boats depart daily from the docks around Pier 19 and the yacht basin, and several commercial piers and numerous rock groin piers extend well into the Gulf from the beachfront. Most of the commercial piers charge about $2 for their use, and are lighted for night fishing. Charter boats also operate out of Freeport, 40 miles southwest of Galveston. **Captain Elliot's Party Boats** offers group deep-sea trips for about $55 per person per day **(1021 W. 2nd St., in Freeport, 409-233-1811).**

Parks and Camping

Bolivar Peninsula

This is a long, narrow strip of territory just across the Houston ship channel from Galveston. To get there, take the Bolivar ferry from the north end of Ferry Road in Galveston. The only road on the peninsula is State Hwy. 87, which goes along the coast from Port Bolivar to the town of Sabine Pass. Four tiny towns sit on the peninsula: Crystal Beach, Gilchrist, High Island, and Port Bolivar. Fishing and other beach activities are the main things here. I've been told that the best fishing is at Port Bolivar and at Rollover Pass, a narrow canal that cuts across the peninsula near Gilchrist. **1-800-386-7863; cofcbolivar@yahoo.com; www.infotexas.com/bolivar1.html, www. crystalbeach.com/chamber.htm.**

Fort Travis Seashore Park

A former army fort has been converted into a seaside park with camping, fishing, and picnicking. About a mile from the landing on the south side of State Hwy. 87 near Port Bolivar, on the Bolivar Peninsula. **409-684-1333.**

Galveston Island State Park

A 2,000-acre park with a beach on one side and the marshes of Galveston Bay on the other. Surf and wade fishing, camping, swimming, picnicking, bird-watching, and walking on nature trails. **West Beach, Farm Road 3005 near Thirteen Mile Rd.; 409-737-1222; www.tpwd.state.tx.us/park/galvesto/ galvesto.htm.**

RV Parks

Gilchrist, on the Bolivar Peninsula, has two RV parks along State Hwy. 87: **Hazel's (1008 Sams St., 409-286-5228)** and **Las Palmas (1041 Church St., 409-286-5612). Dellanera RV Park** is a city-owned facility in Galveston with fifty full hookups, showers, laundry, a grocery store, and a beach area **(10901 San Luis Pass, just west of Six Mile Rd. off Seawall, 409-740-1390).** Others are **Bayou Heaven (6310 Heards Ln., 409-744-2837)** and **Galveston Island RV Resort (2323 Skymaster Rd., 409-744-5464).**

The Seawall

Starting near the east end of Galveston Island and stretching about 10 miles to the west. After the deadly storm of 1900, the citizens of Galveston decided to raise the elevation of the entire island. It all started with a concrete seawall that rose 17 feet above mean low tide, and it still protects Galveston from raging Gulf waters today. The seawall also provides one of the world's longest continuous sidewalks, which makes it great for strolling, jogging, bicycling, skateboarding, roller-skating, in-line skating, and girl/guy-watching.

Texas City Dike and Marina

Extends 5 miles into Galveston Bay, with a 600-foot fishing pier that offers the deepest water for pier fishing in the state. Visitors will also find a beach, boat launching, and camping facilities. **Texas City Dike Rd., 5 miles northwest of Galveston on I-45; 409-948-8172.**

Wildlife Refuges

Bolivar Peninsula is home to three national wildlife refuges. At **Anahuac National Wildlife Refuge,** you can usually see a sea of snow geese between October and March. They also have some of the last red wolves in existence. Primitive camping is permitted. The refuge is **by Gilchrist, across from East Galveston Bay; 409-267-3337; www.gorp.com/ gorp/resource/us-nwr/tx_anahu.htm. McFaddin National Wildlife Refuge,** covering 41,000 acres, is a major winter habitat for migratory waterfowl. Alligators are all around in the marshes and bayous, but they're usually hard to see. Free camping is permitted along the 12 miles of beach facing the Gulf. The McFaddin Refuge is **about 60 miles northeast of Galveston, almost to Sabine Pass; 409-971-2909. Texas Point National Wildlife Refuge** is **at the northernmost part of Bolivar Peninsula, almost to Sabine Pass; 409-971-2909.**

Surfing

Galveston is popular among Texas surfers for its seawall breaks. Surfing is allowed wherever there are signs that read "No Swimming." The best surf generally breaks along the granite jetties. Experienced surfers say the 61st Street jetty usually provides the big waves, but it varies from day to day. Shops along the east end of Seawall Boulevard rent boards by the hour or the day. The community of Surfside, 40 miles south of

The seawall and beach in Galveston. Photo courtesy of Texas Highways *magazine.*

Galveston on Farm Road 3005, is a well-known hangout for surfers.

Swimming

There are more than 30 miles of Gulf beaches on Galveston Island, and every mile is public. Lifeguards are stationed at designated areas, and some of the parks charge admission. Rest rooms and other facilities are available at these parks: **R. A. Apffel Beach Park (Seawall Blvd. and Boddecker St. at the extreme east end of the island, 409-762-3278); Stewart Beach Park,** with a pavilion and amusement park **(Seawall Blvd. near Broadway St.); Galveston County Beach Pocket Parks (at Farm Road 3005 at Seven Mile Rd., Nine Mile Rd., and Eleven Mile Rd., 409-770-5355); Galveston Island State Park (on Farm Road 3005 near Thirteen Mile Rd., 409-737-1222).** You can also take in human-made **Palm Beach (at Moody Gardens, 1 Hope Blvd., 1-800-582-4673, www.moody gardens.com).**

Where to Eat

Galveston is loaded with great seafood places. Take your pick.

Benno's on the Beach

It looks like a fast-food place, but it is much, much more. One of the few real bargains on the beachfront is Benno's boiled shrimp served with corn. Everything comes with a Cajun flavor. **Seawall Blvd. at 12th St.; 409-762-4621.**

Christie's Beachcomber

The luncheon buffet here finds tourists fighting over the food with locals. **Stewart Beach, Seawall Blvd. and 4th St.; 409-762-8648.**

El Nopalito

Galveston's answer to Mexican food. If you like Tex-Mex, you'll love huevos rancheros for breakfast. **614 42nd St.; 409-763-9815.**

Gaido's

A family restaurant that has survived since 1911. Something must be good here if they can stay in business this long. Expect long lines on weekends. **3828 Seawall Blvd.; 409-762-9625.**

Hill's Pier 19

Two eating places in one. You can sit down to eat in the big building and watch the boats go by, or grab a seafood po-boy at the serving counter if you are in a hurry.

Their specialties are the shrimp po-boys. Ummmmm good! **20th and Wharf Sts.; 409-763-7087.**

The Santa Fe Chew Chew

Two restored dining cars that are a part of Galveston's Railroad Museum and serve seafood, as well as beef, veal, and fowl. **25th and Strand Sts.; 409-765-5700.**

Shirley's Bait Camp

Serves up seafood and plate lunches to take out and eat on picnic tables on the grass. **In Port Bolivar at 15th St. and the Intracoastal Canal; 409-684-9251.**

Stingaree Restaurant

One of the better seafood places on the Bolivar Peninsula. The specialty is crab cooked Cajun-style. Open daily for lunch and dinner. **1295 Stingaree Rd. in Crystal Beach; 409-684-2731.**

Where to Stay

The bed-and-breakfast phenomenon has taken hold in Galveston's historic districts, and every season the number of B&Bs increases. A lot of beach houses, mostly in the West Beach area, also go up for rent during the busy season; some are rented for as short a time as 2 nights, but most rent by the week or the weekend. The **Galveston Island Convention and Visitors Bureau (1-888-425-4753, 409-763-4311)** has a listing of bed-and-breakfasts and beach houses for rent.

Flagship Over the Water Hotel

A seven-story hotel built entirely over the Gulf. It has its own fishing pier. **2501 Seawall Blvd.; 1-800-392-6542; flagship@galveston.com; www.galveston.com/accom/flagship.**

Hotel Galvez

This place is often called the Grand Old Lady of Galveston. It was built in 1911 and has been restored to recapture its glorious past. **2024 Seawall Blvd.; 1-800-392-4285, 409-765-7721; www.galvez @hotelgalvez.com.**

The Tremont House

A historical restoration of an 1870 hotel with Victorian-inspired rooms. **2300 Ship's Mechanic Row between 23rd and 24th Sts.; 409-763-0300; www.galveston.com/accom/tremont.**

The Golden Triangle

A lot of Texans truly believe that the Golden Triangle region that includes Beaumont, Port Arthur, and Orange ought to be part of Louisiana, and that the section of Louisiana around Shreveport and Bossier City ought to be part of Texas. I'm one of them. There are more Cajuns than Texans in the Golden Triangle, and more Texans than Cajuns in Shreveport.

But when it comes right down to it, it's probably best that the geography of the two states stays the same. The Golden Triangle offers a Louisiana flavor—with all its syrupy coffee, zydeco music, and language that sounds a little like French and a lot like the ol' South—that can be found nowhere else in Texas. And they do, indeed, know how to party in the Golden Triangle. It's grass-roots fun, and if you can visit whenever a festival is scheduled, you won't want to miss it.

In the late 1970s, a large number of Vietnamese immigrated to Port Arthur because of opportunities in the shrimping business. Today the Vietnamese make up a large part of the population in the town, which is a year-round delight for fishers. The **Port Arthur Convention and Visitors Bureau** (listed below) sells an area waters guide showing locations for catching many varieties of freshwater and saltwater fish in the region.

Visitor Information

Beaumont Convention and Visitors Bureau
Open Mon.–Fri. 8 A.M.–5 P.M. In the city hall at **801 Main St., P.O. Box 3827, Beaumont, 77704; 1-800-392-4401, 409-880-3749; bmtcvb@beau montcvb.com; www.bmtcoc.org, www. beaumontcvb.com.**

Orange Convention and Visitors Bureau
1012 Green Ave.; 409-883-3536; www.org-tx.com/chamber/index.html.

Port Arthur Convention and Visitors Bureau
In the Civic Center at **3401 Cultural Center Dr.;**

1-800-235-7822, 409-985-7822; pacvb@port arthurtex.com; www.portarthurtexas.com.

Texas Travel Information Center
One of the centers provided by the state at key highway entrances to Texas is located on I-10 at the Texas–Louisiana state line. This is a good place to get information about any place you want to visit in Texas. **1-800-452-9282, 409-883-9416.**

Seeing and Doing

Beaumont

MUSEUMS AND HISTORIC SITES

Babe Didrikson Zaharias Museum
Home of one of the greatest female athletes of our time. Mildred Didrikson—Babe, as she came to be called—was a three-time basketball All-American, an Olympics champ, and a pioneering woman golfer. Open daily 9 A.M.–5 P.M. **1750 I-10 and Martin Luther King Parkway; 409-833-4622.**

The John Jay French Museum
The city's first two-story house and the first built with lumber instead of logs. Today it is a museum operated by the Beaumont Heritage Society. Open Tues.–Sat. 10 A.M.–4 P.M. **2985 French Rd.; 409-898-3267.**

McFaddin-Ward House

Colonial architecture dating back to 1906, displaying antiques collected over a 75-year period. Open Tues.– Sat. 10 A.M.–4 P.M. and Sun. 1 P.M.–4 P.M. **1906 McFaddin Ave.; 409-832-2134; info@mcfaddin-ward.org; www.mcfaddin-ward.org.**

Old Town

Historic Beaumont, with many of the old homes turned into establishments selling jewelry, antiques, and clothing. A 36-block area **between Laurel, Harrison, 2nd, and 10th Sts.; 1-800-392-4401.**

OTHER SIGHTS

Crawfish and Alligator Farms

Here are some to visit: **Doguet's Crawfish Farm** (near the town of China, about 16 miles west of Beaumont at **1801 U.S. Hwy. 90, 409-752-5514**); **H & L Crawfish Farm** (near China, on **S. China Rd., 409-752-5514**); and **Alligator Island,** the largest gator-breeding farm in the state and home to Big Al, largest gator in captivity (near Fannett, 20 miles southeast of Beaumont; **State Hwy. 365 and I-10; 409-794-1995**). Crawfish season is January to June.

Port of Beaumont Observation Deck

Located on the deepwater Neches River ship channel. The deck offers a nice overview of one of the busiest ports in the state; tours by reservation. **1255 Main St.; 409-832-1546; info@portofbmt.com; www.portofbmt.com.**

Spindletop/Gladys City Boomtown

The world's first oil boomtown, re-created with clap-board buildings and wooden oil derricks of the era. The Lucas Gusher Monument honors the beginnings of the modern petroleum industry that blew in on January 10, 1901, when a gusher drilled by Anthony F. Lucas, an Austrian immigrant, changed the economic face of the state. Open Tues.–Sun. 1 P.M.–5 P.M. **University Dr. at U.S. Hwy. 69; 409-835-0823.**

Port Arthur

MUSEUMS AND HISTORIC SITES

Museum of the Gulf Coast

An old three-story bank building that has been converted into a museum, displaying the history and development of southeastern Texas and the southwest Louisiana Gulf Coast. Open Mon.–Sat. 9 A.M.–5 P.M. **701 4th St.; 409-982-7000.**

Pompeiian Villa

Built in 1953, mimicking an A.D. 79 home in Pompeii. The house is built around a three-sided courtyard with a Roman fountain in the center, and each room opens into the courtyard. Open Mon.–Fri. 9 A.M.–4 P.M. **1953 Lakeshore Dr.; 409-983-5977.**

Rainbow Bridge

An amazing two-lane bridge spanning the Neches River between the Gulf and the Port of Beaumont that was built in 1938 to accommodate the USS *Patoka*, a U.S. Navy dirigible tender. The navy quit using dirigibles long before the bridge was finished, but it was completed anyway. Today it is a sightseeing experience to drive over this bridge, which rises 177 feet above the water. Rainbow Bridge is **on State Hwy. 87, joining Bridge City on the north with Port Arthur on the south; 1-800-235-7822.**

Sabine Pass Battleground State Historical Park

The site of a rare Civil War battle in Texas in which the Confederates devastated the Union forces. Sixty-five Federals were killed or wounded and 315 were taken prisoner by the Confederates, who suffered no casualties. This is a day-use park. **Fifteen miles south of Port Arthur on Farm Road 3322, just off State Hwy. 87; www.tpwd.state.tx.us/park/sabine/sabine/htm.**

Getting There

From Houston, take I-10 east for about 60 miles. From that point you can get to Beaumont by staying on I-10 for another 27 miles. Or to reach Port Arthur from that point, take State Hwy. 73 due east for 23 miles. Orange is 24 miles east of Beaumont via I-10, or 18 miles north of Port Arthur via Hwy. 73.

Sydney Island, a bird refuge in the Golden Triangle.

Tex Ritter Park

Commemorates the hometown boy and country singing superstar. Also in the park is the **Dutch Windmill Museum,** which displays Tex Ritter memorabilia, and **LaMaison Acadienne Museum,** a replica of an early southern Louisiana Cajun home. Open Tues.–Sun. afternoons from March until Labor Day, Thurs. Sun. afternoons the rest of the year. **1500 Boston Ave., in Nederland, between Port Arthur and Beaumont; 409-772-0279.**

White Haven

Victorian elegance in a southern / Greek-revival mansion in the city's historic district, featuring porcelains from the eighteenth century. Open for tours Mon.–Fri. 9 A.M.–4 P.M. and on most weekends. **2545 Lakeshore Dr.; 409-982-3068.**

Orange

MUSEUMS AND HISTORIC SITES

Heritage House Museum

A 1902-era rambling two-story structure built as a residence, but today serving as a museum depicting the history and traditions of the area. Open Tues.–Fri. 10 A.M.–4 P.M. **905 W. Division St.; 409-886-5385.**

W. H. Stark House

Fifteen-room Victorian mansion, offering period furnishings and a glimpse of how the wealthy lived in East Texas in those pioneer years. The Stark family name still claims a high profile in Orange. Tours Tues.–Sat. at 10:00, 11:00, and 11:30 A.M., and at 1:00, 2:00, and 3:00 P.M. **620 W. Main St.; 409-883-0871.**

OTHER SIGHTS

Chemical Row

Miles-long complex of modern plants that produce a myriad of products connected with the petroleum industry. An impressive sight, day or night. **On Farm Road 1006 south and southwest of Orange.**

TOURS

Super Gator Airboat Tour

An airboat ride through the beauty of the swamplands, with giant cypress trees, Spanish moss, swamp flowers, and birds. Tours May–Sept. 10 A.M.–7 P.M. and Oct.–April 10 A.M.–4 P.M. **106 E. Lutcher Dr.; 409-883-7725.**

WAGERING

Delta Downs

Thoroughbred and quarterhorse racing year-round. It can be a unique experience to visit a horse track in Cajun country. Check out the announcer's version of "They're off" in Cajun. **Ten miles east of Orange in Louisiana, on State Hwy. 3063; 1-800-737-3358, 318-589-7441; downs@valuweb.net; www.deltadowns.com.**

WINERIES

Pineywoods Country Wines

One of the only wineries in East Texas, specializing in muscadine and fruit wines, including plum, pear, peach, mayberry, strawberry, and orange. Open for tasting year-round, Mon.–Sat. 9:30 A.M.–5:30 P.M., Sun. 1:30–5:30 P.M., but the hours are flexible depending on the season and the crowds; call ahead to confirm. **3408 Willow Dr.; 409-883-5408.**

Festivals and Events

January

Janis Joplin's Birthday

On-again, off-again event, usually celebrated with a concert to honor the hometown girl, born January 19, 1943, who rose to stardom with her voice and then died in a world of drugs. **In Port Arthur.**

February

Mardi Gras

Weekend before Ash Wednesday. **In Port Arthur.**

March

Taste of Gumbo

Usually mid-month. Local restaurants compete for the best-tasting gumbo in the Golden Triangle. **At Port Arthur Civic Center.**

April

Neches River Festival

At the end of the month, with art shows, flower shows, museum tours, and speedboat races. **In Beaumont.**

Pleasure Island Music Festival

On the last weekend in the month, with continuous music, plus arts and crafts, contests, and games. **At Pleasure Island Park in Port Arthur.**

May

Cajun Festival

Last weekend in the month, featuring Cajun music, dancing, crawfish races, food, and a carnival. **In Port Arthur at the Bishop Bryne Wellness Center.**

International Gumbo Cookoff

First weekend in the month. Brings Cajun food and fun with gumbos made from just about any critter that flies, runs, or swims. **In Orange at the old Navy base.**

Kaleidoscope

Mid-month. The Art Museum of Southeast Texas hon-ors local and international artists and their work. **In Beaumont.**

June

Juneteenth

The Golden Triangle has one of the largest black populations in the state, so you might expect that June 19, the date that news of the Emancipation Proclamation reached Texas, would be a big event. In typical East Texas style, there is plenty of gospel and zydeco music to enjoy. **In Beaumont at Riverfront Park.**

September

The Cayman Island Fest

A joint effort with Port Arthur and Cayman Island in the Caribbean; a planeload of Cayman Islanders fly in for the festival, which features a soccer match, Caribbean music, and plenty of Cajun and Caribbean food.

Texas Rice Festival

Near the end of the month. Features a beauty pageant, parade, and carnival. **In downtown Port Arthur.**

October

Cav-Oil-Cade Celebration

Celebrates the city's lifeblood, the oil industry. **At Port Arthur Civic Center.**

Shrimpfest

On the last weekend of the month. Brings fun that includes a cook-off and "shrimp calling." **At Pleasure Island concert park outside Port Arthur.**

Roseate spoonbill, one of the rare coastal creatures that attract birders to the Gulf Coast.

December

Christmas Reflections
Elaborate lighting displays in the Area of Peace in Port Arthur and on Pleasure Island, where the lights seem to dance off the waters of the Intracoastal Waterway.

Recreation

Bird-Watching
Port Arthur is located on the Central Flyway for waterfowl, so during the migratory season birds are everywhere. Pleasure Island (just across the Gulf Intracoastal Waterway from Port Arthur) is a good place to watch for them, and of course there is excellent bird-watching in most of the managed wildlife refuges.

For a well-organized tour for watching birds or wildlife in the Golden Triangle—or almost anywhere else, for that matter—check with **Vic Emanual Nature Tours (P.O. Box 33008, Austin, 78764; 1-800-328-8368).** These tours are not inexpensive by any means, but they are wonderful and are run by real professionals.

Fishing
Fishing is a big sport in these parts. The Port Arthur area is a prize freshwater and saltwater fishing region. Taylor and Cow Bayous are excellent for freshwater anglers. The Neches and Sabine Rivers are good for bass, bream, crappie, catfish, and gar.

Saltwater fishing spots include the Sabine ship channel, Sabine Lake, the lower reaches of the Neches River just east of Rainbow Bridge, the Taylor Bayou outfall, and Cow Bayou south of I-10. Saltwater fishing offers speckled trout, drum, flounder, croaker, redfish, and sheepshead. The Gulf of Mexico is easily reached from Sabine Pass or the Bolivar Peninsula for offshore and deep-sea fishing.

There are boat-launching facilities at **Pleasure Island Marina** on Sabine Lake **(520 Pleasure Pier Blvd., Port Arthur, 409-982-4675)** and at **Rainbow Marina** on the Neches River **(7069 Rainbow Ln., Port Arthur, 409-962-9578).** Taylor Bayou has a few private landings on the west side of the State Hwy. 73 bridge and one public landing on the east. At Cow's Bayou, LeBlanc's Landing is on the east side of the State Hwy. 87 bridge at Round Bunch Road.

Parks and Camping

J. D. Murphree Wildlife Management Area
On State Hwy. 73 about 5 miles west of Port Arthur; 409-736-2551.

High Island Boy Scout Wood and Smith Oaks Nature Sanctuaries
A series of bird sanctuaries located on a salt dome owned by the Houston Audubon Society and offering a great spot for birders to the area. The spring migration is usually mid-March to mid-May. The fall migration is from August to October. **About 40 miles south of Beaumont on State Hwy. 124; 281-932-1639.**

Pleasure Island
A thin barrier island just across the Gulf Intracoastal Waterway at Port Arthur. Features **Jep's RV Park (409-983-3822)** and **J&C RV Park (409-985-3638)** as well as a golf course, marina, boat ramps, and miles and miles of free roadside fishing levees from which anglers can take redfish, drum, speckled trout, croakers, and other fish. This is also an excellent crabbing area year-round.

Roy E. Larson Sandyland Sanctuary
Six miles of trails through 2,200 acres of pine and hardwood forest. The creek offers an easy 1-day canoe trip. **The sanctuary is 25 miles north of Beaumont, outside Silsbee on State Hwy. 327; 409-385-4135.**

RV Parks
Lazy L Campground has tent sites and RV sites with full hookups **(west of Port Arthur at Farm Road 365 and I-10, 409-794-2985). East Lucas RV Park** offers RV spaces on shaded grounds **(2590 E. Lucas Dr. off U.S. Hwy. 69 on the outskirts of Beaumont, 409-899-9209). Oak Leaf Park KOA** offers RV sites and cabins **(off I-10 in Orange, 409-886-4082).**

Sabine Lake
At the common mouth of the Sabine and Neches Rivers. The main body of the lake is 19 miles long and 7.5 miles wide at its greatest width. There is fishing from 2-mile-long levees for saltwater speckled trout, redfish, flounder, and other species. Crabbing is also

popular here. **Accessible from Port Arthur and Orange on State Hwy. 87; richmond@iamerica.net; www.pwpd.com.**

Sea Rim State Park

A total of 15,000 acres of marshland with 5 miles of coastline makes this park one of the most popular in the state for airboat riding. It is a birder's paradise and a photographer's dream, with nature trails, beachfront, and easy access to the marsh. There is camping, fishing, and swimming here, but Sea Rim is seen best in an airboat or a marsh buggy. **On the Bolivar Peninsula about 14 miles southwest of Port Arthur via State Hwy. 87; www.tpwd.state.tx.us/park/searim/searim.htm.**

Tyrrell Park

A 10-acre garden center with a Japanese garden, rose garden, azalea wall, and display plantings. Also includes 500 acres of woodland with a golf course, playground, archery, and bridle and hiking trails, plus opportunities for jogging, biking, bird-watching, and wildlife photography. **6090 Tyrrell Park Rd., off State Hwy. 124, in Beaumont; 409-842-3135.**

Village Creek State Park

A 942-acre park with tent and RV sites, 10 miles of hiking trails, a playground, and a canoe launch. Village Creek is one of the few undammed streams in East Texas. **Off State Hwy. 96 in Lumberton, 12 miles north of Beaumont; 409-755-7322; www.pwd.state.tx.us/park/park/village/village.htm.**

Where to Eat

Beaumont

In Beaumont, **Don's Seafood** is my pick for Cajun and Creole seafood **(2290 South I-10, 409-842-0686).**

Sartin's is another notable seafood restaurant in Beaumont **(6725 Eastex Freeway, 409-892-6771).** **Patillo's BBQ** is an informal over-the-counter place with two locations **(2775 Washington Blvd., 409-833-3154, and 610 N. 11th St., 409-832-2572).** The **Green Beanery Cafe** is where the ladies eat while they're shopping in Old Town Beaumont **(2121 McFaddin Ave., 409-833-5913).**

David's Upstairs is tricky to find, but offers imaginative continental cuisine (above the Gaylynn Theater at **11th St. and Calder Ave., 409-898-0214**). Then, of course, there are the famous **Texas Pig Stands** (in Beaumont, the one still open today is at **612 Washington Blvd., 409-835-5153**).

Port Arthur

Percy's Cafe serves up shrimp gumbo and chicken-fried steak, and displays John Wayne collectibles **(5891 Jade Ave.). Charlie's** serves up "boudain balls" and live music at dinnertime **(8901 U.S. Hwy. 69).** **Ester's Seafood and Oyster Bar** is on a barge **at the foot of Rainbow Bridge off State Hwy. 87; 409-962-6288.**

Channel Inn is a commercial fisher's answer to an eating place. They offer what they call "platter service" here, which is all you can eat from platters of crabs, frog legs, catfish, stuffed crab, fried shrimp, and gumbo. **In Sabine Pass, about a dozen miles south of Port Arthur, at 5157 S. Gulfway Dr.; 409-971-2400.**

Dorothy's Front Porch specializes in catfish, cooked just about any way you like and a couple of ways you might not have thought of. **In Nederland, 5 miles northwest of Port Arthur on U.S. Hwy. 69/287, at 119 Holmes Rd.; 409-722-1472.**

Orange

Someplace Special has some of the best soups, salads, and sandwiches in the area. Ask about the sandwich of the day. **Bates Plaza, at 6521 I-10; 409-883-8605.**

Where to Stay

Aside from the Hiltons, the Holiday Inns, the Roadrunner, and the Red Carpets, the Golden Triangle has more than its share of local establishments where you can spend the night. If you are not prone to reservations, it shouldn't be difficult to find a clean motel along I-10. However, if you are more into local flavor, you might like Beaumont's first bed-and-breakfast, the **Grand Duerr Manor,** a New Orleans–style southern mansion that will make you feel right at home **(2298 McFaddin Ave., 409-833-9600).** Another choice would be the **Cajun Cabins (on Pleasure Island at 1900 State Hwy. 82, 409-982-6050).**

Corpus Christi and the Middle Coast

The state's earliest ports were in the middle coastal area between Freeport and Corpus Christi, including Matagorda, Palacios, Point Comfort, Port Lavaca, Indianola, and Port O'Connor. The latter community was where deadly Hurricane Carla came ashore back in 1961, bringing destruction to the coast from Port O'Connor to Galveston.

Indianola is another memorable place along the Texas Middle Coast. Many of the early German immigrants to Texas arrived by boat at Indianola, then traveled on foot to the Texas Hill Country to establish new homes. Others built their homes and communities along the coast, but moved inland after discovering the horrors of Gulf Coast hurricanes. Some homes now in inland cities like Cuero and Victoria were actually moved there intact from Indianola. The only evidence left at the original site of Indianola today indicating that anybody ever lived there is a monument on the beach that honors French explorer René Robert Cavelier, Sieur de la Salle, who proclaimed this region French property back in 1682. Even the monument is not so easy to find anymore, blending in with the sandy beaches and the murky Gulf Coast waters.

The most dynamic city on the Middle Coast is Corpus Christi. The Corpus Christi coastal area doesn't live up to its marketing hype as the Texas Riviera, but it is a fun and pleasant place to spend time. A drive over the Harbor Bridge at Corpus Christi reveals a sparkling city where sailboat masts mix with downtown skyscrapers. Nearby Mustang Island and northern Padre Island offer many miles of sandy Gulf beaches—the best, by far, along the Texas coast.

Corpus Christi is windy, with an average year-round wind speed of 12 miles per hour. That's why you'll find so many sailboats in Corpus Christi Bay. Average temperatures range from 46 to 67 degrees in January and from 76 to 94 degrees in July. The annual rainfall is about 27 inches. Over the last 90 years, only two hurricanes have struck Corpus—one in 1919 and the other, Hurricane Celia, in 1970. I made it to Corpus to cover that hurricane for TV, and I bunked in the top floor of the Hilton Hotel until the glass shattered and the storm's waters ran me off.

Attracted by Corpus Christi's cultural appeal and mild climate, increasing numbers of "snowbirds" are settling into the area each winter. It's still not as popular as the Rio Grande Valley, but it has become a comfortable alternative. Retirement magazines cite the Corpus area as one of the best places in the United States to spend the winter.

Mount Rushmore sculptor Gutzon Borglum designed the 2-mile downtown seawall that runs along Shoreline Boulevard, with a sidewalk and benches along the top and wide steps leading down to the water. The sidewalk is a favorite track for joggers, roller skaters, and bicyclists, as well as strollers.

Getting Around

Gray Line Tours (361-289-7113) offers a city tour that takes 2.5 hours, or a loop tour that lasts about 4 hours and goes around the bay through Padre Island, Port Aransas, and Aransas Pass.

Corpus Christi Yacht Basin. Photo courtesy of Texas Highways *magazine.*

Visitor Information

Corpus Christi Convention and Visitors Bureau

1201 N. Shoreline Blvd., Corpus Christi, 78401; 1-800-766-BEACH, 361-881-1888, fax 361-888-5627; www.cctexas.org, www.corpuschristi.com.

Tourist Information Center

In Nueces River Park at the Nueces River crossing of I-37 at the west edge of Corpus Christi. 361-241-1464.

Visitor Center

9405 S. Padre Island Dr.; 361-937-2621.

Major Attractions

Padre Island National Seashore

Each end of 110-mile-long Padre Island is developed with parks and resorts, but in between, Padre Island National Seashore has preserved an unblemished 80-mile stretch. The southern end of Padre Island—South Padre Island—is where most of the action is on the beaches along the southern Texas coast. South Padre is covered in detail in The Lower Coast chapter.

The northern end of Padre Island—North Padre Island—is relatively more "undiscovered" and private and, in spots, offers more solitude for coastal visitors. There are two approaches by motor vehicle from the north end: a causeway goes from Corpus Christi to North Padre Island (Park Road 22), and another route goes from Port Aransas down Mustang Island to North Padre Island (Park Road 53).

The **visitor center** is located several miles south of the junction of Park Roads 22 and 53 **(9405 S. Padre Island Dr., 361-937-2621).** Also in this area is **Malaquite Beach,** the only beach area in the national seashore that has lifeguards, though swimming is permitted anywhere along the Gulf. A paved campground is located a half mile north of Malaquite Beach and has fresh water, rest rooms, showers, and a dump station.

No-fee primitive camping is allowed on the beach south of the visitor center. Campfires are allowed between the dunes and the beach. **South Beach, Bird Island Basin,** and **Yarborough Pass** are areas along the shoreline where no-fee primitive camping is permitted, but in some areas you must hike or travel in a four-wheel-drive vehicle to get there. Camping is

Getting There

Corpus Christi is easily reachable on major highways from both Houston and San Antonio. From Houston take U.S. Hwy. 59 southwest for 129 miles to Victoria, where it intersects with U.S. Hwy. 77. Then take Hwy. 77 south for 74 miles to Robstown, where you pick up I-37 to Corpus Christi, 15 miles to the east. From San Antonio, I-37 takes you directly to Corpus Christi; it's about 140 miles. **Corpus Christi International Airport** is located about 15 minutes southwest of downtown via Agnes Street. American, Continental, Delta, Southwest, and Conquest airlines operate daily flights from there to several other Texas cities as well as to selected destinations in the United States and Mexico.

allowed on the beaches only, not on the dunes or in the grasslands, and there is a 14-day limit.

The paved road that leads into the park ends just after the visitor center. Beyond this point, you can drive only on the beach—and after 4 or 5 miles, you'll want a four-wheel-drive vehicle. Only serious hikers should attempt backpacking the entire length of the island. There is no fresh water and no shade along the way. You're allowed to hike only on the beach, and that makes for slow walking. A more reasonable goal might be to hike to **Yarborough Pass** at milepost 15, or to **Cuba Island,** a tiny offshore island on the Laguna Madre side at Milepost 21. If all this sounds intriguing to you, don't forget sunscreen, insect repellent, a broad-brimmed hat, sunglasses, a backpacking stove, tent, food, and at least a gallon of water per person per day. The most popular backpacking season is winter, when it is somewhat cooler.

The national seashore has one boat launch: at **Bird Island Basin** on Laguna Madre, which is the shallow saltwater lagoon that separates Padre Island from the Texas mainland. This is also a popular spot for serious windsurfers. A 7-day pass into Padre Island National Seashore costs $5 per vehicle. For further information on swimming beaches, camping, or trails,

contact **Padre Island National Seashore at 9405 S. Padre Island Dr., Corpus Christi, 78418; 361-949-8068; www.nps.gov.pais.**

Seeing and Doing

Gardens and Arboreta
Corpus Christi Botanical Gardens
One hundred acres of gardens along the banks of Oso Creek. A good place for bird-watching. **8500 S. Staples, at Yorktown; 361-882-2100.**

Museums and Historic Sites
Centennial House
The oldest house in Corpus Christi. It was built in 1849 and used as a hospital by both Union and Confederate forces in the Civil War—at different times, of course. **411 N. Upper Broadway; 361-992-6003.**

Columbus Fleet
In 1992 the Spanish government built full-scale replicas of the *Niña, Pinta,* and *Santa Maria* to commemorate the 500th anniversary of the voyage by Columbus to the New World. The three ships, smaller than you might expect, are open for tours at Cargo Dock 1 at the **Port of Corpus Christi, 1900 N. Chaparral; 361-883-2862.**

Heritage Park
A collection of eight historic local homes that have been moved to this spot. Four of the homes are open for public tours. **Along N. Chaparral between Fitzgerald and Hughes; 361-883-0639.**

International Kite Museum
What better place for a kite museum than in the windiest city in Texas? It's a unique museum at the Best Western Sandy Shores Resort, on Corpus Christi Beach. **3200 Surfside; 361-883-7456.**

USS Lexington
The 910-foot-long, 16-deck aircraft carrier USS *Lexington* now serves as a floating naval museum permanently docked at the south end of Corpus Christi Beach. It was known as the Blue Ghost by the Japanese

in World War II because it kept showing up in battle after having been reported sunk. **2914 N. Shoreline Blvd.; 1-800-LADYLEX, 361-888-4873; lady lex@usslexington.com; www.usslexington. com.**

Other Sights

Harbor Bridge
This bridge, 620 feet long and 250 feet high, spans the ship channel and connects downtown Corpus Christi with much of the rest of the city. Built in 1959 at a cost of $20 million, the bridge has a pedestrian walkway with about the best bird's-eye view of the beach, the city, and the whole area.

Parks

Texas State Aquarium
An attractive addition to Corpus Christi Beach. It is the largest seashore aquarium in the country, featuring more than 2,000 marine animals in 350,000 gallons of seawater. Big attractions here are the rare Ridley sea turtles. **2710 N. Shoreline Blvd.; 1-800-477-GULF, 361-881-1200.**

Tours

Flagship and Gulf Clipper Sightseeing Cruises
Morning, afternoon, evening, and moonlight cruises on a scaled-down version of an old Mississippi showboat; a 90-minute tour of the bay and the harbor. **361-643-7128.**

Wagering

Corpus Christi Greyhound Race Track
Year-round racing on a 60-acre facility, plus simulcast races from other tracks. **5302 Leopard St.; 361-289-9333.**

Festivals and Events

April

Buccaneer Days
A 10-day festival commemorating the discovery of Corpus Christi Bay in 1519.

June

Fiesta de Corpus Christi
A celebration of the city's Hispanic heritage. **Water Garden in Bayfront Park.**

July

Texas Jazz Festival
Fourth of July celebration featuring 3 days of jazz performances around the city.

September–October

Bayfest
Fall festival at the **Bayfront Arts and Science Park.**

December

Harbor Lights
A celebration of Christmas, Corpus Christi–style, with a bayfront parade and the lighting of the boats.

Recreation

Diving
There are a number of jetty complexes in Aransas Bay, some 30 miles north of Corpus Christi, and at Port Mansfield, 80 miles south of Corpus Christi, that offer artificial reef viewing, as do some offshore oil rigs. You can rent equipment, take a guided trip, or arrange overnight dive trips at **Copeland Dive Shop (4041 S. Padre Island Dr., 361-854-1135).**

Fishing
Corpus Christi is loaded with fishing piers and jetties, making fishing an easy sport here. Surf fishing is good from the beaches of Padre and Mustang Islands. For wade fishers, the Laguna Madre and Cayo del Oso, near the Naval Air Station (Ocean Dr. and Ave. J, east of Corpus Christi), are both excellent. Party boats for bay fishing operate from the People's Street T-Head at Corpus Christi Marina in the heart of downtown, and usually run 4-hour trips during the day. Charter boats are also available for a price. Most deep-sea charters operate out of Port Aransas. You can get a list of party and charter boats and fishing guides from the

Corpus Christi Convention and Visitors Bureau (1-800-766-BEACH, 361-881-1888).

Parks and Camping

City Parks

Ten major city parks offer a variety of outdoor attractions and facilities, including picnicking, playgrounds, swimming, tennis, softball, and other sports. This includes **Cole Park (on the bay front at 1526 Ocean Dr.)** and the **Hans A. Suter Wildlife Park,** which features a viewing tower for bird-watching, a boardwalk, hiking and biking facilities, and a jogging trail **(along Oso Bay, 361-884-7275).**

Corpus Christi Beach

Old-timers still call this North Beach and remember the 1930s when there were casinos and amusement parks here. Hotels, motels, and condos now line much of the beachfront here. **North of downtown Corpus Christi, off U.S. Hwy. 181 across Harbor Bridge.**

Corpus Christi Marina

Hundreds of pleasure craft moor here. Water-sports equipment can be rented in season. Excursion boats and fishing boats all dock here. It offers an excellent view of sailboat races Wednesday evenings. Near the heart of downtown. **400 Lawrence St.; 361-882-7333.**

County Parks

Among the county parks are **John J. Sablatura Park,** with picnic, barbecue, and camping facilities and a small zoo **(near Banquete on State Hwy. 44); J. P. Luby Surf Park,** with a surf pier **(on Park Road 22); Padre Balli Park,** with overnight camping, covered picnic areas, a pavilion, and a 1,200-foot fishing pier **(15820 Park Road 22, 361-949-8121); Packery Channel Park,** an excellent day-use park with good fishing **(on Padre Island near the junction of State Hwy. 361 and Park Road 22); Padre Island Park,** with a bathhouse, sandy swimming beaches, overnight camping, fishing pier, and a small beachcomber's museum in the park office **(on the Gulf side from Park Road 22);** and **Port Aransas Park (at the northeast end of Mustang Island, on the Gulf side).** For park information,

call the **Nueces County Parks and Recreation Department** at **361-949-8122.**

Lake Corpus Christi State Park

A 14,000-acre lake featuring campsites, screened shelters, fishing, swimming, and boating. **The park is 35 miles northwest of Corpus Christi, near Mathis; 361-547-2635; tpwd.state.tx.us/park/ lakecorp/lakecorp.htm.**

Mustang Island State Park

A total of 3,400 acres of sand dunes, sea oats, and beach morning glory with 5 miles of Gulf beach frontage. Probably the best camping, surfing, fishing, swimming, and shell collecting in the area. Also, there is a large beach area for primitive camping, bird-watching, and walking on nature trails. **Ten miles east of Corpus Christi, near Port Aransas; 361-749-4573; www.tpwd.state.tx.us/park/mustang/mustang.htm.**

Shoreline birds at Mustang Island State Park near Corpus Christi.

Welder Wildlife Refuge

The largest privately endowed wildlife refuge in the world; tours by reservation. **Off U.S. Hwy. 77 in Sinton, about 25 miles north of Corpus Christi; 361-364-2643.**

Sailing

Corpus Christi Bay and Laguna Madre are excellent places to learn how to sail. The **Corpus Christi International School of Sailing** offers instructions for sailing every weekend; for more intensive instruction, there are 3- and 5-day courses **(on the L-head at Corpus Christi Marina, 361-881-8503)**.

Windsurfing

The U.S. Open Pro Am windsurfing tournament is held annually on Corpus Christi Bay. The wind is almost always blowing somewhere around the bay. The most popular windsurfing spot within the city limits is Oleander Point at the south end of Cole Park **(1526 Ocean Dr., 361-884-7275)**. Farther east along Ocean Drive are Ropes Park and Poenisch Park, also good places to windsurf. Corpus Christi Beach, at the north end of Harbor Bridge, gets its share of windsurfers as well.

Rare whooping cranes have made Aransas National Wildlife Refuge famous. Photo courtesy of Texas Highways magazine.

Where to Eat

Catfish Charlie's

Although the only seafood on the menu is shrimp, oysters, and catfish, low prices and Cajun cooking make this place noteworthy. **5830 McArdle Rd.; 361-993-0363.**

Che Bello

Homesick New Yorkers will surely be appeased at this downtown eatery. **320 Williams St.; 361-882-8832.**

Elmo's City Diner and Oyster Bar

This 1950s-style diner serves up blue-plate specials and seafood. **622 N. Water St.; 361-883-1643.**

Joe Cotton's Barbecue

Many barbecue experts say this is, without a doubt, the best barbecue in the South. **Eight miles southeast of Corpus Christi at Robstown on Business U.S. Hwy. 87, across the street from the John Deere tractor dealer; 361-767-9973.**

The Lighthouse Restaurant and Oyster Bar

Has a terrific view of the bay. At the end of the Lawrence Street T-Head. **444 N. Shoreline Blvd.; 361-883-3982.**

Old Mexico

You'll find the city's best all-around Mexican food at this local operation, run by the same family for 35 years. **3329 Leopard St., at Nueces Bay Blvd.; 361-883-6461.**

Snoopy's Pier

The menu is simple. The decor is "old fisherman's hangout," and the food is pleasant. You can enjoy an evening breeze and watch the sun set over the water. **13313 S. Padre Island Dr.; 361-949-8815.**

Water Street Seafood Company

A fancy seafood place with fancy food. **309 N. Water St.; 361-882-8684.**

Where to Stay

There are a number of fine places to bed down for the night, including **Best Western Sandy Shores Resort (3200 Surfside Dr. near the Texas State Aquarium, 361-883-7456)** and the **Holiday Inn– North Padre Island (15202 Windward Dr., 361-949-8041)**. The **Corpus Christi Convention and Visitors Bureau** has a list of agencies in the Corpus Christi area that handle condominium and beachhouse rentals **(1201 N. Shoreline Blvd., 1-800-766-BEACH, 361-881-8888)**.

Towns in the Area

Port Aransas, Rockport, and Fulton

These three communities are popular fishing and bird-watching sites along the Middle Coast. In summer, visitors swell the population by the thousands. The communities are located along the Great Texas Coastal Birding Trail, which extends up the entire Texas Gulf Coast from Brownsville northward to Orange.

GETTING THERE

To get to any of these three places, start in the town of Aransas Pass, which is some 24 miles northeast of Corpus Christi. (From Corpus Christi, take State Hwy. 35 for about 12 miles to Gregory, then turn east onto State Hwy. 361 and go another 12 miles to Aransas Pass.) To get to Port Aransas from Aransas Pass: Simply stay on Hwy. 361 and take the free car ferry across to Port Aransas. To get to Rockport and Fulton from Aransas Pass: Go north on State Hwy. 35 for about 15 miles to Rockport and an additional 3 miles to Fulton.

VISITOR INFORMATION

Port Aransas Chamber of Commerce, 421 W. Cotter Ave., Port Aransas, 78373; 361-749-5919, 1-800-452-6278. Also, **Rockport–Fulton Area Chamber of Commerce, 404 Broadway St., Rockport, 78382; 361-729-9952; www.rock port-fulton.org.**

SEEING AND DOING

Texas Maritime Museum

Displays showing the rich maritime heritage of Texas from Spanish exploration to the search for offshore oil and gas. **1202 Navigation Circle, near the center of Rockport; 361-729-1271.**

FESTIVALS AND EVENTS

March—Fulton Oysterfest

A gumbo cook-off, plus oyster-shucking and oyster-eating contests. **At Fulton harbor.**

October—Rockport Seafair

A land parade, boat regattas, water show, and other water-related events honoring the coast, its industry, and its critters. **Downtown and at Rockport harbor.**

RECREATION

Aransas National Wildlife Refuge

Noted as a principal wintering ground for the whoop-

ing crane. The U.S. Fish and Wildlife Service runs this place as a preserve for many endangered critters that fly and walk. About 300 species of birds have been seen here, along with plenty of white-tailed deer, raccoon, and javelina. November through March is the best period for visiting, and the best way to see the whoopers is on a chartered boat that will take you out to where they and other birds nest. **Captain Ted's Whooping Crane Tours** makes two trips daily (from the Sandollar Pavilion at **918 N. Fulton Beach Rd. in Fulton, 361-729-2381**). The refuge is **35 miles northeast of Rockport off State Hwy. 35; 361-286-3559; www.refugenet.com/aransas.htm.**

Birding

Texas has four of the country's top twelve bird-watching sites, and the Port Aransas–Rockport–Fulton area is one of the best. Local and migrating birds find the wetlands a perfect habitat. Vegetation pockets attract hummingbirds as they migrate in the spring and fall. Brochures listing species of birds that can be viewed here are available from the **Port Aransas Chamber of Commerce (361-749-5919).**

Connie Hagar Cottage Sanctuary

The home and gardens of the lady who first discovered that this part of Texas was a paradise for bird watchers. I met Connie Hagar just before she died, and never have I met a kinder person. She only wanted to let the world know that "birds are beautiful." As long as she could walk, she fed birds every day outside her tiny cottage; she loved them and they loved her. And so did the community of Rockport. A section of wetlands near her house has been named the Connie Hagar Wildlife Refuge. The cottage is **at 1st and Church Sts. in Rockport.**

Copano Bay Causeway State Park

Good fishing pier on the old highway that used to span Copano Bay, **immediately north of Fulton on State Hwy. 35; 361-790-9111.**

Goose Island State Park

Three hundred acres located on a peninsula between Copano and St. Charles Bays. Good fishing, and the site of what some people say is the largest oak tree in Texas; they say it's a thousand years old. This is a huge tree—35 feet around—but communities all over the state claim the largest tree. Still, the Goose Island landmark, officially known as Big Tree, is impressive. **Twelve miles north of Rockport off State Hwy. 35; 361-729-2858.**

Mustang Island State Park

A total of 3,400 acres along 5 miles of shoreline, with camping, surfing, fishing, swimming, birding, and shell collecting. **Fourteen miles south of Port Aransas on State Hwy. 361; 361-749-4573; www.tpwd.state.tx.us/park/mustang/mustang.htm.**

WHERE TO EAT

Boiling Pot

Provides crab, shrimp, and crawfish, all dumped on butcher paper; eat to your heart's delight. **Fulton Beach Rd. just north of Fulton Mansion; 361-729-6972.**

Charlotte Plummer's Sea Fare

Serves seafood in a family-style setting—nothing fancy, just good seafood. **Fulton Beach Rd. and Cactus; 361-729-1185.**

WHERE TO STAY

The **Rockport–Fulton Area Chamber of Commerce (404 Broadway St., Rockport, 78382; 361-729-6445; www.rockport-fulton.org.)** offers a list of apartments, condos, and homes that are in a rental pool.

Laguna Reef Hotel

Offers hotel rooms and condo apartments, plus a 1,000-foot lighted fishing pier. **1021 S. Water St., Rockport; 361-729-1742.**

Sandollar Resort

Forty-five motel rooms, plus a playground, marina, and a lighted fishing pier. **Five miles north of Rockport on State Hwy. 35; 361-729-2381.**

Tarpon Inn

This vintage wooden structure, dating back to 1886, looks more like a seacoast motel nowadays. Franklin D. Roosevelt used to fly in here secretly to get away from the complexities of life as president and to fish. Cake-mix king Duncan Hines spent his honeymoon here as well. **In Port Aransas; 361-749-5555.**

The Lower Coast

There are adventurers today who still believe buried treasure is to be found on the Lower Coast of Texas. In the 1980s I spent some time with a crop duster named Jeff Burke, who insisted he knew where Spanish gold was hidden in the shallow waters off South Padre Island. We flew along the coast and Jeff pointed out silhouettes of sunken ships, and I believed he might be on to something. When last I saw Jeff, he was still looking for buried treasure.

In the sixteenth and seventeenth centuries, Spaniards spent time in and around the Lower Coast. The area had a bad reputation among ship captains, and history records that at least twenty Spanish galleons ran aground in the uncertain waters. All of them carried valuables of one sort or other, and many stories have been told over the years about the current whereabouts of those valuables.

In 1847 a man named John Singer built a driftwood home on the beach about 25 miles from the southern tip of Padre Island. When the Civil War broke out, he is said to have buried $65,000 in gold coins and jewelry in the sand dunes and fled. When the war was over, he returned, but never found the loot. Singer went on to develop the Singer sewing machine and turned that discovery into a fortune. But treasure hunters continued to come to the coast with their shovels and their metal detectors, hoping to find John Singer's first fortune.

Padre Island is only a few blocks wide from east to west, but is more than 100 miles long from south to north. The entire island reaches 110 miles from Port Isabel all the way north to Corpus Christi, but there is no developed road except at the two ends. There are spots where the Gulf waters cut through the island, and there is no bridge or ferry between the northern and southern parts of Padre.

During most of the 1900s, the southern end of Padre Island—South Padre Island—remained untouched and undeveloped. That's all changed now. South Padre has become a major resort, with hotels, high-rise condos, and commercialism as far as the eye

can see. I'm not complaining, mind you. I'm just pointing out that the southern end of Padre Island is different from the northern end, which is relatively quieter and less developed. Of course there's that big stretch in the middle that's not developed at all and that makes up the Padre Island National Seashore (described in detail in the Corpus Christi and the Middle Coast chapter).

But if you prefer activity to solitude, and people to birds, South Padre is the place to be, and offers the best beaches in the state, with white sand and blue water. South Padre is known for water sports, including jet-skiing, fishing (bay, surf, and deep-sea), sailing, windsurfing, and parasailing. A lot of tourists also come to the Lower Coast for bicycling, jogging, sunning, shelling, and horseback riding on the beach.

Port Isabel is the gateway to South Padre Island. The area was a supply base for General Zachary Taylor's army in the Mexican War. In 1848, gold seekers from the eastern United States landed at Port Isabel to begin an overland journey to California.

Gray Line Tours (956-761-4343) offers a tour of Port Isabel and South Padre Island; also daily sightseeing and shopping tours to nearby Matamoros, Mexico, and weekend tours to Monterrey, Mexico.

Visitor Information

South Padre Island Visitor Center

Information on accommodations and activities. **600**

Padre Blvd.; 1-800-SOPADRE; www.sopadre.com.

Visitor Center
421 Queen Isabella Blvd., Port Isabel; 1-800-527-6102, 956-943-2262; www.portisabel.org.

Seeing and Doing

Museums and Historic Sites

Port Isabel Lighthouse State Historic Site
This lighthouse built in 1853 was in use until the early 1900s. Today it offers a wonderful overview of the city, the Queen Isabella Causeway, and South Padre Island. **On State Hwy. 100 at the causeway.**

Sea Turtles, Inc.
A living museum to a kindly old lady named Ila Loetscher, who dedicated her life to caring for endangered Ridley sea turtles. The museum has educational shows daily and some remarkable pictures of the giant turtles. Ila was something of a phenomenon herself. Not only did she care for the turtles that were, incidentally, about as big as she was, but she dressed them in doll clothes and gave each of them its own name. I thought she was just another eccentric Texas

> ### Getting There
> Port Isabel and South Padre Island are near Brownsville. **From Brownsville:** Travel 23 miles northeast on State Hwy. 48 to Port Isabel. From Port Isabel, drive across the 2.2-mile Queen Isabella Causeway to get onto South Padre. **From Corpus Christi:** Take I-37 west for 15 miles, then U.S. Hwy. 77 south for about 143 miles, then State Hwy. 100 east for 23 miles to Port Isabel.

character back when I first met her. I didn't realize she was probably more instrumental than anyone else in saving the Ridley turtles of Texas. **5805 Gulf Blvd., South Padre Island; 956-761-1720; www.south padre-island.com/seaturtle/sti.html.**

Other Sights

Queen Isabella Causeway
This 2.2-mile-long causeway across Laguna Madre Bay between Port Isabel and South Padre Island is the longest bridge in Texas. It's the only bridge I've ever seen that posts warning signs for motorists to watch out

Texas's southern tip, where the Rio Grande meets the Gulf of Mexico. Photo courtesy of Texas Highways magazine.

for flying birds. At the center the span is 73 feet above mean high tide, allowing ships to pass beneath. It was built to withstand much higher than hurricane-force winds. About 5 million vehicles cross it each year. Some years ago, nature enthusiasts were up in arms because a lot of seagulls were being hit and killed by autos crossing the causeway. The bridge offered great wind lifts for the birds, so they naturally gathered there. The community decided it couldn't keep the birds away, so it did the next best thing: it put up signs warning motorists to watch out for the gulls.

The Sons of the Beach

In 1987, during spring break from school, more than 5,000 volunteers came to South Padre Island and built the world's longest sand castle, a structure more than 2 miles in length. The builders became known as the Sons of the Beach. On most summer Saturdays, the SOBs can be found building sand castles with towers, staircases, and gravity-defying arches. It is a sight to behold. **At the Holiday Inn Beach Resort, 100 Padre Blvd.; 956-761-5943; www.unlitter.com.**

Parks

Jeremiah's Landing

A water park that provides a great way to free yourself from all that salt water you got on the beach. Open daily from Memorial Day to Labor Day. **100 Padre Blvd., South Padre Island; 956-761-2131.**

Festivals and Events

March

Spring Break

A big beach bash for tens of thousands of college students from all over the country. There is a big effort to keep everyone happy so they'll come back next year, but there is also a big effort to keep the party safe and sensible. **Various locations on South Padre Island.**

May

South Padre Island Winter Park Blow Out

The largest amateur windsurfing event in the country, this tournament draws boardsailing enthusiasts from all over to compete for trophies in slalom, triangle, long distance, and wave slalom races. **Various locations.**

August

Texas International Fishing Tournament

The second oldest fishing competition on the Gulf Coast, with trophies for bay and offshore fishing. **South Point Marine in Port Isabel.**

October

Lone Star Vegetarian Chili Cookoff

Cooking competition put on by the Rio Grande Valley Vegetarian Society. **South Padre Island Convention Center.**

Recreation

Birding

Laguna Atascosa National Wildlife Refuge

The 46,000-acre refuge marks the southern end of the Central Flyway for birds, with 7,000 acres of marshland. Thousands of waterfowl winter here. **About 17 miles northwest of Port Isabel; 956-748-3607.**

Fishing

From South Padre Island's beaches, piers, and jetties, you may catch redfish, speckled and sand trout, flounder, croaker, skipjack, and drum. Charter boats offer bay and deep-sea fishing for tarpon, sailfish, marlin, kingfish, and others. These include **Captain Jason Ray's Charters (206 W. Swordfish St., 956-761-5453);** the **Island Princess (221 W. Swordfish St., 956-761-7818);** and **Osprey Fishing Trips (1 Padre Blvd., 956-761-6655).**

Horseback Riding

It's great sport in these parts. You can take a romantic horseback ride along a secluded beach and watch the morning glories bloom. Horses are usually available from sunrise to sunset at **Island Equestrian Center, 1 mile west of the Convention Center on Padre Blvd.; 956-761-4677.**

Parks and Camping

Isla Blanca Park provides a mile of clean, white beach for water-related activities, with a fishing jetty, restaurant, full-service marina, and boat ramp **(on the southernmost tip of the island, on Park Road 100, 956-761-5493, www.cameron-county-park.com/iblanca.html).** There is even a nondenominational church at Isla Blanca, the Chapel by the Sea, plus camping facilities. **Andy Bowie Park** features the popular Laguna Madre Nature Trail and beachfront picnic pavilions, and no-fee primitive camping **(3.5 miles north of the causeway at 2300 Padre Blvd., 956-761-2639, www.cameron-county-parks.com/atwood.html).**

Where to Eat

South Padre Island

Blackbeard's
Well known by the beach crowd for its burgers and sandwiches, but they also serve excellent seafood. **103 E. Saturn Ln., off Padre Blvd., 2 miles north of the causeway; 956-761-2962.**

Jake's
Offers seafood, steak, and some Mexican food at moderate prices. **2500 Padre Blvd.; 956-761-5012.**

Ro Van's Bakery
If you're looking for an early-morning breakfast, check out Ro Van's. It opens at 6 A.M. with a variety of breakfasts and baked goods. **5300 Padre Blvd.; 956-761-6972.**

Scampi's
It's an Italian restaurant with a name that, translated, means "shrimp," so take your choice: seafood or pasta. **206 W. Aries Dr. at Laguna; 956-761-1755.**

Port Isabel

Cross-Eyed Pelican
Serves up some good seafood. **823 Garcia St.; 956-943-8923.**

Grill Room at the Pantry
Above-average seafood place in cozy quarters. **708 Padre Blvd. at Franke Plaza; 956-761-9331.**

Mexquito
Garcia serves up Mexican-style seafood. **802 S. Garcia St.; 956-943-6106.**

Pirate's Landing
Good seafood. **100 N. Garcia St.; 956-943-3663.**

The Yacht Club
It hasn't been a yacht club since the depression, but it still takes on the air of a stately club. Food is good and moderately priced. **700 Yturria St.; 956-943-1301.**

Where to Stay

There are more condominium units on South Padre Island than hotel or motel rooms, and many of the condo apartments are available for rent. The **South Padre Island Convention and Visitors Bureau (600 Padre Blvd., 956-761-4412)** has information. Other accommodations include:

South Padre Island
Bahia Mar Resort and Conference Center (6300 Padre Blvd., 1-800-997-2373, res@sbahia mar.com, www.bahiamar.com); Sheraton South Padre Island Beach Resort (310 Padre Blvd., 1-800-325-3535, fax 956-761-6570); Radisson Resort South Padre Island (500 Padre Blvd., 956-761-6511, www.raddisonspi.com); and **Holiday Inn Beach Resort (100 Padre Blvd., 956-761-5401),** where the Sons of the Beach gather regularly to build sand castles (see under Seeing and Doing).

Port Isabel

Yacht Club Hotel
Built in the 1920s and restored with the comforts of today. **700 Iturria; 956-943-1301; jfair@santo cristo.com; www.the-yacht-club.com.**

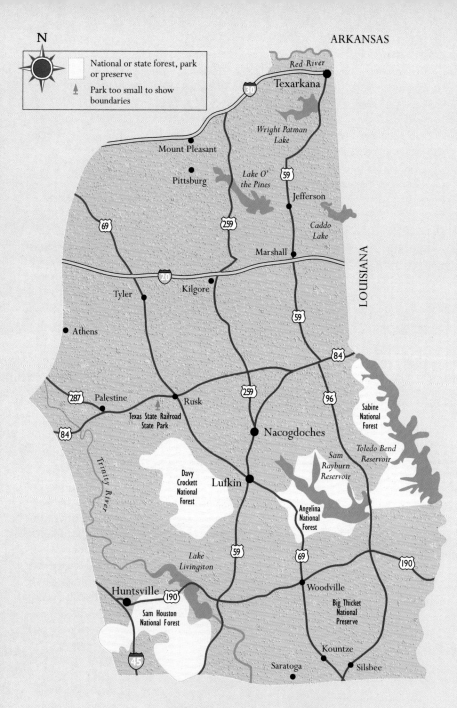

ARKANSAS

N

National or state forest, park
or preserve

Park too small to show
boundaries

Red River

Texarkana

30

Wright Patman
Lake

Mount Pleasant

Lake O'
the Pines

59

Pittsburg

Jefferson

259

Caddo
Lake

69

Marshall

20

Kilgore

Tyler

59

Athens

287   Palestine

Rusk

84

84

Texas State Railroad
State Park

259

96

Sabine
National
Forest

Nacogdoches

Toledo Bend
Reservoir

Trinity River

Davy
Crockett
National
Forest

Lufkin

Sam
Rayburn
Reservoir

Angelina
National
Forest

Lake
Livingston

59

69

190

Huntsville

190

Woodville

Sam Houston
National Forest

Big Thicket
National
Preserve

45

Kountze

Saratoga

Silsbee

LOUISIANA

*East Texas
and the Pineywoods*

East Texas
and the Pineywoods

Reflections in an East Texas lake, near Alto in Cherokee County.

East Texas and the Pineywoods

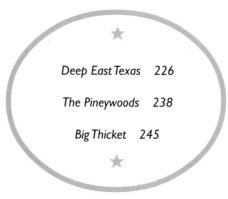

I remember the first time I ever saw East Texas. For a country boy from West Texas, it was a sight to behold. I didn't know Texas had that many trees. I came from a place where people called mesquite bushes "trees," and paved their front yards with concrete and then painted it green to make it look like grass. If you are a fan of plush green grass, tall pines, and towering hardwood trees, East Texas is the place for you.

Before the 1800s most of East Texas was virgin forest inhabited by only small groups of Caddo Indians. Farming and cattle ranching later turned huge tracts of forest into prairies, but then the government got smart. National forests and preserves were set aside, and they proved to be saviors for some 750,000 acres of woodlands.

It would be impossible to list the wide variety of vegetation in East Texas. In the Big Thicket National Preserve alone, there are six forest layers and eight separate plant communities that extend from upland forests to cypress bogs. There are plant species you would never expect to find, including forty species of wild orchids and nine plants that are meat eaters. Some of the common trees in the Big Thicket include loblolly pines, magnolias, sweet gums, dogwoods, and—something you've probably never seen—swamp honeysuckle.

East Texas is also a place of wildlife. Some black bears can be found in the river bottoms. There are a lot of lakes, and a lot of expert bass fishers who take their sport seriously. East Texas is a wonderful place to do some bird-watching. The Pineywoods are a natural attraction for woodpeckers, with several kinds thriving among the tall pines and oaks. The most impressive is the red-crested pileated woodpecker, the largest and loudest woodpecker in the world; East Texans sometimes call them "peckerwoods."

Some of the things that make East Texas so attractive to travelers will run some of them off. The high humidity that keeps the forests green is unbearable during the summer months. Mosquitoes are a serious problem, and chiggers and ticks can be just as bad if you spend much time in the woods. If the lore of the Big Thicket is intriguing enough to bring you here, then the thorny bushes that give the thicket its name may be bad enough to send you away. But all those handicaps can be overcome with some advance planning. East Texas is best visited in the fall, when temperatures and rainfall are moderate. Summer is not a good time to visit. Spring is very comfortable, if you don't mind occasional thunderstorms.

Timber has been big business in this part of the country for generations. There is plenty of rain—about 60 inches annually—and the high humidity keeps the forests moist and helps prevent fires. Growth is profuse. There are huge oil and gas fields in East Texas as well.

East Texas is filled with history and with great stories. There's a town up by Caddo Lake that was named Uncertain, perhaps because its residents never could make up their minds if they were going to stay there. How about the thriving river community of Jefferson? It nearly died because it displeased an early Texas railroad tycoon—and today is better off for it. There are some legendary ghost stories from the Big Thicket that have inspired Hollywood movies. There are people tucked away in the woods and rolling hills of East Texas who will treat you like old friends, if you can find them. It's all just a matter of taking the time and looking around.

Our map of East Texas begins up in the northeast corner of the state at Texarkana and goes all the way south to within about 60 miles of Houston, covering a great swath of territory that lies within about 100 miles of the state's eastern borders. This section of the book divides East Texas into three regions (from north to south): Deep East Texas, the Pineywoods, and the Big Thicket.

Getting There

There aren't many large cities in this part of Texas, but large cities are within driving distance. From Dallas, it's only about 90 miles via I-20 and U.S. Hwy. 69 to Tyler, which leads you into Deep East Texas. It's about 100 miles or so up U.S. Hwy. 59 from Houston to the heart of the Pineywoods. Beaumont is at the southern tip of the Big Thicket.

There are major airports in the Dallas area (Dallas–Fort Worth International Airport and Dallas Love Field) and at Houston (Bush Intercontinental Airport and William P. Hobby Airport). Beaumont has Jefferson County Airport. You can arrange for charter service into smaller airports at a number of East Texas cities, such as Huntsville, Lufkin, Nacogdoches, Tyler, and Marshall. But drive into East Texas and the Pineywoods if you can, to get the real flavor of the region. Drive and take your time. You'll see some amazing scenery and meet some real friendly folks in this part of Texas.

Deep East Texas

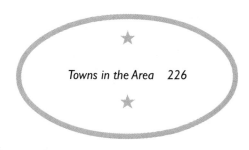

Deep East Texas is the closest you'll get to the look and feel of the Old South in Texas. The land is fertile. The hardwood trees are old and large. The people are hardworking yet laid-back and easy to like. Oil pumps the economy in this part of the state and has replaced timber as the chief money-maker ever since the Kilgore oil boom of the 1930s.

Towns in the Area

To get a feel of Deep East Texas, good places to visit include (from north to south) Texarkana, Mount Pleasant, Pittsburg, Jefferson, Marshall, Kilgore, Tyler, Athens, Rusk, and Palestine. Suggestions on places to eat and to stay are included with most of the towns.

Texarkana

Getting There: Take I-30 northeast from Dallas for about 165 miles to Texarkana. It's right on the Texas border with Arkansas. **Visitor Information: Texarkana Visitors and Convention Bureau, 819 N. State Line Dr.; 903-792-7191; www.texarkana.iamerica.net.** Also, **Travel Information Center, on I-30 just west of U.S. Hwy. 59 near the Arkansas-Texas border; 903-794-2114.**

Caddo Lake, east of Jefferson. Photo courtesy of Texas Highways magazine.

SEEING AND DOING

Four States Fair and Rodeo

Cowboys and cowgirls participate from four adjacent states: Texas, Arkansas, Oklahoma, and Louisiana. **Four States Fairground, at Loop 245 and E. 50th St. in the Arkansas part of Texarkana; 870-773-2941, fax 870-772-0713; info@fourstatesfair.com; www.fourstatesfair.com.**

Oaklawn Opry

Family entertainment every Saturday night, specializing in new and old country music. **Robison and New Boston Rds.; 903-838-3333.**

Perot Theater

A 1,600-seat neo-Renaissance theater restored to its original splendor and used now for performances of all kinds. **3rd and Main Sts., downtown; 1-800-333-0927, 903-792-4992; www.texarkanabond.com/perot.htm.**

Scott Joplin Mural

A painting that colorfully depicts the life and accomplishments of the Pulitzer Prize–winning musical pioneer who was born in Texarkana. In the first two decades of the twentieth century, Joplin was considered the king of ragtime. (His music was used in the movie *The Sting.*) **3rd and Main Sts., downtown.**

Strange Family Bluegrass Festival

Gathering of bluegrass artists from all over, playing music in a natural amphitheater. It always happens on Memorial Day weekend and on Labor Day weekend. **At the Strange Family Park; take U.S. Hwy. 67 west for 4 miles from Texarkana to Farm Road 989, then go south for 6 miles past U.S. Hwy. 59; follow the signs to the park; 903-838-7694.**

Union Station

A major transportation center in the old days. The station was built in 1929 and served Texas and Arkansas for many years. Tours by appointment. **101 W. Front St.; 903-794-0140.**

RECREATION

Crater of Diamonds State Park, Arkansas

A diamond discovery led to establishment of this park. People now pay to wander over the grounds and dig around for diamonds. There have been some big discoveries here, but not by tourists. The park offers sixty sites for camping, picnic sites, a trail, guided walks, and interpretive programs. Also at the park are a laundry, showers, a short-order restaurant, and a gift shop. **Near Murphreesboro, Arkansas, about 50 miles northeast of Texarkana, off I-30; 870-285-3113.**

Crystal Springs Beach

A family-oriented theme park centered around a 12-acre spring-fed lake. Facilities include water slides and paddleboats, a video arcade, and 3 acres for picnicking. They offer camping here too. **Eighteen miles west of Texarkana on U.S. Hwy. 67; 903-585-5246.**

Rolling Water Amusement Park

Fun for the kids, with a wave pool, water slides, and a skating rink next door. Open weekends in May and daily from Memorial Day through Labor Day. **3706 New Boston Rd., Texarkana; 903-832-7572.**

South Haven Golf Course

A pretty and affordable 18-hole golf course. **On Line Ferry Rd. in the Arkansas part of Texarkana; 870-774-5771.**

Wright Patman Lake

A 20,000-acre lake, with commercial facilities and public parks along the shoreline. Water sports, camping, picnicking, hiking trails, and fishing. **Atlanta State Park** is on the south shore **(at Knights Bluff Rd. and Park Road 42; 903-796-6476).** The park has fifty-nine campsites and also offers boating, swimming, fishing, and hiking. **The lake is 12 miles south of Texarkana, off U.S. Hwy. 59; 903-838-8781.**

WHERE TO EAT

Big Jake's Smokehouse

Barbecue is king here. **2610 New Boston Rd.; 903-793-1169.**

Rawleigh's Family Restaurant

Serves up country-style meals. **3002 New Boston Rd.; 903-838-8721.**

WHERE TO STAY

For information on bed-and-breakfast lodgings, call **Book-A-Bed-Ahead at 903-665-3956.**

Mansion on Main

Offers country elegance in Texarkana. **802 Main St.; 903-792-1835.**

Mount Pleasant

Getting There: Take I-30 northeast from Dallas for a little over 100 miles, and then turn south onto U.S. Hwy. 271 and travel a couple of miles to Mount Pleasant. **Visitor Information: Mount Pleasant Chamber of Commerce, 1604 N. Jefferson Ave.; 903-572-8567; www.ci.mount-pleasant.tx.us/citygov.htm.**

Named for its location on beautiful wooded hills, Mount Pleasant is a true "Main Street community," and one of the nicest small towns in the country.

SEEING AND DOING

Dellwood Park

Twenty-five acres of wooded land where a mineral springs resort once stood. Picnicking, a playground, and a small stream. **In the southeast part of Mount Pleasant, off State Hwy. 49.**

Pleasant Jamboree

Housed in a theater that was built in 1913 and for a time was the only theater between Texarkana and Dallas. Every Saturday brings live country music, with a country and western stage show featuring local entertainers. **112 W. 3rd St.; 903-572-2936.**

Tankersley Gardens

A 5-acre garden on Tankersley Creek with more than 100 species of plants, walking paths, footbridges, and sitting areas. Open April–Oct. Tues.–Sat. 9 A.M.–6 P.M. **At I-30 and U.S. Hwy. 271, 8 miles west of Mount Pleasant on Tankersley Rd.; 903-572-0567.**

RECREATION

Bob Sandlin State Park

A 640-acre park offering day-use and overnight camping facilities, with screened shelters, trails, boat ramps, and fishing piers. **Twelve miles southwest of Mount Pleasant, on Farm Road 21; 903-572-5531; www.tpwd.state.tx.us/park/lakebob/lakebob.htm.**

Titus County Park

Boat ramps, camping, and picnic areas. The park is situated between, and offers access to, two of the best bass fishing lakes in the state, Monticello Lake and Lake Bob Sandlin. Boats can be launched into either lake from the park. **About 10 miles southwest of Mount Pleasant.**

WHERE TO EAT

Herschel's Family Restaurant

1612 S. Jefferson Ave.; 903-572-7501.

Pittsburg

Getting There: Pittsburg is about a dozen miles south of Mount Pleasant on U.S. Hwy. 271. **Visitor Information: Pittsburg Chamber of Commerce; 903-856-3442; www.pittsburgtx.com.**

This is one of the top peach-producing areas in Texas, but blueberries and blackberries are also grown here. A lot of growers offer pick-your-own opportunities.

SEEING AND DOING

Ezekiel Airship

In 1902 an inspired preacher-inventor built an airship based on a description in the biblical Book of Ezekiel. It is said to have flown briefly, but was destroyed in a rail accident as it was being shipped to the St. Louis World's Fair in 1904. A full-size replica is on display downtown at **142 Marshall St.**

Scenic Drives

East of Pittsburg on several farm roads between the communities of Hughes Springs, Avinger, and Linden are some nice drives when the wildflowers bloom in spring. Check out **Farm Roads 155, 11, and 49.**

Witness Park and Prayer Tower

A fountain and religious shrine that was a gift to the city from chicken king Bo Pilgrim, whose company headquarters are in Pittsburg. The tower features four Paccard bells from France and a chapel that never closes. **At the intersection of Jefferson and Lafayette Sts.**

WHERE TO EAT

Pittsburg Hot Links

This town is home of the famous Pittsburg Hot Links. Several places around town serve the tasty sausages on butcher paper, with bread and a soft drink. They're greasy, slightly hot, and very tasty. This is the most established outlet in town. **136 Marshall St.; 903-856-5765.**

WHERE TO STAY

Mrs. B's Cottage Guesthouse

512 Quitman St.; 903-856-6232.

Jefferson

Getting There: Jefferson is about 60 miles south of Texarkana on U.S. Hwy. 59. **Visitor Information: Marion County Chamber of Commerce, 118 N. Vale St.; 1-800-467-3529, 903-665-2672; thechamber@jeffersontx.com; www.jeffersontx.com.**

Jefferson has one of the most interesting histories of any Texas city. In the early days, Jefferson was a thriving port community on the Trinity River, moving merchandise and material upriver to Dallas and Fort Worth, and sending cotton and farming goods downriver for shipment around the world. Late in the 1800s, the river level went down, making it impossible for the bigger ships to get upstream. About that time, the railroads expressed an interest in building tracks through town, but the citizens decided against it. They said they would rather see grass grow on the main streets than railroad tracks. So railroad tycoon

Jay Gould laid his tracks around the town. He predicted that Jefferson would dry up and die.

He was right . . . and he was wrong. Grass did grow on the streets of Jefferson, and without the railroad, the town did dry up for about 70 years. Then it staged a miraculous comeback, reborn as a tourist center and a retirement community. Today it is one of the most delightful communities in the state, better off than it would have been if Jay Gould had had his way, and much more entertaining to visit.

The town is filled with arts and crafts shops and special shopping places, and almost every block has a bed-and-breakfast establishment. You'll find food and lodging that will make you want to come back again and again to Jefferson—it's not a river town anymore, and it's not a railroad town as it might have been. Now it's known as "the belle of the bayous."

An interesting historical character with roots in Jefferson was Marion Slaughter. In the early part of the twentieth century people knew him as Vernon Dalhart, and he was one of the great recording artists after Thomas Edison invented the phonograph. Slaughter grew up in the slums of Jefferson, but wound up on the stages of New York as an opera singer.

SEEING AND DOING

Excelsior House

The second oldest hotel in Texas. It was built New Orleans-style in 1858 and has provided overnight lodging for the likes of Rutherford B. Hayes, Ulysses S. Grant, and Oscar Wilde. There are tours of the building. **211 W. Austin St.; 903-665-2513; excelsior@jeffersontx.com; www.jeffersontx.com/excelsior.**

Freeman Plantation

What is left of a once-prominent sugar cane plantation. Open for tours by appointment; listed in the National Register of Historic Places. **One mile west of Jefferson, off State Hwy. 49; 903-665-2320; freeman@jeffersontx.com; www.jefferson tx.com/freeman.**

House of the Seasons

Built in 1872 by Benjamin Epperson, a confidant of General Sam Houston. Guided tours by appointment. **409 S. Alley St.; 903-665-1218; houseofthe seasons@jeffersontx.com.**

Jay Gould's Private Railroad Car "Atlanta"

The plush private railroad car of the railroad guru who predicted the death of the town when its citizens turned down the railroad. **210 W. Austin St., across from the Excelsior House; 903-665-2513.**

Jefferson and Cypress Bayou Railroad

Railroads finally made it to Jefferson. This one is slightly smaller than you might expect. A steam locomotive carries tourists alongside Big Cypress River. **Departs from the depot on E. Austin St.; 903-665-8400.**

Jefferson Pilgrimage

The first weekend in May. One of the best old-home tours in the state. It offers lively entertainment too: The locals put on a play at the Jefferson Playhouse based on the Diamond Bessie murder trial that shocked the country back in 1877. For information, call the **Marion County Chamber of Commerce** at **903-665-2672.**

Pride House

Said to be the very first bed-and-breakfast establishment in Texas, Pride House is a great place to stay, with a lot of history and plenty of friendly faces **(409 E. Broadway St., 903-665-2675).** One of the proudest possessions at Pride House is a painting of a one-eyed rabbit by Floyd Clark. The story of Floyd Clark and his wife, Mildred, is as interesting as any I've run across in my work with the TV program *Eyes of Texas*. A hand-painted sign that read "Oriognal Art for Sale" (that's not a misprint) first led me down the dirt path to the Clark house, a tiny frame building. Mildred was inside, painting childlike pictures on pieces of cardboard. Floyd was on the porch, making picture frames out of rubber bicycle tires. Their whole house was wall-to-wall pictures painted by Mildred. She was 57, but looked about 87; Floyd was 87, going on 100. Mildred did most of the talking between sips of whiskey, while Floyd, a chain smoker, was coughing when he wasn't puffing. They were selling their pictures for $5 apiece and not finding many takers. Six months later, an art specialist from the University of Houston asked me if I had any names to add to her list of "primitive artists," and I told her about Mildred and Floyd. They made the list, and appeared in a book about state artists. About a year later, I heard that Mildred had

The Pride House in Jefferson, identified as the "First Bed & Breakfast in Texas." Photo courtesy of Sandy Spalding.

died and that Floyd had taken up painting. And about a year after that, Floyd passed on—but not before selling a lot of his work to art enthusiasts in East Texas, no doubt for more than $5 a painting. Today a number of people in Jefferson brag about owning a Floyd Clark original or a one-of-a-kind Mildred Clark.

RECREATION

Bayou Riding Stables

Offers a 45-minute narrated horseback tour along the banks of Cypress Bayou. You'll travel amid 100-year-old trees, observe East Texas wildlife, and pass the site of the Diamond Bessie murder. **903-665-7600.**

Caddo Lake State Park

This park is a good introduction to one of the most interesting lakes in all of Texas—a 32,000-acre lake with a maze of channels and bayous and thousands of acres of cypress groves. You'll see spectacular scenery and bird and animal life, and discover why all those Cajuns and East Texans love Deep East Texas so much. The park has an interpretive center, picnic areas, a playground, a fishing pier, a recreation hall, sites for tents and RV camping, pontoon boat tours, and a hiking trail. Bring plenty of mosquito repellent. The park is **about a dozen miles east of Jefferson via Farm Road 134; 903-679-3351; www.tpwd. state.tx.us/park/caddo/caddo.htm.**

If you have ever wanted to ride an airboat, I recommend Caddo Lake and the delightful lakeside community of **Uncertain,** about 3 miles east of the park. At Uncertain, you'll mostly find fishers, bait camps, and a few individuals who will take you on an airboat

ride, for a price. The name of the place may have come from the uncertainty early steamboat captains had about mooring their boats at this spot, or it may have come from the uncertainty residents had about their citizenship before the boundary between the United States and the Republic of Texas was established, or perhaps Uncertain got its name just because the residents could never make up their minds if they were going to stay. In any case, it's a pleasant, secluded spot to visit in Deep East Texas if you're looking to get off the standard tourist trail.

Among the private camping areas available in and around Uncertain are **Crip's Camp (Goose Prairie Dr., 903-789-3233)** and **Shady Glade (449 Cypress Dr., 903-789-3295).** Both offer or have access to airboat tours. Cabins are available at **Johnson's Ranch (E. Cypress Dr., 903-789-3213)** and **Pine Needle Lodge (1 Caddo Lake Ln., 903-665-2911).** A portion of the lake belongs to the **Caddo Lake Wildlife Management Area,** which offers guided boat tours of the lake **(903-679-3743).** **Caddo Lake Steamboat Company** also offers boat tours **(328 Bois D Arcade Ln., 903-789-3978).**

Canoeing Big Cypress Bayou

You can paddle along the southeastern edge of Jefferson or travel to a more remote area on the upper section of the bayou. Check with **Paddler's Post (903-665-3251)** or **Big Cypress Canoe Rental (903-665-7163).**

Lake O' the Pines

An 18,000-acre impoundment of Cypress Creek, set among a pine forest **10 miles west of Jefferson via Farm Road 726.** It's popular for swimming and boating, but mostly for fishing. Campgrounds encircle the lake—including Alley Creek, Buckhorn Creek, Brushy Creek, and Johnson Creek, all of which have tent and camper sites. Cedar Springs, Hurricane Creek, and Oak Valley have primitive campsites. For more information about the lake, call **903-755-2597** or **903-665-2336.** Several commercial concessions operate campgrounds on the lake, including **Big Cypress Marina (off Line St., 903-665-8582), Island View Landing (near Hasty Creek, 903-777-4161), Sunrise Cove (Wisteria Rd. in Ore City, 903-968-4017),** and **Willow Point (in Avinger,**

903-755-2912). All of these have RV hookups, but only Willow Point has a trailer dump station.

Texas Experience

Trail rides, hayrides, and overnight camping with cowboys on the Las Brisas Ranch. They serve campfire meals from a genuine chuckwagon. Overnight cabins are also available. **Six miles outside Jefferson, off U.S. Hwy. 59 in the community of Woodlawn; 903-938-8019.**

Turning Basin River Boat Tour

A 45-minute narrated tour of Big Cypress Bayou. Just below the old trestle across the Polk Street Bridge. **903-665-2222.**

Woodlands Trail

The feature here is a 99-foot state champion yellow poplar tree that survived transplanting from Georgia in 1887. **On U.S. Hwy. 59, about 8 miles north of Jefferson.**

WHERE TO EAT

Diamond Bessie's Saloon

Meals with the flavor of early East Texas. **124 E. Austin St.; 903-665-7454.**

WHERE TO STAY

There are thirty-two bed-and-breakfast accommodations in Jefferson. You can make reservations and get information at **Book-A-Bed-Ahead (903-665-3956).** My favorite is **Pride House (409 E. Broadway St., 903-665-2675)** (see description on page 229).

Marshall

Getting There: Marshall is at the junction of I-20 and U.S. Hwy. 59, about 80 miles south of Texarkana and 140 miles east of Dallas. **Visitor Information: Greater Marshall Chamber of Commerce, 213 W. Austin St.; 903-935-7868; cvd@internet work.net; www.marshalltxchamber.com.** Also, **Travel Information Center, 20 miles east of Marshall on I-20 near Waskom, at the Louisiana state line.**

When Vicksburg fell during the Civil War, Marshall became the wartime capital of the Confederacy west of the Mississippi River. Monuments and old homes,

some now serving as bed-and-breakfast establishments, help trace its history. Marshall is home to East Texas Baptist University, Texas State Technical College, and Wiley College, one of the premier black universities in the nation. The red and white clay in the ground around Marshall is perfect for making stoneware, and accounts for the presence in town of a dozen pottery manufacturers and five pottery stores.

SEEING AND DOING

Ginocchio National Historic District

Three square blocks centered around the 1896 Ginocchio Hotel, one of the state's best examples of Victorian hotel architecture. Next door is the Allen House, a prime example of Texas architecture circa 1877. **Washington St. at the Texas & Pacific Depot.**

Josey's Ranch

Home to the famous Josey Championship School of Calf Roping and Barrel Racing. Students come from every state and some foreign countries to learn from the experts, R. E. and Martha Josey. Visitors are welcome, but the Joseys schedule their tours around classes; school comes first. **Five miles north of Marshall, off State Hwy. 43, near the community of Karnack; 903-935-5358.**

Marshall Pottery and Museum

Established in 1896, this is one of the largest companies in the world producing glazed pottery. They turn out literally millions of red clay pots and hand-turned stoneware items every year. At the main showroom,

Wonderland of Lights, a Christmas tradition in Marshall. Photo courtesy of the Greater Marshall Chamber of Commerce.

visitors can shop for anything and everything that can be made with potter's mud, and usually watch a master potter in action. An RV park next door has eighteen sites, with water, electricity, and a dump station. **4901 Elysian Fields, 2.5 miles southeast of Marshall on Farm Road 31; 903-938-9201.**

Old Courthouse Museum

Displays range from Caddo Indian artifacts to a transportation collection that bills itself as going from "spurs to the space age." An 18,000-year-old Clovis Point arrowhead is on display, along with tributes to many homegrown folks who did all right for themselves, including Lady Bird Johnson (raised in nearby Karnack), journalist Bill Moyers, football's Y. A. Tittle, and boxer George Foreman. **On the square; 903-938-2680.**

Potters Village

A crafts and antiques mall designed, at least in name, to catch some of the spillover crowd from Marshall Pottery. **U.S. Hwy. 59 and Houston St.; 903-935-4320.**

Starr Family State Historic Site

An 1870 home built by the son of Dr. James Harper Starr, who was surgeon general for the Republic of Texas. Construction materials and furnishings were shipped here from New Orleans, making this more of a Louisiana-style home than one of early Texas. **407 W. Travis St.; 903-935-3044.**

FESTIVALS AND EVENTS

May—Stagecoach Days

Third weekend. A celebration of transportation, from the stagecoach to the modern automobile. Activities include a chili cook-off. **On the square.**

September—Central East Texas Fair

Mid-month. A county fair with a livestock show, arts and crafts, food booths, and a carnival. **Fairgrounds at West Houston Street.**

October—East Texas Fire Ant Festival

Second weekend. Leave it to East Texans to honor the dreaded fire ant. They aren't really honoring the critter. It's just another excuse for a Texas celebration, with the usual chili cook-offs, parades, and street

dances, plus the world championship pizza crust-flinging contest. **On the square and around town.**

November–December— Wonderland of Lights

Several years ago one of the city's benefactors gave $1 million to finance the lighting of the town square, and he wasn't disappointed. The city purchased 4.5 million tiny lights and strung them up around town. The result is one of the most spectacular Christmas scenes in all of Texas, particularly around the old courthouse. Choirs sing carols on Tuesday and Thursday evenings, and a Christmas parade is held the first Tuesday in December. **On the square.**

WHERE TO EAT

Friend Home Tea Shop

801 W. Houston St.; 903-938-7467.

WHERE TO STAY

Three Oaks

Bed-and-breakfast. **609 N. Washington Ave.; 903-935-6777.**

Kilgore

Getting There: Take State Hwy. 31 east from Tyler for 26 miles to Kilgore. From Dallas, go east on I-10 for a little over 100 miles, then turn south at the Kilgore exit and travel a couple of miles to the town. **Visitor Information: Kilgore Chamber of Commerce, 813 N. Kilgore St.; 903-984-5022, fax 903-984-4975.**

Kilgore has been one of the state's oil capitals ever since 1930, when the East Texas oil fields blew in. Photographs of the town back then show a sea of wooden oil derricks occupying downtown. It's not that way anymore, but oil is still king here—that is, if you don't count pianist Van Cliburn, who was born in this city, and the Kilgore College Rangerettes, a precision female dance and dance team that has entertained crowds all over the world.

SEEING AND DOING

East Texas Oil Museum

It's a shame this place is called a museum, which seems

to denote a great deal of educating and not much entertaining. But this museum is just the opposite—entertaining from the get-go—and if you become educated along the way, that's good too. This is a living, breathing recollection of those boom years in the East Texas oil fields. A movie here puts you right in the middle of a gusher. The floor shakes and the earth rumbles, and you'll walk away with a smile on your face. **U.S. Hwy. 259 at Ross St., on the campus of Kilgore College; 903-983-8295.**

Rangerette Showcase

A look at the achievements of the Rangerettes, who were the first to introduce show business to the gridiron. **1100 Broadway Blvd., on the campus of Kilgore College; 903-984-8531.**

World's Richest Acre

On this tiny street corner stands one full-size oil derrick and twenty-three miniatures. They represent that time when there were more than a thousand wells drilling in downtown Kilgore. In its heyday this area produced more than 2.5 million barrels of crude oil. **Main and Commerce Sts.; 903-983-8265.**

WHERE TO EAT

Back Porch

Serves good basic East Texas food. **904 Broadway Blvd.; 903-984-8141.**

WHERE TO STAY

Kilgore Community Inn

Near the college. **801 N. Henderson Blvd.; 903-984-5501.**

Tyler

Getting There: Tyler is about 90 miles east of Dallas via I-20 and U.S. Hwy. 69. **Visitor Information: Tyler Area Chamber of Commerce, 407 N. Broadway Ave.; 1-800-235-5712, 903-592-1661; www.tylertx.com.**

Tyler is home to the largest rose garden in the United States—as well as home to football great Earl Campbell and to the Apache Bells, an internationally known dance and drill team from Tyler Junior College.

SEEING AND DOING

Brookshire's World of Wildlife Museum and Country Store

More than 250 specimens of fish, reptiles, and other animals from Africa and North America. The country store looks like one from the 1920s. **1600 W. SW Loop 323 and Old Jacksonville Highway, in the southern park of Tyler; 903-534-2169.**

Caldwell Zoo

It began in 1938 as a backyard menagerie. Today it is one of Tyler's biggest attractions, a free 35-acre facility with everything you might expect in a zoo, plus a native Texas exhibit. **2203 Martin Luther King Dr.; 903-593-0121.**

Camp Ford

In the spring of 1864, this was the largest prisoner-of-war compound west of the Mississippi; at its peak, Camp Ford held 6,000 Union soldiers. **Two miles northeast of Tyler on U.S. Hwy. 271.**

Discovery Science Place

A hands-on children's learning center that is fun for the whole family. **308 N. Broadway St.; 905-533-8011; www.tyler.iamerica.net/discovery.**

Hudnall Planetarium

One of the largest planetariums in the state, with replicas of exploratory space vehicles. **At Tyler Junior College, just east of downtown; 903-510-2249.**

FESTIVALS AND EVENTS

October—Texas Rose Festival

Usually the third weekend. The largest event of the year for Tyler, with a parade, dance, tours of the Municipal Rose Garden, and a show featuring 120,000 roses.

March–April—Azalea and Spring Flower Trail

Last week of March and first week of April. A 7-mile driving trail that winds through residential districts where flowers are thriving. Trail maps are available from the **Chamber of Commerce (903-592-7989).**

September—East Texas Fair
Usually the last week. All the ingredients of a county fair. At the fairgrounds. **903-597-2501.**

RECREATION

Lake Palestine
A 25,000-acre lake with mostly commercial facilities for boating, fishing, and other water sports. Marinas, motels, trailer parks, and camping areas are around the lake. **About 15 miles south of Tyler, off State Hwy. 155; 903-566-2161.**

Lake Tyler and Lake Tyler East
Twin municipal lakes that cover about 5,000 acres and offer boating, fishing, swimming, and camping. **Twelve miles southeast of Tyler, via State Hwy. 110 to Whitehouse, then east on Farm Road 346.**

Tyler State Park
A 1,000-acre scenic playground in one of the state's finest forested areas. Camping, picnicking, fishing, swimming, and boating, plus nature trails. **Ten miles north of Tyler via Farm Road 14 to Park Road 16; 903-597-5338.**

WHERE TO EAT

Tyler Square Antiques and Tea Room
117 S. Broadway Ave.; 903-535-9994.

WHERE TO STAY
Two bed-and-breakfasts are **Woldert-Spence Manor (611 W. Woldert St., 903-533-9057)** and **Mary's Attic (417 S. College Ave., 903-592-5181).**

Athens
Getting There: Athens is at the intersection of U.S. Hwy. 175 and State Hwy. 31, about 70 miles southeast of downtown Dallas and 36 miles southwest of Tyler. **Visitor Information: Athens Chamber of Commerce, 1206 S. Palestine St.; 903-675-5181.** For 24-hour information: **903-677-0775; www.athenstx.org.**

Athens was named for the capital of Greece—or maybe for a city in Georgia. There is a long-lasting local dispute over this matter that has never been rec-

onciled: The city's greatest claim to fame is that it is the home of the hamburger, created, according to local experts, in the late 1800s in a cafe on the courthouse square by a man named Fletcher Davis. True or not, the claim is celebrated every year at the **Uncle Fletcher Davis Home of the Hamburger Cookoff and Trade Fair.** Athens is also known as the black-eyed pea capital, because of its extensive production of the crop in the old days. Today the city pays tribute to the black-eyed pea every July with a jamboree. In May the city puts on its **Old Fiddlers Reunion,** one of the best fiddling events in the state.

SEEING AND DOING

Henderson County Historical Museum
Replica of an early schoolroom, plus memorabilia, displayed in a restored 1896 building. **217 N. Prairieville St.; 903-677-3611.**

New York Texas Cheesecake Outlet
Mouthwatering cheesecake made in New York—New York, Texas, that is—on a farm that overlooks the hills of East Texas. The recipe is so popular that the cake is

This historical photograph captures the grandeur of the Texas State Railroad, which now steams daily through the Pineywoods. Photo courtesy of Charlie Maple, Texas State Railroad.

shipped out all over the country. There is free cheesecake and coffee for visitors, a country gourmet dinner
on Saturday nights, and **bed-and-breakfast accommodations (903-675-2281). Five miles east of
Athens on U.S. Hwy. 175; 1-800-225-6982.**

RECREATION

Cedar Creek Reservoir

A 33,000-acre body of water designed for recreation,
with good fishing, swimming, and boating, plus
attractive campsites nestled among post oaks and pines.
Ten miles west of Athens off State Hwy. 31.

Lake Athens

A popular 1,500-acre impoundment with boat ramps,
a marina, picnic sites, fishing, and a camping area with
RV hookups. **Eight miles east of Athens via State
Hwy. 31 and Farm Road 2495.**

Purtis Creek State Recreation Area

This 1,500-acre park includes a lake, campsites, pic-
nic spots, and room for hiking, fishing, and boating.
**About 15 miles northwest of Athens at 14225
Farm Road 316; 903-425-2332.**

WHERE TO EAT

Bluebonnet Diner

719 E. Tyler St.; 903-677-1800.

WHERE TO STAY

Avonlea

Bed-and-breakfast. **410 E. Corsicana St.; 903-675-
5770.**

Rusk

Getting There: Rusk is 42 miles south of Tyler via
U.S. Hwy. 69. **Visitor Information: Rusk Chamber of Commerce, 415 S. Main St.; 1-800-933-
2381, 903-683-4242; www.rusktexas.com.**

The towns of Rusk and Palestine are in the part of
Deep East Texas I have always enjoyed the most. Maybe
it's because it is so much like my boyhood home in
West Texas—Big Spring—yet different. Rusk has all
the things I grew up with: oil wells, friendly faces,
and a state mental hospital. Big Spring thrived along

A dogwood tree in a pine forest outside Palestine.

the Texas and Pacific Railroad. Rusk and Palestine thrive
today on the Texas State Railroad, which uses a steam
locomotive to offer probably the best-known tourist
train ride in the state. Some of my best friends, the
Whitehead family, live in Rusk. And some of the prettiest scenery in all of Texas lies between Rusk and Palestine, particularly when the dogwoods are blooming.

I met Marie Whitehead when she was running the
newspaper in Rusk, and she became my East Texas
correspondent for the *Eyes of Texas* TV show. She
introduced me to a lady who was raising a cross
between chickens and turkeys; she called them
"turkens." They never caught on in food circles, but
they sure made a good story. Marie's husband,
Emmett, was a state politician, then a county judge,
then mayor of Rusk. Besides the newspaper, the
Whiteheads owned a radio station, a cable TV operation, and a trailer park. Emmett admitted to me that
of the batch, the trailer park was the most profitable.

SEEING AND DOING

Bonner Bank Building

Cherokee County's first bank building, constructed
in 1865. **Euclid St. and U.S. Hwy. 69.**

Footbridge Garden Park

A 546-foot wooden footbridge, said to be the nation's longest, built in 1861 for crossing into town from the south during rainy periods. **Two blocks east of the town square.**

Jim Hogg State Historic Park

This 175-acre scenic forest of lofty pine trees is a memorial to Jim Hogg, one of Texas's more colorful governors. **Two miles northeast of Rusk, off U.S. Hwy. 84; 903-683-4850.**

Sacul and Reklaw

Here are two of the most unusual and delightful East Texas communities you'll ever visit. There is nothing but a couple of traffic signals to point out the towns when you get there, but behind the storefronts you'll discover some of the friendliest people in all of Texas. I've been there for flea markets and for quilting contests, and I can tell you that nobody is a stranger for long in Sacul or Reklaw. The personalities of the towns reflect the personalities of the people who named the places. In the beginning, a couple of guys named Lucas and Walker applied to name the towns after themselves. Both names were taken, so they did the next best thing: they spelled their names backward and reapplied. Wouldn't you? **About 15 miles east of Rusk on U.S. Hwy. 84.**

Texas State Railroad

This popular tourist service is operated by the Texas Parks and Wildlife Department. An antique steam engine powers vintage coaches for 25 miles, from Rusk to Palestine. The trip, through a dense section of East Texas forest, operates weekends from March through May, daily except Tuesday and Wednesday through mid-August, and then on weekends through October. **The depot is in Rusk State Park, which is on U.S. Hwy. 84 about 3 miles west of Rusk.** For reservations, call **1-800-442-8951, 903-683-5126; railroad@rusktexas.com.**

RECREATION

Caddoan Mounds State Historic Site

Three Caddo Indian mounds dating from about A.D. 780 to 1200. Many experts in southwestern history claim this to be the most important historic site in Texas. There isn't a whole lot to view, but there is indeed a lot of history. There are two temple mounds and one burial mound, and a museum and a reconstructed Caddo house. An interpretive trail has exhibits that explain the Caddo way of life. **From Rusk, take U.S. Hwy. 69 south for about 12 miles to Alto, then State Hwy. 21 southwest for about 6 miles; 903-858-3218.**

Fairchild State Forest

A total of 2,700 acres originally part of the state prison system. Most of the area was logged in the early 1900s. There is a small day-use area with fishing, hiking, and picnicking. **Thirteen miles west of Rusk off U.S. Hwy. 84.**

Lake Jacksonville

A 1,300-acre body of water rated by area fishers as one of the best bass lakes in the state. The lake is fun for skiers and boaters alike, and picnicking and camping are popular along a scenic wooded shore. There are screened shelters, camper hookups, dump stations, and fishing guides. **About 10 miles north of Rusk off U.S. Hwy. 69, near Jacksonville.**

Lake Striker

A 2,400-acre lake that is not just an industrial water supply but also a fine recreation area. It's a popular bass lake, with boat launching facilities and marina service, and picnicking and camping areas. **Twenty miles northeast of Rusk off U.S. Hwy. 79, near Henderson.**

Rusk State Park

A 100-acre park built around the Rusk terminal of the Texas State Railroad. It has a group shelter, bathhouse, tennis courts, picnic area, primitive camping, and RV hookups. **Three miles west of Rusk on U.S. Hwy. 84; 903-683-5126.**

WHERE TO EAT

Main St. Crossing

On the square. **102 W. 5th St.; 903-683-4580.**

WHERE TO STAY

Southern Motor Inn

On U.S. Hwy. 69 in Rusk; 903-683-2688.

Palestine

Getting There: Palestine is 47 miles south of Tyler via State Hwy. 155. **Visitor Information: Palestine Convention and Visitors Bureau, in the Carnegie Library building, 502 N. Queen St.; 1-800-659-3484, 903-723-3014.** Also, **Palestine Chamber of Commerce, 502 N. Queen St.; 903-729-6066, fax 903-729-6067; www.palestine-online.org.**

Palestine (PALA-steen) is overflowing with Texas history. Check with the Palestine Chamber of Commerce for brochures detailing self-guided walking tours.

SEEING AND DOING

Eilenberger's Butternut Baking Company

Famous since 1898 for fruit cakes baked from an old-world recipe. They also make and sell pies, cakes, and other specialty items. **512 N. St. John St.; 1-800-788-2996, 903-729-2253.**

Scientific Balloon Base

Operated by NASA. Balloons as large as 300 feet in diameter are periodically launched to study the upper atmosphere and outer space. Tours may be arranged by calling **903-729-0271.**

FESTIVALS AND EVENTS

March–April—Texas Dogwood Trails

Usually the last two weekends in March and the first weekend in April. A fishing tournament and a chili cook-off are just a part of a festival designed to show off Palestine's amazing dogwood trees each year. The focal point of the celebration is **Davey Dogwood Park,** which has more than 200 acres of rolling hills, streams, forest, and meadow, with picnic areas and scenic overlooks from roads that wind through the park. **903-729-7275.**

October—Hot Pepper Festival

Last full weekend. Events usually include a bicycle race, street dance, car show, and arts and crafts shows. **Various locations in downtown Palestine.**

December—Christmas Pilgrimage

First weekend. A tour of some of the fine historic homes in Palestine. **903-729-6066.**

RECREATION

Engeling Wildlife Management Area

An 11,000-acre wildlife habitat with deer, foxes, wolves, squirrels, rabbits, alligators, coyotes, and plenty of birds, along with day-use sites and fishing. **North of U.S. Hwy. 287, 20 miles northwest of Palestine; 903-928-2251.**

Palestine Community Forest

Seven hundred acres of pines and hardwoods, with scenic drives leading to four lakes, fishing, boating, and picnicking. Yaupon and sweetgum trees add brilliant color during autumn. **Just northwest of Palestine near the intersection of State Hwy. 19 and U.S. Hwy. 287.**

WHERE TO EAT

Caddo Creek Cafe

304 E. Crawford St.; 903-729-1198.

WHERE TO STAY

Wiffletree Inn

Bed-and-breakfast. **109 E. Pine St.; 903-723-9565.**

The Pineywoods

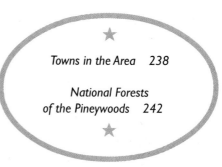

The vast Pineywoods of East Texas are the greatest surprise of all to visitors coming into the state. In most of the stories about Texas, the forest country is left out. The wide-open West is more adventuresome, I guess. But the truth is that Texas is rich in forests that have provided shelter and livelihood for their inhabitants for centuries.

The Pineywoods brought the timber industry to Texas in the nineteenth century and it has grown into an empire. In more recent times, the government stepped in to regulate the industry out of fear the forests would be stripped and then abandoned. Four national forests were created in the region—Sabine, Angelina, Davy Crockett, and Sam Houston—plus the Big Thicket National Preserve, for a combined total of about 750,000 acres of dense forest.

Each of the four Pineywoods national forests have designated recreation areas, many with tent and trailer camping facilities. Primitive camping is allowed anywhere within national forest boundaries except during hunting season from October to mid-January. This chapter gives details on each of these national forests, after taking a look at several of the towns in the region.

Towns in the Area

Among the principal towns in the Pineywoods region are Nacogdoches, Lufkin, and, to the southwest, Huntsville.

Nacogdoches

Getting There: From Tyler, take State Hwy. 64 for 30 miles east to Henderson, then go south on U.S. Hwy. 259 for about 40 miles to Nacogdoches. Or from Houston, go north on U.S. Hwy. 59 for about 135 miles to Nacogdoches. **Visitor Information: Nacogdoches County Chamber of Commerce, 513 North St.; 409-564-7351; www.visitnacog doches.org.**

Nacogdoches is the oldest incorporated town in Texas ("incorporated" is the key word). The area was visited by la Salle in 1687, and there is some evidence that a Spanish mission was here in the early 1700s. For more than 100 years it was a major eastern gateway to Texas.

SEEING AND DOING

El Camino Real
Also known as the King's Highway, it was first blazed in 1691; it's also often called the Old San Antonio Road. **Follows State Hwy. 21.**

La Calle del Norte
Spanish for "The Street of the North," believed to be the oldest public thoroughfare in the United States. Long before Spanish explorers discovered and named it, the route connected the Indian community of Nacogdoches with other Indian villages to the north. For information, call the **Nacogdoches County Chamber of Commerce** at 409-564-7351.

L. T. Barret Memorial
Honors the man who drilled Texas's first oil well—in September 1866. It produced ten barrels a day, but Barret was too early for his time. Oil never made him rich. **On the campus of Stephen F. Austin State University, which is on Business U.S. Hwy. 59 at Griffith St. on the north side of Nacogdoches.**

Millard's Crossing
A group of restored nineteenth-century buildings furnished with antiques and pioneer memorabilia. Guided tours are offered. **6020 North St.; 409-564-6631.**

Oak Grove Cemetery
Cemetery that dates from 1837 and holds the remains

Angelina National Forest near Lufkin. Photo courtesy of Texas Highways magazine.

of prominent Texas pioneers, including Thomas J. Rusk. **At N. Lanana and Hospital Sts.**

Old North Church

One of the oldest Protestant churches in Texas that is still in use; built in 1852. **On U.S. Hwy. 59 about 4 miles north of downtown Nacogdoches.**

Old Stone Fort

Built in 1779 as a Spanish trading post. It was headquarters for four unsuccessful attempts to establish the Republic of Texas, and has had nine flags flown over it in its history. A museum inside features mostly Indian artifacts from the period. **On U.S. Hwy. 59 on the campus of Stephen F. Austin State University, which is on Business U.S. Hwy. 59 at Griffith St. on the north side of Nacogdoches; 409-468-2408.**

RECREATION

Lake Nacogdoches

A 2,000-acre lake with two city parks, boat ramps, picnic shelters, a swimming area, and a floating dock. Boating, sailing, skiing, and fishing are popular here. **Twelve miles west of Nacogdoches on Farm Road 225.**

WHERE TO EAT

Kinfolks

Where the college crowd mingles with the locals. **4817 NW Stallings Dr.; 409-560-9950.**

WHERE TO STAY

Anderson Point

This bed-and-breakfast operates in a beautiful East Texas setting outside Nacogdoches. **29 E. Lake Estates; 409-569-7445.**

Lufkin

Getting There: Lufkin is about 85 miles southeast of Tyler via U.S. Hwy. 69 (and about 115 miles north of Houston via U.S. Hwy. 59). **Visitor Information: Lufkin Visitor and Convention Bureau, 515 S. 1st St.; 409-634-6305, fax 409-634-8726; lufkintx@lcc.net.** Also, **Angelina County Chamber of Commerce, 1615 S. Chestnut St.; 409-634-6644.**

This is the heart of Deep East Texas and the home of a number of lumber and wood-products industries. From Lufkin you have access to outdoor recreation in nearby national forests and the massive Sam Rayburn Reservoir. City parks offer picnicking and sports including golf, fishing, swimming, and tennis.

SEEING AND DOING

Ellen Trout Zoo and Park

One of the best small zoos in East Texas, with a wide variety of animals and birds. This place is known for its breeding programs for West African crowned cranes and Louisiana pine snakes. **North Loop 287; 409-633-0399.**

Museum of East Texas

The art, science, and history of East Texas, housed in an Episcopal church built in 1905. **503 N. 2nd St.; 409-639-4434.**

Renfro's Art Shop

An interesting arts and crafts shop run by David Renfro and his wife, Joyce. There are a lot of really neat things to buy here, but I like the gourds most of all. David raises gourds in his field outside town, picks them, and dries them; then Joyce paints and decorates them. They make great gifts to take back home. Thirty miles southeast of Lufkin on U.S. Hwy. 69 at the community of Zavalla. **301 E. Main St.; 409-897-2802.**

Texas Forestry Museum

Flora and fauna exhibits from the area, plus early logging machinery, antique railroad and sawmill steam engines, and an old railroad depot. There is also a small woodland trail operated by the Texas Forestry Association. **1905 Atkinson Dr.; 409-632-8733.**

FESTIVALS AND EVENTS

September—Texas Forest Festival and Southern Hushpuppy Olympics

Last weekend of the month. Highlighting forest skill contests in which professional lumberjacks compete for prizes and bragging rights. Contestants from all over the country also show up to test their secret recipes for frying up the tastiest hushpuppies in the world. **Angelina County Exposition Center.** For information, call the **Texas Forestry Museum** at **409-632-9535.**

RECREATION

Crown Colony Country Club

One of the best-kept secrets in the state, Crown Colony has a terrific golf course that once was private and reserved solely for those who could afford it. Today it is open to the public. The course is consistently voted among the best in the state. **900 Crown Colony Dr.; 409-637-8800.**

Lake Sam Rayburn

A giant lake in the heart of Angelina National Forest that is one of the most popular recreational lakes in this part of the state. It is the largest body of water that is totally within the state, covering 114,000 acres. The Corps of Engineers and National Park Service have camping, marinas, and recreational areas all along the shoreline. It has open water for all types of boating activities, with enough space left for some excellent fishing. **East and south of Lufkin via State Hwy. 103 and U.S. Hwy. 69.** Two agencies oversee the parks around the lake: the **Corps of Engineers (409-384-5716)** and the **Forest Service (409-639-8620).**

WHERE TO EAT

Fire House Charlie's

Features local specialties. **109 S. 1st St.; 409-637-2151.**

WHERE TO STAY

Executive Suites

103 Harmony Hill Dr.; 409-632-6605.

Huntsville

Getting There: Huntsville is 90 miles north of Houston on I-45. **Visitor Information: Huntsville Chamber of Commerce, 1327 11th St.; 1-800-289-0389, 409-291-9726; www.chamber. huntsville.tx.us/visitor.html, www.hunts villetexas.com.**

The year Texas became a republic, this community was a lonely Indian trading post. Today it has become one of the jewels of the Pineywoods. It is the home of Sam Houston State University. It is also headquarters of the Texas state prison system. Huntsville is filled with turn-of-the-twentieth-century homes, and abounds with Texas history. Sam Houston retired here after serving as a general in the Texas Revolution and as first president of the Republic of Texas. There is a huge mural of this Texas hero on the northeastern edge of the downtown square, and a statue on the outskirts of town that simply cannot be missed if you're traveling on I-45 through town.

SEEING AND DOING

New Zion Barbecue House
In my book, the best barbecue in the whole state. You can see smoke from the grill rising above the tall pine trees. The dining room is modest but the food—especially the ribs—is fantastic. I used to pick up chicken and ribs at the New Zion whenever I was in the area. It's 90 miles from Huntsville to my house. The chicken was too messy to eat on the road, but the ribs were usually gone by the time I got home. They cook here every day except Sunday and Monday. At the New Zion Missionary Baptist Church. **Exit 114 on I-45, then east on Farm Road 1374 for 1 mile; 409-295-7394.**

Oakwood Cemetery
The burial site of Sam Houston, along with some other famous Texans. The Chamber of Commerce offers walking tours. **9th St. and Avenue I.**

Sam Houston Memorial Museum Complex
Includes 15 acres of the land that belonged to General Houston. Buildings here include two period homes and the general's steamboat house, as well as a law office, kitchen, blacksmith shop, and gazebo. This is the site of the General Sam Houston Folk Festival every April. **1836 Sam Houston Ave., across from the Sam Houston State University campus; 409-294-1832.**

Sam Houston Statue
This is the world's tallest statue of an American hero. Huntsville native David Adickes turned 60,000 pounds of concrete and steel into a towering 66-foot statue of General Sam Houston. It is visible for more than 6 miles, and is impressive to say the least. An adjacent visitor center has information on what to see and do in the Huntsville area. **On I-45, 5 miles south of town; 409-291-9726.**

Texas Berry Farm
Acres and acres of berries, where visitors are allowed to pick their own and pay by the pound. The best season is from May to mid-July. They also have vegetables, herbs, and flowers. **Fifteen miles north of Huntsville on Farm Road 980, then 1 mile east on an unpaved county road; 409-294-0416.**

Texas Department of Criminal Justice Institutional Division
Headquarters of the Texas prison system, with several units throughout the city and county. The system received its first convict in October 1849. On different occasions it has been touted as the very best prison system in the nation or one of the worst. The system once held Indian warrior Santana of the Kiowas, who was imprisoned for murdering a mule skinner. Santana jumped to his death from a tower window at the Walls unit; he couldn't stand being cooped up. Authorities eventually gave his remains back to the Kiowa tribe in Oklahoma, but the tombstone marker is still standing at the Peckerwood Hill Cemetery near the Walls prison unit, at **Bowers St. and Sycamore Ln. in Huntsville.**

Texas Prison Museum
If you like Vincent Price horror movies, you'll have a great time touring this place. It documents changes in the state prison system since it opened a century and a half ago. Visitors will see ball-and-chain gear, rifles used by Bonnie and Clyde, and Old Sparky, the official electric chair used between 1924 and 1964. Open daily except Monday. **1113 12th St.; 1-800-289-0389.**

RECREATION

Blue Lagoon
A paradise for scuba divers. Sparkling artesian springs feed an old rock quarry, creating a beautiful environment for underwater exploration. They've sunk a couple of boats in the waters here for you to explore. It's open from March to mid-November. **Eight miles north of Huntsville off I-45 and exit 123; 409-291-6111.**

Golfing
Country Campus, a 9-hole public golf course, is easy to get on **(just off State Hwy. 19 northeast of Huntsville; 409-291-0008).** More challenging

are a couple of courses on Lake Livingston, which is 15 miles or so east of Huntsville: **Waterwood (1-800-441-5211)** and **Cape Royale (713-653-2388).** Waterwood is long and beautiful, built partly along the shores of the lake. Not far from Waterwood, on the southern side of the lake, is Cape Royale: short and tight, with greens that can fool you. Don't bet with any of the residents; knowledge of the greens is worth ten shots per round. And don't let those crazy blackbirds nibble the food in your golf cart, or fly off with any golf balls.

Huntsville State Park

One hundred acres of green in Sam Houston National Forest, complete with camping facilities, a botany trail, hunting, fishing, and swimming on Lake Raven. **Nine miles south of Huntsville on I-45; 409-295-5644.**

National Forests of the Pineywoods

Headquarters for the **U.S. Forest Service** in Texas is in the **Homer Garrison Federal Building, 701 N. 1st St., P.O. Box 756, Lufkin, 75901; 409-639-8620.** Each of the four national forests in East Texas has its own district offices where you can get additional information.

Sabine National Forest

Getting There: District offices are in San Augustine (some 30 miles east of Nacogdoches) and in Hemphill (roughly 25 miles southeast of San Augustine). **Visitor Information: Tenaha Ranger District, 101 S. Bolivar St., San Augustine; 409-275-2632. Also, Yellowpine Ranger District, 201 S. Palm St., Box F, Hemphill, 75948; 409-787-3870.**

The Sabine National Forest extends from just east of Center, Texas, to south of Pineland along the Louisiana border. The forest covers more than 160,000 acres along Toledo Bend Reservoir in Jasper, Sabine, Newton, and Shelby Counties.

RECREATION

Indian Mounds Recreation Site and Wilderness Area

Picnicking, camping, boating, fishing, and hiking. **On

Toledo Bend Reservoir, 5 miles east of Hemphill via Farm Road 93, then 7 miles southeast on Forest Service Road 115 and Forest Service Road 115A.**

Lakeview Recreation Area

Picnicking and camping. **Sixteen miles southeast of Hemphill via State Hwy. 87 and the access road.**

Ragtown Recreation Area

Picnicking, camping, boating, fishing, food concessions, and hiking. **On Toledo Bend Reservoir, 15 miles southeast of Shelbyville via State Hwy. 87, Farm Road 139, Forest Service Road 101, and Forest Service Road 1262.**

Red Hill Lake Recreation Area

Picnicking, camping, boating, fishing, food, and hiking. **On Toledo Bend Reservoir, 3 miles north of Milam via State Hwy. 87.**

Willow Oak Recreation Area

Picnicking, camping, boating, and fishing. **On Toledo Bend Reservoir, 14 miles southeast of Hemphill via State Hwy. 87 and Forest Service Road 117.**

Angelina National Forest

Getting There: The district office is in Lufkin, about 20 miles south of Nacogdoches. **Visitor Information: U.S. Forest Service, Homer Garrison Federal Building, 701 N. 1st St., P.O. Box 756, Lufkin, 75901; 409-639-8620; www.gorp.com/dow/southern/ange.htm.**

Angelina National Forest takes in a large part of Lake Sam Rayburn. From east of Lufkin, it stretches south nearly to Jasper. This forest covers about 156,000 acres surrounding Lake Sam Rayburn in Angelina, Jasper, Nacogdoches, and Augustine Counties.

RECREATION

Bouton Lake Recreation Area

Picnicking, camping, boating (no motors), and hiking. **Fifteen miles southeast of Zavalla via State Hwy. 63 and Forest Service Road 303.**

Sandy Creek Recreation Area

Picnicking, camping, swimming, boating, fishing, and food stores. **On Lake Sam Rayburn, 21 miles southeast of Zavalla via State Hwy. 63 and Forest Service Road 333.**

Townsend Recreation Area

Picnicking, camping, swimming, boating, fishing, and hiking. **On Lake Sam Rayburn, 5 miles northwest of Broaddus via State Hwy. 147, Farm Road 255, and Forest Service Road 335.**

Turkey Hill Wilderness Area

Primitive camping only. **Five miles north of Broaddus via State Hwy. 147 and Forest Service Road 300.**

Davy Crockett National Forest

Getting There: District offices are in Apple Springs (about 15 miles southwest of Lufkin) and in Crockett (about 30 miles west of Apple Springs). **Visitor Information: Trinity Ranger District, on State Hwy. 94, P.O. Box 130, Apple Springs, 75926; 409-831-2246. Also, Neches Ranger District, 1240 East Loop 304, Crockett; 409-544-2046; www.gorp.com/dow/southern/davy.htm.**

Davy Crockett National Forest is located east of Crockett and west of Lufkin. The northern boundary extends to near Alto, while Groveton borders the forest on the south. Encompassing 161,000 acres, this forest is in Houston and Trinity Counties.

RECREATION

Kickapoo Recreation Area

Picnicking and hiking trails. **Three miles southeast of Groveton via U.S. Hwy. 287.**

Neches Bluff Recreation Area

Picnicking and hiking trails. **On Neches River, 7 miles southwest of Alto via State Hwy. 21 and Forest Service Road 511.** The **Big Slough Canoe Trail** offers canoeing on Big Slough and the Neches River and primitive camping. **Two miles north of Ratcliff on Farm Road 227, then east 5 miles on Forest Service Road 314.**

Ratcliff Lake Recreation Area

Picnicking, camping (with electrical hookups), swimming, boating (no motors), and hiking. **Between Kennard and Ratcliff on Forest Service Road 520.** The **4-Cs Hiking Trail,** a 20-mile trail from

Sam Houston National Forest outside Huntsville.

Ratcliff Lake to the Neches Overlook, offers primitive camping.

Sam Houston National Forest

Getting There: The district office is near New Waverly, which is 18 miles south of Huntsville. **Visitor Information: U.S. Forest Service, P.O. Box 393, New Waverly, 77358; located 3 miles west of New Waverly on Farm Road 1375; 409-344-6205; www.gorp.com/dow/southern/samh.htm.**

Sam Houston National Forest is the best known of the East Texas forests. Huntsville is at the northern end of the forest, with the southern boundary following State Hwy. 105 between Conroe and Cleveland. The forest covers 160,000 acres in Montgomery, San Jacinto, and Walker Counties.

RECREATION

Double Lake Recreation Area

Picnicking, camping, swimming, boating (no motors), food concessions, and hiking. **Four miles south of Coldspring via State Hwy. 150 and Farm Road 2025.**

Kelly Pond Recreation Area

Primitive camping, with chemical toilets. **Eleven miles west of New Waverly via Farm Road 1375, then 1 mile south on Forest Service Road 204 and Forest Service Road 271.**

Little Lake Creek Wilderness Area

Primitive camping. **Fourteen miles east of New Waverly via Farm Road 1375, then 4 miles south on Farm Road 149.**

Lone Star Hiking Trail

A popular 26-mile trail that starts west of Lake Conroe off Farm Road 149, then proceeds to Kelly Pond, Stubblefield Lake, Huntsville State Park, and Double Lake, and ends at Farm Road 1725 in Cleveland. Primitive camping along the trail, and drinking water is available at established campgrounds.

Stubblefield Lake Recreation Area

Picnicking, camping, boating, fishing, and hiking. **On the west fork of the San Jacinto River, about 12 miles northwest of New Waverly via Farm Road 1375 and Forest Service Road 208.**

The Big Thicket

When I was a youngster growing up in West Texas, one of my favorite fictional heroes was Br'er Rabbit. He was about the smartest animal I ever read about, and used his wit more than his physical abilities to get out of trouble. He was always talking about the Briar Patch, a dense clump of thorn bushes that made life very uncomfortable for anyone trapped there—anyone, that is, except Br'er Rabbit. The Big Thicket is a lot like that. Native animals get around in the thicket easily, but outsiders usually leave it with thorn bruises and unpleasant memories. The scenery is spectacular, the kind you may never see anywhere else, but the ground cover in the unsettled parts of the Thicket grabs hold and is hard to shake.

If you are driving through Beaumont on I-10, you'll see signs pointing north to Big Thicket National Preserve. Beaumont is the largest Texas city on the fringe of the thicket.

Big Thicket National Preserve

Before the early nineteenth century, the Big Thicket covered 3.5 million acres. But once the lumber and petroleum industries got to work, the Thicket was reduced to about 300,000 acres. In 1974 Congress established Big Thicket National Preserve in order to save 86,000 prime acres. That alerted the rest of the world that a valuable natural resource was here in East Texas, and in the early 1980s the United Nations added Big Thicket National Preserve to its list of 250 International Biosphere Reserves worth protecting worldwide. In 1993 Congress expanded the Big Thicket Preserve to 100,000 acres. Today the preserve encompasses fifteen separate units, consisting of six waterway corridors and nine land tracts. Four of the units are connected by the Neches River and filled with bayous, creeks, and sloughs that feed into the Neches.

There are five basic North American environments here: eastern and Appalachian forests, southeastern swampland, midwestern prairie, and southwestern desert. The rainfall of about 60 inches per year produces more plant communities than in any other area of comparable size on the continent. Temperatures are moderate, with highs in the 60s in January and in the low 90s in July. But the humidity is the key. The relative humidity reaches as high as 94 percent in summer. The humidity, not the temperature, will drive you indoors—if the mosquitoes haven't already done so.

There are more than eighty-five species of trees in the Big Thicket, more than sixty types of shrubs, and nearly a thousand kinds of flowering plants. The dominant trees are the shortleaf, longleaf, and loblolly

Getting There

The fifteen units of Big Thicket National Preserve are located in seven counties in East Texas, but the region starts north of Beaumont. From Beaumont, take U.S. Hwy. 69/287 north for about 10 miles and then follow the signs to the Big Thicket. The nearest large airport is **Jefferson County Airport,** between Beaumont and Port Arthur **(409-722-0251).** Beaumont is also served by **Amtrak (2555 W. Cedar St.; 1-800-USA-RAIL).**

pines, as well as some beech and magnolia. You'll find some bald cypress along the floodplains, and sweetbay and fallberry holly trees in the bogs. There are nine carnivorous plant species in the thicket, and the most common is the pitcher plant. Its leaves are shaped like trumpets, but if you unfold them, chances are you'll find some unsuspecting ant or moth being digested.

Once upon a time, there were plenty of black bears, panthers, and red wolves in this area. Wild ones haven't been sighted for years, but there are still large populations of deer, coyotes, bobcats, beavers, armadillos, alligators, squirrels, turtles, and snakes. More than 300 bird species spend time here throughout the year, including the controversial red-cockaded woodpecker. These birds ordinarily live in diseased and dying trees, but the dying trees eventually fall over, leaving the birds homeless. The National Forest Service has set aside a sizable tract of land in the Thicket and has built homes for the woodpeckers in special trees. Farmers and ranchers say it's a waste of money because the woodpeckers are just pests—and in any case would adjust on their own to living in other trees. The government, in all its wisdom, chooses not to take a chance.

The rare carnivorous pitcher plant in the Big Thicket thrives on ants and other small insects. Photo courtesy of the Texas Department of Tourism.

Visitor Information

Big Thicket Information Station
Open daily and staffed by park rangers, with plenty of free printed information. At the southern end of the Turkey Creek Unit, off Farm Road 420, about 30 miles north of Beaumont via U.S. Hwy. 69/287. The Park Service offers lectures, seminars, guided hikes, and canoe trips. **409-246-2337.** More information can be obtained by contacting **Superintendent, Big Thicket National Preserve, 3785 Milam St., Beaumont, 77701; 409-839-2689; www.nps.gov/bith.**

Camping

BACKCOUNTRY
Camping along riverbanks or on sandbars is permitted in designated backcountry camping areas within the boundaries of the preserve as long as you have a backcountry use permit. Some of the land between preserve units—much of Pine Island Bayou and almost all of Village Creek—is privately owned, but most of the owners don't mind campers unless you abuse the privilege. The few soreheads along the way have "No Trespassing" signs posted. Open fires are not permitted within the preserve except on Neches River sandbars, so bring campstoves for cooking.

Overnight backcountry trips are limited to 5 days. During the hunting season, from October to mid-January, backcountry camping is not allowed except in the Turkey Creek, Upper and Lower Neches, and Loblolly Units. Backcountry use permits are issued free at three locations: the **Big Thicket Information Station,** the **North District Ranger Office** in Woodville, and the **Preserve Headquarters** in Beaumont **(3785 Milam St.).**

OUTSIDE THE BIG THICKET

The Alabama-Coushatta Indian Reservation
Operates a full-service campground. **On U.S. Hwy. 190 between Livingston and Woodville; 409-563-4391.**

Big Thicket RV Park and Campground
A 12-acre facility with tent and RV sites. **Nine miles west of Kountze on Farm Road 1003; 409-246-3759.**

Ceremonial dancers at the Alabama-Coushatta Indian Reservation between Livingston and Woodville. Photo courtesy of the Texas Department of Tourism.

Chain-O-Lakes Campground

A 271-acre facility with tent and RV sites. **Off Farm Road 787 near Romayor; 409-592-2150.**

Martin Dies Jr. State Park

A 700-acre park with tent and camper sites. This place is usually booked solid during the tourist season because of its beauty. It's a great place to visit in the spring when the dogwood trees are in bloom. **On the east side of Steinhagen Lake off U.S. Hwy. 190 near Jasper; 409-384-5231.**

The U.S. Army Corps of Engineers

Maintains three campgrounds at Steinhagen Lake: two on the east side—Sandy Park and East End Park—and one on the west—Magnolia Ridge Park. **409-429-3491.**

Village Creek State Park

74 Park Place in Lumberton, about 12 miles north of Beaumont.

Canoeing

The Big Thicket is best viewed from water level, and it is a favorite destination for canoeists. Even the greenest of greenhorns can negotiate most water routes through the thicket, because there are no rapids and no strong currents. The main requirement is a good map, which can be obtained at the Big Thicket Information Station. The main navigable watercourses are the **Neches River,** 93 miles from Steinhagen Lake near Woodville to Cook Lake in the Beaumont Unit; **Pine Island Bayou,** 49 miles from Saratoga to Beaumont; and **Village Creek,** 37 miles from Village Mills to the Neches River below Silsbee.

You can rent canoes and canoeing equipment, and most suppliers have drop-off and pickup services. Some of the more established businesses are **Eastex Canoe Rentals (in Beaumont, 409-892-3600); H & H Boat Dock and Marina (at Steinhagen Lake, 409-283-3257); Pineywoods Canoe Rental (in Kountze, 409-246-4481);** and **Canoe Rentals Silsbee (in Silsbee, 409-385-6241). Timber Ridge Tours** offer guided pontoon boat tours during summer **(in Kountze, 409-246-3107).**

Hiking

Established hiking trails in the Big Thicket Preserve range in length from less than 1 mile to 18 miles. No permits are required, but the Park Service would like you to register at the trailhead. Comfortable shoes, drinking water, and the strongest insect repellent you can find are necessities. Inquire at the information station for full details on trails.

Big Sandy Horse Trail

An 18-mile round-trip trail designed for horseback riding, hiking, and all-terrain bicycling. The **trailhead is northwest of Dallardsville off Farm Road 1276.**

Kirby Nature Trail

A 4-mile loop that begins at the Big Thicket Information Station and allows a view of hardwood and pine stands.

Pitcher Plant Trail

Only a quarter-mile long, off the Turkey Creek Trail, running east. A surfaced trail takes you through a mixed pine forest to the edge of a wetland savanna, where you can catch a view of a number of meat-eating plants, including the pitcher plant.

Turkey Creek Trail

A 15-mile trail that winds through the most diverse vegetation in the preserve. The main **trailhead is 3.5 miles east of Warren on Farm Road 1943,** about 18 miles northeast of the information station.

Alabama-Coushatta Indian Reservation

Getting There: The reservation is about 60 miles east of Huntsville (on U.S. Hwy. 190, between Livingston and Woodville). **Visitor Information: 409-563-4391; www.livingston.net/chamber/actribe/index.htm.**

If it hadn't been for the tenacity and determination of the people of this tribe, they probably would have lost a place in Texas many years ago. Today the Alabama-Coushatta Indians have 4,800 acres set aside adjacent to the Big Sandy Creek Unit of the Big Thicket National Preserve. This is one of America's few remaining forest Indian reservations.

In the late 1700s the Alabamas and the Coushattas began migrating westward to escape pressure from European immigrants. When the English and French fought for control in these parts, the tribes sided with the French. Bad move. When the English won, the Indians had few friends to turn to, but they insisted on holding on to the land they had occupied in the Big Thicket.

During the Texas Revolution, the tribes were neutral. They always seemed to avoid territorial fights, but in 1839 the Coushattas beat back a Comanche raid on their land at Lon King Creek and won the respect of the Texans.

When Texas joined the Union in 1845, the U.S. Congress formed a plan to move all the Indians to Oklahoma, but the Alabama-Coushatta stood their ground. Eventually they won this battle, and today about 500 of their descendants live and work on the reservation.

SEEING AND DOING

Tribal members now invite tourists to their land and show their cultures, their customs, and their craftsmanship. One fee pays for a **nature bus tour** through the woods, an **Indian village tour,** a narrow-gauge train ride, and **tribal dance performances.** The reservation also operates a **gift shop** and the **Inn of the Twelve Clans restaurant,** which serves fry bread and mainly Tex-Mex food. The tourist complex is open on weekends from mid-March through May, daily in June through August, and then weekends from September to late November. For more information or campsite reservations, contact the **Alabama-Coushatta Indian Reservation, Route 3, Box 640, Livingston, 77351; 409-563-4391.**

Towns in the Area

Interesting towns to visit in the Big Thicket region include Kountze, Silsbee, and Woodville.

Kountze

Getting There: Take U.S. Hwy. 69/287 northwest out of Beaumont for 26 miles to Kountze. **Visitor Information: Kountze Chamber of Commerce, 1015 N. Pine St.; 409-246-3413.**

Kountze is the self-described Big Light in the Big Thicket. It is the closest community of any size to the heart of the Big Thicket, and the major staging area for trips into the preserve.

SEEING AND DOING

Big Thicket Information Station

Can tell you just about anything you want to know about the Big Thicket. Ten miles north of Kountze. **Take U.S. Hwy. 69 north from Kountze for 8 miles, then go east on Farm Road 420 for 2 miles; 409-246-2337.** (A new visitor information center, at the intersection of U.S. Hwy. 69 and Farm Road 420, is planned for completion sometime in 2000.)

Big Thicket Smokehouse

Serves up barbecue and lots more. The place features arts and crafts and barbecue as part of a reconstructed sawmill town, with replicas of a jail, general store, doctor's office, barbershop, trading post, and saloon. **In downtown Kountze at 735 Pine St. (U.S. Hwy. 69); 409-246-4007.**

Indian Springs Camp

Offers guided tours of the thicket and has camping facilities, including an RV park. The camp is **about 15 miles north of Kountze (and about 5 miles northwest of the Big Thicket Information Station) on Holland Cemetery Rd.; 1-800-942-7472, 409-246-2508.**

Timber Ridge Tours

Neches River boat rides exploring the beauty and mystery of the thicket. The operators also offer charter excursions for fishing, camping, nature hiking, and historical tours from mid-February to mid-November. **On U.S. Hwy. 69 in downtown Kountze; 409-246-3107.**

Silsbee

Getting There: Take U.S. Hwy. 96 north out of Beaumont for 26 miles. **Visitor Information: Silsbee Chamber of Commerce, 835 U.S. Hwy. 96; 409-385-5562.**

Silsbee is the largest city in Hardin County and home of the giant Kirby logging empire, created by John Henry Kirby, the son of an East Texas farmer. Kirby was born in 1860 in Peach Tree Village, in Tyler County. His mother taught him to read and write, and his father taught him the value of hard work. In the early 1900s, Kirby created the Kirby Lumber Company and eventually controlled more than 300,000 acres of East Texas pinelands and operated thirteen sawmills.

RECREATION

Village Creek State Park

On a 63-mile-long creek that flows through the Big Thicket. The stream is popular for canoeing enthusiasts and as a float stream as well. The park is dense with softwood and hardwood trees, and is an excellent site for birding. There are RV hookups, tent camping sites, picnic areas, and hiking trails. **Ten miles south of Silsbee near the community of Lumberton, which is just off Farm Road 105; 409-755-7322.**

Woodville

Getting There: Take U.S. Hwy. 69/287 north from Beaumont for 60 miles to Woodville. **Visitor Information: Woodville Chamber of Commerce, 201 N. Magnolia St.; 409-283-2632.**

Woodville, the seat of Tyler County, is known for its annual Dogwood Festival held the first weekend in April, and its proximity to Big Thicket National Preserve.

SEEING AND DOING

Heritage Village

Attracts visitors from all over to see an open-air replica of an early Texas village. Ceramist Clyde Gray built Heritage Village long before it was fashionable to be so interested in regional history. He and his wife lived almost in poverty for many years, waiting for someone to appreciate the work. Now that the Grays are gone, the public appreciates what Clyde did for Woodville. The village is open year-round. **Located on U.S. Hwy. 190 on the western outskirts of town; 409-283-2272.**

WHERE TO EAT

Pickett House Restaurant

Serves up home-style meals every day. The food alone will take you back in time. Located on the **Heritage Village site; 409-283-3371.**

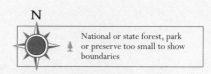

N

National or state forest, park
or preserve too small to show
boundaries

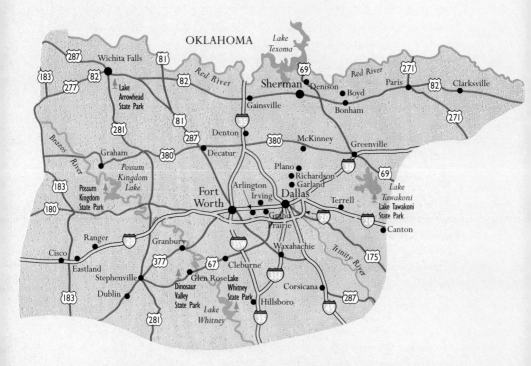

OKLAHOMA

287   Wichita Falls   81

183   82   82   Red River

277   Lake   81
            Arrowhead
            State Park   287

                    81   Denton

281   Graham   380   Decatur   380

Brazos River   Possum
                     Kingdom
                     Lake

183   Possum   Arlington
       Kingdom   Irving
       State Park

180

       Ranger   20   Granbury

Cisco

Eastland   377   67   Cleburne

Stephenville   Glen Rose Lake
                          Dinosaur   Whitney
Dublin   Valley   State Park
                          State Park
                                  Lake
                    281   Whitney

Lake
Texoma

69   Red River   271

Sherman   Denison   Boyd   Paris   82   Clarksville

Gainsville   Bonham   271

McKinney   Greenville   35

Plano   69
Richardson   Lake
Garland   Tawakoni
Dallas   Terrell   Lake Tawakoni
                                State Park
Fort
Worth   Grand   20   20   Canton
         Prairie

Waxahachie   175

35W   Trinity River

Corsicana   287

Hillsboro

35

*The Red River
Valley*

The Red River Valley

Big "D" at night, the magic of the Dallas skyline.
Photo courtesy of Texas Highways magazine.

The Red River Valley

It boggles the mind to think how far we've come since the turn of the twentieth century. When my dad was 3 years old, his family brought him to Texas in a covered wagon. They came south from Indian Territory, which would later be named Oklahoma. They maneuvered the wagon over a crossing in the Red River to a small grove of live oaks on the outskirts of a community called New Boston, not far from Texarkana, where Grandfather Tidwell set up camp for my grandmother and her two sons. It was real pioneering, the stuff of Old West history and of endless Hollywood westerns.

The Red River conjures up images of all those cowboys, on screen and off, who used to drive cattle herds across the waters of the river. The reality is that the mud was a whole lot worse than the water. There never has been that much water there anyway, and that thick, gummy red clay turned out to be great for making pottery but lousy for driving animals through.

Sam Houston crossed the Red River into Mexican-controlled Texas in the 1830s and changed the face of the nation. He saw the Texas territory as a land of promise and led a ragtag army of revolutionaries into war with Mexico. Texas won the war and became a republic. Some say that was the plan all along: that Sam Houston was sent to Texas by then-president Andrew Jackson to steal the territory from Mexico and make it a part of the United States. By 1845, Texas had joined the Union.

The Red River is the namesake for the Red River Valley, the great region of Texas we visit in this section. For purposes of this guidebook, the region is bounded on the north by the Red River border with Oklahoma; on the west by a line from Vernon to just outside Abilene; on the south by a line that runs from near Abilene to Athens, dipping down close to Waco; and on the east by State Hwy. 19 to Sulphur Springs and then I-30 to the outskirts of Texarkana.

The major population center in this region is the Dallas–Fort Worth Metroplex. The region also includes such traveling treats as the resort area around Lake Granbury; the historical route from Gainesville east to Paris; Wichita Falls with its artificial waterfall; Dublin, a city that claims to have staged the very first rodeo; and Eastland, home of the most famous horned lizard of them all, Ol' Rip.

Meteorologists love Texas weather because there is so much of it, and the Red River Valley gets its share. Humidity is lower here than in East Texas, and temperatures are generally warm most of the year but seldom unpleasant. The downside is that it can get cold in winter. The area around Dallas and Fort Worth features a climate that's a cross between the weather in East Texas and South-Central Texas. Heavy rains and occasional tornadoes often appear in late spring, but the rest of the year the weather is fairly moderate. Summers are hot, but not as hot as farther south or east.

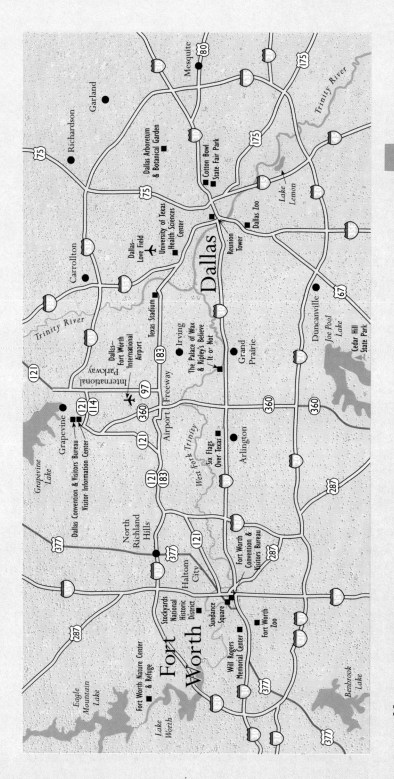

Dallas–Fort Worth

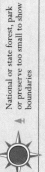

National or state forest, park or preserve too small to show boundaries

N

Dallas
Fort Worth

Mesquite
Garland
Richardson
Carrollton
Dallas Arboretum & Botanical Garden
Cotton Bowl State Fair Park
Lake Lemon
Dallas Zoo
Reunion Tower
University of Texas Health Sciences Center
Dallas–Love Field
Texas Stadium
Irving
The Palace of Wax & Ripley's Believe It or Not
Grand Prairie
Duncanville
Joe Pool Lake
Cedar Hill State Park
Dallas–Fort Worth International Airport
International Parkway
Airport Freeway
Grapevine
Grapevine Lake
Dallas Convention & Visitors Bureau
Visitor Information Center
West Fork Trinity
Six Flags Over Texas
Arlington
North Richland Hills
Haltom City
Fort Worth Convention & Visitors Bureau
Stockyards National Historic District
Sundance Square
Fort Worth Nature Center & Refuge
Will Rogers Memorial Center
Fort Worth Zoo
Eagle Mountain Lake
Lake Worth
Benbrook Lake
Trinity River

Dallas

My mentor in the journalism business, Ray Miller, says promoters created Dallas. He says the city had no industrial base, no reason for being there, except that it was promoted into existence by a bunch of "fat cats" from the East.

He may be right, but if he is, even Ray has to admit that those fat cats did a helluva job of promotion. Today Dallas and the rest of the Metroplex is probably the most dynamic region in the southwestern United States. Dallas didn't have a ship channel to jump-start its economy in the early days. It didn't have thriving cotton, rice, and cattle businesses to draw from. Dallas had to create its own industries, and those industries—like the fashion business, movies, and banking—have done quite well in the past half century. Dallas now ranks third in the United States in the number of headquarters for Fortune 500 companies. It has more shopping centers and more retail space per capita than any other U.S. city. It is home to the two largest Methodist and Baptist churches in the world. It has set aside 60 acres downtown for an art district.

Dallas has quietly lost the age-old battle with Houston to be the largest city in Texas. In fact, the most recent census indicates that San Antonio has moved into second place ahead of Big D, though you'll be hard-pressed to find anybody in this town who'll admit it. But the bottom line is that size doesn't really matter. Dallas is still probably the most recognized and written-about city in the state.

Dallas continues to promote itself. People are still coming to the city to find out where J. R. lives, to examine the grassy knoll around the Texas Schoolbook Depository Building, and to visit Six Flags, the West End, and hundreds of other places available for tourists who choose to live the Big-D experience.

Getting Around

Serious map-users may want to get the **Mapsco** set of maps of the Dallas–Fort Worth area, which cost about $20 and are revised annually. **5308 Maple Ave., Dallas, 75235; 1-800-950-5308, 214-521-2131, fax**

214-559-0081; admin@mapsco.com; www.mapsco.com.

BUSES

Dallas Area Rapid Transit (DART)

The city's main public transportation offers service around town as well as to the two major airports. One of the nice things about Dallas is that they have some buses painted like rabbits, kangaroos, and frogs that circulate downtown and will take you to places like the Arts District, the West End, and the Reunion area for a reasonable price. They are on the "Hop A Bus" high-frequency routes, and they run from sunup to sundown. Hop A Bus route information is available from DART; **214-749-3278; www.dart.org.**

TAXIS

For taxi services, call **Lone Star Cab (214-821-6310)** and **Yellow Checker Cab (214-426-6262).**

TOURS

McKinney Avenue Trolley

Operates from 10 A.M. to 10 P.M. and carries passengers along a 3-mile, 23-stop route along McKinney Avenue, a popular dining and shopping area. **214-855-0006.**

Dallas Gray Line Tours

For $20, take a 3-hour tour of some of the city's main attractions. **214-824-2424.**

Dallas Surrey Services

Offers daily horse-drawn carriage rides through downtown's West End Historic District. **214-946-9911.**

D-Tours

Offers custom, escorted sightseeing of Dallas and vicinity to individuals and groups. **214-241-7729.**

Visitor Information

Dallas Convention and Visitors Bureau

1201 Elm St., No. 2000, Dallas, 75270; **214-571-1000**, fax **214-571-1008; info@dallascvb.com; www.dallascvb.com.**

Dallas Visitors Information Center

The Dallas Chamber of Commerce staffs this booth in the restored 1916 railroad terminal. **West End Marketplace, 603 Munger Ave.; 214-571-1300.**

Major Attractions

Fair Park

The park is home of the annual state exposition, where millions of visitors are entertained for 3 weeks every fall. The facility serves as a popular city park the rest of the year. In October, however, the 200-acre park is home to Broadway musicals, prize livestock and horse-show performances, and a huge midway that features the Texas Star, the largest Ferris wheel in the Western Hemisphere. When I was growing up in West Texas, my birthday present every year from the time I was 7 years old until I was a teenager was a trip on the train to visit my relatives in Dallas and to go to the State Fair of Texas. My uncle never bought us tickets to the annual Cotton Bowl football game, but he would fork over a few cents for a ride on the Texas Star. Fair Park is at **1300 Robert B. Cullum Blvd.**, on the near east side of the downtown Dallas shopping district; from I-30 take the 2nd Ave. exit and follow the signs to the park entrance; **214-670-8400; www.dallascvb.com.**

Among the many attractions in the park is the **Age of Steam Museum**, offering a nostalgic look at the heyday of the railroads **(1105 N. Washington Ave., 214-428-0101, arlington@railroad.net)**. At the park you'll find much, much more: the **Aquarium**, home to more than 375 species of aquatic animals **(1st St. and Martin Luther King Jr. Blvd., 214-670-8443, www.dallas-zoo.org/aquarium.htm); Cotton Bowl Stadium**, site of the annual Texas–Oklahoma college football clash and the annual Cotton Bowl football game **(3750 Midway Plaza Blvd., 214-670-8400); Dallas Horticulture Center (3601 Martin Luther King Jr. Blvd., 214-428-7476, dhort@hotmail.com, www.start-ext.net.homes/dhc); Hall of State**, a majestic shrine that depicts Texas historical figures **(3939 Grand Ave., 214-421-4500);** the **Museum of Natural History (3535 Grand Ave., 214-421-DINO, www.dallasdino.com); Science Place**, with more than 250 hands-on exhibits **(1318 S. 2nd Ave., 214-428-7000, edhelp@scienceplace.org, www.scienceplace.org); Starplex Amphitheater (3800 S. Fitzhugh Ave., 214-421-1100, joey@starplex.com);** and the **State Fair of Texas**

Coliseum, hosting rodeos, horse shows, and sporting events throughout the year **(214-565-9931).**

Reunion Tower

In the nineteenth century, a settlement of French immigrants came to Dallas and established a community in what is now known as the Reunion area. It was the first test of pure socialism in this country, and it didn't work. The community dissolved after a few years, and the people blended into the American way of life.

Several historical markers west of downtown Dallas recognize that effort—and that's where Reunion Tower got its name. The irony of it is that the fifty-story tower is now a major drawing card to downtown Dallas—its success based on pure capitalism. The site draws thousands upon thousands of people to the downtown area year-round for sporting events and for elaborate eating and drinking in a revolving lounge. Located on the southwestern edge of Dallas at **300 Reunion Blvd. E.; 214-939-2770.**

Seeing and Doing

Gardens and Arboreta

Dallas Arboretum and Botanical Garden

Sixty-six acres of natural beauty just minutes from downtown Dallas. Also here is the 21,000-square-foot Everett DeGloyer Mansion, built in 1940 by the Texas oil millionaire, and decorated with antiques and artwork from the sixteenth and seventeenth centuries. The gardens offer blooming plants year-round, but none as colorful as the 2,000 varieties of azaleas in the spring and summer. **8525 Garland Rd., overlooking White Rock Lake; 214-327-8263.**

Museums and Historic Sites

Dallas Memorial Center for Holocaust Studies

Photographs, artifacts, and documentary films recalling a tragic time in world history. **7900 Northaven St.; 214-750-4654.**

Deep Ellum Historic District

In the early 1900s this was a center for African-American business and entertainment, and a center

John Neely Bryan Cabin in Dallas. Photo courtesy of Texas Highways *magazine.*

for blues music and artists. Today it's home to popular shops, restaurants, and clubs that specialize in music from country-western to rock 'n' roll. **Bounded by Elm, Commerce, Oakland, and Good Latimer Sts.; 214-747-3337; www.ondaweb.com/deep_ellum.**

John Neely Bryan Cabin

The reconstructed log cabin of John Neely Bryan, who in 1841 became the first man to settle the area that would someday be Dallas. **In Dallas County Historical Plaza, 600 Elm St.**

Old City Park

A favorite people-place where the nostalgia of yesterday lingers in restored log cabins and turn-of-the-century shops. Just south of downtown, at **1717 Gano St.; 214-421-5141.**

The Sixth Floor

A permanent educational exhibition on the life and death of President John F. Kennedy, featuring photographs, artifacts, and a 30-minute audio tour. There are other Kennedy memorials on Houston Street near Elm Street, which marks the spot where Kennedy was assassinated November 22, 1963. **At the Texas Schoolbook Depository Building, 411 Elm St.; 214-653-6660.**

Swiss Avenue Historic District

European immigrants settled this neighborhood in the 1850s and it became the grandest neighborhood in the city until about 1920. In the 1970s, history buffs started restoring the old houses and today, Swiss Avenue is a showplace once more. **Swiss Avenue is between Fitzhugh and La Vista Sts.**

West End Historic District

Shops and restaurants, and a generally enjoyable place to entertain friends or to be entertained. The "in" place to be seen in Dallas these days. **Area around Market St. from Pacific to McKinney, 301 N. Market St.; 214-720-7107.**

Other Sights

Union Station

An aging railroad facility that outlasted the era of the passenger trains is given new life as Amtrak's Dallas headquarters. A tunnel connects the grand old building to the railroad tracks and on westward to the Hyatt Regency Hotel and Reunion Tower. **401 S. Houston St.; 214-653-1101.**

Parks

Dallas World Aquarium

Showcases sea life from all over the world, featuring sharks, stingrays, and exotic corals. **1801 N. Griffin St.; 214-720-2224.**

Dallas Zoo

Thousands of animals representing more than 1,400 species, with an extremely large rattlesnake collection and a walk-through tropical rain forest. Within the zoo is a 25-acre African exhibit featuring 90 species of birds, mammals, and reptiles. **621 E. Clarendon Dr.; 214-670-5656; dallaszoo@airmail.net.**

Pioneer Plaza

A 4-acre plaza that features the largest bronze monument in the world: of seventy Texas longhorn cattle being driven by three cowboys on horseback. **Between Young and Griffin Sts.; 214-953-1184.**

Thanksgiving Square

A waterfall and landscaping provide a quiet retreat in the center of bustling downtown Dallas. On Thursdays, there often is a special program for the lunch crowd. **Bounded by Award, Bryan, Pacific, and Ervay Sts.; 214-969-1977, fax 214-754-0152; info@ thanksgiving.org; www.thanksgiving.org.**

Shopping

Dallas has 630 shopping centers. Most are like shopping centers anywhere else, but then there are a few special places.

Deep Ellum

A collection of off-the-wall shops that handle goods ranging from custom-made cowboy boots to retro furniture. **Elm Street warehouse district at 2932 Main St.; 214-748-4332; ondaweb.com/deep_ellum.**

Farmer's Market

One of the largest markets in the nation, where upward of 1,000 farmers bring fresh produce to sell. **1010 S. Pearl Expressway; 214-939-2808.**

The Galleria

A supermall with restaurants, hotels, cinemas, year-round ice rink, and 195 stores, including Gucci, Saks Fifth Avenue, and Tiffany & Company. **Dallas Parkway at LBJ Freeway; 972-404-0215.**

Highland Park Village

Claims to be the first shopping center in Texas; it was built in 1931. **47 Highland Park Village, between two fashionable neighborhoods and near the campus of Southern Methodist University; 214-559-2740; www.hpv.com.**

Neiman-Marcus

The original department store that started the American craze for expensive gifts. My mother used to go there just to get shopping bags with "Neiman-Marcus" printed on them. When Stanley Marcus sent out those very first mail-order catalogs in 1959, he advertised black Angus steers for sale; customers could have one delivered alive, or in the form of steaks. A more recent catalog offered a pair of shar-pei puppies for $4,000 and some private-stock barbecue sauce for $14 a bottle. **At Main and Ervay Sts. in the West End Historic District; 214-891-1280.**

Olla Podrida

More than sixty arts, crafts, and antique specialty shops in north Dallas. **5100 Belt Line Rd.; 972-386-6006.**

The Quadrangle

One of the best sidewalk cafe environments in the city, mixed with small specialty shops and pueblo-style stucco buildings. **2800 Routh St. between Cedar Springs and McKinney; 214-871-0878.**

West End Marketplace

One hundred retails shops mixed with restaurants and pubs. **1701 N. Market St.; 214-748-4801.**

Sports

Dallas Cowboys

Once America's *team,* now America's *talk.* They still play exciting Big League football from August through December. **Texas Stadium, 1 Cowboys Parkway, Irving; 972-556-2800; www.dallascowboys.com.**

Dallas Mavericks

A National Basketball Association franchise since 1980. **Reunion Arena, 777 Sports Place; 214-748-1808; www.nba.com/mavericks.**

Malibu Grand Prix and Castle

Entertainment complex featuring sprint racing tracks and vintage racing cars, plus miniature golf and video games. **11130 Malibu Dr.**

Rodeo

Every Friday and Saturday night from the first week in April through the last week in September, the **Mesquite Championship Rodeo** is held. It has been a tradition since 1958. It's a 2-hour rodeo that rivals the pure excitement of a professional football game. The rodeo starts at 8 P.M., but gates open at 6:30 and the barbecue pavilion serves up delicious meals before show time. This is a great experience for anyone who has never seen a professional rodeo before. **Off LBJ Freeway south at the Military Parkway exit; 1-800-833-9339, 972-285-8777, fax 972-289-2999; eddie@mesquiterodeo.com; www.mesquiterodeo.com.**

Texas Rangers

American League baseball action from mid-April to early October. **The Ball Park at Arlington, 1000 Ballpark Way; 817-273-5100; www.texasrangers.com.**

Willow Bend Polo and Hunt Club

Matches are played between the resident team and international opponents in May and June and from September through November. **5845 W. Park Blvd.; 214-248-6298.**

Tours

Dr. Pepper Factory

A tour of the back rooms and the assembly lines that create this made-in-Texas soft drink. Wednesdays only, and reservations are required, but if you're lucky enough to get in, you'll get a free Dr. Pepper. **2304 Century Center Blvd.; 214-721-8315.**

Mrs. Baird's Bread

Tours of this famous Texas bakery are offered every day except Tuesday; reservations required. **5203 Mockingbird Ln.; 214-526-7201.**

Festivals and Events

January

New Year's Day Cotton Bowl Game

Annual college football extravaganza matching two of the nation's top teams. **Downtown and Fair Park.**

February

Tri-Delta Charity Antiques Show

Second weekend in the month. **Dallas Convention Center; 214-939-2700.**

March

Dallas Auto Show

Five-day event that is one of the largest auto shows in the country, with more than 600 vehicles on display. **Dallas Convention Center; 214-939-2700.**

Dallas Blooms

More than 200,000 flowering bulbs; includes plant sales, flower arranging, beekeeping, and more. **Dallas Arboretum and Botanical Gardens, White Rock Lake area; 214-327-8263.**

April

Bryon Nelson Golf Classic
Internationally recognized PGA tour event. **Las Colinas Sports Club, 4900 N. O'Connor Rd., in Irving; 214-541-1141.**

USA Film Festival
Award-winning independent and experimental films and premiers of major motion pictures presented over a 7-day period. **2917 Swiss Ave., Dallas, 75204; 214-821-6364, fax 214-821-6364; www.usa filmfestival.com.**

May

Artfest
Dallas's largest arts and crafts festival. **Cotton Bowl Plaza at Fair Park; 214-421-9600.**

Cinco de Mayo Festival
A festival celebrating one of the most important battles in Mexican history. **Fair Park; 214-421-9600.**

Swiss Avenue Historic Tour
A tour of at least six restored homes in a fancy early-day Dallas residential district. **On Swiss Ave.** For more information, call the **Dallas Visitors Information Center at 214-571-1300.**

June–July

Shakespeare Festival
In June and July. Outdoor performances of Shakespeare plays. **5808 E. Grand Ave. in Samuell-Grand Park; 214-670-4100.**

July

Taste of the West End
A festival of food and live music during weekends in mid-July. **West End Historic District; 414-720-7107.**

September

Montage
A festival of performing arts, plus arts and crafts,

that spans a 3-day weekend. It usually includes the annual Dallas Dance Festival at the Dallas Museum of Art. **Flora St. in the Arts District; 214-922-1200.**

October

Cityfest
A fall festival that celebrates the many cultures that make up the Dallas population: art exhibits, live jazz and pop music, fun runs, chili cook-offs, and more. **City Hall Plaza and various downtown locations.** For more information, call the **Dallas Visitors Information Center** at **214-571-1300.**

State Fair of Texas
The largest exposition in the country, including livestock exhibitions, football games, parades, a rodeo, and a midway of rides and games. **P.O. Box 150009, Dallas, 75315; 214-670-8400; www.dallas cvb.com.**

Vineyard Fair
Dallas's oldest arts and crafts fair, with antiques, art, crafts, music, and other entertainment. **2800 Routh St.** Call the **Dallas Visitors Information Center** at **214-571-1300.**

November

Downtown Dallas YMCA Turkey Trot
A Thanksgiving Day race through the city covering 8 miles; draws up to 12,000 contestants annually. **Starts at City Hall.** Call the **Dallas Visitors Information Center** at **214-571-1300.**

SMU Literary Festival
Writers and poets read from their works and conduct seminars during this week-long event. **Southern Methodist University campus; 214-768-4414.**

December

Old City Park Candlelight Tour
Turn-of-the-century homes and stores are decorated in a traditional Christmas setting. **S. Ervay and Gano, near downtown; 214-421-5141.**

Recreation

Biking

The City of Dallas maintains bike trails all over the city. The two longest and most popular biking trails are **along White Rock Creek** and **around White Rock Lake.** For more information about bike trails, contact the **Dallas Parks and Recreation Department, 7803 Fair Oaks Blvd., 75231; 214-670-8351.**

Golfing

Dallas has a number of very good city-owned golf courses: **Cedar Crest (1800 Southerland Ave., 214-670-7615); Grover C. Keeton (2323 N. Jimm Miller Rd., 214-670-8784); L. B. Houston (11223 Luna Rd., 214-670-6322);** and **Tenison Park (3501 Samuell Blvd., 214-821-1771).**

The Dallas Metroplex area has two notable golf resorts. The Four Seasons Resort and Club in Las Colinas allows its guests to play the **TPC at Las Colinas,** home of the GTE Bryon Nelson Classic **(4200 N. McArthur Blvd., 214-717-2530).** It's difficult to imagine a golf resort at Dallas–Fort Worth International Airport, but one is there: **Hyatt/Bear Creek Resort** rests right underneath the flight path. Bear Creek East has been rated one of the nation's top seventy-five resort courses **(3500 Bear Creek Court, 972-615-6800, fax 214-453-6410).**

The **Radisson North Texas Golf Course** in Denton, about 40 miles northeast of Dallas on I-35, is located right across I-35 from the University of North Texas **(2211 I-35, 940-565-8499).** The course was built just after World War II and was the home course of the four-time NCAA champion North Texas State University team led by Don January and Billy Maxwell.

Hiking

Dallas Nature Center

A 360-acre park in southwest Dallas County near Joe Pool Lake that has 7 miles of hiking trails, picnic areas, a visitor center, and a gift shop. It is a habitat for black-capped vireo and other birds and a variety of Texas mammals, reptiles, fish, and insects. A butterfly garden with wildflowers and reflecting pools attracts a

White Rock Lake, a popular recreation spot near downtown Dallas. Photo courtesy of the Dallas Convention & Visitors Bureau.

variety of native butterflies. **7171 Mountain Creek Parkway; 972-296-1955.**

Nature Trails

The **Mountain View College Nature Trail** winds through 40 acres; open daily; free admission **(off W. Illinois Ave., 23 miles southwest of Dallas, near Grand Prairie, 214-860-8606).** The **L. B. Houston Nature Trail** is part of L. B. Houston Park, a large nature preserve maintained by the Dallas Parks and Recreation Department **(just north of the University of Dallas, on the western edge of the city).**

Horseback Riding

Texas Lil's Diamond A Ranch

Visitors can go horseback riding or swimming, or go on hayrides in a rustic setting. **1125 S. Mukey Ln., in Justin, which is about 40 miles northwest of Dallas via State Hwy. 114, U.S. Hwy. 377, and Farm Road 407; 1-800-545-8455, 817-430-0192; texasslils@texaslils.com; www. texaslils.com.**

Parks and Camping

Bachman Lake

A 205-acre lake ringed by a roller skating and jogging track and featuring a soccer field, playground, and picnic area. Fishing is permitted, and you can rent roller skates and paddleboats. **3500 Northwest Hwy.; 214-670-4100.**

Bachman Recreation Center

A center with a gardenlike atmosphere that is designed to accommodate the disabled, with an indoor swimming pool, auditorium, and arts and crafts areas. **2750 Bachman Dr.; 214-670-6266.**

Bardwell Lake

Has six parks, with camping available at four of them: **Love, Waxahachie Creek, High View,** and **Mott.** There is also a wetlands nature trail on the lake. There are about 200 campsites at Bardwell Lake. The lake is **on State Hwy. 34, 4 miles west of Ennis, which is 34 miles southeast of Dallas on I-45; 972-875-5711.** (Additional information can be obtained through the **Ennis Convention and Visitors Bureau, 100 E. Ennis Ave., 1-888-366-4748.**)

Joe Pool Lake

Joe Pool Lake **(south of I-20 between Fort Worth and Dallas, 817-467-2104)** is the site for several parks.

Loyd Park, operated by the Trinity River Authority, is on the west side of the western arm of the lake **(accessible via Ragland and Arlington Webb Rds., 817-467-2104).** Loyd Park, a part of the Joe Pool Lake Recreational Area, has 200 campsites with water and electricity, 30 walk-in primitive campsites, and 2 group camp areas, plus playgrounds, picnic shelters, and hiking trails.

Lynn Creek Park is a day-use park **(off of Lakeridge Parkway, near the spillway, 5700 Lakeridge Parkway, 817-633-6265).**

Cedar Hill State Park, operated by the Texas Parks and Wildlife Department, has 7.5 miles of frontage of the lake's northeastern shore **(1570 Farm Road 1382, 4 miles south of I-20, 972-291-3900, www.tpwd.state.tx.us/park/cedarhil/cedarhil.htm).** The main access to Cedar Hill is via Farm Road 1382, Belt Line Rd., and Mansfield Rd.

Cedar Hill has 355 campsites with water and electricity, 2 primitive camping areas, and 2 group pavilions with fishing piers, boat docks, and a swimming beach.

Lake Tawakoni

Offers camping facilities in **Arm Point Park, Que Pasa Park,** and **Wind Point Park. Go 34 miles east of Dallas on I-20, then 20 miles east on U.S. Hwy. 80 to Wills Point; the lake is 10 miles north of Wills Point; 903-598-2216.**

Lavon Lake

A 21,000-acre reservoir that has almost two dozen parks, with four camping areas and two hiking trails. **Outside Wylie on State Hwy. 78, 30 miles north of Dallas; 972-442-5711.**

Lewisville Lake

Lewisville Lake **(25 miles north of Dallas, between Dallas and Denton at I-35 and Justin Rd., 972-434-1666)** has 250 miles of shoreline that includes a golf course and a fishing barge. There are sixteen parks around the lake, eleven with camping facilities. The most popular is **Lake Lewisville State Park** on the east-central shore near Wills Point **(903-595-2938),** a 720-acre park with 50 campsites, 38 screened shelters, and room for fishing, swimming, boating, picnicking, and softball.

RV Parks

KOA Kampground Dallas has tent and camper sites, plus cabins and full hookups **(30 miles northwest of Dallas, off I-35, 1-800-562-1893).** Closer in is the **Dallas Hi-Ho Campground,** with full hookups **(18 miles south of Dallas, off I-35 at Bear Creek Rd., exit 412, 214-223-4834).**

White Rock Lake Park

A park surrounding one of the city's oldest and most established lakes. A 12-mile jogging and biking trail along the water's edge encircles the lake. Sailing clubs maintain boat docks on the east side, and paddleboats can be rented on the west side. Old-timers play dominoes on benches around the park, but don't interrupt. They take the game seriously. **8300 Garland Rd.; 214-670-4100.**

Where to Eat

Dallas offers food for just about every taste. Some say it is the gourmet capital of the state. Here's a variety of choices:

8.0 Bar
Health-food dishes with not-so-healthy-sounding names like the Road Kill Platter. The jukebox has more than 1,500 selections. **2800 Routh St.; 214-969-9321.**

Blue Goose Cantina
A favorite Tex-Mex hangout, particularly with the SMU crowd. **2905 Greenville Ave.; 214-823-6786.**

Bubba's
Has all the classics: fried chicken, catfish, biscuits and cream gravy, chicken-fried steak. **6617 Hillcrest Ave.; 214-373-6527.**

The Butcher Shop
A grill-it-yourself steak place; add $2 and they'll cook it for you. **808 Munger Ave.; 214-720-1032.**

Celebration
Down-home cooking in a converted home. **4503 W. Lovers Ln.; 214-904-9911.**

Clark's Outpost
Warren Clark smokes his ribs and brisket for 3 days before it's ready to serve, and people drive from all over North Texas for the barbecue. The walls are lined with pictures of celebrities who have visited the place. It must be good, because a lot of chefs come here for the experience. **U.S. Hwy. 377 and Farm Road 922, 38 miles north of Dallas in Tioga** (Gene Autry's hometown); **940-437-2414.**

Crescent City Cafe
Serves up a great variety of inexpensive New Orleans dishes in the Deep Ellum Historic District. **2615 Commerce St.; 214-745-1900.**

Dakota's
Southwestern cuisine, with an emphasis on mesquite-grilled items. **600 N. Akard St.; 214-740-4001.**

Deep Ellum Cafe
Serves up a creative variety of Texas-American dishes, from Tex-Mex to Cajun. **2708 Elm St.; 214-741-9012.**

Elaine's Kitchen
An up-and-coming Jamaican eating place in South Dallas. **1912 Martin Luther King Jr. Blvd.; 214-565-1008.**

Highland Park Cafeteria
One of the state's best cafeterias, with huge selections of salads, vegetables, and homemade breads. **4611 Cole St., off N. Central Expressway; 214-388-4255.**

La Madeleine
Part French bakery, part restaurant, and all wonderful. **3702 Mockingbird Ln., near Southern Methodist University campus; 214-363-4255.**

Mansion on Turtle Creek
First-class southwestern servings with specialties like quail quesadillas and cheese-filled squash blossoms. **2821 Turtle Creek Blvd.; 214-559-2100; www.mansiononturtlecreek.com.**

Mia's Tex-Mex
Family-run Mexican food establishment where the Dallas Cowboys like to fatten up. You can expect a long line during the peak dining hours. **4322 Lemmon Ave.; 214-526-1020.**

Prince of Hamburgers
A locally famous drive-in that was here before McDonald's and all the other fast-food places took over. They offer burgers like we all grew up with, plus curb service. **5200 Lemmon Ave.; 214-526-9081.**

Sonny Bryan's Smokehouse
Most of the locals say this is the best barbecue in town, but you'd better get there before 2 P.M., because they usually sell out by then. **2202 Inwood Rd.; 214-357-7120.**

Where to Stay

Dallas has all the usual chain hotels but, like Houston, very little in the budget category. When I'm in the area I usually stay in the 'burbs, where the prices are better and you don't have to fight over reservations. But if you can afford it, there are plenty of spots in Dallas that will treat you like royalty, such as: **The Adolphus (1321 Commerce St., 214-742-8200, fax 214-651-3563); Crescent Court (400 Crescent Court, 1-800-654-6541, 214-871-3200); Dallas Grand Hotel (1914 Commerce St., 214-747-7000, fax 214-742-1337, dallasgrand@ earthlink.net, www.dallasgrandhotel.com); Fairmont Hotel (1717 N. Akard St., 214-720-** **2020, www.businesswire.com/cnn/dallas. htm); and The Mansion on Turtle Creek (2821 Turtle Creek Blvd., 214-559-2100, www. mansiononturtlecreek.com).**

Dallas has the largest registry of bed-and-breakfasts in the state, covering not only the Dallas area but also most of the rest of the state. To book a B&B in North-Central Texas, contact **Bed-and-Breakfast Texas Style, 4224 W. Red Bird Ln., Dallas, 75237; 1-800-899-4538; bdtxstyle @aol.com; www.bnbtexasstyle.com.**

Fort Worth

I was in London some years back to attend the World Travel Market, where people from all over the world reserve booths and put up exhibits to promote their countries. Texas was represented by a booth that was larger than the ones put together by most countries. It wasn't difficult to promote Texas. People love Texas and the Texas mystique. And it seemed that every outsider's favorite city in Texas was Fort Worth. Nearly everyone I talked to at the World Travel Market wanted to know what Fort Worth was like. I suspect the Fort Worth Chamber of Commerce had more than a little bit to do with that. They were much better at promoting their town than were Houston, Dallas, or even San Antonio. But for whatever reason, most of the people's fascination with Texas centered on Fort Worth: Cowtown!

Following the Civil War, the great Texas cattle drives began. Between the late 1860s and the mid-1880s, about 10 million head of cattle were driven north along the Chisholm, Dodge City, and Loving-Goodnight Trails. The Chisholm Trail went right by a fort that was built many years before to give settlers some shelter and protection from Indians. This was Camp Worth, later named Fort Worth, but known best by most of the cowboys simply as Cowtown. Fort Worth was the last outpost along the trail to Abilene, Kansas, so cattle drovers always stopped there for supplies and some hell-raising before heading north. It was also the very first stop when they returned with money in their pockets from those long, hard days on the trail.

Cowtown became one of those wild and crazy Texas towns with a gathering of saloons, casinos, and whorehouses. The wildest part of town was Hell's Half Acre, where the Convention Center and Water Gardens are now situated. Needless to say, Cowtown attracted a lot of characters who went on to become famous and infamous. George Parker (Butch Cassidy) and Harry Longabaugh (the Sundance Kid) and a number of other unsavory characters established temporary residence in Fort Worth, until Marshall Jim Courtright was hired to keep peace. But even Courtright couldn't completely do that. Saloon owner Luke Short, who was much of a character himself, outdrew the marshal at the White Elephant Saloon in 1887. It was the last gunfight, western-style, in the city. Now, every February, the gunfight is reenacted for tourists outside the saloon where it happened.

Today, Hell's Half Acre is congested with city traffic, and all the saloons and bawdy houses are long since gone. But Fort Worth has maintained its spectacular image of yesterday. The main part of the downtown business district is known as Sundance Square, and the Fort Worth stockyards still move many thousands of cattle in and out all year long.

A parade of cowboys and cowgirls at the Fort Worth Stockyards. Photo courtesy of Texas Highways magazine.

Getting Around

BUSES

The **Fort Worth Transit Authority** bus system is free in the downtown area **(817-870-6200)**. Elsewhere, there is a small charge, but for about $3 you can buy 2-day visitor passes that give you unlimited use of the buses.

A free **subway (817-877-9999)** runs between the Tandy Center Mall at the north end of Throckmorton Street and a free parking lot across the Trinity River. The subway takes you right into the heart of the downtown shopping district.

TAXIS

Among taxi services is **Yellow Checker Cabs (817-534-5555)**.

TOURS

Antique Carriages (817-870-1464) pulled by Clydesdales make regular stops at the **Worthington Hotel (200 Main St., 817-870-1000)** and the **Radisson Plaza Hotel (815 Main St.**

North Fort Worth Historical Society offers group tours of the stockyards area, and horseback rides are also available **(131 E. Exchange Ave., Suite 115, in the Livestock Exchange Building, 817-625-5082)**. **Gray Line** gives tours of the stockyards, the cultural district, historical buildings, and downtown **(817-625-5887)**.

Visitor Information

Fort Worth Chamber of Commerce

Free street maps of Fort Worth. **777 Taylor St.; 817-625-6427**.

Fort Worth Convention and Visitors Bureau

Brochures on attractions, dining, and accommodations, as well as a map of the cultural district. **In Sundance Square, downtown, at 415 Throckmorton St., Fort Worth, 76102; 1-800-433-5747, 817-336-8791; linda@fortworth.com.**

Fort Worth Visitor Information Center

Brochures on attractions, dining, and accommodations, as well as a map of the cultural district. **131 E. Exchange Ave., opposite the Livestock Exchange in the Stockyards District; 817-624-4741.**

Major Attractions

Fort Worth Stockyards National Historic District

At the turn of the twentieth century, the Fort Worth stockyards were the largest in the world. In 1976 the entire district was added to the National Register of Historic Places. The yards still play a very active role in the Texas livestock industry, and are host to forty-two livestock commission companies that do business here weekly. There are about fifty restaurants, saloons, dance halls, art galleries, and western-wear shops in the immediate area.

The Stockyards District is located about 2.5 miles north of downtown via North Main Street. Turn right onto E. Exchange Ave. to reach the Coliseum, Livestock Exchange, and Visitor Center, where you can sign up for guided tours. Main address for the stockyards is **131 E. Exchange Ave., 100B, Fort Worth, 76106; 817-626-7621; nfuta@fortworth stockyards.org; www.ftworthstockyards. com.**

Among the attractions in the district: **Livestock Exchange Building,** a Mission-style structure that serves as the main building at the stockyards **(131 E. Exchange Ave., 817-624-0679); Cowtown Coliseum,** site of the first indoor rodeo, in 1918 **(111 W. 4th St., 817-336-4475, fax 817-336-2470); National Cowgirl Hall of Fame (across the street from the Coliseum); Stockyards Hotel,** built in 1906—Bonnie and Clyde once stayed here **(109 E. Exchange Ave., 817-625-6427); Billy**

Bob's Texas, world's largest honky-tonk—this place has opened and closed a number of times due to fire and/or financing, so don't schedule your trip to Fort Worth around a trip to Billy Bob's; if it's open when you come, you are likely to see live bands 7 days a week and live bull riding on weekends (**2520 Rodeo Plaza, 817-624-7117, fax 817-626-2340, webmaster@billybobstexas.com; www.billybobstexas.com**).

The stockyards really come alive during the Southwest Exposition and Livestock Show and Rodeo in January, the Chisholm Trail Roundup in June, and Pioneer Days in September. On Sunday mornings during these events, you can even attend a cowboy church in a dirt corral behind the auction arena.

The **Tarantula Steam Train** is housed in a former sheep and hog pen at the stockyards. It's named for an early railroad map of Fort Worth that showed spiderlike rail lines radiating in all directions. This excursion train is operated by the Fort Worth & Western Railroad and carries passengers on a 10-mile round-trip route from the Eighth Avenue Depot downtown at **2318 S. 8th Ave.,** across the Trinity River to the stockyards station at **140 E. Exchange Ave.** It makes three runs daily. **1-800-952-5717; www.tourtexas.com/grapevine/gpvntran.html.**

Sundance Square

The square encompasses 8 historic city blocks, separated by red-brick streets. At the north end of the square is the 1895 **Tarrant County Courthouse,** constructed of pink granite and marble (**100 W. Weatherford St., 817-884-1111**). The oldest building in the square is the **Knights of Pythias Hall,** built in 1881 (**317 Main St., 817-831-1932**). The **Plaza Hotel** came along in 1908 and was one of Fort Worth's last working brothels before it was restored in 1982 (**301 Main St., 817-551-1256**). The **Sid Richardson Collection of Western Art** shows an assortment of sixty paintings by Frederic Remington and Charles Russell (**309 Main St., 817-332-6554**).

Other buildings of interest in Sundance Square include the **Weber Building (400 Main St.),** the **Conn Building (310 Main St.),** the **Jetts Building (400 Main St.),** and **Fire Station No. 1 (2nd and Commerce Sts., www.fortworth.com/sundance),** built in 1907.

Fort Worth Cultural District

Forth Worth has four museums in its cultural district. None charges admission except for special exhibits.

Amon Carter Museum

A collection of western art preserved by the founder of the *Fort Worth Star Telegram.* **3501 Camp Bowie Blvd., between Lancaster and Montgomery; 817-738-1933, fax 817-377-8523; www.cartermuseum.org.**

Kimbell Art Museum

Works by Rembrandt, Monet, Picasso, and many others. **3333 Camp Bowie Blvd.; 817-332-8451, fax 817-877-1264; www.kimbelart.org.**

Modern Art Museum of Fort Worth

The city's first museum. **1309 Montgomery St.; 817-738-9215, fax 817-335-9220; www.mamfw.org.**

Museum of Science and History

Includes the Noble Planetarium and the Omni Theater. **1501 Montgomery St.; 817-255-9300.**

Seeing and Doing

Gardens and Arboreta

Fort Worth Botanic Garden and Japanese Garden

A 114-acre showplace with 2,000 different plants, more than 150 varieties of trees, and 3,500 rose bushes. **3220 Botanic Garden Dr.; 817-870-7686.**

Museums and Historic Sites

American Airlines C. R. Smith Museum

An airline museum, not an aircraft museum; dedicated to the father of American Airlines. **State Hwy. 360 and FAA Road, southwest of Dallas–Fort Worth International Airport; 817-967-1560; www.amrcorp.com.**

Log Cabin Village

Seven restored Texas log cabins built by some of the city's early pioneers. **2100 Log Cabin Village Ln., near Texas Christian University; 817-926-5881.**

Sundance Square in Fort Worth. Photo courtesy of Texas Highways magazine.

Thistle Hill Cattle Baron Mansion

A handsome Georgian Revival mansion built in 1903 that recalls the city back when cattle barons were riding high. Open for hourly tours. **1509 Pennsylvania Ave.; 817-336-1212.**

Will Rogers Memorial Center

Site of Fort Worth's Southwestern Exposition and Livestock Show, and one of the nation's premier equestrian centers. Flanked by a mounted statue of the famous cowboy humorist. **3300 W. Lancaster Ave., in the Cultural District at Amon Carter Square; 817-871-8150, fax 817-871-8170.**

Other Sights

Forest Park Train Ride

The world's longest miniature train ride, carrying passengers 5 miles along the Trinity River in Trinity Park and Forest Park. **University Dr., south of I-30 at the Forth Worth Zoo; 817-336-3328.**

The Last Supper

A life-size wax-figure interpretation of the Last Supper, commissioned by the Southern Baptist Convention. **6350 West Freeway; 817-737-4011.**

Pawnee Bill's Wild West Show

A rootin' tootin' round of trick riders, Indian dancers, singing cowboys, bulldogging, and stagecoach holdups in the grand old tradition of Buffalo Bill. From April to mid-September; tickets $8. **Cowtown Coliseum; 817-654-1148.**

Parks

Fort Worth Water Gardens

Architect Phillip Johnson designed this descending series of terraces and water sculptures. It was built in 1974 and covers 4 city blocks. It's a quiet place to get away from the downtown summer heat. **Between Houston and Commerce Sts. near the Convention Center; 817-871-7698.**

Fort Worth Zoo

A 35-acre zoo with 5,000 animals and almost 1,000 species. I used to come here as a kid, when it was known worldwide as one of the best zoos in the United States; it still is. The aquarium features an extensive collection of freshwater and saltwater fish. The elephant grounds is one of the most successful in the United States for Asian elephant breeding, and the World of Primates exhibit is the only such facility in the nation to feature all four great ape species. **1989 Colonial Parkway off University Dr.; 817-871-7000.**

Heritage Park

Water and a restful park located on a cliff giving you a bird's-eye view of the Trinity River Valley to the north. This marks the site of the original Camp Worth. **E. Belknap St. at Houston St. behind the courthouse; 817-870-8700.**

Shopping

Texas produces more boots than anyplace else in the world. Most come from factories rather than individual bookmakers, but there are still a few individuals left. At **M. L. Leddy's Boots and Saddlery,** boots start at about $400, saddles at $1,400 **(2455 N. Main St., 817-624-3149). Ryon's Saddle and Ranch** also creates custom-made boots; prices are about the same as Leddy's **(2601 N. Main St., 817-625-2391). Justin Boot Company Factory Outlet** sells ready-made factory seconds or overstocks for considerably less than retail **(717 W. Vickery Blvd., 817-654-3103). Luskey's Western Wear** offers ready-made boots and other western apparel and has done so since 1919 **(101 Houston St., 817-335-5833).**

Antique Colony

More than 100 shops selling antiques and collectibles. **7200 Camp Bowie Blvd.; 817-731-7252.**

Maverick Saloon and Trading Post

Southwestern fashions for the whole family. **100 E. Exchange Ave.; 817-626-1129.**

Park Hill Coffee and Tea House

More than 40 coffee and 60 tea varieties from all over the world. **2970 Park Hill Dr.; 817-921-5660.**

Sports

Rodeo

Every Saturday night brings a rodeo as part of a year-round series of contests. Events begin at 8 P.M. and last for about 2 hours. The events can include such entertaining amateur competitions as the Texas High School Rodeo Finals in early June and professional events like the Chisholm Trail Round-up Rodeo in mid-June. **Stockyards Cowtown Coliseum; 817-625-7005.**

Wagering

Trinity Meadows Race Track

About 12 miles west of Fort Worth on I-20 at Aledo, Texas, near Weatherford; **817-441-6819.**

Festivals and Events

January

Southwest Exposition and Livestock Show and Rodeo

Usually late January and early February. This is the largest annual event in the city, with downtown parades, livestock judging, and rodeoing. **Will Rogers Memorial Center, 1 Amon Carter Square; 817-871-8150.**

February

The Last Great Gunfight

Usually the first weekend in the month. A re-creation of the encounter between saloon owner Luke Short and Marshall Jim "Longhair" Courtright, who shot it out in front of the saloon in 1887. Short was quickest on the draw—and he still is every time the shootout is reenacted. **White Elephant Saloon in the Stockyards District.**

The Water Gardens in downtown Fort Worth. Photo courtesy of Texas Highways *magazine.*

March

Main Street Fort Worth Art Festival

Weekends in mid-March. A festival of outdoor art and performances on stage. **Main Street, downtown.**

May

Colonial Golf Tournament

Usually third weekend in the month. Annual PGA golf tournament at the course built by Ben Hogan. **3735 Country Club Circle near University Dr.; 817-927-4243.**

Mayfest

Weekends early in the month. A community picnic honoring the city's rite of spring. Included are art shows, bathtub races, and entertainment. **Trinity Park.**

Van Cliburn International Piano Competition

May–June (every 4 years). In the 1950s a young Texas pianist, Van Cliburn, won the Tchaikovsky International Piano Competition in Moscow, one of the most prestigious in the world. His victory led to the organization of this competition to seek out world-class concert pianists. Now every 4 years the contest marks the beginning of many brilliant concert careers. This is ranked as one of the top three piano competitions in the world. **Landreth Auditorium and Tarrant County Convention Center Theater, 1111 Houston Ave.; 817-738-6536, fax 817-738-6534; www.cliburn.com.**

June

Chisholm Trail Round-up and Chief Quannah Parker Comanche Pow Wow

An annual celebration of the famous cattle-drive trail that helped put Fort Worth on the map. Attractions include chili cook-offs, chuckwagon meals, parades, street dancing, and a Wild West Show—one of the really fun events in the state every year. **N. Main St. at Exchange Ave. in the Stockyards District;** call the **Fort Worth Visitor Information Center** at **817-624-4741.**

Juneteenth Heritage and Jazz Festival

Around June 19. A 3-day jazz, blues, and gospel music festival featuring name artists in their fields, plus Cajun catfish, barbecued goat ribs, fried chicken, and other delicious dishes. **Convention Center, 1111 Houston St.; 817-336-8791.**

Shakespeare in the Park

Two or three weeks in mid-month. Seventy actors, dancers, and musicians put on two Shakespeare plays in the park. **Trinity Park Playhouse; 817-336-8791.**

September

Fort Worth International Air Show

All the things that go with airshows, including fly-bys of World War II and other vintage aircraft, stunt flying, and modern-day barnstorming. **2250 Alliance Blvd.; 817-336-8791.**

Pioneer Days

Late in the month. A celebration of the city's pioneer heritage, with a western wingding. **N. Main St. and Exchange Ave.;** call the **Fort Worth Visitor Information Center** at **817-624-4741.**

October

Oktoberfest

Usually first weekend in the month. A celebration of the city's German heritage, with plenty of German sausage and oompah music. **Convention Center, 1111 Houston St.; 817-884-2313.**

Red Steagal Cowboy Gathering

Third weekend in the month. Cowboy poetry, chuckwagon camping, and western swing music highlight this event sponsored by the Texas Agricultural Extension Service. **In the Stockyards District;** call the **Fort Worth Visitor Information Center** at **817-624-4741.**

November

National Cutting Horse Futurity

Last weekend in the month. One of the richest Cutting Horse Association contests in the country. **Will Rogers Memorial Center, 1 Amon Carter Square; 817-871-8150.**

Recreation

Biking

Free maps showing bicycle and jogging trails are available from the city **Parks and Recreation Department (2222 W. Rosedale St., 817-212-2700). River Ridge Pavilion** rents bikes to ride on the paved bike trail that runs for miles along the Trinity River; they also rent roller skates and paddleboats **(3201 Riverfront Dr., 817-335-7472).**

Golfing

Fort Worth provides a number of public golf courses: **Golf Club at Fossil Creek (3401 Club Gate Dr., 817-847-1900); Lost Horse Golf Club (4101 Lost Creek Blvd., 817-244-3312); Meadowbrook (1815 Jenson Rd., 817-457-4616); Pecan Valley–Lake Benbrook (east of U.S. Hwy. 377 at 6400 Pecan Valley Dr., 817-249-1845); Rockwood (1851 Jacksboro Hwy., 817-624-1771); Sycamore Creek (2401 Martin Luther King Freeway, 817-535-7241); and Z Boaz Golf Course (3200 Lackland Rd., 817-738-6287).**

Hiking

Lake Mineral Wells State Park

Offers an easy day-hike in the cross-timbers back-country that is about 5 miles round-trip; also some rock climbing. A permit is required for camping. **Forty-two miles west of Fort Worth via U.S. Hwy. 180 and Park Road 71; 940-328-1171.**

Ice-Skating

Tandy Center Ice Rink

Tandy Center Shopping Mall on Throck-morton St. between 2nd and 3rd Sts.; 817-878-4800.

Parks and Camping

Benbrook Lake

A 3,700-acre Army Corps of Engineers lake, with six parks for fishing, boating, waterskiing, swimming, picnicking, hiking, and camping. There are horseback riding trails and stables at Dutch Brand Park, and horseback riding trails at Holiday Park. **Six miles southwest of Fort Worth, off Loop 820 at U.S. Hwy. 377; 817-292-2400.**

Eagle Mountain Lake

A 9,200-acre lake providing boating, fishing, swimming, and other water sports. **Twelve miles northwest of Fort Worth, off State Hwy. 199 via Farm Road 1220; www.tpwd.state.tx.us/fish/infish/lkes/eaglemt.**

Fort Worth Nature Center and Refuge

There are buffalo, prairie dogs, and white-tailed deer in this 3,400-acre preserve, with numerous exhibits, plus nature and hiking trails ranging from a half mile to several miles in length. Bird watchers say it's a cross-roads for eastern and western birds. There is a 900-foot boardwalk that makes it possible to walk out into a marsh and keep your feet dry, and a short trail for strollers and wheelchairs. You can fish or picnic, and there's also a 9-mile equestrian trail. **Twenty miles northwest of Fort Worth (2 miles past Lake Worth Bridge on State Hwy. 199, Jackboro Hwy.); 817-237-1111.**

Isle du Bois

A 1,300-acre wooded playground that is a unit of Ray Roberts Lake State Park, with camping, boating, swimming, and fishing. There is an overnight group pavilion and 12 miles of trail for hiking, biking, and horseback riding (you bring the horse). **South side of Ray Roberts Lake; about 50 miles north of Fort Worth (on Farm Road 455, 10 miles east of I-35); 940-686-2148; www.tpwd.state.tx.us/park/rayrob/rayrob.htm.**

Joe Pool Lake

A 7,400-acre lake along the Dallas–Tarrant Counties line, with several parks for camping. (See Parks and Camping in the Dallas chapter for details.)

Lake Worth

A city-owned lake with public and commercial facilities for boating, fishing, picnicking, and other water sports. The *Queen Maria* riverboat **(817-238-9778)** is available for group charters. The lake is **9 miles northwest of downtown Fort Worth on State Hwy. 199; 817-870-7000.**

RV Parks

Sunset RV Park has full hookups **(4921 White Settlement Rd., off Loop 820 east of downtown Fort Worth, 817-738-0567).** Cowtown RV Park also has full hookups **(about 20 miles west of Fort Worth, at 7000 I-20, 817-441-7878).**

Where to Eat

Carshon's Delicatessen

A kosher meat market that grew into a sandwich shop; they specialize in breakfast. **3133 Cleburne Rd.; 817-923-1907.**

Cattleman's Steak House

Has earned a place among the traditions of the stockyards. **2458 N. Main St.; 817-429-8614.**

El Rancho Grande

My favorite is the El Rancho Grande Sampler, with a little bit of everything that is Tex-Mex. **1400 N. Main St.; 817-624-9206.**

Fort Worth Cattle Company

Provides mesquite-broiled steaks and a pleasing view of the Fort Worth skyline. **1900 Ben St.; 817-534-4908.**

Hubba Hubba's Great American Diner

Serves up '50s decor with its burgers, steaks, chicken, seafood, and some Tex-Mex. **8320 State Hwy. 80; 817-560-2930.**

Joe T. Garcia's

Maybe the best-known Mexican food establishment in town, Joe opened part of his home as a Mexican restaurant in 1935. Today the enlarged old house fills half a city block and is still filled with customers during peak hours. **2201 N. Commerce St.; 817-429-5166.**

Juanita's

Means Mexican food and more: beans and rice and tacos, but also quail in tequila or chili-buttered chicken. **115 W. 2nd St., in Sundance Square; 817-534-1499.**

Kincaid's Grocery/Market

A grocery store that developed into a restaurant. Order at the meat counter and eat at some old grocery shelves that have been converted into stand-up counters. Kincaid's serves barbecue, salads, and catfish, but the big thing here is the burgers. This place was recently voted one of the best burger joints in the country. **4901 Camp Bowie Rd.; 817-732-2881.**

Ol' South Pancake House

Good basic food 24 hours a day. They have some tasty dessert crepes. **1507 S. University Dr.; 817-336-0309.**

Paris Coffee Shop

Home-style cooking for the past 60 years. I love their chicken and dumplings, but their specialty is a huge ranchhand-size breakfast. **704 W. Magnolia Ave.; 817-335-2041.**

Reflections

For those who have everything and can afford it. **Worthington Hotel at 200 Main St.; 817-882-1660.**

Star Cafe

This 80-year-old cafe with wooden floors and plastic chairs may serve the lowest-priced good steaks in the stockyards area. That's all they have on the menu, except for bowls of Fort Worth Chili. **111 W. Exchange Ave.; 817-624-8701.**

Where to Stay

Fort Worth Convention and Visitors Bureau (1-800-433-5747) has a complete listing of bed-and-breakfasts in the area.

Miss Molly's Bed-and-Breakfast

Once a bawdy house, now a bed-and-breakfast with eight guest rooms designed around a Cowtown theme. **109 W. Exchange Ave.; 1-800-99MOLLY, 817-626-1522; www.missmollys.com.**

Stockyards Hotel

A good place to stay in the Stockyards District. **109 E. Exchange Ave.; 817-625-6427.**

The Worthington Hotel

Fancy establishment in Sundance Square. **200 Main St.; 817-870-1000; www.worthinghotel.com.**

The Greater Metroplex: Outside Dallas– Fort Worth

The Metroplex takes in a lot more than just the big cities of Dallas and Fort Worth. The area spans 100 miles or more and encompasses a population of close to 4 million people. In this chapter, we take a look at some of the other towns of the Metroplex—both those immediately adjacent to Dallas and Fort Worth, and many of the communities farther out.

Towns in the Adjacent Area

A number of towns hug the borders of Dallas and Fort Worth. The towns covered here (in alphabetical order) are Addison, Arlington, Carrollton, Cedar Hill, Garland, Grand Prairie, Grapevine, Irving, Lancaster, Mesquite, North Richland Hills, Plano, and Richardson. Suggested places to eat and to stay are included with most of the towns.

Addison

Getting There: Addison is at the north edge of Dallas, about 10 miles from the city center, on State Hwy. 289.

SEEING AND DOING

Cavanaugh Flight Museum
History from both world wars and the Korean War, in a display of antique aircraft that have been refurbished to the way they were when they rolled off the assembly line. **4505 Claire Chennault St., north of** Dallas at Addison Airport; 972-380-8800, fax 972-248-0907; cavanaughflightmuseum.com.

WHERE TO EAT

Stadium Cafe
A popular tourist eating place. **4872 Beltline Rd.; 972-701-0030.**

WHERE TO STAY

Wingate Inn
Clean and convenient. **4960 Arapaho Dr.; 1-800-228-1000.**

Arlington
Getting There: Arlington sits on I-20, right between Dallas and Fort Worth. **Visitor Information: Arlington Convention and Visitors Bureau, 1250 E. Copeland Rd., Suite 650, P.O. Box A, Arlington, 76004; 1-800-342-4305, 817-265-7721; visitinfo@acvb.org; www.arlington.org.** Also, **Arlington Visitor Information Center, Six Flags Dr., Suite 123; 817-640-0252.**

Six Flags Over Texas in Arlington. Photo courtesy of the Dallas Convention & Visitors Bureau.

SEEING AND DOING

Antique Marketplace
A number of small antiques shops gathered under one roof (3500 S. Cooper St., 817-468-0689). More than 200 dealers display their wares at the Antique Sampler Mall; check out the Tea Room there, a popular lunch spot (1715 E. Lamar St., 817-461-3030, fax 817-861-4180, www.antique sampler.com). The Upstairs Gallery is Arlington's oldest art gallery, with art in a variety of media (1038 W. Abram St., 817-277-6961).

Antique Sewing Machine Museum
Displays 150 different sewing machines, two dozen dating to during and before the Civil War. Kids get to sew on an old Singer treadle machine. 804 W. Abram St.; 817-275-0971.

Arlington Music Revue
A live country music stage show with a cast of twenty dancers, singers, and musicians. It's a fast-paced performance that offers a dazzling lineup of entertainers; gospel music on Fridays. 224 N. Crester St.; 817-469-9700.

The Ballpark in Arlington
Home of the American League Texas Rangers. It's a great place to tour, especially during baseball season. 15650 Addison Rd.; 817-404-0228.

Kow Bell Rodeo
A regular 2-hour rodeo every Saturday night, with the emphasis on cowboys and bull riding. State Hwy. 157 and Mansfield Hwy., 11 miles south of Arlington; 817-477-3092.

Six Flags Over Texas
A 200-acre theme park, one of the first in Texas, that features fun and fantasy in plush, landscaped settings. The hours vary by season. More than 2.5 million visitors visit the park annually for its shows and its spectacular displays, but mostly for its hundred or so rides that range from an antique carousel to the Texas giant, a 143-foot-tall wooden roller coaster. The park's six main sections reflect the six flags that have flown over Texas. It is hard to see all of Six Flags in one day. On a clear day, and there are plenty of them in this country, you can get a magnificent view of the Dallas–Fort Worth Metroplex from the Six Flags Observation Tower. 2201 Road to Six Flags; 817-530-6000; www.sixflags.com/dallas/index.html.

FESTIVALS AND EVENTS

June—Texas Scottish Festival and Highland Games
Usually the first Saturday and Sunday of the month. The event features bagpipe and drumming competitions, a dance contest, Scottish and Celtic athletic events and demonstrations, a dog show for Scottish breeds, and Scottish foods. At Maverick Stadium, University of Texas–Arlington; 817-654-2293; txscotfest@aol.com.

RECREATION

Lake Arlington
A 2,000-acre city-owned lake with boating, sailing, fishing, and picnicking. Green Oaks Blvd. South, off Loop 303; 817-451-6860.

Golfing
Ditto Golf Course (801 W. Brown Blvd., west of State Hwy. 157, 817-275-5941); Lake Arlington Municipal Golf Course (1516 Green Oaks Blvd. NE, 817-451-6101); Meadow-brook Park (1300 Dugan St., off Abram, 817-275-0221).

WHERE TO EAT

Colter's BBQ
Serves up some popular eats. 3700 S. Cooper St.; 817-417-0988.

Gourmet Gardens
Try this restaurant for more variety. 1115 E. Pioneer Parkway; 817-801-7188.

WHERE TO STAY

Ballpark Inn
Near Texas Stadium. 903 N. Collings St.; 817-261-3621.

Carrollton

Getting There: Carrollton is 13 miles northwest of Dallas city center on I-35. **Visitor Information: Carrollton Chamber of Commerce, 1204 Metrocrest Dr.; 972-416-6600.**

SEEING AND DOING

Sandy Lake Amusement Park
A small lake with paddleboats, miniature golf, amusement rides, and a giant swimming pool. **1800 Sandy Lake Rd.; 972-242-7449, fax 972-242-7452; sandylake@aol.com; www.sandylake.com.**

WHERE TO EAT

Cafe on the Square
1104 S. Elm St.; 972-446-7936.

WHERE TO STAY

Hilton Hotel
Offers comfortable quarters. **2050 Chenault Dr.; 972-875-2307.**

Cedar Hill

Getting There: Cedar Hill is 14 miles southwest of Dallas city center on U.S. Hwy. 67. **Visitor Information: Cedar Hill Chamber of Commerce, 300 Houston St.; 972-291-7817.**

SEEING AND DOING

Penn Farm Agricultural History Center
An interpretive facility that depicts farming just before and after World War II, with exhibits housed in a 1918 barn, a garage, two granaries, and other restored structures. **1570 Farm Road 1382; 972-291-0209; www.tpwd.state.tx.us/park/cedarhil/cedarhil.htm.**

WHERE TO EAT

Longhorn BBQ
Serves up the food of choice around here. **108 W. Beltline Rd.; 972-293-2111.**

WHERE TO STAY

Gingerbread House Bed-and-Breakfast
210 S. Broad St.; 972-291-2066.

Garland

Getting There: Garland is 10 miles northeast of Dallas city center on State Hwy. 78. **Visitor Information: Garland Chamber of Commerce, 914 S. Garland Ave.; 972-272-7551.**

SEEING AND DOING

Texas Queen
A 105-foot paddle-wheel party boat that offers dinner cruises Wednesday through Friday and on Sundays; reservations required. It **departs from Elgin B. Robertson Park on Lake Ray Hubbard at 5 Turtle Cove Blvd.; 972-771-0039.**

RECREATION

Lake Lavon
A 21,000-acre Corps of Engineers reservoir with four large parks, with hookups for campers. Also offers motorcycle riding trails, boat ramps, marina services, swimming beaches, and duck hunting in season in certain areas. **About 3 miles northeast of Garland, off State Hwy. 78.**

Lake Ray Hubbard
A 22,000-acre reservoir on the east fork of the Trinity River, owned by the City of Dallas for a municipal water supply and recreation. Good fishing, boating, and camping. **About 5 miles east of Garland on I-30.**

WHERE TO EAT

Luna de Noche Tex Mex Grill
Mexican food with a local touch. **7602 N. Jupiter Rd.; 972-414-3616.**

WHERE TO STAY

Jupiter Inn
A popular local motel. **2417 Executive Dr.; 972-271-9700.**

Grand Prairie

Getting There: Grand Prairie is halfway between Dallas and Fort Worth, north of I-20 and south of I-30. **Visitor Information: Grand Prairie Convention and Visitors Bureau, 605 Safari Parkway, Suite A-6; 972-263-9588; www.ci.grand-prairie.**

SEEING AND DOING

Palace of Wax and Ripley's Believe It or Not

The usual bizarre and unbelievable displays, plus some stunning scenes from around the world set in wax. **601 E. Safari Parkway; 972-263-2391; www. gptexas.com/ripleys.htm.**

Traders Village

A 106-acre flea market and shoppers bazaar, with hundreds of dealers every weekend. **2602 Mayfield Rd. off State Hwy. 360; 972-647-8205, 972-647-2331.**

RECREATION

Mountain Creek Lake

A 3,000-acre lake popular for fishing and boating. **Off U.S. Hwy. 80, outside Grand Prairie at 1500 Marilla St.; 214-670-4100.**

WHERE TO EAT

Eatumup Cafe

1610 Polo Road; 972-602-3456.

WHERE TO STAY

Homegate Studios & Suites

Clean and comfortable. **1108 N. Hwy. 360; 972-975-0000.**

Grapevine

Getting There: Grapevine is 20 miles northwest of Dallas city center at State Hwy. 114 and Northwest Parkway. **Visitor Information: Grapevine Chamber of Commerce, 200 E. Vine St.; 817-481-1522.**

SEEING AND DOING

Grapevine Opry

A showcase of country and western singers and per-formers. It's a family-style show with a nationwide reputation for entertaining. Every Friday and Saturday night. **308 S. Main St.; 817-481-8733.**

La Buena Vida Vineyards

Locally grown wine. **416 E. College St.; 817-481-9463.**

RECREATION

Wagon Wheel Ranch

A 300-acre ranchland available for horseback riding, group night rides, hayrides, and riding lessons. **816 Ruth Wall Rd.; 972-462-0894, fax 972-573-5277; www.wagonwheel.com.**

WHERE TO EAT

Green Tea Enterprises

Surprisingly good food in a little-known place. **2412 San Jacinto Ln.; 817-424-1586.**

WHERE TO STAY

DFW Lakes Hilton

Upscale lodging. **1800 E. Hwy. 26; 817-481-8444.**

Irving

Getting There: Irving is 9 miles west of Dallas city center at Loop 12 and State Hwy. 183. **Visitor Information: Irving Convention and Visitors Bureau, 3333 N. MacArthur Blvd., Suite 200; 972-252-7476; www.irvingtexas.com.**

SEEING AND DOING

Dallas Cowboys Football Club/ Texas Stadium

Tours Monday through Saturday, unless it's a game day. **Loop 12 at Carpenter Freeway; 972-438-7676.**

Las Colinas Complex

An ultramodern multi-use complex covering 12,000 acres, with an equestrian center, farmers market, business facilities, hotel, restaurant, and shops. Don't miss the **flower clock** at State Hwy. 114 and O'Connor Rd.; it makes for a great photo opportunity. There is also the **Mandalay Canal Walk,** one level below the street. It's a European-style canal featuring Venetian-built water taxis. The focal point of the whole facility is a magnificent sculpture called *Mustangs of Las Colinas.* **Two miles northwest of Texas Stadium on State Hwy. 114; www.dfw metro.com/lascolinas/attract2.htm.**

Studios at Las Colinas

Behind-the-scenes tour of a working motion picture and television sound stage, where major movies were made, including *JFK, Robocop,* and *Silkwood.* **Dallas Communications Complex, 6301 N. O'Connor Rd.; 972-869-3456; tours@studios.gte.net; www.studiosatlascolinas.com.**

WHERE TO EAT

1 Potato 2

Serves up an interesting menu. **3856 Irving Mall; 972-255-0644.**

Slatteryrands Irish Pub

A popular local hangout. **2742 N. O'Connor Blvd.; 972-257-1959.**

WHERE TO STAY

Hilton Garden Inn

Luxurious relaxation. **7516 Las Colinas Blvd.; 972-444-8434.**

Lancaster

Getting There: Lancaster is 8 miles south of Dallas city center on I-35E (Thornton Freeway). **Visitor Information: Lancaster Chamber of Commerce, 100 N. Dallas Ave.; 972-227-2579.**

SEEING AND DOING

Confederate Air Force Wing

This is the Dallas–Fort Worth wing of the CAF, with a prize collection of vintage World War II aircraft. At Lancaster Airport, at **730 Ferris Rd.; 972-227-5721.**

WHERE TO EAT

Amaya's Mexican Grill

Good Tex-Mex. **161 Historic Town Square; 972-227-8911.**

South Fork Ranch, outside Plano, home to J. R. Ewing and the cast of the TV show Dallas. *Photo courtesy of the Dallas Convention & Visitors Bureau.*

WHERE TO STAY

Country Rose

Bed-and-breakfast in a restored old country home. **616 E. Beltline Rd.; 972-218-5017.**

Mesquite

Getting There: Mesquite is 10 miles east of Dallas city center on State Hwy. 352. **Visitor Information: Mesquite Chamber of Commerce, 617 N. Ebrite St.; 972-285-0211.**

SEEING AND DOING

Devil's Bowl Speedway

Half-mile track featuring all types of vehicle races: sprint cars, super-modifieds, modifieds, and motorcycles. **U.S. Hwy. 80, Lawson Rd. exit, at the eastern side of Mesquite; 972-222-2421; www.devilsbowl.com.**

Light Crust Doughboys
Hall of Fame and Museum

Bob Wills, Milton Brown, and all those original musicians who made the Light Crust Doughboys famous in the 1930s are gone now, but their memory lives on at this museum. It was created by a good friend of mine, Art Greenhaw, who can sing like a mockingbird and strum a guitar with the best. Art is the reason that the Light Crust Doughboys are still honored today. He put together the museum himself and has re-created the band and the western swing music that took this country by storm so many decades ago. The museum is in the McWhorter Greenhaw Hardware store on the downtown square at **105 Broad St.; 972-285-5441.** Art and his band of modern-day troubadours keep the good times alive weekly at the Mesquite Opry House, across the street from the hardware store.

RECREATION

Samuell Farm

A 340-acre farm that is maintained to recall the farming days of the 1800s, featuring ponds for fishing, picnic tables, hayrides, hiking, horseback riding, and a variety of animals. This is a wonderful educational facility for teaching young people about life in another

time. **U.S. Hwy. 80, Beltline Rd. exit, on the western edge of Mesquite; 214-670-7866.**

WHERE TO EAT

A & W Family Restaurant

3050 Town East Mall; 972-270-4813.

WHERE TO STAY

Courtyard by Marriott

2300 Hwy. 67; 972-681-3300.

North Richland Hills

Getting There: North Richland Hills is 8 miles northeast of Fort Worth city center on State Hwy. 26. **Visitor Information: North Richland Hills Chamber of Commerce; 817-281-9376; www.ci.north-richland-hills.tx.us/index.html.**

RECREATION

Channel Catfish Ponds

Public fishing. Open daily from daylight until dusk. Ponds are stocked weekly, and you pay by the pound. **7712 Davis Blvd.; 817-428-6608.**

Iron Horse Golf Course

A challenging 18-hole municipal golf course through a hardwood forest, meandering creeks, and under a railroad trestle. **6200 Skylark Circle, Meadow Lakes exit off NE Loop 820; 817-485-6666, fax 817-485-0249.**

WHERE TO EAT

Tippin's Restaurant & Pie

5209 Rufe Snow Dr.; 817-577-0777.

WHERE TO STAY

Lexington Inn DFW West

8709 Airport Freeway; 817-656-8881.

Plano

Getting There: Plano is 25 miles north of Dallas on U.S. Hwy. 75. **Visitor Information: Plano Chamber of Commerce, 1200 E. 15th St.; 972-424-7547.**

SEEING AND DOING

Adventure Balloon Port

Sightseeing balloons give a bird's-eye view of the region at sunrise and just before sunset every day, weather permitting. Balloonists are served champagne on landing and given a flight certificate and balloon pin. **1791 Millard Dr.; 972-422-0212.**

Fairview Farms

A hundred years ago the Haggard family moved to Plano from Kentucky. Today the family is still active in farming and has created an area to bring farm life to the city. They have a farmers market, arts barn, museum, general store, and farm animals. They put on seasonal demonstrations throughout the year, including sheep shearing, horseshoeing, and other activities depicting an earlier way of life. **U.S. Hwy. 75 at Parker Rd.; 972-422-2500, fax 972-578-0607; info@fairview-farms.com; www.fairview farms.com.**

Heritage Farmstead Museum

Built in 1891, this was a working farm until 1972. Today it is listed in the National Register of Historic Places and is open for guided tours from May through August. **1900 W. 15th St.; 972-424-7874; www. heritagefarmstead.org.**

South Fork Ranch

This is the ranch made famous by the TV show *Dallas*. Visitors can tour the mansion and grounds, and see Lucy's wedding dress and the gun that shot J. R. **Take exit 30 off U.S. Hwy. 75, drive east on Farm Road 2514 (Parker Rd.) for about 6 miles, and turn right onto Farm Road 2551 to the ranch; 1-800-989-7800, 972-442-7800, fax 972-442-5259.**

WHERE TO EAT

Gabbs Cafe

2050 W. Spring Creek Parkway; 972-517-1677.

WHERE TO STAY

Carpenter House

Bed-and-breakfast. **1211 E. 16th St.; 972-424-1889.**

Richardson

Getting There: Richardson is 12 miles from Dallas city center on U.S. Hwy. 75. **Visitor Information: Richardson Chamber of Commerce, 411 Belle Grove Dr.; 972-234-4141.**

SEEING AND DOING

Owens Spring Creek Farm

A commercial sausage-making firm maintains a showcase farm and small museum depicting an early North Texas community. **1401 E. Lookout Dr.; 972-235-0192; www.owensinc.com.**

Wineburgh Philatelic Research Library

For stamp-collecting enthusiasts. In the Eugene McDermott Library at the University of Texas–Dallas, **2601 N. Floyd Rd.; 972-883-2570; www.utdallas.edu/library/special/wprl. htm.**

WHERE TO EAT

The Great Outdoors

242 W. Campbell Rd.; 972-437-5038.

WHERE TO STAY

Omni Richardson Hotel

701 E. Campbell Rd.; 972-231-9600.

Other Towns in the Area

Towns big and small are spread throughout the greater Metroplex. Towns included in this section (in alphabetical order) are Boyd, Canton, Cisco, Cleburne, Corsicana, Cresson, Decatur, Denton, Dublin, Eastland, Glen Rose, Graham, Granbury, Greenville, Hillsboro, McKinney, Ranger, Stephenville, Terrell, Waxahachie, and Weatherford. Suggested places to eat and to stay are included with most of the towns.

Boyd

Getting There: Boyd is 30 miles northwest of Fort Worth via U.S. Hwy. 287/81 and State Hwy. 114. **Visitor Information: Boyd City Hall, 101 W. Rock Island Ave.; 940-433-5166.**

SEEING AND DOING

Texas Exotic Feline Foundation

Founded by Robert and Gene Von Reitnauer, who have spent their lives rescuing and providing sanctuary for cats that are no longer wanted by individuals, zoos, or government research facilities. This is a permanent home for animals with nowhere else to go. It offers a walking tour that will let you view more than sixty lions, tigers, jaguars, bobcats, leopards, and other exotic cats. **113 N. Hitt St.; 940-433-5091.**

WHERE TO EAT

Double KK BBQ

For local flavor, check out the Double KK. **115 E. Rock Island Ave.; 940-433-8193.**

Canton

Getting There: Canton is 60 miles east of Dallas at I-20 and State Hwy. 19. **Visitor Information: Canton Chamber of Commerce, 315 First Monday Ln.; 903-567-2991; www.cantontx.com.**

SEEING AND DOING

First Monday Trade Days

The biggest flea market in the Southwest is held the Friday, Saturday, and Sunday prior to the first Monday of each month. The activity began in pioneer days when ranchers brought their livestock into town for auction the first Monday of every month. The horse and cattle auction is still going on, but nowadays it takes a back seat to the flea market across town. Everything imaginable is for sale at the flea market, with booths as far as the eye can see covering more than 100 acres between downtown Canton and I-20. Watch your pocketbooks; the slickest salespeople in the state make good livings at the Canton First Monday flea market. **290 E. Tyler St.; 903-567-6556.**

WHERE TO EAT

Higher Grounds

A popular local spot near the First Monday flea market. **120 W. Dallas St.; 903-567-6551.**

WHERE TO STAY

Bed-and-Breakfast Country Style

Farm Road 859 (Edgewood Rd.), north of Canton; 903-567-2899.

Cisco

Getting There: Cisco is 105 miles west of Fort Worth on I-20. **Visitor Information: Cisco Chamber of Commerce, 309 Conrad Hilton Blvd.; 254-442-2537; www.ciscotx.com.**

Probably the best-known event in Cisco history was the **Santa Claus bank robbery,** which occurred 2 days before Christmas 1927. Four men, led by a man in a Santa Claus costume, robbed the First National Bank of $12,000 cash and $150,000 in non-negotiable securities. They stole a car and kidnapped two young girls. Three people were killed, including the town's most popular law enforcement officers. The robbers were eventually caught: one died of gunshot wounds; one served time in prison and was eventually released; one was executed in the electric chair; and locals lynched the leader of the pack after he shot a jailer while trying to escape. Stories of the robbery are embellished every time they are told, and writers treat this as one of those exciting accounts of life in early Texas, but few people smile when the subject is discussed, even today, in this town. There are still people left who remember that deadly robbery in Cisco, and to this day some carry scars from the incident.

SEEING AND DOING

Mobley Hotel

A restored building that is now the Chamber of Commerce office in downtown Cisco. This is the very first hotel ever bought by Conrad Hilton. He never called it a Hilton; he operated it as the Mobley, and his success here led to his chain of hotels around the country. **309 Conrad Hilton Blvd.; 254-442-2537.**

WHERE TO EAT

White Elephant Restaurant

On the edge of town is where the locals mix with the motorists. **On I-20; 254-442-1520.**

WHERE TO STAY

Gray Bull Guest House
Provides ranch-style living outside town. **Route 2, Box 44D; 254-442-1046.**

Cleburne

Getting There: Cleburne is 30 miles south of Fort Worth via I-35W and State Hwy. 174. **Visitor Information:** Available at **1511 W. Henderson St.; 817-645-2455.**

First known as Camp Henderson, the place was settled in the 1850s. The name was later changed to Cleburne in honor of Confederate general Pat Cleburne. The area is mostly agricultural. The town has a beautiful historical section, with some homes on North Anglin Street and Prairie Street restored to their original 1800s charm.

SEEING AND DOING

Layland Museum
In a restored 1904 Carnegie Library Building, displaying Johnson County relics and artifacts dating from pre-Colombian cultures. **201 N. Caddo St.; 817-645-0940.**

RECREATION

Cleburne State Park
Has 498 scenic acres with camping, picnicking, fishing, swimming, boating, and hiking trails. Boats available for rent. The park also contains a wildlife refuge. **Twelve miles southwest of Cleburne at 5800 Park Road 21; 817-645-1021; www.tpwd.state. tx.us/park/cleburne/cleburne.htm.**

WHERE TO EAT

Lone Star Cafe
A popular local gathering place. **1663 W. Henderson St.; 817-556-3098.**

Corsicana

Getting There: Corsicana is 54 miles south of Dallas on I-45. **Visitor Information: Corsicana Chamber of Commerce, 120 N. 12th St.; 903-874-4731; www.corsicana.org.**

SEEING AND DOING

Corsicana Fruitcake Factory
One of the oldest and best-known fruitcake bakeries in the state. Since 1896 they have been making fruitcakes under the name Deluxe and shipping them all over the world. Business booms during the Christmas season, but the fruitcakes are available year-round and are sold only by mail-order or at the bakery. If you are a fruitcake lover, these are the best. **407 W. 7th St.; 1-800-248-3366.**

Lefty Frizzell Country Music Museum
Dedicated to a local boy who made it big in country-western music. There are mementos of his career, including photos, costumes, and records. A part of Pioneer Village, **915 W. Park Ave., in Beauford Jester Park; 903-654-4846.**

WHERE TO EAT

Bakery Restaurant
Near the Corsicana Fruitcake Factory. **2000 S. U.S. Hwy. 287; 903-874-7413.**

WHERE TO STAY

Colonial Inn
A longtime local motel. **2021 Regal Dr.; 903-874-4751.**

Cresson

Getting There: Cresson is 15 miles southwest of Fort Worth on U.S. Hwy. 377.

SEEING AND DOING

Pate Museum of Transportation
One of the finest antique car collections in the state. Also on display are an antique luxury railroad car and military aircraft. An annual spring swap-meet attracts crowds of collectors and spectators. **840 N. Main St.; 817-332-1161; www.classicar.com/museum/pate/pate.htm.**

Decatur

Getting There: Decatur is 38 miles northwest of Fort Worth on U.S. Hwy. 81/277. **Visitor Information:**

Decatur Chamber of Commerce, 201 E. Main St.; 940-627-3107.

My favorite story about this place involves the courthouse, a traveling salesman, and a couple of old-timers who were resting their bones on the steps outside the courthouse many years ago. The salesman arrived in a taxi and asked if any of the locals would like to earn a dollar carrying his luggage into the courthouse. One old man jumped up and grabbed the luggage. The salesman looked down the street and marveled at a majestic mansion on the corner. He asked the old-timer who owned it, and the man responded, "I do." To which the salesman replied, "How can you afford such a mansion?" The old-timer answered, "By carrying my own damn luggage." They say he was a member of the prominent Waggoner family of Decatur.

SEEING AND DOING

Waggoner Mansion

The large and, at one time, lavish mansion of an early Texas cattle baron. Private, but within eyesight of the courthouse.

Wise County Courthouse

Built in 1895 of pink limestone quarried in Burnet, Texas, this is one of the state's most beautiful courthouses, pronounced a perfect architectural example of its type and era. **101 N. Trinity St.; 940-627-5743.**

Wise County Heritage Museum

Exhibits include Indian artifacts and mementos of early Texas. Housed in the administration building of the old Decatur Baptist College at **1602 S. Trinity St.; 940-627-5586.**

RECREATION

Lake Bridgeport

A 13,000-acre impoundment on the west fork of the Trinity River. Swimming, camping, picnicking, boating, and good year-round fishing. This is the site of the largest wilderness Boy Scout camp in Texas. **Fifteen miles west of Decatur off U.S. Hwy. 380; www.tpwd.state.tx.us/fish/infish/lakes/bridgep/lake_id.htm.**

WHERE TO EAT

Generations Restaurant

For family dining. **600 W. Walnut St.; 940-627-2560.**

WHERE TO STAY

Abercromby Penthouse Suites

Offers comfortable lodging. **103 W. Main St.; 940-627-7022.**

Denton

Getting There: Denton is 35 miles north of Fort Worth on I-35W. **Visitor Information: Chamber of Commerce, 1607 E. McKinney St.; 940-383-2901. Black Chamber of Commerce, 625 Dallas Dr.; 940-484-4404. Convention Bureau, 414 W. Parkway St.; 940-382-7895; www.denton texas.com.**

SEEING AND DOING

Gowns of the First Ladies of Texas

On the Texas Woman's University campus, southeast of downtown Denton; 940-898-3201.

Hangar 10 Antique Airplane Museum

The first airplane museum in Texas was moved here from Brooke Air Force Base in San Antonio. At **Denton Municipal Airport, 5000 Airport Rd.; 940-382-0666.**

Little Chapel-in-the-Woods

Designed by southwestern architect O'Neil Ford in 1939; first lady Eleanor Roosevelt attended the dedication. At **304 Administration Dr., on the campus of Texas Woman's University; 940-898-3601.**

Oak-Hickory Historic District

Victorian homes located on West Oak Street offer good examples of cottages of bygone days. **940-381-1818.**

WHERE TO EAT

Anna's Kitchen

A longtime local favorite. **2217 N. Carroll Blvd.; 940-382-7143.**

WHERE TO STAY

Clayton House
Near Texas Woman's University campus. **1111 W. University Dr.; 940-382-9626.**

Dublin
Getting There: Dublin is 85 miles southwest of Fort Worth on U.S. Hwy. 377. **Visitor Information: Dublin Chamber of Commerce, 213 E. Black-jack St.; 254-445-3422.**

Settled in the 1850s, Dublin was possibly named for the city in Ireland, but more likely it got its name from a common warning cry during Indian raids: "Double in!" The cry told people to squeeze in tight during the battle. Dublin says it's the home of the very first rodeo, but a lot of cities in the Southwest make that claim. It does put on a world championship rodeo every year. It was one of the first communities in Texas to have streetcars, and it's the birthplace of golfer Ben Hogan.

SEEING AND DOING

Dr. Pepper Bottling Company
My favorite place in town. Opened in 1891, this was the very first franchise for the soft drink, and is the only one left that still uses pure cane sugar instead of artificial sweeteners. Bottling is done on Tuesdays only, and you can buy Dr. Pepper in bottles right at the plant. If you prefer the small bottles, though, you'll have to bring your own. **221 S. Patrick St.; 254-445-3466; www.drpep.com.**

WHERE TO EAT

Buckboard Restaurant
Downtown eating spot. **316 N. Patrick St.; 254-445-4107.**

WHERE TO STAY

Dublin's Shamrock Inn
312 N. Patrick St.; 254-445-3334.

Eastland
Getting There: Eastland is 95 miles west of Fort Worth on I-20. **Visitor Information: Eastland**

Chamber of Commerce, 102 S. Seaman St.; 254-629-2332; www.eastland.net/eastland.

Eastland was established around 1875 as a trade center for the surrounding farms and ranches. Current resources include oil, ranching, farming, and manufacturing.

SEEING AND DOING

Kendrick Religious Museum
Thirty diorama scenes from the Bible, with special sound and lighting effects. **Four miles west of Eastland on State Hwy. 6; 254-629-8672.**

Ol' Rip, the Horned Frog
One of the greatest tall tales of Texas is told in Eastland County—though many locals say it's the truth. According to records, a Texas horned frog, officially a horned lizard, was sealed in the cornerstone of an Eastland County courthouse that was built in 1897. In 1927, after a new courthouse was built, the cornerstone from the old building was opened—and the horned frog was found alive. The community named him Ol' Rip, and he's been famous ever since. When he died a year after the discovery, he was placed in a glass-front casket, and is on display today at the courthouse, **100 W. Main St.**

Post Office Mural
National and post office history is depicted in a 6-by-10-foot mural of postage stamps. It took 7 years and about 12,000 stamps to produce the mural. **411 E. Main St.; 254-629-2383.**

WHERE TO EAT

Louise Cafe
Local sandwich shop and country food. **103 S. Lamar St.; 254-629-2949.**

WHERE TO STAY

Eastland B&B
Country and comfortable. **112 N. Lamar St.; 254-629-8397.**

Glen Rose
Getting There: Glen Rose is 57 miles southwest of

Fort Worth via U.S. Hwy. 377 and State Hwy. 144. **Visitor Information: Glen Rose Chamber of Commerce, 108 SW Barnard St.; 254-897-2286.**

Glen Rose is the best place to be in the state if you're looking for dinosaur history.

SEEING AND DOING

Comanche Peak Information Center

Tours of a nuclear power plant site. **Four miles north of Glen Rose on Farm Road 56; 254-897-5554.**

McNeill Ranch Chuckwagon Meals

Served every Friday, Saturday, and Sunday night by reservation from the middle of May through the second weekend in October. They also serve cowboy breakfasts Saturday and Sunday mornings. Two of the nicest people that you'll ever want to meet, George and Ophelia McNeill, run this place. George and Ophelia started cooking chuck wagon–style meals for friends and neighbors, and eventually they just gave their big ranch outside Lubbock to their kids, bought this place outside Glen Rose, and started cooking for a living. As George put it, "There's nothing like a hot cup of coffee on a beautiful Somervell County morning, or enjoying a delicious steak while watching a cowboy sunset." **Off U.S. Hwy. 67 on the eastern outskirts of Glen Rose; 254-897-2221.**

Chuck Wagon cookout at the McNeill Ranch, outside Glen Rose. Photo courtesy of George and Ophelia McNeill.

RECREATION

Dinosaur Valley State Park

This picturesque park contains the best-preserved dino

tracks in Texas. Exhibits give visitors a glimpse of how Texas might have looked 100 million years ago. The 1,200-acre park also offers camping, picnicking, and nature trails. **Five miles west of Glen Rose, off U.S. Hwy. 67 and Farm Road 20; 254-897-4588; www.tpwd.state.tx.us/park/dinosaur/dinosaur.htm.**

Fossil Rim Wildlife Center

This is the best of the exotic wildlife drive-through parks in the state. This is not only an exotic game park for tourists, but it is also a full-fledged research facility. Some of the most difficult creatures in the world to raise and care for, like cheetahs and the rare black rhino, live quite well here. You can see ostriches, giraffes, wolves, talking parrots from South America, and hundreds of other creatures as well. There's a petting pasture, restaurant, nature store, picnic area, nature trail, education center, horseback trail rides, and an overnight horse camp. The center also offers its Foothills Safari Camp, a 3-day, 2-night safari; reservations needed. **Off U.S. Hwy. 67, 3.5 miles west of Glen Rose; P.O. Box 2189, Glen Rose, 76043; 254-897-2960; www.fossil rim.com.**

RV Parks

Facilities in the Glen Rose area include **Tres Rios RV Park and Campground,** a 55-acre site providing tent camping, cabins, canoeing, tubing, and fishing **(2322 County Road 312, 254-897-4253).** Other camping sites are **Cedar Ridge RV Park (Rural Route 1, off U.S. Hwy. 67, 254-897-3410); Midway Pines Cabins (254-573-0869); Oakdale Park (1016 Barnard St., 254-897-2321, across from Big Rocks Park); and Squaw Creek Park (2300 Coates Rd., 817-573-7053).**

Squaw Valley Golf Course

Owned and operated by the county, and one of the best courses in the region. **U.S. Hwy. 67 outside Glen Rose; 254-897-7956.**

WHERE TO EAT

Fossil Rim Wildlife Restaurant

Elegant dining. **2155 County Road 2008; 254-897-3805.**

WHERE TO STAY

Popejoy Haus

This bed-and-breakfast captures the flavor of an early German community. **1943 County Road 321; 254-897-3521.**

The **Glen Rose Chamber of Commerce** can provide a list of other bed-and-breakfasts **(254-897-2286).**

Graham

Getting There: Graham is 80 miles northwest of Fort Worth via State Hwy. 199, U.S. Hwy. 281, and U.S. Hwy. 380. **Visitor Information: Graham Chamber of Commerce, 608 Elm St.; 940-549-3355.**

Located in southeastern Young County, this community was founded along the Chicago, Rock Island, and Gulf Railroad lines in 1872. Graham, the hub of agribusiness in the area, has the oldest newspaper in northwestern Texas, the *Graham Leader.* The city has one of the few remaining drive-in theaters in the state, and it is home to one of my great disappointments in the broadcasting business: there used to be a company in town called Praise the Lord Oil Company, but the owners never would allow me to do a story on the place.

SEEING AND DOING

Robert E. Richeson Memorial Museum

Memorabilia from World War II, donated by former military men and their families. **At Graham Municipal Airport, 1810 Jacksboro Hwy.; 940-549-6150.**

RECREATION

Graham and Eddleman Lakes

An impoundment of more than 2,500 acres, with fishing, boating, and plenty of lakeside campsites. **Two miles northwest of Graham on Salt Creek, just off U.S. Hwy. 380.**

Possum Kingdom Lake

This is among the state's most popular outdoor recreation destinations for swimmers, skin divers, boaters, and fishers. It is dotted with lakeside resorts and camps. **Possum Kingdom State Park** is located on

Granbury Opera House in the resort town of Granbury.

the southwestern shoreline. Scenic woodlands surrounding the lake offer good hunting in season. **Twelve miles southeast of Graham via State Hwy. 16; 1-888-779-8330, 940-549-1803, fax 940-779-4631; www.possumkingdomlake.com.**

WHERE TO EAT

Aunt Kay's Country Kitchen

1429 4th St.; 940-549-1771.

Granbury

Getting There: Granbury is 33 miles southwest of Fort Worth via U.S. Hwy. 377. **Visitor Information: Granbury Convention and Visitors Bureau, 100 N. Crockett St.; 817-573-5548; www.granbury.org.**

Granbury offers some of the most scenic landscapes in all of Texas, occupied by people with some of the most vivid imaginations. A few old-timers claim **John Wilkes Booth** escaped to Texas after killing Abraham Lincoln and lived out his life as a saloonkeeper in Granbury. Others say **Jesse James** spent time in these parts. Down the road a ways, in Hico, is the grave of a fellow known as Brushy Bill, said by some to be **Billy the Kid.**

SEEING AND DOING

Acton State Historical Park

This is the smallest state park in Texas, and is the grave site of Elizabeth Crockett, second wife of Davy Crockett. She settled in this area after Crockett was killed at the Alamo. **Six miles east of Granbury on U.S. Hwy. 377.**

Granbury Opera House
Built in 1886, restored in 1975. Plays, musicals, and historic reenactments, like the story of John Wilkes Booth, are presented on weekends, February through December. On the square at **133 E. Pearl St.; 817-573-9191.**

Lewisville Lady
Sightseeing cruises on Lake Granbury on a 73-foot replica of a Mississippi River paddle wheeler. **2211 S. Morgan St.; 817-573-6822.**

RECREATION

Lake Granbury
An 8,700-acre lake that almost completely surrounds the city. It is 30 miles long and has 103 miles of shoreline, with public and commercial facilities for fishing, swimming, boating, and other water sports. Lake Granbury is what makes this area a true resort in North Texas. The weather seems always pleasant, the people are friendly, and something is going on either here or in Glen Rose or Stephenville year-round. **The lake is both south and east of town; 817-573-5548; www.tpwd.state.tx.us/fish/infish/lakes/granbury/access.htm.**

WHERE TO EAT

Chris-Mill German Restaurant
3317 Glen Rose Hwy.; 817-573-2517.

Nutt House
A noted restaurant and restored country inn dating from 1893; family-style meals with old-time favorites like hot-water cornbread and chicken and dumplings. **On the square at 121 E. Bridge St.; 817-573-5612.**

WHERE TO STAY

Iron Horse Inn
Bed-and-breakfast. **616 Thorpe Springs Rd.; 817-579-5535.**

Nutt House
121 E. Bridge St.; 817-573-5612.

Greenville
Getting There: Greenville is 55 miles northeast of Dallas via I-30. **Visitor Information: Greenville Chamber of Commerce, 2713 Stonewall St.; 903-455-1510; www.greenville-chamber.org.**

SEEING AND DOING

Audie Murphy Room
Mementos of America's most-decorated soldier in World War II. **Walworth Harrison Public Library, 3716 Lee St.; 903-457-2992.**

Puddin' Hill Bakery
World-famous pecan fruitcakes and chocolate delicacies, made on the premises. They have a great lunch menu too, with homemade soups, sandwiches, and desserts served Monday through Saturday. **I-30 at Division St.; 903-455-6931.**

WHERE TO EAT

Puddin' Hill Store
Has terrific sandwiches and local flavor. **I-30 at Division St.; 903-455-6931.**

Two Señoritas
An above-average Mexican restaurant. **6103 Wesley St.; 903-455-4881.**

WHERE TO STAY

Iron Skillet Inn
Bed-and-breakfast. **664 Forrester St.; 903-455-0074.**

Hillsboro
Getting There: Hillsboro is 53 miles due south of Fort Worth, on I-35. **Visitor Information: Hillsboro Chamber of Commerce, 115 N. Covington St.; 817-582-2481; www.hillsboro.net.**

A rich agricultural region and the gateway to Lake Whitney, Hillsboro is known for its many restored Victorian homes and about 200 antique dealers that open their doors on weekends. There is also a huge Southwest Factory Outlet Center on I-35 that attracts many shoppers.

SEEING AND DOING

Confederate Research Center and Gun Museum

Historic artifacts, arts, and firearms are on display at the center, which is dedicated to the Civil War era, particularly Hood's Texas Brigade. **Campus of Hill College at 112 Lamar Dr.; 254-582-2555.**

RECREATION

Lake Whitney

A 23,000-acre Corps of Engineers impoundment on the Brazos River, one of the most popular water recreation areas in the state. Campsites, marinas, parks, recreation areas, and leisure home developments. Fishing is excellent. The lake is **20 miles southwest of Hillsboro, off State Hwy. 22; 940-694-3793; www.lakewhitneytexas.com. Lake Whitney State Park** offers camping, trailer hookups, screened shelters, with fishing, boating, swimming, and hiking. The park is **on the eastern shore of the lake, off Farm Road 1244; 254-694-3793; www.tpwd. state.tx.us/park/lakewhit/lakewhit.htm.**

WHERE TO EAT

Carl's Corner

A truck stop on the northern outskirts of Hillsboro, with good food, friendly conversation, and plenty to talk about. Carl has an eighteen-wheeler and an airplane displayed on top of his gas station/restaurant. How he got them up there is a story only Carl can tell. But even if he's not around when you stop, the food is good—served in heaping portions, truckerstyle. **2959 I-35; 254-582-8433.**

Texas Boys BBQ

Another good place to get a meal. **610 W. Elm St.; 254-582-2440.**

WHERE TO STAY

The Tarlton House of 1895

Bed-and-breakfast. **211 N. Pleasant St.; 817-582-7216.**

McKinney

Getting There: McKinney is 33 miles north of Dallas via U.S. Hwy. 75. **Visitor Information: McKinney Chamber of Commerce, 1801 W. Louisiana St.; 972-542-0163; www.mckinneytx.com.**

SEEING AND DOING

Bolin Wildlife Exhibit

Mounted animal trophies from several states and foreign countries, along with turn-of-the-century memorabilia. **1028 N. McDonald St.; 972-562-2639.**

Chestnut Square

Five Victorian and Greek Revival homes on display. **311 S. Chestnut St., south of the square; 972-562-8790; www.mckinneytx.com/chestnut-square/index.htm.**

Heard Natural Science Museum and Wildlife Sanctuary

Offering natural-history exhibits and native live-animal exhibits. Nature trails wind through a 275-acre wildlife sanctuary, and there is a scenic picnic area. **1 Nature Place, 2 miles south of McKinney on State Hwy. 5; 972-542-5566, fax 972-548-9119; heardmuseum @texoma.net; www.heardmuseum.org.**

WHERE TO EAT

Brazos Cattle Co.

Popular local steak house. **401 S. Central Expressway; 972-727-1614.**

WHERE TO STAY

Amerihost Inn

Clean and convenient. **407 S. Central Expressway; 972-396-9494.**

Ranger

Getting There: Ranger is 95 miles west of Fort Worth via I-20 and Farm Road 101. **Visitor Information: Ranger Chamber of Commerce, 121 S. Commerce St.; 254-647-3091.**

Ranger was one of the genuine oil boomtowns in Texas in the early part of this century. When McClesky No. 1 blew in 1917, it touched off an economic explosion in the petroleum industry, and in 1 year, Ranger's population grew from 1,000 to 30,000. Farmers became millionaires, and four railroad companies raced to Texas to compete for the transportation business.

SEEING AND DOING

McClesky No. 1
Site of the 1,700-barrel-per-day gusher that started all the excitement in 1917.

Roaring Ranger Museum
Artifacts and photos of the boom days; also serves as the Chamber of Commerce. **Main and Commerce Sts. downtown.**

Thurber Ghost Town
The town of Thurber was founded by the Texas and Pacific Coal Company in 1888 and maintained as a company town for years. It was one of the first cities in the world with complete electric service. Bricks from clay taken out of the mines at Thurber paved Congress Avenue in Austin and Camp Bowie Boulevard in Fort Worth. Thurber was positioned to develop into a great Texas city, until the coal played out. One grocery store in town had thirteen checkout counters—unheard of at the time. Today, Thurber is just a ghost town, with a few old structures still standing and historical markers telling stories of the good ol' days. An annual Thurber reunion is held on the second Saturday in June. **Sixteen miles east of Ranger, on I-20.**

WHERE TO EAT

Bobby's Burger
Old-fashioned West Texas hamburgers. **1000 West Loop; 254-647-5401.**

Stephenville
Getting There: Stephenville is 64 miles southwest of Fort Worth on U.S. Hwy. 377. **Visitor Information: Stephenville Chamber of Commerce, 187 W. Washington St.; 254-965-5313; www. stephenville.com.**

SEEING AND DOING

All Creatures Small Farm
This is a pet livestock farm that raises miniature Mediterranean donkeys, miniature sheep, pygmy goats, and other small animals. Open on Saturdays. **Off U.S. Hwy. 377, outside Stephenville; 254-965-7224.**

WHERE TO EAT

Cutting Horse Restaurant
A local steak house. **2865 W. Washington St.; 254-968-5256.**

WHERE TO STAY

Oxford House
Bed-and-breakfast. **563 N. Graham St.; 254-965-6885.**

Terrell
Getting There: Terrell is 34 miles east of Dallas on I-20. **Visitor Information: Terrell Chamber of Commerce, 1314 W. Moore Ave.; 972-524-5703.**

SEEING AND DOING

Silent Wings Museum
Dedicated to airborne personnel of World War II, with special emphasis on the men who flew gliders into some of the deadliest battles of the war. **At the Municipal Airport, 2 miles north of I-20 via State Hwy. 34, at 119 Silent Wings Blvd.; 972-563-0402.**

WHERE TO EAT

All Country Cafe
801 E. Main St.; 972-551-1760.

A likeness of a local girl, Mabel Frame, carved on the sandstone walls of the Ellis County Courthouse in Waxahachie by Italian sculptor, Harry Hurley. Photo courtesy of Texas Highways magazine.

WHERE TO STAY

Bluebonnet Inn
Bed-and-breakfast. 310 W. College St.; 972-524-2534.

Waxahachie
Getting There: Waxahachie is 29 miles south of Dallas on I-35E. **Visitor Information: Waxahachie Chamber of Commerce, 102 YMCA Dr.; 972-937-2390; www.waxahachie.org.**

SEEING AND DOING

Ellis County Courthouse
One of the grandest courthouses in Texas from an architectural standpoint, and there is an intriguing story about its construction. An Italian sculptor by the name of Harry Hurley was imported to carve images of faces in the red sandstone on the exterior walls. This Italian fell madly in love with Mabel Frame, the local telegraph operator and daughter of the woman who ran the boardinghouse where he was staying. Mabel displayed little affection for Harry and eventually married another man. Harry took out his disappointment, it is said, by carving ugly images on the courthouse columns. It was a sad ending for a Texas love story, but it did produce a truly unique courthouse for the state. **101 W. Main St.; 972-923-5000.**

Scarborough Faire
A springtime Renaissance fair featuring arts and crafts and foods, mixed with medieval entertainment. For eight weekends, from mid-April through early June. **On Farm Road 66, 1.5 miles west of I-35E; 972-938-3247; www.scarboroughfairerenfest.com.**

WHERE TO EAT

Crazy Horse Cafe
103 E. Main St.; 972-938-9818.

WHERE TO STAY

Bonnynook Inn
414 W. Main St.; 972-938-7207.

Weatherford
Getting There: Weatherford is 28 miles west of Fort Worth on I-20. **Visitor Information: Weatherford Chamber of Commerce, 401 Fort Worth St.; 817-594-3801.**

SEEING AND DOING

First Monday Flea Market
Evolved from old-time trade days, when farmers and ranchers brought livestock and products to town to sell on the first Monday of each month. The event is now held over the weekend preceding the first Monday of the month. **At U.S. Hwys. 80 and 180, 3 blocks east of the courthouse.** For more information, call the **Weatherford Chamber of Commerce** at 817-594-3801; **www.firstmonday.com.**

Oliver Loving's Grave
Resting place for the dean of Texas trail drivers, Oliver Loving, who came to Parker County in 1855. His career inspired the book and television movie *Lonesome Dove.* He was wounded by Indians during a cattle drive with his partner, Charles Goodnight, and died at Fort Sumner in 1867. Loving's son and Goodnight returned his body over 600 miles by wagon for burial in Weatherford. Loving's grave is **in Greenwood Cemetery, Front and Mill Sts.**

Peter Pan Statue
Bronze statue sculpted by artist Ronald Thomason honors Weatherford native Mary Martin, who created the role of Peter Pan on Broadway. The statue and other displays honoring the city's most famous daughter are at the **Weatherford Public Library (1214 Charles St.).**

WHERE TO EAT

Iron Skillet Restaurant
2001 Santa Fe Dr.; 817-594-0245.

WHERE TO STAY

Two Pearls Bed-and-Breakfast
804 S. Alamo St.; 817-596-9316.

The Red River Border

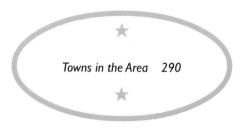
Texas and Oklahoma disputed the land along the Red River border until the early 1900s, but finally agreed to set the line dividing the two states right in the middle of the river. Some of the state's real characters grew up in this environment, plowing fields in the rich, fertile farmland from Wichita Falls east to Red River County.

Other native sons, like Sam Rayburn of Bonham, used their background and upbringing to carry them to more flamboyant heights in the nation's capital. Dwight Eisenhower, thirty-fourth president of the United States, was born here.

This chapter visits a group of towns that are near the Red River border: Wichita Falls, Gainesville, Sherman, Denison, Bonham, Paris, and Clarksville. The listings start with Wichita Falls and move eastward along the Red River. Suggested places to eat and to stay are included with most of the towns.

Towns in the Area

Wichita Falls

Getting There: From Fort Worth, travel northwest on U.S. Hwy. 81/287 for 114 miles. **Visitor Information: Texas Travel Information Center, 900 Central Freeway; 940-723-7931.** Also, **Wichita Falls Convention and Visitors Bureau, 1000 5th St.; 940-716-5550; www.wichita falls.org.**

Wichita Falls grew up around a rail stop in the 1880s. It had more than its share of transient cattle drovers and quickly became a city of saloons and dance halls. There was a time when it was referred to as Whiskeytaw Falls. Today you can still walk into most drinking establishments in town and order a Red Draw, a local invention consisting of beer and tomato juice.

SEEING AND DOING

Wichita Falls Waterfall

The waterfall that gave the town its name was destroyed by a flood in 1886, but 100 years later the city built its own artificial waterfall to take its place—except that this 54-foot-high fall is five times larger than the original. The water in the falls is recirculated at 3,500 gallons a minute. It faces north on I-44 and is **immediately north of downtown.**

Wichita Theater and Opry House

Home of the Texas Gold country music show every Saturday night, featuring old-fashioned family entertainment. **924 Indiana Ave.; 940-723-9037.**

FESTIVALS AND EVENTS

The city has two large events every August: the **Hotter 'n Hell One Hundred,** the largest 100-mile bicycle race in the United States, and the **Texas Ranch Roundup,** where hands from all over the state compete in events that display ranch skills, like saddle bronc riding, horseshoeing, chuck-wagon cooking, fiddling, and guitar picking. The ranch of the team that accumulates the most points is awarded the title Best Ranch in Texas—quite an honor.

RECREATION

Lake Arrowhead State Park

Open 7 days a week for day use. The lake covers about 13,500 acres and has 106 miles of shoreline. The lake lies over what used to be an oil field, and some of the old derricks have been left in the water, providing great hideouts and feeding areas for the fish—and terrific fishing. The park is **18 miles southeast of Wichita Falls on Park Road 63; 940-528-2212; www.tpwd. state.tx.us/park/lakearro/lakearro.htm.**

WHERE TO EAT

Fat McBride's Steakhouse
A popular eating spot. **4537 Maplewood; 940-696-0250.**

Kemp Street BBQ
A favorite with locals. **2500 Kemp Blvd.; 940-723-7204.**

WHERE TO STAY

Harrison House Bed-and Breakfast
This B&B is a spacious prairie-style home with 10-foot ceilings and narrow-board oak floors. **2014 11th St.; 940-322-2299.**

Spur Hotel
Part of *The Last Picture Show* was filmed here. **110 N. Center, U.S. Hwy. 79, in Archer City, 25 miles south of Wichita Falls; 940-574-2591.**

Gainesville
GettingThere:Take U.S. Hwy. 287 east from Wichita Falls for 19 miles to Henrietta, then go left on U.S. Hwy. 82 for about 65 miles to Gainesville. **Visitor Information: Travel Information Center, about 5 miles north of town on I-35; www.gainesville. tx.us.** Also, **Gainesville Chamber of Commerce, 101 S. Culberson St.; 940-665-2831.**

SEEING AND DOING

Frank Buck Zoo
Named in honor of adventurer Frank Buck, who was born in Gainesville. Monkeys, zebras, flamingos, bears, and elephants provide hours of enjoyment for the whole family. **In Leonard Park, just south of I-35; 940-668-4533; www.cooke.net/zoo/html.**

Gainesville Factory Outlet Shops
Bargain-shopper's delight. **4321 N. I-35; 940-668-1888.**

WHERE TO EAT

Cary's Tea Room
111 W. California St.; 940-665-6540.

WHERE TO STAY

Rose House Bed-and-Breakfast
An 1898 Queen Anne Victorian home fewer than 2 blocks from the courthouse. **321 S. Dixon St.; 940-665-1010.**

Sherman and Denison
Getting There: Sherman is 33 miles due east of Gainesville on U.S. Hwy. 82. Denison, its sister city, is 10 miles north of Sherman on U.S. Hwy. 69/75. **Visitor Information: Sherman Chamber of Commerce, 307 W. Washington St.; 903-893-1184. Denison Chamber of Commerce, 313 W. Woodard St.; 903-465-1551.Travel Information Center, 2 miles north of Denison on U.S. Hwy. 75; 903-687-2548; www.shermantex.com, www.denisontx.com.**

The Sherman and Denison area is an educational, medical, commercial, and industrial center, with a number of Fortune 500 industries. Denison is the birthplace of Dwight D. Eisenhower. Sherman took its name from General Sidney Sherman, the Republic of Texas cavalry officer credited with the slogan "Remember the Alamo." This area gets my vote as the most unchanged region in the state. The people are still friendly here, and a handshake is as good as a contract.

SEEING AND DOING

Eisenhower Birthplace
A restored 1890s home where Dwight David Eisenhower was born. The son of a railroad worker, he became this country's top military leader in World War II and eventually its president. **208 E. Day St. in Denison; 903-465-8908, fax 903-465-8988; eisenhower@texoma.net; www.eisenhower birthplace.org.**

Grayson County Frontier Village
A collection of eighteen rustic buildings dating from 1840 to 1900. Open from mid-May through October. **In Loy Park on Loy Lake Rd. in Denison; 903-463-2487.**

Kelly Square
Shopping opportunities in a beautifully restored,

Possum Kingdom Lake near Denison. Photo courtesy of Texas Highways *magazine.*

three-story, turn-of-the-century building. **115 S. Travis St. in Sherman; 903-868-1771.**

Munson Vineyards

Named for T. V. Munson, whose development of hybrid grape varieties is acclaimed worldwide. Many of the varieties he discovered are on display on a 5-acre tract on the property. **On the west campus of Grayson County College at 6101 Grayson Dr. in Denison; 903-786-4382.**

Red River Historical Museum

Displays 1933 WPA murals and the history of Grayson County in pictures and artifacts. In the old Carnegie Library at **301 S. Walnut St. in Sherman; 903-893-7623.**

RECREATION

Hagerman National Wildlife Refuge

Includes 11,300 acres of land and water offering food and rest for migrating and wintering waterfowl. About 300 bird species have been recorded here. The refuge is visited by hundreds of thousands of birders each year. **From U.S. Hwy. 75 between Sherman and Denison, take Farm Road 691 west of the county airport, then Farm Road 1417 north 1.5 miles and follow the signs; 903-786-2826.**

Lake Texoma

A huge reservoir along the border between Texas and Oklahoma. A shoreline of 580 miles includes scenic coves and inlets. This is one of the most popular Army Corps of Engineers lakes in the nation, logging more than 9 million visitors a year. There are 57 campgrounds, scores of trailer parks, 110 picnic areas, more than 100 shelter buildings, and more than 80 boat ramps. There are superb marinas and luxury resorts, and room for every kind of boating activity. Lake Texoma is **about 5 miles north of Denison, off U.S. Hwy. 75.** An office of information for Lake Texoma is at **101 E. Main St. in Denison; 903-463-9888; www.laketexoma.com.**

WHERE TO EAT

Buckaroo BBQ
2601 U.S. Hwy. 75 in Sherman; 903-892-7427.

Cotton Patch Cafe
500 U.S. Hwy. 75 in Denison; 903-484-0097.

WHERE TO STAY

Best Western Grayson House
2105 Texoma Parkway in Sherman; 903-892-2161.

Molly Cherry Victorian
Bed-and-breakfast. 200 W. Prospect St. in Denison; 903-465-0575.

Bonham
Getting There: Take U.S. Hwy. 287 southeast from Wichita Falls for 19 miles to Henrietta, then go left on U.S. Hwy. 82 for 125 miles to Bonham. **Visitor Information: www.bonhamtx.com.**

Bonham, named for Alamo hero James Butler Bonham, is best known as the birthplace and home of Sam Rayburn—Mister Sam—who ruled with an iron hand as Speaker of the U.S. House of Representatives for more years than any other Speaker in American history.

SEEING AND DOING

Fort Inglish Park
A replica of a log blockhouse and stockade built as a personal fort by Bailey Inglish in 1837. This was the nucleus of homesteads that eventually became the town of Bonham. **At State Hwy. 56 and Chinner St.; 903-583-3943.**

Ivanhoe General Store
About 10 miles north of Bonham on Farm Road 273 is the community of Ivanhoe. It's only a speck on the map, with a general store that also serves as a post office and cafe. But I'm here to tell you that the cafe serves the best doggone hamburgers in the territory. Farmers drive in straight from the field in the middle of the day to get a hamburger at the Ivanhoe General Store. What a sight it is to see all those John Deere tractors parked out front at lunchtime. **On U.S. Hwy. 273 in Ivanhoe; 903-583-5377.**

Oliver Store
A few miles east of Bonham, between Bonham and Paris on U.S. Hwy. 82, is another interesting eating place. The community is Windom, and the establishment is Oliver Store. At a glance it looks like most other general stores up by the Red River, selling whatnots and whatever, and it is not at all unusual to see tractors parked out front when farmers make quick trips into town for things they need. What is unusually good are the homemade pies Loretta Oliver makes at her home every morning before dawn and brings in to decorate the lunch counter at the rear of the store. A slice of her chocolate pie, and it's a man-size slice, sells for $1 at Loretta's place, and you have to be there early to get some. **414 Main St., Windom; 903-623-4188.**

Sam Rayburn Home
Mister Sam's home, built in 1916 and restored to 1961 condition, the year Sam Rayburn died. **U.S. Hwy. 82, 1.5 miles west of Bonham; 903-583-5558.**

Sam Rayburn Library
An elegant structure, of white Georgia marble, that Mister Sam would not have approved of, because he was a very modest man. When he retired as Speaker, he moved back to Bonham and lived in his family home. The Sam Rayburn Library includes an exact duplicate of the Speaker's office in the U.S. Capitol. **Four blocks west of downtown at 800 W. Sam Rayburn Dr.; 903-583-2455.**

WHERE TO EAT

Jace's Feed Mill Restaurant
Features Tex-Mex and chicken-fried steak. **201 N. Main St.; 903-961-2711.**

The town square in Paris, Texas, designed to resemble the real Paris. Photo courtesy of Texas Highways *magazine.*

WHERE TO STAY

Granny Lou's
This bed-and-breakfast is a three-story Victorian home near downtown. **317 W. Sam Rayburn Dr.; 903-583-7912.**

Paris
Getting There: Paris is 37 miles east of Bonham, and approximately 182 miles east of Wichita Falls, on U.S. Hwy. 82. **Visitor Information: Paris Chamber of Commerce** offers walking and driving tour maps that include thirty-four points of interest in the area; **1651 Clarksville St.; 903-784-2501; www.paristexas.com.**

I was at a cafe in Paris some years ago and, as usual, made a fool of myself. I wanted soup and asked the waitress if their soup was homemade. She replied, "All our soup is homemade," and pointed out the window to the **Campbell Soup factory** across the street. The factory at **500 NW Loop 286** is still turning out "homemade" soup daily; **903-784-3341.**

SEEING AND DOING

Evergreen Cemetery
Dating from 1866, this cemetery contains more than 40,000 graves, including many early Texas patriots. There are many unusual, handsome carved headstones and monuments. If you are a grave rubber, you'll enjoy this visit. **506 Evergreen St.**

Sam Bell Maxey State Historic Structure
Victorian-style mansion built by Confederate General Sam Bell Maxey in 1868 and occupied by the family for almost a century. Guided tours Wed.–Fri. by appointment. **812 S. Church St.; 903-785-5716.**

WHERE TO EAT

German Sausage Place
You can taste the old country here. **1308 Clarksville St.; 903-785-7608.**

TaMolly's Mexican Restaurant
Serves fine south-of-the-border food. **1934 Bonham St.; 903-785-1989.**

WHERE TO STAY

Cane River
Bed-and-breakfast. **441 12th St. SE; 903-784-7402.**

Clarksville
Getting There: Clarksville is 213 miles east of Wichita Falls via U.S. Hwy. 287 and U.S. Hwy. 82. **Visitor Information: Clarksville Chamber of Commerce, 101 N. Locust St.; 903-427-2645.**

SEEING AND DOING

Colonel Charles DeMorse Home
The home of the man known as the father of Texas journalism. DeMorse founded the *Northern Standard* newspaper. **One block north of the town square.**

Fiberglass Artist Bert Holster
Bert works out of his house in Clarksville. He's one of the most popular fiberglass artists in the world, and his work is in demand. Once when I visited him, he was working on the head of what turned out to be a 40-foot gorilla.

If you drive by his house, near downtown, you may see him working on a larger-than-life-size Hereford bull for a client in California. Bert says it's one of the strangest assignments he has ever embarked on, because the guy wants wings on the bull. **307 W. 2nd St.; 903-427-3055.**

Golden Gals' Pralines
A cottage industry specializing in gourmet pralines, handmade with Texas pecan halves. They also sell woven baskets, made in Clarksville. **1101 S. Donoho St.; 903-427-3148.**

Red River County Courthouse
Dates from 1885, with massive walls, yellow stone, and a remarkable clock tower. The clock ran smoothly until 1961, when the town decided to convert it to run on electricity. Soon after, the clock, referred to by locals as Old Red, began striking gongs, on and on, until someone unplugged it. Today the people in these parts refer to the experience as "the night it got later than ever before" in Clarksville. **400 N. Walnut St.; 903-427-3761.**

Sam Houston Park

The park has a marker indicating the site of General Sam Houston's entry into Texas when he came to fight against Mexico. **About 40 miles north of Clarksville via State Hwy. 37 and Farm Road 410.**

WHERE TO EAT

Coleman BBQ
604 North M. L. King Dr.; 903-427-5131.

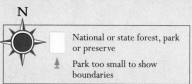

N

| National or state forest, park or preserve
| Park too small to show boundaries

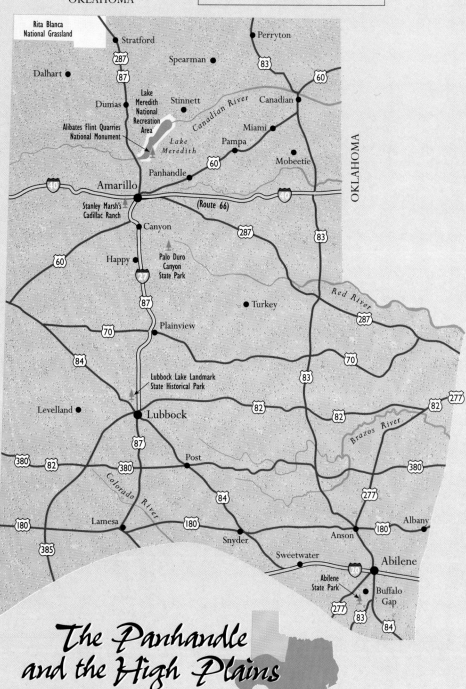

OKLAHOMA

Rita Blanca
National Grassland

Stratford

Perryton

287

Spearman

83

87

Dalhart

60

Lake
Meredith
National
Recreation
Area

Stinnett

Canadian River

Canadian

Dumas

Alibates Flint Quarries
National Monument

Lake
Meredith

Miami

Pampa

60

Mobeetie

OKLAHOMA

Panhandle

40

Amarillo

(Route 66)

40

Stanley Marsh's
Cadillac Ranch

Canyon

287

83

NEW MEXICO

60

Happy

27

Palo Duro
Canyon
State Park

87

Turkey

Red River

287

70

Plainview

84

Lubbock Lake Landmark
State Historical Park

83

82

277

Levelland

Lubbock

82

82

82

Brazos River

87

380

82

380

Post

Colorado River

84

277

380

Albany

277

180

Lamesa

180

Snyder

Anson

180

385

Sweetwater

Abilene

20

Abilene
State Park

277

Buffalo
Gap

83

84

*The Panhandle
and the High Plains*

The Panhandle
and the High Plains

The Lighthouse, a natural formation in Palo Duro Canyon.
Photo courtesy of Texas Highways magazine.

The Panhandle and the High Plains

Amarillo is considered the capital of the Panhandle by virtue of being the largest city. Lubbock is known as the capital of the High Plains for the same reason. The Panhandle and the High Plains region are filled with small communities, all feeding off the two larger cities—and, in turn, the two major cities depend on the work and sweat of the men and women in the smaller towns to boost the economy of the region.

Most of this area is dedicated to farming and ranching. A farming friend of mine in Hereford, Dave Dziuk, made quite a killing a few years ago when he came up with the unique idea of "popcorn on the cob." He raised it right there in his fields and sold it to supermarkets all over the country. Most of the farming done in the Panhandle involves wheat—with plenty of oil and gas production thrown in for variety. They also grow cotton, sorghum, vegetables, and sunflowers. In the Lubbock area, wineries have received international recognition for some excellent wines.

A large part of the Panhandle and High Plains region is desolate and empty, but there is a lot of beauty too. On one memorable trip, I flew over the land in an old Stearman biplane with my lifelong friend Dave Stirton at the controls. The aerial views of the patterns of the wheat fields were as beautiful as anything I've ever seen.

Summers in the Panhandle and the High Plains are warm during the day and cool at night. Rainfall averages about 20 inches a year, with the wettest months usually being May, June, and August. Late fall, winter, and early spring are blustery. Winter in the Amarillo area can often produce beautiful snowfall. Most of the snow that falls south, though, near Lubbock, turns to slush and just makes life miserable for anyone who works outdoors.

The terrain is mostly flat, and winds can sweep across the region with considerable force. I think anybody who has grown up in this part of Texas has a permanent earache, caused by the incessant blowing of the wind. The region is not entirely flat, though. In several places, most notably southeast of Amarillo, are deep canyons. Palo Duro Canyon attracts droves of tourists.

Amarillo

Amarillo ("yellow" in Spanish, but pronounced am-uh-RILL-oh) is literally the center of the Texas Panhandle. The city and the region offer a true western heritage, with wide-open spaces and breathtaking sunrises and sunsets. Amarillo is also the gateway to 120-mile-long Palo Duro Canyon, America's second largest canyon. With its relatively mild climate, Amarillo is rated as having some of the cleanest air in the country. Take it from a longtime traveler of the Lone Star State: Amarillo has more than its share of friendly people and outrageous characters.

Getting Around

BUSES
Amarillo City Transit handles city bus service **(806-378-3094).**

TAXIS
For taxis, call **Bob's Taxi Service (806-373-1171), Checker Cab (806-376-8211),** or **Dependable Cab (806-372-5500).**

TOURS
In conjunction with the Amarillo Convention and Visitors Bureau, **Old West Tours** offers a wide range of tours of the city and the area **(806-374-1497).** Shuttles to the annual Texas Outdoor Musical Drama at Palo Duro Canyon are available through **Amarillo Tours (806-655-9637).** (For more information on the outdoor musical, see Palo Duro Canyon State Park, under Major Attractions.)

Visitor Information

Amarillo Convention and Visitors Bureau
Downtown in the Bivins Home, 1000 S. Polk St.; 806-374-1497, 1-800-692-1338; amar@ arn.net; www.amarillo-cvb.org. The city also maintains an information booth at Amarillo International Airport.

Camara de Comercia Hispana
900 S. Jefferson St.; 806-379-8800.

Texas Information Center
Information and maps about places throughout the state. **I-40 at the airport; 1-800-452-9292.**

Major Attractions

Cadillac Ranch
Amarillo's most famous attraction, just west of the city on I-40, was created by one of the city's eccentric millionaires, Stanley Marsh III. It's a row of Cadillac cars, dating from 1949 to 1963, planted nose first in the ground along the highway. Stanley says it's a monument to the golden age of automobiles—to "petro-power." The attraction has been there since the 1970s. Now and then Stanley changes it a bit, and when he does, he invites the whole town to join in. A few years back, at a time when the O. J. Simpson case was in the headlines, Stanley repainted all the cars and invited people in to add modern-day graffiti. The most popular phrase written on the cars turned out to be "Save O. J."

Cadillac Ranch is not the only unusual piece of art Stanley Marsh has created in the area. He also dreamed up a **"floating mesa"** on a mountaintop west of Amarillo. Stanley hired workers to haul hundreds of 4-by-8 sheets of plywood to the top of the mesa. They painted them sky-blue and put them up just below the top of the mountain. What motorists see when approaching the place is a mountain and a blue sky—and then overhead, the true top of the mesa, then the real sky. It's hard to explain, but if you drive by it on a day when the sky is blue, it will honestly amaze you. It looks like the top of the mountain is detached from the earth and floating in the sky. For a good view of the "floating mesa," **go north on Bell Ave. from I-40 in Amarillo to Tascosa Rd. (Farm Road 1061); turn left (west) onto Road 1061 and travel about 8 miles.** When you pass the Bishop Hills subdivision, look to the left, and in the distance you'll see Stanley Marsh's creation.

Route 66

Amarillo has long been famous for its location along old Route 66, which once connected East with West in this country. Now the old route has become Interstate 40. All you baby boomers remember the TV show in the '70s about two good-looking guys, played by George Maharis and Martin Milner, traveling across the country in their Chevy Corvette. All us old-timers remember that grand old Nat King Cole song that tells us, "Get your kicks on Route 66."

Part of the fun of traveling with my family when I was a kid was checking out the tourist courts (that's old-time talk for motels) along Route 66. Most of

Early 1950s gas station along Route 66 in Shamrock.

them were old and rundown even then, but it was entertaining to stay in them because of the architecture. Some of them looked like service stations; some were built to look like log cabins. Some *were* log cabins. Along the way we would find drive-in theaters, snake pits, and souvenir shops. A few of the old buildings that made Route 66 so memorable are still standing—monuments to a time when Route 66 carried Americans from one end of this country to the other. A group helping to keep memories of the highway alive is the **Route 66 Association, P.O. Box 4117, Amarillo, 79116; 806-372-US66.**

Amarillo is working to restore the part of Route 66 that went through town, and other Texas communities along the route are starting to preserve the old buildings. You'll have to follow I-40 if you want to see Route 66 today. Check out the towns as you come to them. If you exit the interstate at the towns, you might be surprised at what you'll find.

The town of **Shamrock,** near the eastern end of the Texas portion of Route 66, has one of the last great examples of the old gas stations that once were so prolific. Right in the middle of town on old Route 66 and U.S. Hwy. 83 is a service station that looks like the builder couldn't make up his mind whether he was putting up a gas station or a castle. He compromised and got something in between.

Heading west from Shamrock, you'll come to **McLean,** with its downtown restoration of one of the old Phillips 66 gas stations. McLean also has the **Devil's Rope Museum (100 S. Kingsley St., 806-779-2225),** with a history of the old highway. Route 66 continues west through **Alanreed** and **Jericho,** then on to **Groom,** before reaching Amarillo. West of Amarillo you'll pass through **Bushland, Vega,**

Adrian, and Glenrio before crossing into New Mexico. In each of these communities you may find some interesting old buildings that are remnants of the days when Route 66 powered these towns.

Palo Duro Canyon State Park

Palo Duro is a 120-mile-long canyon that drops 1,200 feet from rim to floor. You can drive past millions of years of geologic time on a park road that winds through the canyon along the Prairie Dog Fork of the Red River. Other activities include camping, hiking, horseback riding, picnicking, and riding the **Sad Monkey Miniature Train (806-488-2222)** through the canyon. The park has six camping areas and a total of 116 sites.

Palo Duro Park has a few developed trails, but visitors are free to wander anywhere along the river. The park is particularly scenic in late October when the leaves are turning, and in April when wildflowers bloom. Exploring the side canyons can be exciting as well, because some rock climbing is usually required. Don't get too close to the edge of cliffs; the limestone and sandstone crumble easily.

A hiking and equestrian trail, the **Lighthouse Trail,** leads south into Sunday Canyon. It's about 3 miles round-trip, and may be closed during heavy rains. Horses and riding equipment can be rented at the park stables, next to Goodnight Trading Post. The **Capitol Peak Mountain Biking Trail** makes a 4-mile loop through the park. The visitor center has maps.

In summer, the granddaddy of all Texas outdoor musicals is presented at Palo Duro Park: a historical drama called *Texas.* It is usually sold out every year. That's the good news. The bad news is that it started out as an amateur event involving local people, generally bad acting, and mainly mediocre singing, but it was a lot of fun. Today, mostly professional singers, dancers, and actors are brought in to put on the event. The play and the music are much better now, but the drama seems to have lost some of that homespun flavor that brought people here in the beginning. Play information: **806-655-2181.**

Palo Duro Canyon State Park is **22 miles southeast of Amarillo via I-27 and State Hwy. 217; 806-488-2555; 512-389-8900 (camping reservations); pdc@palodurocanyon.com; www. palodurocanyon.com.**

Seeing and Doing

Art Galleries and Museums

James M. Haney Gallery

Western and southwestern art. **4500 W. I-40; 806-358-3653.**

Museums and Historic Sites

American Quarter Horse Heritage Center and Museum

A facility with hands-on displays, laser movie presentations, a library and research archives, and works of art focusing on quarter horses. Outside is a demonstration arena with occasional riding programs and a store that sells leather tack, southwestern jewelry, books, art, and toys. **2601 E. I-40; 806- 376-5181.**

Cal Farley's Boys Ranch and Old Tascosa

The town of Tascosa boomed in the very old days, but busted in the late 1800s when the railroad passed it by. During its heyday, the likes of Billy the Kid, Pat Garrett, and Len Woodruff, who deposited three of his victims in the nearby Boot Hill Cemetery, hung out in these parts. In 1939 prizefighter Cal Farley built a boys ranch here to rescue orphans and troubled boys and give them a fresh start in life. Today, Boys Ranch is a self-contained community for more than 400 residents. The Boys Ranch Rodeo each September attracts some 10,000 visitors. Boys Ranch is about **35 miles northwest of Amarillo, via Farm Road 1061; 1-800-657-7124, 806-372-2341; www.calfarleysboysranch.org/ boysranch.html.** Girlstown, USA, in Whiteface, 45 miles west of Lubbock, is part of the same organization (also at 1-800-657-7124).

Helium Monument

Amarillo has been a cattle center and an oil center. Until 1930, when Arabian oil deposits were discovered, the Amarillo area had the largest known oil deposits in the world. In 1929 helium was extracted from gas in Amarillo for the first time, and the area is now the source for 99 percent of the world's helium, valuable in aerospace technology, welding, cryogenics, and more. **1200 Streit Dr., adjacent to the**

Don Harrington Discovery Center; 806-355-9547.

Sterquell Collection

An intriguing collection of vehicles from before the age of the automobile, featuring about fifty horse-drawn carriages, wagons, and sleighs. Also on display are milk wagons, farm vehicles, a hearse, and a photographer's wagon. **5501 Everett St.; 806-372-7522; sterquell-collection@amaonline.com; www.amaonline.com/sterquell.**

Other Sights

Amarillo Livestock Auction

Amarillo is headquarters for an immense ranch and cattle feedlot area and the state's largest livestock auction. More than 600,000 cattle move through the auction arena at the stockyards each year. Auctions are held Tuesdays. **100 S. Manhattan St.; 806-373-7464.**

Parks

Don Harrington Discovery Center

A 51-acre park with a lake, picnic area, museum, and planetarium. The exhibits encourage hands-on activity, with a giant aquarium, the Black Hole, a large kaleidoscope, and more. The planetarium has star shows and films with some spectacular effects. **1200 Streit Dr.; 806-355-9548.**

Shopping

Boot and Saddle Shops

At the **Rancher and Farmer Supply Company,** you can get custom-made boots and other things **(8048 River Rd., 806-383-2181); Horse & Rider** makes saddles for working cowboys, as well as leather tack and chaps **(2500 Coultier Dr., 806-352-5544); Oliver Brothers Saddle Shop** also does custom saddle and leather work **(3016 Plains Blvd., 806-372-7562).**

Boots 'n Jeans

The best price and selection in town for western wear. **2225 S. Georgia St.; 806-353-4368.**

Old San Jacinto

A string of shops along old Route 66. Antiques shops, coin and bottle shops, used-book dealers, record stores, crafts, odds and ends, and a couple of eating places line the route, making it a shopper's paradise. **On 6th Ave. from the 2700 block to the 3900 block.**

Tours

Boot Steps Guest Ranch

A guest ranch close to town, offering meals, a barn dance, hayrides, and even a little horseshoe pitching. They call it "gentle" roughing it. The dining hall is air-conditioned. **4512 Gem Lake Rd., 5 miles west of Amarillo; 806-355-1405.**

Cowboy Morning/Evening

From April 15 to October 15, you can get Old West–style chuckwagon breakfasts on the open range at the rim of Palo Duro Canyon. Who in your group would not enjoy scrambled eggs, ranch sausage, sourdough biscuits, brown gravy, and campfire coffee? The dinner consists of steaks and all the trimmings, plus wagon rides and a chance to watch real cowboys at work. **Figure 3 Ranch, about 25 miles southeast of Amarillo; 1-800-658-2613.**

Creekwood Ranch Old West Show and Chuck Wagon Supper

Wagons take visitors to a campsite for an old-fashioned country meal and entertainment by cowboys; Thurs.–Sun. **Creekwood Ranch, 8 miles south of Amarillo at 2433 W. I-40; 1-800-658-6673, 806-356-9256.**

Festivals and Events

May

Funfest

Memorial Day weekend. A 3-day family festival of games, entertainment, and food that attracts more than 70,000 people every year who come to hear top-notch entertainment. There is a Funfest marathon and half marathon, volleyball and golf tournaments, bicycle races, a talent contest, and numerous kiddie activities. **Thompson Park, Amarillo, off U.S. Hwy. 87.**

Greater Southwest Music Festival

First week in May. Junior and senior high school musicians from seven states compete in a 3-day contest. **Civic Center at 3rd and Buchanan Sts. and at Amarillo College.**

September

Tri-State Fair

Usually the week beginning the third Monday in September. The usual variety of state fair activities, plus big-name country and western stars and livestock competition. **Fairgrounds at 10th and Bell Sts.**

November

National Old-Timers Rodeo

Usually 4 days early in the month. This is the finals for rodeo cowboys over the age of forty. They compete in about fifty rodeo events around the country, and the top sixty cowboys make it here. **Civic Center.**

Recreation

Parks and Camping

Alibates Flint Quarries

Distinctive for its varied colorations in the rock outcroppings of the Canadian River. There is evidence here that early humans quarried flint in the region. The site is magnificent to behold, but accessible only on ranger-led tours. **Thirty miles north of Amarillo, off State Hwy. 136, about 10 miles south of the community of Fritch** (there is a **visitor center** in Fritch; **806-857-3151**).

Buffalo Lake National Wildlife Refuge

One of the major waterfowl refuges on the Central Flyway. This 7,600-acre refuge is a winter home for a million ducks and 80,000 geese. The refuge draws visitors for its 5-mile interpretive auto route and its interpretive walking trail. There is picnicking, sightseeing, birding, nature tours, photography opportunities, and campsites (but without drinking water or electricity).

About 30 miles southwest of Amarillo, outside the town of Umbarger; 806-499-3382.

Campgrounds

Amarillo KOA (off U.S. Hwy. 60, 3 miles east of Amarillo at 1100 Folsom Rd., 806-335-1792); Longhorn Trailer Inn (17010 E. I-40, 806-359-6302).

Lake McClellan

A small lake of 325 acres that provides water for several towns in the region. It's a very popular recreation spot in the Panhandle because of its accessibility, wooded picnic areas, and camping with RV hookups. **Fifty-five miles due east of Amarillo on I-40, between Jericho and Alanreed.**

Lake Meredith

Built by the U.S. Bureau of Reclamation. This lake reaches out among the colorful buttes and cliffs of the Canadian River Valley. There are eight public parks with boating, fishing, camping, and picnicking. Park headquarters is at **419 E. Broadway St. in Fritch, which is 51 miles northeast of Amarillo on State Hwy. 136; 806-857-3151; www.tpwd. state.tx.us/fish/infish/lakes/meredith/ lake_id.htm.**

Where to Eat

The Big Texan Steakhouse

You can't miss this place: billboards tell about it well before you get to Amarillo. They advertise a 72-ounce steak—four and a half pounds—and if you can eat the entire thing, it's free. (But watch out: You have to eat all the side dishes as well, and that includes shrimp cocktail, baked potato, salad, and roll, and you have to eat it all in 1 hour.) I've seen some people collect on the deal—mostly Dallas Cowboys football players. Most people wind up paying the $30 for the meal. The Big Texan also offers barbecue, chicken, and a few West Texas specialties like jackrabbit, rattlesnake, buffalo burgers, and calf fries (if you have to ask what this is, you don't want it). **7701 E. I-40; 806-372-6000.**

Calico Country

They'll chicken-fry anything here, from steak to

Palo Duro Canyon, near Amarillo.

chicken gizzards—even corn on the cob—and then serve it as you please. One of their salads is made from the fixings of a pig sandwich—without the bread, of course. **2410 Paramount Blvd.; 806-358-7664.**

Doodles
The best burgers in town, great fries, and cobbler for dessert. **3701 Olsen Blvd.; 806-355-0064.**

La Fiesta
This is the place for Tex-Mex, steaks, and chicken dishes after visiting the American Quarter Horse Museum. **2200 Ross St.; 806-374-3689.**

OHMS Gallery Cafe
A popular gathering place for artists and musicians. The food, with a British flavor, is served buffet-style. **619 S. Taylor St.; 806-373-3233.**

Ruby Tequila's Mexican Kitchen
Is that a great name, or what? Tex-Mex in liberal portions. **2108 Paramount Blvd.; 806-358-7829.**

Stockyard Cafe
You can enjoy down-home meals while rubbing elbows with cowboys and ranchers from the nearby stockyards. **110 S. Manhattan St.; 806-374-6024.**

Where to Stay

Amerisuites
A two-story hotel/motel with 126 suites. **6800 W. I-40; 806-358-7943.**

Big Texan
A colorful two-story motel with a western motif. **7703 E. I-40; 806-372-5000.**

Galbraith House
A restored old home that is now a B&B with five rooms and private baths. **1710 S. Polk St.; 806-374-0237.**

Hotel Harvey
A ten-story hotel with 266 rooms. **3100 W. I-40; 806-358-6161.**

Parkview House
A 1909 home turned B&B with three rooms and a shared bath. **1311 S. Jefferson St.; 806-373-9464.**

Towns in the Area

Interesting towns in this part of Texas include Panhandle,

Pampa, Miami, Canadian, Mobeetie, Canyon, and Happy. Suggested places to eat and to stay are included with most of the towns.

Panhandle

Getting There: Panhandle is 30 miles northeast of Amarillo on U.S. Hwy. 60. **Visitor Information: Panhandle City Hall, 1 Main St.; 806-537-3517.**

The people produce wheat, cattle, and petroleum in this area, but the biggest attraction for tourists is the scenery. Along Farm Road 293 west to State Hwy. 136 are some spectacular views of the High Plains.

SEEING AND DOING

Square House Museum

One of the best-kept small museums in the state, with displays and dioramas that interpret the history of the Panhandle. Open daily **at Pioneer Park, on State Hwy. 207; 806-537-3524.**

Thomas Cree's Little Tree

On this site was what is said to be the first tree planted in the Texas Panhandle. In 1888 settler Thomas Cree hauled a sapling of bois d'arc from beyond the Cap Rock and planted it by his dugout home. The tree thrived until 1969, when it was killed by an agricultural chemical. Natural seedlings are growing today at the site, set behind a protective fence **at the southern edge of U.S. Hwy. 60, about 5 miles southwest of Panhandle.**

WHERE TO EAT

The Butter Churn Restaurant
On State Hwy. 207; 806-537-5274.

WHERE TO STAY

Texan Hotel
117 E. Broadway St.; 806-537-3372.

Pampa

Getting There: Take U.S. Hwy. 60 northeast of Amarillo for about 60 miles. **Visitor Information: Pampa Chamber of Commerce, 200 N. Ballard St.; 806-669-3241; www.pampa-texas.com.**

Founded in 1888 on the Santa Fe Railroad line, Pampa today is a city of beautiful churches, large parks, and fine homes. There are fourteen city parks and three lakes.

SEEING AND DOING

Pickin' Shack

Eudell and Mary Ann Gifford don't have a telephone, but they do have a lot of friends who enjoy bluegrass and country music. Almost any evening, if you're passing through the community of Lefors, you are apt to hear some of that music if your window is down. Just follow the sound. The only thing the Giffords enjoy more than down-home country music is an audience. **About 10 miles southeast of Pampa on State Hwy. 27 in the community of Lefors.**

White Deer Land Museum

Period rooms and documents of the White Deer Land Company that was established in 1882. Exhibits recall early ranching days. Open Tues.–Sun. 1:30–4 P.M. **116 S. Cuyler St.; 806-669-8041.**

WHERE TO EAT

Dyer's BBQ

Serves up Panhandle barbecue. **At U.S. Hwy. 60 west, in Pampa; 806-665-4401.**

Furr's Family Dining
1200 N. Hobert St., in Coronado Shopping Center; 806-665-3321.

WHERE TO STAY

Davis Hotel

One of several mom-and-pop motels in the area. **116 ¹/₂ W. Foster Ave.; 806-669-9115.**

Miami

Getting There: Take U.S. Hwy. 60 northeast for about 60 miles to Pampa, then just continue on for 23 miles farther to Miami. **Visitor Information: Miami Chamber of Commerce; 806-868-4791.**

Miami (my-AM-uh) is an Indian word for "sweetheart." Miami was first a construction camp along the railroad line, and it grew into a town. Today it is popular as a hunting and fishing area.

SEEING AND DOING

Roberts County Museum

Housed in a restored old Santa Fe Railroad depot. It has pioneer artifacts and Indian relics, along with a blacksmith shop, chuckwagon, and half-dugout home. Part of the Meade Collection of prehistoric archaeological artifacts and fossils is here. **U.S. Hwy. 60 downtown; 806-868-3291.**

WHERE TO EAT

Granny's Place

The down-home cooking here attracts locals and tourists alike. **122 Water St.; 806-868-5561.**

WHERE TO STAY

Howerton House

This bed-and-breakfast offers views of the magnificent scenery around Miami. **112 W. Commercial; 806-868-4771.**

Canadian

Getting There: Canadian is 110 miles northeast of Amarillo via U.S. Hwy. 60. **Visitor Information: Canadian Chamber of Commerce, 216 S. 2nd St.; 806-323-6234; www.webtex.com/canadian.**

Located on the Canadian River, one of the state's pretty rivers, Canadian is supported by oil and ranching enterprises. Early settlers in this community held one of the very first rodeos in Texas.

SEEING AND DOING

River Valley Pioneer Museum

The usual local museum, featuring memorabilia on the history of Canadian and Hemphill County. Open Tues.–Fri. 10 A.M.–noon and 1–4 P.M., Sun. 2–4 P.M. **118 S. 2nd St.; 806-323-6548.**

RECREATION

Black Kettle National Grasslands

Nature trails that are popular during fall foliage, and

opportunities to see wild turkey, deer, and waterfowl. The site offers camping, picnic grounds, and fishing at Lake Marvin. **Twenty miles southeast of Canadian on Farm Road 2266.**

WHERE TO EAT

Alexander's Grocery & Deli

It's not much to look at, but the sandwiches will turn you on. **959 S. 2nd St.; 806-323-8853.**

Paula's Custom Cakes

A local favorite for folks who have a thing for desserts. **402 N. 2nd St.; 806-323-9825.**

WHERE TO STAY

Bed-and-breakfast choices include:

Emerald House
103 N. 6th St.; 806-323-5827.

Thicket B&B
On Farm Road 2266 on the outskirts of Canadian; 806-323-8118.

Mobeetie

Getting There: Take U.S. Hwy. 60 northeast from Amarillo to Pampa for 60 miles; from there, continue on Hwy. 60 for about 6 more miles, then turn right onto State Hwy. 152. From there it's about 30 miles to Mobeetie. **Visitor Information: Mobeetie City Hall; 806-845-3581.**

Just a dot on the map, but known for its unusual name. Old-timers say early settlers chose to name their town Sweetwater, but wanted to use the Indian translation of the word. The local Indians told them the translation was *Mobeetie*, so that was the name the community took. Years later, and too late to change the name, it was discovered that the Indians had pulled a prank, and that *Mobeetie* actually meant "cow chip." To this day nobody knows if the tale is true, but it makes a good story.

SEEING AND DOING

Mobeetie Jail Museum

One of the best museums in this part of the state,

housed in an old jailhouse. It includes an authentically restored sheriff's quarters. **806-845-2028.**

WHERE TO EAT

Sally's Cafe
1701 W. Main St.; 806-845-1014.

Canyon

Getting There: Canyon is 15 miles south of Amarillo on I-27. **Visitor Information: Canyon Chamber of Commerce, 1518 5th Ave.; 806-655-7815.**

Canyon is the gateway to **Palo Duro Canyon State Park.** (See Major Attractions earlier in the chapter for details on the park.)

SEEING AND DOING

Panhandle Plains Historical Museum
One of the finest museums and historical research facilities in the state. The museum honors the pioneers of Texas in a limestone building that is historic in its own right. This is really five museums in one, with sections dedicated to petroleum, western heritage, paleontology, transportation, and art. The oldest known cabin in the Panhandle is on display here. Among my favorites at the museum is the Bob Wills music library. **On the campus of West Texas State A&M University; 806-656-2244, fax 806-651-2250.**

WHERE TO EAT

Cowboy Cafe
1410 U.S. Hwy. 60; 806-655-1124.

Texas Star Restaurant
2200 4th Ave.; 806-655-9379.

WHERE TO STAY

Country Home
Bed-and-breakfast. **On 8th St.; 806-655-7636.**

House of Kathleen
Bed-and-breakfast. **4270 White Fence Rd.; 806-655-9436.**

Ranch House
Bed-and-breakfast. **On Rural Road 1 on the outskirts of Canyon; 806-655-0339.**

Happy

Getting There: Happy is 45 miles south of Amarillo on I-27. **Visitor Information: Happy City Hall, 106 N. Talley Ave.; 806-558-2121.**

This town bills itself as the "happiest little place in Texas." The town is friendly, but I suspect you'll be happiest seeing Happy in your rear-view mirror. There is a giant cattle feedlot just off the thoroughfare, and you can smell it long before you get to Happy and long after you leave it.

WHERE TO EAT

Methad Corporation
It's an odd name, but the food is good. **In downtown Happy; 806-764-3352.**

The Northern Border

The northern border of the Texas Panhandle, north of Amarillo, is the stuff of legends. All the old-time cattle drives that originated in Texas wound through this land. It's not uncommon to wander upon old trail markers that designated some of the cattle drives headed up by the likes of Charles Goodnight and Oliver Loving. Communities like Stinnet and Spearman were the site of Indian battles. In more modern times, the northern border has been known for its wheat farmers and its windmill collectors. The land is beautiful, and is rich in Texas history, with people who are among the friendliest you'll find in the Lone Star State.

Towns in the Area

Towns that we'll visit along the northern border are Dalhart, Dumas, Stratford, Stinnett, Spearman, and Perryton. Suggested places to eat and to stay are included with most of the towns.

Dalhart

Getting There: Take U.S. Hwy. 87/287 north from Amarillo for about 50 miles to Dumas, then follow U.S. Hwy. 87 west for 24 miles and then north for

J. B. Buchanan Windmill Farm in the Texas Panhandle. Photo courtesy of Irene Snider, Spearman Chamber of Commerce.

15 miles to Dalhart. **Visitor Information: Dalhart Chamber of Commerce, 102 E. 7th St.; 806-249-5646; www.dalharttx.com.**

Some people say this is about as far north as you can get and still be in Texas, but actually the Oklahoma and New Mexico borders are still about 45 miles away. Dalhart grew up at the junction of the Denver City and Rock Island Railroad lines. First it was known as Twist, then later Denrock. Finally the founders settled on the current name, which is a combination of the names of two counties, Dallam and Hartley.

SEEING AND DOING

Empty Saddle Monument

A favorite photo opportunity for travelers. The monument stands at the north end of Dalhart's V-shaped underpass. A cowboy designed it after a widow asked that a horse bearing an empty saddle appear in the annual reunion parade, in tribute to her dead husband, who was a former XIT Ranch cowboy. **On U.S. Hwy. 87.**

Junior Gray's Saddle Shop

The saddlemaker does most of his jobs for working cowboys, but he can be persuaded to make fancy saddles too, for tourists. Junior's wife does other leatherwork, such as chaps and belts. **310 E. 7th St.; 806-249-2054.**

XIT Ranch

The XIT was once the world's largest fenced ranch: Three million acres in the 1880s. The state of Texas gave the land to a Chicago corporation in 1882 in exchange for construction of the state capitol. An English company, the Capitol Freehold Land and Investment Company of London, operated the spread for many years. The ranch took in parts of ten present-day Texas counties. The north fence was 200 miles from the south fence, and 3,000 miles of barbed wire were put up around the place. The initial herd of cattle totaled almost 111,000 head. Over the years, XIT lands have been split up and sold to smaller ranchers. The **Dallam-Hartley Counties XIT Museum** displays a wealth of artifacts, circa 1900, from the days when the grand old ranch was operating under one company, including railroad antiques, Indian artifacts, frontier firearms, cowboy clothing, saddles, and tack. **108 E. 5th St.; 806-249-5390.**

FESTIVALS AND EVENTS

August—XIT Rodeo and Reunion

This may just be the best darned cowboy gathering in the state. It is the world's largest amateur rodeo, and has been held annually for more than a half century. XIT old-timers are honored. **At Rita Blanca Park; 806-249-5646.**

RECREATION

Lake Rita Blanca Wildlife Management Area

Remarkable views of various species of birds and other wildlife that gather in this region from time to time. In October, migrating geese stop over to rest—upward of 100,000 at one time. A pond northwest of the wildlife management area offers fishing. **On Farm Road 281 at U.S. Hwy. 385/87, just south of town; 1-800-792-1112.**

WHERE TO EAT

Country Heart Bakery

A great morning place. **518 W. 7th St.; 806-249-2822.**

Nursanickel Restaurant

A longtime name in the restaurant business in the Dalhart area. **U.S. Hwy. 87 S.; 806-249-8040.**

WHERE TO STAY

Best Western Nursanickel

102 Scott Ave.; 806-249-5637.

XIT Ranch Motel

209 Liberal St.; 806-249-4589.

Dumas

Getting There: Dumas is 50 miles north of Amarillo on U.S. Hwy. 87/287. **Visitor Information: Dumas Chamber of Commerce, 524 S. Porter Ave.; 806-935-2123.**

The town is named after its founder, Louis Dumas. People like to believe this is the place that Phil Harris meant when he wrote the song "Ding Dong Daddy from Dumas." The truth is, he was really singing about a town named Dumas in the southern United States.

Recreation areas include eight city parks and the rugged canyons and hills of the Canadian River area.

SEEING AND DOING

Moore County Historical Museum

Local history exhibits and memorabilia donated by pioneer families. **8th St. Dumas Ave.; 806-249-5390.**

WHERE TO EAT

Cathy's Kitchen

A popular gathering place. **900 S. Dumas Ave.; 806-935-9356.**

Chuck Wagon Cafe

Offers family-style meals and good chicken-fried steak. **10 E. 1st St.; 806-934-9757.**

WHERE TO STAY

Serendipity House

This bed-and-breakfast offers a taste of early Texas living. **On U.S. Hwy. 287 S.; 806-935-0339.**

Stratford

Getting There: Take U.S. Hwy. 87/287 north from Amarillo for about 50 miles to Dumas, then continue north on Hwy. 287 for 34 miles to Stratford. **Visitor Information: Stratford Chamber of Commerce, 520 N. 3rd St.; 806-396-2260.**

Stratford was established in secrecy in the middle of the night in May 1901, when Sherman County records were moved from the former county seat at Coldwater to land along the Rock Island Railroad route. Texas Rangers were called in to settle the dispute, which Stratford won. (Coldwater has long since disappeared.) The town was named either for Stratford-on-Avon, England, or for the Virginia plantation where Robert E. Lee was born. Nobody knows for sure.

SEEING AND DOING

Sherman County Depot Museum
A good local history museum displaying farm and ranch memorabilia, Indian artifacts, prehistoric fossils, and other things from the Panhandle. **17 N. Main St.; 806-396-2582.**

Stinnett and Spearman
Getting There: Take U.S. Hwy. 60 northeast from Amarillo for 31 miles, then go north on State Hwy. 207 for 35 miles to Stinnett. Spearman is another 30 miles up Hwy. 207. **Visitor Information: Stinnett City Hall, 609 Mackenzie St.; 806-878-2422. Spearman Chamber of Commerce, 211 Main St.; 806-659-5555.**

Stinnett was established around the turn of the twentieth century as a trade center and livestock shipping point at the northern edge of the Canadian River Valley. Spearman came along in 1917 in anticipation of the completion of the North Texas and Santa Fe Railway. World War I delayed completion of the railway for 2 years, but not the growth of Spearman. Like its neighbor, Stinnett, Spearman thrived on the sudden influx of settlers. The stark beauty of this region is displayed in the flowing wheat fields of the region.

SEEING AND DOING

Battle of Adobe Walls
If the story of this battle sounds a bit familiar, take note that many Hollywood movies have been based, in part, on the events at Adobe Walls in 1874. A gathering of Indians under the command of Quanah Parker—a white man who was kidnapped as a child and raised with the Indians—and another Indian leader, Lone Wolf, attacked a group of buffalo hunters camped in the area. A fierce dawn attack opened the siege. The Indians outnumbered the buffalo hunters and were set to wipe out the twenty-eight men and one woman in the camp, but the attack was repulsed that first day. On the second day, a group of Cheyenne Indi-

ans appeared on a mesa overlooking the camp. They were almost a mile away, and were assured by the medicine man traveling with them that they were in no danger. Then the strangest thing happened. From the camp, cowboy Billy Dixon fired his buffalo rifle and shot dead one of the Indians on horseback. The Indians were so shocked that they retreated. The medicine man was proclaimed an outcast and permanently banned from the tribe. Stories told in these parts today say that descendants of that medicine man are still considered outcasts, more than 100 years after Billy Dixon fired off that lucky shot at Adobe Walls. To get to the site, **travel north from Stinnett on State Hwy. 207 (Main St.) for about 15 miles, and then look for the sign pointing you to Adobe Walls—it's about 3 miles off the highway.** At the site are plenty of historical markers, but not much else. The **Panhandle Plains Historical Museum (806-656-2244)** at West Texas State A&M University, in the town of Canyon, has lots of information on Adobe Walls.

J. B. Buchanan Windmill Farm
J. B. Buchanan has spent a lifetime preserving and restoring old windmills, and he's got most of them blowing in the wind just outside his farmhouse **about 10 miles north of Stinnett, off State Hwy. 207.** An expert from the Panhandle Plains Museum in Canyon told me he thought Buchanan's collection was the best-kept, most extensive collection of windmills in the country. The nice folks at the Buchanan farm are happy to show you around, if they are not working the wheat fields and if you don't take advantage of their pleasant nature. The city of Spearman, about 20 miles north of the Buchanan house, has shown an interest in preserving some of J. B.'s windmills, so he has allowed some of his old machines to be moved to a site next to the Spearman courthouse.

Isaac McCormick Pioneer Cottage
The restored home of the area's first settlers, built in 1899 and furnished in pioneer style. **On the town square in Stinnett.**

WHERE TO EAT

Cactus Cafe
A place where the cowboys and the wheat farmers

A lonely marker in an open field is all that remains at the Adobe Walls Battlefield. Photo courtesy of Gina Gillespie, Spearman Chamber of Commerce.

come for coffee and meals in Stinnett. **612 N. Main St.; 806-878-3181.**

Ivey's Hungry Cowboy
Turns out good family meals in Spearman. **1020 S. Hwy. 207; 806-659-5151.**

Paloduro Supper Club
An upscale dining place in Spearman. **22 Archer St.; 806-659-2232.**

WHERE TO STAY

Newcomb House Bed-and-Breakfast
A B&B in Spearman. **122 S. Hazelwood St.; 806-659-3287.**

Perryton

Getting There: From Amarillo, take U.S. Hwy. 60 for about 60 miles to Pampa, then go north on State Hwy. 70 for 65 miles to its intersection with U.S. Hwy. 83. From there it's only another 7 miles to Perryton on Hwy. 83. **Visitor Information: Perryton Chamber of Commerce, 9 SE 5th St.; 806-435-6575; www.perryton.com.**

This is the northernmost county seat in Texas—550 miles from the state capitol in Austin. Perryton is in one of the nation's top wheat-producing regions.

SEEING AND DOING

Museum of the Plains
Features exhibits on the history of the Texas and Oklahoma Panhandles, with a railroad depot and an old store. **1200 N. Main St.; 806-435-6400.**

RECREATION

Fryer Lake
An extremely pleasant recreation spot along beautiful Wolf Creek, encompassing a 700-acre county park that is popular with fishers, boaters, swimmers, and picnickers. There are RV campsites. **Twelve miles southeast of Perryton, off U.S. Hwy. 83** (Fryer Lake is not shown on most maps).

WHERE TO EAT

Money's Barbecue and Steak
14 SE 3rd Ave.; 806-435-3945.

WHERE TO STAY

Ambassador Inn
210 SE 24th St.; 806-435-9611.

Lubbock and the Plains

Established in the 1890s as a ranching center for the south plains area of the Panhandle, Lubbock gave root to some of the state's largest ranch empires, including the 3-million-acre XIT spread. It's also a farming town. And it's a college town, with Texas Tech, one of the state's four major universities. In addition, Lubbock is an important military outpost, with nearby Reese Air Force Base, a training center for jet pilots.

Getting Around
Citibus operates the city buses (806-762-0111). Taxi service is provided by City Cab (806-765-7474) and Yellow Cab (806-765-7777).

Visitor Information

Lubbock Chamber of Commerce
1500 Broadway St.; 806-763-4666.

Lubbock Convention and Visitors Bureau
1120 14th St.; 806-747-5232; www.interoz.com/lubbock.

Major Attractions

Ranching Heritage Center
The center is a 14-acre outdoor museum, featuring some thirty structures brought to the site from their original locations throughout the region and restored as nearly as possible to their original condition. The buildings illustrate ranching from the 1830s through the 1920s, and represent the best heritage museum in the state. From time to time the center puts on special events, such as a candlelight Christmas, when craftspeople in costume demonstrate frontier skills, from blacksmithing to candle dipping. 4th St. and Indiana Ave.; 806-742-2482; www.lubbock legends.com/ranching_heritage_center.htm.

Museum of Texas Tech University
An educator's dream, this is an academic and research facility that teaches people about the land and about the way of life in these parts. Among recent museum acquisitions is the Diamond M Collection, from Snyder, which focuses on art of the American West and includes the world's most extensive collection of N. C. Wyeth paintings. Part of the collection is a fascinating exhibit of jades and ivories. 4th St. and Indiana Ave.; 806-742-2490, fax 806-742-1136; www.cs.ttu.edu/~museum.

Lubbock Lake Landmark State Historical Park
This park is the only place in North America that contains deposits related to all the cultures known to have existed on the southern plains. Artifacts, tools, and remains of humans and mammals dating back 12,000 years have been uncovered here.

At the park you'll find an interpretive center with exhibits, and a three-quarter-mile self-guided trail around a 20-acre excavation site. The rest of the 300-acre site may be seen along a 3-mile trail that meanders through Yellowhouse Draw, with shaded shelters, exhibits, and picnic areas along the way. 2202

Landmark Ln., at the northeastern edge of Lubbock, near Loop 289 and Clovis Rd.; 806-741-0306.

Seeing and Doing

Antiquing

Antique Mall

Fifty antiques dealers in one spot, about 3 miles west of Loop 289, at **7907 W. 19th St.; 806-796-2166.**

Museums and Historic Sites

Buddy Holly's Statue and Walk of Fame

Visitors arrive from all over the world to visit the hometown of pioneer rock star Buddy Holly. Holly sang his way to fame in the 1950s and then was killed in an airplane crash at the peak of his career in 1959. Paul McCartney of the Beatles said Buddy Holly's music inspired his career. Along with Holly, the Walk of Fame honors other West Texans who have contributed to music, including Mac Davis, Jimmy Dean, and Waylon Jennings. **8th St. and Avenue Q, on a traffic island at the entrance to the Civic Center.**

Dan Blocker Museum

Tribute to a hometown boy, one of the stars of the long-running TV series *Bonanza*. Blocker grew up in these parts and is still remembered today. **In the community of O'Donnell, 40 miles south of Lubbock on U.S. Hwy. 87.**

Lubbock Memorial Civic Center

A complex of modern buildings replaced the structures destroyed in a killer tornado in May 1970. A memorial at the center honors the citizens who died in the tragedy. **1501 6th St.; 806-765-9441.**

Parks

Texas Water Rampage

A water park with two 63-foot water slides, a wave pool that creates its own waves, and the Rio Rampage, a 72-foot lazy river for tubing. **U.S. Hwy. 82 and Spur 327 at the southwest edge of Lubbock; 806-796-0701.**

Shopping

Cactus Alley

A gathering of shops around a courtyard, selling everything from stuffed bears to eggshell art. **2610 Salem St.; 806-796-2999.**

Western Wear

For things western, stop at **Boot City (6645 19th St., 806-797-8782); Branding Iron (3320 34th St., 806-785-0500); Dean Leonard Custom Hats (3215 34th St., 806-791-0550); and Luskey's Western Store (2431 34th St., 806-795-7106).**

Wineries

Llano Estacado Winery

One of the oldest wineries in the state, Llano Estacado has won more national and international awards than any other winery in Texas. Complimentary tours and tasting Mon.–Sat. From Lubbock, **travel south on U.S. Hwy. 87 to Farm Road 1585, then go east for 3 miles; 806-745-2258; llanowine@aol.com; www.llanowine.com.**

Festivals and Events

April

Lubbock Arts Festival

Three-day weekend in the latter part of the month. A celebration of the arts, including crafts demonstrations, continuous entertainment, and evening shows by nationally known performers. **Civic Center, 1501 6th St.; 806-775-2244.**

September

Buddy Holly's Birthday

Holly was born September 7, 1936, so this event is held the first week of the month, with the main purpose being to display, trade, buy, and sell Buddy Holly memorabilia. For location and schedule, call **806-799-4299.**

Fiestas del Llano

Three days in mid-September. This is the local version of Mexican Independence Day, featuring plenty of music and Mexican food. **Civic Center, 1501 6th St.**

National Cowboy Symposium

The largest event of its kind in the country, this conference is a mixture of academics and entertainment, attracting people from all walks of life. Everyone from working cowboys to Ph.D.s gather to articulate the heritage of the cowboy through storytelling, poetry, music, demonstrations, and panel discussions. **Civic Center, 1501 6th St.**

South Plains Fair

One week in late September or early October. All you might expect from a big fair, with a midway, horse and livestock shows, a flower festival, and lots of competition. Top country and western entertainers perform at the Coliseum every night. **At Fair Park and Fair Park Coliseum.**

Texas International Wine Classic

One weekend late in the month. Tastings and competition among local, national, and international wine makers, plus seminars, lectures, and gourmet meals. **Civic Center, 1501 6th St.**

October

Texas Tech Intercollegiate Rodeo

Usually on a weekend late in October, but sometimes early in November. Rodeoing is a big sport at Texas Tech, having started here in 1940. Teams from more than a dozen colleges in Texas and New Mexico compete in everything from bareback bronc to bull riding, putting on a rodeo that's better than most. **Livestock Pavilion at Fair Park.**

December

Festival of Lights

Thousands of lights mark the season, along with the singing of Christmas carols and other special events. **Along Broadway from the Texas Tech campus to downtown.**

Recreation

Parks and Camping

Buffalo Springs Lake Recreational Area

This pleasant recreation area on a 1,200-acre lake offers boating, fishing, waterskiing, and paddleboat riding. Along 7 miles of shoreline are picnic areas and sites for tent and RV camping. There are two sandy beaches and a water slide, plus a 2-mile self-guiding nature trail and interpretive center. The trail descends 155 feet from the rim of a canyon to a stream. **Four miles east of Lubbock on Farm Road 835; 806-747-3353.**

MacKenzie Park

Named for Colonel R. S. "Three Fingered" MacKenzie, who figured prominently in the Indian wars, this 500-acre park has picnic and camping facilities, along with fishing, swimming, a golf course, and a prairie dog town. Visitors can observe the cute little critters, along with burrowing owls and an occasional rabbit, in an enclosed area of the park. The bottom of the enclosure is concrete-lined to keep the prairie dogs confined; they are pests to farmers and ranchers in these parts. The park is part of Yellowhouse Canyon Lakes, which have waterfalls, boating facilities, fishing piers, picnic tables, and hiking and biking trails. Every summer the Great Yellowhouse Canyon Raft Race draws rafting enthusiasts on homemade boats. **4th St. and Ave. A; 806-762-6418.**

Where to Eat

Abuelo's

Lubbock's most upscale Mexican food restaurant. A courtyard makes for pleasant outdoor dining when the weather cooperates. **4401 82nd St.; 806-794-1762.**

Barton House, circa 1909, at the Ranching Heritage Center in Lubbock.

County Line

Barbecue with all the fixings in an atmosphere that allows you to stroll along a lake and admire the ducks, peacocks, and other not-so-wild fowl. **Farm Road 2641, north of town; 806-763-6001.**

The Depot

A 1928 railroad depot that is now one of Lubbock's most popular restaurants, with Victorian decor, antique furniture, and a beer garden. **1801 Ave. G at 19th St.; 806-747-1646.**

Gardski's Loft

A favorite lunch spot, with fancy sandwiches and gourmet burgers. **2009 Broadway; 806-765-8217.**

Grapevine Cafe and Wine Bar

A favorite with the Texas Tech faculty and other local folks. It features seafood, crepes, pasta, soups, and salads. **2407 19th St., near the university; 806-744-8246.**

Great Scotts

Barbecue smoked with oak. This place attracts crowds on weekends for socializing and playing washers, a game that's a bit like horseshoes. **At U.S. Hwy. 87 and Farm Road 1585, south of town; 806-745-9353.**

Jazz

In the hospital district, this is one of the few Cajun food restaurants in town. **3703-C 19th St.; 806-799-2124.**

Josie's

Modest, low-priced Mexican food at a place that is almost always crowded. Check out the breakfast burritos. **212 University Ave.; 806-747-8546.**

Mesquites

Down the alley and across the street from Texas Tech, this is a popular spot with students. The menu includes barbecue, burgers, and some Tex-Mex. The onion rings are excellent. **2419 Broadway St.; 806-763-1159.**

Old Town Cafe

Renowned for its hearty, home-style breakfast and lunch buffets. **2402 Ave. J; 806-762-4768.**

Where to Stay

Barcelona Court

Total of 151 suites in a three-story hotel. Very nice. Very expensive. **5215 Loop 289; 806-794-5353.**

Holiday Inn Civic Center

A six-story hotel with almost 300 rooms. **801 Ave. Q; 806-763-1200.**

La Quinta Inn & Suites

A high-rise hotel near the Texas Tech campus and the hospital district that is built around a full atrium. Rooms are large and offer pleasant views. **4115 Brownfield Hwy.; 806-792-0065.**

Towns in the Area

The towns to be visited are Levelland, Post, Plainview, and Turkey.

Levelland

Getting There: Levelland is 32 miles due west of Lubbock on State Hwy. 114. **Visitor Information: Levelland Chamber of Commerce, 1101 Avenue H; 806-894-3157, fax 806-864-4284; levellandcoc@door.net.**

The town, named for its wide-open, level terrain, was surveyed by cereal king C. W. Post in 1912. Levelland is in Hockley County, once one of the largest cotton-producing counties in the state. It is consistently one of the top ten oil-producing counties in Texas, and is situated on the migratory path for several species of birds and the monarch butterfly.

SEEING AND DOING

City of Mosaics
This is a name recently attached to the town, with its acquisition of several large, colorful outdoor mosaics. They are visible **on the Chamber of Commerce building, on several buildings at South Plains College,** and **on the hospital building;** a freestanding mosaic is on display **in Carver Park.**

South Plains College
The college has a fine music department, providing degrees in the art of bluegrass music. Musicians like Heath Wright and Lee Ann Womack got their training here, and if you are a bluegrass buff, you'll recognize names of other former students, such as Alan Munde, Joe Carr, and Ed Marsh. Country and western star Tom T. Hall is perhaps the most recognized name associated with this very special college. **1401 College Ave.; 806-885-3048, 806-894-9611.**

WHERE TO EAT

Cattlelacs Steak & Grill
106 College Ave.; 806-894-3608.

Tienda's Tortilla Factory
510 Houston St.; 806-894-7691.

WHERE TO STAY

Levelland Motel
Provides clean rooms near the college campus. **304 College Ave.; 806-894-7335.**

Post
Getting There: Post is 41 miles southeast of Lubbock on U.S. Hwy. 84. **Visitor Information: Post Chamber of Commerce, 106 S. Broadway St.; 806-495-3461; www.posttx.com.**

The town is named for C. W. Post, the cereal manufacturer who founded the town in 1907 as an experiment to demonstrate his economic ideas. Post developed the town around spacious streets and bou-

levards, and hoped to convince the rest of the nation that this is how towns should be built. Post's town never caught on nationally, but today it is an amazing sight to behold this thoroughly planned downtown area with wide streets in a small town in the wide-open plains—as if someone built a downtown for a major city, but no one ever showed up.

Between 1910 and 1930, Post was the scene of another elaborate C. W. Post experiment. He set off a number of atmospheric explosions in the area as part of rainmaking experiments. They failed to produce any positive results.

Main Street is lined with gift and clothing stores and restored historic structures.

SEEING AND DOING

Algerita Art Center
The work of area artists is on display in a restored old hotel. **129 E. Main St.**

City-County Park
A small lake for fishing, with walking trails and picnic areas, is **at the southern edge of town on U.S. Hwy. 84.**

Familiar sign outside the community center in Turkey, the hometown of Bob Wills, who introduced the world to his "Country Swing" music. Photo courtesy of Gary Johnson.

Llano Estacado Tourist Marker
The marker provides details on the surrounding country. Stretching across the horizon as a range of flat-topped mountains is the Cap Rock escarpment, the eastern boundary of the vast Llano Estacado, or "staked plains." The marker is **between Post and Justiceburg on U.S. Hwy. 84.**

WHERE TO EAT

George's Restaurant
202 S. Broadway St.; 806-495-3777.

Fort Justice
With specialties like steaks and buffalo burgers. **In Justiceburg, 13 miles south of Post on U.S. Hwy. 84.**

L D's Daughters Cafeteria
In Post at U.S. Hwy. 380 east; 806-495-2078.

WHERE TO STAY

Deluxe Inn
215 N. Broadway St.; 806-495-2883.

Plainview
Getting There: Take I-27 north from Lubbock about 50 miles. **Visitor Information: Plainview Chamber of Commerce, 710 W. 5th St.; 806-296-7431.**

The town was founded in 1887 and named for its magnificent view of the Plains. Plainview is in Hale County, unique to the region because of its abundant underground water supply and its leadership in grain and cotton production. Oil is also a big boost to the economy in these parts.

SEEING AND DOING

Llano Estacado Museum
Hale County exhibits, with artifacts from an archaeological site dating to 8000 B.C. and remains of the Easter Elephant, a prehistoric skull and tusks uncovered near the community of Easter in 1988. Open weekdays 9 A.M.–5 P.M.; also on weekends March–Nov., 1–5 P.M. **On the campus of Wayland Baptist University; 806-296-5521.**

Running Water Regional Park
The park includes a wonderful area for youngsters called Kidsville, featuring state-of-the-art playground equipment. **4th and Ennis Sts.**

WHERE TO EAT

Carlito's Mexican Restaurant
Serves up old-fashioned, basic Mexican food. **3105 Olton Rd.; 806-296-9222.**

Chuckwagon BBQ
A local favorite. **2105 Dimmitt Rd.; 806-296-7033.**

Elk's Restaurant
A longtime family eating establishment. **908 North I-27; 806-293-8770.**

WHERE TO STAY

Harman-Y House B&B
815 Columbia St.; 806-296-2505.

Turkey
Getting There: Take I-27 north from Lubbock about 75 miles to Tulia, then go east on State Hwy. 86 for 55 miles to Turkey (don't blink, or you'll miss it). **Visitor Information: Gary and Suzie Johnson at the Hotel Turkey** serve as the community's greatest diplomats and promoters; **806-423-1151.**

Turkey was first called Turkey Roost, named for all the wild turkeys the first settlers found in the region. Later the name was shortened to Turkey by the U.S. Post Office because it saved paper space. Today Turkey is best known as hometown of the king of western swing, Bob Wills.

SEEING AND DOING

Bob Wills Monument
A larger-than-life-size monument honors the barber who went on to become the most successful country and western musician of his day. The monument is located **on the west side of town adjacent to Bob Wills Park.** Bob Wills introduced the nation to his unique brand of western swing music and captured the hearts of millions during the depression. He was part of the original group called the **Light Crust**

Doughboys, created by the dough company, and went on tour around the country to advertise their products and to entertain. A fellow named W. Lee O'Daniel led the group, but Bob was the musical genius. The gig led Wills and his band to Hollywood and stardom, and led O'Daniel to the Texas governor's mansion.

The annual **Bob Wills Reunion** takes place the last Saturday in April. Turkey's population is small, but upward of 15,000 people show up for the reunion.

Also look in at the **Bob Wills Museum.** Open Mon.–Tues. 9–11:30 A.M. and 1–5 P.M., and Wed.–Fri. 8–11 A.M. and 1–5 P.M.; **6th and Lyles Sts.; 806-423-1253.**

WHERE TO EAT

Peanut Patch

A great place for sandwiches or a meal. **2nd and Main Sts.; 806-423-1051.**

WHERE TO STAY

Hotel Turkey

One of my favorite rest stops in the Texas Panhandle, this restored hotel has been turned into a bed-and-breakfast establishment. The people are friendly and the restaurant here serves up Texas-size meals. **At the corner of 3rd and Alexander Sts.; 806-423-1151; www.llano.et/turkey/hotel.**

Abilene

The land from the Abilene area westward is truly what outsiders think of as the Old West. It is wide-open country, with farming and ranching, and some oil wells sprinkled in. The people have somehow managed to hold on to the past in a quiet sort of way. Things may not seem so flashy in this part of Texas, but the people are honest and genuine, and big deals are still sealed with a handshake. You'll find friendly folks who will invite you in at the drop of a hat—or sit back and make fun of your city ways if you cross them.

Abilene got its name from Abilene, Kansas, and there's been a lot of confusion about the two cities ever since. Abilene, Kansas, was a rootin' tootin' Wild West town, a lawless community that sprang up in the cattle-driving days. Abilene, Texas, was founded in 1881 as a railhead for the Texas and Pacific Railroad, which cut short those long cattle drives that previously had to go on to Dodge City. Unlike the Kansas town, the Abilene in Texas gained the reputation of being the buckle of the Bible Belt—a title it still holds today, with three church-affiliated colleges and a large number of churches located here. But the town has had some difficulty escaping a Wild West image, because tourist-oriented businesses seem to like it that way.

Getting Around

BUSES

Bus service in the area is provided by **CityLink** (1189 S. 2nd St., 915-676-6287); **Greyhound** (535 Cedar St., 915-677-8127); **Sun Set Stages** (324 Sycamore St., 915-677-5151); and **Howard Little Charters** (155 Cedar St., No. 1, 915-676-3913).

TAXIS

Taxi service is available from **A-1 Yellow Checker Cab** (915-677-2446), **Abilene Yellow Cab** (915-677-4334), **Classic Cab** (915-677-8294), and **Presidential Cab** (915-677-7775).

Visitor Information

Abilene Convention and Visitors Bureau
1101 N. 1st St., Abilene, 79601; 1-800-727-7704, fax 915-676-1630; visitors@abilene.com; www.abilene.com.

Visitor Information Center
On I-20 and Farm Road 600.

Seeing and Doing

Antiquing

The place called **Under One Roof** has about three dozen antiques vendors (244 Pine St., 915-673-1309). On **Historic Hickory Street**, more antiques are for sale (500 to 700 block of Hickory Street).

Historic Sites

Dyess Air Force Base

Established as a Strategic Air Command base in 1952, during the Korean War. Today it serves as headquarters for the Air Combat Command's 7th Wing, which flies B-1 bombers and C-130 transport planes. During World War II, the 7th Wing bombed Japanese supply lines in Southeast Asia, including the famous bridge over the River Kwai. Dyess is a closed base; you need permission to enter. On display at the base are twenty-five aircraft from World War II, the Korean War, and the Vietnam War. Dyess holds an annual open house in late April or early May that features air shows and open cockpits to the old planes. Located **on the western outskirts of Abilene off I-20; 915-696-5609; www.dyess.af.mil.**

Fort Phantom Hill

The ruins of the old fort are on private property, but the owner makes them accessible to the public. Watch out for the Texas longhorns that sometimes graze here. The place is just a pile of rubble now, but once this fort housed five companies of U.S. infantry. It was one of many forts built in Texas in the 1850s to protect settlers from Indians. The problem was that the fort was manned with foot soldiers, not horse soldiers, and thus the fort was never very effective against the great Comanche warriors, legendary for their horsemanship. The fort was more productive in later years as an outpost for the Texas Rangers, then the Confederate army. Eventually it became a station on the Butterfield Stagecoach Line. **On Farm Road 600 about 14 miles north of Abilene.**

Parks

Abilene Zoo

More than 900 animals inhabit this 13-acre zoo. The Texas Plains section of the facility is home to bison, pronghorns, javelina, coyotes, and wild turkeys. **In Nelson Park, State Hwy. 36 at Loop 322; 915-676-6085, 915-672-9771.**

Performing Arts

Paramount Theatre

A restoration by the Abilene Preservation League, this classic-style movie house from the 1930s is used today for such things as a classics film series and other special performances, including dance and opera. **352 Cypress St.; 915-676-9620.**

Shopping

Boots and Saddles

Bell Custom Made Boots specializes in boots and

> ### Getting There
>
> *Near the geographic center of Texas, Abilene is easily accessible by major highways. Abilene is about 160 miles due west of Fort Worth on I-20.*
> ***Abilene Regional Airport*** *is a fairly small facility that offers very little service from the major carriers, but does have eight to ten flights daily to and from Dallas–Fort Worth International Airport via* ***American Eagle (1-800-433-7300).*** *The airport is at* ***2733 Airport Parking Circle; 915-676-6367.***

---

belts; boots start at about $400 and go up to about $2,500 **(2118 N. Treadaway Blvd., 915-677-0632); James Leddy Boots** is one of the better-known boot makers in Texas, with stores in several cities; you can also get a tour of the shop **(1602 N. Treadaway Blvd., 915-677-7811); Art Reed Custom Saddles** makes saddles from scratch; working saddles start at about $1,500 **(361 E. South 11th St., 915-677-4572).**

Festivals and Events

March

Abilene Railroad Festival

Second weekend in the month. Includes a Hobo Cook-off and a model train exhibit. **Downtown.**

April

Buffalo Gap Arts Festival

Usually the last weekend of the month. Arts, an arts auction, and a variety of musical events, benefiting the museums of Abilene. **At the Perini Ranch, 3002 Farm Road 89, about 1.5 miles outside Buffalo Gap, which is 20 miles southwest of Abilene on Farm Road 89; 915-572-3339.**

May

Western Heritage Classic and Ranch Rodeo

Second weekend in the month. An event celebrating

Panhandle snow storm, near Lamesa.

both the Old West and the ranches of today, with a rodeo, campfire cook-off, blacksmith competition, trail ride, and more. **Taylor County Expo Center, Abilene.**

September

Chili Superbowl

Held every Labor Day weekend **at the Perini Ranch, outside Buffalo Gap, which is 20 miles southwest of Abilene on Farm Road 89.**

West Texas Fair and Rodeo

Starts the first Friday after Labor Day. A livestock and horse show and rodeo, with exhibits and tractor pulls and other contests. **Taylor County Expo Center.**

Recreation

Abilene State Park

A 500-acre park that offers facilities for picnicking, tent and trailer camping, and hiking on a nature trail. Next door, 595-acre **Lake Abilene** offers day fishing and boating. **About 20 miles south of Abilene, off U.S. Hwy. 83; 915-572-3204.**

Johnson Park

A 37-acre camping area **(at Lake Phantom Hill, 6 miles north of Abilene on Farm Road 600).**

RV Parks

Full hookups are available at **Abilene RV Park (6195 E. I-20, at exit 2920B, 915-672-0657)** and **KOA Kampground (4851 W. Stamford St., 915-672-3681).**

Seabee Park

Camping facilities spread out over a 40-acre area **(3 miles north of Abilene on Farm Road 600).**

Where to Eat

Gardski's

A touch of everything from gourmet burgers to steaks. **3370 N. 1st St.; 915-676-8279.**

Harold's Bar-B-Que

The decor at Harold's leaves something to be desired, but it's wall-to-wall people come lunchtime. Harold's features oakwood-cooked barbecue and hot-water cornbread. **1305 Walnut St.; 915-672-4451.**

Joe Allen's Pit Bar-B-Que

This is a popular eating spot opened by a former Taylor County Extension Agent. **1233 S. Treadaway Blvd.; 915-672-6082.**

John Zentner's Daughter Steak House

The most popular steak house in town. There are several of these eating places in the western part of the state. The people out here say they have the best steaks around; you be the judge. **4358 Sayles Blvd.; 915-695-4290.**

Where to Stay

Aside from these listings, there are a number of motels along I-20 on the outskirts of town from which to choose.

Bolin Prairie Bed-and-Breakfast

Offers antiques-furnished rooms in a 1902 setting.

1742 S. 12th St., just west of downtown; 915-675-5855.

La Quinta Motor Inn
3501 Farm Road 600 at I-20; 915-676-1676.

Mulberry House
A fine old restored home put to use as a bed-and-breakfast establishment. **1042 Mulberry St.; 915-677-7890.**

Towns in the Area

Among the towns that reward a visit are Albany, Buffalo Gap, Anson, Sweetwater, Snyder, and Lamesa.

Albany
Getting There: Albany is 33 miles northeast of Abilene via State Hwy. 351 and U.S. Hwy. 180. **Visitor Information: Albany Chamber of Commerce, 2 S. Main St.; 915-762-2525; www.albanytex.com.**

Albany was an early supply point on the western trail to Dodge City. It is still important as a ranching community, but the oil industry has grown here as well. Albany is perhaps best known as the home of the Hereford, the place where the Hereford cow was introduced to the state.

SEEING AND DOING

Fort Griffin Fandangle–Prairie Theater
This theater continues to present one of the best outdoor cowboy shows in the state—an outdoor extravaganza put on by townsfolk. Of the town's 2,500 people, about 300 help put on the annual show. The resulting musical makes the heritage of early West Texas come alive. One of the chief attractions here is deafening: It's an old steam calliope that is wheeled in every year for the performances, which are given the last two weekends in June. The calliope is so loud it hurts the ears, but it's worth the experience because there are only a few people left who can play one of these old dinosaurs, and few who can say they've heard one. **On Cook Field Rd., about a mile west of the courthouse; 915-762-3642; albanytex.com/events/fandangle.html.**

Fort Griffin State Historical Park
Fort Griffin is another fort established to protect settlers from Indians. This one was built in 1867 and abandoned in 1881. Fort Griffin is also home of the state longhorn herd started by author J. Frank Dobie, which continues to produce some of the famed mascots for the University of Texas at Austin. There are twenty sites for camping in the park, plus picnic tables, playgrounds, and a nature trail. **Fifteen miles north of Albany, off U.S. Hwy. 283; 915-762-3592.**

Georgia Monument
Georgia was the only state in the Union to supply arms to the people who fought in the Texas Revolution. In 1855 the Georgia Legislature sent a claim for $3,000 for the guns it sent, but later waived payment if Texas would build a monument to Georgia. This is it. **City Park at S. Main and S. 1st Sts.**

Old Jail Art Center
The people of Albany are all wrapped up in the arts and are appreciative of good work. They have it here, including works of Picasso, Modigliani, Klee, and others. **201 S. 2nd St.; 915-762-2269.**

Shackelford County Courthouse in Albany.

Shackelford County Courthouse
In my humble opinion, this is the best-looking courthouse in Texas. It was built for less than $50,000 in 1883, and is the focal point of an entire downtown district that is registered as a National Historic Landmark. **At S. Main and S. 2nd Sts.**

Buffalo Gap
Getting There: Buffalo Gap is 20 miles southwest of Abilene, via Farm Road 89. **Visitor Information: Buffalo Gap Historic Village, P.O. Box 818,**

Buffalo Gap, 79508; 915-572-3365;
www.abilene. com/art/bgap.

Buffalo Gap is a tiny town that has hardly changed since the turn of the twentieth century, with one exception: Now it caters to tourists rather than frontier people.

SEEING AND DOING

The main attraction is **Buffalo Gap Historic Village,** a collection of 100-year-old buildings, including the original Taylor County Courthouse and jail built in 1879 of sandstone blocks. Civil War cannonballs still can be found in the community. **133 Williams St.; 915-572-3365.**

Anson

Getting There: Anson is 20 miles north of Abilene on U.S. Hwy. 83. **Visitor Information: Anson Chamber of Commerce, 1132 W. Court Plaza; 915-823-3259.**

Here is a typical West Texas community with a beautiful courthouse and a wide main street. Anson is best known for its annual **Cowboy Christmas Ball** that attracts West Texans from far and wide. This event is particularly exciting in this part of the Bible Belt, where most people don't believe in dancing the rest of the year.

SEEING AND DOING

Opera House

Built in 1907 and once considered the fanciest showplace between Fort Worth and El Paso. Hosted musical and dramatic productions, public and civic activities, silent and talking movies, and even wrestling and bare-fist fighting events until the 1930s. Today it is used for occasional stage productions, including a country-western musical usually presented on the third Saturday of each month. On the north side of the square at **1104 11th St.; 915-823-2669.**

Sweetwater

Getting There: Take I-20 for 38 miles west of Abilene. **Visitor Information: Sweetwater Chamber of Commerce, 810 E. Broadway St.; 915-235-5488; swater@camalott.com; www. camalott.com/sweetwater.**

The town began as a dugout store in a buffalo hunter's camp. Today it is the seat of Nolan County and has ninety buildings and sites listed in the National Register of Historic Places.

SEEING AND DOING

Pioneer City-County Museum

More than a dozen displays of life and times in early Nolan County, with extensive photographs and ranching exhibits. **610 E. 3rd St.; 915-235-8547.**

Sweetwater Rattlesnake Roundup

The largest in the world, where experts get together to honor, recognize, and make life miserable for thousands of rattlesnakes who live in the area. They kill, cook, eat, and even stuff hundreds of them every year in March, but there are always plenty more the following year. Several residents capture and milk rattlesnake venom for a living out here; the venom is shipped all over the world for research purposes. For more information, call the **Sweetwater Chamber of Commerce** at **915-235-5488.**

Snyder

Getting There: Take I-20 west from Abilene for 45 miles (several miles past and west of Sweetwater), then turn north onto U.S. Hwy. 84 and travel 30 miles to Snyder. **Visitor Information: Snyder Chamber of Commerce, 2302 Ave. R; 915-573-3558; www.snydertex.com.**

Founded as a trading post in 1878, Snyder grew to 12,000 people in 1950 after discovery of the Canyon Reef oil field, now the center of one of the largest oil fields in the world. Some say the Snyder oil field made Bob Hope and Bing Crosby wealthy. They were among the first investors in the operation, and royalties are still being paid to the families.

SEEING AND DOING

Scurry County Museum

County history rich in lore and legends of the Old West. **6200 College Ave. on the campus of Western Texas College; 915-573-6107.**

Towle Park

Playgrounds, swimming pool, picnic areas, and more:

a fishing lake for the kiddies, and an old steam locomotive that was used by the Roscoe, Snyder, and Pacific Railroad, once proclaimed the shortest short-line railroad in the country. Probably the best park in the state for watching prairie dogs. There's an enclosed prairie dog town where the critters can be seen close-up. They are really fun to watch. South side of Snyder, **on the Big Spring Hwy. (State Hwy. 350); 915-573-3313.**

White Buffalo Statue

The statue recalls frontier days when a rare albino buffalo was killed near here. **On the Courthouse Square.**

Lamesa

Getting There: From Abilene, take I-20 west for 110 miles to Big Spring, then turn north onto U.S. Hwy. 87 and travel 45 miles to Lamesa. **Visitor Information: Lamesa Chamber of Commerce, 123 Main Ave.; 806-872-2181.**

Part of the High Plains, Lamesa (la-MEE-suh) got its name from the Spanish words meaning "the table." The economy is oil and agriculture based, and the town is in one of the state's largest cotton-producing counties.

SEEING AND DOING

Dal Paso Museum

Specializing in early West Texas history. Open June–Aug. daily except Mon., 2–5 P.M.; open Sept.–May on Tues., Thurs., and Sat. 2–5 P.M. **306 S. 1st St., in the restored Dal Paso Hotel; 806-872-5007.**

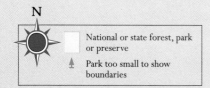

N

| | National or state forest, park or preserve |
| | Park too small to show boundaries |

NEW MEXICO

El Paso   Dell City

Ciudad
Juárez

Salt Flat

Guadalupe
Mountains
National Park

285

Kermit

Wink

Monahans
Sand Hills
State
Park

385

Big Spring

87

20

Midland

Odessa

Big
Spring
State Park

385

87

Colorado River

277

83

Pecos

Pecos River

Monahans

385

San Angelo
State Park

67

San Angelo

87

Rio Grande

10

Balmorhea

290

10

Fort
Stockton

67

Iraan

190

Twin
Butte
Reservoir

MEXICO

Fort Davis

67

290

10

Davy Crockett Monument

90

Alpine

285

Ozona

Marfa

Ruidosa

90

Devil's River
State Natural
Area

277

Shafter

Presidio Big Bend Ranch
State Natural Area

Terlingua

Lajitas

Study
Butte

Big Bend
National
Park

Rio Grande

Seminole
Canyon State
Historical Park

Amistad
Reservoir

377

Amistad
National
Recreation
Area

The Far West

The Far West

*The Salt Flats at the base of the Guadalupe Mountain Range in West Texas.
Photo courtesy of Texas Highways magazine.*

The Far West

The Far West is what people expect to see when they visit Texas. It's the wide-open spaces. The cacti. The cowboys. And the cattle ranches. But it's much much more than that. It has metropolitan areas like Midland/Odessa, San Angelo, and El Paso and some of the most magnificent scenery you'll ever want to see. The Far West is what brings people to Texas. (The rest of the state is where they all seem to move to after they get here.)

When I was traveling for the TV show *Eyes of Texas,* people were forever asking me where they should retire, and about the so-called best place to live in Texas. I always told them I had two candidates. My first choice was the land around Fort Davis, in the Far West. The air is cleaner there, the people are friendlier there, and the scenery is unbeatable. But there are no big hospitals out there either, and it's 200 miles from the nearest real airport. My second favorite place to retire in Texas would be Wimberley, in the Hill Country. It has most of the attributes of Fort Davis, and it's only a stone's throw from San Antonio and Austin.

But no part of Texas has the characters that come out of the Far West. Like Hallie Stillwell of Big Bend, who came to this country as a young bride and stayed here to keep her ranch intact after her husband was killed. Like Ramon Bartnett, a chuckwagon cook who follows the cattle drives. Like Connie Edwards of Big Spring, who made a living as a movie stunt pilot and, when last I checked, was building castles out in Howard County.

Then there's Buck Newsome. Buck is one of the cowboys who helped civilize the Far West. He was a lawman and border patrolman for most of his life, but by the time I met him, he was retired and could be found in the company of friends most days exchanging stories in the coffee shop at El Paisano Hotel in Marfa. I used to enjoy listening to his stories about tracking down outlaws in Big Bend country. The way he told his tales was captivating. Buck said an old-time lawman in West Texas required a great deal of patience. Traveling from town to town on horseback took days, even weeks, and often it could take months just to catch up with the bad guys. In one memorable story, Buck tracked some rustlers from out near El Paso and caught up with them just before they were about to cross over the Rio Grande into Mexico at Castalon. Buck Newsome and people like him are what make the Far West so special.

The climate measures hot and even hotter for most of West Texas. It's a dry heat with little humidity, so 95 degrees in West Texas is not as bad as you might think. Sun-worshipers love the Far West, but beware of getting too much sun. Take hats and plenty of water if you plan to be outdoors for any length of time. There is still a lot of wide-open country in this part of the state, and the stretches between rest stops and gas stations are often long—so travel prepared. In the summer you can fry eggs on the freeway between Midland and El Paso, but turn south to the Davis Mountains and you may have to sleep under cover at night. Fort Davis is about a mile high, the same elevation as Denver, and it can be downright cool at times.

San Angelo

San Angelo is the garden spot of West Texas, blessed with more trees and flowers than most cities out here. San Angelo has a lot going for it, and many of my friends and relatives have retired here. When I was growing up in the region, we used to attend Boy Scout Camp on a ranch outside San Angelo, on the Concho River. The city has now established its own River Walk along the Concho where it goes through downtown. The quaint little shops and gardens of San Angelo help this town stand out in the crowd of West Texas communities.

Getting Around

San Angelo Street Railroad Company provides transportation throughout most of the city. The trolley service runs Mon.–Fri. 6:30 A.M.–6:30 P.M., Sat. 9:30 A.M.–6:30 P.M. Headquarters are at the **Santa Fe Depot, 703 S. Chadbourne St.; 915-655-9952.**

Visitor Information

San Angelo Visitor Information Center **500 Rio Concho Dr., San Angelo, 76903; at the Convention Center; 1-800-375-1206, 915-653-1206, fax 915-658-1110; cvb@sanangelo-tx.com; www.sanangelo-tx.com.** The **San Angelo Chamber of Commerce** is at the same address but with a different telephone number: **915-655-4136.**

Seeing and Doing

Gardens and Arboreta

Civic Park Lilypond

Rare and exotic water lilies grow here, including the ancient blue lotus of the Nile. **Beauregard Ave. and Park Dr.**

Museums and Historic Sites

Aermotor Windmill

Home of the last American windmill manufacturer, Aermotor. The first Aermotor windmill was the result of more than 5,000 steel-windmill experiments conducted by Thomas Perry in Chicago in the 1880s. His wheel was more efficient than the best wooden wheels. By 1892 the Aermotor windmill was synonymous with the pumping of water in this country. The company made a fortune until the 1960s, when windmills fell out of fashion. In 1969 the Aermotor company moved to Argentina, and 10 years later it moved back to the United States, to Arkansas. In 1986 investors brought the company to San Angelo. Visitors are welcome to tour the plant, but you must call ahead. **4277 Dan Hanks Ln.; 915-651-4951; www.aero motorwindmill.com.**

Fort Concho

Among the best-preserved of the frontier military forts, this 40-acre National Historic Landmark comprises twenty-three original and restored old buildings. The fort was established in 1867 to protect settlers and wagon trains from Indians. It was closed in 1889 after the bureaucrats in Washington decided the area was civilized. There are several museums on the property: **Robert Wood Johnson Museum of Frontier Medicine,** with memorabilia from a nineteenth-century frontier hospital **(in the old north ward of the post hospital); San Angelo Museum of Fine Arts,** with changing exhibits of different media **(704 Burgess St., 915-658-4084);** and **E. H. Danner Museum of Telephony,** displaying telephones including Alexander Graham Bell's "gallows frame phone," wooden phones and push-button phones from the 1880s, and present-day instruments **(213 E. Ave. D, 915-653-0756).** The fort is within the city limits, **just east of S. Oakes St., between Ave. C and Ave. D; 915-657-4441; www.fortconcho.com.**

Miss Hattie's Museum

A restored saloon/brothel that was a landmark in these parts for decades. Restored with original furnishings and fashions to display the living style of the ladies who entertained soldiers, ranchers, and cowboys from the mid-1800s to 1946, when the Texas Rangers closed the place down. **18 E. Concho Ave.; 915-658-3735.**

Nature Centers

San Angelo Nature Center

Exhibits of natural sciences and history, detailing the Edwards Plateau region. Displays include native wildlife, live reptiles and amphibians, an aquarium, and a glass-enclosed beehive and ant farm. In the former Rangers Headquarters building at **7409 Knickerbocker Rd.; 915-942-0121.**

Other Sights

Producers Livestock Auction Company

The second largest livestock auction in the state. **1131 N. Bell St.; 915-653-3371.**

Parks

Concho River Walk

More than 6 miles of jogging and walking trails along the river where it winds through downtown. There are also flowing fountains, an outdoor stage, a 9-hole golf course, and a small amusement park.

El Paseo de Santa Angela

This is a footpath from Fort Concho, once used by soldiers stationed here to walk to the village across the river. The landscaped trail covers the heart of downtown, including the river, several frontier buildings, the railroad area, and Celebration Bridge. The trail is good for joggers and walkers. **Between Fort Concho and Concho Ave.**

Getting There

San Angelo is about 200 miles southwest of the Dallas–Fort Worth Metroplex, at the junction of two major U.S. highways, 87 and 277. The highways are wide and mostly straight in this part of the state, making for relatively easy driving. **San Angelo Regional Airport/Mathis Field** welcomes seven flights a day from Dallas–Fort Worth International Airport, flown by **American Eagle Airlines (1-800-433-7300). Enterprise Air Charter (915-896-2356)** operates one of the larger charter services out of Mathis Field. The airport is **8 miles southwest of downtown San Angelo, off Knickerbocker Rd.; 915-659-6409; mathsfld@wcc.net.**

Concho River running through downtown San Angelo. Photo courtesy of Texas Highways *magazine.*

Shopping

Eggemeyer's General Store
An unusual store with a variety of country items for sale. **35 E. Concho Ave.; 915-655-1166.**

Hatatorium Hat Shop
They've been making hats here since the 1940s, and the "Angelo hats" are famous in the state. You can visit the factory in the rear of the store during business hours Mon.–Fri. **25 N. Chadbourne St.; 915-653-7716.**

Ingrid's Custom Woven Rugs
San Angelo is a wool center, and saddle blankets are popular items. Ingrid's has probably the best selection. Ingrid's is in the little community of **Paint Rock, 32 miles east of San Angelo on Farm Road 380; 915-732-4370.**

Jewelry
Concho pearl jewelry and Bart Mann originals are available at **Legend Jewelers (105 S. Irving St., 915-653-2902). Holland Jewelry** is where they make the famous spurclip, a miniature western spur with a turning rowel fashioned into a piece of jewelry for tie bars, cuff links, ladies' pins, necklaces, and earrings; prices start at about $90 **(11 W. Beauregard Ave., 915-655-3135).**

Old Chicken Farm Art Center
A chicken farm converted into studios for about a dozen artists working in various media, including painting, photography, fiber, metal, glass, clay, and wood. **2505 Martin Luther King Blvd.; 915-653-4936.**

Sam Lewis and Associates
Jalapeño Sam Lewis is one of those genuine West Texas characters I was telling you about. I went with him to the World Travel Market in Europe several years ago. I carried my camera; he brought his live armadillos. Needless to say, Sam stole the show. In San Angelo, you can stock up on his jalapeño-flavored lollipops, jalapeño-stuffed olives, jalapeño peanut brittle, and a large selection of food items made with Sam's fiery pepper. And if Sam's around, chances are he'll let you pet one of his armadillos. **420 N. Van Buren St.; 915-655-0485.**

Festivals and Events

March

San Angelo Stock Show and Rodeo
First weekend in the month. Entries come from all over Texas to this stock show. There's a rodeo most nights. **Coliseum Fairgrounds.**

May

Sabers, Saddles, and Spurs
The Fort Concho Equestrian Review, featuring polo, cavalry drills, and displays of horsemanship. The San Angelo Saddle Club has one of the best polo teams in the state. **Fort Concho Parade Grounds.**

June

Fiesta del Concho
Usually the third week in the month. A river parade with many floats to provide a nighttime extravaganza, plus talent shows, a fiddling contest, a dance under the stars at Fort Concho, arts and crafts, and armadillo races. **Various locations in town center along the river.**

September

Fiestas Patrias
During the second week of the month. A celebration of Mexican independence, with parades, music, dances, and Mexican food. **Various locations.**

November

Cowboy Roping Fiesta
First weekend in the month. Some of the best calf and steer roping in the country. A lot of world-champion calf ropers come from this part of Texas. **Coliseum Fairgrounds.**

December

Christmas at Old Fort Concho
First weekend. A great Christmas celebration in this part of Texas, with twenty historic buildings lit up for the

season. Each building is decorated to represent Christmas at a different time in the past. **Fort Concho.**

Recreation

Lake Nasworthy

A 1,500-acre city lake that provides the water supply for the city. There is camping, picnicking, fishing, swimming, and other water sports. You can fish in fresh water for some fish normally associated with salt water: redfish and speckled trout. **Six miles southwest of San Angelo, off U.S. Hwy. 277; 915-944-1311; www.tpwd.state.tx.us/fish/infish/lakes/nasworth/access.htm.**

Paint Rock Pictographs

For thousands of years, nomadic Indians lived in the limestone cliffs, and created a gallery of Indian art on the walls. Tribal artists used a mixture of red colors from bear or buffalo fat, yellow from geodes, and black from charcoal to create more than 1,500 images at the site, including serpents, running bison, and Spanish missionaries. **Paint Rock Excursions** has an office at the intersection of Farm Road 380 and U.S. Hwy. 83 **(915-732-4418);** it's the only company that offers tours to the site. The tour takes about an hour and involves a bit of walking. **Outside the community of Paint Rock on a private ranch. Paint Rock is 32 miles east of San Angelo on Farm Road 380.**

RV Parks and Camping

Twin Buttes Marina, with a campground and full hookups, boat ramps, a marina, and dumpsite **(4 miles west of San Angelo, 915-949-2651); Spring Creek Marina,** offering full hookups and cable TV **(45 Fisherman's Rd., on Lake Nasworthy, 915-944-3850);** and **KOA Kampground,** offering campsites, and RV sites with and without hookups **(off Knickerbocker Rd., 3 miles west of Loop 306, 915-949-3242).**

San Angelo State Park

Offers 7,000 acres of excellent facilities for the outdoor enthusiast. This park is built around O. C. Fisher Reservoir, with boating, fishing, hiking, bird-watching, nature trails, and archaeological areas, plus plenty of space for camping. Two entrances: off U.S. Hwy. 87 to the north entrance, and off U.S. Hwy. 67 to the south entrance. **3900 Mercedes St.; 915-949-4757, 915-389-8900; www.tpwd.state.tx.us/park/sanangel/sanangel.htm.**

Twin Buttes Reservoir

An impoundment on the Concho River that has one of the longest earth-fill dams ever built by the Bureau of Reclamation—8 miles long, with a maximum height of 131 feet. There is boating, swimming, fishing, and other water sports, along with lakeside camps. **Eight miles southwest of San Angelo off U.S. Hwy. 277.**

Where to Eat

Dun Bar East

Catfish, chicken-fried steak, and liver and onions are the specialties. Near the Producers Livestock Auction Barn, at **1728 Pulliam St.; 915-655-8780.**

Fuentes Original Cafe

Good and basic Mexican food. **9 E. Ave. K; 915-658-4081.**

Mejor Que Nada

Excellent, basic Mexican food served West Texas-style; popular for Tex-Mex meals. **1911 S. Bryant Blvd.; 915-655-3553.**

Twin Mountain Steakhouse

They offer good steaks and also serve chicken and seafood. **Two miles west of San Angelo at 6534 U.S. Hwy. 67; 915-949-4239.**

Zentner's Daughter Steak House

A favorite in this area. **1901 Knickerbocker Rd.; 915-949-2821.**

Where to Stay

Holiday Inn Convention Center

441 Rio Concho Dr.; 915-658-2828.

La Poulet-Villa Bed-and-Breakfast

2503 Martin Luther King Blvd.; 915-659-1440.

The Permian Basin

The geography of Texas is amazing to examine. It has mountains and canyons, dense woods, open plains. Those of us who grew up in West Texas were astonished the first time we saw the Pineywoods of East Texas—and many East Texans have never seen the vastness of West Texas. Some people say that if Texas does have a shortness of scenery, it's in the Permian Basin—named for the region's abundance of oil-bearing rocks from the Permian geological period. Others believe the flat plains and oil fields of the Permian Basin make this the most beautiful part of the state. The heat can be miserable at times, and often the wind seems to blow on forever, but the people are friendly—and beauty, as they say, is in the eye of the beholder.

My sharpest memories of childhood in West Texas are of blowing dust and storm shelters. Mom was forever standing at the back door, trying unsuccessfully to sweep away the dust. During tornado season, we spent about 3 nights a week in the backyard storm shelter that Dad dug for us, supplied with everything we needed to spend the night—and we did just that a few times as twisters passed overhead.

The geographical center of the Permian Basin is Big Spring. But when the region first boomed with oil, folks in Big Spring didn't like the idea of all those outsiders moving to town, so they discouraged industrial growth. Industry went down the road to Midland and Odessa. With few exceptions, the oil companies built their administrative buildings in Midland, while the oil-field workers built their homes in Odessa.

Visitor Information

Big Spring Area Chamber of Commerce
215 W. 3rd St.; 1-800-734-7641, 915-263-7641, fax 915-264-9111; www.bigspringtex.com.

Downtown Midland Inc.
214 W. Texas Ave.; 915-683-7111; www.ci.midland.tx.us.

Midland Convention and Visitors Bureau
109 N. Main St.; 1-800-624-6435, 915-683-3381.

Odessa Convention and Visitors Bureau
700 N. Grant Ave., No. 200; 1-800-780-4678; www.ci.odessa.tx.us.

Towns in the Area

Midland

Midland got its name by being the midway point between Fort Worth and El Paso on the Texas and Pacific Railroad line. It was little more than a tiny farming community until the Permian Basin oil fields were discovered in the 1920s. It then became one of the most prosperous communities in West Texas. When I was growing up, I heard there were more millionaires per capita in Midland than anyplace else. Many of the oilmen here kept offices in Houston and commuted between the two cities. These men wore boots and smelled of oil. Their wives shopped by mail-order from the exclusive Neiman-Marcus store in Dallas, drove Cadillacs, and wore mink stoles.

SEEING AND DOING

Confederate Air Force and American Airpower Flying Museum

The original home of the Confederate Air Force (CAF) was in the South Texas Valley, but several years ago when the economy of that area could no longer support it, the members who collect and restore vintage aircraft moved their headquarters and airplanes to Midland. The CAF now has more than 140 aircraft representing sixty-one different models from the United States, Britain, Germany, and Japan. The museum is open Monday through Saturday, and the CAF puts on air shows throughout the year. **At Midland International Airport, which is halfway between Midland and Odessa on I-20; 915-563-1000, fax 915-567-3047.**

Midland Man

Anthropologist Fred Wendorf authenticated the remains of what is now known as the Midland Man and proved the existence of humans in this region 22,000 years ago. The upper skull was discovered at a site on the Scharbauer ranch south of town. A reproduction of the remains is on display in the **Midland County Museum at 301 W. Missouri Ave.; 915-688-8947.**

Museum of the Southwest

Some of the most prized southwestern art in the country is housed in a 1934 mansion that takes up an entire block. The house itself is as much of an attraction as the valuable items on display inside. **1705 W. Missouri Ave.; 915-683-2882.**

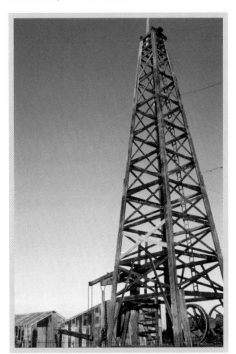

Permian Basin Petroleum Museum in Midland showcases the history of the oil industry in West Texas. Photo courtesy of Texas Highways *magazine.*

Getting There

The three major cities of the Permian Basin—Big Spring, Midland, and Odessa—are located along I-20. Big Spring is about 270 miles west of Dallas–Fort Worth, and Midland is 40 miles west of Big Spring. Odessa is 20 miles west of Midland—although the two cities are almost growing together. **Midland International Airport (915-560-2200)** sits between Midland and Odessa. Regular service is offered by Southwest Airlines, Continental Airlines, American Eagle, and United Express.

Nita Stewart Haley Library

The collections at this research library emphasize Texas and southwestern history, including photographs by historian J. Evetts Haley and artifacts relating to the horseback tradition of the range country. **1805 W. Indiana Ave.; 915-682-5785, fax 915-685-3512.**

Parks

In a city of fine parks, there are four that are exceptional: **Dennis the Menace Park (at Garfield St. and Missouri Ave.),** a 3-acre duplicate of the original in Monterey, California, with bright colors, wading pools, walks, slides, playhouses, and fountains; **Hogan Park (3600 N. Fairgrounds Rd.),** with playgrounds, a pool, and picnic areas, plus a 27-hole golf course and the Sibley Nature Center and Trail; **Chris Davidson Memorial Park (at Ventura and A Sts.),** totally accessible to wheelchairs; and **Centennial Plaza** in the center of town **(100 Lorraine St.),** a tribute to the pioneers who settled this land, with waterfalls, terraced landscaping, and seating for outdoor picnic lunches.

Permian Basin Petroleum Museum

This place ranks in my book as one of the two best petroleum museums in the state (the other being in Kilgore). It has an interesting display of early oil-field equipment outside the main building, and relics inside of those early boom years. One nice touch is the main street of an early West Texas boom community, with audio recordings of people telling what it was like growing up in this part of Texas. One old-timer tells about driving a Model T along the dirt road from Midland to a small community south of town—and having twelve flats on the way. He fixed the flats with bubble gum. Another display explains the procedures for discovering and drilling for oil. It's a game that costs many millions and seldom pays off, except for a fortunate few. **1500 W. I-20, at State Hwy. 349; 915-683-4403.**

Pliska Aircraft

This airplane, which may be the very first built and flown in Texas, now hangs from the ceiling of a glass-walled enclosure, poised in perpetual flight. John Pliska, a local blacksmith, built it about 3 years after the Wright Brothers' first flight at Kitty Hawk. Pliska and a friend, Gary Coggins, flew the aircraft several times, but gave up flying when it failed during a demonstration in Odessa. A rowdy cowboy crowd of spectators demanded their money back and ran Pliska and Coggins out of town. They later returned and rescued the plane, but never flew it again. It's on display **in the main terminal building of Midland International Airport, which is halfway between Midland and Odessa on I-20; 915-560-2200.**

FESTIVALS AND EVENTS

May—Celebration of the Arts

First weekend of the month. An arts festival featuring arts and crafts and more than a hundred visual and performing artists. **Midland Center and Centennial Plaza.**

June—Summer Mummers

Every weekend during the summer, put on by the Midland Community Theater. This is an outrageous annual musical filled with fun and satire. One year featured three guys dressed to look like the Andrews Sisters, lip-syncing music from the post–World War II era. The main act was a kid from the local high school peeling a banana to the music from *2001: A Space Odyssey.* See what I mean? If the crowd likes the act, they scream and toss handfuls of popcorn up on stage. If they don't like the act, they boo and toss handfuls of popcorn.

September—Septemberfest

Usually second weekend. Artists and craftspeople from

all over the country exhibit and sell their art. Also featured is a variety of music, such as polkas, mariachis, and bluegrass. **Museum of the Southwest, 1705 W. Missouri Ave.; 915-683-2882.**

October—Confederate Air Force "Airsho"

Second weekend. Major air battles of World War II are re-created in this show put on by the Confederate Air Force Ghost Squadron. Battles include Pearl Harbor, Wake Island, and the Battle of Britain. **Midland International Airport, 9506 LaForce Blvd.; 915-560-2200.**

October—Midland Jazz Classic

A 4-day festival that features some of the best jazz musicians in the country. **Various locations in Midland; 915-683-5208.**

WHERE TO EAT

Cattleman's Steakhouse

An above-average steak place, with the walls decorated with pictures of western scenes and of the Confederate Air Force. **3300 N. Big Spring St.; 915-682-5668.**

Santa Fe Grill

Upscale southwestern cuisine that includes Tex-Mex delights, including jalapeño-sauteed shrimp. **117 W. Wall St. in the Midland Hilton; 915-683-6131.**

Wall Street Bar and Grill

Ordinarily I would be reluctant to recommend seafood this far from the Gulf, but Midland is full of high rollers, and they can afford to import their seafood. **115 E. Wall St.; 915-684-8686.**

WHERE TO STAY

Hilton Hotel

117 W. Wall St.; 915-683-6131.

Top O the Mark Bed-and-Breakfast

112 S. Lorraine St.; 915-682-4560.

Odessa

Russian rail workers named the town, originally a way station on the Texas and Pacific Railroad, after the

Ukraine city of Odessa. When I was growing up, Odessa was a hard, tough-talking town occupied mostly by roughnecks. It has cleaned up its act. Some of that Midland money apparently made its way into Odessa, and there are now fewer trailer parks and more residential subdivisions, and several very nice shopping malls and parks.

SEEING AND DOING

Art Institute for the Permian Basin
Three art galleries, with the emphasis on contemporary artists. **4909 E. University Ave.; 915-368-7222.**

Globe of the Great Southwest Theatre
A replica of England's Globe Theatre, and designed specifically for performances of William Shakespeare's dramas. A Shakespeare Festival is held every year in April. **2308 Shakespeare Rd., just west of U.S. Hwy. 385; 915-332-1586; hamlet@ globesw.org; www.globesw.org.**

Jackrabbit Statue
A 10-foot-high statue—the world's largest jackrabbit. A popular photo spot. **802 N. Sam Houston Ave.**

Odessa Meteor Crater
The second largest meteor crater in the United States and the sixth largest in the world. A large meteor shower struck this region more than 20,000 years ago. One meteor, estimated to have weighed a thousand tons, produced a hole 550 feet in diameter. Of course the hole is not as impressive as it once was, because over the years it has filled to within 6 feet of the top with accumulated sediments. The ancient meteor shower also made other craters in the area, with diameters of 15 to 70 feet. A nature trail leads across the center of the main crater and along one side of the rim. **Ten miles west of Odessa on Business I-20, near its intersection with Farm Road 1936; look for the signs.**

Presidential Museum
A museum dedicated to the U.S. presidency, with campaign memorabilia, presidential medals, inaugural gowns, and other relics. **622 N. Lee Ave.; 915-332-7123.**

White-Pool House
The oldest existing house in Ector County, restored to reflect the lifestyles of the 1880s ranching period and the 1920s oil-boom era. **12 E. Murphy St.; 915-333-4072.**

FESTIVALS AND EVENTS

January—Sandhills Hereford and Quarter Horse Show and Rodeo
First week in January. This is the beginning of year-long competition on the Professional Rodeo Cowboys Association circuit. **Ector County Coliseum, 4201 Andrews Hwy.; 915-366-3541.**

April—Odessa Shakespeare Festival
Held for two weeks in mid-April. A celebration of Shakespeare's work, with professional and collegiate productions. **Globe of the Great Southwest Theatre, 2308 Shakespeare Rd.; 915-332-1586.**

May—Renaissance Fair
Uusually the first week in the month. An outdoor show representing the festivities of fourteenth-century England. **Globe of the Great Southwest Theatre, 2308 Shakespeare Rd.; 915-332-1586.**

September—Permian Basin Fair and Exposition
Mid-month. An old-fashioned country fair with livestock shows, quilt and food judgings, arts and crafts, a carnival, and outdoor stage entertainment. **Ector County Coliseum, 4201 Andrews Hwy.; 915-366-3541.**

WHERE TO EAT

The Barn Door and Pecos Depot
A lively nineties-style restaurant that serves all kinds of food. Each entree comes with soup, fresh hot bread, and a block of cheddar cheese. This is the original Santa Fe Railroad depot, moved to Odessa from Pecos. **2140 Andrews Hwy.; 915-337-4142.**

Dos Amigos
A horse barn that has been turned into a Tex-Mex eating establishment. The owner puts on bull-riding exhibitions once a month. **520 W. 47th St.; 915-368-7556.**

Harrigan's

Mesquite-grilled prime rib, plus chicken, seafood, and Tex-Mex. **2701 John Ben Shepperd Parkway; 915-367-4185.**

WHERE TO STAY

K-Bar Ranch Hunting Lodge

Bed-and-breakfast. **15448 S. Jasper Ave., Odessa; 915-580-5880.**

Radisson Hotel

5200 E. University Blvd., Odessa; 915-368-5885.

Big Spring

The town is named after a natural water hole that was about the only wet spot in West Texas for centuries. Big Spring remained little more than a tent village until the coming of the railroad, and then grew through the years with the oil boom.

Big Spring is also noted for being the home of the first of the big Texas spenders. The Earl of Aylesford, an Englishman, moved here in 1883, bringing along an entourage of assistants, associates, and servants. The local hotel didn't have room for his group, so he bought the hotel. He bought a saloon to throw a party, then built a butcher shop so he could get the choice cuts of meat he wanted. In the mid-1880s the earl initiated a Christmas celebration that lasted into January—and before it was over, the Englishman died of overindulgence. He was 36 years old. His old butcher shop is still standing at **121 Main St.**

SEEING AND DOING

Heritage Museum

Featuring artifacts and memorabilia from early Texas. An old-time windmill stands outside, while a collection of longhorn cattle horns, the largest in the region, is on display inside. **510 S. Scurry St.; 915-267-8255.**

Potton House

A restored Victorian home built of Pecos sandstone in 1901, with fish-scale shingles and an iron fence. **Gregg and 2nd Sts.; 915-263-0511.**

The Record Shop

This place may now be just another record store, but it used to be known worldwide. Antique-record collectors would make special trips to Big Spring to meet Oscar Glickman, the man who started the business. I remember him from my childhood as a gruff old man who glared at me if I spent too much time in his shop without buying something. But I never really knew Oscar until I returned years later to Big Spring to do a story on him and his shop. In the basement of his building, Oscar stored all his old 78 rpm records; he never threw one away. So years later, when it became fashionable to collect some of these classics, Oscar was one of the few people to have any for sale. Eventually people from all over were contacting him about the records. And the amazing truth is that he never sold one of those classic 78s for more than $1.19, no matter how valuable it was to a collector. He refused to gouge anyone on the price. "Why not?" I asked him. "That's the price I put on 'em when I bought 'em," he replied, "and that's what I'll sell 'em for." Oscar Glickman of Big Spring is gone now, but they still sell records at The Record Shop. However, I don't think they have any classic 78s left, and it's just not the same without Old Man Glickman guarding the store. **211 S. Main St.; 915-267-7501.**

Big Spring's favorite son, Bob "Tumbleweed Smith" Lewis's syndicated radio show features Texans at their best. Photo courtesy of Bob Lewis.

The Stampede

A popular warehouse-like dance hall built by western singing sensation Hoyle Nix and his West Texas Cowboys in 1954. Hoyle was best known for his song "Big Balls in Cowtown." He was also among the first to record "Orange Blossom Special." Hoyle died in 1985, but his son, Jody, still opens the Stampede for dancing on Saturday nights when his band is in town. Some of the old-timers in town claim that Lawrence Welk used to play regularly at The Stampede during the early part of his career. **About 2 miles north of Big Spring on State Hwy. 350 (Snyder Hwy.); 915-267-9268.**

Dune jumpers at Monahans Sandhills State Park. Photo courtesy of Texas Highways *magazine.*

Tumbleweed Smith

Not a historical site, not a place, but a real-life Texas character. Tumbleweed Smith is a writer, a storyteller, a poet, and a communications expert. Chances are good that if you witness some celebration during your trip to West Texas, Tumbleweed Smith will be a part of it. In real life he is Bob Lewis, and he can often be found on the lecture circuit or out doing other work in West Texas. Bob worked with me in Houston for many years as a radio newsman. He now lives in Big Spring and produces the program *Sounds of Texas,* heard on hundreds of radio stations, with vignettes on Texans. He decided he needed a real Texas name, so he goes by the moniker Tumbleweed Smith. Bob likes you to think he's a real down-home Texas boy, but actually he's pretty sophisticated—a college graduate, a published author, and the best interviewer I've ever known. He makes his subjects the stars of his program, and he always makes people feel comfortable. **915-263-3813.**

FESTIVALS AND EVENTS

March—Rattlesnake Roundup

Usually the middle of the month. They hunt them, demonstrate how to handle them, milk them, and skin them, then use the parts for everything from hatbands and belt buckles to fried snacks. **Howard County Fairgrounds, eastern city limits.**

June—Big Spring Cowboy Reunion and Rodeo

Usually late in the month. Parades, street dances, cowboy poetry, and a professional rodeo with top competitors. World-champion calf ropers Toots Mansfield and Sonny Edwards came from Big Spring. **Howard County Rodeo Bowl and Fairgrounds.**

September—Howard County Fair

Usually the first week of the month. A county fair with livestock shows, flower shows, carnivals, a chili cook-off, and nightly entertainment. **Fairgrounds.**

RECREATION

Big Spring State Park

A 370-acre park atop the limestone-capped mesa known as Scenic Mountain, providing a bird's-eye view of Big Spring and the whole area. I used to park at night on Scenic Mountain in my 1939 Mercury and listen to a radio station broadcasting from Dallas. As the highest point around, it was the only place the radio could pick up a signal from 300 miles away. **Off Farm Road 700 west of downtown Big Spring, at 1 Scenic Dr.; 915-263-4931; www.tpwd. state.tx.us/park/bigsprin.bigsprin.htm.**

Comanche Trail Park

The site of the original big spring that gave Big Spring its name. This is a 500-acre Big Spring city park with a swimming pool, tennis courts (where I first met the woman who was to become my wife), and an 18-hole golf course. The park also has hiking, biking, nature trails, campsites, and a 7,000-seat amphitheater built of hand-cut native limestone during the depression. **Southern limits of Big Spring, off U.S. Hwy. 87; 915-263-8311.**

Lake Colorado City

A 1,600-acre lake with fishing sites, boat ramps, picnic spots, and camping areas. Includes the 500-acre Lake Colorado City State Park. **About 50 miles east of Big Spring, south of I-20 at Colorado (col-uh-RA-duh) City; 915-728-3931.**

Lake J. B. Thomas

This is a large lake for West Texas. It's on the Colorado River, with 75 miles of shoreline for swimming, boating, skiing, fishing, and camping. **About 40 miles northeast of Big Spring via State Hwy. 350 and Farm Road 1298.**

Moss Creek Lake

Water supply and recreational facility for Big Spring, with fishing, boating, and camping. It's also a good area for bird-watching. **Ten miles southeast of Big Spring at 10,000 E. Moss Lake Rd.; 915-393-5246.**

RV Parks

Midessa KOA, offering tent sites, cabins, and full hookups **(off I-20 at exit 126, between Midland and Odessa, 915-563-2368); Comanche Trail Park (off U.S. Hwy. 87, south of Big Spring, 915-263-8311);** and the **Whip In Campground (7 miles east of Big Spring, off I-20, 915-393-5242).**

Sandhill Crane Sanctuary

One of a series of shallow lakes, filled mainly with rainwater, that provides nesting and feeding grounds in winter for thousands of sandhill cranes. Better known as One Mile Lake because of its distance from downtown Big Spring. **Off U.S. Hwy. 80 going west.**

WHERE TO EAT

Carlos Restaurant and Bar

The definitive Mexican food restaurant in West Texas. Nothing fancy; just good basic Mexican food. When I was growing up around here and had the money, I usually went to Carlos's for tacos, burritos, and cheese enchiladas. They didn't know what fajitas were back then. Nobody had even heard of flautas—and what's all this about a Meximelt or a tostada? Although Carlos has compromised a bit for the outside crowd—he now offers fajitas and such—his family recipes remain the

same. If you go there, he'll still serve you basic Mexican food, and he won't bring out the sour cream unless you dudes request it. **308 NW 3rd St.; 915-267-9141.**

Casa Blanca Restaurant

A great place for Mexican food in Big Spring if Carlos Restaurant and Bar is packed. **1005 Lamesa Hwy.; 915-263-1162.**

Herman's Restaurant

A good choice for breakfast. **1601 Gregg St.; 915-267-3281.**

WHERE TO STAY

Best Western

I-20 at U.S. Hwy. 87, Big Spring; 915-267-1601.

Other Towns in the Area

Other towns of note in the Permian Basin include Monahans, Kermit, Wink, Pecos, Fort Stockton, and Iraan.

Monahans

Getting There: From Odessa, take I-20 west for about 35 miles to Monahans. **Visitor Information: Monahans Chamber of Commerce, 401 S. Dwight Ave.; 915-943-2187; www.monahans. org.**

Spanish explorers examined this land more than 400 years ago, but nobody seriously settled the place until the 1880s, when the Texas and Pacific Railroad arrived. Today it's a ranching and oil center. Some of the oil wells on the outskirts of town are slanted to draw oil from beneath city hall, the courthouse, and several other downtown buildings.

SEEING AND DOING

Million Barrel Museum

Built in 1928 as a giant concrete drum that would hold a million barrels of oil for storage. It never worked. The oil seeped through the concrete and leaked out into the ground. In 1987 the drum was converted into a museum that displays old homes and other relics of the past. This unusual museum includes an amphitheater, the first jail in Ward County, a collection of antique oil-field equipment, and Holman House, a hotel that stood in town early in the twentieth century. **400 Museum Blvd., on U.S. Hwy. 80, a mile east of Monahans; 915-943-8401.**

Monahans Sandhills State Park

A thousand acres of windblown sand dunes, making this place look like the Sahara Desert. The park has a museum and interpretive center, plus space for picnicking, camping, and sand surfing (don't knock it till you try it). **On I-20, 5 miles east of Monahans; 915-247-3903.**

Rattlesnake Bomber Base and Pyote Museum

The old base was home to the World War II 19th Bomber Group, and the bomber *Enola Gay* departed from this base on its mission to drop an atomic bomb on Hiroshima. The Rattlesnake Bomber Base site is now the property of the University of Texas; it's used as a research facility and is not open to the public. A nearby museum in a county park in the town of Pyote has photos of some of the men who flew the bombers. The park also has space for picnicking and camping, plus a 3-hole golf course. The museum is open Sat. 9 A.M.–6 P.M. and Sun. 2–6 P.M. The park and the base are **off I-20, 15 miles west of Monahans, at Pyote; 915-389-5548.**

Windmill Collection

Lefty Christopher was once a telephone company lineman, and in his retirement he put together one of the most interesting windmill collections I've ever seen. He did all this in the front yard and backyard of his house just east of downtown. Lefty had West Texas written all over him. He was about the friendliest person you'd ever want to meet. Lefty is gone now and is most likely tending to those giant windmills in the sky, but his widow, Nancy, who is just about as colorful, is still showing off the windmill collection at **1404 S. Calvin Ave.; 915-943-4525.** If you can't catch Nancy at home, some of Lefty's windmills are on display at the **Million Barrel Museum.**

Kermit

Getting There: From Odessa, take State Hwy. 302 west for 46 miles to Kermit. **Visitor Information:**

Kermit Chamber of Commerce, 112 N. Poplar St.; 915-586-2507.

In 1926 only eighty-one people lived in Winkler County; it was wide open and empty. Then oil was discovered in the Permian Basin. Kermit today is a center for oil-related companies.

SEEING AND DOING

Kermit Sandhills Park

There is overnight camping at Sandhills Park. Off-road vehicles are welcome. The sand will stick to your body and seemingly never come off, but running around on the white hills of blowing West Texas sand can be an entertaining experience for the youngsters. **Ten miles east of Kermit at State Hwy. 115 and Farm Road 874.**

Medallion Home

This is Kermit's oldest existing structure, built in 1907. Lumber was brought in by rail to build the house, because there aren't many trees in this area. (In fact, 25 miles east of Kermit is a community called Notrees.) The house is furnished with antiques from the period. **At 200 School St., in Pioneer Park, directly north of Winkler County Park.** Open by appointment only: call the **Kermit Chamber of Commerce** at **915-586-2507.**

Wink

Getting There: From Odessa, take State Hwy. 302 west for 46 miles to Kermit, then State Hwy. 106 south for 6 miles to Wink. **Visitor Information: Wink Chamber of Commerce, 210 N. Hendricks Blvd.; 915-527-3441.**

Ranching and oil made Wink into a fairly prosperous but dull West Texas town. Rock music star Roy Orbison put the city on the map.

SEEING AND DOING

Roy Orbison Boulevard and Marker

Wink is the hometown of Roy Orbison. The town celebrates his name today, although it laughed at him while he was growing up. In the 1950s as a teenager, Roy traveled with Little Johnny and the Wink Westerners, playing for pennies at sock hops around West Texas. Little Johnny was the star and Roy was just one of the backup singers. Little Johnny eventually faded into oblivion, while Roy went on to compose and record some of the most popular music of his generation, and ranked with stars like Elvis Presley and Buddy Holly for many years.

Roy Orbison Museum

Memorabilia from Orbison's boyhood and his long career on the music scene. **In downtown Wink on State Hwy. 115.** For tours, call **915-527-3622.**

Pecos

Getting There: From Odessa, take I-20 west for 75 miles to Pecos. **Visitor Information: Pecos Chamber of Commerce, 111 S. Cedar St.; 915-445-2406.**

Established along the Texas and Pacific Railroad line, this community had a reputation for being a hangout for rowdy cowboys and fast-drawing lawmen during those early years. Today it's a ranching and oil center and also is touted as a place for hunting, with a hefty supply of mule deer, javelina, and upland game birds.

SEEING AND DOING

Maxey Park and Zoo

A real Texas zoo with buffalo, longhorns, javelina, mountain lions, and antelopes. There is a picnic area, a full-facility campground and RV park, and a botanical garden with regional flowers and shrubs. **On the I-20 access road between U.S. Hwy. 285 and State Hwy. 17 just south of town.**

Pecos Cantaloupes

Pecos is the home of the sweetest cantaloupes in the world. Just ask any expert. They are grown in irrigated fields outside Pecos and are enjoyed by gourmets all over the United States. The quality is derived from a natural combination of alkali soil, western sunlight, and altitude.

Many people believe Pecos cantaloupes enjoy a comparable status with Maine lobsters, French wines, and Swiss cheese—but beware of the distributors: A lot of them grow their cantaloupes in places like California, then ship them through Pecos and call them Pecos cantaloupes. The real Pecos beauties are harvested from late July through September.

West-of-the-Pecos Museum and Park

A museum in one of the town's fine old hotels, with ornate displays of life in the late 1800s and the site where two outlaws were gunned down by bartender Barney Riggs, who was a quick-draw artist. The fifty rooms in the building showcase West Texas history. A park next door contains the first building in Pecos, the grave of Clay Allison (known as the gentleman gunfighter), and a replica of Judge Roy Bean's saloon (the real one is in Langtry—see the Rio Grande Border chapter). Open Mon.–Sat. 9 A.M.–5 P.M. and Sun. 2–5 P.M. **120 E. 1st St.; 915-445-5076.**

Fort Stockton

Getting There: From Odessa, take U.S. Hwy. 385 south for 53 miles, travel west on U.S. Hwy. 67 for 32 miles, then go west on I-10 for the final 14 miles to Fort Stockton. **Visitor Information: Pecos Visitor Information Center, I-10 and U.S. Hwy. 285; 915-336-8052.** Also, **Pecos Chamber of Commerce, 1000 E. Railroad Ave.; 915-336-2264.**

Established as a military post in 1859, this city was located on the Butterfield Overland Mail Route at the crossing of the Old San Antonio Road and an ancient Comanche war trail.

The area was popular with Indians long before white men arrived, because of its abundant natural springs. Today the main highway through town is lined with motels and restaurants catering to travelers between El Paso and San Antonio, and between Big Bend country and San Angelo.

SEEING AND DOING

Annie Riggs Hotel Museum

A popular stop on the stage route, this old hotel was built in 1899 and has been restored by the local historical society. **301 S. Main St.; 915-336-2167.**

Comanche Springs Pool

Site of the **Fort Stockton Water Carnival** every July. Water may be scarce in this part of Texas, but Fort Stockton flaunts its water supply with a show and pageant that has been going on annually since 1936. The park also offers picnicking and tennis. In **James Rooney County Park, off Spring Dr., on the southern edge of Fort Stockton; 915-336-2751.**

Historic Fort Stockton

A typical frontier military post, established in 1858 and in service until 1886. The fort consisted of thirty-five buildings made of adobe and hand-hewn limestone. Four original buildings are still standing, and some of the other buildings have been reconstructed. **300 E. 3rd St.; 915-336-2400.**

Old Fort Cemetery

One of the most startling stories of the Old West came out of this town. It involves Sheriff A. J. Royal, a Fort Stockton lawman who is buried at Old Fort Cemetery. Royal helped civilize the town, and when the townspeople eventually voted him out of office, he couldn't accept their judgment. He wouldn't turn over his position, and most people were afraid to confront him on the subject. So the city commissioners met in secret and drew straws to see who would remove him from office. The removal was permanent: the commissioner who drew the shortest straw shot the sheriff dead behind his desk. Nobody was ever tried for the 1894 murder of Sheriff Royal, whose headstone reads "assassinated." The cemetery is located at a crossroads in the center of town, at **U.S. Hwy. 290 and Main St.**

Paisano Pete

A 20-foot-long, 11-foot-tall monument to the Texas roadrunner. It's a popular photo spot in town. U.S. Hwy. 290 at Main St.

WHERE TO EAT

Sarah's Cafe

A must-visit eating spot and the oldest restaurant in Fort Stockton. If you are uncertain about what to order, just ask for the Sarah's Cafe special. My choice is cheese enchiladas, the best I've ever tasted. **106 S. Nelson St.; 915-336-7700.**

Iraan

Getting There: From Odessa, take U.S. Hwy. 385 south for 53 miles, then travel east on U.S. Hwy. 67 for 15 miles, go south on State Hwy. 349 for 22 miles, and finally go east on U.S. Hwy. 190 for 4 miles to Iraan. **Visitor Information: Iraan Chamber of Commerce, 502 W. 6th St.; 915-639-2232.**

Iraan is the site of a huge oil discovery some years ago. The oil wells here are natural-flow, meaning you don't need pumps to pull the oil out of the ground; the oil just naturally flows to the surface when a hole is drilled.

The name of the town has an interesting history. The land where the oil discovery was made belonged to pioneer Ira Yates, so the oil field came to be known as the Yates Field. When it came time to name the town that grew up here, Ira decided to share the name with his wife, Ann, resulting in Iraan (EYE-ruh-ANN).

SEEING AND DOING

City Park

A 40-acre park at the western edge of Iraan offers places for picnicking, barbecuing, and camping. A historical marker in the park notes that Iraan's **Discovery Well A No. 1** blew in more than a half century ago. It's still one of the largest-producing oil wells in North America. There must have been plenty of commotion when the well came in; a stream of oil from the gusher sprayed a tent city 4 miles away.

Fantasyland

One of the early-day roughnecks who worked the oil fields in this area was V. T. Hamlin, a loner of sorts from the East who showed up one day for work, stayed for a while, then suddenly moved on. Some say the land around here inspired Hamlin to create a comic strip character that lives on today, Alley Oop. Fantasyland is a park inspired by Hamlin's characters, with giant statues of Oop, his girlfriend, Ooola, and his dinosaur, Dinny. Dinny is 65 feet long and 16 feet tall, and weighs 80,000 pounds. Also on the Fantasyland site is the **Iraan Archaeological Museum,** with its collections of fossils, Indian artifacts, ranching antiquities, and oil-field relics. **1000 Park Side St.; 915-639-8895.**

The Davis Mountains

The Davis Mountains are unique among West Texas mountain ranges because they are mostly smooth-topped and grassy. It's no secret in the Lone Star State that this region has what many agree is the best year-round climate. The cool summers are mostly thanks to the elevation, which averages about 5,000 to 6,000 feet. The Davis Mountains average more than 20 inches of rain a year—and that constitutes a wetland to folks out here. The air is clear. The stars are bright at night.

Visitor Information

See the individual towns in this chapter.

Towns in the Area

Among the interesting towns in this region are Balmorhea, Fort Davis, Marfa, and Alpine.

Balmorhea

Getting There: Balmorhea is on State Hwy. 17, just off I-10—about 50 miles west of Fort Stockton and 185 miles east of El Paso. **Visitor Information: Balmorhea City Office, 4th and San Antonio Sts.; 915-375-2307.**

Balmorhea was established by land promoters in 1906, who set up a townsite on a 14,000-acre tract by San Solomon Springs and sold off lots.

SEEING AND DOING

Balmorhea State Park

Facilities include a motel, camping and trailer sites, picnic area, playground, and one of the world's largest spring-fed swimming pools. It's worth the trip just to swim in this huge walled pool that is fed by the springs at the rate of 22 million gallons a day. The springs were an important watering place for buffalo, Indians, and pioneers. Today the springs supply the irrigation needs of the area. The park is **4 miles south** of Balmorhea, on State Hwy. 17, at San Solomon Springs; 915-375-2370; www.tpwd. state.tx.us/park/balmorhe/bal-morhe.htm.

WHERE TO EAT

Dutchover Restaurant
State Hwy. 17 in Balmorhea; 915-375-2628.

Fort Davis

Getting There: From Balmorhea, travel south on State Hwy. 17 for about 40 miles to Fort Davis. **Visitor Information: Fort Davis Chamber of Commerce, 1 Town Square; 915-426-3015; www. fortdavis. com.**

Named for a frontier fort founded in 1854 near the Chihuahua Trail and the San Antonio–El Paso Trail, Fort Davis now caters more to tourists than anyone else. It's probably the most pleasant town in Texas to live in if you don't mind the isolation. During hunting seasons, hunters have the opportunity to go for pronghorn antelope and some of the largest mule deer in the state.

SEEING AND DOING

Chihuahuan Desert Research Institute
Founded in 1974 for the study of the Chihuahuan Desert, this institute covers 580 acres dedicated to saving, researching, and showing off native plants. There are nature trails, an arboretum, and a botanical garden with more than 500 regional species. The last week in April is usually the best time for viewing. Open May–Aug., Mon.–Fri. 1–5 P.M. and Sat.–Sun. 9 A.M.–5 P.M. The institute is **3.5 miles south of Fort Davis on State Hwy. 118; 915-364-2499; manager@ cdri.org; www.cdri.org.**

Fort Davis National Historic Site
I believe this site exhibits the best restoration work of

all the Texas forts, with a visitor center located in what used to be the company barracks. A small museum chronicles the history, and there is a self-guiding tour. In summer the park staff and volunteers dress in period costumes and give free guided tours, and an 1895 Retreat Parade is reenacted twice a day. At the rear of the officers' quarters is the trailhead for the **Tall Grass Nature Trail,** a 1.2-mile loop to a viewpoint in the hills above the site. Check out the legend of Indian Emily; a marker near the base of the hills tells the story. **On the northern outskirts of Fort Davis on State Hwy. 17; 915-426-3224.**

Indian Lodge

The best-kept secret in the state. This is the only motel located in Davis Mountains State Park, and it's operated by the State of Texas. Of course, the state doesn't want to compete with other motels for business, so it simply does not advertise. But if you are able to reserve a room, this is the place to stay on your trip to Fort Davis. The lodge is a thirty-nine-room pueblo-style facility built by the Civilian Conservation Corps in the 1930s. The adobe walls are 18 inches thick, and many of the interior furnishings are original. Indian Lodge is near many great places to visit, including the park, the city, and McDonald Observatory. **Off State Hwy. 118, west of Fort Davis; P.O. Box 786, Fort Davis, 79734; 915-426-3254.**

McDonald Observatory

This University of Texas astronomy research center on Mount Locke is rated one of the top ten observatories in the world. The Davis Mountains are a good location because of the lack of light pollution (there aren't many cities out here), the large number of cloudless nights, and the concentration of native plants and trees that filter dust and radiation. When it was built in 1938, its telescope was the second largest in existence. In 1969 the observatory added a 107-inch telescope, which is in heavy demand year-round by scientists. Guided tours of the dome and the grounds are conducted daily, or you can look around by yourself. Once a month the observatory allows visitors to view the sky through the big scope; a schedule of public viewing nights is available at the **W. L. Moody Jr. Visitors Information Center (915-426-3640),** at the foot of Mount Locke. Visitors are asked to check in at the center before proceeding up the mountain to

the observatory. The center has good exhibits and a gift shop. Every Tuesday, Friday, and Sunday in the evenings, the Moody Center puts on a star party, giving visitors an opportunity to view the skies through 8- and 14-inch telescopes. The observatory itself is high atop Mount Locke, **16 miles northwest of Fort Davis via State Hwy. 118 and Spur 78; 915-426-3263.**

Neill House Doll Museum

Displays of more than 400 antique dolls and toys. Open June–Labor Day daily 10 A.M.–5 P.M. **Seven blocks west of the Fort Davis courthouse; 915-426-3969.**

Getting There

There is no commercial airline service to the Davis Mountains region. It is between El Paso and Midland–Odessa, so if you are flying in, your best bet is one of those two places. Then you can rent a car for the 130-mile trip from Midland–Odessa or the drive of close to 200 miles from El Paso. From Midland, I-20 takes you southwest through Monahans and Pecos. The land is flat and wide open, and filled with mesquite. But when you turn south near Pecos onto State Hwy. 17, suddenly you get a glimpse of the mountains in the distance. For the next 32 miles, the scenery changes dramatically. Once you reach Balmorhea, the fauna will capture your heart, and as you continue south to Fort Davis, you'll see why I think this is the prettiest part of Texas. From El Paso, the drive is not nearly so spectacular, although the first 100 miles or so east on I-10 take you parallel to the Rio Grande and the Mexican border. At Van Horn, you can take U.S. Hwy. 90 south for 80 miles or so to Marfa, the western entrance to the Davis Mountains region. Or from Van Horn, you also have the choice of continuing straight on I-10 for about another 70 miles to Balmorhea.

Panoramic view of the Davis Mountains in Big Bend Country. Photo courtesy of Texas Highways magazine.

Prude Ranch

It was first a cattle ranch; then in the 1930s, cabins were constructed here for workers building the McDonald Observatory. Today it is a combination dude ranch, mountain resort, RV park, and campground. **Six miles northwest of Fort Davis on State Hwy. 118; 1-800-458-6232, 915-426-3202, fax 915-426-3502; prude@overland.net; www.pruderanch.com.**

Scenic Loop

Beginning at Fort Davis, **State Hwys. 166 and 118** form a 74-mile loop through the lower third of the Davis Mountains, circling Mount Livermore and passing Madera Canyon, Mount Locke, and Davis Mountains State Park. This is a beautiful drive, especially at sunset or sunrise.

RECREATION

Davis Mountains State Park

One of the most beautiful parks in the state, centered on a canyon formed by Limpia Creek. The park offers hiking trails, fishing, swimming, a longhorn herd, a scenic drive with overlooks, and an interpretive center. From June through August, rangers conduct campfire programs. At certain times of year, astronomers from nearby McDonald Observatory bring telescopes to the park for stargazing parties. There are plenty of areas for tent, trailer, or RV camping inside the park, with all facilities. From Fort Davis, **travel 1 mile north on State Hwy. 17, turn west onto State Hwy. 118 and travel 3 miles, then turn south onto Park Road 3 and into the park; 915-426-3337; www.tpwd.state.tx.us/park/davis/davis.htm.**

Horseback Riding

Davis Mountains Horseback Tours (915-426-3022) offers guided half- and full-day trail rides.

WHERE TO EAT

Fort Davis Drug Store

Offers good sandwiches and good company. **On Main St. next to the town square; 915-426-3118.**

Hotel Limpia Restaurant

An upscale menu, with prices to match. **On Main St., on the town square; 915-426-3254.**

Indian Lodge Restaurant

At Indian Lodge. **Just west of town, off State Hwy. 118; 915-426-3254.**

WHERE TO STAY

Boynton House Guest Lodge
Outside Fort Davis, on Dolores Mountain; 915-426-3123.

Limpia Hotel
A restored country inn, circa 1912, with turn-of-the-century furnishings and a boardinghouse restaurant. **Main St., on the square; 1-800-662-5517, 915-426-3241, fax 915-426-3983; frontdesk@hotellimpia.com; www.hotellimpia.com.**

Veranda Country Inn Bed-and-Breakfast
210 Court Ave.; 915-426-2233.

Marfa

Getting There: From Balmorhea, travel south on State Hwy. 17 for about 40 miles to Fort Davis, then continue on Hwy. 17 for another 21 miles to Marfa. **Visitor Information: Marfa Chamber of Commerce, 200 S. Abbot St.; 915-729-4942; www.marfalights.com.**

Established in 1881 as a water stop for the Texas and New Orleans Railroad, Marfa today is a trading center for many of the large ranches in the area. Marfa's climate attracts vacationers, while its wild game attracts hunters. Soaring is a popular sport out here, and it's not uncommon to spot sailplanes winging silently over mesas and mile-high peaks.

SEEING AND DOING

Chinati Foundation
Includes some large-scale sculpture by contemporary artists, notably that of the man responsible for it all, Donald Judd. Judd moved to town years ago, bought up a lot of property, and started creating his unusual art. The townsfolk never really accepted Judd, but his work is honored in art circles around the country. **On the grounds of historic Fort D. A. Russell on the southern edge of the city, at 1 Cavalry Rd.; 915-729-4362.**

El Paisano Hotel
A restored 1929 hotel listed on the National Register of Historic Places. The hotel has become somewhat of a shrine for fans of James Dean, who made his final movie, *Giant*, in this territory. A glass case in the lobby of the hotel contains autographed pictures of cast members and news clippings about the production. However, Dean didn't stay at the hotel. The shooting took place on a ranch west of town, and the big stars—Dean, Rock Hudson, and Liz Taylor—were put up in rented private homes in Marfa. The hotel is downtown at **207 N. Highland Ave.; 915-729-3145.**

Marfa Mystery Lights
First reported by settlers in 1883, these lights still defy explanation. There is a marker at the prime viewing area **9 miles east of town on U.S. Hwy. 90,** but don't expect to be dazzled. I've been out there at least a dozen times and have yet to see a thing. Skeptics believe the lights are merely reflections of lights in some city far away, because the air is so clean and the sky so clear out here.

RECREATION

Marfa Country Club
The 9-hole golf course here is touted as being at the highest elevation (4,688 feet) of any course in the state. It stays in remarkably good shape when you consider that water is a rare commodity in this region. It's the only golf course I've ever played where they tell you to keep the golf carts on the fairway and out of the rough; the rough is so rough that it will damage the cart. The air around Marfa is clean and thin, and I finally found a par five I could hit with a driver and a 7 iron. Watch out, Tiger Woods, here I come. **On Golf Course Rd.; 915-729-4043.**

Balmorhea State Park contains the state's largest natural swimming hole. Photo courtesy of Texas Highways magazine.

WHERE TO EAT

El Paisano Restaurant
207 N. Highland Ave.; 915-729-3040.

WHERE TO STAY

Arcon Inn
Bed-and-breakfast. **215 N. Austin St.; 915-729-4826.**

El Paisano Hotel
207 N. Highland Ave.; 915-729-3145.

Alpine

Getting There: From Balmorhea, travel south on State Hwy. 17 for about 40 miles to Fort Davis, then 23 miles southeast on State Hwy. 118 to Alpine. **Visitor Information: Alpine Chamber of Commerce, 106 N. 3rd St.; 915-837-2326; www.alpinetex.com.**

Alpine, established in the 1880s, is the seat of Brewster County—at 5,900 square miles, it's larger than the state of Connecticut. This is ranching country that is also rapidly growing as a tourist center, with the climate and the location making it a popular vacation area. Visitors enjoy golfing, mountain climbing, horseback riding, rock and mineral collecting, hunting, and camping amid spectacular vistas.

SEEING AND DOING

Apache Trading Post
The post has a large collection of topographical, geological, and raised relief maps of the Big Bend region of Texas; also regional handicrafts and books on West Texas. **2701 W. Hwy. 90, Alpine; 915-837-5506, fax 915-837-9216.**

Museum of the Big Bend
Showcases the history of the area in panels, dioramas, and paintings. **On the campus of Sul Ross State University on U.S. Hwy. 90 in Alpine; 915-837-8143; www.sulross.edu/~museum.**

Scenic Drive
U.S. Hwy. 67 between Alpine and Marfa offers beautiful views of the Big Bend region and the Davis Mountains. Keep your eyes open and you may see some Texas antelope.

Woodward Agate Ranch
Years ago a couple of old-timers of the Woodward name opened up their ranch to rockhounds for a price. The land was loaded with beautiful stones—jasper, labradorite, feldspar, calcite, precious opal, and other minerals—and they sold rock off the place by the pound. The Woodwards are gone now, but the ranch is still in the family, and the business of rock hunting is paying off for the descendants. Rough agate sells for 50 cents a pound, and the price goes up from there. **Eighteen miles south of Alpine on State Hwy. 118; 915-364-2271.**

RECREATION

Campgrounds and RV Parks
Just outside Alpine are three RV parks with full hookups: **Pecan Grove RV Park (1902 U.S. Hwy. 90 W., 915-837-7175); Danny Boy Camper Park (2305 U.S. Hwy. 90 E., 915-837-7135);** and **B.C. Ranch RV Park (State Hwy. 118 N., 915-837-5883).** There are also campsites at the **Woodward Agate Ranch (18 miles south of Alpine on State Hwy. 118, 915-364-2271).**

WHERE TO EAT

Gallegos Mexican Food
This is the best basic Mexican eating place in town. 1102 E. Holland Ave.; 915-837-2416.

WHERE TO STAY
Choose among a stream of motels that line the eastern limits of the city.

Sunday House Motor Inn
U.S. Hwy. 90 in Alpine; 915-837-3363.

Big Bend National Park

Big Bend is a corner of West Texas where the Rio Grande takes a sharp turn: From heading southeast, it suddenly makes a big bend to the northeast. Indians say the Great Spirit placed all the leftover rocks here after creating the earth. In this area the Rio Grande cuts through three mountain ranges, creating some spectacular canyons.

The good news is that Big Bend is an isolated area, far away from the population centers of Texas, thus making it difficult for humans to contaminate the countryside. The bad news is that Big Bend is an isolated area, so if you want to get there, you need to allow yourself plenty of time.

The Big Bend area is composed of two parts: the National Park, and the rest of the area. Most of this chapter deals with the park. But don't make the long trip to Big Bend country and visit only the park. There is much more to see.

Visitor Information

Park headquarters is at **Panther Junction** in the north-central part of the park **(915-477-1158).** Other ranger stations/visitor centers are at **Persimmon Gap**, on U.S. Hwy. 385 at the northern entrance to the park **(915-477-2393); Castolon**, in the southwest part of the park **(915-477-2225); Chisos Basin**, in the center of the park **(915-477-2264);** and **Rio Grande Village**, at the southeast edge of the park **(915-477-2271).** For additional information, contact **Superintendent, Big Bend National Park, 79834; 915-477-2251.**

The park staff at Big Bend conducts daily activities that include guided interpretive walks, slide presentations, and lectures. The **Big Bend Natural History Association** sponsors seminars from mid-April through late August on subjects such as Trans-Pecos archaeology, wildlife photography, and the history of the region. **P.O. Box 68, Big Bend National Park, 79834; 915-477-2236; www.big.bend.national-park.com.**

Big Bend National Park

Big Bend National Park is one of North America's great national parks, a territory of nearly a million acres that is part desert and part mountain range, and includes a big chunk of the Rio Grande. The elevation in Big Bend National Park starts at 1,800 feet at the Rio Grande and reaches 7,800 feet in the Chisos Mountains. That makes it very diverse in terms of climate, from scorching summers on the park's western edge to some snow in the mountains. But on the whole, most people don't enjoy Big Bend country in the heat of the summer.

Annual rainfall varies from 5 inches in the desert to 15 inches in the mountains. Visitors can usually count on a generous supply of sun, even during the wetter months. Overall the best times to visit Big Bend are October through November and March through April. The area's popularity in March means you may have trouble finding lodging or campsites. Fall is best for river running; spring is best for birding and wildflower viewing. Even in the height of summer, the park can be comfortable if you stick to the mountains. August usually is the coolest summer month, thanks to afternoon rains.

People who have never visited a living desert imagine sand dunes and vultures. There is some of that out here, but for the most part Big Bend Country is quite beautiful with the subtle colors of desert plants. In season, Texas wildflowers burst upon the horizon with magnificent colors that may reach from mountain to mountain. If you've come to Big Bend to see cacti,

Getting There

Two main highways lead into Big Bend Park: U.S. Hwy. 385 from Fort Stockton and Marathon to the northern entrance to the park; and State Hwy. 118 from Alpine through Study Butte to the western entrance. There is no public transport into the park, but **bus service** is available between Alpine and Study Butte **(915-424-3471)**. One of the most scenic approaches to the park is from the west via Farm Road 170, along the Rio Grande from Presidio to Lajitas, Terlingua, and then Study Butte. Major airlines fly into the airports at San Angelo, Midland–Odessa, and El Paso, and you can rent a car at any of those places.

you won't be disappointed. No other national park has so many species—more than seventy. In spring, many of them produce beautiful flowers. In the highlands are plenty of trees, from scrub oaks to ponderosa pines, plus some cypress, fir, aspen, and big-tooth maple trees at the southern and western extremes of the park.

About seventy-five species of mammals make their home in Big Bend National Park. White-tailed deer hang out in the high country. Mule deer, easily identifiable by their long and floppy ears, live below 5,000 feet. You are likely to see fox, armadillo, javelina, maybe even a coyote or two. Most of the mountain lion sightings have been, surprisingly, on park roads, not hiking trails. They are nocturnal animals, so you're not likely to see them unless you're out at night. If you happen to encounter a lion, don't run or hide. Hold your ground, talk loudly, and wave your hands: the lion will most likely move on because he may be as afraid of you as you may be of him. If you have small children, pick them up. That will make you look bigger and when you're in the wild, the old saying "bigger is better" is definitely true.

There has been an increase in Mexican black bear sightings in the park. The creatures are moving north out of the mountains in Mexico in search of food. And tourists bring food into the park. Rangers recommend storing your food away when not eating.

Big Bend is a mecca for birds, because it's at the southern end of the Central Flyway. More than 400 species have been recorded here, more than in any other national park in the United States or Canada. Birders from all over the world flock to Big Bend. The Big Bend Natural History Association publishes a bird checklist that is distributed by the National Park Service. **Big Bend Birding Expeditions (915-371-2356)** arranges $1/_2$-day, 1-day, and 2-day bird-watching trips in the park.

The park also is home to many species of amphibians, snakes, lizards, and turtles. My favorite critter, the horny toad—or, more correctly, the Texas horned lizard—thrives in the grassy areas of the northernmost part of the park. You may run across a few ornery animals, such as the tarantulas sometimes found on highways in the summer; these spiders are not deadly, but they will bite. Big Bend also has about fifteen species of scorpions, which inject painful venom by means of a stinger in the tail. If you see any of these, have fun watching them, but keep your distance.

Recreation

The park has three kinds of roads: paved roads, dirt roads, and back roads. An ordinary passenger car can handle the first two except during heavy rains. The back roads demand high-clearance vehicles; four-wheel drive is not a must, but it's nice to have. No off-road travel is allowed in the park, even with motorcycles. Most RVs can handle the paved and improved dirt roads, but vehicles more than 24 feet long should not use Basin Drive because of the tight curves.

Start off every trip with a full tank of gas. Gas is available only at Panther Junction and Rio Grande Village. Travel with a spare tire, jack, and plenty of water, for yourself and for your radiator. If you get stuck in the sand, don't spin your wheels. That just makes it worse. Deflate your tires a bit and then slowly accelerate out of the sand. If that doesn't work, stay with your car until someone shows up. It may take a while. If you can get to a phone, call **915-477-2251** for towing service.

CAMPING

There are three drive-in camping areas: **Chisos Basin Campground,** with 63 sites for tents and campers **(at Chisos Basin, 915-477-2291); Rio Grande Village,** with a 25-site RV park and a 100-site campground **(in the southeast corner of the park,**

Yucca plant at the base of the Big Bend Mountain Range.

915-477-2271); and **Cottonwood Campground,** with 35 sites that are usually less crowded than the others because the campground is more remote **(at Castolon, 915-477-2251).** From mid-May to mid-November, no fees are collected at the Rio Grande Village and Cottonwood Campgrounds. Free backcountry campsites are scattered throughout the park; you need a permit. Outside the park, there are campgrounds and RV parks in the Study Butte–Terlingua–Lajitas area (see Towns in the Area).

HIKING

There are more than 200 miles of hiking trails in the park. You can walk in Boquillas Canyon at 1,800 feet elevation or on Emory Peak at 7,800 feet where the air in thin. The Panther Junction Visitor Center distributes the *Hikers' Guide to Trails in Big Bend National Park.* Rangers issue the usual warnings to hikers: carry plenty of water; if you get water out of streams, be sure to boil or filter it before drinking; wear sturdy hiking boots; carry a first-aid kit. For long hikes, bring a flashlight, compass, and map.

Here are a few examples of hikes in the park, but there are plenty more.

Outer Mountain Loop

Thirty-one miles round-trip, a real adventure that takes in parts of the Dodson, Juniper Canyons, Pinnacles, Laguna Meadows, and Blue Creek Trails. Whichever route you choose, this trail takes you through more different kinds of Big Bend terrain than any other hike.

Pine Canyon Trail

Four miles round-trip. Begins at the end of Pine Canyon Road, which is about 5 miles from Panther Junction. This is one of the park's prettiest trails, showcasing ponderosa pines, big-tooth maples, and some Texas madrone trees. The trail ends at the base of a 200-foot waterfall during the rainy season.

Santa Elena Canyon Trail

Two miles round-trip. Begins where Ross Maxwell Scenic Drive ends. This is the easiest way to get a close-up view of some remarkable canyon scenery.

South Rim Loop

Fourteen miles round-trip, along the southwestern edge of the Chisos Mountains, about 2,500 feet above the desert. This trail offers the best mountain viewing of all, but you'll have to work for it. There are thirteen backcountry campsites along the way for those who wish to spread the trip out over 2 days.

HORSEBACK RIDING

Big Bend National Park no longer has a stable and riding concession, but riders are permitted to bring in their own stock for use on two trails: **Laguna Meadow Trail** and the **Window Trail.** The only park facility dedicated to equestrians is a corral at the Government Springs backcountry campsite off Grapevine Hills Road. Reservations for the campsite and corral: **915-477-2251.**

RIVER RUNNING

The part of the Rio Grande that wraps around Big Bend National Park wasn't successfully navigated until the latter part of the nineteenth century. By the time the river reaches the canyons of Big Bend, its currents are strong and deep. But it's not nearly as treacherous today as it used to be. Before the dam at Lake Amistad backed up the Rio Grande, the waters through Big Bend were shallower, and few sections of the river were without jagged rocks that shot up in the midst of the rapids. However, riding the river can still be a memorable experience.

Anyone with determination and the assistance of local experts can float down 245 miles of Rio Grande wilderness in a couple of weeks. The river forms the southern boundary of the park and travels for 118 miles through three major canyons: Santa Elena, Mariscal, and Boquillas. The Park Service also has jurisdiction over an additional 127 miles downstream from Boquillas designated as the Rio Grande Wild and Scenic River.

River use permits can be obtained from the ranger stations at Panther Junction, Persimmon Gap, or Rio Grande Village. You can use canoes, kayaks, or inflatable rafts, and they can be rented at the **Lajitas Trading Post (in Lajitas, 915-424-3234)** or at **Rio Grande Outfitters (in Terlingua, 915-371-2424).** The river guide-booklets available at the ranger stations contain valuable information about the river and navigation tips.

Licensed river runners hire out their services for trips through the canyons. The oldest outfitter is **Far Flung Adventures (in Terlingua, 915-371-2489).** Others include **Big Bend River Tours (in Lajitas, 1-800-545-4240); Outback Expeditions (in Terlingua, 915-371-2490); Texas River Expeditions (out of Houston, 1-800-839-7238); Rio Grande Outfitters (in Terlingua, 915-371-2424);** and **Scott Canoe Livery (in Marathon, 1-800-613-5041).**

The following are principal canyons for river running in Big Bend.

Boquillas Canyon

A 33-mile trip that **puts in near Rio Grande Village and takes out at La Linda,** Mexico. The Mexican authorities allow river runners to drive vehicles across the bridge at La Linda for boat pickups and launches. Rapids are Class II and III.

Colorado Canyon

West of the park, this day-trip is relatively short and easy, a 10-mile run from the Rancheras Canyon put-in to the Teepees Roadside Park take-out. Whitewater stretches are Class II. **Both are off Farm Road 170 and easy to reach by car.**

Lower Canyons

An 83-mile run that in sheer distance is definitely not for novices. This 5-day run takes you through the Rio Grande Wild and Scenic River region. There are some Class IV rapids. You **put in at La Linda and take out at Dryden Crossing.**

Mariscal Canyon

An easy day-trip that covers about 10 miles. Mariscal features the Rock Pile, about 100 yards long, with Class II and III rapids. **Put in at Tally and take out at Rio Grande Village.**

Santa Elena Canyon

An 18-mile descent, the classic Big Bend river run and the most popular. The scenery is spectacular, ranging from sandy banks to stone walls 1,500 feet high. The Rockslide rapids offer a Class IV run through house-size boulders. **The put-in is at Lajitas, with the take-out at the mouth of Santa Elena Canyon.**

SCENIC DRIVES

Some roads that are open for all vehicles offer spectacular scenery, including the 20-mile drive from Panther Junction to Rio Grande Village and the 9-mile drive from Panther Junction to the Chisos Basin. But if you have to pick just one, take the 22-mile **Ross Maxwell Scenic Drive** to Castolon and the mouth of Santa Elena Canyon, offering views of mountains, canyons, and desert.

High-clearance vehicles have more fun. There is an additional 150 miles of backcountry dirt roads, of which four are recommended: **Old Ore Road,** 26 miles long; **Glenn Spring Road,** 15 miles long; **River Road,** 50 miles long; and **Paint Gap Road,** 4 miles long. River Road is my choice as the most scenic, beginning at Castolon and proceeding east along the bottom edge of the park to Rio Grande Village. On that trip you'll pass old ranches, mining camps, the Mariscal Mountains, and fifteen designated backcountry campsites. The Panther Junction Visitor Center carries copies of the *Road Guide to Paved and Improved Dirt Roads* and the *Road Guide to Backcountry Dirt Roads,* containing detailed descriptions of the routes.

WHERE TO STAY

Chisos Mountain Lodge
Built more than a half century ago by the Civilian Conservation Corps, this is the park's only indoor accommodation. It offers thirty-four guest rooms in either a motel setting or in stone cabins that sleep three to six people. Reservations are a must. **National Parks Concession, Chisos Mountain Lodge, Big Bend National Park, 79834; 915-477-2291.**

Towns in the Area

Towns to visit in Big Bend country include Study Butte, Terlingua, Lajitas, Presidio, and Ruidosa. First we take a look at a place that's not exactly a town, but a spot with great memories of a remarkable woman.

Stillwell Store
Getting There: Take U.S. Hwy. 385 north from Panther Junction for 29 miles, then turn right onto a dirt road and go about 5 miles to Stillwell Store. **Visitor Information: Stillwell Store; 915-376-2244.**

We lost a giant when Hallie Stillwell died, only 2 months shy of her 100th birthday. Hallie was a bright-eyed girl from the city who came to Big Bend as a young bride and never left. Her husband was killed in a freak accident when he was a young man, and Hallie had every reason to move back to civilization, but she stayed and helped settle this land. She survived Indian

attack, drought, and money woes, and did everything, from teaching school to driving cattle, to keep the ranch and family intact.

Stillwell Store today is a little community that's not on most maps, and consists only of the general store, a trailer park, and a little museum dedicated to Hallie. It's a shame you never met Miss Hallie. If you had driven by as recently as the middle of 1997, she would have been there, resting in a chair, surrounded by friends and visitors listening to her stories about the Old West. Miss Hallie was friendly to everyone and would have treated you like a member of the family.

SEEING AND DOING

Hallie Stillwell Hall of Fame
A collections of photos and writings about one of the true pioneers to this part of Texas, complete with life-size pictures of Hallie and her friends. **At Stillwell Store; 915-376-2244.**

Jeep Tours
Just a simple general store out in the middle of the desert—but it's actually more than that. It's also headquarters to one of the best guided trips in the Big Bend area. Hallie's daughter, Dadie Stillwell Potter, organizes jeep rides to the nearby Maravillas Mountains, where visitors see Indian wall paintings, and maybe even a black bear or two. **From Stillwell Store; 915-376-2244.**

Study Butte and Terlingua
Getting There: Study Butte is 2 miles from the western entrance to Big Bend National Park, on State Hwy. 118. Terlingua is 4 miles west of Study Butte, via State Hwy. 118 and Farm Road 170. **Visitor Information: Chamber of Commerce, at the junction of State Hwy. 118 and Farm Road 170; 915-371-2320.**

Terlingua had its heyday around the turn of the century when mercury mines were big business in the area. The town prospered until the price of mercury dropped in the 1940s. Then Terlingua slowly dried up and became a ghost town, which is now being resurrected. Both Terlingua and Study Butte have their characters, so my advice is to check out every store and just watch and listen. Some of the people may look a little unfriendly, but they're not.

The Rio Grande between Lajitas and Presidio, separating Texas and Mexico.

SEEING AND DOING

Perry Mansion

Private and not open for tours, but easy to spot. It's the most impressive residence in these parts, located on a rock hill just beyond the Terlingua Trading Company. The mansion was built shortly after the turn of the twentieth century by one of the men who developed the area for mercury mining. Bill Ivy, who runs the Trading Post, now lives in the mansion.

Starlight Theater

A restored movie house with a new lease on life as a dinner theater, serving steaks, chicken, burgers, and some Mexican delights in adobe surroundings. **On the main drag, Terlingua; 915-371-2326.**

Study Butte Store

A popular hangout on State Hwy. 118. Every time I've been there it seemed to have new owners. One couple who ran the place didn't have a freezer, so the husband got on his Harley Davidson every morning and made the 160-mile round-trip to Alpine for perishables. They fried their hamburgers and they were terrific. **915-371-2231.**

Terlingua Cemetery

The best bargain in town—a free walk through an old cemetery. Some of the tombstones are intriguing.

Terlingua Trading Company

Located in the former headquarters of the Chisos Mining Company, this is a souvenir store with books, jewelry, T-shirts, and all sorts of Mexican imports. **At**

the top of the hill on a main street that is only 1 block long; 915-371-2234.

RECREATION

RV Parks and Camping
BJ RV Park, 915-371-2259; and Terlingua Oasis RV Park, 915-371-2218.

WHERE TO EAT

La Kiva Steak House
On Farm Road 170 in Terlingua; 915-371-2250.

Roadrunner Deli
On State Hwy. 118 in Study Butte; 915-371-2364.

WHERE TO STAY

Big Bend Motor Inn
Just a basic motel, but good clean rooms. **At the intersection of State Hwy. 118 and Farm Road 170 in Study Butte; 915-371-2218.**

Lajitas

Getting There: From the western entrance to Big Bend National Park, take Farm Road 170 west for about 20 miles to Lajitas (la-HEE-tuss). **Visitor Information: Badlands Hotel, on the boardwalk in Lajitas; 915-424-3471; www.lajitas.com.**

Lajitas began in 1915 as an army post, getting its name from the large outcroppings of flagstones in the region (the name means "flagstones" in Spanish). The army was sent there to protect citizens from the Mexican bandito Pancho Villa. After Villa's demise, Lajitas became just another sleepy little border village on the Rio Grande. Lajitas was still that way in the 1960s, when David Mischer came to town. Mischer made his fortune building streets, curbing, and parking lots for developers in the Houston area. But he always wanted to do more, and Lajitas gave him the chance. He had visions of building a resort out here, and that's what he did.

Today, aside from Big Bend National Park, Lajitas is probably the most-visited place in Big Bend country. It has motels and hotels, condos, a restaurant, and all kinds of shops. It has swimming pools, tennis courts, horseback riding, river rafting, and one of the greenest golf courses you'll ever lay eyes on. I remember reaching the 18th hole one morning at Lajitas when a little old man, who had been watching me and my friend play, graciously walked up and tended the flag stick while we putted. As I was lining up my putt, my friend leaned over and said, "Don't blow it, Gary. That's the highest-priced caddie you'll ever see." It was David Mischer.

SEEING AND DOING

Lajitas on the Boardwalk
A full-service bike shop with mountain bike rentals and guided tours of Big Bend National Park, the Chihuahuan Desert, and San Carlos, Mexico. **915-424-3366.**

Lajitas on the Rio Grande
The resort development that David Mischer built includes eighty-one rooms in a small hotel and three motels, plus a group bunkhouse. Individual houses and condos are also for rent. The resort has a restaurant, RV and tent camping spaces, swimming pool, golf course, and tennis courts—even its own airstrip. **1 Main Place; 915-424-3471.**

Lajitas Stables
Guided trail rides ranging from day-trips to overnight journeys. Wagon rides and steak cookouts are also available. **On State Hwy. 170 at the eastern edge of town; 915-424-3238.**

Lajitas Trading Post
It's as old as the town, and located on a dirt road that leads to the Rio Grande crossing. It's the only place in the area that sells gasoline, and is still a popular hangout for local workers. But John Henry, the goat that used to drink beer out of a bottle at the trading post, is no longer with us. **915-424-3234.**

Warnock Environmental Education Center
The center serves as one of the two entry points to Big Bend Ranch State Park (described in the section on Presidio later in this chapter). Exhibits offer an archaeological, historical, and natural history profile of the Big Bend region. The center has information about vehicle, hiking, and river raft access, along with

Lajitas, an oasis in the desert of West Texas, in Big Bend country.

maps, books, and other informational material. Outside is a 4-acre desert garden with cacti and other plants native to the Chihuahuan Desert. **Farm Road 170 on the eastern outskirts of Lajitas; 915-424-3327.**

WHERE TO EAT

Badlands Restaurant
Typical hotel food, but convenient for anyone staying in Lajitas. **On the boardwalk in Lajitas; 915-424-3471.**

WHERE TO STAY

Badlands Hotel
Resort living, with comfortable quarters—and scenery that will take your breath away. **On the boardwalk in Lajitas; 915-424-3471.**

Presidio

Getting There: From the western entrance to Big Bend National Park, take Farm Road 170 west for 87 miles to Presidio. **Visitor Information: Presidio Chamber of Commerce, on U.S. Hwy. 67 downtown; 915-229-3199.**

Presidio is an isolated village on the Rio Grande, west of Lajitas. One of the finest scenic drives in the state is along Farm Road 170 between Lajitas and Presidio. The narrow 65-mile route takes you past breathtaking vistas of desert terrain and deep canyons. On the south is the Rio Grande, separating Texas and Mexico. On the north is part of one of the state's newest acquisitions, Big Bend Ranch State Park. Drive cautiously: the road has some steep grades, sharp curves, and low-water crossings, and you may encounter loose livestock.

SEEING AND DOING

Fort Leaton State Historic Site

This is one of the state's most unusual historic sites, featuring an adobe fortress built by frontiersman Ben Leaton in 1848, immediately after the Mexican War. Leaton was an Indian trader, so the fort was as much a storage place for goods he brought in to sell to Apaches and Comanches as it was a safe haven for people running from hostile Indians. In fact, Leaton was often accused of encouraging Indian raids on settlements in nearby Mexico by supplying the guns. The old fort has more than forty rooms still intact, and twenty-four of them have been restored. **Four miles southeast of Presidio on Farm Road 170; 915-229-3613.**

RECREATION

Big Bend Ranch State Park

The visitor center at Fort Leaton State Historic Site (4 miles southeast of Presidio on Farm Road 170) introduces you to Big Bend Ranch State Park, with information on bus tours of the area that are offered the first and third Saturdays of each month. The center also offers information about vehicle, hiking, and river raft access to the vast, primitive region. There are no developed facilities in this park. If you drive the 33-mile route from Fort Leaton to the Sauceda headquarters of the park, take your time so you can soak up the kind of scenery found only in West Texas. You'll pass rock formations, clear flowing springs, canyons, and flatlands. The Big Bend Ranch State Park road is dirt, and high-clearance vehicle are recommended but not entirely necessary. You can camp in a primitive area at the Sauceda headquarters or spend the night indoors at the Big House, a comfortable ranch home that sleeps a maximum of eight people in three bedrooms. The cost is $40 per night. Big Bend Ranch, operated by the state, has outdoor programs year-round, including trail rides, desert survival workshops, longhorn cattle drives, rock art seminars, and hikes. For information, call **915-229-3416.**

WHERE TO EAT

El Alamo

Mexican food. **On U.S. Hwy. 67 at Presidio; 915-229-4763.**

Ruidosa

Getting There: From the western entrance to Big Bend National Park, take Farm Road 170 west for about 125 miles to Ruidosa.

Ruidosa is another sleepy little village along the Mexican border. There is little more than an intersection here, and most of the streets are dirt, but the trip is worth it if you favor Big Bend scenery. The road from Lajitas to Ruidosa follows the legendary Rio Grande, and if you turn east at Ruidosa onto Farm Road 2810, you'll see some of the most striking scenery in all of West Texas.

SEEING AND DOING

Chinati Hot Springs Resort

This little-known oasis in the middle of the Chihuahuan Desert is nestled deep in the Chinati and Cuesto del Burro Mountains. People from both sides of the Rio Grande have used the healing waters for hundreds of years. The mineral-rich waters are at a temperature of about 110 degrees. The atmosphere is quiet and peaceful—the perfect spot for relaxation. There's a bathhouse, rustic adobe cabins, and a campground (no RV hookups). You can also do some birding, explore for arrowheads, and visit some of nature's unspoiled land at this isolated resort. **Twenty-five miles east of Ruidosa, via Farm Road 2810; 915-229-4105.**

Scenic Drive

The dirt road between Ruidosa and Marfa, **Farm Road 2810,** provides more than a scenic drive, it offers an experience. The trip is only about 50 miles, but it may take 2 or 3 hours. You'll drive through a number of dry creekbeds, negotiate around a lot of sharp rocks in the road, and I'll bet you'll see at least one rattlesnake and an antelope before you reach Marfa. Check with the locals before you go, and ask plenty of questions.

Guadalupe Mountains National Park

The Guadalupe Range splits the Texas–New Mexico border in the Far West, rising high above the surrounding Chihuahuan Desert. The north end of the range descends gradually into New Mexico's Carlsbad Plains. The south drops abruptly into a huge salt basin in Texas.

You can see the peaks of the Guadalupe Mountains from 50 miles away, but tourists have long ignored the area. Guadalupe Mountains National Park is not easy to get to, and the main attractions are not accessible by road. There are no hotels or lodges in or near the park. The nearest motel is in Whites City, New Mexico, near Carlsbad Caverns National Park, and neither of the two drive-in campgrounds in Guadalupe Mountains National Park have RV hookups.

Visitor Information

Headquarters Visitor Center

The center provides brochures and maps and a schedule of ranger-guided walking tours. The center also sells books with historical and natural history information about the area and topographic maps for hikers. **At Pine Springs, on U.S. Hwy. 62/180, 110 miles east of El Paso; 915-828-3251; www.nps.gov/gumo. Mailing address: Guadalupe Mountains National Park, HC 60, Box 400, Salt Flat, 79847-9400.**

Guadalupe Mountains National Park

Temperatures vary from very hot to very cool in the Guadalupe Mountains. In January, the high averages 53 degrees, and the low averages 30. But in July, the average high is 88, while the average low is 63. High winds are not uncommon in the highlands. August and September are the rainiest months, but it can rain at any time, and snow is not unusual in the high country during winter. The best time to visit the park is during the cooler months: in October, when there is the fall change of colors, and in April.

The Guadalupes support an unusually diverse community of plant and animal species. On the floor of the lower canyons are typical desert plants like yucca, prickly pear cactus, and sotol. As you get higher in elevation you'll pass by Douglas fir, ponderosa pines, and the Texas madrone. About sixty species of mammals make their home in the Guadalupe Mountains, including bats, coyotes, mule deer, some descendants of Rocky Mountain elk, and even some porcupines. At last count there were 255 bird species in the park, including wild turkeys, red-tailed hawks, killdeer, woodpeckers, and roadrunners. You may spot a bald eagle or two in the summer. The golden eagle can be seen year-round.

Recreation

CAMPING

Nine designated wilderness camping sites are accessible only on foot in the park. A no-fee backcountry use permit is required and can be obtained from the visitor centers or at Dog Canyon Campground. A topographic map is recommended for backpackers.

Dog Canyon Campground

This is the second drive-in camping facility in the park. It's slightly cooler, at an elevation of 6,300 feet. Camping facilities include 18 walk-in tent sites and 5 RV

Getting There

Guadalupe Mountains National Park is 110 miles east of El Paso on U.S. Hwy. 62/180, 75 miles north of Van Horn on State Hwy. 54, and 55 miles southwest of Carlsbad, New Mexico. Most people who do not camp in the park stay at motels in Carlsbad or in Whites City, New Mexico, 20 miles south of Carlsbad.

El Capitan, the focal point of Guadalupe Mountains National Park. Photo courtesy of Texas Highways magazine.

parking spaces; no RV hookups or dump stations. A ranger station, picnic area, rest rooms, and horse corrals are close at hand. Two major trailheads, **Tejas Trail** and **Bush Mountain Trail,** are near the Dog Canyon Campground. **Access to Dog Canyon Campground is from the north via New Mexico State Hwy. 137.**

Pine Springs Campground

Pine Springs is the largest of the two drive-in campgrounds in the park, with 19 tent sites and 29 RV sites; there are no RV hookups or dump stations. Mescalero Apache Indians were here before the land was settled by whites. Before and after the Civil War, the U.S. Army camped here, and in the 1850s the Butterfield Overland Mail established a stage station at the site. The Pine Springs area just off U.S. Hwy. 62/180 is located **at Guadalupe Pass, 9 miles north of the junction of State Hwy. 54 and Hwy. 62/180.**

HIKING

Unless you are a hiker, you'll never see the real beauty of the park. There are no scenic overlooks to drive to, and none of the canyons are accessible by car. But there are more than 80 miles of hiking trails. The only sources of drinking water are at Headquarters Visitor Center, McKittrick Canyon Visitor Center, Pine Springs Campground, and Dog Canyon Campground.

Following are just a few of the many trails in the park. Check the maps provided by the Park Service for full details.

Bush Mountain Trail

Twelve miles one-way. This trail runs parallel to the Tejas Trail from Dog Canyon Campground to the top of Pine Springs Canyon. It also runs as far west into the Guadalupes as established trails will take you, following the western escarpment over Bush Mountain, the second highest peak in the park. It offers access, and can be traveled from either direction.

Devil's Hall Trail

Two and a half miles one-way. Leads to the upper end of Hiker's Staircase, a canyon formed by Pine Springs. Devil's Hall refers to the narrow walls along the way. Because of the pools of water that usually collect in the canyon, this is a good hike for viewing wildlife and vegetation. It is also a relatively cool hike, even on hot days.

Guadalupe Peak Trail

Four and a half miles one-way, to the highest point in Texas—Guadalupe Peak (8,749 feet)—where the view is outstanding.

McKittrick Canyon Trail

Ten miles one-way. Begins at the McKittrick Canyon Visitor Center and continues along the canyon floor to Pratt's cabin and McKittrick Ridge. This is one of the most scenic areas in the canyon.

Tejas Trail

Twelve miles one-way, extending the length of the park between Pine Springs Campground and Dog Canyon Campground. This is one of the main access routes to the high country and has elevation changes of about 2,000 feet. The hike affords wonderful canyon views, plus vistas of Guadalupe, Bartlett, and Shumard Peaks.

HORSEBACK RIDING

About 80 percent of the park trail system is open for equestrian use, mostly along the north-to-south ridges that run through the center of the park. There are no horses for hire, so all saddle stock must be brought in. Riders must get a free permit from a visitor center before taking horses on any trail. The visitor centers also distribute a free saddle-stock access guide.

Towns in the Area

Dell City

Getting There: From El Paso, go east on U.S. Hwy. 62/180 for about 75 miles, then turn north onto Farm Road 1437 and go a dozen miles or so to Dell City.

The biggest attraction in Dell City appears during the Christmas season. I call it tumbleweed art, and it's put up around town by Mary and Jim Lynch, a couple of old-timers who run the local paper and have a ranch on the outskirts of town. Mary is the artist. She creates all sorts of Christmas characters with dead tumbleweeds that Jim gathers out on the farm. Mary decorates them with hats, coats, snow shovels, and such. It has given Dell City something to be proud of, and it makes this hot, dry, and almost deserted West Texas community light up every year when Santa comes calling.

WHERE TO EAT

There's no place to spend the night in Dell City, but at the **Dell Junction Cafe** on the main drag, they serve darn good burgers and Mexican food. Cowboys drive in from nearby ranches daily at noon for the hamburgers.

Salt Flat

Getting There: From El Paso, go east on U.S. Hwy. 62/180 for about 85 miles.

This tiny community got its start with the discovery of huge salt deposits left by intermittent lakes in Hudspeth County, west of the Guadalupe Mountains. The area was the sight of a bloody dispute in the 1860s known as the Salt War, whose assassinations and revenge killings went on for years. A part of the sea of salt is still visible from U.S. Hwy. 62/180.

Salt Flats, south of Guadalupe Mountain Range, east of El Paso.

El Paso

El Paso, with a population of some 600,000, is the largest Texas city on the U.S.–Mexico border and the fourth largest city in Texas. It is tucked away in a pocket where Texas, Mexico, and New Mexico meet and, some say, it is practically in the middle of nowhere. It is closer to three other state capitals—Santa Fe, Phoenix, and Chihuahua City—than it is to the Texas capital of Austin, so a lot of people out here think they've been forgotten by the state government. El Paso is closer to Los Angeles than it is to Houston and, unlike the rest of Texas, is in the mountain time zone.

The name El Paso evokes images of the Old West. Check out its history and you'll discover that the images may not be far off. A lot of memorable western characters spent time here. Others passed through here heading farther west.

The Europeans first discovered El Paso del Norte ("the Pass of the North") in the 1500s. They stood on the relatively flat land that would someday be El Paso and looked north toward a mountain range that would someday be called the Franklin Mountains, and they saw what they described as a pass that would provide access to the north for Spanish colonists. They called this new land El Paso del Norte. In later years, the city that grew up along this route became known as El Paso, and an east-west trail was established as well.

In the 1680s, Spanish and Tigua Indian refugees flocked to this area. They were running from the Pueblo Indian revolt in Ysleta, New Mexico, and they called their new home Ysleta del Sur ("Ysleta of the South"). This was most likely the first organized settlement in the land that we now know as Texas. In the 1800s, Anglo-Americans started arriving. By 1840, there were five Anglo settlements north of the Rio Grande. One of them was called Franklin and provided the base for the city of El Paso.

When the Southern Pacific Railroad finally reached El Paso in 1881, the town boomed. For the next 40 years or so, gunfighters, soldiers of fortune, cattle rustlers, banditos, Texas Rangers, and Mexican revolutionaries gave the town its reputation as the "six-shooter capital" of the United States. Marshals like

Wyatt Earp, Bat Masterson, and Pat Garrett spent time here, and so did some notorious outlaws, like John Wesley Hardin, said to be the fastest gun in the West.

It was a wild ride for a lot of characters, but it all ended in 1916 when General Blackjack Pershing's troops were sent here to get rid of the Mexican bandit Pancho Villa. Pershing never caught the elusive Villa, but the expanded military presence at nearby Fort Bliss was enough to establish law and order in the region. The Wild West days were over.

El Paso features a desert climate and sits at an elevation of 3,700 feet. Average annual rainfall is about 7 inches, and the air is dry. High temperatures rest in the 90s about a third of the year, mostly between May and September. Due to the desert environment, nights are usually cool. Summer days are usually bearable because of the low humidity, but don't let anybody fool you: when it's 100 degrees, even in low humidity, it's still hot. Best months to visit El Paso are March, April, May, October, and early November, when it is neither too hot nor too cold, and the air is usually clear.

Getting Around

BUSES
Sun Metro (915-533-3333), bus line for the city, operates during the day. It is mainly convenient for the downtown area.

TAXIS

Reliable cab service in the city is offered by **Checker (915-532-2626)** and **Yellow Cab (915-533-3433)**. In addition, at either side of the bridges that cross the Rio Grande are fleets of taxis that ferry passengers back and forth between El Paso and Juarez, Mexico.

TOURS

Several companies in El Paso conduct bus tours, including half-day or full-day sightseeing or shopping or visits to the Juarez racetrack or bull ring. Most motels and hotels can arrange the tours, or you can contact a company directly: **Around and About Tours (915-833-2650); Golden Tours (915-779-0555); Si El Paso Tours (915-581-1122); Rio Grande Tours (915-564-0493);** and **Sunland Park Charter (915-533-8300). El Paso/Juarez Tours** provides an easy and fairly inexpensive way to cross the border for shopping and sightseeing in Juarez; air-conditioned trolleys depart from the Civic Center on the hour **(915-544-0062). Fiesta Tours** offers trips across the border for shopping and to the racetrack in mini-coaches, and hotel pickup is available **(915-544-4646).**

Visitor Information

El Paso Convention and Visitors Bureau

Arranges group tourism and conventions. **1 Civic Center Plaza, El Paso, 79901; 1-800-351-6024, 915-534-0696, fax 915-532-0263; elpaso@ huntleigh.net.**

El Paso Tourist Information Centers

One center is in Civic Center Plaza downtown; another is at El Paso International Airport. **915-534-0653.**

Mexican Consulate in El Paso

If you are a U.S. citizen planning to enter Mexico as a tourist, without a private vehicle and for less than 180 days, you don't need to check with the Mexican consulate at all. Citizens from other countries may need to apply. Any non-Mexican citizen intending to take a vehicle into Mexico must apply for the necessary papers at the consulate or at the border. **910 E. San Antonio Ave.; 915-533-3644.**

Mexico Tourist Information Center

The English-speaking staff has travel information for

> **Getting There**
>
> **El Paso International Airport** *is the gateway to West Texas, southern New Mexico, and northern Mexico. Eight commercial airlines operate out of the airport, which handles 200 combined arrivals and departures per day. The airport is 5 miles northeast of downtown El Paso, at* **6701 Convair Dr.; 915-772-4271. Sun Metro (915-533-3333)** *runs a 7-day-a-week schedule between the airport and the Downtown Plaza, with an intermediate stop at Bassett Center.*

Juarez and Mexico. They can also assist if you have a problem, such as theft, while in Juarez. **In Juarez in the Municipal Building, just across the border on Avenida Colegio Militar; phone 011-52-16-152301.**

U.S. Consulate in Juarez

Phone 13-40-48. After business hours, you may call **915-525-6066** in El Paso.

Travel Information Center

On I-10 at the Texas–New Mexico state line; **915-886-3468.**

Websites

www.elpasotexas.com; www.citi-guide.com/ ep-index.htm; www.elpaso-juarez.com.

Major Attractions

The Old Missions

In the lower valley in the El Paso area are several Spanish missions that predate the better-known missions of California. They are open daily. Information on the Mission Trail is available at **915-534-0630. Mission Tour (915-544-0062)** provides a $4^1/_2$-hour trolley tour of the missions, starting at the El Paso Civic Center.

Nuestra Señora del Carmen

Established in 1681 and later renamed Ysleta Mission,

Scenic drive overlooking downtown El Paso. Photo courtesy of Texas Highways *magazine.*

this is the oldest mission in Texas. It was built for the Tigua Indians. When the mission was established, it was south of the Rio Grande, putting it in Mexico. But with the changes in the river channel, it's now on the U.S. side. Ysleta is 10 miles southeast of downtown El Paso, at **100 Old Pueblo Rd. (Zaragoza Rd. exit from I-10).**

Nuestra Señora de la Concepcion del Socorro

Established in 1682 as a mission for Piros, Thanos, and Jemes Indians, this mission was physically moved to Socorro after a threatened revolt by a group of Indians. It too used to be on the Mexican side of the Rio Grande until the river channel changed. **In the community of Socorro,** which is adjacent to southeast El Paso, off **Farm Road 258.**

San Elizario Presidio Chapel

Founded in 1777 to serve the Spanish military garrison and the government, this chapel is still in use today. **In the old community of San Elizario** just beyond Socorro, off **Farm Road 258.**

Juarez, Mexico

Juarez is Mexico's fourth largest city—population 1.5 million—and the largest city on the U.S.–Mexico border. It is linked to El Paso by three bridges over the Rio Grande. Tourism is big business, and visitors are treated to exciting times, with shopping malls, markets, night clubs, a racetrack, and a bull ring.

You'll find the **Lincoln Statue** in Juarez, just south of Chamizal Federal Park. President Lincoln and President Juarez of Mexico were of the same era. This

statue honors the common bonds between the two men and the two countries. Also at Chamizal is a beautiful garden maintained by the Mexican government, where American visitors are welcome to browse through a forest of colorful flowers. (Later in this chapter is information on other Juarez attractions, including restaurants and shopping.)

The **Chamizal National Memorial** in El Paso commemorates an amicable settlement of a long-standing border dispute between the United States and Mexico. There is a visitor center, exhibits, and films in Spanish and English on Chamizal and border history. Open daily 8 A.M.–5 P.M. **800 S. San Marcial St.; 915-532-7273; www.nps.gov/cham.**

Seeing and Doing

Museums and Historic Sites

Concordia Cemetery

John Wesley Hardin is buried here, along with other notable gunslingers. I suggest you look around for a copy of *The Shooters,* by an old friend of mine, western historian Leon Metz. This book about gunmen in the early West includes fascinating stories of life and death in early El Paso. I could listen to him for days talking about the likes of Billy the Kid, Wild Bill Hickok, Butch Cassidy, and some of the other notorious characters who spent time in the state. The cemetery is **just north of I-10 at the Gateway North and U.S. Hwy. 54 interchange.** Easiest access to the cemetery is from Yandell Dr., which runs parallel to I-10. Coming west on I-10, take the Copia St. exit, make a right on Stevens, and another right on Yandell.

Fort Bliss

A U.S. Army post established in 1848 as a defense against hostile Indians. It remained active after the Mexican War to maintain U.S. authority over the land that was acquired from Mexico. Bliss was headquarters for Confederate forces in the Southwest during the Civil War, and today it is an Army Air Defense Center. Its long and varied history makes for interesting visits to several museums on the base: **Air Defense and Artillery Museum,** with hands-on exhibits **(in building 5000, 915-568-4518); Fort Bliss Cavalry Museum,** a replica of the original adobe fort during the frontier military era **(Pleasanton Rd. and Sheridan Dr., 915-568-1922); and Museum for the Noncommissioned Officer,** with artifacts dating from the Revolutionary War **(Barksdale and 5th Sts., 915-568-8646).**

Magoffin Home State Historic Structure

A home that was the political and social center of Magoffinville (now the site of downtown El Paso). This home was built in 1875 as a replica of an earlier home destroyed in a great flood in 1868. **1120 Magoffin St.; 915-533-5147.**

Sierra del Cristo Rey

At a point where Texas, New Mexico, and Mexico intersect, atop a 4,700-foot peak, a statue of Christ overlooks El Paso. Sculptor Urbici Soler carved the figure out of limestone in 1938. It is identical in style and scale to the Christ statue that overlooks Rio de Janeiro. On the final Sunday in October, Sierra del Cristo Rey is the site of an annual procession in which hundreds of worshipers climb 2.5 miles along a winding footpath to reach the top. The peak is **visible from I-10 as you drive west from El Paso into New Mexico.**

Tigua Indian Reservation

Located at Ysleta, oldest community within the present boundaries of Texas. The mission church is still the focal point of the community, but there is also much more to see. The reservation has **a museum, restaurant, and arts and crafts center** in an extensive adobe complex. Descendants of those first Indians in the region craft beautiful pottery and pull fresh Indian bread out of adobe ovens. The restaurant features *gorditas*—Indian tacos with spicy filling and a special brand of Tigua Indian chili. For the adults, the Tigua operate a handsome **bingo hall (122 Old Pueblo Rd., 915-860-7777),** next to Ysleta Mission. Ysleta is **10 miles southeast of downtown El Paso, via I-10 to the Zaragoza Rd. exit; 915-859-3916 (for the reservation).**

Other Sights

Indian Cliffs Ranch

A daytime dude ranch for families on 23,000 acres of desert. Activities include hayrides, trail rides, a children's petting zoo, and a replica of a frontier fort. Groups can also arrange overnight hayrides, and those chuckwagon meals are worth the trip. **From El Paso, take I-10 east for about 30 miles to Fabens, then go 5 miles north on Farm Road 793 to the ranch; 915-544-3200; www.cattlemanssteak house.com.**

Parks

El Paso Zoo

Exhibits more than 700 animals, including about 200 species. Featured is an Asian section, plus animals from North, Central, and South America. An 8,000-square-foot aviary allows visitors to walk among the birds. Open daily except Thanksgiving, Christmas, and New Year's Day. **4001 E. Paisano St., near the Bridge of the Americas; 915-544-1928.**

Shopping

El Paso–Juarez is a major trading center for the Southwest, and hundreds of manufacturers and importers look to this area to unload their goods. Some of the

A Tigua Indian Fiesta in El Paso. Photo courtesy of Texas Highways magazine.

better buys are Tarahumara Indian blankets, Casas Grandes pottery, Pueblo Indian jewelry, and cowboy boots. You can get real bargains on rustic southwestern-style furniture. Beware of the junk; shop around before reaching for your pocketbook.

In **Juarez,** as in most border towns, the shops that cater to English-speaking tourists are clustered along the streets leading from the bridges that lead into the city. **Avenida Juarez** extends from the Santa Fe Bridge; **Avenida Lincoln** is at the Cordova crossing near Chamizal. There are also a lot of shops along **Avenida 16 Septiembre.** Border towns are hagglers' paradises, and Juarez is no exception. You won't get a discount unless you ask. A couple of must-visit places are the **ProNAF** and the **Centro Artesanal** on Avenida Lincoln. These are government-owned shops that offer authentic art from all over Mexico, but there's no bargaining here because the prices are already fixed.

Boots, Jeans, and Western Gear

More cowboy boots are made in El Paso than anywhere else in the world. All the major Texas boot makers maintain factory outlets here. Prices are usually about 20 to 40 percent below retail: **Justin (7100 Gateway Blvd. E., 915-779-5465); Tony Lama (1137 Tony Lama St., 915-778-8311);** and **Dan Post and Lucchese (6601 Montana Ave., 915-778-3066).** For those of you with a yearning for custom boots and the money to spend, try **Rocketbuster Boots (115 S. Anthony St., 915-541-1300)** or **Botas Santa Fe (738 Ave. de las Americas, in Juarez).** Levi's and Wrangler both have large plants in El Paso, so there are some good buys on those brands. **El Paso Trading Post** sells custom saddles, and they also sell western wear **(1060 Doniphan Park Circle, 915-585-1174).** Another good place for saddles and tack is **Cowboy Trading Post (301 E. Borderland Rd., 915-581-1984).**

El Paso Saddleblanket

Leather goods, local antiques, southwestern pottery, and handwoven blankets. About everything in the store comes from Mexico and Central America, and although it may be more fun to ferret out the bargains in the marketplace at Juarez, if you are short on time and bargaining skills, this place is a great compromise. It costs slightly more here, but this place is a lot more

organized. **601 N. Oregon St., downtown El Paso; 915-544-1000.**

Pueblito Mexican

An enclosed multilevel mall that is designed to look like a colonial Mexican village, devoted to the arts, crafts, and history of Mexico. It has areas set aside for silver, hand-woven tapestries, rustic furniture, and pottery. **Avenida Lincoln, south of the Cordova crossing, in Juarez.**

Susan Eisen Fine Jewelry

Jewelry, paintings, and prints for sale, displayed in a turn-of-the-century home. **7500 N. Mesa St. at La Promenade Shopping Center; 915-584-0022.**

Ysleta and Socorro

The Mission Trail through these communities is lined with specialty shops that are open mostly on weekends. Among them are the **Bosque Trading Post (10167 Socorro Rd.); El Mercadito (10189 Socorro Rd.);** and the **Riverside Trading Post (10300 Socorro Rd.).** The nearby **Tigua Indian Reservation Cultural Center** specializes in Tigua Indian art, and the pottery is something to behold **(119 S. Old Pueblo Dr., 915-859-7913).**

Sports

Bullfighting

Juarez is on the major professional bullfighting circuit. Fights are usually held early on Sunday evening between Easter and Labor Day. **At the Plaza Monumental de Toros in Juarez.**

El Paso Diablos

The Diablos are a team in the Texas League. You've never witnessed a baseball game until you see these guys play. The franchise is dedicated to putting some life into a slow-moving sport, and they've succeeded. They had mascots roaming the bleachers long before the Big Leagues had them. They have funky music playing at the appropriate times, and a screaming PA system pumps up the fans throughout the game. Diablos fans know every player by name and nickname and are quick to pull a dollar or two out of their pockets to reward a player who slams one over the fence. A lot of the things dreamed up to enhance attendance at this park have been adopted by major league teams, but in El Paso you can get the same entertainment for under $4. **Cohen Stadium, 9700 Gateway N.; 915-755-2000, fax 915-757-0671; www.diablos.com.**

El Paso Speedway Park

Auto racing every Saturday night from mid-April to mid-October on a half-mile semi-banked clay oval track. Events feature everything from mini-stocks to IMCA-type modifieds. Twelve miles east of El Paso International Airport at **14900 Montana Ave.; 915-857-3478.**

Rodeo

At the **Charreada Mexican Rodeos** in Juarez, costumed cowboys perform feats of horsemanship most Sunday afternoons. Most times these rodeos are more exciting than the ones held in the states. **At Lienzo Charro Lopez Mateos Arena, on the Pan American Highway at Avenida del Charro.**

Wagering

Juarez Racetrack

Greyhound racing in a place billed as the Taj Majal of racing, Wednesday though Sunday year-round. **On Avenida 16 de Septiembre near Boulevard Lopez Mateos and the Pan American Highway, in Juarez; phone 011-52-16-131656.**

Sunland Park Racetrack

Thoroughbred and quarter horse racing, Wednesdays and on weekends from October through May. **Ten miles west of El Paso, off I-10, in Sunland Park, New Mexico; 505-589-1131.**

Festivals and Events

February

Southwest International Livestock Show and Rodeo

First week in the month. Three thousand animals and 700 cowboys and cowgirls take to the arena for one of the most exciting rodeos in the country. **El Paso County Coliseum, 4100 E. Paisano Dr.; 915-534-4229.**

March

Siglo de Oro Drama Festival

Usually first two weeks in the month. An international cultural festival celebrating the Hispanic golden age of the arts, with presentations from theater groups from Spain, Mexico, Central and South America, Puerto Rico, New Mexico, New York, and El Paso. **Chamizal National Memorial Theater, 800 S. San Marcial St.; 915-534-6668.**

Transmountain Run

A 10-mile footrace sponsored by the American Heart Association. **On Trans Mountain Rd. in the Franklin Mountains; 915-833-1231.**

April

Juan de Onate First Thanksgiving Reenactment

Costumed actors reenact the very first feast of thanksgiving in the New World. In 1598, Juan de Onate and a band of settlers bound for New Mexico reached the Rio Grande after crossing the desert of northern Mexico. This annual event marks the celebration of that thanksgiving 400 years ago. **Chamizal National Memorial, 800 S. San Marcial St.; 915-534-6668.**

May

International Balloon Festival

Hot-air balloonists from all over the country meet for what they call a border balloon crossing. Also features music, dancing, food, and fireworks. **915-886-2222.**

June

Feast of St. Anthony

The most important religious holiday for the Tigua tribe. The celebration involves ceremonies at the mission, then feasting and dancing. Visitors are welcome. Ysleta Mission, Tigua Indian Reservation. **In Ysleta at 119 Old Pueblo Dr.; 915-859-7913.**

The Franklin Mountains when the wildflowers are in bloom. Photo courtesy of the Texas Department of Tourism.

July–August

International Festival de la Zarzuela

Last weekend in July and first two weekends in August. A Spanish operetta and a festival. **Chamizal National Memorial, 800 S. San Marcial St.; 915-534-6668.**

Viva! El Paso

A lavish outdoor summer production celebrating the 400-year history of the border area. **McKelligon Canyon Amphitheater, 3 McKelligon Rd.; 915-565-6900.**

September

Diez y Seis de Septiembre Celebration

A festival and parade marking the anniversary of Mexico's independence from Spain. **At Chamizal National Memorial, 800 S. San Marcial St.,** and also on the Juarez side of the border.

Paso del Norte Street Festival

Usually early in the month. A 5-day birthday party for El Paso that has grown into a major summer festival. **El Paso Civic Center Grounds, 1 Civic Center Plaza; 915-534-0609.**

October

Amigo Airsho

Early in the month. Promoted as a circus in the sky, this airshow features professional and military precision flying teams, aerobatic acts, and parachute jumping. **Biggs Army Airfield at Fort Bliss, 125 Slater Rd.; 915-568-4518.**

Border Folk Festival

Early in the month. Folk music, dancing, and crafts to celebrate the peaceful settlement of the Rio Grande area. **Chamizal National Memorial, 800 S. San Marcial St.; 915-534-6668.**

Kermezaar

Mid-month. A major arts and crafts show with participants from all over the Southwest. **The Grand Hall at the El Paso Convention and Performing Arts Center, 1 Civic Center Plaza; 915-534-0609.**

November

NARC World Finals Rodeo

The grand finals of the North American rodeo season. **El Paso County Coliseum, 4100 E. Paisano Dr.; 915-534-4229.**

Sun Carnival Parade

Thanksgiving Day. A celebration that kicks off a series of sports-related events in the area leading up to the Sun Bowl on Christmas Day. **Downtown.**

December

John Hancock Sun Bowl Football Classic

Post-season college football game. **At the Sun Bowl on the campus of the University of Texas, El Paso.**

Recreation

Golfing

Ascarate Golf Course, 18-hole county course **(6800 Delta Dr., 915-772-7381); Cielo Vista Municipal Course (1510 Hawkins Blvd., 915-591-4927); Emerald Springs Golf Club (16000 Asford St., 915-852-9110); Juarez Country Club,** 18-hole course on the Mexican side of the river **(phone 011-52-16-173439); Painted Dunes (12000 McCombs St., 915-821-2122).** Check with the **El Paso Tourist Information Center** for information on these and other courses **(915-534-0653).** And watch out for sandbaggers when you play; it looks like a lot of good golfers out here make a living from "friendly" games of golf.

Horseback Riding

Blue Sky Outfitters (915-855-3845) organizes equestrian trips in the Guadalupe Mountains and southwest New Mexico. **Cowboy Trading Post** arranges day and overnight horseback trips into the Franklin Mountains and other places around El Paso **(301 E. Borderland Rd., 915-581-1984).**

Parks and Camping

Franklin Mountains State Park

A 16,000-acre park that's undeveloped, but hardy hikers may want to give it a try. The only constructed trail in the park is **Ron Coleman Trail,** about 3.5 miles long, which has Smugglers Pass on one end and McKelligon Canyon on the other. You'll need a day-use permit. **4838 Montana Ave. in El Paso; 915-566-6441; www.tpwd.state.tx.us/park/franklin/franklin.htm.**

Hueco Tanks State Park

For centuries, Hueco Tanks was a strategic travel stop in this arid region, because precious water collected in the hollow rocks. There are ancient Indian pictographs to see here, plus names of some of the '49ers who stopped here on their way to the gold rush in California. There are picnic grounds and plenty of room for hiking, camping, and rock climbing. The park is **26 miles east of El Paso, on U.S. Hwy. 62/180; 915-857-1135.**

McKelligon Canyon Park

A park in the heart of the Franklin Mountains, with facilities for picnicking. You can hike on the 3-mile-long **Senda Mañana Trail.** A cliff-enclosed amphitheater here is the summer home of the musical *Viva! El Paso.* **McKelligon Rd. off Alabama St. in El Paso; 915-534-0609.**

RV Parks

Mission RV Park is the largest and most modern of the local RV sites **(I-10 and Americas Ave., 915-859-1133).** Several others are located east of El Paso, off I-10 or U.S. Hwy. 62/180: **Roadrunner Travel Trailer Park (915-598-4469); Western Horizon Campground (915-852-3388); Samson RV Park (915-859-8383); Cotton Valley RV Park (915-851-2137);** and **Desert Oasis Park (915-855-3366). Starlight Mobile Home Park** is near the eastern edge of the Franklin Mountains **(915-755-5768).**

Rock Climbing

Hueco Tanks State Park is the place. The best season for rock climbing is late October to early February, although any time is good except for the hot days of June through August. Climbers with permits, obtained at the park entrance, may climb anywhere they like except on rock art. No bolts, pitons, or other equipment with a potential for damaging the rock are allowed. A booklet available at the park office, *Hueco Tanks: A Climber's and Boulderer's Guide,* details the climbing routes. Better yet, talk to the climbers who hang out at Pete's, in the Quonset hut on the left side of Ranch Road 2775 as you approach the park. Pete's is owned and operated by Pete Zavala, who treats climbers like part of the family. Besides providing them with a cheap place to camp, he also sells food, drinks, and climbing chalk. Information and tips on rock climbing is free. The park is **26 miles east of El Paso, on U.S. Hwy. 62/180; 915-857-1135.**

Where to Eat

El Paso and Juarez jointly claim the title of Mexican Food Capital of the World, but there is a lot more here than just Mexican food. Up until a few years ago, the locals went to Juarez for Asian food and seafood and to El Paso for barbecue, steaks, and Italian, and to either side for Mexican food, but that rule is no longer so rigid. New restaurants on both sides of the border have opened the area for all types of cuisine.

El Paso

Avilla's
Probably El Paso's best-known Mexican restaurant, serving Tex-Mex food daily. Two locations: **6232 N. Mesa St. at Sunland Park Dr. on the west side of El Paso (915-584-3621)** and **10600 Montana Ave. on the east side (915-598-3333).**

Bill Parks Bar-B-Q
The local choice for barbecue, with southern-style veggies like black-eyed peas, fried okra, and greens. They also have sweet potato pie. **3130 Gateway; 915-542-0960.**

Cattleman's Steakhouse
You have to want the steaks because it's a long drive to get there, but this is still my favorite steak house in West Texas. The decor is Old West, and you can eat your steak as you watch the sunset. **At Indian Cliffs Ranch; from El Paso, take I-10 east for about 30 miles to Fabens, then go north 5 miles on Farm Road 793 to the ranch; 915-544-3200; www.cattlemanssteakhouse.com.**

Cooks Steak House
You can cook your own steak or order it up. **1204 Airway Blvd.; 915-779-5080.**

Dona Lupe Cafe
This was a drugstore in the 1960s, but today it is one of the most popular Mexican food restaurants in the city. **2919 Pershing Dr.; 915-566-9833.**

Forti's Mexican Elder Restaurant
Forti's has been serving up West Texas–style Mexican food for generations. **321 E. Chelsea St., 915-772-0066.**

Juarez

Casa del Sol
A restaurant of choice on the Mexican side, serving up beef dishes and fillet of fish, plus tortilla soup. **At ProNAF, on Avenida Lincoln.**

Chihuahua Charlie's Bar and Grill
Entertains you with tequila shrimp, huachinango veracruzano, and homemade tortillas. **2525 Paseo Triunfo de la Republica.**

Julio's Cafe Corona
One of the best-known Mexican food places on the Mexican side of the border. Specialties include black bass a la Vera Cruz, and spicy chicken soup with avocados. (Some argue that Julio's on the American side, at 8050 Gateway, has better food.) **In the Artesanal Building on Avenida Lincoln; phone 011-52-135509.**

Martino's
An old-timey seafood place that has maintained its reputation for good food over the years. Stuffed black bass is a favorite. **412 Ave. Juarez.**

Shangri-la
One of the best Chinese restaurants on either side of the river. **133 Ave. de las Americas.**

Where to Stay

El Paso has all the standard motels, and most of the newer ones can be found along I-10 east or near the airport. It's not hard to find a place to spend the night here, but among the more interesting are:

Cowboys and Indians Bed-and-Breakfast
This is a real western hacienda. A half-hour drive from downtown El Paso, just over the border into New Mexico. **505-589-2653.**

Park Place
Another well-known El Paso hotel. **325 N. Kansas; 915-533-8241.**

Sunset Heights
This bed-and-breakfast offers a taste of early El Paso in one of the city's old subdivisions. **717 W. Yandell Dr.; 915-544-1743.**

Westin Paseo del Norte
Built in 1912, this landmark hotel has been restored and offers comfortable, pleasant surroundings for travelers. Seventeen floors, with 375 rooms and suites. Across from the Convention Center, **101 S. El Paso; 915-534-3000.**

One of the naturally formed pools at Hueco Tanks State Park, east of El Paso. Photo courtesy of the Texas Department of Tourism.

Index

About the Author

For more than 30 years, **GARY JAMES** has traveled Texas, meeting the people and developing stories for his award-winning syndicated TV show *Eyes of Texas*. During his tenure with KPRC-TV in Houston, he coauthored 6 travel books on the state based on his TV program.

Over the years he has won numerous awards for his writing and his photography, particularly in the field of television documentaries, including two Emmy awards for news specials about pollution in the Gulf of Mexico and about the plight of a mentally disturbed youngster in Houston. Gary is also the proud winner of the George Foster Peabody award for dinstinguished journalism for his efforts in a TV documentary about a black man who grew up in the ghettos of Houston and went on to become the president of a prominent black college in East Texas.

The owner of a video production company, he now devotes his time to developing his own videos about the state he calls home. Married to his childhood sweetheart, Gary is the father of three children. He and his wife live in Sugar Land, Texas.